Business Law and Ethics

Pearson

At Pearson, we have a simple mission: to help people make more of their lives through learning.

We combine innovative learning technology with trusted content and educational expertise to provide engaging and effective learning experience that serve people wherever and whenever they are learning.

We enable our customers to access a wide and expanding range of market-leading content from world-renowned authors and develop their own tailor-made book. From classroom to boardroom, our curriculum materials, digital learning tools and testing programmes help to educate millions of people worldwide — more than any other private enterprise.

Every day our work helps learning flourish, and wherever learning flourishes, so do people.

To learn more, please visit us at: www.pearson.com/uk

Business Law and Ethics

Fourth Edition

Selected chapters from:

Essentials of Business Law
Fourth Edition
Ewan MacIntyre

Business Ethics and Values: Individual, Corporate and International Perspectives
Fourth Edition
Colin Fisher, Alan Lovell and Néstor Valero-Silva

 **Pearson**

Harlow, England • London • New York • Boston • San Francisco • Toronto • Sydney • Dubai • Singapore • Hong Kong
Tokyo • Seoul • Taipei • New Dehli • Cape Town • São Paulo • Mexico City • Madrid • Amsterdam • Munich • Paris • Milan

Pearson
KAO Two
KAO Park
Harlow
Essex CM17 9NA

And associated companies throughout the world

Visit us on the World Wide Web at:
www.pearson.com/uk

© Pearson Education Limited 2015 – 2018
This new edition published 2018

Compiled from:

Essentials of Business Law
Fourth Edition
Ewan MacIntyre
ISBN 978-1-4479-2362-6
© Pearson Education Limited 2007, 2009, 2011 (print)
© Pearson Education Limited 2013 (print and electronic)

Business Ethics and Values: Individual, Corporate and International Perspectives
Fourth Edition
Colin Fisher, Alan Lovell and Néstor Valero-Silva
ISBN 978-0-273-75791-7
© Pearson Education Limited 2003, 2006, 2009 (print)
© Pearson Education Limited 2013 (print and electronic)

ISBN 978-1-78726-448-9

Printed and bound in Great Britain by Ashford Colour Press, Gosport, Hampshire.

CONTENTS

1

The legal system

Introduction

An English trial is a peculiar process. The achievement of justice is not the main aim of the lawyers or of the judge. The lawyers are adversaries, arguing with every means at their disposal to win the case for the client they represent. If they exchanged clients, they would argue the opposing case with equal enthusiasm. The judge is not an inquisitor searching for truth and justice. He is there to apply the law, regardless of whether or not this leads to the fairest outcome. His job is to obey the rules and see that everyone else does the same.

Despite its adversarial nature, the English legal system seems to achieve justice as effectively as any other. Indeed, English business law, the subject of this text, is one of the United Kingdom's invisible exports. When two foreign businesses make a contract with each other, perhaps a German company buys goods from a Japanese company, it is common for a term of the contract to state that, in the event of a dispute, English law should apply.

Most people have little idea of how a lawyer argues a case. It is commonly assumed that the strongest argument in a lawyer's armoury is that a decision in favour of his or her client would be the fairest outcome to the case. In English law this is far from true.

Once the facts of a civil case have been established (and in many cases they are not even in dispute), the lawyers will try to persuade the judge that he or she is bound to decide in favour of their client, whether this is fair or not. The judge is, of course, in a superior position to the lawyers, being in charge of the proceedings. What is often not realised, however, is that judges are bound by very definite legal rules and that it is their duty to apply these rules, no matter how much they might wish not to do so.

These legal rules might well be contained in a statute, an Act of Parliament. Alternatively, they might be found in the growing body of European EU law. However, the heart of English law is the system of judicial precedent. As we shall see, the courts are arranged in a hierarchical structure and the system of precedent holds that judges in lower courts are bound to follow legal principles which were previously laid down in higher courts.

Most of the law examined in this text was made by judicial precedent rather than by statute. This is the case even though some of the areas of law have a strong statutory framework. Amongst other subjects, this book examines company law, partnership law and sale of goods law. The Companies Act 2006 provides the framework for company law, the Partnership Act 1890 for partnership law and the Sale of Goods Act 1979 for sale of goods law. These statutes are the basis of the law in the areas of law concerned. But, when studying company law, partnership law and sale of goods law, it is soon seen that the framework laid down by the various statutes is constantly refined by the process of judicial precedent. The higher-ranking courts make decisions as to how these statutes should be interpreted, and these decisions immediately become binding upon lower courts. In this way the law remains alive, constantly being refined and updated.

So, having seen that courts must follow legal rules, this chapter begins by considering where those rules are to be found.

Sources of law

Legislation

Legislation is the name given to law made by Parliament. It can either take the form of an Act of Parliament, such as the Sale of Goods Act 1979, or take the form of delegated legislation, such as the Unfair Terms in Consumer Contracts Regulations 1999. The difference lies in the way the legislation was created. To become a statute, a draft proposal of the legislation, known as a Bill, must pass through both Houses of Parliament and then gain the Royal Assent. Many Bills achieve this without significant alteration. Others have to be amended to gain parliamentary approval, and some Bills fail to become statutes at all. Once the Bill has received the Royal Assent, it becomes a statute which the courts must enforce.

Delegated legislation is passed in an abbreviated version of the procedure needed to pass a statute. Once delegated legislation has been passed, it ranks alongside a statute as a source of law which is superior to any precedent. The courts cannot declare a statute void, but they do have the power to declare delegated legislation void. However, this can be done only on the grounds that the delegated legislation tries to exercise powers greater than those conferred by the Act of Parliament which authorised the delegated legislation to be created.

Effect of legislation

A statute is the ultimate source of law. The theory of parliamentary sovereignty holds that the UK Parliament can pass any law which it wishes to pass and that no Parliament can bind later Parliaments in such a way as to limit their powers to legislate. In order to secure the UK's entry into what is now the European Union, Parliament had to pass the European Communities Act 1972. This statute accepted that in certain areas the UK had surrendered the right to legislate in a way which conflicted with European law. (European law is examined later in this chapter.) While the European Communities Act 1972 remains in force, Parliament is therefore no longer truly sovereign. However, parliamentary sovereignty is preserved, in theory at least, because Parliament still retains the power to pass a statute which would remove the limitations imposed by the European Communities Act. To pass such a statute would mean the UK leaving the European Union, and at the present time it seems most unlikely that this will happen.

Judges may not consider the validity of statutes, and they are compelled to apply them. In **British Railways Board *v* Pickin (1974)**, for example, a person whose land had been compulsorily purchased under the British Railways Act 1968 tried to argue that the statute was invalid, on the grounds that Parliament had been fraudulently misled into passing it. The House of Lords, now the Supreme Court, ruled that such an argument could not be raised in any court.

Furthermore, statutes remain in force indefinitely or until they are repealed. A statute loses none of its authority merely because it lies dormant for many years. In **R *v* Duncan (1944)**, for example, a defendant was convicted of fortune-telling under the Witchcraft Act 1735, even though the statute had long since fallen into disuse.

A judge, then, must apply a statute, and in the vast majority of cases he or she will find no difficulty in doing so. However, some statutes are ambiguous. When faced with an ambiguous statute a judge must decide which of the two or more possible interpretations to apply.

Rules of statutory interpretation

Literal rule of statutory interpretation

The literal rule of statutory interpretation says that words in a statute should be given their ordinary, literal meaning, no matter how absurd the result. An example of this rule can be seen in **IRC *v* Hinchy (1960)**, in which the House of Lords was considering the effect of the Income Tax Act 1952. Section 25 of the ITA stated that any tax avoider should pay a £20 fine and 'treble the tax which he ought to be charged under this Act'. Hinchy's lawyers argued that this meant a £20 fine and treble the amount of tax which had been avoided. Unfortunately for Hinchy, the House of Lords decided that the literal meaning of 'treble the tax which he ought to be charged under this Act' was that a tax avoider should pay a £20 fine and treble his whole tax bill for the year. The outcome of the case was that Hinchy had to pay £438, even though the amount he had avoided was only £14.

It is almost certain that the meaning applied by the House of Lords was not what Parliament had in mind when the Income Tax Act 1952 was passed. The statute was badly worded. The blame for this must lie with the parliamentary draftsmen. At the same time, however, it must be realised that they have a near impossible task. Skilled lawyers though these draftsmen are, they cannot possibly foresee every interpretation of the statutes they prepare. Once the statute has become law, every lawyer in the land might be looking for an interpretation which would suit his or her client. In **Hinchy's case** the Revenue lawyers, with typical ingenuity, spotted a literal meaning that had not been apparent before. They then managed to persuade the House of Lords judges that it was their duty to apply this meaning.

Judges who adhere to the literal rule approach do so in the belief that less harm is done by allowing a statute to operate in a way in which Parliament had not intended for a short time, until Parliament has time to pass another amending statute, than would be done by allowing the judges to take over the law-making role altogether, as they would be in danger of doing if they interpreted statutes in any way they saw fit.

The golden rule (or purposive approach)

Other judges, though, perhaps the majority, adopt the purposive approach to statutory interpretation. Using this approach, the judges use the golden rule to give the words in a statute their ordinary, literal meaning as far as possible, but only to the extent that this would not produce an absurd result.

In **R *v* Allen (1872)**, for example, the defendant's lawyers argued that although Allen had married two different women he could not be guilty of bigamy because the crime, as described in the Offences Against the Person Act 1861, was impossible to commit. Section 57 of the Act provides that 'whosoever, being married, shall marry any other person during the life of the former husband or wife', shall be guilty of bigamy. Allen's lawyers argued that this crime was impossible to commit because one of the qualifications for getting married is that you are not already married. Therefore, 'whosoever, being married, shall marry . . .' has already defined the impossible. They contended that the section should have read, 'whosoever, being married, shall *go through a ceremony of marriage* during the life of the former husband or wife' shall be guilty of bigamy.

If the judges in this case had used the literal rule they might well have acquitted. Unfortunately for Allen, they used the purposive approach and convicted him. They decided that the literal approach would have produced an absurd result, that they had not the slightest doubt as to what Parliament had meant when it passed the statute, and that Allen was therefore plainly guilty.

It is never possible to say in advance which rule a court will adopt, although the golden rule is currently more in favour than the literal rule. It is also commonly the case that a court uses elements of both approaches.

The mischief rule

The mischief rule holds that the judge can take into account what 'mischief' the statute set out to remedy. In **Smith v Hughes (1960)**, the Lord Chief Justice, Lord Parker, had to consider whether prostitutes who were soliciting from balconies and from behind windows were soliciting 'in the street' within the meaning of s. 1 of the Street Offences Act 1959. Using the mischief rule, he had little difficulty in deciding that they were. The prostitutes were not literally soliciting 'in the street', but their behaviour was just the kind which the Act sought to prevent.

The Court of Appeal recently applied the mischief rule in **Wolman v Islington LBC (2007)**. A GLC bye-law made it a criminal offence to park a vehicle with one or more wheels 'on any part of' a pavement. The claimant, a barrister, parked his motorbike on a stand in such a way that its wheels were above the pavement but not actually on it. He therefore claimed not to have committed the offence. Applying the mischief rule, the Court of Appeal held that the offence was committed if one or more of the bike's wheels were either on or over the pavement.

Whichever rule the judges adopt, there is no doubt that, in theory, a statute is the strongest source of law. A lawyer who has a statute on his or her side holds the most powerful card in the game. The lawyer may appear to be inviting the judge to apply the statute, but in effect is ordering the judge to do so. However, we shall shortly see that in practice even the power of a statute can be subject to EU law or subject to another very important statute, the Human Rights Act 1998.

Minor rules

Other, less important, rules of statutory interpretation are applied by all judges. The *ejusdem generis* rule (of the same kind rule) holds that general words which follow specific words must be given the same type of meaning as the specific words. For example, the Betting Act 1853 prohibited betting in any 'house, office, room or other place'. In **Powell v Kempton Racecourse Company (1899)**, the court held that the Act did not apply to a racecourse. The specific words 'house, office, room' were all indoor places, and so the general words 'or other place' had to be interpreted as applying only to indoor places.

The rule *expressio unius est exclusio alterius* (to express one thing is to exclude another) holds that if there is a list of specific words, not followed by any general words, then the statute applies only to the specific words mentioned. For example, in **R v Inhabitants of Sedgeley (1831)**, a statute which raised taxes on 'lands, houses, tithes and coal mines' did not apply to other types of mines.

Until relatively recently, a judge interpreting a statute was not allowed to consider the speeches which MPs made when the statute was being debated. However, in **Pepper v Hart (1993)**, a landmark decision, the House of Lords held that *Hansard*, which records the debates in Parliament, could in some circumstances be consulted if this was the only way to solve an ambiguity.

Judicial precedent

As already mentioned, the doctrine of judicial precedent holds that judges in lower courts are absolutely bound to follow decisions previously made in higher courts.

The hierarchy of the courts

The court structure is examined in more depth in a later chapter. (See Figures 17.1, 17.2 and 17.3.) For the purposes of understanding the system of precedent, we need only to know that the courts are arranged in a hierarchical structure and that there are five levels in the hierarchy.

The Supreme Court

The Supreme Court is the highest court in Great Britain and Northern Ireland. It replaced the House of Lords on 1 October 2009, when the 11 Law Lords who used to sit in the House of Lords became the first Supreme Court justices. The court now has a full complement of 12 justices. The Supreme Court justices, five of whom sit in most cases, are not bound by any previous precedents. Furthermore, their decisions are binding on all courts beneath them. In practice, the Supreme Court justices do tend to follow their own previous decisions unless there is a good reason not to. Supreme Court justices also hear appeals from some Commonwealth countries. When they sit in this capacity, the justices are known as the Privy Council. Technically, decisions of the Privy Council are not binding on English courts, but in practice they are usually regarded as having the same authority as Supreme Court decisions. In some particularly important cases seven, or even nine, Supreme Court justices sit, rather than the usual number of five. Seven Law Lords sat in **Pepper v Hart (1993)**, the effect of which we have already considered. In 2008, nine Law Lords sat in a case to decide whether foreign nationals suspected of terrorism could be held in prison without trial. The Supreme Court has no power to overturn a statute.

The Court of Appeal

The Court of Appeal is the next rung down the ladder. Its decisions are binding on all lower courts. They are also binding on future sittings of the Court of Appeal. In **Young v Bristol Aeroplane Co Ltd (1944)** it was decided that the Court of Appeal could refuse to follow its own previous decisions in only three circumstances:

- First, where there were two conflicting earlier Court of Appeal decisions, it could decide which one to follow and which one to overrule.
- Second, if a previous Court of Appeal decision had later been overruled by the House of Lords (now the Supreme Court), the Court of Appeal should not follow it.
- Third, a previous Court of Appeal decision should not be followed if it was decided through lack of care, ignoring some statute or other higher-ranking authority such as a previously decided House of Lords (now the Supreme Court) case.

Although the principles set out apply to both the Civil and Criminal Divisions of the Court of Appeal, it is generally recognised that the Criminal Division has slightly wider powers to depart from its own previous decisions. It can do so where justice would otherwise be denied to an appellant.

In terms of precedent, the Court of Appeal is the most important court. The Supreme Court hears only about 100 cases a year. The Court of Appeal hears several thousand.

However, the Supreme Court hears cases of greater public importance, and there is no doubt that its decisions have the greatest authority. Generally, the 38 Court of Appeal judges sit in courts of three judges. Sometimes there are five judges sitting, but this does not increase the extent to which the decision must be followed or give any greater power not to follow previous Court of Appeal decisions.

The Divisional Courts

There are three Divisional Courts of the High Court. These courts are appeal courts in which two or three High Court judges sit. Their decisions are binding on other Divisional Courts, subject to the **Young *v* Bristol Aeroplane Co Ltd** exceptions, and on all courts below. They are not binding on the Court of Appeal or the Supreme Court.

The High Court

Judges in the High Court are bound by decisions of the Supreme Court and the Court of Appeal. High Court decisions are binding upon all courts beneath the High Court. If there is only one judge sitting in a High Court case, the decision is not binding on other High Court judges. In a Divisional Court of the High Court more than one judge sits. The decisions of Divisional Courts are therefore binding on future sittings of the High Court.

Inferior courts

The decisions of inferior courts (the Crown Court, the county court and the magistrates' court) are not binding on any other courts. Judges sitting in these courts do not make precedents.

Figure 1.1 shows an overview of which courts bind which other courts.

The binding part of a case

The *ratio decidendi*, loosely translated from the Latin as 'the reason for the decision,' is the part of the case which is binding on other judges. It is the statement of law which the judge applied to the facts and which caused the case to be decided as it was. Despite the great length of most cases, the *ratio* is often quite simple. For example, the *ratio* of **Partridge *v* Crittenden (1968)** (the facts of which are set out in Chapter 2), might be that 'magazine advertisements, which describe goods and the price for which they will be sold, are not contractual offers but only invitations to treat'. As you will see when you consider the law of contract, this is a relatively straightforward statement of law.

Ultimately, the *ratio* of a case will be decided by future courts when they are considering whether or not they are bound by the case.

Partridge *v* Crittenden was decided by a Divisional Court of the High Court. It would not therefore be binding on the Supreme Court or on the Court of Appeal. However, later sittings of the High Court, as well as county courts, Crown Courts and magistrates' courts, would be compelled to follow it, unless they were confronted with a statute or higher-ranking precedent to the contrary.

Statements of law which did not form the basis of the decision are known as *obiter dicta* (other things said). Examples of *obiter dicta* can be found in most cases. For example, in **Partridge *v* Crittenden** Ashworth J said that the fact that the appellant's advertisement did not directly use the words 'offers for sale' made it less likely that Partridge was guilty of the crime with which he was charged – offering for sale a bramblefinch hen contrary to s. 6(1) of the Protection of Birds Act 1964. This statement of law is *obiter*, not *ratio*, because it was not the reason for deciding that Partridge was not guilty.

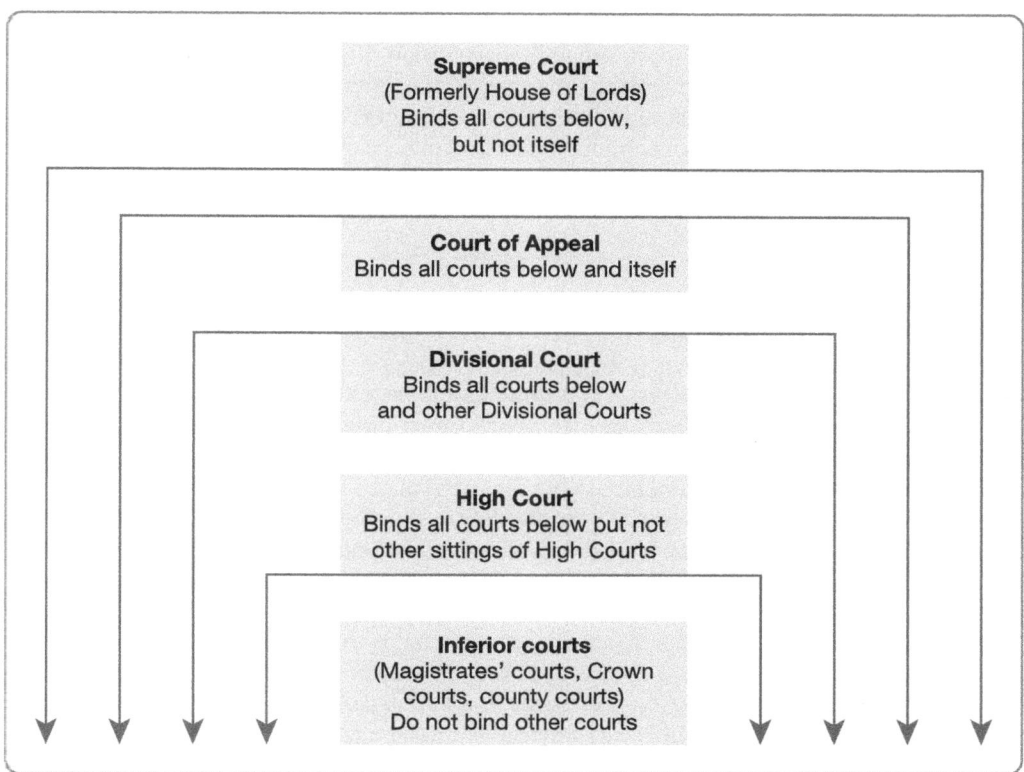

Figure 1.1 Which courts bind which other courts? An overview

Obiter dicta are not binding on judges, no matter what court they were made in. However, if the judges in the Supreme Court all express the same *obiter*, then a lower court judge would almost certainly follow the *obiter* in the absence of a precedent which he or she was compelled to follow.

Courts which hear appeals (appellate courts) usually have more than one judge sitting. Fortunately, it is an odd number of judges rather than an even number. A majority of judges will therefore decide for one of the parties or for the other. If the decision is unanimous, for instance the Court of Appeal decides 3:0 for the defendant, then the *ratio* of the case can be found in the judgments of any of the three judges. If the court decides for the defendant 2:1, then the *ratio* must be found in the decisions of the two judges in the majority. The decision of the judge in the minority may be persuasive as *obiter*, but it cannot form a *ratio* which will bind future courts.

Overruling and reversing

A higher-ranking court can **overrule** a *ratio* created by a lower-ranking court. The Supreme Court, for example, could overrule **Partridge v Crittenden** and hold that magazine advertisements stating the price at which goods will be sold are always offers. (This is most unlikely, it is merely an example.) If the Supreme Court were to overrule the decision, then the *ratio* of **Partridge v Crittenden** would be deemed to have been wrongly decided, and so it could no longer be a binding precedent. When overruling a case, the superior court specifically names the case and the rule of law being overruled. A statute may overrule the *ratio* of a particular case, but the statute will not mention the case concerned.

Many cases are **reversed** on appeal. Reversing is of no legal significance. It merely means that a party who appeals against the decision of an inferior court wins the appeal. No rule of law is necessarily changed. For example, in the fictitious case **Smith *v* Jones**, let us assume that Smith wins in the High Court and Jones appeals to the Court of Appeal. If Jones's appeal is allowed, for whatever reason, the Court of Appeal have reversed the judgment of the High Court.

Disadvantages of the system of precedent

There are currently 108 High Court judges, 38 Court of Appeal judges and 12 Supreme Court justices. Every sentence of every judgment they make might contain a precedent which would be binding on future judges. It is an impossible task for anyone to be aware of all of these potential precedents. In fact, so many High Court judgments are made that most are not even reported in the Law Reports.

Law reporting is not a government task but is carried out by private firms. The law reporters are barristers and they weed out the vast number of judgments which they consider to be unimportant. Even so, as students become aware when they step into a law library, the system of precedent does mean that English law is very bulky. There are hundreds of thousands of precedents and it can be very hard for a lawyer to find the law he or she is looking for.

Precedent suffers from another disadvantage, and that is that bad decisions can live on for a very long time. Before 1966, a House of Lords decision was binding on all other courts, including future sittings of the House of Lords. If a bad decision was made, then it could be changed only by Parliament, which was generally far too busy to interfere unless grave injustice was being caused. Sometimes a superior court says, *obiter*, that it thinks a binding precedent should be changed. However, the court cannot change the precedent until it hears a case where such a change would be the *ratio* of that case. The court cannot choose to hear such a case, it has to wait for such a case to be brought before it.

These disadvantages of the system of precedent are thought to be outweighed by two major advantages.

Advantages of the system of precedent

The first advantage is that the device of **distinguishing** a case means that the system of precedent is not entirely rigid. A judge who is lower down the hierarchy can refuse to follow a precedent by distinguishing it on its facts. This means that the judge will say that the facts of the case he or she is considering are materially different from the facts of the case by which he or she appears to be bound. This device of distinguishing gives a degree of flexibility to the system of precedent. It allows judges to escape precedents which they consider inappropriate to the case in front of them. For example, if a county court judge strongly wanted to hold that a television advertisement was an offer to sell, it is possible that he or she might distinguish **Partridge *v* Crittenden** on the grounds that a television advertisement is materially different from an advertisement in a magazine. Similarly, a county court judge might distinguish **Partridge *v* Crittenden** if the wording of an advertisement suggested that a definite contractual offer had been made.

The second and more important advantage of precedent is that it causes high quality decisions to be applied in all courts. Judges in appellate courts have the time and the experience to make very good decisions, often on difficult or philosophical matters. These decisions can then be applied by much busier and less experienced lower court judges, who do not have to consider whether the legal principles behind the decisions are right or wrong.

Until recently, judges were chosen only from the ranks of barristers. Now solicitors too can become judges. The Bar is a career, rather like acting, which has extremes of success, and very many talented young people enter it. If a barrister gains promotion and becomes a circuit judge, he or she will sit in the Crown Court or the county court. This is an honour and an achievement. Even so, the judge will make no law. He or she will supervise proceedings, decide who wins civil cases, award damages and sentence criminals. However, no matter how brilliant the judge's analysis of the law might be, it will not form a precedent.

High Court judges are a different matter. They make the law of England from the very first case in which they sit. Every word of their reported judgments is open to scrutiny by the other judges, by lawyers and by academics. If they were not very able, this would soon be noticed.

Almost 50 judges are promoted beyond the High Court to the Supreme Court or Court of Appeal. These days it seems unthinkable that any but the very able should go this far.

It is not only on the grounds of ability that the Supreme Court ought to come to very high quality decisions. Unlike the lower court judges, the justices who sit in the Supreme Court do not decide a case there and then. They read the facts of the case, and hear the arguments of the barristers, and then reserve their judgment. They talk to each other informally to see whether there is a consensus of opinion. If there is a consensus, one of the judges is chosen to write the judgment. If there is no consensus, the minority will write their own dissenting judgments. In a particularly difficult case the process of writing the judgment can take a very long time.

The system of precedent has a further advantage in that it can lead to certainty as to what the law is. If an appellate court makes a clear decision on a particular matter, then lawyers will advise their clients that the law on the matter is settled, and that there is no point in pursuing a contrary argument.

Alternatives to the system of precedent

As already stated, most other countries do not use a system of precedent. France, which is fairly typical of European countries, has a codified system of law known as a civil law system. All of the civil law is contained in the Civil Code, which originated in the late eighteenth century.

French judges, who choose a career as a judge early on, do not feel compelled to interpret the Code according to previous decisions until those decisions have for some time unanimously interpreted the Code in the same way.

Scotland has a mixed legal system. It is based on the civil law system, but has strong common law influences. In Scotland the system of precedent is used, but a precedent does not have quite the same force as in England.

European Union Law

In 1952 the European Coal and Steel Community was set up with the object of preventing any European country from building up stockpiles of steel and coal, the raw materials needed to wage war. Following the success of this, the European Economic Community (EEC) came into existence in 1957. The six original Member States signed the Treaty of Rome. This used to be called the EC Treaty but is now called the Treaty on the Functioning of the European Union. These six original countries were Germany, France, Italy, Belgium, the Netherlands and Luxembourg. Part of the founding philosophy of the Community was to provide an appropriate response to the Soviet Bloc countries to the East. However, the motivation was also economic, in that there seemed to be obvious advantages to the creation of a free market in Europe. The EEC is now known as the European Union (EU). At the time of writing, there are 27 Member States, the original six having been joined by Austria, Bulgaria, Cyprus, the Czech Republic, Denmark, Estonia, Finland, Greece, Hungary, Ireland, Latvia, Lithuania, Malta, Poland, Portugal, Romania, the Slovak Republic, Slovenia, Spain, Sweden and the United Kingdom. Croatia, Macedonia, Serbia and Turkey are candidate countries, meaning that their application to join has been officially accepted by the European Council. Five other Balkan states are potential candidate countries.

The United Kingdom joined the EU in 1973. In order to be admitted as a member, the UK Parliament passed the European Communities Act 1972. This statute agreed that Community law should be directly effective in UK courts.

In 1986 the EU consisted of 12 Member States, all of whom signed the Single European Act. This Act was designed to remove all barriers to a single market by 1992. In addition, the Act introduced a system of qualified majority voting in the European Council, thereby reducing the power of any single State to block developments.

In 1992 the Treaty on European Union (the Maastricht Treaty), was signed by all 15 States which were at that time Member States. The Treaty was more of a statement of political intention than a statement of precise obligations. It proposed co-operation on matters other than purely economic matters, envisaging the creation of a European Union with the three following pillars: the European Community; a common foreign and security policy; and co-operation in the fields of justice and home affairs. The Treaty also envisaged that economic and monetary union would be achieved in three stages. However, the UK and Denmark opted out of the third stage. The UK also opted out of participation in the social chapter, which set out employment and social rights.

The Treaty of Amsterdam was signed in October 1997 and came into force in May 1999. This Treaty aimed for closer political co-operation between Member States. It incorporated much of the Justice and Home Affairs pillar into the original EC Treaty and gave Member States a greater power to veto proposals which would affect their vital national interests.

The Treaty of Lisbon was signed by all EU leaders in December 2007. However, it could not become effective until all Member States ratified it. In June 2008 Irish voters rejected the Treaty in a referendum. In October 2009, at the second time of asking, they voted in favour of the Treaty. The Treaty became effective in December 2009, although other EU countries have not asked their voters to ratify it by way of referendum.

The Treaty of Lisbon amended the existing treaties, incorporating them into a new treaty called the Treaty on the Functioning of the European Union. This has four main aims: to make the EU more democratic and transparent; to make it more efficient; to promote rights, values, freedom, solidarity and security; and to make the EU an actor on the global stage.

The first of these aims involves increasing the power of the European Parliament so that it will be placed on an equal footing with the Commission. As regards most EU legislation, the Parliament and the Commission will approve legislation using a co-decision procedure. A greater role in making EU law will be given to national parliaments in areas where they can achieve better results than the EU. A Citizens' Initiative will allow 1 million citizens from several Member States to ask the Commission to introduce new policies. The relationship between the EU and Member States will be clarified, and States which wish to do so will be allowed to withdraw from the EU.

Great efficiency will be achieved by extending qualified majority voting. From 2014, a qualified majority will be achieved if a dual majority of 55 per cent of Member States, and Member States representing 65 per cent of the EU's population, vote in favour. The EU Commission will be reduced in size and a new President of the European Council will be elected by national governments for a period of office lasting two and a half years. The European Council will be separate from the Council of Ministers, the leaders of which will continue to be elected on a six-month rotating basis. The European Council will not have legislative powers but will guide policy.

The promotion of rights, values, freedom, solidarity and security will be achieved by guaranteeing the principles set out in the Charter of Fundamental Rights, and by giving them legal force. This charter set out principles of human rights to be applied throughout the EU but at present it has no legal force. In addition, the EU will be given a greater role in fighting crime and preventing terrorism. The EU will be made a stronger actor on the global stage by creating a High Representative for Foreign Affairs and Security Policy, and by encouraging the EU to act as a single legal personality.

The provisions of the Treaty of Lisbon will be introduced gradually, and may take about ten years to become fully adopted.

The institutions of the EU

The original EEC Treaty set up four main institutions. These institutions are now known as: the Council of the European Communities; the European Commission; the European Parliament; and the European Court of Justice.

The Council of the European Communities

The Council of the European Communities, generally known as the Council, is not a permanent body. It consists at any given time of the President of the European Commission and one Minister from the government of each Member State. Which Government Ministers will constitute the Council of Ministers depends upon the nature of the measures which the Council is considering. For example, if the measures relate to agriculture, then it will be the relevant Ministers of Agriculture. Often the Council is made up of Heads of Government or the Member States' Foreign Ministers. Up to four times a year the Presidents or Prime Ministers of all of the countries along with the President of the European Commission, hold meetings as the 'European Council'. At these meetings overall EU policy is set and issues which could not be settled at a lower level are settled.

The Council is the main policy-making body of the EU. It passes legislation, co-ordinates EU policy, concludes international agreements, approves the EU budget and develops the EU Common Foreign and Security Policy. When the Council passes legislation, generally in conjunction with the European Parliament, it does so under a system of qualified majority voting. However, a Treaty might require unanimity for votes on certain matters, such as the common and foreign security policy, police and judicial co-operation in criminal matters, asylum and immigration policy, economic and social cohesion policy or taxation. Under this system each country is allocated a certain number of votes in relation to its population. The United Kingdom is one of four countries having the maximum of 29 votes. Malta has the fewest votes, with just three. There are 345 votes in total. A qualified majority is reached in two circumstances. First, if 255 (73.9 per cent) votes are in favour. This means that 91 votes can defeat a proposal and so at least four countries must vote against. Second, if a simple majority of Member States approve. However, if a matter which was not based on a proposal from the Commission is being voted upon, a two-thirds majority of Member States must approve. Additionally, any Member State can require confirmation that votes representing at least 62 per cent of the total population of the EU were in favour. If it is discovered that this figure was not reached, then the proposal voted upon will not be regarded as having been accepted.

Article 11 of the Treaty of Amsterdam gives effect to the Luxembourg Accord and allows any Member State to argue that unanimity, rather than a qualified majority vote, should be required on any particular proposal. When such an argument is raised, the Council will delay taking a vote in order to allow the dissenting State to gain the support of other Member States. However, if it is unsuccessful in this, the issues will in any event be resolved by a qualified majority vote.

The European Commission

Twenty-seven individual commissioners are appointed by the Member States to serve in a full-time capacity for a term of five years. When these commissioners act collectively they are known as the European Commission, which is generally abbreviated to the Commission. Each commissioner also has individual responsibility for a particular matter, such as agriculture. The Commission is supported by large executive and administrative systems. The commissioners are expected to act completely independently of their Member States, but in practice tend to guard the independence of their Member States. They are selected on political grounds, and all UK commissioners have previously played a leading role in UK politics.

The most powerful position in the EC is the President of the Commission. The President is the figurehead of the EC and has a strong political influence upon it. The Council selects the President and the appointment must then be approved by the European Parliament.

The Commission is involved in broad policy-making. It prepares specific proposals to be submitted to the Council. It also manages and implements EU policies and the EU budget, it acts jointly with the Court of Justice to enforce EU law and it acts as the EU's representative when dealing with other countries. It is politically accountable to the European Parliament, which can demand that the whole Commission resigns. Individual commissioners can be forced to resign if the President of the Commission demands this and the other commissioners agree. In addition to its major roles, the Commission also commissions research and prepares reports on matters which concern the Community and negotiates with non-Member States on these matters. It also prepares the draft Community budget.

The European Parliament

Members of the European Parliament (MEPs) are elected directly by Member States, using a system of proportional representation. Elections are held every five years. The UK elects 72 out of the 736 MEPs who make up the Parliament. The MEPs do not sit in blocks representing their Member States, but in blocks representing seven Europe-wide political groups. It is perhaps surprising that the European Parliament does not have the power to initiate and pass legislation on its own. Generally, the power to pass legislation is shared by the Parliament and the Council. One of the Parliament's most significant powers is to approve or amend the EC budget. The Commission prepares a draft budget, which is submitted to the Council and then to the Parliament. The Parliament must approve, amend or reject the budget within 45 days.

The Parliament must approve the Commission when it is first appointed and must also approve the new President. It must also approve the accounts of the Commission and new appointments to the Commission. Article 234 of the Treaty on the Functioning of the European Union (TFEU) gives the Parliament the power to pass a vote of censure to dismiss the Commission. Such a vote must be passed by a two-thirds majority. In January 1999 a vote to remove the Commission on account of nepotism and corruption failed. Two hundred and thirty-two MEPs voted for removal, 293 voted against. However, the whole of the Commission resigned in March 1999, on publication of a report made by an investigative committee.

Initially the Parliament had few real powers. It had to be consulted about EC legislation but had no powers to block any legislation. The EU Parliament still does not have the power to legislate in the way that the UK Parliament has. It passes law by 'co-decision' with the Council. On many matters the Parliament and the Council have equal standing, but on others the Council has the power to legislate after consulting the Parliament. The Parliament also has the power to ask the Commission to put forward proposals for legislation.

The European Court of Justice

The European Court of Justice (ECJ), which sits in Luxembourg, is made up of 27 judges. These judges are assisted by advocates-general. The judges and advocates are appointed by common consent of the Member States and hold office for a six-year term which may be renewed.

The decisions of the court are signed by all the judges, without any indication that some may have dissented. It is comparatively rare for the full court to sit. Eighty per cent of cases are referred to one of the six chambers, where either three or five judges sit. The number of judges sitting is always odd, so that a majority decision can always be reached. The more important the issues involved, the greater the number of judges sitting. The judgments of the Court are available free on its website, but cases typically take between 18 months and two years to be heard.

The advocates-general must act with complete impartiality and independence, in open court, making reasoned submissions on cases brought before the Court. They do not therefore argue the case for one or other of the sides involved. Each case has an advocate-general assigned to it. The advocate-general makes a summary of the facts, an analysis of all the relevant Community law and a recommendation as to what the decision of the Court should be. The parties cannot comment on this and the judges deliberate upon it in secret. The Court has no obligation to agree with the advocate-general's recommendation.

When ready to vote, the most junior judges vote first and then the other judges vote in order of reverse seniority. The Court does not use a system of precedent: it can and does depart from its own previous decisions.

Certain matters may be referred to the Court of First Instance rather than to the European Court of Justice. These matters tend to concern competition law or cases brought by private individuals. The Court of First Instance operates in a very similar way to the way in which the ECJ operates. There is an automatic right of appeal on a point of law from the Court of First Instance to the ECJ.

Jurisdiction of the ECJ

Apart from hearing appeals from the Court of First Instance, the ECJ has three separate areas of jurisdiction. First, it can express an authoritative opinion on EC law, if requested to do so by a national court, so that EU law is applied uniformly across the EU. Once the ruling has been made by the ECJ, the case returns to the court which asked for the ruling so that that court can apply the ruling. Article 267 TFEU allows a national court to request an authoritative ruling as to three types of matters: the interpretation of EU legislation; the validity and interpretation of acts of institutions of the Community; and on the interpretation of statutes of bodies established by an act of the Council, where those statutes so provide. Any national court or tribunal may refer a matter within Article 267 to the ECJ if it thinks this necessary to give judgment. Most of the ECJ's work involves preliminary rulings. The ruling is sought by the court, not by the parties to the case. Although a national court has a discretion to seek a preliminary ruling, a court of final appeal has an obligation to do so where a relevant point of EU law is at issue and where there has been no previous interpretation of the point by the ECJ. However, there is no such obligation where the point is so obvious as not to require a ruling.

The second area of jurisdiction arises under Articles 263 and 264 TFEU, which allows the ECJ to review the legality of acts done by the European Parliament or other Community institutions. The ECJ can also review a community institution's failure to act. This review process is similar to the process of judicial review whereby the High Court ensures that the Government and others do not exceed their powers.

The third area of jurisdiction arises under Article 258, which allows the ECJ to bring actions against Member States to make sure that they fulfil their Community obligations. Article 259 allows Member States to take other Member States to the ECJ for failure to live up to their Treaty obligations.

Sources of EU law

Applicability and effect

In order to understand the effect of EU law, it is necessary to understand the distinction between the terms 'direct applicability' and 'direct effect'. If EU legislation is directly applicable, it automatically forms part of the domestic law of Member States, without those States needing to do anything to bring the law in. However, this would not necessarily mean that individuals could directly rely upon the legislation in the domestic courts of their own countries. In order for such reliance to be possible, the legislation would have to be capable of having direct effect. Where EU legislation has direct effect an individual can directly rely upon the legislation, either as a cause of action or as a defence, in the domestic courts of his or her country. The Articles of the Treaty on the Functioning of the European Union are always directly applicable, as are EU Regulations, but, as we have seen, this does not necessarily mean that they have direct effect.

No EU legislation can have direct effect unless it satisfies the criteria laid down by the European Court of Justice in **Van Gend en Loos v Nederlands Administratie der Belastingen (1963)**. These criteria will be satisfied only if the legislation is sufficiently clear, precise and unconditional, and if the legislation intends to confer rights. Many Treaty Articles do not meet these criteria as they are mere statements of aspiration. Even if Community legislation does meet the **Van Gend** criteria, it may have only direct vertical effect, rather than direct horizontal effect. If it has direct vertical effect it can be invoked by an individual only against the State and against emanations of the State, such as health authorities. A provision which has direct horizontal effect can be invoked against other individuals as well as against the State and emanations of the State.

If an EU law does not have direct effect it might nevertheless have indirect effect. An indirectly effective EU law could not be enforced in national courts. However, these courts would be obliged to interpret their own national law, to the extent that this is possible, in such a way that it did not conflict with the indirectly effective EU law.

Treaty Articles

The Treaty on the Functioning of the European Union has over 350 Articles. These are directly applicable. Whether or not a Treaty Article has direct effect depends first upon whether it satisfies the criteria in **Van Gend**. As we have seen, some will not satisfy these criteria as they are merely statements of aspiration. Some of the Articles are much more significant than others. Article 157 TFEU requires Member States to ensure and subsequently maintain the application of the principle that men and women should receive equal pay for equal work, and the effect of this Article has been highly significant.

Some Treaty Articles, like Article 157, have both direct horizontal and vertical effect, others have only direct vertical effect. Whether or not they have direct horizontal effect will depend upon the wording of the Article and the interpretation of the Article by the ECJ. For example, Article 34 TFEU, which prohibits restrictions on the free movement of goods, only has direct vertical effect. It can therefore only be invoked by an individual against the State or against an emanation of the State. One private company could not invoke Article 34 against another private company which was not an emanation of the State.

Regulations

Regulations are binding in their entirety and are directly applicable in all Member States without any further implementation by Member States. Regulations have direct effect, sometimes both vertically and horizontally, providing the **Van Gend** criteria are satisfied. Even if these criteria are not satisfied, a Regulation may have **indirect effect**. This means that, although an individual cannot invoke the Regulation, the courts of Member States are bound to take account of it.

Directives

Directives, which are addressed to the governments of Member States, are not directly applicable. It is therefore left to each individual Member State to implement the objectives of the Directive in a way that is best suited to its own particular political and economic culture. All Directives are issued with an implementation date and Member States are under a duty to implement by this date. If the Directive is not implemented by the due date, the Commission has the power to take proceedings against the Member State in question.

Before the implementation date has been reached, Directives have no effect at all. However, in the **Wallonie ASBL case (1997)** the European Court of Justice held that a Member State should not enact legislation or implement measures that significantly conflict with the objectives of a Directive that has yet to meet its implementation date. Generally, the UK Government will implement EC Directives by delegated legislation. Several statutory instruments which we consider in this book, such as the Commercial Agents (Council Directive) Regulations 1993, were enacted to give effect to Directives. (It is slightly confusing that these statutory instruments are usually called Regulations, given that EC Regulations are a quite different matter.) Once an EC Directive has been implemented by UK legislation then, obviously, an individual can invoke the domestic legislation against another individual. For example, the Commercial Agents (Council Directive) Regulations 1993 are regularly invoked by individuals against other individuals.

There can, however, be a problem if the UK Government either fails to implement a Directive at all, or does not implement the Directive properly. Once the implementation date has been reached, whether or not an unimplemented Directive has direct effect depends first upon whether the Directive satisfies the **Van Gend** criteria, and second upon the relationship between the parties involved. Where the parties to a legal action are in a vertical relationship (for example, patient and health authority), the Directive is capable of having direct effect. Where the parties are in a horizontal relationship (for example, a consumer suing a shop), the Directive does not have direct effect. In other words, Directives which should have been implemented are capable of having direct vertical effect, but not direct horizontal effect. (This can mean that a person employed by an emanation of the State, such as a worker in the NHS, night have more rights against his employer than a person employed by a person who is not an emanation of the State.) However, when dealing with a case between two individuals, the domestic courts are under a duty to try, as far as possible, to interpret the domestic legislation so as to give effect indirectly to the objectives of the Directive. In situations where it is not possible for the domestic court to give direct or indirect effect to an EC Directive, the remedy of last resort is for the aggrieved individual to sue the Member State for failure to implement. If found to be in breach, the Member State could be ordered to pay compensation to the aggrieved individual.

In **Francovich and Bonifaci v Republic of Italy (1993)** the ECJ held that an individual could be compensated on account of a Directive not having been implemented if certain criteria were satisfied. **Brasserie du Pêcheur SA v Germany (1996)** subsequently established that the three necessary criteria are as follows. First, the rule of law in question must confer rights upon individuals. Second, the breach must be sufficiently serious. Third, there must be a direct causal link between the breach and the damage.

The legal effect of the Treaties, Regulations and Directives is shown in Figure 1.2.

Decisions

Decisions are addressed to one or more Member States, to individuals or to institutions. They are binding in their entirety, without the need for implementation by Member States, but only on those to whom they were addressed. In practice, decisions are of little practical importance.

Recommendations and opinions

The Commission has the power to make recommendations and opinions. These have no binding legal force. However, where a Member State passes legislation to comply with a decision or an opinion, a national court may refer a case to the ECJ to see whether or not the decision or opinion applies and how it should be interpreted.

Supremacy of EU law

EU law can only be effective if it overrides national law. If every Member State were free to pass legislation which conflicted with EU legislation, the EU would be rendered ineffective. In **Costa v ENEL (1964)** the ECJ stated that the Treaty on Rome, as amended, had become an integral part of the legal systems of Member States and that the courts of Member States were bound to apply the Treaty. It also stated that Member States had, by signing the Treaty, limited their sovereign rights, within limited areas, and created a body of law which bound both their citizens and themselves. The case specifically decided that Italian legislation which was incompatible with Community law, and which had been passed after Italy had signed the Treaty, could have no effect.

In **R v Secretary of State for Transport, ex parte Factortame (No. 2) (1991)**, Spanish companies sought judicial review of the Merchant Shipping Act 1988, which they claimed breached two Articles of the EC Treaty. The companies asked for an injunction to suspend that part of the Act which was in breach of the relevant Treaty Article. The House of Lords held that injunctions could not be effective against the Crown and refused to grant the injunction. However, the case was referred to the ECJ, which held that UK limitations on the availability of remedies should be overruled and that the injunctions should be available. Subsequently, the House of Lords immediately suspended the operation of the offending part of the Act. A few years after **Factortame**, in **Equal Opportunities Commission v Secretary of State for Employment (1994)**, the House of Lords suspended the operation of a section of employment legislation on the grounds that it was in breach of the EU Equal Treatment legislation. However, it should be noted that this power of UK courts to suspend

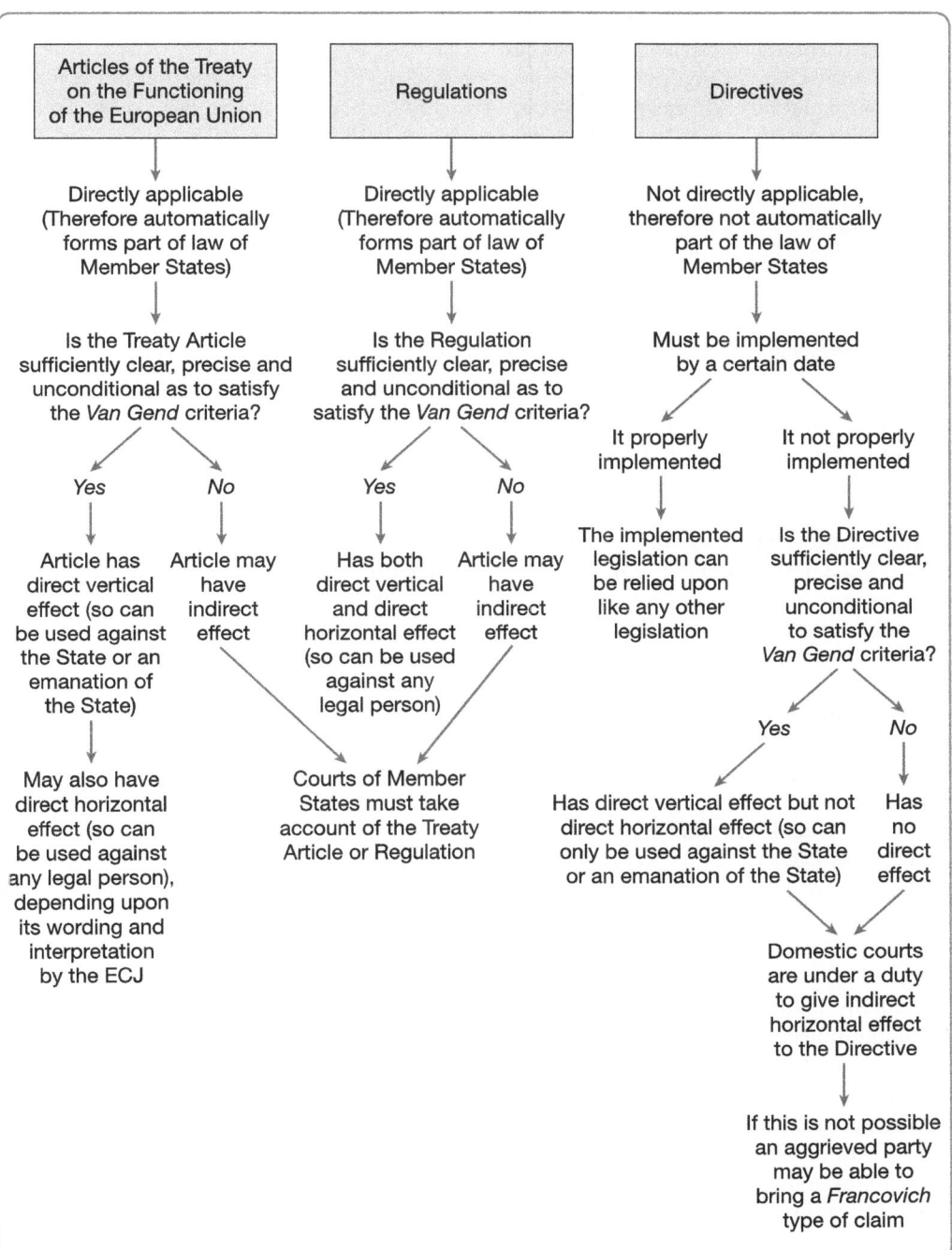

Figure 1.2 The legal effect of Treaty Acticle, Regulations and Decisions

conflicting domestic legislation will only be used sparingly in cases involving serious breaches of directly effective EU legislation.

Whilst the United Kingdom remains a member of the EU, it is arguable that it has surrendered parliamentary sovereignty. However, two points should be noted. First, other Treaties such as those which provided that the United States had direct command over US soldiers based in the United Kingdom, have at some time or other meant that the United Kingdom did not have true parliamentary sovereignty. Second, the UK Parliament could vote to repeal the European Communities Act 1972 and leave the EU. It must be said, however, that this option becomes increasingly unlikely and would become virtually impossible if full monetary union were ever achieved.

The Human Rights Act 1998

First, it should be noted that the European Convention on Human Rights is not a creation of the EU. The Convention was drawn up in 1950, before the EU was created. The United Kingdom ratified the Convention in 1951. Before the Human Rights Act 1998 (HRA 1998) came into effect, in October 2000, the Convention could not be directly enforced in the UK courts. It could be enforced only by taking a case to the European Court of Human Rights in Strasbourg.

Section 2 of the Human Rights Act 1998 now requires any court or tribunal which is considering a question which has arisen in connection with a Convention right to take into account any decision of the European Court of Human Rights. This court sits in Strasbourg and is quite separate from the European Court of Justice, which sits in Luxembourg. Section 2 of the Act preserves parliamentary sovereignty because the UK courts merely have to take into account decisions of the European Court of Human Rights. The UK courts are not absolutely bound by these decisions. This point was emphasised by Lord Phillips, the President of the Supreme Court, in **R v Horncastle (2009)**. He said that when senior UK judges had concerns about whether a decision of a Strasbourg Court sufficiently appreciated or accommodated particular aspects of the UK process, a UK court could decline to follow the decision of the Strasbourg Court, giving reasons for this course of action. Lord Phillips thought that, if this happened, the Strasbourg Court would then be given the opportunity to reconsider the aspect of its decision which had caused the problem.

Section 3 HRA 1998 requires that all legislation is read and given effect in a way which is compatible with the Convention rights, but only in so far as it is possible to do this. Any precedent-making court has the power in any legal proceedings to make a declaration of incompatibility, stating that any legislation is incompatible with Convention rights. However, such a declaration would not invalidate the legislation in question. It would give the relevant minister the option to revoke or amend the legislation. The minister could, however, leave the incompatible legislation in place. If the European Court of Human Rights delivers an adverse ruling the relevant minister has the same powers to revoke, amend or leave in place the incompatible legislation. Any court can declare delegated legislation, but not statutes, invalid on the grounds of incompatibility. However, this is not the case if the Parent Act, which authorised the legislation in question, provides that the legislation should prevail even if it is incompatible. Whenever a new Bill is introduced into Parliament, s. 19 HRA 1998 says that the relevant minister must make a statement to Parliament, before the second reading, declaring that the legislation either is compatible or is not. If the minister states that the legislation is incompatible, he or she must state that the Government intends to proceed with it anyway. The minister does not need to state the way in which the legislation is incompatible.

Section 6(1) HRA 1998 provides that it is unlawful for a public authority to act in a way which is inconsistent with a Convention right, unless the public authority could not have acted differently as a result of a UK Act of Parliament. This section will have a major effect on many UK businesses, as a public authority is defined as including persons whose functions are functions of a public nature. It follows that businesses such as private schools, private nursing homes and private security firms will all be regarded as public authorities for the purposes of the HRA 1998. If a public authority breaches a Convention right, a victim of the breach may bring legal proceedings against it for breach of a new public tort.

The rights conferred by the Convention are as follows.

- The right to life (Art. 2).
- The right not to be subjected to torture or inhumane or degrading punishment (Art. 3).
- The right not to be held in slavery or servitude or required to perform forced or compulsory labour (Art. 4).
- The right to liberty and security of the person (Art. 5).
- The right to a fair trial (Art. 6).
- The right not to be convicted of a criminal offence which was created after the act was committed (Art. 7).
- The right to respect for a person's private and family life, home and correspondence (Art. 8).
- The right to freedom of thought, conscience and religion (Art. 9).
- The right to freedom of expression (Art. 10).
- The right to freedom of peaceful assembly and to freedom of association with others (Art. 11).
- The right to marry and form a family (Art. 12).
- The right to have the Convention applied without discrimination (Art. 14).

Article 15 allows departure from the Convention in time of war. Articles 1 and 13 have not been incorporated into UK law.

The United Kingdom has also agreed to be bound by protocols, which give the right to peaceful enjoyment of possessions, and outlaw the death penalty.

Forty-seven States have signed the Convention on Human Rights and there are 47 judges in the plenary Court of Human Rights, one judge representing each State. This plenary court almost always delegates the hearing of complaints to Chambers. Each Chamber has seven judges plus an additional judge who represents the State against which the complaint is being made. The Chambers themselves set up Committees of three judges. These Committees sift through complaints and dismiss as soon as possible those which are completely unfounded. The European Court of Human Rights is very much a court of last resort. Article 35 of the Convention requires an applicant to the court to prove four things:

(1) that the complaint involves a breach of the Convention by a country which has ratified it;

(2) that the breach happened within that country's jurisdiction;

(3) that all domestic remedies have been exhausted; and

(4) the application has been made within six months of these being exhausted.

However, if domestic remedies are unsatisfactory, then the court can deem them to have been exhausted. The court cannot enforce its judgments but can order 'just satisfaction' amounting to the payment of compensation and costs. The court does not use a system of precedent. The Human Rights Act 1998 has already had a significant impact on many areas of UK law. Both government ministers and senior judges who supported the passing of the HRA 1998 have recently said that it is being applied too widely, both by judges and those in official positions.

Civil law and criminal law

The distinction between civil and criminal liability is fundamental to English law. The courts themselves are divided into civil courts and criminal courts, and the two sets of courts have quite different purposes. The civil courts are designed to compensate people who have been injured by others. The criminal courts are designed to punish people who have committed a crime.

Table 1.1 shows the essential differences between civil and criminal law.

Despite the differences shown in Table 1.1, it is quite possible that the same wrongful act will give rise to both civil and criminal liability. For example, if a motorist injures a pedestrian by dangerous driving, then both a crime and a tort (a civil wrong) will have been committed.

The State might prosecute the driver for the crime of dangerous driving, and if the driver is found guilty he or she will be punished. The driver would probably be banned from driving, and might also be fined or imprisoned. The injured pedestrian might sue the driver in the civil courts for the tort of negligence. If the driver is found to have committed the tort, then he or she will have to pay damages to compensate for the pedestrian's injuries.

Table 1.1 The differences between civil and criminal law

	Criminal	Civil
Purpose of the case	To punish a wrongdoer	To compensate a person injured by an unlawful act
The parties	The state prosecutes a defendant, e.g. **R v Smith**	An individual (the claimant) sues an individual (the defendant), e.g. **Smith v Jones**
The outcome	The defendant is either acquitted or convicted	The claimant either wins the case or does not
The consequences	If convicted, the defendant will be sentenced	If the claimant wins, he or she will be awarded a remedy
The courts	The case will first be heard in the magistrates' court or the Crown Court	The case will first be heard in either the county court or the High Court
The facts	Decided by the magistrates or by a jury	Decided by the judge
The law	Decided and applied by the judge or by the magistrate, on the advice of the clerk to the court	Decided and applied by the judge
Burden and standard of proof	The prosecution must prove the defendant's guilt, beyond reasonable doubt	The claimant must prove his or her case on a balance of probabilities
Examples	Murder, theft, false trade descriptions, misleading price indications	Negligence, trespass, breach of contract, disputes as to ownership of property

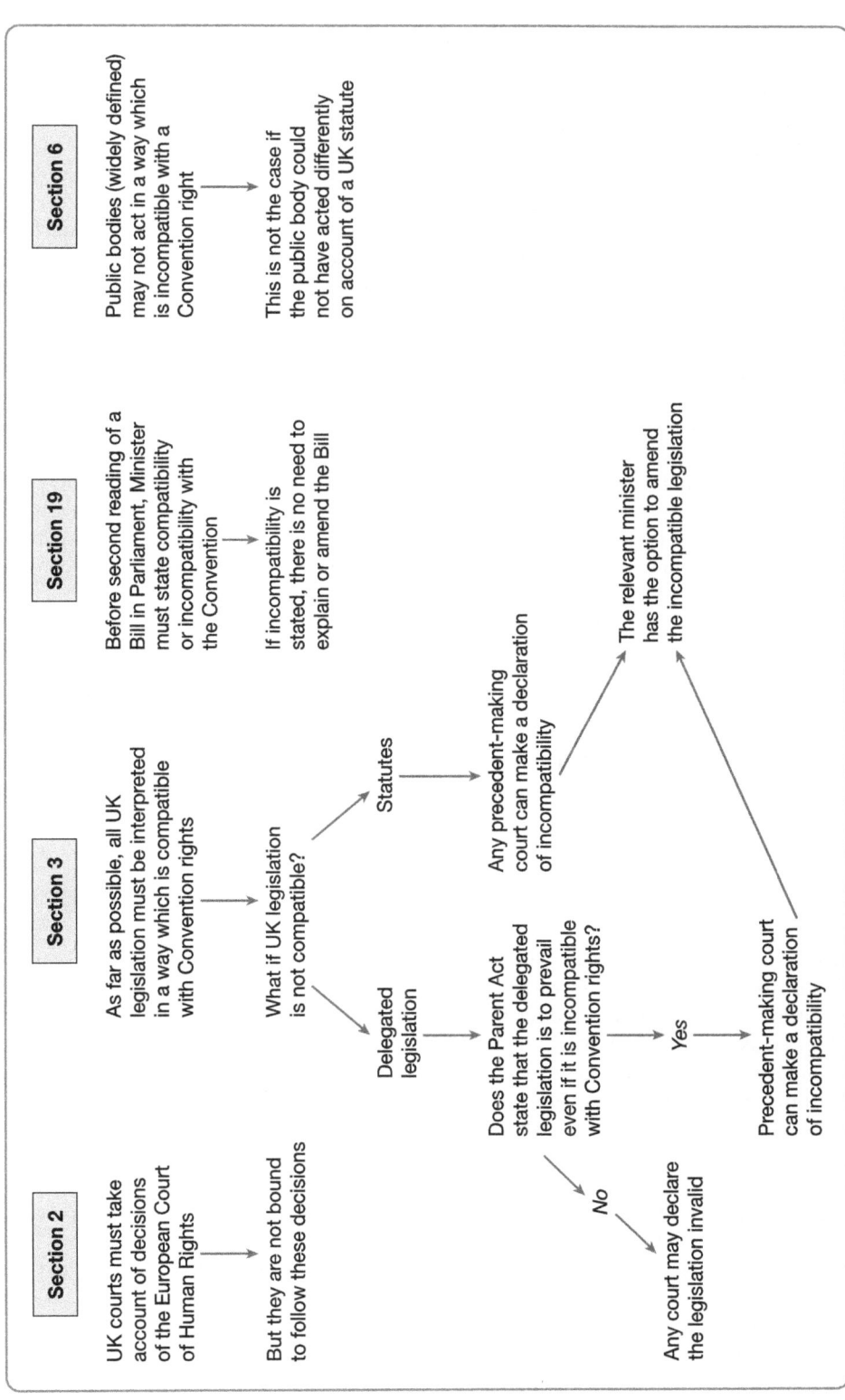

Figure 1.3 An outline of the effect of the Human Rights Act 1998

The different functions of the civil and criminal courts can be further demonstrated if we consider what would have happened if the driver's behaviour had been much worse.

Let us now assume that the driver was very drunk, driving very badly, and that the pedestrian was killed. Under the criminal law the driver would be charged with the more serious offences of causing death by reckless driving and of driving with excess alcohol. The purpose of charging the driver with these more serious offences would be to punish him or her more severely. If convicted, the driver would almost certainly be imprisoned.

However, the civil courts would not order the defendant to pay more damages merely on account of his or her behaviour having been worse. In fact, if the pedestrian was killed, the damages might well be less than if he or she had been badly injured. Damages payable to a pedestrian injured so badly that nursing care would be required for the rest of his or her life might well exceed £1 million. They would take account of the cost of the claimant's nursing care, as well as pain and suffering and loss of earnings. If the driver was killed instantly, no damages would be paid in respect of nursing care or pain and suffering. A pedestrian who was not injured at all could bring no claim for damages.

This example demonstrates the different purposes which the two sets of courts are trying to achieve. The criminal courts are designed to punish bad behaviour. The worse the behaviour, the greater the punishment. Once it has been established that the defendant's behaviour has been such as to incur civil liability, the civil courts are not concerned with the heinousness of the defendant's behaviour. They are concerned with the extent of the injuries or losses which the claimant has suffered.

Crimes which cause injury to a victim will also give rise to a civil action. However, 'victimless' crimes will not. Possessing a controlled drug, for example, is a crime, but the fact of the defendant's possessing the drug does not directly injure anyone else.

Most civil wrongs are not crimes. A person who breaks a contract or trespasses on another's property might well be sued, but will not have committed a crime. Notices on private land which state that 'trespassers will be prosecuted' are misstating the law. Trespassers commit a tort and might be sued for it. However, they generally do not commit a crime and so they cannot be prosecuted.

Common law and equity

A hundred years after the Norman conquest, King Henry II began the process of applying one set of legal rules, the common law, throughout the country. The decisions of judges began to be recorded, and subsequent judges followed them, in order to provide a uniform system of law known as the common law.

The common law grew to have several defects and, to counter these, people seeking a remedy could petition the Chancellor, the highest-ranking clergyman, to ask him to intercede. This justice dispensed by the Chancellor, and later by judges under the Chancellor's control, became known as equity.

Equity was not designed to be a rival system to the common law system. Originally, it was intended to supplement the common law, to fill in the gaps. Gradually, however, equity developed into a rival system.

The Judicature Acts 1873–75 merged the two systems of law. These Acts created the modern court structure, designed to apply common law and equity side by side in the same courts. Even today, however, equity still has an influence on English law. The administration of law and equity was fused, but the separate rules of each branch of the law lived on.

From a student's point of view it is sufficient to say that certain matters are still 'equitable' and that there are two main consequences of this. First, certain remedies are equitable in nature and are therefore awarded only if the court considers it equitable to award them. Second, some relationships, such as the relationship between partners in a firm, are governed by equitable principles and therefore require very high standards of honesty and openness.

Features of the English legal system

The English legal system is unlike that of any other European country.

Antiquity and continuity

English law has evolved, without any major upheaval or interruption, over many hundreds of years. The last successful invasion of England occurred in 1066, when King William and his Normans conquered the country. King William did not impose Norman law on the conquered Anglo-Saxons, but allowed them to keep their own laws. These laws were not uniform throughout the kingdom. Anglo-Saxon law was based on custom, and in different parts of the country different customs prevailed.

In the second half of the twelfth century, one set of legal rules, known as 'the common law', began to be applied throughout England. Since that time, English law has evolved piecemeal. For this reason the English legal system retains a number of peculiarities and anomalies which find their origins in medieval England.

English law does not become inoperative merely because of the passage of time. When we study the law of contract we shall see that two ancient cases, **Pinnel's case (1602)** and **Lampleigh v Brathwaite (1615)**, are still important precedents. Although these cases have been refined and developed by subsequent cases, there would be no reason why a modern lawyer should not cite them in court. In the same way, statutes remain in force indefinitely or until they are repealed.

Occasionally, a litigant springs a major surprise by invoking an ancient law. In 1818 the defendant in **Ashford v Thornton (1818)**, who was accused of murder, claimed the right to have his case settled by battle. Trial by battle had been a method of resolving disputes shortly after the Norman Conquest (as described below) but had fallen into disuse before the end of the thirteenth century. In **Ashford v Thornton** the offer of trial by battle was declined and so the defendant was discharged. The Appeals of Murder Act 1819 was hurriedly passed. Until Parliament passed this Act, trial by battle still existed as a possible means of settling some types of legal disputes.

The adversarial system of trial

The English system of trial is adversarial. This means that the lawyers on either side are adversaries, who 'fight' each other in trying to win judgment for their clients. The judge supervises the battle between the lawyers, but does not take part. Recent reforms of the civil justice system now require the judge to manage the case rather than to leave this to the lawyers. The judge will therefore set timetables for the completion of certain stages of litigation and try to encourage co-operation on certain issues. Despite this judicial case management, a trial is still conducted on adversarial lines. Today the battle is metaphoric, but in the early Middle Ages many disputes were resolved with a Trial by Battle. The parties would fight each other, both armed with a leather shield and a staff, and it was thought that God would grant victory to the righteous litigant. If either of the parties was disabled, or too young, or too old, he could hire a champion to fight for him. This was no doubt considerably more entertaining than a modern trial, but eventually it came to be realised that it was not the best way to achieve justice. Lawyers replaced the champions. However, the idea of a battle survived, and a trial is still a battle between the lawyers, even if the shields and staves have given way to witnesses and precedents.

Most other countries have an inquisitorial system of trial, where the judge is the inquisitor, determined to discover the truth. A French examining magistrate, for example, has enormous powers. He or she takes over the investigation of a criminal case from the police and can interrogate witnesses. He or she can also compel witnesses to give evidence and can surprise witnesses with other witnesses, hoping that the confrontation will point the finger of guilt.

When a French case reaches court, it is often all but decided. By contrast, no-one can ever be certain of the outcome of an English trial. The lawyers will fight each other on the day and either side might win. The judge should be disinterested in the outcome, merely ensuring that the lawyers fight by the rules.

Absence of a legal code

In most European countries the law has been codified. This means that the whole of the law on a particular subject, for example the law of property, can be found in one document or code. As we have seen in this chapter, the bulk of English law has been made by judges in individual cases.

Occasionally, Parliament codifies an area of law with a statute such as the Partnership Act 1890. Such an Act aims to take all the relevant case law on a particular subject and to codify it into one comprehensive statute. However, as we shall see, the vast majority of English law remains uncodified. Nor does Britain have a written constitution, as most other democratic countries have.

The law-making role of the judges

In most European countries the judges interpret the legal code. In doing this they do not themselves deliberately set out to create law. Earlier in this chapter, when we studied the doctrine of judicial precedent, we saw that the decisions of judges in the High Court, the Court of Appeal and the House of Lords must be followed by lower-ranking judges. So these senior judges are constantly creating the law.

Importance of procedure

In the Middle Ages a claim would fail if the correct court procedure was not rigidly adhered to, even if the substance of the claim was perfectly valid. To some extent this is still true today. If a litigant fails to follow the correct procedure, it is possible that his claim will be struck out. Recent reforms of the judicial process have attempted to reduce the importance of procedure. However, in cases which involve a substantial claim there is no doubt that procedure remains very important.

Absence of Roman law

The Romans occupied England from 55 BC to AD 430. Roman law was extremely sophisticated by the standards of its day. The other European countries which were part of the Roman Empire have retained elements of Roman law. However, English law has almost no Roman law influence, although Roman law is still taught as an academic subject at some English universities.

Other features

Two other features of the English legal system are worth mentioning. First, the legal profession is divided, lawyers being either barristers or solicitors. Second, in almost all criminal trials the innocence or guilt of the accused is decided by laymen, rather than by lawyers or judges. If the accused is tried in the Crown Court, it will be a jury which decides whether the accused is guilty. If the crime is tried in the magistrates' court, it is generally a bench of lay magistrates who make this decision.

The legal profession

Unlike other European countries, England has two different types of lawyers – barristers and solicitors. There are slightly over 12,000 practising barristers, about 32 per cent of whom are female and 11 per cent of whom are from ethnic minorities. The main job of barristers is to argue cases in court. However, the role of the practising barrister is much wider than merely acting as an advocate. Barristers spend a considerable amount of time giving written opinions, in which they state what they consider the law to be. They also draft statements of case, the formal documents which the parties must exchange before a case is heard in court. Barristers tend to specialise either in criminal law or in a particular branch of civil law. They have rights of audience in all civil and criminal courts. Until 1990, barristers had an exclusive right to be heard in the higher courts, but now some solicitors also have rights in such courts.

About 1,250 senior barristers are known as Queen's Counsel, and they generally appear in court with a junior barrister assisting them. Since June 2005 they have been appointed by a Queen's Counsel selection panel. Queen's Counsel, or QCs as they are usually known, can charge higher fees than other barristers, in recognition of their expertise.

Traditionally, barristers operate from chambers, which are offices where several barristers are allocated work by a barrister's clerk, who also negotiates the barrister's fees. Under the 'cab rank' rule a barrister, like a taxi, is supposed to provide his services to any client. Theoretically, therefore, any barrister is available to any client whose solicitor asks that the barrister should be engaged. This is not always true, as some barristers' fees are beyond the means of many clients and because barristers' clerks, who arrange what cases a barrister can take, are skilled at deflecting unwanted cases. It often happens that when a particular barrister has been engaged, he is not available when the case starts because another case in which he is appearing has not finished in time. The client is then allocated a different barrister. Many barristers do not practise, but work in industry or commerce or for local government or the Civil Service. The Legal Services Act 2007 has allowed barristers and solicitors to work together in partnership.

There are about 118,000 practising solicitors, almost 11.5 per cent of whom are from ethnic minority groups. Almost 45 per cent of practising solicitors are women, a percentage which is increasing annually. Solicitors, many of whom work in very large partnerships, are the first point of contact for a client with a legal problem.

A solicitor in a one-person business should have a good idea of most areas of law and should know where more information could be found if needed. In the larger firms solicitors would tend to specialise in one particular area of law. Solicitors routinely give their clients legal advice, enter into correspondence on their behalf, draft wills, and draw up documents which transfer ownership of land.

Until 1990, solicitors were allowed to argue cases only in the magistrates' court and the county court. Now the barristers' monopoly right to appear in the Crown Court and appellate courts has been removed by statute, and solicitors who have gained the necessary advocacy qualifications can represent clients in any court. However, barristers still perform the vast bulk of advocacy work in these courts. Whereas solicitors have gained rights of audience since 1990, they have lost their monopoly rights to perform conveyancing and to obtain grants of probate. The Administration of Justice Act 1985 allowed licensed conveyancers to practise. It was widely predicted that this would be disastrous for many small firms of solicitors, but this does not seem to have been the case. However, the Legal Services Act 2007 has allowed non-lawyers to own law firms, and many have suggested that this will be very damaging to small high-street firms.

The Legal Services Act 2007

The Legal Services Act (LSA) received Royal Assent in 2007. However, it will not fully come into force until 2012. The Act sets up a new framework of regulation for legal services in England and Wales and is probably the most significant reform of legal services ever to have been made. Part 1 of the Act sets out the Act's eight regulatory objectives, namely:

(1) protecting and promoting the public interest;

(2) supporting the constitutional principle of the rule of law;

(3) improving access to justice;

(4) protecting and promoting the interests of consumers;

(5) promoting competition in the provision of services;

(6) encouraging an independent, strong, diverse and effective legal profession;

(7) increasing public understanding of the citizen's legal rights and duties; and

(8) promoting and maintaining adherence to the professional principles, which are set out in s. 1(3).

The professional principles set out in s. 1(3) require 'authorised persons', that is to say those who can offer 'reserved legal services', to act with independence, integrity and confidentiality; to maintain proper standards of work; to act in the best interests of clients; and to act in the best interests of justice when litigating in court.

Part 2 of the Act has created a Legal Services Board (LSB), which aims to maintain and develop standards relating to the legal profession. The LSB has a duty to promote the eight regulatory objectives set out in Part 1 of the Act, and to establish a Consumer Panel. It is independent from the Law Society and the Bar Council, which are now called 'front-line' legal regulators.

Part 3 of the Act sets out the 'reserved legal activities' which can be carried out only by lawyers. These matters are advocacy in court, formally conducting litigation, and charging for the preparation of probate papers. Other, minor, reserved legal activities can be carried out by notaries or commissioners for oaths.

Part 5 of the Act, which came into force in 2009, allows Legal Disciplinary Practices (LDPs) to be set up as companies, partnerships or limited liability partnerships. Within LDPs, solicitors can be in business with non-solicitor partners and non-lawyer managers. (However, managers must be solicitors, barristers, notaries, licensed conveyancers, legal executives, patent agents, trade mark agents or law costs draftsmen.) This allows expertise to be brought into a business, increasing its ability to provide a one-stop service to customers. It also allows non-solicitors to provide capital to businesses which provide legal services. As from September 2012, all LDPs with non-lawyer managers have needed to register as Alternative Business Structures (ABS).

In an ABS lawyers and those without legal qualifications can work together to provide both reserved legal activities and other services. In such businesses non-lawyers are able to exercise professional, management and ownership roles. As long as an ABS has been licensed by an approved regulator, such as the Law Society, it can offer 'reserved legal activities', which need to be carried out by lawyers. However, any other activities can be carried out by those who are not legally qualified. It seems very likely that many non-traditional legal services providers will employ non-lawyers to carry out much of the background work which was traditionally carried out by lawyers. This has caused several distinguished commentators to fear that lawyers, if they are to be able to compete, will have to give up much of the work which they have traditionally done, or accept much reduced salaries for doing it. The legal services market is estimated to be worth about £19 billion annually. It seems very likely that banks, insurance companies and large retailers will try to take over a large share of the market. Lawyers will probably have to change their outlook and their business structures to compete effectively. However, it should be remembered that the LSA does not provide for complete deregulation of legal services providers. Any new ABS still needs to apply for a licence if any non-lawyer has a material interest in the ABS or is able to control it. A licence will be granted only to businesses which are competent to provide legal services. Furthermore, any non-lawyer who owns more than 10 per cent of an ABS is subject to a fitness-to-own test. It should also be remembered that the demise of the legal profession was widely predicted, not least by the profession itself, when in the late 1980s solicitors lost their monopoly rights to write wills and practise conveyancing. Such predictions have been proved spectacularly wrong.

The LSA 2007 is intended to allow non-lawyers to do much of the work currently done by lawyers and thereby to lead to innovation, price reductions and greater access to legal services. The extent to which it will achieve these objectives will not be known for some years.

The judiciary

There are five main levels in the judicial hierarchy. Supreme Court Justices sit as judges in the Supreme Court. Lords Justices of Appeal sit in the Court of Appeal. There are currently 38 Lords Justices of Appeal and 12 Supreme Court justices. There are also 108 High Court judges, who sit in the High Court and sometimes in the Crown Court.

It is convenient to consider the judges who sit in the High Court, the Court of Appeal and the Supreme Court as distinct from judges who sit in lower courts. The High Court is generally not an appeal court. The Court of Appeal and Supreme Court do not try cases but only hear appeals. The further up the hierarchy the judge is sitting, the more importance he is likely to attach to the precedent which he is creating.

There are currently 680 circuit judges, who try criminal cases in the Crown Court and civil cases in the county court. In the Crown Court these circuit judges are assisted by some 1,300 part-time judges called recorders. In the county court they are assisted by around 450 district judges and 800 deputy district judges. Circuit judges and district judges do not create precedents. Their role is therefore confined to trying the cases which they hear. They supervise the proceedings in court, and in civil cases decide the facts of the case if they are in dispute and award damages and costs. In criminal cases in which a judge sits the facts will be decided by the jury, but the judge will supervise the proceedings. He will also sum up the law to the jury, so that they can reach the correct verdict, and pass sentence if the accused is convicted.

Twenty-two per cent of judges are female and five and a half per cent are of minority ethnic origin. In the precedent-making courts the judges are almost exclusively white and male. Only three such judges are from a minority ethnic background and only nineteen are female.

Ninety-seven per cent of all criminal cases are decided in the magistrates' court, rather than in the Crown Court. Most magistrates are lay magistrates, meaning that they are not legally qualified. However, there are currently 134 district judges (magistrates' court) and they are assisted by 103 deputies.

There are somewhere around 30,000 lay magistrates, who are not paid a salary. Although they are not legally qualified, upon appointment lay magistrates do receive training on matters such as decision-making, stereotyping and avoiding prejudice. Magistrates generally sit as a bench of three, and are advised about the law by the legally qualified clerk of the court. As well as deciding whether or not a person accused of a crime is granted bail, magistrates try cases, deciding whether an accused is innocent or guilty and passing sentence on those who are convicted. They also conduct committal proceedings when a defendant is committed for trial to the Crown Court. Lay magistrates must live or work in the area in which they serve, must have a good knowledge of the local community, must be of good character and have personal integrity. Generally, they must be between the ages of 27 and 65. Most people are eligible to become magistrates, but those in the police or the armed forces are not.

Judicial review

Judicial review is a legal procedure which allows the Administrative Court to examine whether a public law decision, or the exercise of discretionary power by a public body, is legal. The definition of public body includes government ministers and has been held to cover decisions of private bodies which make decisions that affect the public.

The court can grant one or more of the following remedies:

- An order that overrules the original decision.
- An order that forces the decision-maker to do something.
- An order which prevents a decision-maker from doing something which is not legal.
- State the legal position between the parties.

Judicial review has become increasingly important in recent years as the number of applications has increased dramatically. Businesses are increasingly either applying for judicial review or are subject to judicial review proceedings. A business might apply, for example, on the grounds that a decision taken by a government minister affects the running of the business.

Juries

In the Crown Court the jury decides whether the accused is guilty or not guilty. This decision is based on the judge's summing up, which explains the relevant law to the jury. It is therefore said that juries decide the facts of the case. A judge can direct a jury to acquit an accused, but cannot direct them to convict. Juries do not give an explanation for their decisions. If a jury acquits, an appeal cannot overturn this acquittal. This enables juries to bring in 'perverse acquittals' if they think that the circumstances of the case so demand.

Juries play little part in civil cases. The absolute right to trial by jury in the Crown Court for an indictable (serious) offence has also been breached. In March 2010 four men were convicted of armed robbery in the Crown Court, without a jury, because there were serious concerns about jury nobbling. Since then, two other trials for indictable offences have been earmarked for trial in the Crown Court without a jury. However, in the near future it is highly unlikely that more than a handful of such trials will be tried without a jury each year.

In the past few years problems have arisen because jurors have used the Internet to help them with their deliberations. In **R v Thompson and others (2010)** the Court of Appeal held that, at the beginning of a trial, jurors should be specifically told not to use the Internet but to base their verdict on the evidence presented to them in court. In June 2011 a juror who contacted via Facebook a defendant who had already been acquitted, thereby causing a multi-million pound drug trial to collapse, was jailed for eight months for contempt of court.

Essential points

- Legislation is the name given to law made by Parliament.
- The literal rule of statutory interpretation says that words in a statute should be given their ordinary, literal meaning, no matter how absurd the result.
- The golden rule gives the words in a statute their ordinary, literal meaning as far as possible, but only to the extent that this would not produce an absurd result.
- The mischief rule holds that the judge can take into account what 'mischief' the statute set out to remedy.
- The doctrine of judicial precedent holds that judges in lower courts are absolutely bound to follow decisions previously made in higher courts.
- The *ratio decidendi*, loosely translated from the Latin as 'the reason for the decision', is the part of the case which is binding on other judges.
- Statements of law which did not form the basis of the decision are known as *obiter dicta* (other things said).
- A higher-ranking court can overrule a *ratio* created by a lower-ranking court.
- The United Kingdom joined what is now the EU in 1973. In order to be admitted as a member, the UK Parliament passed the European Communities Act 1972. Under this statute the United Kingdom agreed to apply EU law in UK courts.
- The Human Rights Act 1998 requires that all legislation is read and given effect in a way which is compatible with the Convention rights, but only in so far as it is possible to do this.
- The English courts are divided into civil courts and criminal courts, and the two sets of courts have quite different purposes.
- The civil courts are designed to compensate people who have been injured by others. The criminal courts are designed to punish people who have committed a crime.
- Unlike other European countries, England has two different types of lawyers – barristers and solicitors.
- Judicial review is a legal procedure which allows the Administrative Court to examine whether a public law decision, or the exercise of discretionary power by a public body, is legal.
- In the Crown Court the jury decides whether the accused is guilty or not guilty.

Practice questions

1 What are the three main rules of statutory interpretation? What is the effect of these rules?

2 What is the effect of the *ejusdem generis* rule and the rule *expressio unius est exclusio alterius*?

3 What is meant by the doctrine of judicial precedent?

4 What are the five main levels of the courts, for the purposes of precedent?

5 What is meant by *ratio decidendi* and *obiter dicta*? What is the significance of the distinction? What is meant by overruling, reversing and distinguishing?

6 Find a case concerning the Human Rights Act 1998 either in a newspaper or on the Internet. Which articles of the Convention did the case concern? Describe the outcome of the case or, if it has not yet been decided, state what you think the outcome of the case might be.

7 Describe how the system of judicial precedent operates. Do you consider that the advantages of the system outweigh the disadvantages?

Task 1

Draw up a report for your employer, briefly explaining the following matters:

(a) The main rules of statutory interpretation.

(b) The way in which the system of judicial precedent operates.

(c) The ways in which EU law is created and the effect of EU law in the United Kingdom.

(d) The effect of the Human Rights Act 1998.

mylawchamber

Visit **www.mylawchamber.co.uk/macintyreessentials** to access tools to help you develop and test your knowledge of business law, including interactive multiple choice questions, practice exam questions with guidance, weblinks, glossary, glossary flashcards, legal newsfeed and legal updates.

mylawchamber
unrivalled support for legal education

2

Making a contract

Definition of a contract

A contract is a legally binding agreement. In order for a contract to be created, one of the parties must make an offer to the other party and the other party must accept this offer. Furthermore, the circumstances in which the offer and acceptance were made must indicate that the parties intended to enter into a legal relationship. A final requirement, which distinguishes contracts from gifts, is that the two contracting parties must both give some benefit (known as consideration) to the other. There are then four requirements of a contract. There must be an offer, an acceptance of that offer, an intention to create legal relations and consideration given by both parties. In this chapter we consider these four requirements, which are shown in Figure 2.1.

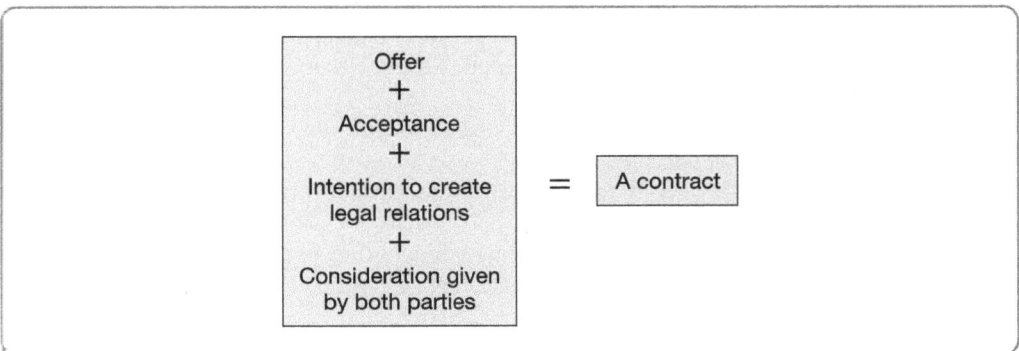

Figure 2.1 The requirements of a contract

Once a contract has been made, both sides will be bound to honour its terms or take the legal consequences. A party who does not stick to what was agreed in a contract is said to have breached the contract. Whenever one of the parties breaches a contract, legal remedies will be available to the other party.

Offer

A person who makes an offer is known as an offeror. A person to whom an offer is made is known as an offeree. An offer is made when an offeror proposes a set of terms to an offeree, with the intention that if the proposed terms are accepted they will create a binding contract between the two parties. By accepting the terms proposed, the offeree would also agree to become legally bound by them. This acceptance would therefore form a contract. As a contract is a legally binding agreement, neither an offer nor an acceptance should be made without a willingness to accept the legal consequences.

Neither the offer nor the acceptance need to be made in writing, or even in words. For example, when goods are sold at an auction a contract is formed even though both the offer and the acceptance are made by conduct. Each bidder makes an offer to buy the particular lot being auctioned by making a gesture which the auctioneer recognises as a bid. The auctioneer accepts the highest bid by banging the gavel on the table. At that moment the contract is created, even though both the offer and acceptance were made without the use of words.

Invitation to treat

It is important to make a distinction between an offer and an invitation to treat. An invitation to treat is not an offer. It is an invitation to negotiate or an invitation to make an offer.

An offer should not be made by a person who is not fully prepared to take the legal consequences of its being accepted. For example, I should not offer to sell you my car for £100 unless I am fully prepared to go through with the deal, because if you accept my offer, I will either have to go through with the contract which will have been created or take the legal consequences. A response to an invitation to treat, however, cannot result in a binding contract. It is quite safe for me to ask you how much you would give me for my car. You might name a price (thereby making an offer) but I would have no obligation to agree to the deal.

A court decides whether or not one of the parties has made an offer by looking objectively at what it thinks that both of the parties intended. All the circumstances of the case will be considered in reaching this decision.

Advertisements can amount either to offers or to invitations to treat. If an advertisement is an offer, then a person who accepts the offer makes a contract with the person who advertised. If an advertisement is only an invitation to treat, then it cannot be accepted in such a way that a contract is thereby formed.

In the following two cases the court had to decide whether or not an advertisement was merely an invitation to treat or whether it was in fact an offer.

 Partridge v Crittenden (1968)

The defendant had advertised bramblefinches in a magazine at £1.25 each. A customer sent the defendant £1.25 and a bramblefinch was sent to him. The defendant was charged with offering for sale a wild live bird, contrary to the Protection of Birds Act 1964.

Held The defendant was not guilty because his advertisement was an invitation to treat, not an offer. As the advertisement was not an offer, the defendant had not 'offered for sale' a wild bird. (The defendant had committed a different crime, selling a wild bird. However, he had not been charged with this offence.)

Comment This was a criminal case but it was decided upon a point of civil law. Several criminal offences are committed by offering goods for sale. Whether or not an offer has been made is decided by analysing the law of contract.

At first sight it seems as if the defendant in **Partridge *v* Crittenden** did make an offer. However, the court reasoned that this could not be the case. If the advertisement had been an offer, then the defendant would have had to supply a bird to everyone who wrote in accepting the offer. The defendant had only a limited supply of birds and so could not have intended that any number of customers would be supplied with one. Therefore, his advertisement was an invitation to treat, not an offer.

Although the vast majority of advertisements will amount to no more than invitations to treat, some advertisements do amount to offers. The following case shows that if all advertisements were only invitations to treat then this would lead to unfairness.

 ### Carlill *v* The Carbolic Smoke Ball Co (1893) (Court of Appeal)

The defendants manufactured smoke balls. They claimed that the use of these smoke balls cured many illnesses and made it impossible to catch flu. A large advertising campaign stated that if anyone used a smoke ball correctly, but still caught flu, they would be paid £100 reward. One advertisement stated that the defendants had deposited £1,000 in a Regent Street bank to show that they meant what they said. The claimant, Mrs Carlill, was persuaded by this advertisement to buy a smoke ball. Despite using the smoke ball properly, she still caught flu. When Mrs Carlill claimed the £100 reward the defendants refused to pay, arguing that their advertisement was not an offer.

Held The advertisement was an offer of a unilateral contract (see below). The claimant had accepted this offer by using the smoke ball in the correct way and catching flu. She was therefore entitled to the £100 reward.

Comment If the advertisement had been held not to have been an offer, this would unfairly have allowed the Smoke Ball Company to break its promise. In reaching their decisions the Court of Appeal judges considered what the reasonable person would have made of the advertisement.

In **Carlill *v* The Carbolic Smoke Ball Co** the offer was made to the whole world. Offers are more usually made to just one person or to a limited number of people. Only a person to whom an offer was made, an offeree, can accept an offer. For example, an offeror might offer to sell a car very cheaply to one particular person, a friend. Only the person to whom the offer was made, the offeree, could accept the offer.

Offer of a unilateral contract

The vast majority of contracts are bilateral (two-sided) because both parties make a promise to the other. Let us assume, for example, that Martin phones John and asks whether or not he wants to buy a consignment of goods. John accepts the offer. This is a bilateral contract because both of the parties have made a promise to the other. Martin has promised to deliver and give ownership of the goods at the price agreed. John has promised to pay the price and take delivery of the goods. A bilateral contract such as this is made up of an exchange of promises. When one of the parties makes an offer of a unilateral contract, as happened in **Carlill *v* The Carbolic Smoke Ball Co**, only one promise is made. The party making the offer promises that *if* the offeree performs some specified act then the offeror promises to do something in return. The offeree makes no promises. The offeree either performs the specified act, thereby creating a contract, or does not. For example, in **Carlill v The Carbolic Smoke Ball Co** the Smoke Ball Co promised that if Mrs Carlill, or anyone else, properly used a smoke ball but still caught flu, they would be entitled to the £100 reward. Mrs Carlill did not promise to use a smoke ball and catch flu. Furthermore, she could not have accepted the offer by promising to do these things. The only way in which she could accept the offer was by doing the acts requested. Whenever a reward is offered, this is usually the offer of a unilateral contract.

Goods in shops

Customers who buy goods in shops make contracts to buy those goods. In the following case the court had to analyse exactly when the offer and acceptance were made when goods were purchased in a self-service shop.

Pharmaceutical Society (GB) *v* Boots Cash Chemists Ltd (1953) (Court of Appeal)

The Pharmacy and Poisons Act 1933 made it a criminal offence to sell listed drugs without a pharmacist being present. The defendants displayed listed drugs on a supermarket shelf in an area of their supermarket where no pharmacist was present. However, a pharmacist was present near the till. It therefore had to be decided *where* the drugs were sold, that is to say *where* the contract to sell the drugs was made. If the contract was made in the area of the supermarket where the drugs were displayed, then the defendants would have been guilty of the offence. If, however, the contract was made at the till, then the defendants would not have been guilty. The prosecution argued that the displayed drugs amounted to an offer and that this offer was accepted when customers put the drugs into their baskets.

Held The defendants were not guilty. The display of goods on supermarket shelves amounts only to an invitation to treat. A customer makes an offer to buy the goods displayed by selecting the goods and taking them to the till. The cashier can accept this offer by ringing up the price. However, the cashier has no obligation to accept the offer and can refuse to sell. So the defendants were not guilty of the offence because any contract to sell the listed drugs was made at the till and would therefore have been made in the presence of a pharmacist.

A display of goods in a shop window does not amount to an offer to sell the goods displayed. The display is only an invitation to treat.

Fisher *v* Bell (1961)

The defendant was charged with offering for sale an offensive weapon, contrary to the Restriction of Offensive Weapons Act 1959. He had displayed a flick knife in his shop window and a ticket behind the knife had said, 'Ejector knife – 4 shillings'.

Held The defendant was not guilty. The display of the knife amounted only to an invitation to treat and not to an offer to sell. The defendant had not therefore 'offered for sale' the offensive weapon. Lord Parker said: 'the display of an article with a price on it in a shop window is merely an invitation to treat. It is in no sense an offer for sale the acceptance of which constitutes a contract. That is clearly the general law of the country.'

Acceptance

As we have already seen, a contract comes into existence as soon as an offer is validly accepted. Generally, the acceptance of an offer is regarded as complete only when it is received by the offeror, as the following case shows.

 Entores Ltd *v* Miles Far East Corporation (1955) (Court of Appeal)

The claimants, who were in London, telexed an offer to buy goods to the defendants, who were in Holland. (Telex is a form of near instantaneous communication, whereby a message typed in one place is received on a different typewriter in another place.) The defendants telexed acceptance of the offer back to the claimants. A dispute later arose and the defendants were sued on the contract in an English court. The defendants argued that the contract was made in Holland, not England, and that the English courts therefore did not have the jurisdiction to hear the case. This defence was based on the argument that the acceptance was effective as soon as it was typed out in Holland.

Held The acceptance only became effective once it was received. Therefore, the contract was made in England, where the acceptance was received, and so the English courts had jurisdiction to hear the case.

An acceptance cannot be made by doing and saying nothing, even if the offeror specifies that the acceptance should be made in this way. For example, in **Felthouse *v* Bindley (1862)** the claimant wanted to buy a horse from his nephew for £30.75. The claimant was fairly sure that his nephew would want to sell at this price. He therefore wrote a letter saying that if he heard no reply he would take it that the horse was sold at this price. The nephew wanted to sell at £30.75 and so he did not reply. Later, a dispute arose when an auctioneer sold the horse by mistake. The court held that there had been no acceptance and so there was no contract.

Although **Felthouse *v* Bindley** established that a person cannot accept an offer by doing and saying nothing, some businesses try to sell goods by sending them to people who have not requested them. They then follow this up with a letter demanding the return of the goods or payment for them.

Regulation 24 of the Consumer Protection (Distance Selling) Regulations 2000 provides that if unsolicited goods are sent, the recipient may keep them and regard them as an unconditional gift after six months have passed. (If the recipient gives written notice, stating the place from where the goods can be collected, they become an unconditional gift after 30 days have passed.) The Consumer Protection from Unfair Trading Regulations 2008 make it a criminal offence to demand payment for unsolicited goods.

An acceptance can be made by conduct, as happens when goods are sold by auction. The following case provides an example in a commercial context.

 Photolibrary Group Ltd *v* Burda Senator Verlag Gmbh (2008)

For some years the claimants had supplied the defendants with non-digital photographic transparencies, along with a delivery note. The defendants sent the transparencies to Germany where clients of theirs might choose to pay to use them. The defendants lost nearly 2,000 of the claimants' transparencies. The claimants claimed over £1.2 million under a clause in the delivery note. The defendants argued that the delivery note was not part of the contract as they had never signed it. Nor had they signed any of the identical delivery notes which had previously been delivered. On the other hand, they had never done anything to indicate that they did not regard the delivery note as binding.

Held The delivery note was part of the contract between the claimants and the defendants. This conclusion could be arrived at in three different ways. First, delivery of the transparencies, along with the delivery note, was an offer which was accepted by keeping the transparencies and sending them to Germany. Second, the defendants' act of asking for the transparencies was, in the light of the previous course of dealing between the parties, an offer to supply them subject to the terms in the delivery note. This offer was accepted by sending the transparencies and the delivery note. Third, regardless of who made the offer and the acceptance, the terms in the delivery note were simply incorporated through the previous course of dealing between the parties. (See **Kendal v Lillico** in Chapter 3.)

A court may decide that as soon as a person does an act which makes payment for goods or services inevitable, that act must be an acceptance (if no earlier act was acceptance). For example, in **Thornton v Shoe Lane Parking Ltd (1971)** (Court of Appeal) Lord Denning MR held that once a customer had driven into a multi-storey car park the contract had been concluded. By this time the customer was committed beyond being able to change his mind.

The postal rule

Whenever an acceptance is made by posting a letter, the possible effect of the postal rule has to be considered. If the rule applies, then the acceptance is effective when the letter is *posted*, not when it is received. The rule originated in the following case.

 Adams v Lindsell (1818)

On 2 September 1818 the defendants posted an offer to sell some wool to the claimant. The offer asked for a reply by return of post. The letter containing the offer was misdirected because it was not properly addressed. It therefore arrived on 5 September, whereas if it had not been misdirected it would have arrived on 3 September. The claimant posted a letter of acceptance by return of post. This letter arrived on 9 September. If the first letter had not been misdirected, a reply by return of post would have reached the defendants by 7 September. On 7 September the defendants sold the wool to someone else because they had not received a reply to their offer. The claimant sued for breach of contract.

Held The defendants were in breach of contract. The claimant's acceptance was effective on 5 September, as soon as it was posted.

The postal rule has been developed by subsequent cases. In **Household Fire Insurance Co v Grant (1879)** it was applied even when the letter of acceptance was permanently lost in the post. (The Court of Appeal accepted evidence that the letter of acceptance had been posted.) In **Henthorn v Fraser (1892)** the Court of Appeal held that the rule would apply whenever it could reasonably be expected that acceptance would be made by post, even if the offer was not made by post. However, in **Re London and Northern Bank (1900)** it was held that the rule could apply only if the letter of acceptance was properly posted. Handing it to a postman to post was held not to be good enough. A letter handed to a postman would be properly posted only when the postman actually did post it.

In the following case the Court of Appeal reviewed the postal rule.

 Holwell Securities Ltd v Hughes (1974) (Court of Appeal)

On 19 October 1971, Dr Hughes gave the claimants an option to purchase his house for £45,000. This option amounted to an offer to sell and was to be exercisable 'by notice in writing' within six months. The claimants posted a letter of acceptance on 14 April 1972, but this letter was never delivered. After the option had expired the claimants sued for specific performance (a court order requiring Dr Hughes to honour the contract and sell the house to them. The nature of this remedy is explained in Chapter 5). The claimants argued that the postal rule applied and that a contract had therefore been made as soon as the letter of acceptance was posted.

Held There was no contract. The postal rule did not apply because the offer, by asking for 'notice in writing', had expressly stated that an acceptance had to reach the offeror. The postal rule would not apply where all the circumstances of the case indicated that the parties did not intend there to be a binding contract until an acceptance was actually received. Furthermore, the court stated that the rule would never apply where its application would produce 'manifest inconvenience and absurdity'.

Despite the decision in **Holwell Securities Ltd v Hughes**, the postal rule is still very much alive and can still apply. It is, however, important to remember that the rule can apply only when *acceptance is made by posting a letter*. As we saw when considering **Entores Ltd v Miles Far East Corporation**, the rule does not apply to acceptance by telex. Nor will it apply to acceptance by any other means such as fax or email. The rule will never apply to revocation (withdrawal) of an offer, even when the revocation is made by posting a letter. The rule is confined to acceptance of an offer by posting a letter. An outline of the effect of the postal rule is shown in Figure 2.2.

Acceptance of the offer of a unilateral contract

We have seen that, the postal rule apart, an acceptance of a bilateral contract is effective when it is received rather than when it is sent. However, acceptance of an offer of a unilateral contract is effective as soon as the act requested is fully performed, even if the offeror does not yet know that the act has been performed. This can be demonstrated by considering the decision in **Carlill v The Carbolic Smoke Ball Co**. Mrs Carlill could not have accepted the offer by promising that she would buy a smoke ball and then catch flu. She accepted by actually doing these things. Furthermore, her acceptance was complete as soon as she had done the acts requested, even though the company did not yet know that she had done them. This was not unfair to the Smoke Ball Company. It made the offer and chose to make the reward payable when the acts requested were completed.

Counter offer

A counter offer rejects the offer to which it responds and replaces it with a different offer. Having rejected the original offer, an offeree who responded with a counter offer can no longer accept the original offer.

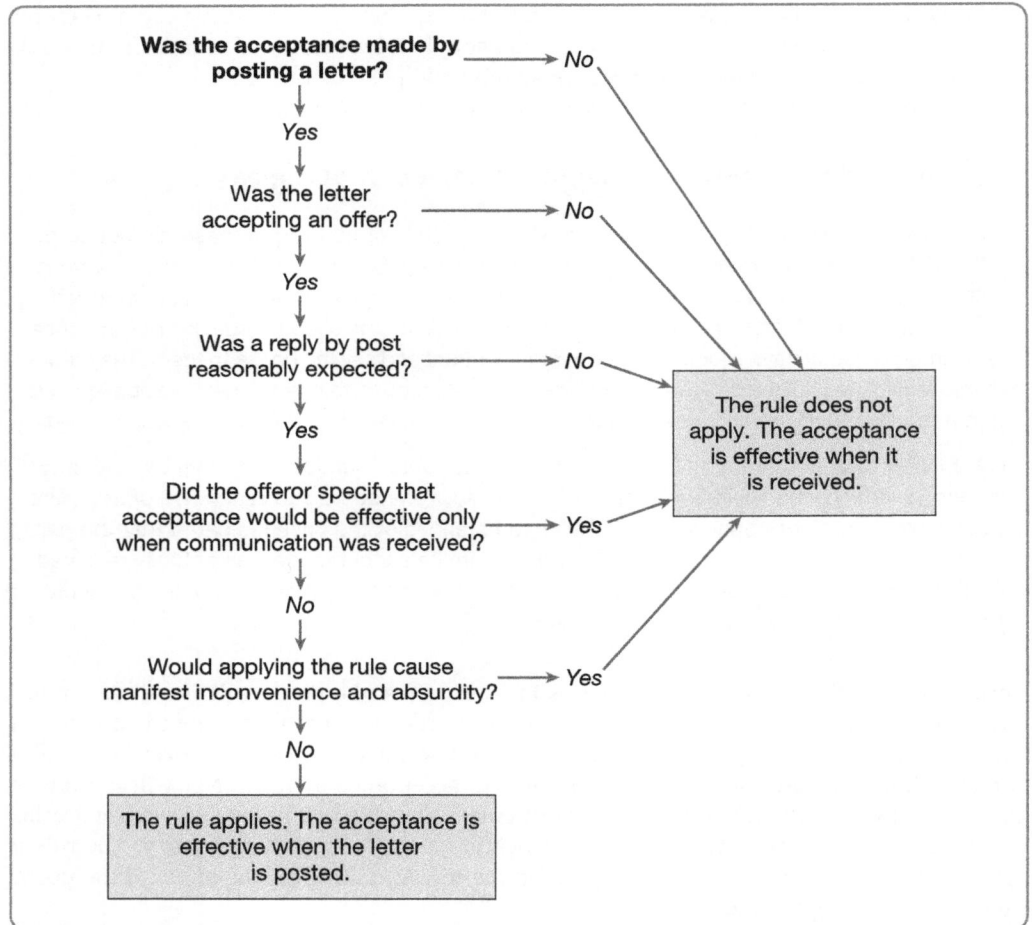

Figure 2.2 An outline of the postal rule

⚖️ **Hyde *v* Wrench (1840)**

The defendant offered to sell his farm to the claimant for £1,000. The claimant offered £950 for the farm. The defendant wrote to the claimant declining the counter offer of £950. The claimant immediately wrote back, saying that he accepted the original offer to sell the farm for £1,000. The defendant refused to sell the farm at this price.

Held There was no contract. The defendant's original offer had been revoked by the claimant's counter offer. The original offer had therefore ceased to exist and could not later be accepted.

The decision in this case makes good sense. If a business offers an asset for sale at a certain price and receives a counter offer, then the counter offer is in effect a refusal of the offer to sell. The business wishing to sell might therefore reasonably enough sell the asset to someone else. If the original offeree could then accept the original offer, and make the business liable for breach of contract, this would be very harsh.

Auctions

As we have seen, a lot at an auction is sold when the auctioneer's gavel hits the table. Before such an acceptance is made, any bid can be withdrawn. When a person makes a new bid, all previous bids lapse. As soon as the gavel hits the table, a contract is formed and the highest bidder has bought the lot which is up for sale. A bid can be withdrawn before the gavel falls, but not after the gavel has hit the table.

If an auction is advertised as being 'without reserve', this means that the auctioneer makes a definite promise that if the auction of any particular lot is commenced, that lot will be sold to the highest genuine bidder. This is the case no matter how low the highest genuine bid might be. Furthermore, the person who put the goods into the auction, the owner of the goods, cannot make a genuine bid. These principles are demonstrated by the following case.

Barry *v* Davies (trading as Heathcote-Ball & Co) (2000) (Court of Appeal)

Two machines were put up for auction without reserve. The machines were each worth £14,000 and the auctioneer tried to get a bid of £5,000. The claimant bid £400 for the machines but the auctioneer refused to accept the bid.

Held The auctioneer was in breach of contract and the claimant was awarded damages of £27,600. (This was the difference between what the claimant had bid and the amount he would have had to pay to buy the machines elsewhere.) The auctioneer's promise that the machines would be sold without reserve was the offer of a unilateral contract, given in exchange for the claimant's attending the auction and making the highest bid.

The fact of advertising that an auction will take place 'without reserve' does not amount to a promise that the auction will actually take place, or that any goods will actually be included in the auction. For example, in **Harris *v* Nickerson (1873)** an auctioneer placed advertisements in London newspapers, stating that office furniture was to be sold by auction, without reserve, in Bury St Edmunds. Some of the furniture in question was not included in the auction. A dealer, who had travelled to the auction from London, sued the auctioneer on the grounds that he had wanted to buy the furniture which was not auctioned. It was held that the auctioneer had committed no breach of contract as the advertisement was just an invitation to treat.

It must be remembered that most auctions do allow reserves. At such auctions the auctioneer will take bids in the normal way but refuse to sell if the highest bid does not exceed the reserve. For example, when goods are auctioned on eBay there is often a reserve price below which the goods will not be sold.

Tenders

Goods can be either bought or sold by tender. This is perhaps best explained by considering an example. Let us assume that a business will need a very large quantity of a particular type of paper. The business might place an advertisement, asking for tenders to supply the paper needed. This advertisement could either be an offer or an invitation to treat, depending upon the words it used. If the advertisement merely asked for tenders to supply the paper, without anywhere including a statement that the lowest tender would definitely be accepted, then the advertisement would be just an invitation to treat. Those who responded by putting in tenders to supply the paper would be making offers. The business which asked for tenders could choose to accept one of these offers but would have no obligation to do so. It might accept the lowest offer, or any other offer, or just not accept any of the offers. However, if the advertisement stated that the tenderer who submitted the lowest price would definitely be awarded the contract to supply the paper, then the advertisement would amount to an offer of a unilateral contract. This offer could be accepted by submitting the lowest price.

'Referential tenders' refer to other tenders. In **Harvela Investments Ltd *v* Royal Trust Co of Canada Ltd (1986)** the House of Lords held that referential tenders can have no effect because to give them effect would destroy the whole idea behind fixed competitive tendering. The facts of the case were that two people had been invited to put in tenders to buy a parcel of shares and it was promised that the highest bid would get the shares. Both invitees put in a tender. One tender offered to pay $2,175,000. This tender was successful because the other tender, which had agreed to pay $101,000 more than any other tender, was held to be invalid.

Certainty of agreement

Even if an offer is accepted, a contract will be created only if the reasonable person could state with certainty exactly what it is that has been agreed.

The courts use the device of the reasonable person because this gives an objective view of what the parties intended. If the court looked at what the parties actually intended, the subjective views of the parties might well be of little benefit. (One of the parties would claim that the agreement was definite enough to be a contract; the other party would claim that it was not.)

In the following case the House of Lords had to decide whether or not a written agreement was sufficiently certain to amount to a contract.

 Scammel *v* Ouston (1941) (House of Lords)

A firm of furnishers agreed to take a van from the defendants. It was agreed that the price should be £288 and that £100 should be allowed against an old van which was traded in. The agreement then said: 'this order is given on the understanding that the balance of the purchase price can be had on hire-purchase terms over a period of two years.' The parties began to disagree. Later, the defendants refused to supply the van, arguing that there had never been an agreement which was certain enough to amount to a contract.

Held There was no contract. The agreement was not certain enough to amount to a contract because the reasonable person would not have known exactly what had been agreed.

A contract may contain a price variation clause, which allows the price to be adjusted to take account of matters such as a rise in the cost of raw materials. Such a term will not make the contract void for uncertainty, as long as the contract agrees a definite procedure for setting how the price will change.

Meaningless terms

It is not unusual for a written business contract to contain one or more meaningless terms. Such terms can be ignored and will not therefore invalidate the contract. For example, in

Nicolene Ltd v Simmonds (1953) the defendants agreed to sell 3,000 tons of reinforced steel bars to the claimants. It was agreed that 'the usual conditions of acceptance apply'. There were no usual conditions of acceptance and the defendants therefore claimed that there was no enforceable contract. However, the Court of Appeal held that if the words were meaningless they could be ignored, leaving behind an enforceable contract.

Lord Denning explained that if a party to a contract could escape from it on account of having discovered a meaningless term, anyone who did not want to be bound by a contract could be found looking through it for a meaningless term which would provide an escape from liability.

When the parties have previously dealt with each other, their previous dealings might well indicate what has been agreed. For example, if in **Nicolene Ltd v Simmonds** the two parties had made similar contracts on several previous occasions, it might well have been certain what the usual conditions of acceptance were. The decision in **Scammel v Ouston** might also have been different if there had been previous dealings between the parties. If the furnishers had previously taken vans from the defendants on hire purchase terms, the words 'the balance of the purchase price can be had on hire-purchase terms over a period of two years' might have been sufficiently certain to mean that there would have been a binding contract.

Offer and acceptance when dealing with machines

It has become common for people to buy goods (or tickets which entitle them to services) from machines. At first sight this seems to cause considerable difficulty in finding the offer and the acceptance. The customer cannot make both the offer and the acceptance so the machine, on behalf of the supplier of the goods or services, must make either the offer or the acceptance.

In **Thornton v Shoe Lane Parking Ltd (1971)** (Court of Appeal) Lord Denning MR analysed the position when a customer is given a ticket by a machine. He concluded that the contract was completed not when the customer received the ticket, but as soon as the customer became irrevocably committed to the contract. In the case of a machine which did not have a coin refund this would be as soon as he put his money into the machine. He said:

> The customer pays his money and gets a ticket. He cannot refuse it. He cannot get his money back. He may protest to the machine, even swear at it. But it will remain unmoved. He is committed beyond recall. He was committed at the very moment when he put his money into the machine. The contract was concluded at that time. It can be translated into offer and acceptance in this way: the offer is made when the proprietor of the machine holds it out as being ready to receive the money. The acceptance is made when the customer puts his money into the slot.

Earlier in this chapter we considered **Entores Ltd v Miles Far East Corporation (1955)**, and saw that an acceptance by telex will generally be effective when it is received. However, difficulties with contracts concluded by machines may arise where the acceptance is received out of office hours or in the middle of the night. In **Brinkibon Ltd v Stahag Stahl und Stahlwarenhandelsgesellschaft GmbH (1983)** (House of Lords) Lord Wilberforce, dealing with communication by telex, made it plain that the courts will take a practical, flexible approach.

> The message may not reach, or be intended to reach, the designated recipient immediately: messages may be sent out of office hours, or at night, with the intention, or on the assumption, that they will be read at a later time. There may be some error or default at the recipient's end which prevents receipt at the time contemplated and believed in by the sender . . . And many other

variations may occur. No universal rule can cover all such cases; they must be resolved by reference to the intentions of the parties, by sound business practice and in some cases by a judgment where the risks should lie.

It does seem fairly certain that if an acceptance by telex or fax is received during office hours it is effective when received and not when it is noticed. In **Brinkibon** Lord Fraser said: 'Once the message has been received on the offeror's telex machine, it is not unreasonable to treat it as delivered to the offeror, because it is his responsibility to arrange for prompt handling of messages within his own office.' Lord Fraser also made the point that the acceptor by telex can generally tell if his message has not been received, whereas the offeror would not know that an unsuccessful attempt had been made to send an acceptance.

Offer and acceptance made over the Internet

As yet there have been no significant decisions by the courts as to when a contract is concluded over the Internet. There are two main ways in which such a contract might be formed. First, a contract could be made by exchange of emails. Second, a customer might visit a website and buy goods or services described there.

The position where emails have been exchanged should be catered for by the common law rules already considered in this chapter. The courts will take an objective view of an email and consider whether it was an offer, an acceptance or an invitation to treat. An offer might or might not be of a unilateral contract. The difficulty most likely to arise will be deciding precisely when an acceptance by email is effective. The general principles laid down in relation to telex seem likely to be applied. However, email differs from communication by telex in that a person who sends an email does not immediately know whether or not it has been received. In some ways acceptance by email is more similar to acceptance by letter than to acceptance by telex. However, it seems very unlikely that the postal rule will apply. The approach of the courts has been to restrict the rule rather than to expand it. It seems much more likely that the statement of Lord Wilberforce in **Brinkibon**, set out above, will apply to acceptance by email. This statement does not provide a cast-iron answer applicable to all situations. It indicates that the court will be flexible and will look at the intentions of the parties, sound business practice and a judgment as to where the risks should lie.

In general, websites which describe goods and services and the prices at which they are available will be making invitations to treat rather than offers. This would be particularly true if the material on the website makes it plain that it is the customer who makes the offer and that his offer might or might not be accepted. The customer might make the offer by clicking on a button. Any acceptance would be effective when the customer was informed that his offer had been accepted. However, there is no reason why a website should not make the offer of a unilateral contract. If this were the case, then the contract would be concluded as soon as the customer had performed the stipulated act of acceptance (generally by clicking on an acceptance button).

As we have seen, the key question when dealing with the conclusion of contracts is the time when the acceptance is effective. The Electronic Commerce (EC Directive) Regulations 2002 are concerned with the formalities which must be complied with when a contract is concluded by electronic means. They do not deal, as such, with the time at which the contract is concluded. In any event (as we shall see in Chapter 5), the question is often of little relevance in consumer contracts because the Consumer Protection (Distance Selling) Regulations 2000 give consumers the right to cancel concluded distance contracts. However, the Regulations give no such right to non-consumers.

Termination of offers

As soon as an offer is accepted, a contract is created. However, an offer which has been made might cease to exist in various ways, and once an offer has ceased to exist it can no longer be accepted.

Revocation

If an offer is revoked, it is called off by the offeror. Once an offer has been revoked it can no longer be accepted. A revocation is effective when it is received rather than when it is sent. We have already seen that acceptance of an offer is also effective when received. Therefore, cases involving revocation often amount to discovering which of the parties managed to communicate with the other first. Was the acceptance communicated before the revocation was communicated? If so, there will be a contract. Or was the revocation communicated before the acceptance was communicated? If so, there will be no contract. The following case provides an example of this type of dispute and also demonstrates that revocation can be communicated by an unauthorised third party, if he can be regarded as reliable.

 Dickinson v Dodds (1876)

On Wednesday 10 June the defendant wrote a letter to the claimant offering to sell his house. The letter stated that the offer would be kept open until 9 a.m. on Friday 12 June. On Thursday the defendant sold the house to a third party, Allen. Yet another person, Berry, found out about this and told the claimant. At 7 a.m. on Friday 12 June the claimant accepted the defendant's offer. The defendant told the claimant that he was too late to accept. The claimant sued for breach of contract.

Held There was no contract because the offer to sell had been revoked by Berry when he told the claimant that the house had been sold to Allen. Therefore, the offer no longer existed when the claimant attempted to accept it.

Comment It might seem unfair that the offer could be revoked before the deadline. This was allowed because no consideration was given in return for the promise to keep the offer open, that is to say nothing of any value was given in return. Consideration is examined later in this chapter.

The postal rule, which we examined earlier, has always been confined to acceptance of offers and has never applied to revocations. Revocations are always effective when received, whether sent by letter or not.

 Byrne & Co v Van Tienhoven & Co (1880)

On 1 October 1879 the defendants, who carried on business in Cardiff, posted an offer to sell 1,000 boxes of tinplate to the claimants in New York. On 8 October the defendants posted a revocation of their offer. The defendants' offer was received by the claimants on 11 October and a telegram of acceptance was sent the same day. On 20 October the defendants' letter of revocation reached the claimants.

Held A good contract came into existence on 11 October. The revocation was not effective until it was received on 20 October.

An offer of a unilateral contract can be revoked before the offeree has begun to accept it. If the offer was made to the whole world by means of an advertisement it can be revoked in two ways: first, by direct communication with an offeree; second, by another advertisement likely to reach the same audience as the advertisement which made the original offer. However, it is not possible to revoke the offer of a unilateral contract once the offeree has begun to perform the act which was requested as acceptance.

In **Errington *v* Errington & Woods (1952)**, for example, a man bought a house for £750, taking out a mortgage of £500. He promised his daughter-in-law that if she paid all of the mortgage instalments, she could have the house when the mortgage was paid off. This unilateral offer could not be revoked once the daughter-in-law started to pay the mortgage instalments as they became due. In **Daulia Ltd *v* Four Millbank Nominees (1978)** Goff LJ confirmed this approach, saying: 'Until [the offeree starts to perform] the offeror can revoke the whole thing, but once the offeree has embarked on performance it is too late for the offeror to revoke his offer.'

Refusal

If an offeree refuses an offer, then, as far as that offeree is concerned, the offer is terminated and cannot later be accepted. We saw earlier, when we considered **Hyde *v* Wrench**, that a counter offer is regarded as a refusal of the original offer and that it therefore ends it. Difficulties may arise in distinguishing a counter offer from a request for more information about the offer. As a request for more information does not imply a rejection of the offer, it does not terminate it. For example, in **Stevenson, Jacques & Co *v* McLean (1880)** the defendant offered to sell a quantity of iron at £2 a ton. The offeree asked if he could have credit. The defendant did not reply, but instead sold the iron to a third party. Then the offeree accepted the offer to sell at £2 a ton. The defendant was in breach of contract because the offeree had only made a request for more information. Unlike a counter offer, this request did not revoke the original offer.

Lapse of time

If a time limit is put on an offer, then the offer will end when the time limit expires. However, even where there is a time limit, the offeror can revoke the offer before the expiry time (unless some consideration was given for keeping the offer open). We saw an example of this in **Dickinson *v* Dodds**. When no time limit is placed upon an offer, it will remain open for a reasonable time. The amount of time which is reasonable will depend upon all the circumstances of the case. If, for example, a business made two offers, one to sell a boatload of ripe fruit and the other to sell a lorry, the offers would not remain open for the same length of time.

Subject to contract

Houses and land are often said to be sold 'subject to contract'. It has become established that this means that no contract has yet been concluded. This principle is not confined to contracts for the sale of land and houses. If goods are sold 'subject to contract', then a court would be likely to infer that no definite contract had yet been concluded.

Condition not fulfilled

An offeror might expressly or impliedly state that an offer is to remain open only until a certain condition is fulfilled. For example, when an offer to buy goods is made, it is implied that the offer will lapse if the goods are damaged before acceptance.

Alternatively, it might be agreed that a contract will become operative only if a condition is fulfilled. If A and B make a contract of sale, and agree that C will fix the price, this agreement is sufficiently certain to amount to a contract. However, if C refuses to fix a price, then the agreement will be avoided.

Battle of the forms

We shall see later (in Chapter 3) that many businesses use their standard terms and conditions when buying or selling goods. This can cause difficulties when both the buyer and the seller of goods insist that a contract is made upon their own particular standard terms. If the parties refuse to agree whose terms are to apply, then there will be no contract. If the parties do agree, so that a contract is formed and the goods are sold and delivered, a court might need to discover which set of terms was agreed to. This would be done by applying the ordinary principles of offer and acceptance, as the following case demonstrates.

 Butler Machine Tool Co Ltd v Ex-Cell-O Corporation Ltd (1979) (Court of Appeal)

On 23 May the claimants offered to sell a machine to the defendants. This offer was made on the claimants' standard terms and conditions, which said that they were to prevail over any terms and conditions contained in the buyer's order. On 27 May the defendants ordered a machine. This order said that it was made on the defendants' terms and conditions. The claimants' terms and conditions contained a price variation clause whereas the defendants' terms and conditions did not. The defendants' terms and conditions contained a tear-off slip at the bottom of the order. This said: 'We accept your order on the Terms and Conditions stated thereon.' On 5 June the claimants signed this slip and returned it to the defendants. They also added that the order 'is being entered in accordance with our revised quotation of 23 May'. After the machine had been delivered the claimants argued that their terms and conditions prevailed and that they were entitled to an additional £2,892 under their price variation clause.

Held The claimants were not entitled to the extra money. The price variation clause did not apply as the contract was made on the defendants' terms and conditions. On 23 May the claimants made an offer. On 27 May the defendants made a counter offer. On 5 June the claimants accepted this counter offer when they signed the acknowledgement slip and returned it to the defendants.

Comment In **Tekdata Interconnections Ltd v Amphenol Ltd [2009]** the Court of Appeal held that in a 'battle of the forms' case the party who fired the last shot would generally win, but that his would not always be the case. The question would always depend upon what the parties must be taken, objectively, to have intended when the contract was made. This should be determined, objectively, on the basis of a proper interpretation of the documents.

Intention to create legal relations

The acceptance of an offer will create a contract only if the offeror and offeree *appeared to intend* to create a legally binding agreement. It is therefore said that it is a requirement of a contract that there must be an intention to create legal relations. This requirement can be demonstrated by considering an example. Let us assume that one motor dealer says to another, 'I've got to sell that Ford Ka you were interested in. If you want it, you can have it for £5,500', and that the other motor dealer replies, 'Thanks a lot. I'll definitely take it.' If this conversation took place in a business context, for example if the dealers were speaking on the phone during office hours, then there would be a contract. All of the circumstances would indicate that by making the offer and the acceptance the parties did intend to enter into a legally binding agreement. However, if the offer and acceptance were made jokingly, for example in a pub as part of a long-standing joke between the parties, then there would be no contract. The circumstances would indicate that the parties did not intend to enter into a legal relationship.

In deciding whether or not there was an intention to create legal relations, the court takes an *objective* view of the parties' intentions. The court does not ask what the parties actually intended, but looks at what they appeared to the reasonable person to intend.

Agreements made in a business or commercial context

If an agreement is made in a business or a commercial context, there is a presumption that the parties did intend to make a contract. As this is only a presumption, it is not a cast-iron rule but only a starting point. It will therefore be up to the party who is claiming that there was no intention to create legal relations to introduce evidence to rebut the presumption (to show that it was not correct). It might be possible to do this, but if the presumption is not rebutted then there will be a contract.

In **Esso Petroleum Ltd *v* Commissioners of Customs and Excise (1976)** Esso advertised that they would give a World Cup coin to any motorist who bought at least four gallons of petrol at an Esso garage. (The coins showed the images of one of the England players taking part in the 1970 World Cup.) For tax reasons it became necessary to know whether or not the coins were supplied under a contract. The House of Lords held that there was an intention to create legal relations and so there was a contract to supply the coins.

In the **Esso** case the advertisement made a definite promise which motorists were entitled to believe would be kept. Many claims made in advertisements, such as that a particular type of beer refreshes the parts that other beers cannot reach, are regarded as mere 'sales puffs'. These sales puffs do not make any definite binding promise and are not intended to be taken seriously. They are either obviously untrue or incapable of being proved true or false. So even though sales puffs are made in a commercial context, the reasonable person would not think that they were intended to be legally binding.

It is quite possible to make an agreement, even a business agreement, on the understanding that it will have no legal effect at all. In such cases there will be no contract because the parties will have shown that they did not intend to create legal relations.

Agreements made in a social or domestic context

Social agreements are made between friends. Domestic agreements are made between the members of a family. When either a social or a domestic agreement is made, the courts begin with the presumption that the parties do not intend to make a contract. A party who claims that such an agreement is a contract will need to introduce evidence to show that this is what both parties intended. This may well be possible. For example, if friends or family members contributed money to buy a lottery ticket, a court would almost certainly decide that they intended that any prize should be shared. In **Wilson and another *v* Burnett (2007)** the Court of Appeal considered whether or not three friends had made a contract to share a bingo prize of over £100,000. On the evidence, the Court of Appeal agreed with the trial judge that they had not. May LJ gave the only judgment and said that the case depended upon whether the friends had made a sufficiently certain binding agreement. He was prepared to accept that this might have happened, but said there would always be 'intrinsic problems . . . on the question of whether a necessarily casual conversation could be elevated into an agreement binding and enforceable in law.'

The approach which a court will take is shown in Figure 2.3.

Figure 2.3 Intention to create legal relations

Consideration

A contract is a bargain under which each party must give some benefit, known as consideration, to the other. The consideration of one party is given in return for the consideration of the other. For example, let us assume that I visit a garage and agree to buy a new car for £9,999. A contract has been made. My consideration is the promise to pay £9,999 to the garage. The garage's consideration is its promise to pass ownership of the car to me. In bilateral contracts, such as the one used in this example, the consideration of both parties consists of a promise to do something. The one promise is given in return for the other.

In unilateral contracts the consideration of only one of the parties consists of a promise to do something. The consideration of the other party consists of actually performing the act requested by the promisor. For example, if I offered a £100 reward to anyone who found my lost dog, and you found the dog, a unilateral contract would have been created. My consideration would have been the promise to pay the reward. Your consideration would have been the act of finding the dog.

If only one of the parties gives some consideration, then a contract will not be created. Instead, any agreement will be a gift. So if a garage offered to give me a car for nothing, and I accepted this offer, there would be no contract. The garage would have provided some consideration to me, by promising to give me the car. But I would have provided no consideration to the garage because I would not have promised anything in return. Therefore, there would be no contract and the garage would not have to give me the car.

Later in this chapter we shall see that the promise of a gift is not enforceable unless the promise was made by a deed. When an agreement is made by a deed, it is enforceable as a specialty contract even if no consideration was received by one of the parties.

Consideration can be defined as a benefit given by one party or a loss suffered by the other. Usually, consideration is both a benefit to one party and a loss to the other. For example, if I buy a car from a garage, the garage's promise to give me ownership of the car is a benefit to me and a loss to the garage. Conversely, my promise to pay the money is a benefit to the garage and a loss to me.

Executed, executory and past consideration

Executory consideration consists of a promise to do something in the future. The consideration is called executory because when the contract is made the promisor has not yet performed (executed) his consideration. If we examine a typical bilateral contract, for example **Nicolene Ltd v Simmonds** (earlier in the chapter), we see that the consideration of both parties was executory. The defendants promised that they would deliver the 3,000 tons of steel bars, and the claimants promised that they would pay the price.

Executed consideration occurs when one of the parties makes the offer or the acceptance in such a way that he has completely fulfilled his liability under the contract. The only contractual liability remaining is that of the other party. A seller of goods, for example, might ask the buyer to send cash with his order. If the buyer does this, then his consideration is executed. Executed consideration is found in the acceptance of unilateral offers, where the acceptance is made by performing some action rather than by promising to do something in the future. For example, in **Carlill v The Carbolic Smoke Ball Company** Mrs Carlill's consideration was executed. She did not promise to use a smoke ball and catch flu, she just did it. The consideration of the smoke ball company, being a promise, was executory.

It is not possible to give as consideration a promise to do some act which has already been done. **Past consideration** is no consideration. This seems sensible enough, because to promise to do something which has already been done is to promise nothing at all. For example, in **Re McArdle (1951)** the claimant lived in a house which she did not own, and spent a considerable amount of money on having the house repaired. The owners had not asked her to do this. After the claimant had done this, the owners of the house signed an agreement to pay the claimant £488 in consideration of her having had the repairs done. The owners did not have to pay. When the promise to pay was made the claimant had already had the repairs done.

Despite the rule that past consideration is no consideration, a past act can be good consideration if two conditions are satisfied. First, the other party must have requested that the act be performed. Second, both parties must all the time have contemplated that payment would be made. The following case provides an example.

 Lampleigh v Brathwaite (1615)

The defendant had killed another man and needed to get a pardon from the King. He asked the claimant to get him a pardon. The claimant managed, at considerable personal expense, to obtain the necessary pardon. Upon hearing that the pardon had been granted, the defendant agreed to pay the claimant £100 for what he had done. Later, the defendant grew less grateful and refused to pay. The claimant sued for breach of contract.

Held The defendant had to pay the £100. Both of the conditions were satisfied. First, the defendant had asked the claimant to get the pardon. Second, both parties had contemplated that the claimant would be paid for his services.

Comment This case demonstrates the principle that a past act can amount to good consideration if the two conditions are satisfied. The amount of money payable would now be governed by s. 15(1) of the Supply of Goods and Services Act 1982. Section 15(1) implies a term that where the price of a service supplied under a contract is not fixed by the parties, a reasonable price will be paid.

Sufficiency and adequacy

A well-known principle of the law of contract holds that consideration must be sufficient but does not need to be adequate. At first sight this can seem puzzling, as in everyday language the words 'sufficient' and 'adequate' have a very similar meaning. However, in the context of the law of contract the two words have quite different meanings:

- By saying that consideration must be *sufficient* it is meant that consideration must be of some recognisable value, however small.
- By saying that consideration does not need to be *adequate* it is meant that consideration does not have to be of the same value as the other party's consideration.

An example demonstrates what is meant. If I agree to buy a new television from a shop for its ordinary selling price of £299.99, then my consideration, like that of the shop, is sufficient and adequate. My consideration is sufficient because it has some recognisable value. It is adequate because my promise to pay the money is worth much the same as the shop's promise to give me ownership of the television. If the shop and I had agreed that I could have the television for £1, then my consideration would have been sufficient but would not have been adequate. That is to say, my promise to pay £1 would have been worth something, but would not have been worth as much as I was getting in return. However, a contract would still have been formed, because consideration does not need to be adequate. If the shop had agreed to give me the television for nothing, then no contract would have been formed. I would not have given any consideration to the shop in return for the promise to give me ownership of the television. The shop would therefore not need to give me the television, unless its promise to do so had been made in a deed.

There are two main reasons why the law is not concerned with the adequacy of consideration. The first is that it is not always possible to say what something is worth. A thing is worth what someone will give for it, and this will depend on all of the circumstances. The second reason is that a business which makes bad contracts should not be allowed to escape from these contracts.

The performance of a trivial act can amount to good consideration as long as it confers an economic benefit on the other party. For example, in **Chappell & Co v The Nestlé Co Ltd (1959)** the defendants advertised that they would 'give away' records to members of the public who sent in 7.5p, which was one-fifth of the usual price, and three chocolate bar wrappers. For copyright reasons it became necessary to know whether or not the sending in of the wrappers was part of the customers' consideration. The House of Lords held that it was. Customers who sent in 7.5p without the wrappers would not have received a record. The principle in this case is important. As consideration does not need to be adequate, a trivial act could be given as consideration in any contract, as long as it conferred an economic benefit on the other party. In **Chappell & Co v The Nestlé Co Ltd** the defendants benefited through the publicity generated.

Performing an existing duty

Sometimes, a person claims to have given as consideration a promise to perform an existing duty. Whether or not such a promise amounts to good consideration depends upon how the duty arose in the first place. Three possibilities must be considered: first, that the duty arose under the general law of the land; second, that the duty arose under a previous contract with a third party; third, that the duty arose under a previous contract with the same person.

The duty arose under the general law

It is not good consideration to promise to perform a duty which is imposed by the general law of the land.

 Collins *v* Godefroy (1831)

The claimant was subpoenaed to attend a trial and give evidence. This means that he had a legal duty to attend the trial, this duty having arisen under the general law. The defendant agreed to pay the claimant six guineas (£6.30) if he actually did attend the trial.

Held The claimant was not entitled to the payment of any money. He could not give as consideration his promise to attend the trial. The general law of the land already obliged him to do this.

However, it is good consideration to promise to *exceed* a duty which has arisen under the general law of the land.

 Glasbrook Bros *v* Glamorgan County Council (1925) (House of Lords)

During a strike by coal miners the police were doing their best to protect collieries. The defendants asked the police to provide extra protection for their colliery, by stationing policemen on the colliery premises. The police superintendent in charge said that this would not be necessary. However, 100 policemen were stationed on the colliery premises when the defendants agreed to pay the wages of these policemen. After the strike the defendants refused to pay the £2,300 bill for the policemen's wages, arguing that the police had provided no consideration.

Held The defendants had to pay the £2,300. The police had a duty to protect property under the general law of the land. However, the extra protection provided was in excess of that which the police were obliged to provide under the general law of the land. Providing the extra protection therefore amounted to good consideration for the promise to pay the policemen's wages.

The duty arose under a previous contract with a different person

The same consideration can be given to two different people, so that two contracts are validly created. The following case provides an example.

Shadwell v Shadwell (1860)

The claimant was engaged to marry Ellen Nicholl. In those days, such an engagement amounted to a contract. If the claimant had breached the contract, by not marrying Ellen Nicholl, then she could have sued him. The claimant's uncle was pleased that the marriage was going to take place, and agreed that after it had he would pay the claimant £150 a year until the claimant's income as a barrister amounted to £630 a year. This agreement was to last for the whole of the uncle's life. The uncle died 18 years after the marriage had taken place. He had paid the full allowance for 12 of the 18 years and part of the allowance for one year. The claimant sued for the amounts of the allowance which had not been paid.

Held The claimant was entitled to the allowance which had not been paid. He had already made a contract with Ellen Nicholl that he would marry her. However, he was entitled to give exactly the same consideration (marrying Ellen Nicholl) in a separate contract with his uncle.

Comment A modern example of this principle can be seen in **New Zealand Shipping Co v A. M. Satterthwaite & Co (1974)** (Privy Council). A business which had agreed with a ship-owner that it would unload a ship (contract 1) could give the same promise to unload the ship to the owner of the goods on the ship (contract 2).

The duty arose under a previous contract with the same person

Until recently it was not possible to create two contracts by giving the same person the same consideration twice. The following case established this principle.

 Stilk v Myrick (1809)

The claimant signed a contract, agreeing to be a sailor on a ship for wages of £5 a month. The ship had a crew of only eleven men. When two of the crew deserted, the captain promised the remaining nine that if they continued with the voyage, as they had originally agreed to do, they could have the wages of the two deserters shared amongst them. The claimant and the other eight remaining crew agreed to this and completed the voyage. However, the captain refused to pay any more than the £5 a month originally agreed. The claimant sued for his share of the extra money which had been promised.

Held The men were not entitled to the extra money which they had been promised. At the start of the voyage they had promised the captain that they would do their duty in return for £5 a month. They could not later give the captain the same promise as consideration for a new contract.

Comment It might be thought that the nine remaining crew were doing more than they had originally agreed. However, the court thought that they had agreed to do whatever was necessary to complete the voyage. Lord Ellenborough said: 'They had sold all their services till the voyage be completed.'

The facts of **Hartley v Ponsonby (1857)** were very similar, except that half of the crew had deserted. To carry on with half a crew would have been dangerous. It was held that the sailors who agreed to continue the voyage were entitled to the extra payment which the captain had promised. They were regarded as having exceeded their duty because they had not originally agreed to work on a dangerous ship.

In the following case the Court of Appeal again considered this area of the law.

⚖️ Williams *v* Roffey Bros Ltd (1990) (Court of Appeal)

The defendants had contracted to refurbish a block of flats. They subcontracted the carpentry work to the claimant, who was to be paid £20,000 for doing the carpentry on 27 flats. Soon after starting work, the claimant realised that he had priced the job too low. He told the defendants that he would not be able to afford to finish the job if he were not paid more. If all the work on the flats was not finished on time the defendants would have become liable to pay huge damages to the owner of the block of flats. The defendants were so concerned about this that they agreed to pay the claimant an extra £575 per flat if he carried on and did the carpentry work as originally agreed. Happy with this agreement, the claimant carried on with the work. The claimant was not paid the extra money which he had been promised and so he sued for breach of contract.

Held The defendants were in breach of contract, and so had to pay the extra £575 per flat which they had agreed to pay. By agreeing to complete the carpentry work on time, the claimant had conferred a benefit on the defendants. This was the case even though he had already agreed with the defendants that he would do this work at the original contract price. By agreeing to do the work in return for the extra payment, the claimant had enabled the defendants to avoid paying the damages to the owner of the flats and had saved them the trouble of finding a different carpenter. This was a benefit to the defendants. Therefore, the claimant had provided fresh consideration for the defendants' promise to pay the extra £575 per flat.

In **Williams *v* Roffey Bros Ltd** the Court of Appeal claimed to have refined **Stilk *v* Myrick**, rather than to have overruled it. However, it is not easy to see how the two cases differ in principle. It is of some relevance that there was no such concept as economic duress when **Stilk *v* Myrick** was decided. If there had been, it seems likely that the contract would have been voidable because the sailors pushed the captain into the agreement in such a way that he did not really agree to it. **Williams *v* Roffey Bros Ltd** was different, in that it was the defendants who suggested the extra payment. Economic duress is considered in a later chapter (Chapter 4).

The following table shows the extent to which a promise to perform an existing duty can amount to good consideration.

Table 2.1 Whether a promise to perform an existing duty amounts to consideration

How duty arose \ Extent to which duty was promised to be performed	Promise to perform the duty	Promise to exceed the duty
Under the general law	No consideration	Good consideration
Under a previous contract with the same person	Maybe consideration **Stilk *v* Myrick** – no (but consider economic duress) **Williams *v* Roffey** – possibly yes	Good consideration
Under a previous contract with a third party	Good consideration	Good consideration

Settling out of court

A dispute is settled out of court when a person agrees not to pursue a legal action in return for the payment of a sum of money. By way of example, let us assume that Sajjid has been injured in an accident and has a claim against Tom. It is possible that if Sajjid and Tom cannot agree on the correct amount of compensation, the dispute will go to court. It is much more likely that Sajjid will take an amount of money offered by Tom, and in return will promise never to bring any legal claim against Tom in respect of the accident. If such an agreement were made, the dispute would have been settled out of court. (Sajjid and Tom would generally make such an agreement through their solicitors.) Once made, such an agreement would be binding upon both of the parties because it is a contract. The consideration of Tom would consist of paying the sum of money agreed. The consideration of Sajjid would consist of promising not to sue. Most legal disputes are settled out of court. It is obviously good public policy that, once a dispute has been finally settled, it cannot be reopened.

Part payment of a debt

If one person owes a sum of money to another, the debt can be extinguished in two ways. First, obviously enough, the debt is extinguished if the debtor pays the sum owing in full. Second, the debt is extinguished if the debtor and creditor agree that the creditor will take anything other than money instead of the amount owing. For example, if Harry owes Bill £10,000, the debt can be extinguished either by Harry paying the full £10,000 or by Harry and Bill agreeing that Bill should take Harry's car in full settlement of the debt. If Harry and Bill do agree that Bill should take the car in full settlement of the debt, the court would not be concerned with how much the car was actually worth. As we have seen, the courts are not concerned with the adequacy of consideration. So no matter what Harry's car might be worth, the full debt would be extinguished.

Difficulties arise where the parties agree that the creditor should take a sum of money which is less than the amount owing, in full settlement of the debt. Let us assume, for example, that Harry owes Bill £10,000 and that Bill agrees that if Harry pays £9,000 the debt will be extinguished and Bill will never ask for the rest of the money. **Pinnel's Case (1602)** held that a lesser sum of money cannot be consideration for a greater sum owed. Bill would therefore be able to sue Harry for the balance of £1,000, even though he had promised that he would not do this. The promise which Bill gave does not create a contract because no consideration was received in return for it. The promise made by Harry, to pay £9,000 in full settlement of the debt, could not be consideration to extinguish the whole debt of £10,000 because a lesser sum cannot be consideration for a greater sum owed. In this area the law does seem to be concerned with the adequacy of the consideration. It is saying that £9,000 is not enough consideration for a debt of £10,000. The reason for this is that the only thing which can always be given a definite monetary value is money itself. In extreme circumstances, a pen, a bicycle or a car might be worth £10,000. However, in no circumstances could £9,000 be worth £10,000. The decision in **Pinnel's Case** was directly approved by the House of Lords in the following case.

 Foakes v Beer (1884) (House of Lords)

Mrs Beer had successfully sued Dr Foakes, who had been ordered to pay her £2,090 damages. Dr Foakes was unable to pay all of this immediately. Mrs Beer agreed in writing that if Dr Foakes paid the full amount by instalments she would not 'take any proceedings whatever' on the judgment in her favour. Dr Foakes paid the full amount in instalments, as he had agreed to do. Mrs Beer then sued him for £360 interest. (Interest is always payable on a court judgment which is paid in instalments.)

Held Dr Foakes had to pay the £360 interest. A lesser sum of money cannot be consideration for a greater sum owed. Therefore, £2,090 payable by instalments without interest (the lesser sum) could not be consideration for £2,090 payable by instalments with interest (the greater sum owed).

Comment **Foakes *v* Beer** is an important case because in it the House of Lords directly approved the decision in **Pinnel's Case**. As House of Lords decisions are binding upon all other courts, the decision gave great strength to the rule that a lesser sum of money cannot be consideration for a greater sum owed.

Despite the decision in **Foakes *v* Beer**, the rule that a lesser sum of money cannot be consideration for a greater sum owed has always been subject to some exceptions:

- If the creditor agrees to take anything else instead of, or as well as, a lesser sum of money, then the debt is extinguished.
- If the creditor asks for a lesser sum to be paid before the debt is actually due, then the debtor's paying the lesser sum early can amount to good consideration.
- If the creditor requests that a lesser sum be paid in a different place, perhaps a different country, then the debtor's agreeing to this could possibly amount to good consideration.
- If there is a dispute as to the amount owed, and the creditor agrees to settle for less than he thinks he is owed, this agreement will be binding. (The parties will have settled out of court.)
- Another possible exception, promissory estoppel, is considered below.

Promissory estoppel

The concept of promissory estoppel arose in the following case.

Central London Property Trust Ltd *v* High Trees House Ltd (1947) (the High Trees Case)

In 1937 the defendants took a lease on a block of flats in London at a rent of £2,500 a year. During the Second World War (1939–45), many people moved away from London as it was being bombed. In 1940 the defendants found that they could not sublet the flats and could not therefore pay the claimants the full rent. The claimants accepted that this was the position and agreed that the defendants should pay a reduced rent of £1,250 a year. It was not agreed for how long the reduced rent should be paid. In 1945 the claimants were once again able to fully sublet the flats. However, the claimants were still paying a rent of only £1,250 a year. In September 1945 the claimants sued for the full rent in the future and the full rent from the time when the flats had once again become fully sublet.

Held The claimants were entitled to the full rent both in the future and from the date on which the flats had become fully sublet.

The decision in the **High Trees Case** was not particularly surprising. However, the judge who heard the case, Denning J, caused considerable controversy by saying that, if the claimants had asked for the full rent for the years when the flats were not fully sublet, they would not have got it. This statement is at odds with the decision in **Pinnel's Case** (i.e. that a lesser sum of money cannot be consideration for a greater sum owed). Denning's theory became known as promissory estoppel. It said that if a person made a promise, and the person to whom it was made was intended to rely on the promise and did rely on it, then the promise would be binding. This would be the case even if no consideration was given in return for the promise. However, promissory estoppel will apply only if the following four conditions are satisfied:

(1) There must have been an existing legal relationship between the parties.

(2) The promisor must have intended to enter into legal relations, by promising not to insist on his strict legal rights.

(3) The promisor must have known that the promisee would act upon this promise.

(4) The promisee must actually have acted upon the promise.

If the claimants in the **High Trees Case** had sued for the full rent for the years when the flats were not fully sublet, the four conditions would have been satisfied. According to Denning J, the claimants would therefore have been defeated by promissory estoppel.

Three further points about promissory estoppel must be made. First it is 'a shield not a sword' and this means that it can only be used as a defence. A claimant cannot use promissory estoppel to sue somebody with. Therefore, the decision in **Stilk v Myrick** would not be changed by promissory estoppel. In order to get their extra money, the sailors needed to sue the captain for it.

Second, there is no certainty as to whether promissory estoppel acts so as to permanently extinguish the right to sue, or whether it merely suspends the right to sue until reasonable notice of the intention to reintroduce the right to sue has been given. It is probably the case that where there is a continuing obligation it merely suspends the right to sue, unless the claimant indicated that he was permanently giving up his rights, but where there is a one-off obligation, such as to pay a debt, promissory estoppel could possibly extinguish the right to sue. However, in **Re Selectmove (1995)** the Court of Appeal held that it was bound by **Foakes v Beer**, which was still good law, and that part payment of a debt could not amount to good consideration.

Finally, it is certain that promissory estoppel is an equitable doctrine. It will therefore only act so as to prevent a claimant from breaking a promise where it would be inequitable (unfair) of the claimant to break the promise. In the following case promissory estoppel did not apply because it was not inequitable for the claimants to break the promise to accept a lesser sum of money.

 D & C Builders v Rees (1966) (Court of Appeal)

The claimants were a small firm of builders. The defendant owed the claimants £482 for work which the claimants had properly done. The defendant's wife knew that the claimants were very short of money. She told them that they would have to accept £300 in full settlement of the debt or they would be paid nothing. She knew that if the claimants refused to accept this, and sued for the full amount, they would be bankrupt before the case came to court. The claimants reluctantly agreed to take the £300, in full settlement of the debt. Once they had received this money, the claimants sued for the remaining £182.

Held The claimants were entitled to the remaining £182. **Foakes *v* Beer** applied and the lesser sum of money could not be satisfaction for the greater sum owed. The defendant could not use promissory estoppel as a defence. It was not inequitable for the claimants to break their promise to accept £300 in full settlement of the debt because they had been pressurised into making this promise.

Comment Since this case, the law on economic duress has changed a great deal. If such a case were to arise today the agreement to accept the lesser sum of money would be voidable for economic duress. (See Chapter 4.)

An outline of the requirements of promissory estoppel is set out in Figure 2.4. However, it must be remembered that the doctrine is surrounded by considerable uncertainty.

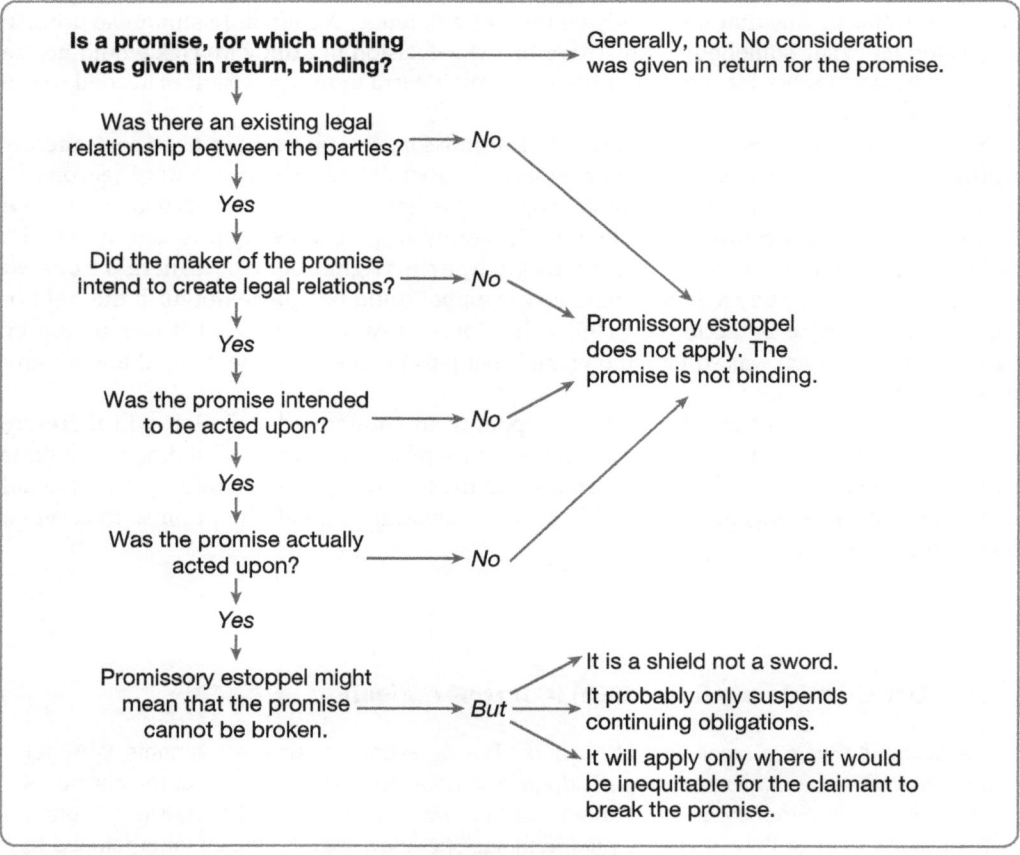

Figure 2.4 An outline of the effect of promissory estoppel

Privity of contract

The doctrine of privity of contract holds that a contract is private between the parties who made it. Anyone who did not make the contract cannot sue on the contract or be sued on it. The Contracts (Rights of Third Parties) Act 1999 has created an exception to the privity rule. However, privity is perhaps best understood if it is considered before the effect of the 1999 Act is considered. The following case provides a classic example of the privity rule.

 Tweddle v Atkinson (1831)

William Guy and John Tweddle made a contract with each other that William Guy would pay the claimant £200 and in return John Tweddle would pay the claimant £100. The claimant was the son of John Tweddle, who was marrying the daughter of William Guy. The contract between William Guy and John Tweddle said that the claimant should be able to sue either of them to enforce the contract. John Tweddle paid the money he had promised to pay but William Guy died before paying the money he had promised. The claimant sued William Guy's personal representatives to make them pay. The personal representatives took over William Guy's affairs and would have had exactly the same obligation to pay as William Guy would have had.

Held The claimant could not sue on the contract because he did not make the contract.

The privity rule was affirmed by the House of Lords in the following case.

 Dunlop Pneumatic Tyre Co Ltd v Selfridge & Co Ltd (1915) (House of Lords)

Dunlop sold car tyres to Dew & Co, who were dealers in motor accessories. In return for being given a 10 per cent discount on the price, Dew & Co agreed that they would obtain a written undertaking from any person to whom they resold the tyres that the tyres would not be sold below a certain price. Dew & Co resold the tyres to Selfridge & Co. Dew & Co gave Selfridge & Co a discount on the price of the tyres in return for the written agreement not to resell below the agreed price. Selfridge & Co resold the tyres below the agreed price and Dunlop sued them on the written agreement not to do this.

Held Dunlop could not sue Selfridge on the agreement as there was no contract between them. Dunlop had given no consideration to Selfridge & Co in return for the promise not to sell below the agreed price. The discount which Selfridge & Co had been given in return for their agreement had been given by Dew & Co and not by Dunlop.

Figure 2.5 shows how privity operated in **Tweddle v Atkinson** and **Dunlop Pneumatic Tyre Co Ltd v Selfridge & Co Ltd**.

Privity could cause particular injustice when one person bought unsafe goods or services on behalf of another. The following case provides an example.

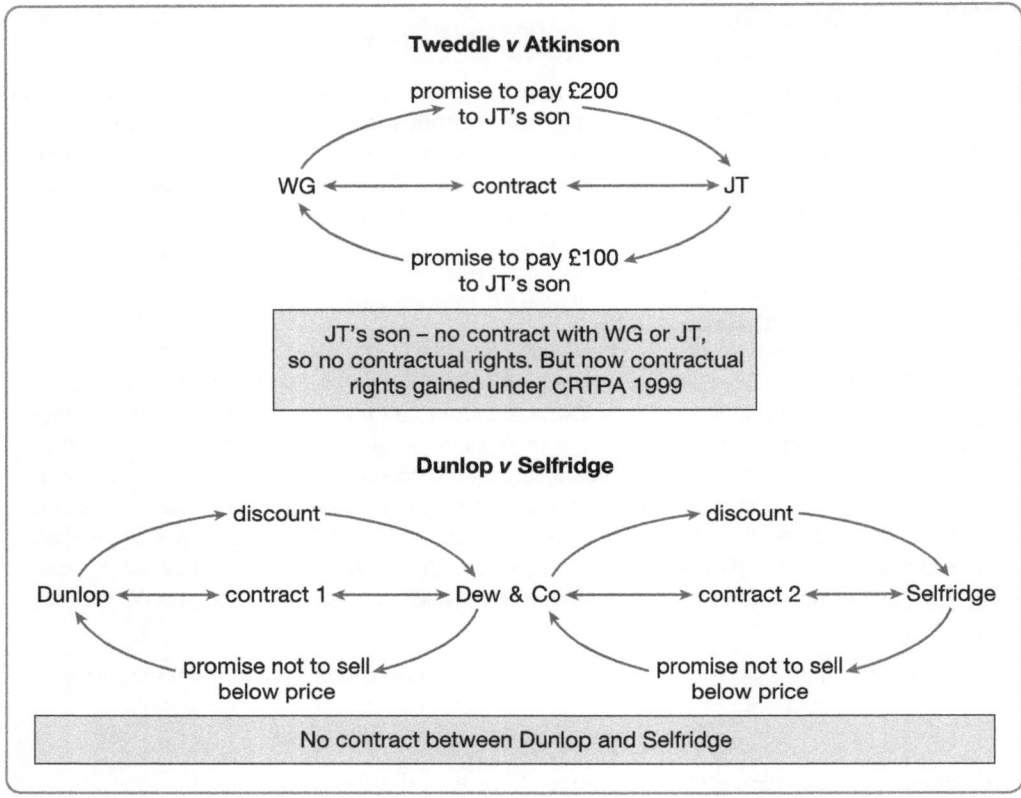

Figure 2.5 Tweddle *v* Atkinson and Dunlop Pneumatic Tyre Co Ltd *v* Selfridge & Co

---

⚖️ **Daniels and Daniels *v* R White & Sons Ltd and Tarbard (1938)**

Mr Daniels bought a bottle of lemonade. Both Mr and Mrs Daniels drank the lemonade, which was contaminated with carbolic acid. They were both injured by this and both sued the manufacturers of the lemonade for the tort of negligence. Mr Daniels also sued the retailer of the lemonade for breach of contract.

Held The manufacturers were not liable for the tort of negligence. They showed that they operated a 'fool proof' system and so it could not be proved that they had failed to take reasonable care. Mr Daniels succeeded in his claim for breach of contract. The retailer had to pay damages to compensate Mr Daniels for his injuries, but did not have to pay damages in respect of Mrs Daniels's injuries. The damages for breach of contract were only to compensate for the loss caused to Mr Daniels. Mrs Daniels could not sue the retailer for breach of contract because she had no contract with the retailer.

Comment If the case were to arise today, Mrs Daniels would succeed against the manufacturers under the Consumer Protection Act 1987 Part 1, which is considered in Chapter 8. However, this does no affect the contractual liability of the retailer.

In **Jackson *v* Horizon Holidays Ltd (1975)** the Court of Appeal allowed a husband who had booked a holiday for himself and his wife to recover substantial damages for both himself and his wife when the holiday proved to be disastrous. The House of Lords later commented that this decision was correct and suggested that some contracts, such as those to provide holidays or to book a taxi, call for special treatment. As regards package holidays, the Package Travel, Package Holidays and Package Tours Regulations 1992 now provide that damages can be awarded to holidaymakers who do not get the holiday contracted for, even if they did not themselves make the contract. However, these Regulations are confined to package holidays and do not change the principles of the general law of contract.

The Contracts (Rights of Third Parties) Act 1999

The Contracts (Rights of Third Parties) Act 1999 has changed the privity rule but not abolished it. The Act provides that a third party can in two circumstances sue on a contract which he or she did not make:

(1) A third party can sue on the contract if the contract expressly provided that he should be able to sue. (The s. 1(1)(a) route.)

For example, a man might buy a car for his son and the contract might state that if the car was not of satisfactory quality the son could sue the seller on the contract. (**Tweddle v Atkinson** would now therefore be differently decided.)

(2) A third party can sue on the contract if the contract intended to confer a benefit on the third party. (The s. 1(1)(b) route.)

However, the s. 1(1)(b) route does not apply if the other party to the contract can show that the parties to the contract did not intend the contract to be enforceable by the third party.

Section 1(3) requires that the third party must be expressly identified in the contract by name, as a member of a class or as answering a particular description. This is the case for both routes. Express identification by name needs no explanation. Express identification by class could arise in many ways: for example, if a contractual provision was made for the benefit of all the members of a particular club, or for the benefit of the contracting party's brothers and sisters. Express identification of the third party as his or her answering a particular description could also arise in many ways: for example, if a contractual provision was made for the benefit of 'my youngest brother' or for the benefit of the Sheriff of Nottingham. Applying the Act to **Daniels v White and Tarbard**, we can see that the Act would not have allowed Mrs Daniels to sue on the contract with the retailer unless Mr Daniels had expressly identified Mrs Daniels as a person for whose benefit the contract was being made.

When a benefit is conferred on a third party by the Act, the third party gets any remedy which would have been available to him if he had made the contract. The third party can also avail himself of exclusion or limitation clauses. Any rights conferred on the third party are additional to rights conferred on the person who made the contract. However, s. 5 protects the promisor from double liability.

If a party to the contract has any defences arising from the contract, these are as available against the third party as they would have been available against the other party to the contract.

Example

A contract is made between Bert and Chas. Bert is to sell 50 bicycles to Chas, and a term of the contract provides that Chas should pay the price to Dan. Bert delivers only 30 bicycles to Chas. Chas accepts the 30 bicycles. Chas will not need to pay the whole contract price to Dan, but will need to pay only the price of 30 bicycles.

The promisor (in the above example Chas) will also have available defences, rights of set-off and counterclaims which did not arise in connection with the contract, if these would have been available against the third party if the third party had been a party to the contract.

> **Example**
>
> Bert agrees to sell 50 bicycles to Chas. A term of the contract provides that Chas is to pay the price of £5,000 to Dan. Bert delivers 50 bicycles to Chas. Dan owes £1,000 to Chas in connection with a contract made last month. Chas is entitled to set-off the £1,000 and pay Dan only £4,000.

Figure 2.6 gives an overview of the Contracts (Rights of Third Parties) Act 1999.

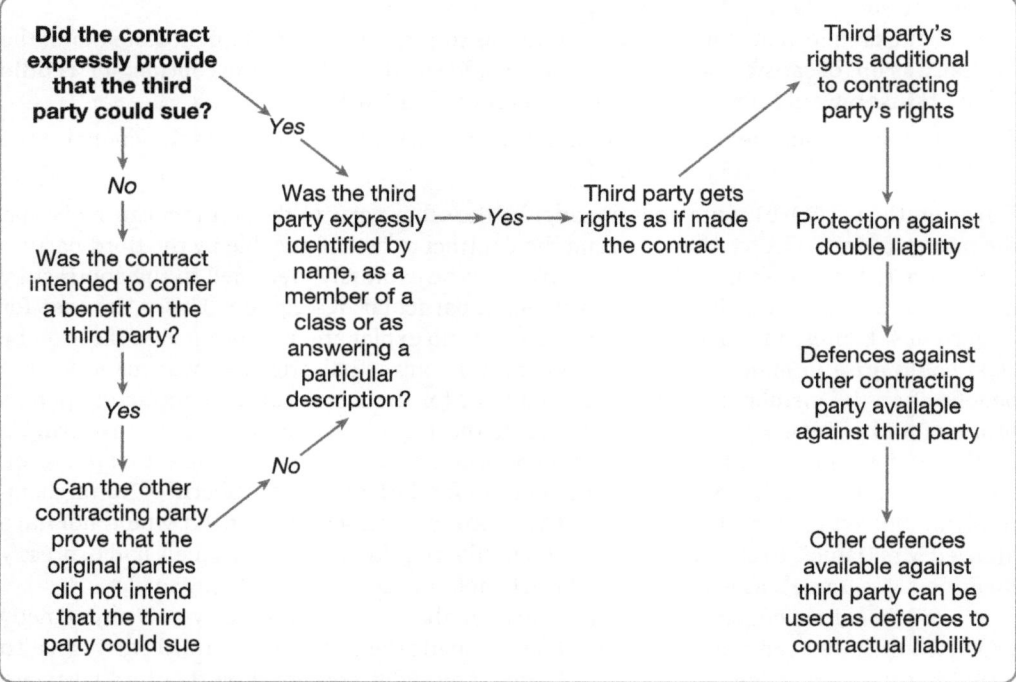

Figure 2.6 The effect of the CRTPA 1999

Formalities

In general, contracts can be created without the need for any special formalities. The types of contracts which can be made only if certain formalities are observed are as follows.

Contracts which must be made by a deed

A conveyance of a legal estate in land must be made by a deed. Also, a lease of land of over three years' duration must be made by a deed or no legal estate will be created.

Earlier in this chapter we saw that gifts are not contracts and that the promise of a gift is not enforceable as a contract. However, if a gift is made by a deed it is enforceable as a contract. This is because the act of making the deed is regarded as providing the required consideration.

Deeds must be made in writing and must be signed by the maker of the deed in the presence of a witness. The witness must sign the deed to indicate having witnessed the signature of the maker of the deed. The deed must also indicate that it is intended to be a deed. This can be done if the deed states that it is signed as a deed by the maker in the presence of the witness. For example: 'This document is signed as a deed by Jane Smith in the presence of Mary McGuire.'

Later (in Chapter 5), we shall see that the Limitation Act 1980 provides that the right to sue on a simple contract is lost after six years have passed from the time when the right to sue arose. When a contract is made by a deed, this time limit is increased to 12 years after the right to sue arose.

Contracts which must be in writing

Contracts to sell or dispose of an interest in land must be made in writing. The written contract must incorporate all the terms of the contract in one document, or in both contracts where contracts are exchanged, and must be signed by both of the parties. If these formalities are not complied with, the contract will be void and therefore of no effect. There is, however, one exception. A lease of land for a period of three years or less will be valid if made orally, as long as the lease takes effect immediately.

Regulated consumer credit agreements cannot be enforced unless they were made in writing and unless the other requirements of the Consumer Credit Act 1974 have been complied with. An agreement is a regulated consumer credit agreement whenever an individual (who can be in business, but cannot be a company) is provided with credit.

Contracts which must be evidenced in writing

Contracts of guarantee must be evidenced in writing, and signed by the person giving the guarantee, or they will be unenforceable. When a contract of guarantee is made, one person agrees to undertake secondary liability to settle the debts or liabilities of another person. Although the contract under which the guarantee is given needs to be evidenced in writing, the contract which created the debt which is being guaranteed does not. An example might make this more clear.

Let us assume that Paint Ltd agrees to buy a new van from a garage for £10,000 and that Sarah guarantees to pay the price if Paint Ltd should fail to do so. The contract under which Paint Ltd buys the van does not need to be in writing nor evidenced in writing. However, the contract under which Sarah guarantees to pay the price if Paint Ltd should fail to do so does need to be evidenced in writing.

A contract which is evidenced in writing does not need to be a written contract as such. However, there must be some written evidence that the contract has been made. This written evidence, which might for example be in a letter or a note, must be signed by the person giving the guarantee and must contain all the material terms of the contract of guarantee.

Minors

A person who is capable of making contracts is said to have capacity to make contracts. Adults have full contractual capacity, but special rules apply to minors (persons who are under the age of 18). Contracts made by minors might be either valid, voidable or void, depending upon the type of contract made.

Valid contracts

Section 3 of the Sale of Goods Act 1979 provides that minors must pay a reasonable price for necessary goods sold and delivered to them. They must also pay a reasonable price for necessary services supplied. Therefore, contracts to supply minors with either necessary goods or necessary services are valid contracts. Goods are regarded as necessary if they are suitable to the minor's position in life and are actually required by him. This obviously varies from person to person. It is worth noticing that the amount which minors must pay is a reasonable price, which might not always be the same as the price agreed in the contract.

A minor can also validly make a contract of employment, as long as the contract is beneficial overall to the minor.

Voidable contracts

Contracts which impose a continuing liability on a minor are voidable by the minor. This means that the contracts are valid, except that the minor has the option to avoid the contract (call the contract off). (The way in which a voidable contract can be avoided is considered in Chapter 4.) A minor who is to avoid these types of voidable contracts must do so either before reaching the age of 18 or within a reasonable time of having reached the age of 18. The main types of contracts voidable by a minor are contracts of partnership, contracts to buy shares and contracts to take a lease of property.

Void contracts

Minors are not bound by contracts to buy unnecessary goods or services. A minor who makes such a contract may be entitled to regain any money paid under the contract, but only if the minor has not received any benefit under the contract. Nor are minors bound by contracts to borrow money. For this reason it would be most unusual for a bank or other commercial lender to lend money to a minor unless repayment of the loan was guaranteed by an adult. Agreements by the minor to repay the loan will be of no effect if they were made before the minor had reached the age of 18. Agreements to repay which were made after the minor had reached the age of 18 will compel the minor to repay the loan. If a minor acquires property under an unenforceable contract, s. 3(1) of the Minors' Contracts Act 1987 allows a court to order the minor to give the property back to the supplier. This remedy is available at the court's discretion and would not be applied if the minor had paid for the property.

Essential points

- A contract is a legally binding agreement.
- A contract is formed when an offer is accepted.
- An invitation to treat is not an offer, but an invitation to negotiate or an invitation to make an offer.

- As soon as an acceptance of an offer is received, a contract is created.
- If the postal rule applies, an acceptance made by posting a letter is effective when it is posted.
- An offer of a unilateral contract can be accepted only by performing the act requested.
- A counter offer is not an acceptance and revokes the original offer.
- A contract can be created only if the reasonable person could state with certainty exactly what it is that has been agreed.
- An offer which has been revoked cannot be accepted.
- Revocation of an offer is effective when it is received. (The postal rule never applies to revocations.)
- A contract will only be created if the parties appeared to intend to create a legal relationship.
- Consideration consists of a right given to one party, or a loss or detriment suffered by another.
- A past act cannot be given as consideration.
- Most contracts do not need to be made in writing.
- Minors (persons under 18) are bound by contracts to buy necessary goods or services.
- Minors must pay a reasonable price for necessary goods or services which they have contracted to buy, if the goods or services are supplied to them.
- If minors make contracts to buy goods or services which were not necessary, the contract will be void.

Practice questions

1 On 10 July Ace Ltd posted an offer to sell a consignment of 1,000 widgets to Brian, a retailer. The offer said that the price was £10,000 and that the offer would remain open until 31 July. On 12 July Brian telephoned Ace Ltd and asked whether he would be allowed three months' credit. Ace Ltd's manager replied that payment would have to be made in cash, upon delivery. On 29 July Ace Ltd sold the consignment of widgets to a third party, Charles. On 30 July Brian posted a letter accepting Ace Ltd's offer. This letter arrived on 1 August. Upon opening the letter, Ace Ltd's manager telephoned Brian and told him that the consignment of widgets had been sold and that further similar widgets were not available. Advise the parties as to whether or not a contract has been created.

2 Acme Supastore advertised its 'price promise' heavily in the Nottown Evening News. This promise stated that Acme was the cheapest retailer in the city of Nottown and that it would guarantee that this was true. The advertisement stated: 'We are so confident that we are the cheapest in the area that we guarantee that you cannot buy a television anywhere in Nottown cheaper than from us. We also guarantee that if you buy any television from us and give us notice in writing that you could have bought it cheaper

at any other retailer within five miles of our Supastore on the same day we will refund twice the difference in price. Offer to remain open for the month of December. Any claim to be received in writing within 5 days of purchase.' Belinda saw the advertisement and was persuaded by it to buy a television from Acme Supastore for £299. The contract was made on Monday 3 December. On Friday 7 December Belinda found that a neighbouring shop was selling an identical model of television for £289 and had been selling at this price for the past six months. Belinda immediately telephoned Acme Supastore to say that she was claiming her money back. She also posted a letter claiming her money back. The letter arrived on Monday 10 December. Acme Supastore are refusing to refund any of the purchase price. Advise Belinda as to whether or not any contract has been made.

3 A large department store advertised its January sale on a local radio station and in a local newspaper. The advertisement said that the first customer to enter the store when it opened on 2 January would be able to buy a new video recorder for just £1. The advertisement showed the model of video recorder which could be bought. Joanne decides to try to be the first in the department store so that she can buy the video recorder. She camps outside the shop at midday on 1 January, relieved to see that nobody else is yet queuing. At 7 a.m. on 2 January the manager of the department store tells Joanne that the offer has been called off. Joanne refuses to accept this. At 8 a.m. the manager shows Joanne an advertisement in the morning edition of the local newspaper. This advertisement says that the offer has been called off. Again, Joanne refuses to leave. When the department store opens, at 9 a.m., Joanne enters the shop and tells the manager that she is the first customer and that she is buying the video recorder for £1. The manager refuses to accept the money and says that the video recorder is only available at its usual price of £299.99. Advise Joanne as to whether or not a contract has been created.

4 **Brogden *v* Metropolitan Railway Co (1877)** concerned a dispute between a coal merchant and a railway company. The House of Lords had to decide whether a contract existed and if so, what the terms of the contract were. The facts of the case can be set out as the following four statements.

   (a) After the railway company had taken coal from Brogden for many years, the company sent Brogden a written agreement which set out the position as regards future supplies of coal.

   (b) Brogden altered the written agreement, then signed it and sent it back to the company.

   (c) The company filed the agreement in a drawer, leaving it there for two years.

   (d) Brogden delivered coal, which the company had ordered, in accordance with the altered agreement.

   Each of the four statements above amounts to one of the following: an offer; an invitation to treat; an acceptance; a revocation; a counter offer; a contract; or nothing at all. Decide which of these matters each of the statements amounts to. (In reaching your decision you should apply at least three of the cases which we have considered in this chapter.)

5 A company which deals in gold and jewellery employs two private security guards to guard the premises each night. The security guards are both self-employed, providing their services under two separate contracts. One night, one of the security guards

phones in to say that he will not be able to work for the rest of the week, as he is ill. The company tells the other security guard that he must work single-handed for the remainder of the week. The security guard manages to do this, although it involves a certain amount of extra work. At the end of the week the company tells the security guard who worked alone that he will be paid double wages for the week. Now the company has changed its mind and pays the guard only his normal amount. Advise the security guard as to whether or not he will be entitled to the extra amount promised.

6 With reference to decided cases, explain the difference between an offer and an invitation to treat. Why does the distinction matter?

Task 2

A friend of yours, Rory, works as self-employed painter and decorator. Rory has heard that materials can often be bought more cheaply at auction or by tender than from wholesalers. Rory has asked you to write a brief report, indicating the following matters:

(a) The way in which a contract is made by the process of offer and acceptance.

(b) How an offer differs from an invitation to treat.

(c) How the offer and acceptance are made when goods are bought at auction.

(d) How the offer and acceptance are made when goods are bought by tender.

(e) The extent to which offers can be withdrawn after they have been made.

(f) What is meant by an intention to create legal relations.

(g) What is meant by consideration.

(h) Whether all contracts can be made without the need for writing.

mylawchamber

Visit **www.mylawchamber.co.uk/macintyreessentials** to access tools to help you develop and test your knowledge of business law, including interactive multiple choice questions, practice exam questions with guidance, weblinks, glossary, glossary flashcards, legal newsfeed and legal updates.

Use **Case Navigator** to read in full some of the key cases referenced in this chapter with commentary and questions:

Carlill *v* The Carbolic Smoke Ball Co (1893)

Pharmaceutical Society (GB) *v* Books Cash Chemists Ltd (1953)

Williams *v* Roffey Bros Ltd (1990)

Central London Property Trust Ltd *v* High Trees House Ltd (1947)

3

The terms of the contract

The terms of a contract define the obligations which the parties to the contract have undertaken. This chapter begins by examining the ways in which terms can arise, and explains the difference between express and implied terms. Next the different types of terms are considered. Breach of some types of terms gives the injured party the right to terminate the contract, whereas breach of other types does not. Breach of any term always gives a right to sue for damages.

Exclusion clauses are terms which attempt to exclude liability for breach of contract or for breach of a tortious duty of care. This chapter concludes by considering the special rules which apply to exclusion clauses.

Nature of terms

A contract is made up of terms. All of the promises which the contract contains, whether they were made expressly or impliedly, will be terms. If any of these promises are not kept, one or more terms of the contract will have been breached. The injured party will then always have a remedy for breach of contract.

Terms can find their way into contracts in one of two ways: they can be expressed, in either speech or writing, or they can be implied. Express terms are actually agreed by the parties in words. Implied terms are implied either by the court (on the grounds of the presumed intention of the parties) or by a statute. Figure 3.1 shows the ways in which terms arise.

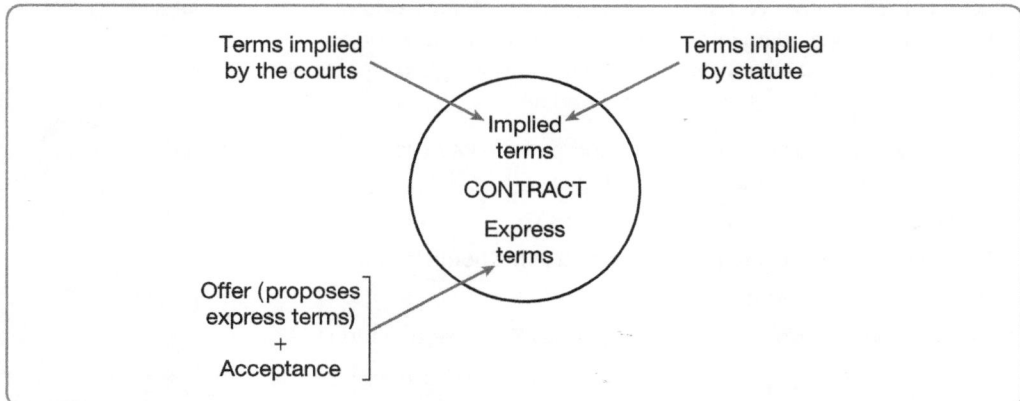

Figure 3.1 The ways in which terms arise

Express terms

A contract is formed when an offer is accepted. The offeror proposes a set of terms. If the offer is accepted by the offeree, these proposed terms become legally binding as the terms of the contract. Oral contracts usually contain very few express terms. Written contracts, especially business contracts, usually contain far more. If there is any conflict between an express term and an implied term the express term will prevail, unless the implied term is a statutory one which cannot be changed. (See later in the chapter.)

Terms implied by the courts

The courts have the power to imply terms into contracts. Despite having this power, the courts have always made it plain that they are not prepared to make a contract for the parties. The courts will imply a term on only two grounds. First, that it was so obviously intended to be a part of the contract that the parties felt no need to mention it. Second, that the term must be implied as a matter of law.

Terms based on intentions of the parties

 The Moorcock (1889) (Court of Appeal)

A jetty owner made a contract which allowed a shipowner to moor his ship at the jetty. Both parties knew that the ship would be grounded at low tide. When the ship did touch the ground it was damaged because there was a ridge of rock beneath the mud. The shipowner asked the court to imply a term that the jetty owner had taken reasonable care to ensure that the jetty was a safe place to unload a ship.

Held The term was implied by the court. The jetty owner had breached the term and was therefore in breach of contract. It was obviously intended by both parties that the mooring should be safe.

Care must be taken when looking for terms implied by the courts, as the courts do not imply them freely.

Lord Pearson said in **Trollope *v* NWRHB (1973)**:

> An unexpressed term can be implied if and only if the court finds the parties must have intended that term to form part of their contract . . . it is not enough for the court to find that such a term would have been adopted by the parties as reasonable men if it had been suggested to them . . . it must have been a term which went without saying, a term necessary to give business efficacy to the contract.

If the courts were prepared to imply terms freely, they would move towards making a contract for the parties rather than giving effect to what the parties had themselves agreed.

Customary terms

Terms may be implied by the courts on the grounds that they are customary in a particular trade, customary in a particular locality or customary between the parties.

Many trades have customs, and these customs will be implied into contracts made within the context of those trades. In the bakery trade, for example, a dozen used to mean 13, and a baker who sold 20 dozen loaves would be deemed to have sold 260, not 240.

In a similar way, customs of a particular locality will be implied into contracts made in that locality. A term can become customary between the parties to the contract if they regularly make contracts which include such a term.

In **Kendall v Lillico (1969)** the parties had often dealt with each other. Whenever an oral contract was made, the same 'sold note' containing a large number of terms was always sent the following day. The House of Lords held that the terms in the 'sold note' had become customary between the parties and were therefore incorporated into an oral contract which was made. (See also **Photolibrary Group Ltd v Burda Senator Verlag Gmbh (2008)** in Chapter 2.) However, the course of dealing must be well established. In **Hollier v Rambler Motors Ltd (1972)** the claimant had signed the same exclusion clause three or four times in the previous five years when he had had his car repaired at the defendant's garage. The car was damaged while being repaired under a contract made orally. The garage tried to rely on their exclusion clause but the court held that they could not do so. The exclusion clause was not incorporated into the oral contract. Salmon LJ said: 'I am bound to say that, for my part, I do not know of any other case in which it has been decided or even argued that a term could be implied into an oral contract on the strength of a course of dealing (if it can be so called) which consisted at the most of three or four transactions over a period of five years.'

Terms implied as a matter of law

The courts imply terms into particular types of contracts as a matter of law. These terms are not implied because the parties must have intended them to be a part of the contract; they are implied because, as a matter of law, such terms are always implied into the type of contract in question. For example, in **Liverpool City Council v Irwin (1977)** the House of Lords implied a term that the landlord of a block of flats would keep the flats in reasonable repair and reasonably usable. This term was implied because such a term would be implied generally into contracts between landlord and tenant.

Later it will be seen that certain terms are implied generally into contracts of employment (see Chapter 13).

Exclusion of implied terms

Later in this chapter we shall see that the terms implied by statutes can never be excluded in consumer cases and can be excluded in non-consumer cases only where this is reasonable. However, terms implied by the court on the basis that they are customary, or are what the parties obviously intended, can always be excluded by an express term.

Types of terms

If any term is breached the injured party will always have a remedy for breach of contract. The nature of that remedy will depend upon what type of term was breached.

Conditions and warranties

Traditionally, all terms could be classified as being either conditions or warranties.

A condition is a term which seemed vitally important when the contract was made (a term which went 'to the root of the contract'). If a condition is breached, then the injured party can terminate the contract and claim damages.

A warranty is a term which did not seem vitally important when the contract was made (a term which did not go 'to the root of the contract'). If a warranty is breached, the injured party can claim damages but cannot treat the contract as terminated. Figure 3.2 shows an outline of the different types of terms.

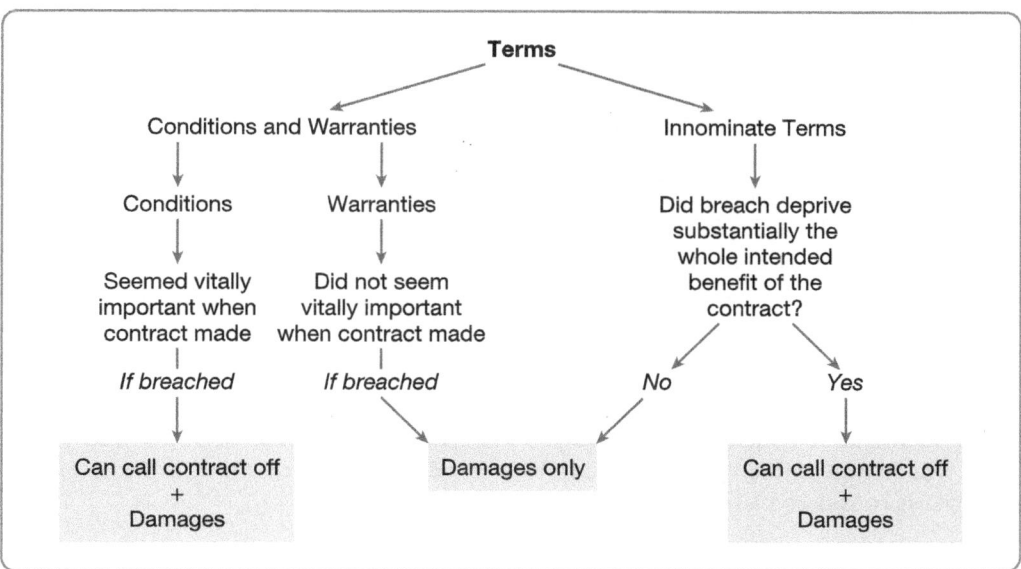

Figure 3.2 Types of terms

Example

Packaging Ltd bought 1,000 cardboard boxes from Box Ltd. A term of the contract provided that the boxes would weigh a certain amount. This term is breached because the boxes do not weigh the correct amount. If the term was a condition, Packaging can terminate the contract. If they did terminate, they could reject all of the boxes, refuse to pay for the boxes, and claim damages. If the term was a warranty, Packaging cannot terminate the contract. So they could not reject the boxes, or refuse to pay the price, but they could claim damages. Even if the term was a condition, Packaging could treat it as a warranty if they chose to do this. So Packaging Ltd would not be compelled to reject the boxes if the term was a condition. The important point to note is that they could do this if they wanted to.

It might be thought that the right to terminate a contract is of little importance if damages are always available. However, the right to terminate can be very important when one of the parties has made what has turned out to be an ongoing bad bargain.

Innominate terms

In the **Hong Kong Fir Case (1962)** the Court of Appeal invented a new category of term, the innominate or intermediate term. In deciding whether or not breach of such a term gives the injured party the right to terminate the contract, the court does not consider how important the term seemed when the contract was made. Instead, the court asks whether or not the breach deprived the injured party of substantially the whole benefit of the contract. If the breach did do this, the injured party can treat the contract as terminated and claim damages. If the breach did not do this, the injured party can claim damages but cannot treat the contract as terminated. Innominate terms have not replaced conditions and warranties. Some terms can now be classed as conditions or warranties, others are innominate terms.

There may be some uncertainty as to whether a court will classify a particular term as either a condition, a warranty or an innominate term. Generally, the position is as follows.

- A statute, such as the Sale of Goods Act 1979, or a rule of law might establish that a term is a condition or a warranty.

- The parties themselves might agree that certain terms will or will not give the right to terminate if they are breached. The court will give effect to such an agreement. However, the mere labelling of a term as a condition or a warranty will not of itself be enough to indicate such an agreement.

- If no term of the contract or rule of law stipulates that a particular term will or will not allow termination, the courts will regard the term as an innominate term. Breach of such a term will allow the injured party to terminate the contract only if the breach deprived the injured party of substantially the whole benefit of the contract.

It should also be remembered that damages will always be available for any breach of contract, whether the injured party has the right to terminate the contract or not. The subject of damages is considered later (see Chapter 5).

Terms implied by statute

Terms are implied into contracts by three statutes: the Sale of Goods Act 1979; the Supply of Goods (Implied Terms) Act 1973; and the Supply of Goods and Services Act 1982. The terms which these statutes imply are inserted into certain types of contracts without the parties needing to agree to them. Indeed, as we shall see, in consumer contracts the terms can be implied even if the parties expressly agree that they should not be.

The Sale of Goods Act 1979

The Sale of Goods Act 1893 was the first statute to imply terms into contracts. The 1893 Act has been replaced by the Sale of Goods Act 1979 (SGA 1979). The implied terms contained in the SGA 1979 are virtually identical to those contained in the original 1893 Act. The terms implied by the other two statutes, the Supply of Goods (Implied Terms) Act 1973 (SGITA 1973) and the Supply of Goods and Services Act 1982 (SGSA 1982), are also very closely modelled on the terms implied by the Sale of Goods Acts 1893 and 1979. Almost all of the case law on statutory implied terms is concerned with terms implied by the Sale of Goods Acts. We therefore consider the terms implied by the Sale of Goods Act 1979 before we consider the terms implied by the SGITA 1973 and the SGSA 1982.

Scope of the Sale of Goods Act 1979

The SGA 1979 applies only to contracts of sale of goods. Such contracts are defined by s. 2(1) of the Act:

> A contract of sale of goods is a contract by which the seller transfers or agrees to transfer the property in goods to the buyer for a money consideration, called the price.

Reading s. 2(1), we can see that a sale occurs when a buyer pays money in return for ownership of goods. It does not matter whether the buyer pays cash, by cheque or by credit card.

A free gift, however, where the buyer pays no money, cannot be a sale. Nor is it a sale where goods are bartered (exchanged) for other goods.

Note also that the seller must transfer the property in goods (ownership of the goods) to the buyer. This requirement rules out contracts to hire or to lease, where possession of the goods is transferred but ownership is not.

As long as there is a definite commitment to pass ownership in return for money, either immediately or in the future, it does not matter that the money is paid later or that ownership is transferred later. If the contract agrees that the property in the goods should be transferred at some future date, or when some condition has been satisfied, then this is an agreement to sell goods rather than a sale of goods. Agreements to sell goods are governed by the SGA 1979 and become sales of goods when the time elapses or the condition is fulfilled. For example, a merchant might agree to sell 100 tonnes of wheat of a certain type, to be delivered on 1 August next year. This is an agreement to sell goods and is governed by the SGA 1979. On 1 August next year the agreement becomes a sale of goods.

Meaning of goods

Section 61(1) of the SGA 1979 defines goods as 'all personal chattels other than things in action'.

A personal chattel is a physical thing which can be touched and moved, for example a car, a cup or a computer. Land and houses cannot be moved and are real property rather than personal chattels.

A thing in action is a right which can be enforced only by suing (taking legal action). A guarantee, for example, is a thing in action. A guarantee may be written on a piece of paper but the paper is not the property. The property is the right which the guarantee gives and, ultimately, that right can only be enforced by suing the person who gave it. Debts and intellectual property rights are other examples of things in action.

The terms implied by the Sale of Goods Act 1979

Sections 12–15 of the SGA 1979 contain five major implied terms, all of which are conditions. These terms do not need to be mentioned by the buyer or the seller, as the Act will automatically imply them into contracts of sale of goods. The five conditions implied by the SGA 1979 are as follows.

(1) Section 12(1) implies a condition that the seller has *the right to sell the goods*.
(2) Section 13(1) implies a condition that the goods *will correspond with any description by which they were sold*.
(3) Section 14(2) implies a condition that the goods are of *satisfactory quality*.
(4) Section 14(3) implies a condition that the goods are *fit for the buyer's purpose*.
(5) Section 15(2) implies a condition that where goods are sold by sample *the bulk will correspond with the sample*.

The terms implied by ss. 14(2) and (3) are implied only into sales of goods which are made in the course of a business. The other terms are implied into all contracts of sale of goods.

These implied terms are vitally important and each one must be examined closely.

The right to sell (s. 12(1))

Section 12(1) of the SGA 1979 provides that unless the circumstances show a different intention:

> There is an implied [condition] on the part of the seller that in the case of a sale he has a right to sell the goods, and in the case of an agreement to sell he will have such a right at the time when the property is to pass.

This term, like the others, is a condition. As we have seen, when a condition is breached the injured party can treat the contract as terminated and also claim damages. If a seller breaches a condition and the buyer chooses therefore to treat the contract as terminated, the buyer will get all of the purchase price back.

 Rowland *v* Divall (1923) (Court of Appeal)

A thief stole a car from its owner and sold the car to the defendant. The claimant, a motor dealer, bought the car from the defendant for £334. The claimant did the car up and sold it to a customer for £400. On discovering that the car was stolen, the police took it from the customer and returned it to its original owner. The customer complained to the claimant who returned his £400. The claimant asked the defendant for the return of the £334 he had paid. The defendant refused to pay, saying that he had no idea that the car was stolen.

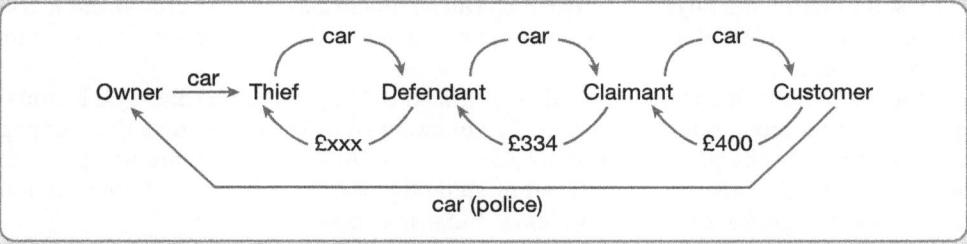

Figure 3.3 Rowland *v* Divall

Held The claimant got all of his money back. Section 12(1) provides that the seller must have the right to sell, and when the defendant sold the car to the claimant he did not have this right because he did not own the car. The thief never owned the car. He therefore could not pass ownership to the defendant, who could not pass ownership to the claimant, etc. None of the parties except the original owner ever had the right to sell the car.

Atkin LJ held: 'It seems to me that in this case there has been a total failure of consideration, that is to say that the buyer has not got any part of that for which he paid the purchase price. He paid the money in order that he might get the property, and he has not got it.'

Where there is a chain of innocent sellers, the loser will generally be the person who bought from the thief, as in **Rowland *v* Divall**. Of course, this person could successfully sue the thief, but in practical terms this would probably be a waste of money as it is most unlikely that the thief could be found and would have the money to pay when the case reached court.

However, if any of the the sellers in the chain has become insolvent, then the person who bought from that seller will be the one with no practical remedy.

For example, let us assume that a thief has stolen a car from its owner and then sold the car to A, who sold it to B, who sold it to C, who sold it to D. As can be seen from Figure 3.4, A will be the loser.

But now let us further assume that B has become insolvent. D can recover from C, but C cannot recover from B. Nor can C leapfrog B and sue A – there is no contract between the two of them.

Section 12(2) implies two warranties. First, that the goods are free from encumbrances, meaning that no-one has a mortgage or charge over the goods. Second, that no person will

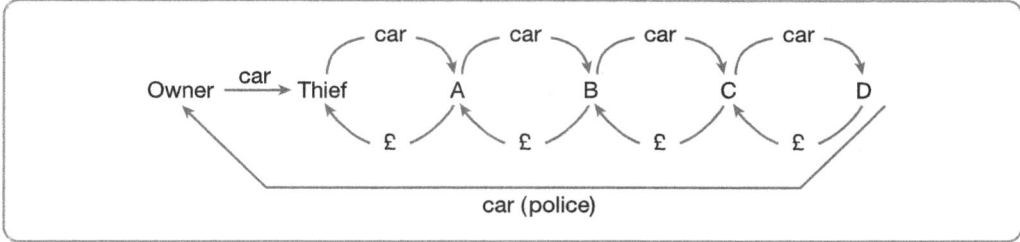

Figure 3.4 Who is the loser?

interfere with the buyer's right to enjoy quiet possession of the goods. This term would be important if the seller owned the goods sold and had the right to sell them, but the buyer was later prevented from using the goods because a third party had acquired a property right, such as a patent, in the goods. The term will not be implied if the seller reveals before the sale that the buyer will not enjoy quiet possession of the goods. As we have seen, when a warranty is breached the injured party can claim damages for breach of contract, but cannot treat the contract as terminated.

Correspondence with description (s. 13(1))

Section 13 of the SGA 1979 provides that:

> Where there is a contract for the sale of goods by description, there is an implied [condition] that the goods will correspond with the description.

A seller has no obligation to describe the goods sold. Furthermore, the fact that the seller has made a description does not necessarily mean that the goods were sold by that description so as to bring in s. 13.

Several hurdles must be overcome before s. 13 is satisfied. First, there must actually have been a description of the goods. Second, the description must have been intended to be a term of the contract. Section 13 will not apply if the description was intended to be a representation or intended to have no legal effect. Third, the goods must have been sold by reference to the description. So it must have been reasonably intended that the buyer would rely on the description. For example, in **Harlingdon & Leinster Enterprises Ltd v Christopher Hull Fine Art Ltd (1991)** the Court of Appeal held that two paintings had not been sold by description. The paintings had been described as being by a German expressionist called Munter. The buyer was an expert in German expressionist painting, but the seller had made it plain that he was not. In fact, the paintings were fakes and were worth only 1 per cent of the price which the buyer paid. Section 13(1) provided no help to the buyer. The paintings were not sold by description because the description was not an important term of the contract on which the buyer relied. The buyer did not rely on the term, he relied on his own expertise. However, when unascertained goods are sold in a commercial context, it is presumed that the buyer does rely on any description of them. **Unascertained goods** are identified *only* by description, so that any goods matching the description can be supplied under the contract. They are contrasted with **specific goods**, which are identified and agreed upon, before the contract is made, as the particular goods which must be supplied. (For further detail, and an example of the two types of goods, see Chapter 7.) Finally, the description must be a substantial ingredient in the identity of the thing being sold, so that it identifies the commercial characteristics of the goods which are being bought. However, when unascertained goods are sold in bulk, it is likely that s. 13 will require exact correspondence with all aspects of the description.

Arcos Ltd *v* EA Ronaasen & Son (1933) (House of Lords)

The seller contracted to sell a quantity of wooden staves which were to be used for making cement barrels. The goods were unascertained. The staves had been described as 'half an inch thick'. Ninety per cent of the staves were between half an inch and five-eighths of an inch, but 10 per cent were over five-eighths of an inch. The buyer rejected all of the staves, even though they were perfectly fit for making cement barrels. He did this because the market price of such staves had dropped.

Held Section 13(1) was breached because the staves did not correspond with the description by which they were sold. The buyer could therefore treat the contract as terminated and was entitled to all of his money back.

Comment This case differs from **Harlingdon & Leinster Enterprises Ltd *v* Christopher Hull Fine Art Ltd** in that the contract was for the sale of unascertained goods and so the buyer had to rely on the seller's description. In **Harlingdon** the goods were specific and the buyer did not rely on the seller's description.

Since s. 13 can apply only where the description is a term of the contract, the real significance of s. 13 is that it makes the term a condition, rather than a warranty or an innominate term. So breach of s. 13 will always give the buyer a right to terminate the contract and get his money back (subject to ss. 15A and 35 considered below). Breach of a warranty would not give this right and breach of an innominate term might not.

Having decided that a sale was made by description, we then need to examine how closely the description must be adhered to. A rule expressed in Latin, *de minimis lex non curat* (the law is not concerned with trifles) has always been a general principle of the common law. The effect of the rule here is that if the failure to match the description was very trivial the seller will not breach s. 13(1). However, the following case shows that where goods are sold by description in a commercial context the description must be very closely adhered to.

 Re Moore & Co and Landauer & Co (1921) (Court of Appeal)

A consignment of 3,100 tins of peaches was sold. The goods were to be shipped from Australia to a buyer in London. The buyer rejected the consignment on the grounds that whereas the peaches had been described as packed 30 tins to a case, about half of the tins were packed 24 to a case instead of 30. The correct number of tins were delivered.

Held The buyer could reject all of the tins. Section 13(1) had been breached because the goods did not correspond with the description by which they had been sold.

Comment The principle in this case, that where unascertained goods are sold in a commercial context then any description is likely to be within s. 13, has not changed. However, s. 15A would now force the buyer to treat the breach of condition as a breach of warranty. Therefore, he could not terminate the contract if the case were to arise today, but could only claim damages. (Section 15A is considered later in this chapter, after all of the statutory implied terms have been considered.)

Section 13(2) provides that goods can be sold by both sample and description. If they are, they must correspond with both the description and the sample. Section 13(3) provides that goods can still be sold by description even if, being exposed for sale or hire, they are selected by the buyer. So the fact that a buyer chooses goods, perhaps in a supermarket for example, will not prevent the goods from having been sold by description.

Figure 3.5 shows how s. 13 operates.

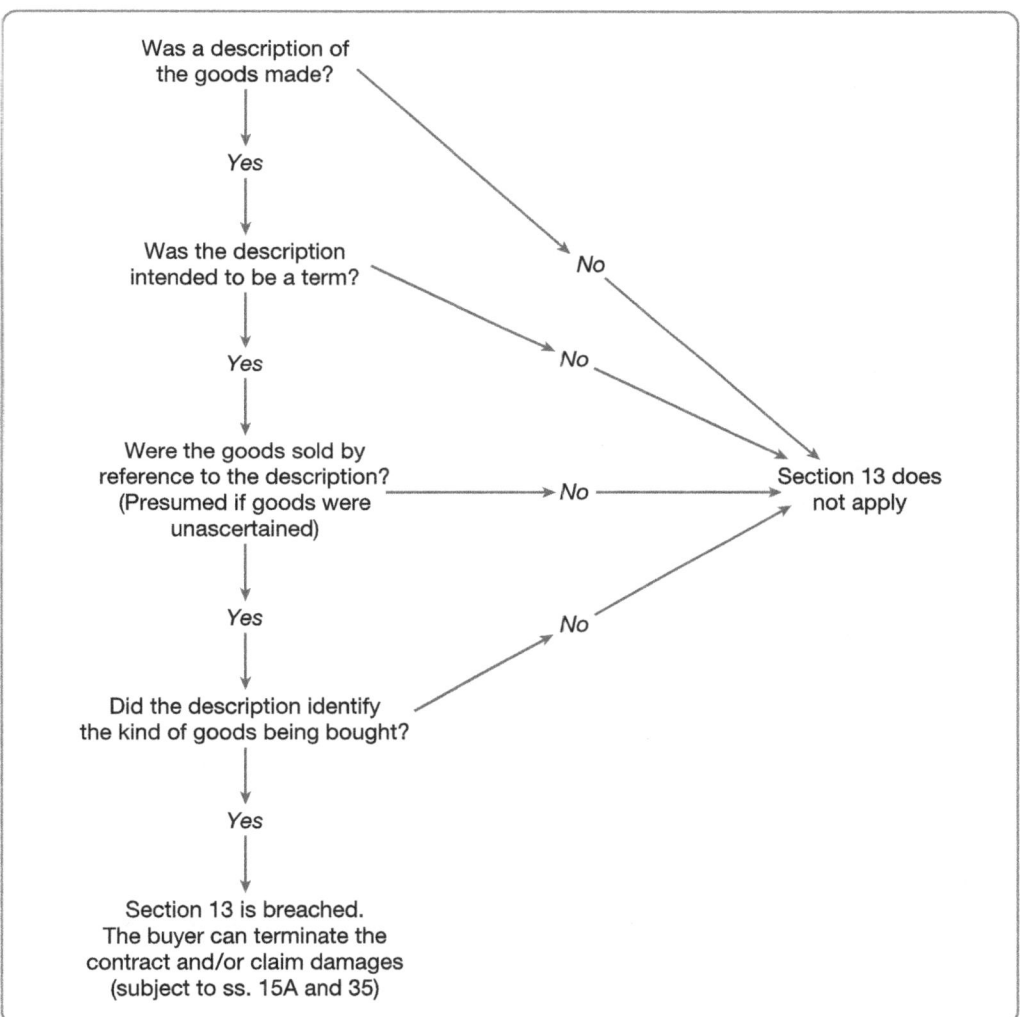

Figure 3.5 Section 13 SGA 1979

Quality and fitness in business sales (s. 14)

Section 14(2) of the SGA 1979 implies a term that goods sold in the course of a business are of satisfactory quality.

Section 14(3) of the SGA 1979 implies a term that goods sold in the course of a business are reasonably fit for the buyer's purpose.

Business sales

The terms as to satisfactory quality and fitness for purpose are implied only where goods are sold in the course of a business. Neither section will apply where goods are sold by a private seller. The following case considered the circumstances in which goods are sold in the course of a business.

  Stevenson _v_ Rogers (1999) (Court of Appeal)

The defendant had been in business as a fisherman for 20 years. He sold an old fishing boat when he wanted to buy a new one. The boat sold, which was not of satisfactory quality, was not being used as part of the stock in trade of the business at the time of sale. The defendant argued that no term as to satisfactory quality should be implied as the boat was not sold in the course of a business.

Held The boat was sold in the course of the defendant's business. For the purposes of s. 14 of the SGA 1979, the words 'in the course of a business' should be taken at face value. Section 14 applies to any sale made by a business, even if what is sold is not the stock in trade which the business exists in order to sell. Even a one-off sale by the business is a sale in the course of a business. However, purely private sales which are made outside the limits of the business would not be made in the course of a business.

Satisfactory quality (s. 14(2))

Section 14(2) of the SGA 1979 provides that:

> Where the seller sells goods in the course of a business, there is an implied [condition] that the goods supplied under the contract are of satisfactory quality.

Circumstances in which s. 14(2) will not be implied

Even where goods are sold in the course of a business, s. 14(2C) indicates that the term as to satisfactory quality will not be implied in two circumstances:

(1) It will not apply as regards defects which were specifically pointed out to the buyer before the contract was made.

(2) Where the buyer examines the goods before buying them, it will not apply as regards defects which _that examination_ ought to have revealed.

If a defect is specifically pointed out to the buyer, then that particular defect cannot make the goods unsatisfactory. This is the case even if the defect proves to be more serious than the buyer imagined.

 Bartlett _v_ Sidney Marcus Ltd (1965) (Court of Appeal)

A dealer sold a second-hand car and pointed out to the buyer that the car had a defective clutch. The buyer negotiated a reduced price to take account of the defect. Repairing the clutch cost far more than the buyer had anticipated, and he claimed to reject the car under s. 14(2).

Held The defect had been pointed out to the buyer and so it did not cause s. 14(2) to have been breached.

A buyer has no obligation to examine goods before buying them. If, however, the buyer does examine the goods, the goods cannot be rendered unsatisfactory on account of defects which that examination ought to have revealed. However, even the most glaringly obvious defects will make the goods unsatisfactory if the buyer chooses not to examine the goods.

Meaning of satisfactory quality

This requirement that the goods supplied under the contract must be of satisfactory quality is relatively recent. The Sale of Goods Act 1979 was amended in 1995. Before the amendment, the 1979 Act implied a term that goods sold in the course of a business had to be of merchantable quality. However, the meaning of merchantable quality had become unclear, and so the requirement was changed to one of satisfactory quality. Section 14(2A) of the SGA 1979 now provides the following definition of satisfactory quality.

> Goods are of satisfactory quality if they meet the standard that a reasonable person would regard as satisfactory, taking account of any description of the goods, the price (if relevant) and all the other relevant circumstances.

We should note three things about this definition. First, the standard required is objective, being that which a reasonable person would regard as satisfactory. Second, any description of the goods may be taken into account. (There is no requirement here that the goods are sold by description, as there was in the case of s. 13(1).) Third, any other relevant circumstances, which may include the price, can be taken into account. It is also worth noticing that it is not only the goods sold which must be of satisfactory quality. Section 14(2) requires that 'the goods supplied under the contract' must be of satisfactory quality and this would include any packaging.

Section 14(2B) lists five factors which can be taken into account in assessing the quality of the goods.

> For the purposes of this Act, the quality of goods includes their state and condition and the following (among others) are in appropriate cases aspects of the quality of the goods
>
> (a) fitness for all the purposes for which goods of the kind in question are commonly supplied,
>
> (b) appearance and finish,
>
> (c) freedom from minor defects,
>
> (d) safety, and
>
> (e) durability.

It is important not to get carried away with s. 14(2B). The five matters listed are not absolute requirements of quality. They are *aspects of quality in appropriate cases*.

Example

A car which has been written off in an accident is sold by a business for scrap. The car will be of satisfactory quality even though it might be unfit to be driven, badly battered and completely unsafe. Taking into account the description, the price and all the other relevant circumstances, the reasonable person would regard such a car as being of satisfactory quality.

The liability imposed on the seller by s. 14(2) is strict and does not depend upon the seller having been at fault. Shops which sell defective goods will breach s. 14(2) even if the goods were sold in packaging which prevented the defect from being discovered.

In **Darren Egan *v* Motor Services (Bath) Ltd (2007)** Lady Justice Ward, giving the only significant judgment of the Court of Appeal, considered the extent to which a minor defect would make an expensive new car of unsatisfactory quality. She said,

. . . it seems to me unlikely that a buyer will be entitled to reject goods simply because he can point to a minor defect. He must also persuade the judge that a reasonable person would think that the minor defect was of sufficient consequence to make the goods unsatisfactory. Of course, if a car is not handling correctly, one would expect any reasonable person to say that it is not of satisfactory quality . . . But the mere fact that a setting is outside the manufacturer's specification will not necessarily render the vehicle objectively unsatisfactory. The reasonable person may think that the minor defect is of no consequence.

In **Thain v Anniesland Trade Centre 1997** a Scottish court held that durability was not an appropriate aspect of quality when a five- or six-year-old Renault 19, which had done 80,000 miles, was bought for slightly under 30 per cent of the price of a new model. Within two weeks of purchase the car's gear box developed a fault which soon made the car undrive-able. The court was satisfied that this fault had not been present when the car was bought. It held that the car was of satisfactory quality. Durability was not a quality which a reason-able person would have expected of this particular car.

In the following case the Court of Appeal considered whether a new motor home was of unsatisfactory quality because it was, technically, too wide to be legally driven on UK roads.

 Bramhill v Edwards (2004) (Court of Appeal)

E was a specialist dealer in motor homes imported from the USA. He imported a 'Dolphin' motor home which was 102 inches wide. Vehicles over 100 inches wide cannot legally be used on the UK roads, although insurance companies are prepared to insure them. B and his wife were enthusiasts who knew that vehicles over 100 inches wide could not legally be used. They saw the Dolphin at a show in Malvern where E was displaying it. Shortly afterwards, after living in the Dolphin for a few days, B bought it for £61,000. B had ample opportunity to measure the width of the Dolphin before purchasing it but there was no evidence that he actually did this. After some seven months using the vehicle, B measured it and found it to be 102 inches wide. B complained to E about this. E said that the width would not cause a problem and B continued to use the Dolphin. After another four months B complained to E that he thought he had bought a 100-inch wide vehicle, not an illegal 102-inch wide one. Two months later B asked E to take the Dolphin back in part exchange for one of two other vehicles, one of which was also 102 inches wide. When these requests were refused he sued E.

Held B had not proved that s. 14(2A) had been breached on account of the vehicle being too wide. There was plenty of evidence that the authorities turned a blind eye to the use of vehicles which were 102 inches wide and enthusiasts for such vehicles knew this. Consequently, B had not proved, on a balance of probabilities, that a reasonable person would regard the vehicle as unsatisfactory.

Comment Auld LJ gave the only judgment. When considering the excessive width of the vehicle, he said that the test of satisfactory quality was an objective test which focused on the attitude of the reasonable person. However, he went on to say that this meant the reason-able person in the position of the buyer with the buyer's knowledge, and that it would not be appropriate to consider a reasonable third-party observer who was not acquainted with the background of the transaction. '*The reasonable buyer must be attributed with knowledge of all background facts . . . such facts in this case would include that: . . . a sig-nificant number of vehicles of greater width than permitted in this country were in use on its roads; and the authorities were turning a blind eye to that illegal use.*' Recognising that there were arguments both for and against a reasonable person thinking that the Dolphin was of satisfactory quality, Auld LJ held that B had failed to prove that the reasonable person would think that the Dolphin was not of satisfactory quality. B had therefore not discharged his obligation to prove his case on a balance of probabilities.

Public statements on the specific characteristics of the goods

Section 14(2D) provides that where the buyer deals as a consumer, the relevant circumstances in s. 14(2A) include any public statements on the specific characteristics of the goods made about them by the seller, the producer or his representatives, particularly in advertising or labelling. (Producer means the manufacturer of the goods, or the person who imported them into the EU or a person who put his own name, trade mark or other distinctive mark on the goods.) So if a car manufacturer advertised that a certain model of car did 45 miles per gallon, a customer who bought such a car new from a garage, and found that it did not achieve this mileage, might be able to claim that the car was not of satisfactory quality. However, s. 14(2E) provides that a public statement is not by virtue of s. 14(2D) to be considered a relevant circumstance if the seller can show one of three things:

(1) that at the time of the contract the seller was not, and could not reasonably have been, aware of the statement; or

(2) that the statement had been withdrawn in public or corrected in public before the contract was made; or

(3) that the consumer's decision to buy the goods could not have been influenced by the statement.

The circumstances in which a buyer deals as a consumer are considered below, in relation to the Unfair Contract Terms Act 1977 (see later in the chapter). It will be seen there that a company can deal as a consumer when buying goods.

Figure 3.6 gives an overview of the circumstances in which s. 14 will apply.

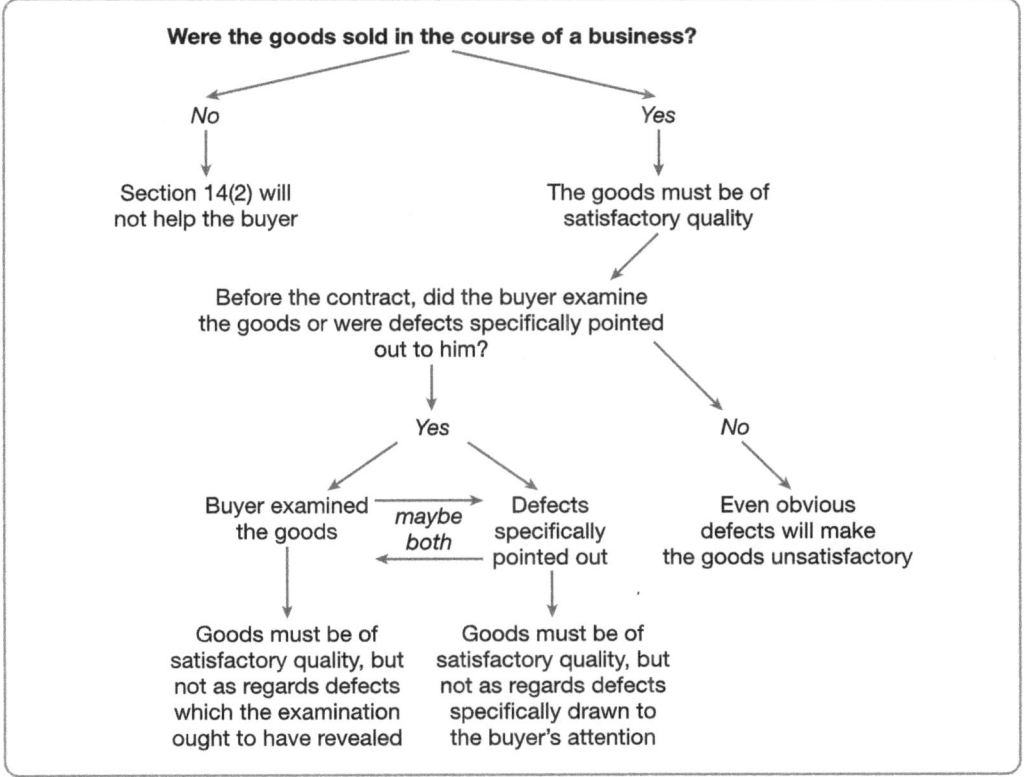

Figure 3.6 The circumstances in which s. 14(2) SGA 1979 will apply

Fitness for purpose (s. 14(3))

Section 14(3) of the SGA 1979 states that if the buyer expressly or impliedly makes known to the seller any particular purpose for which the goods are being bought, then there is an implied condition that the goods are reasonably fit for that purpose. This is the case whether or not the purpose made known by the buyer is the purpose for which goods of that particular type are commonly supplied.

However, s. 14(3) will not apply if the circumstances show either that:

- the buyer does not rely on the skill and judgement of the seller; or
- it was unreasonable for the buyer to rely on the skill and judgement of the seller.

The following example shows how s. 14(3) might operate.

> **Example**
>
> Hannah visits a shop and buys a cake. Before buying the cake, Hannah asks the seller whether or not the cake contains nuts, explaining that she is allergic to nuts. The seller says that it does not. Relying on this, Hannah buys the cake and eats it. Hannah is made ill by the cake, because it did contain nuts. Section 14(3) will have been breached even though there was nothing wrong with the general quality of the cake.

If the purpose for which goods are to be used is perfectly obvious, then the buyer does not need to state the purpose. The terms as to satisfactory quality and fitness for the buyer's purpose will both be implied.

> **Grant *v* Australian Knitting Mills Ltd (1936) (Privy Council)**
>
> A customer who bought a pair of underpants from a shop contracted dermatitis because a chemical used in the manufacture of the underpants had not been rinsed out properly. The customer sued under s. 14(3), as well as under s. 14(2), because the purpose for which he bought the underpants was perfectly obvious.
>
> *Held* The buyer won under both sections.

The term in s. 14(3) will not protect a buyer who does not make known, expressly or impliedly, the particular purpose for which the goods are bought.

> **Griffiths *v* Peter Conway Ltd (1939) (Court of Appeal)**
>
> A customer with abnormally sensitive skin contracted dermatitis from a tweed coat which she bought from a shop. The coat would not have affected most people.
>
> *Held* The shop were not liable under s. 14(2) because there was nothing wrong with the coat. The shop were not liable under s. 14(3) because the customer had not made her condition known.

When defective goods are bought for their usual purpose, it is common for the buyer to sue under both s. 14(2) and s. 14(3), as **Grant v Australian Knitting Mills** demonstrates. However, the terms are not implied in identical circumstances. Section 14(2) applies even if the buyer did not make any purpose known to the seller or rely in any way on the seller's skill and judgement. However, s. 14(2) does not apply where the buyer examined the goods and ought to have noticed a defect. Nor does it apply where the defect was specifically pointed out to the buyer. Section 14(3) applies only where the buyer makes a particular purpose known to the seller and relies on the skill and judgement of the seller (although both of these matters can be done impliedly). It can apply even as regards defects which the buyer noticed or which were specifically pointed out. (If, for example, the seller wrongly said that the defect would cause the buyer no problems.)

Figure 3.7 shows how s. 14(3) operates.

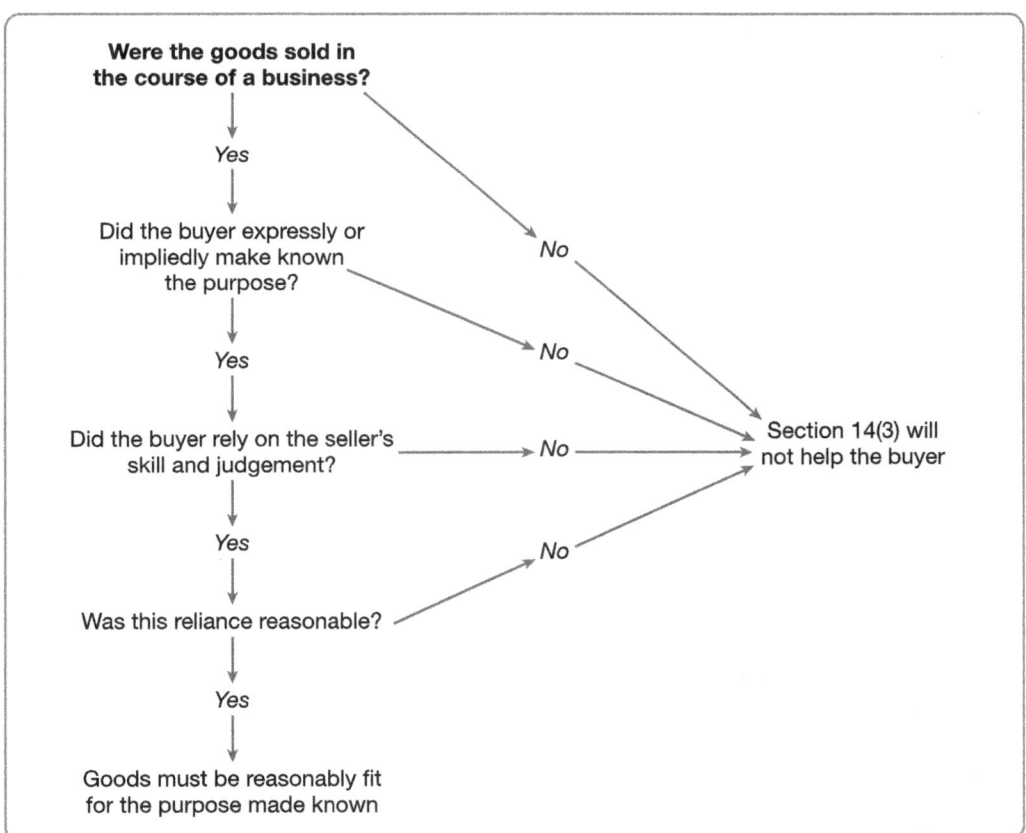

Figure 3.7 Section 14(3) SGA 1979

Sale by sample (s. 15)

Section 15 provides that if goods are sold by sample the following two conditions are implied:

(1) the bulk of the goods must correspond with the sample in quality; and

(2) the bulk must be free from hidden defects, which would render the goods unsatisfactory, if these defects would not be discovered on a reasonable examination of the sample.

These two terms are implied into all sales by sample, even those which were not made in the course of a business. The first term is similar to sale by description, with the sample acting as the description. The buyer should look at the sample to assess the quality of the goods, knowing that the bulk must be of the same quality. The second term is similar to s. 14(2). However, s. 14(2) does not require the buyer to examine the goods. A sample is there to be examined, so s. 15 regards the buyer as having examined the sample. If the bulk of the goods contain a defect which renders the goods of unsatisfactory quality, the outcome will depend upon whether this defect would have been apparent on a reasonable examination of the sample. If the defect would have been apparent, then neither s. 14(2) nor s. 15 will have been breached. This is the case even if the buyer did not examine the sample or notice the defect. If the defect would not have been apparent, then s. 15 will have been breached.

 Godley v Perry (1960)

A six-year-old boy bought a catapult which snapped in use and caused the boy to lose an eye. The boy sued the shopkeeper under s. 14(2) and won. The shopkeeper sued the wholesaler under s. 15 because, before buying the catapults, he had tested a sample catapult by pulling back the elastic, and this sample had not snapped.

Held The shopkeeper won under s. 15. The defect was not apparent on a reasonable examination of the sample.

If a sale is made by both sample and description, the bulk of the goods must correspond with both the sample and the description. For example, in **Nichol v Godts (1854)** oil was sold by sample and was also described as 'foreign rape seed oil'. The goods not only had to correspond with the sample but also had to correspond with the description.

The Supply of Goods (Implied Terms) Act 1973

As we have seen, the terms implied by the Sale of Goods Act have given excellent protection to buyers of goods since 1893. However, for many years people who acquired goods under contracts which could not be classed as contracts of sale of goods had to rely on case law for protection.

In the 1970s Parliament passed two statutes which extended the Sale of Goods Act implied terms into other types of contract.

The first of these statutes was the Supply of Goods (Implied Terms) Act 1973 (SGITA 1973), which extended the implied terms into contracts of hire-purchase. The terms implied, which are virtually identical to the terms implied by ss. 12–15 of the Sale of Goods Act 1979, are contained in the following sections.

Section 8	Right to pass ownership
Section 9	Correspondence with description
Section 10(1)	Satisfactory quality (business contracts only)
Section 10(2)	Fitness for purpose (business contracts only)
Section 11	Correspondence with sample

A contract of **hire-purchase** is one whereby a customer agrees to hire goods for a certain period, and is given an option to purchase the goods for a small sum at the end of that period.

> **Example**
>
> Mr Smith takes a fridge on hire-purchase from a shop. The fridge would have cost £350 to buy, but Mr Smith takes it on hire-purchase for three years at £17 a month. Until the final payment is made, Mr Smith is merely hiring the fridge. The last payment he makes will include a nominal purchase price and when Mr Smith makes the final payment he then buys the fridge.

The SGITA 1973 implies terms as to the right to pass ownership, description, quality, fitness and sample as soon as the hire-purchase agreement begins.

Section 10, which implies the terms as to satisfactory quality and fitness for the hirer's purpose, applies only if the owner of the goods makes the hire-purchase agreement in the course of a business. The other sections apply to all contracts of hire-purchase. In almost all hire-purchase agreements the owner will make the agreement in the course of a business.

The Supply of Goods and Services Act 1982

Part I of the Act

Part I of the Supply of Goods and Services Act 1982 (SGSA 1982) implies terms equivalent to the terms in the SGA 1979 into two types of contracts. First, the terms are implied into contracts for the transfer of property in goods. Second, the terms are implied into contracts of hire. The terms are implied by the following sections.

Contracts for the transfer of property in goods

Section 2	Right to transfer the property
Section 3	Correspondence with description
Section 4(2)	Satisfactory quality (business contracts only)
Section 4(3)	Fitness for purpose (business contracts only)
Section 5	Correspondence with sample

A contract will be a contract for the transfer of property in goods if it is any contract which involves the passing of ownership of goods (except a contract of sale of goods or a contract of hire-purchase). It would therefore include contracts under which goods are bartered for other goods. It would also cover the supply of goods in a contract under which services are supplied. For example, it would cover the supply of oil when a car is serviced.

Contracts of hire

Section 7	Right to hire
Section 8	Correspondence with description
Section 9(2)	Satisfactory quality (business contracts only)
Section 9(3)	Fitness for purpose (business contracts only)
Section 10	Correspondence with sample

Table 3.1 shows the terms implied by the SGA 1979, SGITA 1973 and SGSA.

Table 3.1 The terms implied by SGA 1979, SGITA 1973 and SGSA 1982

Type of contract Term implied	Sale of goods	Hire-purchase	Transfer of property in goods	Hire
Right to sell	SGA 1979 s. 12(1)	SGITA 1973 s. 8	SGSA 1982 s. 2	SGSA 1982 s. 7
Quiet possession and freedom from encumbrances	SGA 1979 s. 12(2)	SGITA 1973 s. 8	SGSA 1982 s. 2	SGSA 1982 s. 7
Correspondence with description	SGA 1979 s. 13	SGITA 1973 s. 9	SGSA 1982 s. 3	SGSA 1982 s. 8
Satisfactory quality in business sales	SGA 1979 s. 14(2)	SGITA 1973 s. 10(2)	SGSA 1982 s. 4(2)	SGSA 1982 s. 9(2)
Fitness for purpose in business sales	SGA 1979 s. 14(3)	SGITA 1973 s. 10(3)	SGSA 1982 s. 4(3)	SGSA 1982 s. 9(3)
Correspondence with sample	SGA 1979 s. 15	SGITA 1973 s. 11	SGSA 1982 s. 5	SGSA 1982 s. 10

Under a contract of hire, a hirer is given temporary possession of goods but not ownership, by the owner of the goods.

Part II of the Act

Part II of the Supply of Goods and Services Act 1982 implies three terms into contracts under which a service is supplied. These terms are as follows:

Section 13   Reasonable care and skill (business services only)
Section 14   Reasonable time (business services only)
Section 15   Reasonable price

Reasonable care and skill (s. 13)

SGSA 1982 s. 13 provides that:

> In a contract for the supply of a service where the supplier is acting in the course of a business, there is an implied term that the supplier will carry out the service with reasonable care and skill.

First, it is important to note that this term will be implied only where the service is supplied in the course of a business. Second, and very important, it must be realised that this term does not impose strict liability. It imposes a tort standard of reasonable care and skill. For example, in **Thake and another v Maurice (1986)** a patient sued a surgeon who had carried out a vasectomy which did not have the desired effect. The surgeon was not liable because he had used reasonable care and skill. (The effect of a very few vasectomies can be reversed naturally.) If the surgeon had guaranteed that the vasectomy would be successful, then he would have been liable. In the absence of such a guarantee, however, s. 13 implies a term only that the provider of a service in the course of a business will use reasonable care and skill.

The test of whether the service provided was carried out with reasonable care and skill is objective, not subjective. A person who professes to have a certain level of skill must show the level of skill which the reasonable person would expect. Professionals, such as solicitors and accountants, and tradesmen, such as plumbers and roofers, would be expected to show the level of skill which is normal in that profession or trade. The government has indicated that a new Consumer Rights Act will be passed by December 2013 to give effect to an EU directive, the Consumer Rights Directive. Under the new Act, the standard required when a business provides a service to a consumer will be made closer to the Sale of Goods Act s. 14 requirements of satisfactory quality and fitness for purpose. As regards some types of service there will be a statutory guarantee of the quality of the service, with statutory remedies if this quality is not met.

It is also important to realise that a contract can still be a contract for the supply of a service even though it is a contract under which possession of goods or ownership of goods is transferred.

Example

A contract is made under which a motorist buys new tyres, to be fitted by the garage. This is both a contract of sale of goods and a contract for the supply of a service. In such cases two sets of terms are implied. Sections 14(2) and 14(3) of the Sale of Goods Act 1979 imply terms as to satisfactory quality and fitness for purpose. Section 13 of the Supply of Goods and Services Act 1982 implies a term that the service is carried out using reasonable care and skill. So if the tyres fitted were worn at the time of sale, the buyer would sue under SGA 1979 s. 14(2) because the tyres were not of satisfactory quality. If the tyres were fitted badly and came off the car, causing the driver to be injured, the driver would sue under SGSA 1982 s. 13 because the tyres were not fitted with reasonable care and skill. If the contract had merely been to service the car, this would not have been a sale of goods but would have been a contract to supply a service. If the service was performed negligently, liability would arise under s. 13 SGSA 1982. However, if through no fault of the garage the oil put into the engine was not of satisfactory quality, then the buyer would sue under SGSA 1982 s. 4(2).

Reasonable time of performance (s. 14)

Section 14 SGSA 1982 applies only to services which are supplied in the course of business. It provides that if no time for completion of the service was either expressly or impliedly fixed, then the service should be performed within a reasonable time. The length of a reasonable time will depend upon all the circumstances of the case.

Reasonable price (s. 15)

Section 15 SGSA 1982 provides that if no price for a service was expressly or impliedly fixed, then the customer should pay a reasonable price. This section applies to all services, whether supplied in the course of a business or not.

The status of the statutory implied terms

The term contained in s. 12(1) of the Sale of Goods Act 1979 is always a condition. If this term is breached, the buyer is always therefore entitled to treat the contract as terminated and/or claim damages. The term is a condition because if the seller does not have the right to sell, this amounts to a total failure of consideration. The corresponding terms contained in the SGITA 1973 s. 8 and the SGSA 1982 ss. 2 and 7 are also always conditions.

The term contained in s. 12(2) of the Sale of Goods Act 1979 is a warranty. If this term is breached, the buyer will therefore be able to claim damages but will not be entitled to treat the contract as terminated. The corresponding terms in the SGITA 1973 and the SGSA 1982 are also always warranties.

The terms contained in ss. 13–15 of the Sale of Goods Act 1979 are conditions. So are the corresponding terms in the SGITA 1973 ss. 9–11 and the SGSA 1982 ss. 3–5 and 8–10. Where the person buying or acquiring the goods is a consumer, all of these terms are always conditions. However, **s. 15A** of the Sale of Goods Act 1979 (and corresponding terms in the SGITA 1973 and in the SGSA 1982) provides that a buyer who does not deal as a consumer cannot treat the contract as terminated where breach of one of these implied terms is so slight that it would be unreasonable to allow the buyer to treat the contract as terminated. Instead, the buyer must treat the breach of condition as a breach of warranty and therefore cannot terminate the contract but can still claim damages. Section 15A does not apply if the parties showed an intention that the person acquiring the goods should be able to treat the contract as terminated even where the breach was so slight as to make this unreasonable.

Example

A car dealer bought a new car from a car manufacturer and sold the car on to a consumer. The car had a very slight defect, which was just enough to mean that it was not of satisfactory quality, both when the manufacturer sold it and when the dealer sold it. Section 14(2) of the SGA 1979 has therefore been breached as regards both sales. The consumer can treat this breach as breach of a condition and will be entitled to reject the car and treat the contract as terminated (as well as to claim damages). The car dealer will not be able to treat the contract as terminated if the breach is so slight as to make this unreasonable. As he did not deal as a consumer when buying the car, s. 15A requires him to treat the breach of condition as a breach of warranty. So the car dealer will not be able to reject the car, but will be able to claim damages for breach of warranty. The car dealer would therefore be likely to repair the car, or have it repaired, and then claim damages from the manufacturer. These damages might reflect the cost of the repair and any profit which the dealer lost as a result of the sale to the consumer falling through.

Section 15A applies only where the buyer does not 'deal as a consumer'. The SGA 1979, like the SGITA 1973 and the SGSA 1982, decides whether or not a person is dealing as a consumer by applying the definition set out in s. 12 of the Unfair Contract Terms Act 1977. This definition is complex and is considered later in this chapter, where a flow chart shows how the section should be applied.

The Sale of Goods Act 1979 s. 11(4) makes one further important rule. It provides that where a seller of goods breaches a condition, a buyer who has 'accepted' the goods must treat the breach of condition as a breach of warranty. Therefore, such a buyer cannot terminate the contract but can still claim damages. Acceptance by the buyer has a technical meaning (which is examined in detail in Chapter 7). Here it is enough to say that a buyer will be deemed by s. 35 to have accepted the goods if he:

- keeps them for more than a reasonable time without rejecting them; or
- indicates acceptance of them; or
- does an act which is inconsistent with the seller continuing to own the goods.

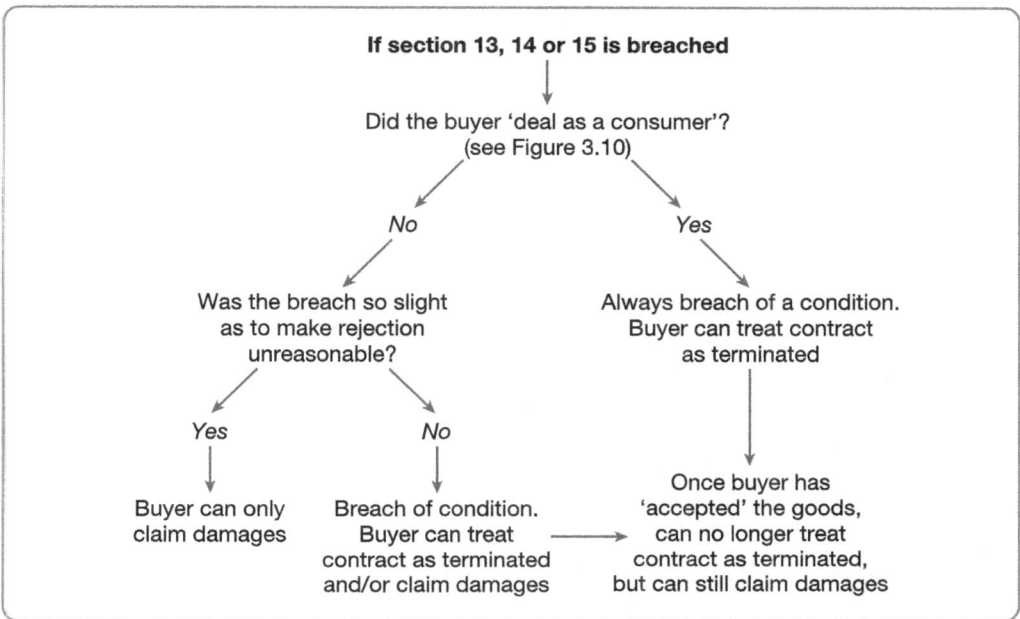

Figure 3.8 Effect of breach of sections 13, 14 and 15, SGA 1979

Additional rights of the buyer in consumer cases

The Sale and Supply of Goods to Consumers Regulations 2002 amended the SGA 1979 by adding ss. 48A–48F. These new sections confer significant new rights on buyers who deal as consumers when the goods bought do not conform to the contract of sale. Before considering the new rights in detail, it is important to note that the new rights are additional to any other rights which the consumer might have. They do not replace the statutory implied terms or any other remedies which might exist.

The circumstances in which the new rights apply

Two requirements must be satisfied before the new rights will apply:

(1) The buyer must have dealt as a consumer.

(2) The goods bought must fail to conform to the contract of sale at the time of delivery.

For the purposes of ss. 48A–48F, the definition of dealing as a consumer set out in the Unfair Contract Terms Act 1977 (UCTA 1977) is applied. This definition, which is complex, is considered later in this chapter in relation to the UCTA 1977. Figure 3.10 gives an overview of how the definition should be approached.

Section 48F provides that the goods do not conform to the contract of sale if either an express term of the contract is breached or if one of the statutory terms implied by ss. 13–15 of the SGA 1979 is breached. Furthermore, s. 48A(3) provides that if the goods fail to conform to the contract within six months of the date of delivery, they are to be presumed not to have conformed on the date of delivery. Section 48A(4) allows this presumption to be overturned if:

- it is established that the goods did conform to the contract at the date of delivery; or
- the presumption is incompatible with the nature of the goods or the nature of the lack of conformity.

The hierarchy of rights

Once it has been established that the buyer dealt as a consumer, and that the goods did not conform to the contract at the time of delivery, the buyer acquires a hierarchy of rights. The two primary remedies of the buyer are to have the goods repaired or replaced. The two secondary remedies are to gain a reduction of the price or to rescind the contract.

Section 48B allows the buyer to require the seller to either repair or replace the goods. It also requires the seller to carry out the repair or replacement within a reasonable time and without causing significant inconvenience to the buyer. The seller has to bear any costs in doing this, including the costs of labour, materials and postage. However, a buyer cannot insist on repair or replacement if the remedy requested would be disproportionate in relation to one of the other three remedies. A remedy is disproportionate if the costs which it imposes on the seller are unreasonable, taking into account:

- the value which the goods would have if they did conform to the contract of sale;
- the significance of the lack of conformity; and
- whether the other remedy could be effected without significant inconvenience to the buyer.

For example, if a consumer bought a very cheap digital watch which did not work at all, repair of the watch would be disproportionate in relation to rescinding the contract or taking a replacement watch. Where the buyer does request repair or replacement of the goods, s. 48D requires the seller to be given a reasonable time to perform the remedy requested. Until this reasonable time has passed, the buyer cannot ask for any other remedy, whether the remedy arose under ss. 48A–48F or in some other way.

Section 48C deals with the secondary remedies, that is to say it deals with requiring the seller to reduce the contract price by an appropriate amount and with rescission of the contract. In this context, rescinding the contract means treating it as if it had never been made and claiming the return of the contract price. However, this amount can be reduced to take account of any use of the goods which the buyer has had. These two remedies are regarded as secondary because they cannot be claimed as of right, but only in two circumstances. The first circumstance is that the buyer cannot require repair or replacement because both of these remedies are impossible or are disproportionate in relation to one of the secondary remedies. The second circumstance is that the buyer has required the seller to repair or replace the goods but the seller has not done so within a reasonable time and without significant inconvenience to the buyer.

Section 48E gives the court additional powers when a claim is made by a buyer under ss. 48A–48F. The court can order the seller to specifically perform an obligation to repair or replace the goods as requested by the buyer. If the buyer requests one of the remedies set out in the new sections, the court can instead award a different one of these remedies if it decides that the other remedy is more appropriate. The court also has the power to adjust any of the new remedies on such terms and conditions as it sees fit, perhaps by ordering that damages also be paid.

Earlier in this chapter we saw that a buyer who has 'accepted' goods can no longer reject those goods for breach of a condition. We also saw that s. 35 SGA deems a buyer to have accepted goods in three circumstances: first, where the buyer indicates to the seller that the goods are accepted; second, where the buyer does any act which is inconsistent with the seller still owning the goods (such as consuming the goods); and third, where the buyer keeps the goods for more than a reasonable time without letting the seller know that the goods are rejected. It seems probable that ss. 48A–48F will be most useful to a buyer who cannot reject for breach of a condition on account of having accepted the goods. Figure 3.9 shows an outline of the additional rights of the consumers which are conferred by SGA ss. 48A–F.

Example

Mary, a teacher, bought a new radio from a shop in January. Mary did not use the radio until she went on holiday in May. She then found that the radio did not work properly because it could not pick up FM. Despite this problem, Mary continued to use the radio to listen to AM stations. Section 14(2) SGA would have been breached if Mary could prove that the radio was not of satisfactory quality when she bought it. However, as Mary kept the radio for more than a reasonable time without rejecting it, she would be too late to reject under s. 14(2). (She could, of course, still claim damages for the breach of s. 14(2).) Mary dealt as a consumer and the radio did not conform to the contract of sale. (As the radio did not conform to the contract within six months of the date of delivery, it is presumed that it did not conform to the contract at the date of delivery.) Mary's primary remedies under ss. 48A–48F would be to have the radio either repaired or replaced. Mary could choose which remedy she wanted. If the shop did not give Mary the remedy which she asked for within a reasonable time, and without causing significant inconvenience to her, then Mary could require one of the secondary remedies, rescission of the contract or a reduction of the price. Rescission of the contract would seem to be the more appropriate remedy. Mary would then be entitled to get the purchase price back, but perhaps not the whole of the price if the court deducted an amount to take account of any use of the radio which Mary had had.

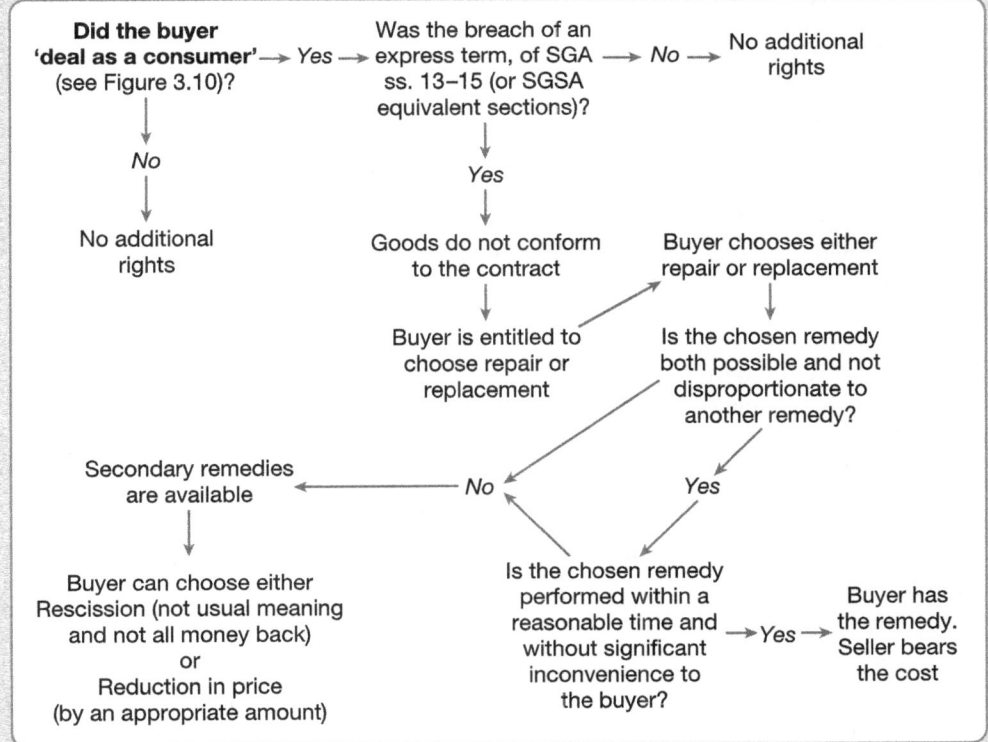

Figure 3.9 The additional rights of consumers conferred by SGA ss. 48A–48F

The Supply of Goods and Services Act 1982 was amended at the same time as the SGA 1979. Amendments which are virtually identical to those made to the SGA 1979 were made to the SGSA 1982, in so far as it relates to contracts for the transfer of goods. Goods do not conform to the contract if an express term is breached or if any of the statutory implied terms as to description, satisfactory quality, fitness for purpose or correspondence with sample are breached. In addition, if installation forms part of the contract the goods do not conform to the contract if they are not installed properly. The consumer is given the same hierarchical rights as those given by ss. 48A–48F of the SGA.

Consumer guarantees

The Sale and Supply of Goods to Consumers Regulations 2002 have brought in new rules which apply to consumer guarantees. There is no need for a guarantee to be given when goods are sold. However, Regulation 15(1) provides that where goods are sold or otherwise supplied to a consumer, and a consumer guarantee is given, the guarantee takes effect as a contractual obligation under the conditions set out in the guarantee and associated advertising. So the guarantee and associated advertising become terms of the contract. Before the Regulations came into force, there was considerable doubt as to whether or not a consumer could enforce a guarantee.

A 'consumer' is here defined as a natural person (and therefore not a company) who is acting for purposes outside his trade, business or profession. It should be noticed that this EU definition of a consumer is quite different from the SGA 1979 and UCTA 1977 definition of 'dealing as a consumer'. A 'consumer guarantee' is defined as any undertaking to a consumer, given without extra charge by a person acting in the course of his business, to reimburse the price paid or to replace or handle consumer goods in any way if they do not meet the specifications set out in the guarantee or in the relevant advertising. This definition takes account of the fact that many guarantees do not offer to refund the price. They might merely agree to repair the goods and might require the consumer to pay costs such as postage and packing. So when goods bought by a consumer are defective, the primary remedy will be under s. 14(2) of the SGA 1979. However, a guarantee will be useful if the goods were of satisfactory quality when delivered but have become defective within the guarantee period, or if the consumer cannot reject the goods on account of having accepted them. The Regulations do not apply to contracts to provide services. They do apply to contracts to supply goods, whether the supply is by way of sale, lease, hire or hire-purchase.

Regulation 15(2) requires that the guarantee is written in plain, intelligible English and that it contains a statement that the consumer has statutory rights which are not affected by the guarantee. It also requires the guarantee to set out the essential particulars necessary for making claims, including the length of the guarantee period, the name and address of the guarantor and the countries in which the guarantee is effective. If the consumer requests a copy of the guarantee from either the retailer or the person giving the guarantee, then a copy must be supplied in writing. Trading standards officers can apply for injunctions to enforce the Regulations.

Exclusion clauses

Exclusion clauses, or exemption clauses as they are sometimes known, are clauses which try to exclude or limit one party's liability. Usually, the liability in question will have arisen as a result of an express or implied term of a contract. However, exclusion clauses can go further and can exclude other types of liability, such as liability arising in tort.

We shall see that Parliament has restricted the effect of exclusion clauses. The following case demonstrates how unfairly exclusion clauses could operate before Parliament intervened.

⚖ L'Estrange *v* Graucob (1934) (Court of Appeal)

A café owner bought a cigarette vending machine and signed a sales agreement which she did not read. A term of this agreement which was 'in regrettably small print but quite legible', said that the machine did not need to work and that all statutory implied terms were not to apply. The machine did not work. The café owner sued to get her money back, claiming that s. 14(2) of the Sale of Goods Act had been breached.

Held The café owner failed, even though s. 14(2) of the Sale of Goods Act had clearly been breached. The claimant had signed the agreement and so she was bound by it.

Because of the unfairness of such cases, Parliament felt the necessity to intervene. In 1977 it passed the Unfair Contract Terms Act (UCTA 1977). We shall examine UCTA 1977 later in this chapter. When faced with an exclusion clause, however, the first step is to consider whether the exclusion clause was a term of the contract. If the clause was not a term of the contract, then it would not have any effect anyway, and it would not be necessary to consider the Act.

Is the exclusion clause a term of the contract?

It is always necessary when considering the effect of an exclusion clause in a contract to first decide whether or not the clause was a term of the contract. As we saw in **L'Estrange *v* Graucob**, a person who signs a document will be bound by its contents. Written, signed documents therefore present little difficulty in deciding whether or not an exclusion clause was a term of the contract. However, a person who misrepresents the effect of an exclusion clause may not be able to rely on it, even if the other party does sign the document which contains the clause. An example can be seen in **Curtis *v* Chemical Cleaning and Dyeing Co Ltd (1951)**, in which a customer who took her wedding dress to a dry cleaners was asked to sign a 'receipt'. The customer asked what it said and was told that it just covered liability for damage to beads and sequins. She signed the document, which in fact excluded all liability on the part of the dry cleaners. The wedding dress was badly stained and the dry cleaners tried to rely on their exclusion clause. The Court of Appeal held that they could not do so because they had misrepresented the effect of the clause.

If an exclusion clause is contained in a document, such as a train ticket, which the reasonable person would think was a part of the contract, then the term will be binding. If the clause was contained in a document, such as a receipt, which the reasonable person would not think contained the terms of the contract, then the clause will not be binding. Sometimes what the reasonable person would have thought is obvious enough. In other cases it can be very hard to tell.

Chapelton *v* Barry UDC (1940) (Court of Appeal)

The claimant hired a deck chair for 2d (1p). When he sat in the chair it collapsed and he was injured. The hirers of the chair relied on an exclusion clause, which said that they were not liable for any accident or damage resulting from the hire of the deck chair. This clause had been printed on a slip of paper which the attendant issued to hirers of the chairs. It was possible to sit on a chair for an hour or two before the attendant took the money and issued the slip.

Held The clause was not a part of the contract because it was contained in a mere receipt. The reasonable person would not have expected the terms of the contract to be contained in such a receipt.

This case must be contrasted with **Thompson *v* London, Midland and Scottish Railway Co (1930)**, in which the Court of Appeal held that a train passenger who could not read was bound by an exclusion clause in the railway's timetables. The ticket was for a cheap excursion, and was said to be available subject to the company's timetable and regulations. The timetable was not free but was available to be purchased. It contained an exclusion clause. It was held that the passenger had been given reasonable notice of the exclusion clause.

An exclusion clause will be effective only if it was agreed as a term of the contract, or if reasonable notice of it was given before the contract was made. A term cannot later be put into a contract which has already been made.

 Olley *v* Marlborough Court Hotel Ltd (1949) (Court of Appeal)

A married couple booked into a hotel for one week and paid their bill in advance. During their stay at the hotel the wife's fur coat was stolen from their room. The hotel denied liability because a notice in their room said that the hotel were not liable for lost or stolen property, unless it had been handed in to reception for safe custody.

Held The notice was too late to be effective. The contract was made when the couple booked into the hotel.

 Thornton *v* Shoe Lane Parking Ltd (1971) (Court of Appeal)

The claimant was badly injured in the defendants' car park, the accident being partly caused by the defendants' negligence. The claimant had driven into the car park and passed a notice at the entrance which said that cars were parked at the owner's risk. When the claimant stopped at a red light he was issued with a ticket. The ticket said on it that it was issued subject to notices displayed inside the car park. These notices, which could only be read once fully inside the car park, said that the defendants were not liable for damage to goods or for injuries to customers. The defendants denied liability for the claimant's injuries, saying that the conditions displayed inside the car park were a part of the contract.

Held The notices inside the car park were not a part of the contract. By the time the claimant had been given the ticket which referred to these notices the contract had been made. (The contract was made either at the time the claimant had put his money into the machine or when he drove past the point at which he could no longer change his mind about entering the car park.)

Earlier in this chapter we saw that a term can be implied into a contract because of a course of dealing between the parties. We considered **Kendall v Lillico**, in which the House of Lords held that an exclusion clause was a part of an oral contract. This was because the parties had often made similar oral contracts, and on each occasion the seller had sent a 'sold note' which always contained exactly the same terms. All the terms in the sold note, including several exclusion clauses, were therefore implied into the oral contract. We also saw that terms can be implied on the basis that they are customary in a particular trade or industry. **British Crane Hire Corpn Ltd v Ipswich Plant Hire Ltd (1975)** provides an example. The claimants needed a crane in a hurry and made an oral contract to hire one from the defendants. This contract was made subject to all the terms in the 'Contractors' Plant Association Form' because both sides knew that whenever cranes were hired they were hired subject to the terms contained in this form.

Does the exclusion clause cover the breach which occurred?

An exclusion clause will not exclude liability for a breach of contract unless the court is satisfied that the wording of the clause has this effect. When considering the effect of exclusion clauses the courts interpret them *contra preferentum* (against the wishes) of the party who wants to rely on them. So the wording will need to clearly exclude liability or it will not do so.

Only if the court does decide that the exclusion clause was a term of the contract and that it excluded liability for the loss which arose will it be necessary to move on to consider the effect of the Unfair Contracts Terms Act 1977 and the Unfair Terms in Consumer Contracts Regulations 1999.

The Unfair Contract Terms Act 1977

Contracts covered by the Act

The important sections of UCTA 1977 apply only to business liability. This is defined by s. 1 of the Act as liability which arises:

- from things done or to be done by a person in the course of a business; or
- from the occupation of premises used for the business purposes of the occupier.

So, in general, a person who is not in business will not be subject to the Act. However, s. 12(1) SGA 1979 (the implied term as to the right to sell) can never be excluded. Nor can the corresponding terms in SGITA 1973 and SGSA 1982. Furthermore, a person who is not in business will be subject to s. 6 UCTA 1977, the effect of which is explained below.

The effect of the Act

Section 2 – Excluding liability arising from negligence

Section 2(1) provides that no contract term can exclude liability for death or personal injury arising from negligence.

Section 2(2) provides that liability for other types of loss or damage arising from negligence, such as damage to goods, can be excluded if the term excluding liability was reasonable.

(Schedule 2 to the Act and s. 11 define what reasonable means, and we will look at these later in this chapter.)

Smith _v_ Eric S Bush (1989) (House of Lords)

The claimant applied to a building society for a mortgage to buy a house. The building society employed the defendants to make a survey of the house. The claimant paid £40 to the building society, who agreed to supply her with a copy of the report. A disclaimer said that neither the building society nor the surveyors would be liable for any inaccuracies. The report itself also carried a similar disclaimer. The report said that the house was worth £16,000 and that no major building work was necessary. Eighteen months later the chimneys fell through the roof because a chimney breast had been removed without proper supports being fitted. The claimant sued the defendants for negligence.

Held The defendants were liable to the claimant in the tort of negligence. The disclaimer which excluded liability had to be reasonable under UCTA s. 2(2). It was not reasonable and so it did not apply.

Comment If the claimant had been killed or injured by the falling chimneys, then s. 2(1) UCTA 1977 would have applied. It would not have been possible for any term to exclude liability for the death or injury if it was caused by negligence. It would not therefore have been necessary to consider whether or not any term which tried to do so was reasonable.

Earlier in this chapter we examined s. 13 SGSA 1982. It provides that where a service is supplied in the course of a business, a term is implied that the service is supplied using reasonable care and skill. Whenever s. 13 SGSA 1982 is breached, the UCTA 1977 regards this as negligence. Therefore, s. 2 UCTA 1977 will determine the extent to which liability for breach of s. 13 SGSA 1982 can be excluded, if it can be excluded at all.

Section 3 – Liability arising in contract

Section 3 protects two classes of people who make a contract:

(1) those who 'deal as a consumer'; and

(2) those who deal on the other party's written standard terms.

Before considering what protection s. 3 offers, we should be clear about exactly who is protected.

The Act makes a very important distinction between a person who deals 'as a consumer' and a person who does not.

Section 12(1) UCTA defines dealing as a consumer by saying that a person deals as a consumer if:

● he neither makes the contract in the course of a business nor holds himself out as doing so; and

● the seller does make the contract in the course of a business.

Unfortunately, the words 'in the course of a business' do not have the same meaning here as they have in s. 14 SGA 1979. When we considered s. 14, earlier in this chapter, we saw that **Stevenson _v_ Rogers** held that whenever a business sells anything it does so in the course of a business, for the purposes of s. 14 SGA. When considering the meaning of the words 'in the course of a business' in s. 12 UCTA 1977, the test set out in **R & B Customs Brokers Ltd v United Dominions Trust Ltd (1988)** must be used. This test allows a business to buy goods without buying them 'in the course of a business'. It regards a buyer as acting in the course of a business only if the contract is an integral part of the business. The case also explains what this means. A purchase by a business will be made as an integral part of the business in only three circumstances:

(1) If the goods the business bought are the type of goods which the business is in business to sell. For example, if a car dealer buys a car this contract will be an integral part of the business and so the dealer will not deal as a consumer.

(2) If the goods are not the type of goods the business usually sells, but they were bought with the intention of selling them at a profit. For example, if a car dealer bought a yacht, intending to sell it at a profit.

(3) If the goods are the type of goods which the business buys fairly regularly. For example, if a car dealer bought petrol to be used in demonstration cars.

It does seem unfortunate that the words 'in the course of a business' have different meanings, depending upon whether they are used in s. 14 SGA or s. 12 UCTA. However, in **Feldaroll Foundry plc v Hermes Leasing (London) Ltd (2004)** the Court of Appeal confirmed that this was the case.

If the buyer is a company, then a further requirement is added by s. 12(1)(c) UCTA. This requirement is that the goods supplied under the contract must be of a type ordinarily supplied for private use or consumption. In **R & B Customs Brokers** this condition was satisfied when an import and export company bought a car. If the company had bought a JCB digging machine, then it could not have dealt as a consumer because this is not a type of goods which are ordinarily used for private use or consumption. A JCB is a type of goods ordinarily bought only for business use.

Figure 3.10 shows how to decide whether or not a person deals as a consumer for the purposes of UCTA 1977. Since the SGA 1979 uses the UCTA definition of dealing as a consumer, the figure also applies to the SGA. We have already seen that s. 15A SGA applies only where the buyer deals as a consumer. We have also seen that the new remedies in SGA ss. 48A–48F apply only where a buyer deals as a consumer.

A person deals on the other party's written standard terms when the same written terms are used whenever the business deals with this person or whenever it deals with customers generally. Matters such as the price and quantity may of course be different. Contracts to hire tools or cars are usually made on standard terms, as are terms referred to on bus or train tickets.

Having decided that a person is either dealing as a consumer or dealing on the other party's written standard terms, the protection given by s. 3 is as follows:

- an exclusion clause cannot protect a party against liability for breach of contract unless this is reasonable; and

- an exclusion clause cannot protect a party who fails to perform the contract at all, or who performs in a manner different from what was reasonably expected, unless this is reasonable.

Sections 6 and 7 – Exclusion of statutory implied terms

Sections 6 and 7 of the Unfair Contract Terms Act 1977 deals with exclusion of liability for breach of the terms implied by ss. 12–15 SGA 1979 and the corresponding terms implied

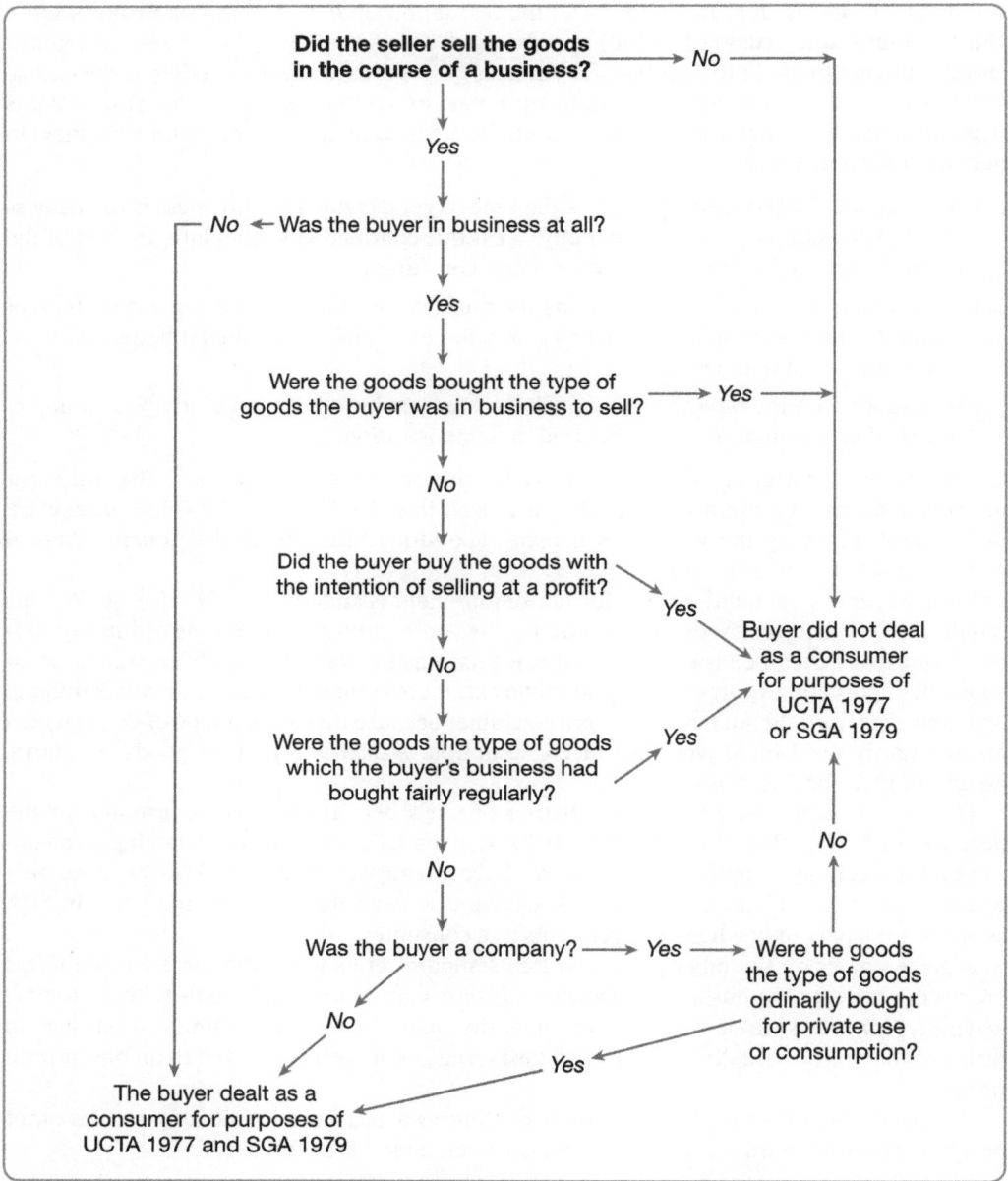

Figure 3.10 Did the buyer deal as a consumer for purposes of UCTA and SGA?

by the SGITA 1973 and the SGSA 1982. These implied terms were considered earlier in this chapter.

Sections 6 and 7 UCTA 1977 provide that no term can exclude liability for breach of the implied term as to the right to sell, contained in s. 12(1) SGA 1979. Nor can any term exclude liability for breach of the corresponding terms contained in the SGITA 1973 or the SGSA 1982.

The terms implied by ss. 13–15 of the Sale of Goods Act 1979 (and the corresponding terms implied by the SGITA 1973 and the SGSA 1982) are treated differently. As regards these terms, ss. 6 and 7 UCTA 1977 make two rules.

(1) If the buyer deals as a consumer, none of the statutory implied terms can be excluded by any contract term.

(2) If the buyer does not deal as a consumer, the statutory implied terms can be excluded, but only to the extent that the term which does exclude them satisfies the UCTA 1977's requirement of reasonableness.

One further point should be noted. A person who buys at an auction or by tender is never to be regarded as dealing as a consumer.

Section 8 – Excluding liability for misrepresentations

Section 8 UCTA 1977 provides that no term can restrict liability for misrepresentation, unless the term satisfies the requirement of reasonableness.

The effect of UCTA 1977 is undoubtedly rather complex. Figure 3.11 might make it more easily understood.

The meaning of reasonableness

Most of the sections of the UCTA 1977 which we have considered do allow an exclusion clause to be effective if the clause satisfies the Act's requirement of reasonableness.

Section 11 says that the requirement is satisfied if:

> the term shall have been a fair and reasonable one to be included having regard to the circumstances which were, or ought reasonably to have been, known to or in the contemplation of the parties when the contract was made.

Schedule 2 to the Act says that regard must be had to the following, in deciding whether or not a term was reasonable:

(1) The relative strength of the parties' bargaining position relative to each other, which will include whether or not the customer could find another supplier.

(2) Whether the customer was given any inducement to agree to the term, or could have made a similar contract with a different supplier without agreeing to such a term.

(3) Whether the customer knew or ought to have known that the term existed.

(4) If the term excludes liability unless some condition is complied with, whether or not it was reasonably practicable to comply with that condition.

(5) Whether the goods were manufactured, altered or adapted at the customer's request.

So, for example, a term would be more likely to be reasonable if:

- the parties were of equal bargaining power; or if the customer could have bought from plenty of other people; or

- if he was given money off to agree to the term; or

- if he could have dealt with someone else who would not have insisted on a similar term; or

- if the term was pointed out to him; or

- if the goods were changed to suit the customer's special needs.

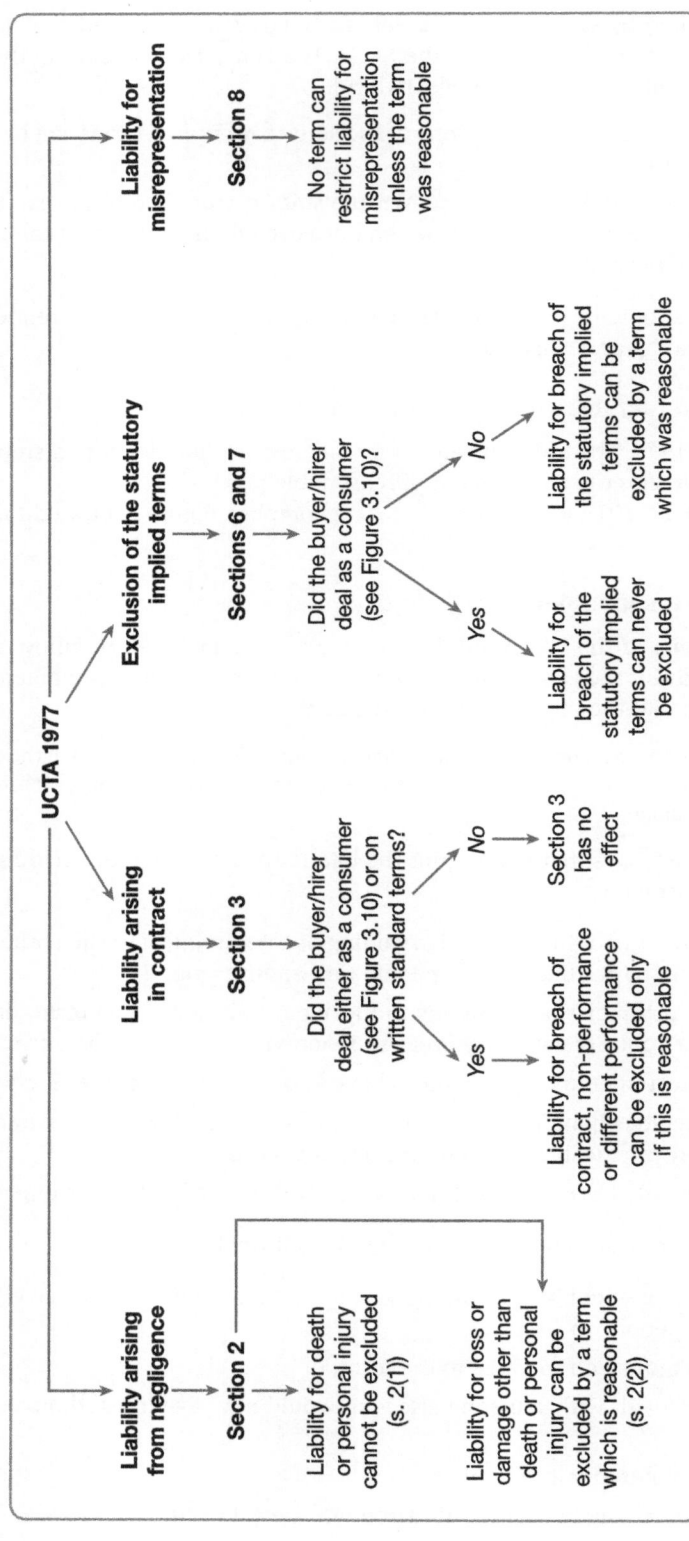

Figure 3.11 The effect of UCTA 1977

The Unfair Terms in Consumer Contracts Regulations 1999

Figure 3.12 gives an overview of the Regulations.

These Regulations were passed to give effect to an EC directive. The Regulations do not replace the Unfair Contracts Terms Act 1977, but run alongside it.

The Regulations apply only to contracts made between a 'seller' or 'supplier' and a 'consumer' (reg. 4(1)). A consumer is defined as a natural person who does not make the

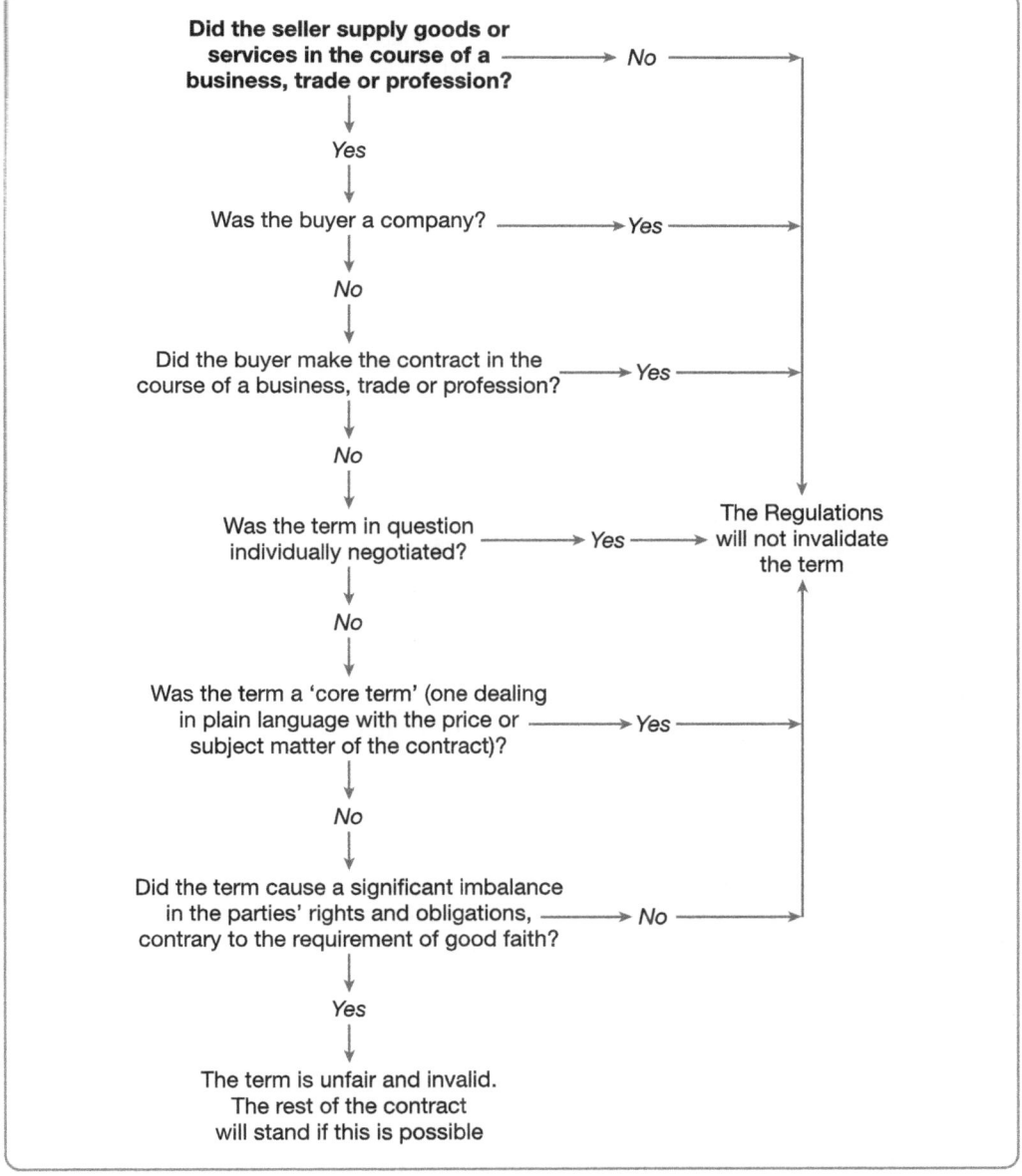

Figure 3.12 Will the UTCC Regulations 1999 invalidate a term?

contract in the course of a business, trade or profession. (Notice that this test is quite different from the UCTA 1977 test as to whether or not a buyer deals as a consumer.)

In **Evans _v_ Cherry Tree Finance Ltd (2008)** the Court of Appeal held that a loan taken partly for a business purpose and partly for a non-business purpose was covered by the regulations.

A company is not a natural person and so a company can never be a consumer for the purposes of the Regulations. Sellers and suppliers are defined as people who supply goods or services in the course of a business, trade or profession. The Regulations apply to contracts to supply goods or services and are not limited to dealing with exclusion clauses.

Regulation 5(1) provides that:

> A contractual term which has not been individually negotiated shall be regarded as unfair if, contrary to the requirement of good faith, it causes a significant imbalance in the parties' rights and obligations arising under the contract, to the detriment of the consumer.

A term will not have been individually negotiated if the contract was drafted in advance and the consumer had no chance to influence the substance of the term (reg. 5(2)). This is obviously a similar concept to the UCTA 1977 concept of 'written standard terms'. It is for the seller or supplier to prove that a term was individually negotiated (reg. 5(4)). In deciding whether or not the requirement of good faith has been breached, the court will consider all relevant circumstances. In **Director General of Fair Trading _v_ First National Bank (2001)** Lord Bingham said that 'the requirement of significant imbalance is met if a term is so weighted in favour of the supplier as to tilt the parties' rights and obligations under the contract significantly in his favour'. Lord Bingham also said that good faith required fair and open dealing, so that there were no hidden traps for the consumer. If terms were disadvantageous to the consumer they should be given prominence, and if the consumer was in a disadvantageous position the supplier should not take advantage of this.

If a term is regarded as unfair, then it is not binding upon the consumer, although the rest of the contact will stand if this is possible without the unfair term (reg. 8).

Schedule 2 to the Regulations sets out examples of the types of terms which may be regarded as unfair. The list is far too long to be reproduced here, but includes:

- making the consumer subject to terms which he had no real opportunity to find out about before the contract was made;
- making a consumer in breach of contract pay too much by way of compensation; and
- making the consumer bound by the agreement when the supplier is not.

The Regulations can consider the effect of any term in a contract except a 'core' term which was written in plain and intelligible language. A 'core' term sets out the contract price or the main subject matter of the contract. The Regulations are not therefore confined to dealing with exclusion clauses. Potentially, they could have a very wide effect. In **Office of Fair Trading _v_ Abbey National and others (2009)** the Supreme Court held that terms which allowed for bank charges to be made when customers overdrew their accounts without permission were core terms, as they set out the price of having a bank account. They could not therefore be assessed for fairness under the Regulations. The price of having an account with the bank was not the same for all customers. Banking services to customers were a package. Customers who overdrew paid a higher price than those who did not.

In addition to making unfair terms not binding upon consumers, the Regulations also allow the Director General of Fair Trading to apply for an injunction to prevent an unfair term from being used in contracts made with consumers.

Essential points

- The terms of a contract define the obligations which the parties to the contract have undertaken.
- A breach of contract occurs whenever a term of the contract is breached.
- Express terms are agreed in words by the parties to the contract.
- Terms may be implied into a contract either by the court or by a statute.
- The Sale of Goods Act 1979 implies five major terms into contracts of sale of goods. The implied terms are:
  - that the seller has the right to sell the goods;
  - that the goods correspond to any description by which they were sold;
  - that goods sold in the course of a business are of satisfactory quality;
  - that goods sold in the course of a business are fit for the buyer's purpose;
  - that, where goods are sold by sample, the bulk of the goods corresponds with the sample in quality.
- A consumer who buys goods which do not conform to the contract is given a hierarchy of rights, these rights being additional to any other rights which the consumer might have.
- Exclusion clauses are clauses which try to exclude or limit one party's liability for breach of contract or for liability arising in tort.
- The Unfair Contract Terms Act 1977 provides that no contract term can exclude liability for death or personal injury arising from negligence.
- In non-consumer deals, liability for breach of the statutory implied terms as to satisfactory quality, fitness for purpose, correspondence with description and correspondence with sample can be excluded only by a term which is reasonable. When a buyer deals as a consumer these implied terms can never be excluded.
- Only a term which is reasonable can restrict or exclude liability for misrepresentation.
- The Unfair Terms in Consumer Contracts Regulations 1999 apply only to consumer contracts.

Practice questions

1 Janice, who owns a garden centre, agreed to buy a second-hand tractor from Gerald, a farmer, for £6,500. Janice also agreed to buy 100 sacks of King Edward seed potatoes from Giles, another farmer. Gerald delivered the tractor to Janice. Eighteen months later the police took the tractor away from Janice, explaining that it had been stolen from Oswald two years ago. Gerald had bought the tractor at an auction and had no idea that it was stolen. At the time when the police took the tractor away it was worth about £2,000 as Janice had used it very extensively. The seed potatoes which Giles delivered were Maris Piper, not King Edwards. Janice was not very bothered about this, as she thought that customers were as likely to buy Maris Piper seed potatoes as they

were to buy King Edwards. However, the day after the seed potatoes were delivered, Janice saw a documentary on the television saying that Maris Piper potatoes had been linked to a certain type of cancer. In the light of the documentary Janice does not think that she will be able to sell any of the potatoes once they have been grown. Advise Janice of her legal position as regards both Gerald and Giles.

2   Keith, a market trader, bought ten portable CD players from CDMaker Ltd. The following day Keith sold three of these on his market stall. All three customers have returned the CD players which they bought to Keith's stall and demanded a refund. They claim that the CD players do not work properly as they spring open when being played. Keith finds that this is true, but that the problem can easily be fixed by tightening a screw. The customers refuse to accept this repair and are demanding their money back. Advise Keith of his legal position as regards both his customers and CDMaker Ltd.

3   Manufacturer Ltd pay Service Co £2,000 to service their two boilers. After the service has been completed, Manufacturer Ltd find that neither boiler can be used. The problem with the first boiler was caused by Service Co inserting a replacement valve which did not work properly. Service Co could not have discovered in advance that the valve was faulty because it had been bought as new and looked perfectly all right. The problem with the second boiler was caused by an unknown problem. No parts were supplied or changed and Service Co say that they serviced the boiler while adhering strictly to a code of practice which is widely accepted in the boiler servicing trade. The boiler did not work before the service was carried out and nor did it work afterwards. Advise Manufacturer Ltd of their legal position as regards the defects in the two boilers.

4   A retailer buys a television from a manufacturer. The retailer hires the television to a consumer for a three-month period. The television was badly manufactured, so that its back casing is not tightly fitted together. The retailer could easily have tightened several screws and fixed this defect but did not do so before hiring the television to the consumer. As regards both the sale by the manufacturer and the contract of hire by the retailer, explain which sections of which statutes have been breached and the remedies available.

5   Service Co service a boiler for Buildem Ltd. The contract is made on Service Co's new written standard terms. One term of the contract states that: 'Neither Service Co nor any of its employees can be liable in any way for any loss, injury or damage caused by faulty workmanship.' The Service Co employee who services the boiler forgets to fasten a plate securely. This problem causes the boiler to explode. The explosion badly burns the managing director of Buildem Ltd, completely destroys the boiler and causes extensive damage to Buildem Ltd's factory. Advise Buildem Ltd of their legal position.

6   Satvinder is a keen ballroom dancer and often stays at the Dance Hotel. A prominently displayed notice at the entrance to the Dance Hotel states that: 'All hotel guests are warned that the management cannot be held responsible for the loss of items left in hotel rooms.' Satvinder leaves her handbag in her room while she goes dancing. When she returns she finds that her handbag has been stolen. A chambermaid opened Satvinder's room but then forgot to lock it. An opportunistic thief then slipped into the room and stole the handbag. Advise Satvinder of her legal position.

7   Explain the protection which the requirement of satisfactory quality, set out in Sale of Goods Act 1979 s. 14(2), gives to buyers of goods. Explain also the remedies available to a buyer of goods if s. 14(2) is breached.

Task 3

A friend of yours who is visiting the country from abroad is thinking of setting up a trading company in the United Kingdom. Your friend is keen to understand English law as it relates to contractual terms, and has asked you to draft a report explaining the following matters:

(a) How the express terms of a contract come to be included in the contract.

(b) The circumstances in which a court will imply terms into a contract.

(c) The terms which are implied into contracts of sale of goods by the Sale of Goods Act 1979.

(d) Other types of contracts into which statutes imply terms similar to those implied by the Sale of Goods Act 1979.

(e) The terms which are implied into a contract to provide services by the Supply of Goods and Services Act 1982.

(f) The effect of the Unfair Contract Terms Act 1977.

(g) The effect of the Unfair Terms in Consumer Contracts Regulations 1999.

mylawchamber

Visit **www.mylawchamber.co.uk/macintyreessentials** to access tools to help you develop and test your knowledge of business law, including interactive multiple choice questions, practice exam questions with guidance, weblinks, glossary, glossary flashcards, legal newsfeed and legal updates.

Use **Case Navigator** to read in full some of the key cases referenced in this chapter with commentary and questions:

Hong Kong Fir Case (1962)

Stevenson *v* Rogers (1999)

4

Misrepresentation, mistake, duress and illegality

This chapter deals with matters which can invalidate a contract. The first of these matters is misrepresentation. A misrepresentation is made when a statement which is not a part of the contract, but which induced the making of the contract, proves to be false. Remedies are available to the party who was induced by the misrepresentation to make the contract. However, as we shall see, these remedies can easily be lost.

Sometimes the parties make a contract while they are mistaken as to some fundamental fact. Depending upon the nature of the mistake made, it is possible for a contract to be rendered void on account of a mistake having been made.

A contract is made under duress when a party is pushed into it in such a way that he or she did not really consent to it. When a contract is made under duress, or where it is made on account of the undue influence of someone else, the contract can be avoided by the victimised party.

This chapter concludes by examining the grounds on which a contract may be void or illegal.

The difference between terms and representations

A contract is made up of terms and the express terms are inserted into the contract by the parties (see Chapter 3). The offeror proposes a set of terms in the offer. If the offeree accepts the offer, the proposed terms become the terms of the contract. If any term is breached, the injured party will always have a remedy for breach of contract.

Frequently, however, a person is persuaded to make a contract by a statement which is not a part of the contract. Such a statement cannot be a term. If this statement turns out to be untrue, the injured party might or might not have a remedy for misrepresentation. To sue for misrepresentation, however, is not the same as to sue for breach of contract. Not only are the remedies different, but also the whole basis of the action is different. It is therefore necessary to distinguish terms and representations.

Written contracts

In written contracts the express terms will be contained in the written document. Statements which are not contained in the written document cannot be terms but can be representations.

> **Example**
>
> Sarah buys a car from a dealer, and the terms of sale are spelt out in a standard form contract. When both parties sign this contract they expressly agree to all of its terms. If any of the terms are breached, then the injured party will always have a remedy for breach of contract. However, if Sarah was persuaded to sign the standard form contract because the dealer made an untrue statement (perhaps saying that all the cars would be going up in price the following week, when this was not true), then the dealer has not breached a term, but has only made an untrue representation. As no term has been breached, Sarah will not be able to sue for breach of contract. She might, however, have a remedy for misrepresentation.

Similarly, it might have been Sarah who made an untrue statement which caused the dealer to make the contract. A customer who pays with a cheque impliedly makes the statement that the cheque will be honoured. If this implied statement was untrue, because the cheque was stolen and would be dishonoured, the customer would not be breaching a term of the contract. The customer would, however, be making an untrue representation, and the dealer might have a remedy for misrepresentation.

So when both parties have signed a written contract, there is not too much difficulty in telling a term from a representation. Statements included in the written contract will be terms, statements not included can only be representations.

Oral contracts

Where a contract is made orally it is much harder to tell a term from a representation. It is still the case that a term is a part of the contract and a representation is not. However, it can be much harder to tell exactly which statements were included in the contract.

By way of example, let us assume that a farmer, Giles, orally offered to sell his combine harvester to Javed for £1,000. Javed accepted, because shortly before the sale Giles said that the harvester had recently had a new engine fitted. After the contract was made Javed discovered that the harvester had not had a new engine fitted. Was Giles's statement about the new engine a term of the contract, or only a representation?

The courts decide questions such as this by asking whether the reasonable person would have thought that the parties intended the statement to be a term or a representation.

This objective test is necessary because once again there is no point in looking for the opinions of the parties themselves. If the court asks Giles whether he thought that the statement about the new engine was a term or a representation, Giles is likely to say that he thought it was just a representation. If the court asks Javed, he is likely to say that he thought it was a term.

Over the years the courts have devised various tests to decide what the reasonable person would have thought.

Strong statements are likely to be terms

The stronger the statement made, the more likely it is to be a term.

Schawel *v* Reade (1913) (House of Lords)

The claimant was considering buying a horse to be used for stud purposes. The defendant said: 'You need not look for anything; the horse is perfectly sound. If there was anything the matter with the horse I would tell you.' Three weeks later the claimant bought the horse, which turned out to be utterly useless for stud purposes.

Held The defendant's statement was a term. It was so strong that it was the basis on which the offer and acceptance were made.

The weaker the statement, the more likely it is to be a representation.

 Ecay *v* Godfrey (1947)

The claimant bought a boat for £750. Before selling the boat, the defendant said that the boat was sound and capable of going overseas. However, he also advised the claimant to have it surveyed before making the purchase. The claimant bought the boat, without having it surveyed, and soon discovered that it was not at all sound.

Held The statement that the boat was sound was only a representation. It was not a part of the contract because it was a very guarded statement.

The reliance shown to be placed upon the statement

If one of the parties demonstrates that the statement is considered to be vitally important, then the statement is likely to be a term.

 Bannerman *v* White (1861)

The claimant, a merchant who traded in hops, sent around a circular to all the hop farmers with whom he dealt. The circular said that the claimant would no longer buy hops which had been treated with sulphur, because the Burton-upon-Trent brewers would not use them. When later buying a consignment of hops from the defendant, the claimant asked if they had been treated with sulphur, adding that if they had he would not buy them at any price. The defendant said that they had not been treated with sulphur, but in fact some of them had.

Held The defendant's statement was a term. The claimant had demonstrated that he considered the statement to be vitally important.

Comment The defendant's statement was not a term just because the claimant considered it to be vitally important. It was a term because the claimant demonstrated that he considered the term to be vitally important. The reasonable person cannot objectively deduce what the parties are thinking unless the circumstances give some indication of what they are thinking.

The relative knowledge of the parties

A party who has more knowledge about the subject matter of the contract is likely to make terms. A party with less knowledge is likely to make representations. For example, in **Oscar Chess Ltd v Williams (1957)** a customer traded in a car to a car dealer, saying that the car was a 1948 model. In fact, the car was a 1939 model. The customer did not know this because the car's documents said that it was a 1948 model. The customer's statement was only a representation because the dealer was as well placed as the customer to know the true age of the car. By contrast, in **Dick Bentley (Productions) Ltd v Harold Smith (Motors) Ltd (1965)** a motor dealer sold a car to the claimant, saying that the car had only done 20,000 miles since having a new engine fitted. In fact the car had done 100,000 miles. The dealer's statement was a term. The dealer, with his greater knowledge of cars, had much more chance of knowing that the statement was untrue than the claimant had.

It is important to remember that the tests we have used to distinguish terms and representations are useful only to indicate what the parties seemed to have intended. In **Heilbut, Symons & Co v Buckleton (1913)** Lord Moulton said that the various tests were valuable but not decisive. The real test is the apparent intentions of the parties, which can be deduced only by looking at all of the evidence.

Figure 4.1 gives an overview of how terms and representations are distinguished.

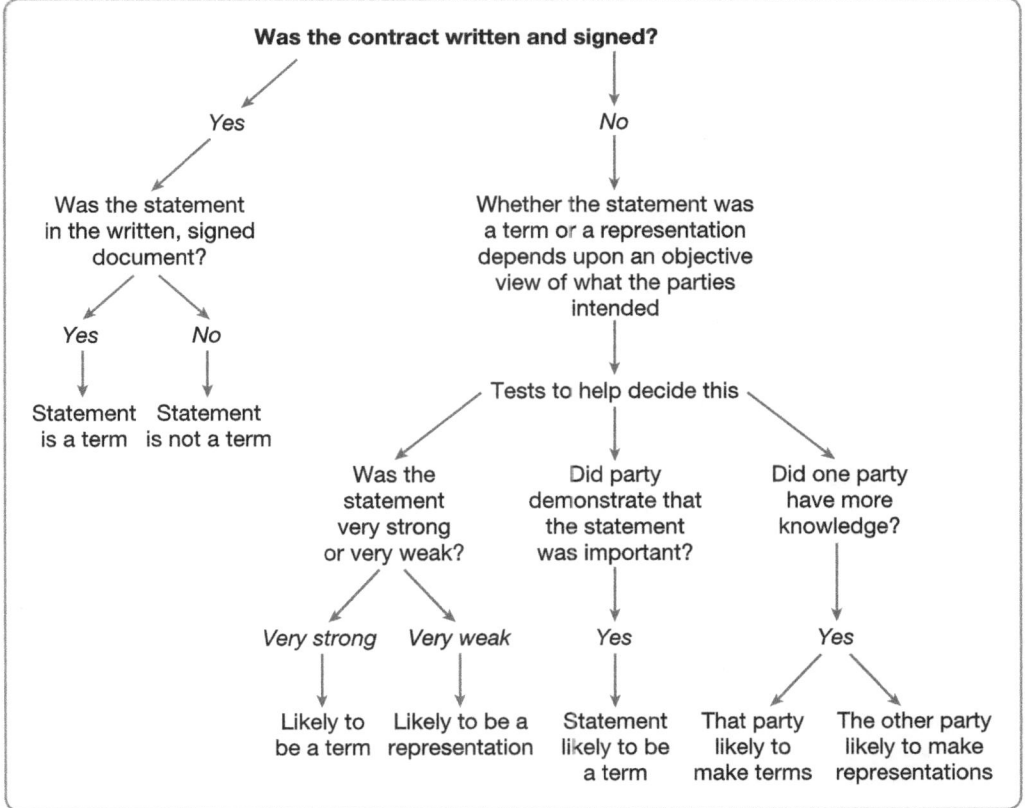

Figure 4.1 Was a statement a term or a representation?

Actionable misrepresentation

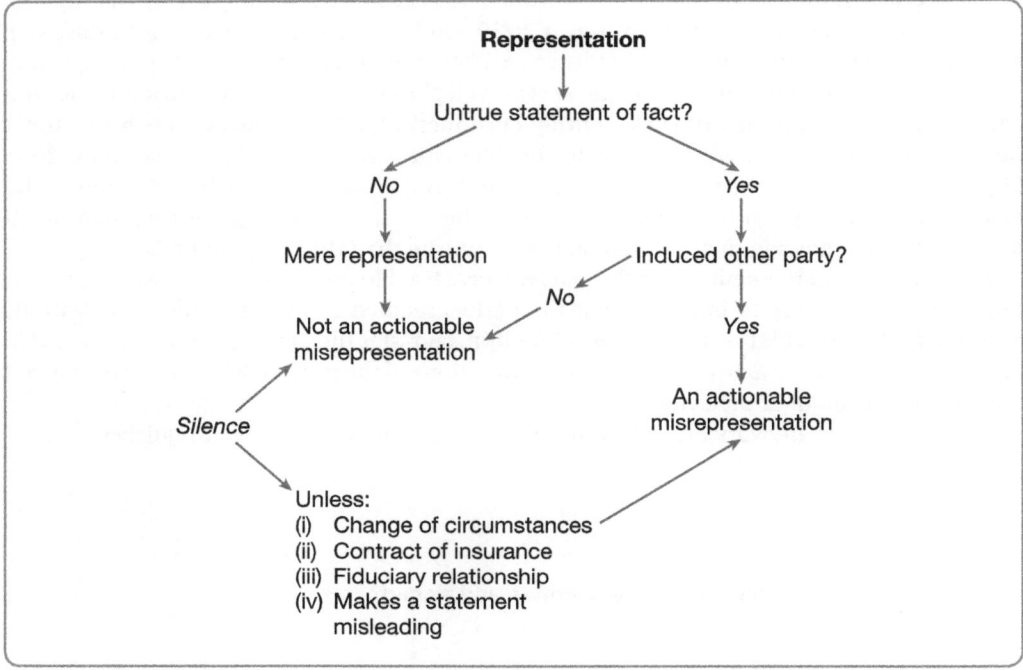

Figure 4.2 How a representation becomes an actionable misrepresentation

A breached term always gives the injured party the right to a remedy for breach of contract. An untrue representation will lead to a remedy if it amounts to an actionable misrepresentation. If, however, the representation does not fit within the definition of an actionable misrepresentation, then it will be a mere representation and no remedy will be available. Figure 4.2 provides an overview of how a representation becomes an actionable misrepresentation.

Definition of a misrepresentation

An actionable misrepresentation is an untrue statement of fact which induced the other party to make the contract.

The statement must be one of fact

Statements of mere opinion are not capable of being misrepresentations.

 Bisset _v_ Wilkinson (1927) (Privy Council)

The claimant bought a farm because the defendant told him that the farm would support 2,000 sheep. The claimant knew that the farm had never before been used for sheep farming. In fact the farm, no matter how well managed, could not support anything like 2,000 sheep.

Held The statement was just an opinion and could not therefore amount to a misrepresentation.

However, some statements of opinion imply statements of fact, as the following case shows.

 Smith *v* Land and House Property Corporation (1884) (Court of Appeal)

The claimants offered their hotel for sale, stating that it was occupied by 'Mr Frederick Fleck (a most desirable tenant)'. Before the sale went through, Mr Fleck went bankrupt. The defendants discovered that for some time Mr Fleck had been badly in arrears with his rent. They refused to go ahead with the purchase of the hotel, claiming that the statement that Mr Fleck was a most desirable tenant amounted to a misrepresentation.

Held The statement was a misrepresentation. It sounded like a mere statement of opinion, but it implied facts (such as the fact that the tenant paid the rent) which justified the opinion.

Bowen LJ said: '. . . if the facts are not equally known to both sides, then a statement of opinion by the one who knows the facts best involves very often a statement of a material fact, for he impliedly states that he knows facts which justify his opinion.'

Misrepresentations made without words

In **Spice Girls Ltd *v* Aprilia World Service BV (2000)** a company representing a pop group, the Spice Girls, made an advertisement for another company. All of the Spice Girls took part in the filming of this advertisement. Shortly afterwards, one of the Spice Girls left the group. When the contract for the advertisement was signed, all of the group knew that one of them was about to leave the group. It was held that the act of taking part in the filming amounted to a representation by the company that it did not know at that time, and had no reasonable grounds to believe, that one of the group intended to leave.

The statement must induce the other party to make the contract

A statement can amount to a misrepresentation only if it was one of the reasons why the claimant made the contract. If a person makes a contract without checking the truth of a statement, this suggests that the statement did induce the making of the contract.

 Redgrave *v* Hurd (1881)

The claimant, a solicitor, advertised for a partner who would also buy the solicitor's house and solicitor's practice. The defendant answered the advertisement and was told that the practice made about £300 p.a. The claimant produced papers which he said would prove that his statement about the value of the practice was true, but the defendant did not read the papers. If he had done so, he would have discovered that the practice made only £200 p.a. When the defendant did discover that the practice made only £200 p.a. he refused to go ahead with the purchase.

Held The claimant's statement about the value of the practice was a misrepresentation. It could therefore be used as a defence for not going ahead with the contract. The fact that the defendant did not check the papers showed that the claimant's statement did induce the defendant to make the contract.

A person who checks the truth of a statement cannot later say that the statement induced the making a contract.

Attwood *v* Small (1838) (Court of Appeal)

The claimant bought a mine because the defendant greatly exaggerated the capacity of the mine. Before buying the mine the claimant got his own experts to check the defendant's statement. The experts mistakenly agreed that the defendant's statement was true.

Held The statement about the mine's capacity was not a misrepresentation because the claimant did not rely on it. By appointing his own experts to check the statement, the claimant proved that he did not rely on it.

Silence as a misrepresentation

Generally, silence cannot be a misrepresentation. The old rule *caveat emptor* (let the buyer beware) applies.

 Fletcher *v* Krell (1873)

The claimant applied for a job as a governess without revealing that she was divorced. In those days she would have been well aware that she stood no chance of getting the job if her secret had been discovered. The employer did not ask the claimant whether she was divorced, so she did not reveal that she was. The claimant was given a three-year fixed term contract to work in Buenos Aires at a salary of £100 a year. When the employer discovered that the claimant was divorced he ended the contract.

Held The claimant's silence did not amount to a misrepresentation. She was therefore entitled to sue for breach of contract. (The employer had argued that the claimant had made a misrepresentation, and that this gave him a defence to being sued for breach of contract.)

There are, however, four exceptions to the general rule. Silence will amount to a misrepresentation in the following circumstances.

(1) If there has been a change of circumstances.

(2) In contracts of insurance.

(3) If there is a fiduciary relationship between the parties.

(4) If the silence makes another statement misleading.

These exceptions need to be examined individually.

A change of circumstances

If a person makes a statement which is true, but due to a change of circumstances the statement becomes untrue before the contract is made, then it may be a misrepresentation not to reveal that the circumstances have changed.

 With *v* O'Flanagan (1936) (Court of Appeal)

A doctor who was selling his practice said that it had a turnover of £2,000 a year. This was true, but when the sale went ahead three months later the practice was virtually worthless because the doctor had been ill.

Held The doctor's failure to reveal the change was a misrepresentation.

Contracts of insurance

Contracts of insurance are contracts *uberrimae fidei* (of the utmost good faith). In such contracts, everything which could affect the price of the premium is a material fact. A person taking out insurance must reveal all material facts, whether asked about the matter or not.

 Lambert *v* Co-op Insurance Society Ltd (1975) (Court of Appeal)

The claimant insured her own and her husband's jewellery. She did not mention that her husband had been convicted of a small theft some years earlier. When the claimant renewed the policy she did not reveal that her husband had recently been sent to prison for 15 months for theft. The insurance company did not ask about convictions so the claimant felt no need to mention them. Over £300-worth of the insured jewellery was later stolen, and the claimant claimed on her insurance.

Held The insurance company did not need to pay on the policy. The convictions were a material fact and the claimant should have revealed them. Not to do so amounted to a misrepresentation.

Where there is a fiduciary relationship between the parties

A fiduciary relationship is a relationship of great trust. When the parties in such a relationship make a contract with each other, everything must be revealed. If this is not done, the silence will amount to a misrepresentation. Promoters and directors of companies owe fiduciary duties to their companies, and partners in a firm owe fiduciary duties to each other.

Silence makes a statement misleading

Even a statement which is literally true can amount to a misrepresentation if the statement conveys a misleading impression.

 Nottingham Patent Brick and Tile Co *v* Butler (1886) (Court of Appeal)

The defendant's solicitor, who was selling land on behalf of the defendant, was asked whether there were any restrictive covenants attached to the land. (The buyer would generally not want restrictive covenants. If there were any, they would be included in documents which the solicitor should have read.) The solicitor replied that he was not aware of any restrictive covenants. This was true, but the reason why the solicitor was not aware of any was that he had not read the documents which he should have read. The claimant agreed to buy the land but pulled out of the contract when he discovered that there were restrictive covenants.

Held The solicitor's statement, although literally true, was a misrepresentation. Therefore the claimant was entitled to withdraw from the contract.

Remedies for misrepresentation

There are three types of actionable misrepresentation. Each type gives rise to different remedies. Table 4.1 shows an outline of the types of actionable misrepresentations and their remedies.

Table 4.1 Types of actionable misrepresentations and their remedies

	Type of misrepresentation		
	Fraudulent	Negligent	Wholly innocent
Definition	Made (i) Knowingly false, or (ii) without belief, or (iii) recklessly, not caring whether it is true or false	Made Honestly, but the maker cannot prove reasonable grounds for believing it was true	Made Honestly, and the maker can prove reasonable grounds for believing it was true
Remedies	Rescind and damages for tort of deceit (time does not run)	Rescind and damages for tort of deceit (time runs from date of contract)	Rescind. Usually no damages (time runs from date of contract)

RESCISSION

Contract is affirmed ◄——— Lost if ———► Cannot be restored
to pre-contract
position

▼

Third party has rights

Fraudulent misrepresentation

Fraudulent misrepresentation was defined by **Derry v Peek (1889)** as a misrepresentation made either:

(1) knowing that it was untrue; or

(2) not believing that it was true; or

(3) recklessly, not caring whether it was true or false.

> **Example**
>
> Jason sells a lorry to Harjinder and makes a misrepresentation to the effect that the lorry has had a new engine fitted. The misrepresentation will be fraudulent if either: Jason knows that a new engine has not been fitted; or Jason does not think that a new engine has been fitted; or Jason has no idea whether or not a new engine has been fitted.

Remedies for fraudulent misrepresentation

A fraudulent misrepresentation allows the injured party to rescind the contract (call it off) and sue for damages for the tort of deceit. If the contract is to be rescinded for fraudulent misrepresentation, this must be done within a reasonable time of the innocent party becoming aware of the misrepresentation.

Damages for the tort of deceit are usually much greater than contract damages as a claim can be made for all expenses and losses caused by the deceit, even if these were not reasonably foreseeable.

Negligent misrepresentation

Section 2(1) of the Misrepresentation Act 1967 defines a negligent misrepresentation as one made by a person who cannot prove that he honestly believed that the facts represented were true and that he had reasonable grounds for this belief.

> **Example**
>
> Daniel sells a printer to Bill and makes a misrepresentation to the effect that it is a colour printer. Daniel believes this to be true. The misrepresentation will be negligent unless Daniel can prove that he had reasonable grounds for believing that the printer was a colour printer. (Notice that the burden of proof is on Daniel.)

Remedies for negligent misrepresentation

A negligent misrepresentation allows the injured party to rescind the contract and to sue for damages for the tort of deceit. If the contract is to be rescinded for negligent misrepresentation, this must be done within a reasonable time of the misrepresentation having been made.

A person to whom a false statement was made might try to recover damages for negligent misstatement at common law (see Chapter 8). However, if an action for negligent misrepresentation is possible, a claim for negligent misstatement is rarely made. There are three disadvantages to such a claim. First, the claimant will need to prove that there was a 'special relationship' between the parties. Second, the burden of proving negligence will be on the claimant. Third, any damages will be for negligence rather than for the tort of deceit. For these reasons a claim under s. 2(1) MA 1967 is almost always preferable.

Wholly innocent misrepresentation

A wholly innocent misrepresentation is one made by a person who can prove that he honestly believed that the facts represented were true and that he had reasonable grounds for this belief.

> **Example**
>
> Minoosh sells a computer to Jill and makes a misrepresentation to the effect that it can operate Apple software. Minoosh believed this to be true. If Minoosh can prove that she had reasonable grounds for believing it was true (perhaps because that is what the shop told her when she bought the computer), then she will have made a wholly innocent misrepresentation. If Minoosh cannot prove this, then she will have made a negligent misrepresentation. (Again, notice that the burden of proof is on Minoosh.)

Remedies for wholly innocent misrepresentation

The injured party can rescind but has no right to claim damages. However, as regards both negligent and innocent misrepresentation, s. 2(2) of the Misrepresentation Act 1967 allows the court to award contract damages instead of rescission where the court considers it 'equitable to do so'. It is rare for the courts to use this section to award damages for an innocent misrepresentation, but they sometimes do so when the misrepresentation was so trivial that rescission would be too drastic a remedy.

William Sindell *v* Cambridgeshire County Council (1994) provides an example. In 1989 building land was sold for £5 million. The purchasers alleged that there had been a misrepresentation made by the sellers of the land, on account of there being a sewage pipe on the land. By this time the land was worth only £2.5 million because the property market had collapsed. The purchasers claimed that they were rescinding the contract for misrepresentation. The Court of Appeal found that there had been no misrepresentation. However, they said that if there had been a misrepresentation, damages would have been awarded under s. 2(2) instead of rescission. These damages would have compensated for the relatively small cost of removing the sewage pipes. Rescission would have been too drastic a remedy.

The burden of proof

The person who has the burden of proof must prove what he alleges. In civil cases the claimant must prove what he alleges on a balance of probabilities, meaning that he must prove that it is more likely to be true than untrue. In criminal cases all of the elements of the crime must be proved beyond reasonable doubt. However, an exception to the civil standard of proof is made when a claimant alleges fraudulent misrepresentation. A claimant who alleges fraudulent misrepresentation must prove the fraud on a standard approaching the criminal law standard, because in effect the claimant is alleging that a crime has been committed. Almost all fraudulent misrepresentations also amount to a criminal offence.

If a party alleges negligent misrepresentation then he must prove, on the civil standard of proof, that there has been a misrepresentation. The burden of proof is then shifted to the other party, using the civil standard of proof, to prove that he had reasonable grounds for believing that his statement was true. If he cannot do this, the misrepresentation will have been negligent. Because the remedies for fraudulent and negligent misrepresentation are virtually identical, many victims of fraudulent misrepresentation allege negligent rather than fraudulent misrepresentation. All they have to do is prove that there has been a misrepresentation, and this will then be negligent unless the misrepresentor can prove that he had reasonable grounds for believing that his statement was true. This is much easier than proving fraudulent misrepresentation.

Figure 4.3 shows the burden of proof in cases of non-fraudulent misrepresentation.

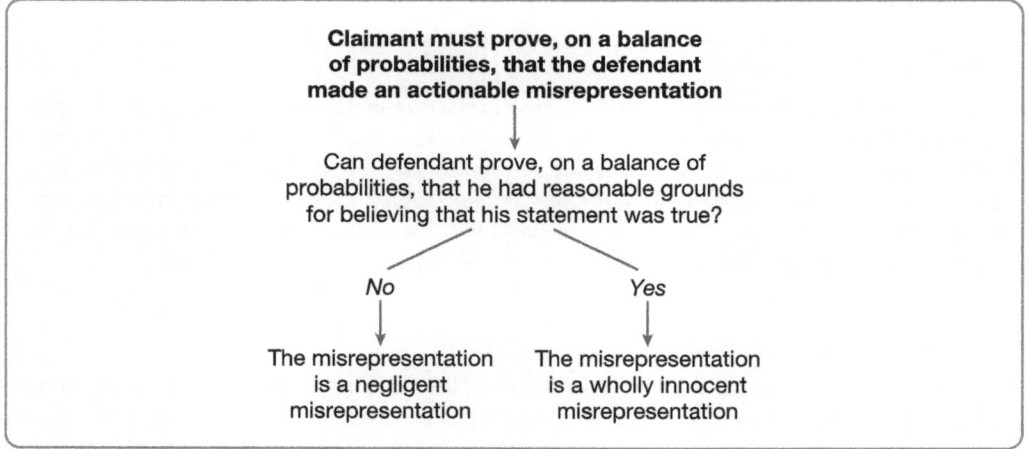

Figure 4.3 The burden of proof in non-fraudulent misrepresentation

Losing the right to rescind

All three types of misrepresentation give the injured party the right to rescind.

Rescission of a contract means that the parties are returned to the position they were in before the contract was made. So the whole of the purchase price will be returned to a purchaser who rescinds. Earlier (see Chapter 3) we saw that s. 48C SGA 1979 allows a secondary remedy of 'rescission' to a consumer who has bought goods which do not conform to the contract. A consumer who does rescind under s. 48C may not get all of the purchase price back as the court may deduct an amount to take account of any use of the goods which the consumer has had. The meaning of rescind under s. 48C is confined to that particular section. In general, a purchaser who rescinds will get all of the purchase price back. A party can rescind merely by letting the other party know that the contract is no longer regarded as binding. Rescission can also be used as a defence to a person who is sued for refusing to perform the contract, as we saw in **Redgrave v Hurd**.

The right to rescind can be lost in the following three ways:

(1) If the contract is affirmed.

(2) If a third party acquires rights.

(3) If the subject matter of the contract no longer exists.

The contract is affirmed

The contract will be affirmed if the claimant decides to carry on with the contract after discovering the misrepresentation. The claimant might indicate affirmation expressly or impliedly. If the claimant does nothing for a considerable period of time, the court might well take the view that the contract has been impliedly affirmed.

 Leaf v International Galleries (1950) (Court of Appeal)

The claimant bought a painting from International Galleries because of a non-fraudulent misrepresentation that the painting was by Constable. Five years later the claimant discovered that the painting was not by Constable and he immediately applied to the court for rescission of the contract.

Held The claimant was too late to rescind. He had affirmed the contract by doing nothing for five years.

Comment If the misrepresentation by the gallery had been fraudulent, time would only have started to run against the claimant from the moment when the misrepresentation was discovered. He would therefore have been able to rescind the contract. This is the main difference between the remedies for fraudulent and negligent misrepresentation.

If a third party has acquired rights

A contract which can be rescinded is said to be a voidable contract, because one of the parties has the option to avoid the contract (call it off). Although a misrepresentation makes a contract voidable, it does not prevent ownership of goods sold under the contract from passing to a person who made the misrepresentation. In such a case the person making the misrepresentation will own the goods unless and until the innocent party avoids the contract. The innocent party has no obligation to avoid and may choose to affirm the contract, despite the misrepresentation, and keep what was gained under the contract.

If the misrepresentor sells goods he received under the contract to a third party *before* the contract is avoided, then the third party can keep the goods forever. This is because, at the time when the goods were sold on, the misrepresentor still owned the goods, and therefore still had ownership to pass on. This rule is confirmed by s. 23 of the Sale of Goods Act 1979, which provides that:

> Where the seller of goods has a voidable title to them, but his title has not been avoided at the time of the sale, the buyer acquires a good title to the goods, provided he buys them in good faith and without notice of the seller's defect of title.

If, however, the goods are sold to the innocent third party *after* the contract has been avoided, then the innocent third party will get no ownership of the goods. This is because, when the goods were sold on, the misrepresentor no longer had any ownership to pass on, the contract having been avoided.

Cases on this matter amount to a dispute about who did what first.

 Lewis *v* Averay (1972) (Court of Appeal)

A rogue bought the claimant's car. The rogue paid with a bad cheque, pretending to be a famous actor called Richard Greene. (The rogue therefore made a fraudulent misrepresentation.) At first, the claimant was unwilling to take the rogue's cheque. However, the claimant did take the cheque when the rogue produced a Pinewood Studios pass in the name of Richard Greene, which showed the rogue's photograph. Having got possession of the car, the rogue sold it to the defendant. The defendant paid a reasonable price for the car and believed that the rogue owned it. The claimant later tried to avoid the contract.

Held Although the contract was voidable for fraudulent misrepresentation, the defendant gained complete ownership of it by virtue of s. 23 SGA 1979. Once the car had been resold by the rogue, the claimant was too late to avoid the contract and had lost ownership of the car.

 Car and Universal Finance Co *v* Caldwell (1965) (Court of Appeal)

A rogue bought a car with a bad cheque, knowing that the cheque would not be honoured. The car was later sold to a third party who bought it in good faith. Before this sale the original seller found out about the rogue's fraudulent misrepresentation. He could not find the rogue to tell him that he was avoiding the contract, so he told the police and the AA.

Held Telling the police and the AA was enough to avoid the contract because it was an action which showed a definite intention to avoid the contract. The original seller therefore got the car back from the third party. If the original seller had not told the police and the AA until *after* the rogue had resold the car, s. 23 of the Sale of Goods Act 1979 would have applied and he would never have got the car back.

Comment The misrepresentation in this case was fraudulent. The Court of Appeal raised the question as to whether or not the contract would have been avoided by telling the authorities if the misrepresentation had been negligent or innocent. Unfortunately, having raised the question, the court said that it did not know the answer. So the case is only an authority where the misrepresentation was fraudulent.

In all of these cases where a rogue buys goods with a stolen cheque one of two innocent parties is bound to suffer a loss. Either the original owner will get the goods back, in which case the purchaser from the rogue will have paid money to the rogue in return for nothing at all, or the original owner will not get the goods back, and will therefore have been deprived of ownership of the goods in return for a worthless cheque. (It should be noticed that s. 23 SGA 1979 will never operate in favour of a third party who did not act in good faith when buying from the misrepresentor.)

Whichever of the two parties suffers the loss will be left with the right to sue the rogue for damages. However, it should be pointed out that this right is likely to be worth very little. First, the rogue might never be identified. Second, rogues who buy goods with bad cheques rarely have enough money to pay damages.

If it is impossible to put the parties back into their pre-contract positions

When a contract is treated as terminated for breach of a term, future performance of the contract is not required. This is the case whether or not the contract has been partly per-formed. However, when a contract is avoided, the parties must be put back into the positions they were in before the contract was made. If this cannot be done, then the contract cannot be avoided. In **Clarke v Dickson (1858)** Crompton J gave the example of a butcher who bought live cattle because a farmer had made a fraudulent misrepresentation about them. He said that once the cattle had been slaughtered and butchered rescission would not be possible. (However, damages for the tort of deceit could have been claimed.) Again, it should be noticed that when s. 48C SGA talks of rescission the word is not used in its usual sense but in a sense which applies only to that section. Under s. 48C a contract can be rescinded even if the parties cannot be put back into the positions they were in before the contract was made.

Mistake

When the parties make their contract, one or both of them might be mistaken as to some fundamental matter. Here we examine the types of mistake which might be made and the effect of these mistakes upon the validity of the contract. First, we consider the position where both parties make the same mistake. (This is known as common mistake.) Then we consider the position where only one of the parties makes a mistake. (This is known as unilateral mistake.) Figure 4.4 shows an outline of the different types of mistake.

Common mistake

There is said to be a common mistake when both of the parties freely reach agreement, but do so while making the same mistake.

Common mistake as to existence of goods

A common mistake might be made about the existence of the subject matter of the contract. For example, let us assume that X Ltd agrees to buy a second-hand machine from Y Ltd. Let us also assume that at the time of the contract, unknown to both parties, the machine does not exist because it has been destroyed in a fire. Section 6 of the Sale of Goods Act provides that, where there is a contract for the sale of specific goods, and the goods, without the knowledge of the seller, have perished at the time the contract is made, the contract is void. Y Ltd will not therefore be in breach of contract for failure to deliver the machine and X Ltd will not have to pay the contract price. If the contract had been for the sale of unascertained goods, such as 100 tonnes of wheat, then Y Ltd would have to find another 100 tonnes of wheat from elsewhere or be in breach of contract. (The difference between specific and unascertained goods is explained in Chapter 7.)

It is important to note here that if specific goods which are sold cease to exist *after* the contract has been made, but before the goods have been delivered to the buyer, the contract will not be void for mistake. Generally, the buyer will have received ownership of the goods

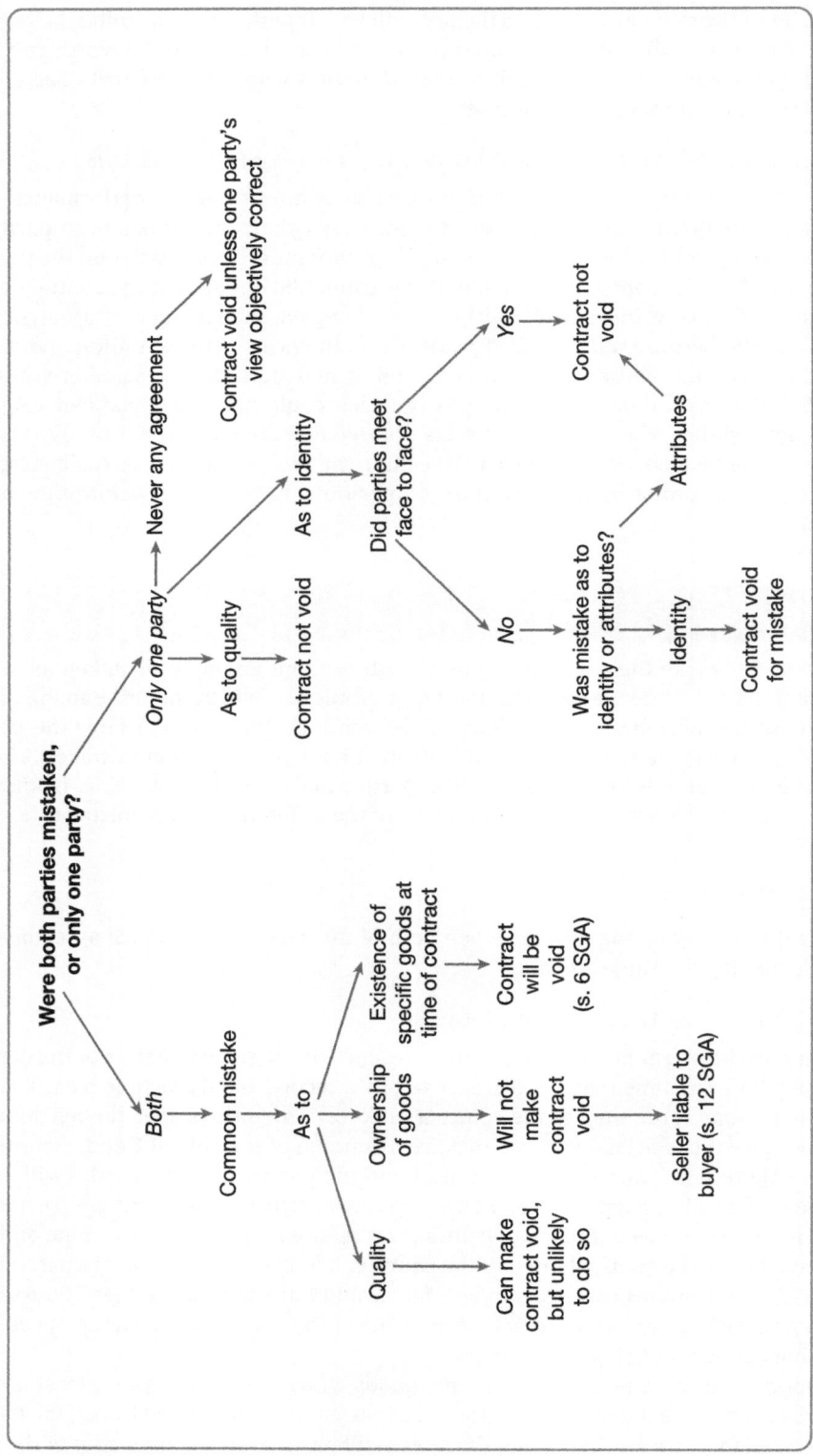

Figure 4.4 An outline of the different types of mistake

as soon as the contract was made and so the goods will then have been at his risk. If this is the case, the buyer will therefore have to pay for the goods. (See SGA 1979 s. 18, rule 1 in Chapter 7.) If, after a contract to sell specific goods was made, the risk had not passed to the buyer at the time when the goods ceased to exist the contract would not be void for mistake; the seller would be in breach of contract.

However, if the goods had perished, s. 7 SGA 1979 would cause the contract to be frustrated (s. 7 is explained in Chapter 7).

Common mistake as to ownership of goods

A common mistake as to the ownership of goods will not generally make the contract void. Earlier (see Chapter 3) we saw that s. 12(1) of the Sale of Goods Act 1979 implies a term that the seller of goods owns the goods. A seller who does not own the goods sold will be in breach of contract, as we saw in **Rowland v Divall**.

Common mistake as to possibility of performance

If the parties agree to make a contract which is, at that time, impossible to perform, then the contract will be void for mistake.

Common mistake as to quality

A common mistake as to the quality of goods sold will not generally make the contract void.

 Bell v Lever Bros (1932) (House of Lords)

A company paid an employee £30,000 in return for him accepting redundancy. Afterwards, it was discovered that the employee could have been dismissed without paying any compensation because he had breached the company's rules. Neither the employee nor the company realised that the employee could have been dismissed without paying compensation when the agreement was made.

Held The agreement was not void for mistake and the employee could keep the money. A common mistake as to quality will make a contract void only if the mistake means that what was being bought was essentially a different thing from what the parties believed it to be. Both parties knew that what was being bought was the right to make the employee redundant. They were mistaken as to how much this was worth, thinking it was worth £30,000 when in fact it was worth nothing. However, they were not mistaken as to what was being bought. Whether it was worth £30,000 or nothing, the thing which was being bought was the same thing, the right to make the employee redundant.

Lord Atkin said: 'A buys B's horse; he thinks the horse is sound and he pays the price of a sound horse; he would certainly not have bought the horse if he had known, as the fact is, that the horse is unsound. If B has made no representation as to soundness and has not contracted that the horse is sound, A is bound and cannot recover back the price. A buys a picture from B; both A and B believe it to be the work of an old master, and a high price is paid. It turns out to be a modern copy. A has no remedy in the absence of a representation or warranty.'

Bell v Lever Bros was applied by the Court of Appeal in the following case.

Great Peace Shipping Ltd v Tsavliris Salvage International Ltd (2002) (Court of Appeal)

The defendants offered salvage services to a ship which was in trouble in the Indian Ocean. A reliable third party told the defendants that the claimants' ship, the *Great Peace*, was the closest ship which could provide salvage. So the defendants booked the *Great Peace* for a minimum of five days. When the contract was made, the defendants thought that the *Great Peace* was within 35 miles of the ship in trouble. In fact, the two ships were 410 miles apart and it would have taken the *Great Peace* 39 hours to arrive. The defendants therefore told the claimants that they wanted to cancel the contract, but not until they had found a closer ship. When the defendants did find a closer ship, they cancelled the contract but the claimants refused to accept this. The defendants argued that the contract was void for common mistake because both parties thought that the *Great Peace* was close to the ship which was in trouble.

Held Applying **Bell v Lever Bros**, the contract was not void for common mistake. The contract would have been void only if the distance between the ships had meant that the services which the *Great Peace* was to provide were essentially different from what the parties had agreed. The fact that the defendants wanted to keep the contract on unless a closer ship could be found indicated that this was not the case.

Unilateral mistake

Unilateral mistake meaning no agreement was made

If the parties to the contract were at cross purposes when making the offer and acceptance, there may have been no real agreement. If the reasonable person could not objectively say which of the parties' views was obviously correct, then there will be no contract. If the reasonable person could say that the view of one or other of the parties was obviously correct, then there will be a valid contract.

 Raffles v Wichelhaus (1864)

A contract was made to buy cotton as soon as it arrived on a ship called *Peerless* which was sailing from Bombay. In fact, two ships called *Peerless* were sailing from Bombay. When the contract was made the defendant was thinking of a ship called *Peerless* which set off in October. The claimant was thinking of a different ship which set off in December.

Held There was no contract because the reasonable person could not say what had been agreed. However, if the reasonable person could have said that one or other of the ships was obviously what the parties seemed to have intended, then there would have been a contract to buy the cotton which arrived on that ship. (This might have happened, for instance, if one of the ships was a world famous carrier of cotton from India, while the other was an unknown ship.)

Unilateral mistake as to the terms of the contract

If one of the parties knows that the other made the contract while making a fundamental mistake as to the terms of the contract, then the contract can be void for mistake. In **Hartog v Colin & Shields (1939)**, for example, sellers of a large quantity of animal skins made a slip of the pen and offered to sell them at one-third of their usual price. The buyer accepted, knowing that a mistake had been made. The contract was void for mistake because the buyer knew that the sellers had made a mistake about the terms of their offer. However, if one party knows that the other is making a fundamental mistake about the quality of what is being sold, then the contract will not be void for mistake. For example, in **Smith v Hughes (1871)** a seller of oats showed a potential buyer a sample of the oats. The buyer thought that the oats were old oats and so he bought them. In fact, they were new oats which were no use to him at all. It was held that even if the seller knew of the buyer's mistake the contract was not void for mistake. This situation differs from the examples given by Lord Atkin in **Bell v Lever Bros** because in those examples both parties were mistaken as to the quality of what was being sold.

Mistake as to the identity of the other contracting party

This is the most important type of unilateral mistake and needs to be considered in a little more detail. Most of the cases concern a rogue who buys goods while pretending to be someone else and who pays for the goods with a bad cheque. We have already seen that a rogue who pays with a bad cheque commits a fraudulent misrepresentation which makes the contract capable of being rescinded, which is also known as making the contract **voidable**. So if the person who sells to the rogue avoids the contract before the rogue sells the goods to a third party there will be no need to argue mistake. It is when the person who sells to the rogue does not avoid in time that it becomes necessary to argue that the contract is **void** for mistake. If this argument is successful the person who sells to the rogue will always get the goods back because a void contract is no contract at all. No ownership of the goods ever passes to the rogue under a void contract, or to anyone else to whom the rogue sells the goods.

Figure 4.5 shows the different effect of good, void and voidable contracts. It assumes that A sells goods to B and that B sells the goods on to C, who buys them in good faith. The figure examines the different positions if the contract between A and B was a good contract, a void contract or a voidable contract.

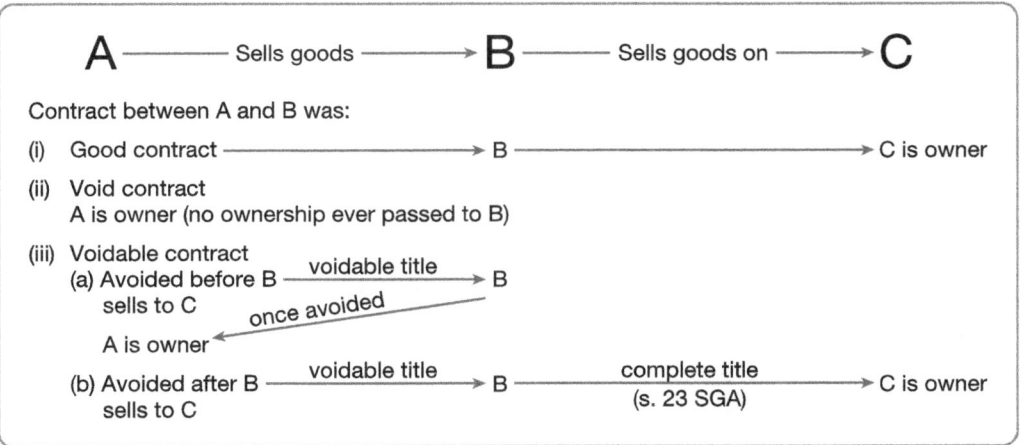

Figure 4.5 The effect of resale after good, void and voidable contracts

Whether or not a mistake as to the identity of the other contracting party will make a contract void depends upon several factors. First, it is necessary that the parties did not meet face to face when making the contract. If the parties did meet face to face, then the contract will not be void for mistake. In **Lewis v Averay**, which we considered earlier in this chapter, the claimant argued that the contract was void for mistake. (If this argument had been successful the claimant would have got the car back.) The Court of Appeal rejected this argument. If the parties meet face to face, then the contract will not be void for mistake.

If the parties did not meet face to face, then it is possible that the contract will be void for mistake. However, this will be the case only where the innocent contracting party was mistaken as to the *identity* of the rogue. If the innocent contracting party was mistaken only as to the rogue's *attributes*, then the contract will not be void for mistake. (Attributes are concerned with a person's qualities or distinguishing features. For example, one of the attributes of Stuart Broad, the cricketer, is that he is a very good fast bowler. This is not the same as his identity. There are other very good fast bowlers.) The following two cases show the difference between being mistaken as to identity and being mistaken as to attributes.

 Cundy *v* Lindsay (1878) (House of Lords)

A rogue ordered a very large quantity of handkerchiefs from the claimants. The rogue pretended to be a reputable firm with whom the claimants had previously dealt. This firm was called Blenkiron & Co of 123 Wood Street, London. The rogue, who was called Blenkarn, disguised his signature to look like Blenkiron & Co, giving his address as 37 Wood Street, where he had hired a room. The trick worked and the claimants sent the handkerchiefs to Blenkiron & Co at 37 Wood Street. The rogue sold 250 dozen of these handkerchiefs to the defendant who bought them in good faith. The claimants sued the defendant to get these handkerchiefs back.

Held The contract was void for mistake because the claimants were mistaken as to the identity of the person with whom they made the contract. Therefore, ownership of the handkerchiefs never moved away from the claimants.

Comment The contract was of course voidable for fraudulent misrepresentation, but the claimants had not avoided it in time. As regards avoiding for misrepresentation, they would therefore have been defeated by s. 23 of the Sale of Goods Act 1979, as explained above.

 Kings Norton Metal Co Ltd *v* Edridge, Merrett & Co Ltd (1897) (Court of Appeal)

A rogue ordered goods from the claimants, who were metal manufacturers. The rogue was called Wallis, but he made the letter appear to come from Hallam & Co, Sheffield. No such company ever existed. However, the claimants made the contract and delivered the goods because the rogue's letter was printed on very impressive notepaper. The rogue sold the goods on to the defendants, who bought them in good faith. The claimants sued the defendants to get the goods back.

Held The contract was not void for mistake and so the claimants were not entitled to the goods. The claimants were not mistaken about the identity of the person they were dealing with. (Unlike the claimants in **Cundy v Lindsay**, the claimants in this case had no prior knowledge of the person with whom they thought they were dealing.) They were mistaken only about the attributes of that person. They thought that they were dealing with someone who was creditworthy and respectable, whereas in fact they were not.

Comment (i) The contract was voidable for fraudulent misrepresentation but the claimants were defeated by s. 23 of the Sale of Goods Act 1979. (ii) The rogue could have been sued for damages for the tort of deceit. However, this rogue (like most other rogues) would not have had enough money to pay any damages.

In the following case the House of Lords thoroughly reviewed the cases on mistake as to the person.

 Shogun Finance Ltd *v* Hudson (FC) (2003) (House of Lords)

The defendant, Hudson, bought a car from a rogue. The rogue had taken the car on hire-purchase from Shogun Finance Ltd, the claimants. If this contract between the rogue and the claimants was a good contract, then the defendant would become owner of the car under s. 27 of the Hire-Purchase Act 1964. (This is a technical provision with which we need not be concerned here. Its effect is examined in Chapter 7.) If the contract was void, then the defendant could not gain a good title. The question for the House of Lords was therefore whether the contract between the rogue and the claimants was void for mistake. The rogue had not met the claimants face to face but had visited a dealer who was not the claimants' agent. At the dealer's showroom the rogue had produced a driving licence stolen from one Durlabh Patel and had filled in one of the claimants' standard hire-purchase forms in Durlabh Patel's name. A copy of this agreement had been faxed to the claimants who had approved the sale.

Held (3 to 2) The contract between the rogue and the claimants was void for mistake and so the defendant never became owner of the car.

Comment (i) The judges in the majority thought it significant that the contract was a written contract which would not have come into existence until a credit check had been carried out. They indicated that the position might have been different if it had been an oral sale of goods because ownership of the goods could then have already passed to the rogue before the time for payment and identification arose. (The time at which ownership of goods passes to a buyer is considered in Chapter 7.) (ii) All five of the judges thought that **Lewis *v* Averay** was correctly decided. (iii) The two judges in the minority thought that **Cundy *v* Lindsay** should be overruled and that a voidable contract existed between the rogue and the claimants. However, the three judges in the majority confirmed **Cundy *v* Lindsay** as being correct.

The final requirement for a contract to be void on account of a unilateral mistake as to the person is that the mistake must have been a material mistake, that is to say it must have been a mistake which induced the making of the contract. For example, in **Mackie *v* European Assurance Society (1869)** the claimant asked a friend to insure him. The claimant thought that the policy would be taken out with one particular insurance company but in fact it was taken out with another. When the claimant claimed on his insurance policy the insurers refused to pay, arguing mistake as to the person. The contract was not void for mistake. It was true that the parties did not meet face to face and that the claimant was mistaken about the identity of the other contracting party. The contract was not void for mistake, however, because the claimant would not have been bothered which of the two insurance companies made the contract of insurance.

Mistake as to the nature of what is being signed

If a person signs a document while making a complete mistake as to what type of document it is, then the contract can be void for a type of mistake known as *non est factum* (it is not my deed).

Saunders *v* Anglia Building Society (1970) (House of Lords)

An elderly woman intended to leave her house to her nephew after her death. The nephew owed money to one Lee. To pay Lee off the nephew visited the elderly aunt with Lee, who asked the elderly woman to sign a document. Lee told her that this gave the house to the nephew but that she would be allowed to live there for the rest of her life. In fact, the document said that Lee had bought the house and paid for it. The elderly woman did not read the document because her glasses were broken. Lee mortgaged the house to the Anglia Building Society but did not pay any of the mortgage instalments. The building society applied to repossess the house.

Held The contract was not void for *non est factum* because there was not a fundamental difference between what the elderly woman signed and what she thought she was signing. (Either way she was transferring her ownership of the house.) Therefore, the contract was valid and the building society could repossess the house.

Non est factum cannot be claimed by a person who was careless in signing. In **United Dominions Trust Ltd *v* Western (1975)** the Court of Appeal therefore held that it was not available to a person who signed a blank document for the figures to be filled in later.

Foster *v* Mackinnon (1869) provides a rare example of a successful plea of *non est factum*. An old man with very poor eyesight signed a document which he was told was a guarantee. In fact, the document was a cheque. *Non est factum* applied and the old man was not liable on the cheque.

Duress and undue influence

Duress

Traditionally, a contract was voidable for duress only if one of the parties was forced into making it by the threat of illegal physical violence. This common law doctrine was so narrow as to be virtually useless. A person who makes a contract because of such threats is unlikely then to go to court to avoid the contract.

More recently, a doctrine of economic duress has developed. A threat of physical violence is no longer necessary. Now a party who was pushed into a contract in such a way that there was no real consent to the contract can avoid the contract. For example, in **The Universe Sentinel (1982)** shipowners were told that if they did not agree to pay money to a seamen's charity a trade union would not allow their ship to leave port. The shipowners agreed to the union's demands and their ship was allowed to sail away. The House of Lords held that the shipowners were entitled to recover the money paid to the charity on the grounds of economic duress. They had not freely agreed to pay this money, they were pushed into the contract in such a way that they did not really consent. The following case provides another example.

Atlas Express Ltd *v* Kafco Ltd (1989)

The defendants, a small company, agreed that the claimants would carry their products to Woolworths shops throughout the country. The price of carriage was agreed at £1.10 a carton. The claimants, through their own error, had miscalculated the size of the cartons. The claimants told the defendants that they would not continue to perform the contract unless the defendants agreed to pay a minimum price per load. The defendants could not find another carrier and so they had to agree to this or they would have lost their contract with Woolworths, which was vital to them. After the cartons had been carried, the defendants refused to pay the extra amount.

Held The defendants did not need to pay. The contract was voidable on the grounds of economic duress.

As the law of economic duress has expanded, some of the old cases on consideration might now be differently decided. For example, the ship's captain in **Stilk *v* Myrick** (which was considered in Chapter 2) was pushed into the contract against his wishes. If the case were to arise today a court might hold that there was a contract but that it was voidable for economic duress.

Undue influence

Undue influence is an equitable doctrine which complements the common law doctrine of duress. It can make a contract voidable if the claimant was unduly influenced by the defendant to make it. If there was a threat, or illegitimate pressure, then the case is likely to be one of duress rather than undue influence.

To establish undue influence the claimant must prove two matters. First, he must prove that there was a relationship of undue influence between himself and the defendant. As regards some types of relationships (such as parent and child, solicitor and client, trustee and beneficiary and solicitor and client), there is a presumption that the dominant party influenced the weaker party. However, the relationship of husband and wife is not one in which there is a presumption of influence. Where there is no relationship in which influence is presumed, the claimant must prove that he actually was influenced to make the contract by the defendant. The second stage, after influence has been proved one way or another, is that the claimant must show that he entered into a transaction which calls for explanation. This transaction does not need to be a contract with the defendant, it could be a contract with a third party. Once the claimant has done this, the burden of proof shifts to the defendant to show that there was in fact no undue influence. The most effective way to do this is to show that the claimant took independent legal advice before entering into the contract. If the defendant cannot prove that there was in fact no undue influence, then the contract will be voidable by the claimant. As with all contracts which are voidable, the right to rescind can be lost, as we saw earlier in this chapter.

Banks tainted with undue influence

A situation which arises quite commonly is that a husband persuades his wife that they should mortgage the matrimonial home in order to get a loan for the husband's business from a bank. If the loan is not repaid, the bank will want to repossess the matrimonial home. This means that they would sell it to recover the amount which they were owed. In **Royal Bank of Scotland plc *v* Etridge (No. 2) (1998)** the House of Lords held that the bank should positively inform the wife that she should get independent legal advice before agreeing to the mortgage. If the bank does this, it will be able to enforce the mortgage. If the bank does not do this, and if agreeing to the mortgage could not readily be explained by the relationship of the parties, then the mortgage cannot be enforced. However, in many cases the mortgaging of the matrimonial home can be explained by the relationship of the parties. In many cases it is a reasonable risk to take to secure the husband's business. The principles in this case apply not only to husband and wife, but also whenever the relationship between the debtor and the person guaranteeing the debt is not a commercial relationship.

Illegal contracts

The following types of contracts are illegal at common law and therefore unenforceable.

- *Contracts tending to promote corruption in public life.* An example is provided by **Parkinson v College of Ambulance Ltd (1925)**. The claimant was promised that he would receive a knighthood if he made a donation to a charity. He made the donation but sued for its return when he did not get the knighthood. His action failed because the contract was illegal.

- *Contracts tending to impede the administration of justice.* A contract to make sure that a person is not prosecuted would be illegal and void. However, a contract not to pursue a civil action is perfectly valid. Disputes are often settled in this way and this is known as settling out of court (see Chapter 2).

- *Contracts to trade with enemy nations.* In times of war, certain nations become enemy nations. A contract to trade with a person voluntarily living in an enemy nation is generally void.

- *Contract to commit a tort, fraud or crime.* A strange example is provided by **Everett v Williams (1725)**. One highwayman tried to sue another on an agreement to rob a stagecoach. The highwayman failed in this action. (Both the claimant and the defendant were hanged and the lawyers were fined £50 for bringing the case!)

- *Contracts tending to promote sexual immorality.* An example is provided by **Pearce v Brooks (1866)**, where a prostitute hired a carriage which the owner knew was to be used for immoral purposes. The prostitute refused to pay for the hire of the carriage but the owner was not allowed to recover the agreed payments.

- *Contracts to defraud the Revenue.* In **Miller v Karlinski (1945)** a contract was made to defraud the Revenue. The claimant sued for ten weeks' wages and £21 travelling expenses. Of the travelling expenses, £17 should have been paid as wages. The claimant and the employer agreed to say they were travelling expenses to avoid paying income tax on the £17. The Court of Appeal held that the whole agreement was unenforceable. Therefore, the claimant could not recover anything, not even the proper wages or the £4 genuine travelling expenses.

Many statutes also make certain types of contracts illegal. The contracts concerned are so numerous that it is beyond the scope of this book to attempt to list them.

Contracts which contravene public policy

A contract which contravenes public policy will be void. The most important type of such a contract is a contract in restraint of trade. Contracts in restraint of trade attempt to prevent a person from working or carrying on a business. Such contracts are void unless they can be proved to be reasonable. They tend to arise where a person who sells a business agrees not to compete with the new owner. When considering whether such agreements in restraint of trade are reasonable or not, the court will consider the length of time for which the agreement was to last, the extent of the area in which competition was prohibited and the type of competition which was prohibited. Contracts in restraint of trade are also found where an employee agrees not to compete with the employer's line of business after leaving the employment. A contract in restraint of trade which attempts to prevent an ex-employee from working for another employer can be valid only if it was necessary to protect trade secrets, trade connections or confidential information.

Essential points

- A term is part of a contract and if a term is breached this is breach of contract.
- A representation is a statement which persuaded another person to make a contract.
- An actionable misrepresentation is an untrue statement of fact which induced the other party to make the contract.
- Generally, silence cannot amount to an actionable misrepresentation.
- A misrepresentation is fraudulent if it was made either: knowing that it was untrue; or not believing that it was true; or recklessly, not caring whether it was true or false.
- A misrepresentation is made negligently if the person who made it cannot prove that he believed that it was true and that he had reasonable grounds for this belief.
- A misrepresentation is made innocently if the person who made it can prove that he believed that it was true and that he had reasonable grounds for this belief.
- If a contract is rescinded the parties are restored to the positions which they were in before the contract was made.
- The right to rescind can be lost if the contract is affirmed, or if a third party has acquired rights, or if it is impossible to put the parties back into their pre-contract positions.
- There is a common mistake when both of the parties freely reach agreement, but do so while making the same mistake.
- A common mistake might be as to the existence of the subject matter of the contract, or as to the ownership of goods sold or as to the quality of goods sold.
- If one party knows that the other is mistaken as to the terms of the contract, this will make the contract void.
- A mistake as to the identity of the other contracting party can make the contract void if the parties did not meet face to face.
- A contract will be voidable for duress if it was made as a result of actual physical violence or the threat of it.
- A contract may be voidable for economic duress if a person was pushed into it in such a way that there was no real consent to the contract.
- Many types of contracts are made illegal by statute.
- Some contracts are illegal at common law.
- Illegal contracts are void.

Practice questions

1   Two months ago, Samikah bought a small bakery for £1 million. The vendor of the bakery, Bill, told Samikah that the average monthly turnover was about £100,000. Bill offered to show Samikah the business records, which he claimed would have proved that his statement about the turnover was true. Samikah declined this offer, saying that she trusted Bill. The written contract of sale made no mention of the business turnover. Since Samikah bought the business, the turnover has been only £30,000 a month. Samikah has now discovered that the monthly turnover of the business has never exceeded £45,000. Advise Samikah of her legal position.

2   Cedric, a manufacturer of jewellery, received an order from a company called Acme (Superjewellers) Ltd. Cedric sent a small amount of jewellery and received prompt payment. Cedric then received a bigger order from Acme (Superjewellers) Ltd and posted jewellery worth £10,000 to Acme (Superjewellers) Ltd. Cedric did not receive payment for this and has since been informed that Acme (Superjewellers) Ltd is a fictitious company, often used as an alias by Edward, a rogue. Edward has been caught by the police and is likely to be sent to prison. The police have discovered that Frederick now has the jewellery which Cedric sent to Acme (Superjewellers) Ltd. Frederick bought the jewellery from Edward. Advise Cedric of his legal position.

3   Gina, a dealer in antiques, visits the premises of Helen, another dealer. Gina buys a painting for £5,000. Helen does not make any claims about the painting. The painting turns out to be a fake and virtually worthless. Advise Gina of her legal position in the following circumstances.

    (a) Helen, like Gina, believed that the painting was genuine and worth about £5,000.

    (b) Helen had a good idea that the painting was a fake.

4   George is a retired teacher. Fay has agreed to buy George's boat, so that she can sail to the Channel Islands. How would the contract be affected if, unknown to both parties:

    (a) The boat did not belong to George?

    (b) The boat was completely unseaworthy?

    (c) The boat had been destroyed by fire five minutes before the contract was made?

5   Sarah buys a painting from a junk shop for £1,000. What would the effect on the contract be if:

    (a) Sarah discovered that the painting was utterly worthless?

    (b) The shop owner had untruthfully said that the painting was by the minor Edwardian artist, René Dulux, and therefore worth at least £1,000? (In fact the painting is worthless.)

6   Jermaine, a carpenter, put in a tender to do the carpentry work on a development which was being built in North Wales. Jermaine's tender was accepted. The work was to be completed in two months and Jermaine was to be paid £5,000. When Jermaine arrived on the site, he was told that there had been a mistake and another carpenter had been employed instead. Jermaine was told that he could still do the work but that he would only be paid £3,500. Jermaine felt that he had to accept these new terms as he had no other work available and had given up his flat so that he could move to Wales. Jermaine has now finished the job on time. Advise Jermaine of his legal position.

7   Explain any remedies which are available to a person who sells goods to a rogue who buys the goods with a bad cheque whilst using a false identity.

Task 4

A friend of yours who is visiting the country from abroad is considering starting a business in England. Your friend has asked you to write a report, briefly dealing with the following matters:

(a) The difference between a contract term and a representation.

(b) The nature of a misrepresentation.

(c) The remedies for misrepresentation.

(d) The types of mistake which can make a contract void.

(e) The circumstances in which a contract can be voidable for duress or undue influence.

(f) The types of contract which are illegal at common law.

mylawchamber

Visit **www.mylawchamber.co.uk/macintyreessentials** to access tools to help you develop and test your knowledge of business law, including interactive multiple choice questions, practice exam questions with guidance, weblinks, glossary, glossary flashcards, legal newsfeed and legal updates.

Discharge of contracts and remedies for breach

Discharge of contractual liability

We have seen (in Chapters 2, 3 and 4) that contractual liability is created when an offer is accepted, and that this liability is to perform the terms agreed upon. When a party's contractual liability is discharged it ceases to exist. This can happen in four ways:

(1) by performance;

(2) by agreement;

(3) by frustration; or

(4) by breach.

In addition, legislation can give a right to conclude certain types of contracts during a 'cooling-off' period. Figure 5.1 gives an overview of how contracts are created and discharged.

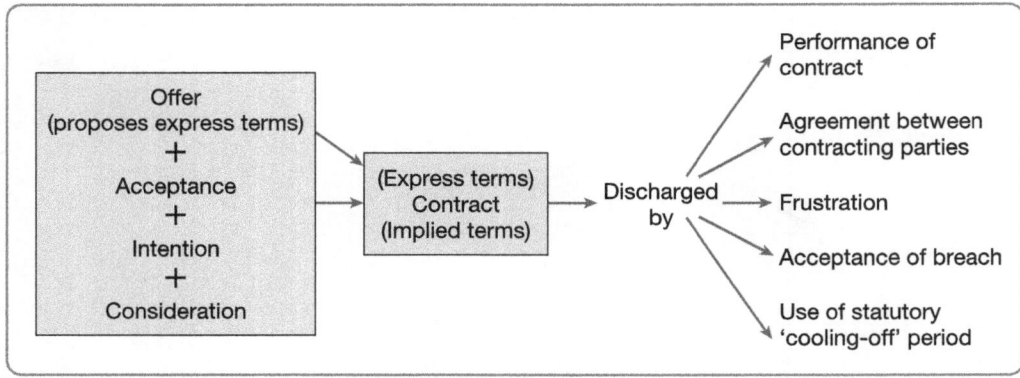

Figure 5.1 How contracts are created and discharged

Discharge by performance of the contract

The Sale of Goods Act 1979 makes special rules about the performance of contracts of sale of goods. These rules are considered later (see Chapter 7). Here we are considering the position as regards contracts other than contracts of sale of goods.

It was seen earlier (in Chapter 2) that a party who makes the offer of a unilateral contract promises to do something if the other party performs an act which has been requested. For example, in **Carlill _v_ The Carbolic Smoke Ball Co (1893)** the company promised to pay any person a £100 reward if they bought a smoke ball, used it properly and caught flu. A party who makes the offer of a unilateral contract needs to keep the promise made only if the other party fully performs the act specified. So if Mrs Carlill had not bought the smoke ball, used it properly and caught flu, there would have been no obligation to pay her any part of the reward.

In bilateral contracts the general rule is that if one party fails to fully perform the contract the other party need not perform the contract at all. The following case demonstrates this general rule.

 Cutter v Powell (1795)

Cutter had agreed to be a ship's mate on a voyage from Jamaica to Liverpool. The contract said that Cutter was to be paid £31.50, 'provided he proceeds, continues and does his duty . . . from hence to the port of Liverpool'. The journey took about two months and usually ship mates were paid about £4 a month. Cutter died after three-quarters of the voyage and therefore did not fully perform his contractual obligations. Cutter's widow sued for payment for the work Cutter had performed.

Held The ship's captain had no obligation to pay anything because Cutter had not completely performed his contractual obligations.

There are four exceptions to this general rule:

(1) Divisible or severable contracts.
(2) Substantial performance.
(3) Acceptance of partial performance.
(4) Prevention of performance.

Divisible contracts

Part payment must be made for partial performance if the contract is regarded as divisible or severable. In **Cutter v Powell** the wording of the contract, and the fact that Cutter was to be paid an unusually large lump sum for completing the contract, made it plain that Cutter's obligation to act as ship's mate was entire. That is to say, it was one obligation which was either performed or not. If a contract is divisible, then it will consist of a number of separate obligations and part payment will be required for each obligation performed. Whether or not a contract is divisible or entire depends upon what the parties intended when they made the contract. In **Ritchie v Atkinson (1808)**, for example, a ship's captain agreed to carry a cargo of hemp at £5 a ton. The captain carried only half the cargo. This contract was divisible because the price was expressed per ton rather than as a lump sum for carrying the whole cargo. The captain was therefore paid for the cargo he did carry (but had to pay damages in respect of the cargo which he failed to carry). If the contract had been entire, then the captain would not have been paid anything at all.

Substantial performance

A second exception to the general rule arises where the partial performance very nearly amounted to total performance. If the partial performance can be regarded as substantial performance, then it will have to be paid for. For example, in **Hoenig v Isaacs (1952)** the contract was to decorate and furnish a flat for £750. Defects in the work would have cost £56 to put right. The Court of Appeal held that there had been substantial performance and so the decorator was paid £750, but then had to pay damages of £56. By contrast, in **Bolton v**

Mahadeva (1972) the contract was to install central heating in a house for £560. Defects in the work would have cost £174 to put right. The Court of Appeal held that there had been no substantial performance and so the installer received no payment at all.

Acceptance of partial performance

A third exception to the general rule arises where partial performance was freely accepted by the other party. However, this acceptance must arise as a matter of choice. For example, in **Sumpter v Hedges (1898)** the claimant had agreed to build two houses for the defendant for £565. After doing work to the value of £333 the claimant was forced to stop work because he had run out of money. The defendant finished the work himself. The court held that the defendant did not have to pay the claimant for the work he had done. The defendant's act of finishing the work did not indicate that he had freely accepted the claimant's partial performance.

Prevention of performance

A final exception to the general rule arises where one of the contracting parties prevents the other from fully performing the contract. The party who is prevented from fully performing will be paid the amount deserved for the work done. This is known as a *quantum meruit* payment. In **Planché v Colburn (1831)**, for example, the claimant had been commissioned by the defendant to write a book. The book was on costumes and armour, part of a series called the Juvenile Library, and the claimant was to be paid £100 on completion. The defendant cancelled the series when the claimant's book was partly written. The claimant was entitled to a payment of £50 for the work he had done.

Figure 5.2 gives an overview of how contracts are discharged by performance.

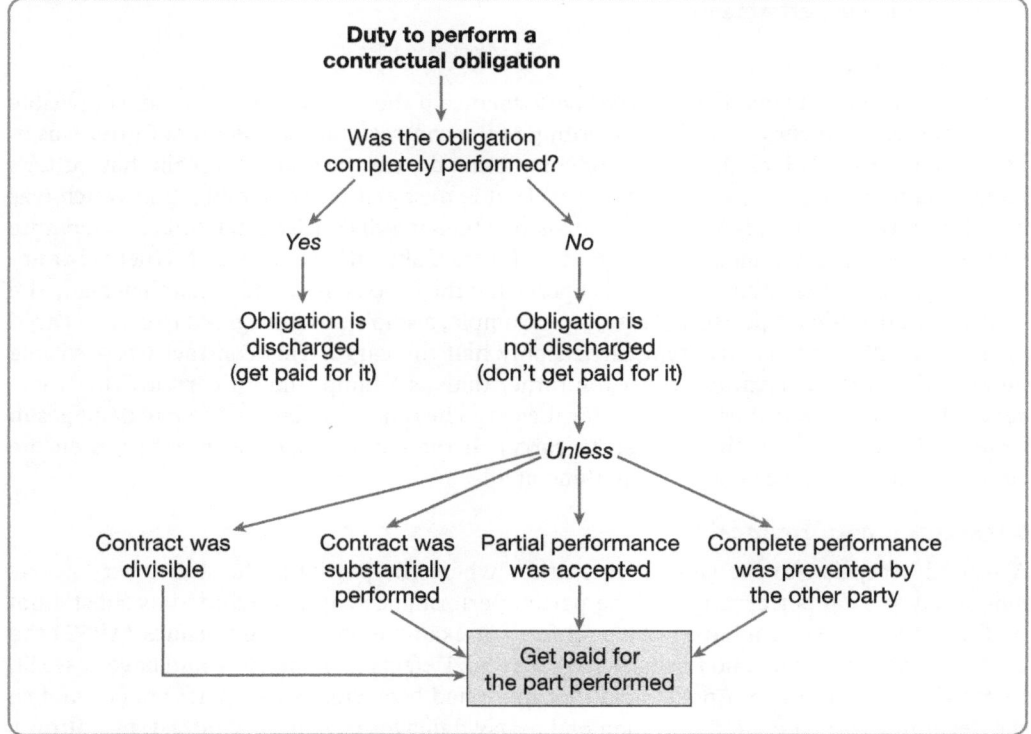

Figure 5.2 Discharge of contractual obligation by performance

Discharge by agreement

Having made a contract, the parties are free to agree to abandon it or to vary it. However, an agreement to do either of these things must amount to another contract. All the requirements of a new contract are therefore necessary. There must be an offer, an acceptance, an intention to create legal relations and consideration moving both ways. As the parties must agree to alter their legal position, there is usually no difficulty in finding the offer and acceptance or an intention to create legal relations. Generally, any problem which arises is caused by the difficulty of showing that consideration has moved from both of the parties. The following extended example shows the possibilities.

Example

John has agreed to service Jim's boiler for £1,000. Several possibilities must be considered.

(1) If both of the parties agree to call the contract off before there has been any performance of it, the contract will be discharged. John has given consideration to Jim by discharging him from the obligation to pay the money. Jim has given consideration to John by discharging him from the obligation to service the boiler.

(2) If John does some of the work, and Jim agrees to pay him a proportion of the money for the work he has done, then the contract is discharged. Jim's consideration is letting John off with finishing the job. John's consideration is letting Jim off with paying the rest of the money.

(3) If John does some of the work and agrees that Jim need not pay him for this work done, then the contract is discharged. John lets Jim off with paying the money. Jim lets John off with finishing the work.

(4) If John finishes the whole job but agrees that Jim need not pay anything, the contract is not discharged. Jim has not provided any consideration for being let off the duty to pay the price.

(5) If John finishes the work and agrees to accept a bicycle instead of the contract price, the contract is discharged. The court will not enquire whether or not the bicycle is worth £1,000. Earlier (in Chapter 2) we saw that consideration must be sufficient (worth something) but need not be adequate (worth the same amount as the other party's consideration).

(6) If John finishes the work but agrees to accept 90 per cent of the contract price, the contract is not discharged. Earlier (in Chapter 2) we saw that (subject to promissory estoppel) a lesser sum of money cannot be consideration for a greater sum owed.

A party may waive (give up) contractual rights by indicating to the other party that the rights will not be insisted upon. If no consideration was given in return for the waiver, the contract is not discharged. However, the rights which were waived can be reintroduced only by giving reasonable notice of this. Until this is done, a party cannot be in breach of contract for failure to perform a waived right.

For example, in **Charles Rickards Ltd *v* Oppenheim (1950)** the claimant agreed to sell the defendant a specially constructed car. The contract provided that the car was to be delivered on 20 March. The claimant did not deliver on time and the defendant kept asking him for delivery. The defendant then said that if the car was not delivered by 25 July he would refuse to accept delivery. The claimant tried to deliver the car in October, but the defendant refused to accept delivery. The Court of Appeal held that the defendant was entitled to refuse to accept delivery. The defendant had waived his right to receive delivery on 20 March, but had given reasonable notice that delivery had to be made by 25 July. If the claimant had tried to deliver at any time before 25 July the defendant would have been bound to accept the delivery.

Discharge by frustration

A contract may become frustrated if it becomes impossible to perform, illegal to perform or radically different from what the parties contemplated. Before we examine these three grounds on which a contract may be frustrated, it is important to notice that we are talking about a valid contract *becoming* illegal, impossible or radically different. If a contract is impossible to perform when it is made, then it may be void for mistake. If a contract is illegal to perform at the time when it is made then it is an illegal contract and will therefore be void. If the contract was, at the time of making the contract, radically different from what the parties intended then it may be void for mistake. Both mistake and illegal contracts were considered earlier (see Chapter 4).

Impossibility of performance

If a contract becomes impossible to perform then it will be frustrated.

 Taylor *v* Caldwell (1863)

A music hall was hired out for four days. Before these days came around the music hall was accidentally burnt down.

Held The contract was frustrated.

Comment The contract would not have been frustrated if the music hall had been sold, not hired, and had burnt down immediately after the contract. The buyer would have got ownership of the hall and his hall would have burnt down. A contract to sell unascertained goods, such as 100 new DVDs, will not be frustrated if the DVDs which the seller intended to use to perform the contract are destroyed before the DVDs are delivered. If the risk had passed to the buyer, then it would be his loss and if it had not yet passed it would be the seller's loss. Either way, the contract would not be frustrated. If specific goods, such as a particular second-hand machine, are sold then it is possible, but very unlikely, that the contract could be frustrated under s. 7 of the Sale of Goods Act 1979. This would depend upon the goods having perished before the risk had passed. Almost always, however, the contract would not be frustrated. The Sale of Goods Act rules on frustration and risk are considered in an earlier chapter (see Chapter 7). There it will be seen that frustration under the SGA is quite different from common law frustration, which we are considering in this chapter.

If a party who has contracted to perform the contract personally dies or becomes too ill to perform, the contract will be impossible to perform. It will therefore be frustrated.

 Condor *v* The Barron Knights Ltd (1966)

When the claimant was 16 he became a drummer with the defendant band. His five-year contract obliged him to work seven nights a week and sometimes to do two performances in one night. One month after joining the band the claimant collapsed and was taken to a mental hospital. Doctors told the claimant that if he worked more than four nights a week he would have a complete mental breakdown. The band dismissed the claimant because they could not arrange to have the claimant drumming for four nights a week and someone else drumming for three nights a week. The claimant sued the band for wrongful dismissal.

Held The claimant had not been wrongfully dismissed because the contract was frustrated. It had become impossible for the claimant to perform the terms of the contract. If the failure to perform the terms had been for a short time only, then the contract would not have become frustrated. However, since it was long-term impossibility, the contract was frustrated.

Comment In **Cutter v Powell (1795)** (earlier in the chapter), the contract was not frustrated because the doctrine of frustration did not evolve until around the year 1850.

Illegality of performance

Where a contract becomes illegal to perform, it will be frustrated. For example, in the **Fibrosa Case (1943)** the House of Lords held that a contract to supply machinery to Poland was frustrated when Germany occupied Poland. Great Britain was at war with Germany, and it is illegal to supply an enemy-occupied country.

The contract becomes radically different

A contract will be frustrated if it becomes radically different from what the parties intended when they made the contract.

 Krell *v* Henry (1903) (Court of Appeal)

King Edward VII was about to be crowned. In celebration, a huge coronation procession was to pass through London on 26 and 27 June. The defendant agreed to hire a room from the claimant for these two days for £75. The written contract did not state the purpose of this. However, both parties understood that the sole purpose was that the defendant and his friends could view the coronation procession from the room. The King was ill and so the coronation procession was cancelled. The claimant sued the defendant for the contract price.

Held The defendant did not have to pay because the contract had become frustrated.

In a similar case, **Herne Bay Steam Boat Co *v* Hutton (1903)**, the defendant had agreed to hire a steamboat for two days in order to take passengers cruising around the fleet so that they could watch the naval review. The King's illness caused the naval review to be cancelled. The Court of Appeal held that the contract was not frustrated. Performance of the contract was different from what the parties intended, but it was not radically different because the defendant could still have taken passengers cruising around the fleet.

Rules about frustration

Before we examine the effects of a contract becoming frustrated, there are several points about frustration which we should notice.

Performance required in a particular way

If a contract states that it should be performed in a certain way, then it will be frustrated if it becomes impossible to perform in that way. For example, if a contract states that a cargo should be carried on a particular ship then it will be frustrated if that ship sinks. This is the case even if other ships could carry the cargo just as well.

Contract becomes more difficult to perform

A contract will not become frustrated merely because it becomes more difficult to perform. For example, in **Davis Contractors Ltd v Fareham Urban District Council (1956)** the House of Lords held that a contract to build 78 houses in eight months was not frustrated when a shortage of labour and materials meant that the contract took 22 months to perform. The builders should have considered that there might be shortages of labour and materials before agreeing to do the job.

Force majeure clauses

If the parties to the contract foresee that there might be difficulties which they cannot control and set out in the contract what should happen if these difficulties arise, the courts will give effect to what has been agreed. Clauses which make such provisions are known as *force majeure* clauses. For example, in **Davis Contractors Ltd v Fareham UDC** the parties might have included a *force majeure* clause dealing with what the position should be if there turned out to be a shortage of labour and materials. Such a clause might have stated that if there was a shortage of labour and materials, then the contract would be frustrated. Or it might have said that, if there was a shortage of labour and materials, the contract should not be frustrated but the builder should be given more time to do the work and paid more money. Whatever the *force majeure* clause agreed, the court would have enforced the clause.

Frustrating event is foreseen

If only one of the parties knows that the frustrating event might happen (or should have known this), then that party cannot claim frustration. For example, in **Walton Harvey Ltd v Walker & Homfrays Ltd (1931)** a hotel owner who had agreed to let the claimant put advertisements on his hotel could not claim that the contract was frustrated when the hotel was compulsorily demolished. The hotel owner was in breach of contract because he knew that the hotel might be compulsorily demolished and the advertisers did not know this.

One party took the risk

If the interpretation of the contract and the surrounding circumstances indicate that one of the parties took the risk of the 'frustrating' event happening, then the contract will not be frustrated. In **Herne Bay Steam Boat Co v Hutton**, for example, the court thought that the commercial venture of hiring the steamboat was at the defendant's risk and this was a factor in deciding that the contract was not frustrated.

Self-induced frustration

A party to the contract who has brought about a certain event cannot claim that this event frustrates the contract. Self-induced frustration is no frustration.

 Maritime National Fish Ltd v Ocean Trawlers Ltd (1935) (Privy Council)

The claimants chartered a ship with an otter trawl (a certain type of fishing net) to the defendants. Both parties knew that it was illegal for a ship to fish with an otter trawl unless a licence had been gained from the Canadian Government. The defendants applied for five licences because they had four other boats fitted with otter trawls. However, the defendants were granted only three licences. They assigned these licences to three of their own boats and claimed that the contract with the claimants was frustrated because it would be illegal to use the chartered boat for fishing.

Held The contract with the claimants was not frustrated. The defendants were the ones who had caused the chartered boat not to have a licence and so they could not argue that the absence of a licence frustrated the contract.

Leases of land

A lease can be frustrated only in the most exceptional circumstances. A lease is more than a contract, it creates an interest in land.

The legal effect of frustration

As soon as the frustrating event happens, the contract comes to an end. The Law Reform (Frustrated Contracts) Act 1943 (LRFCA 1943) then makes the following rules:

- Money owing under the contract ceases to be payable.
- Money which has already been paid under the contract can be recovered. However, the court has a discretion to allow a party who has incurred expenses to be paid for these expenses. The amount of the expenses cannot be more than the money paid or payable before the contract was frustrated.
- If one of the parties has received a valuable benefit under the contract, the court can order that a fair amount is paid to compensate for this.

Example

X Ltd has agreed to supply Y Ltd with 1,000 toy guns. The contract price was £2,000 and half of this was paid in advance, half was to be paid when all of the goods were delivered. Parliament passes a statute making the sale of toy guns illegal. The contract is therefore frustrated. Y Ltd do not need to pay the £1,000 which has not yet been paid. Y Ltd can recover the £1,000 already paid. However, the court could allow X Ltd to keep some of this money to compensate for expenses incurred. If 100 toy guns had already been delivered, then the court could order that Y Ltd make a payment for these. This payment might be 10 per cent of the contract price (because 10 per cent of the guns have been delivered) but would not necessarily be so. The amount payable, if anything, is at the court's discretion.

Difficulties arise when a valuable benefit conferred is destroyed by the frustrating event. For example, where the contract is to put central heating in a house and shortly before this work is completed the house is burnt down. When is the valuable benefit to be valued? If it is valued immediately before the frustrating event, the contractor might be paid close to the whole contract price. If it is valued immediately after the frustrating event, it is worth nothing. In **BP Exploration Co (Libya) Ltd *v* Hunt (No. 2) (1982)** it was held that the value of any benefit is considered immediately after the frustrating event. So in the example above the contractor would receive nothing for the work already done.

Figure 5.3 gives an overview of frustration.

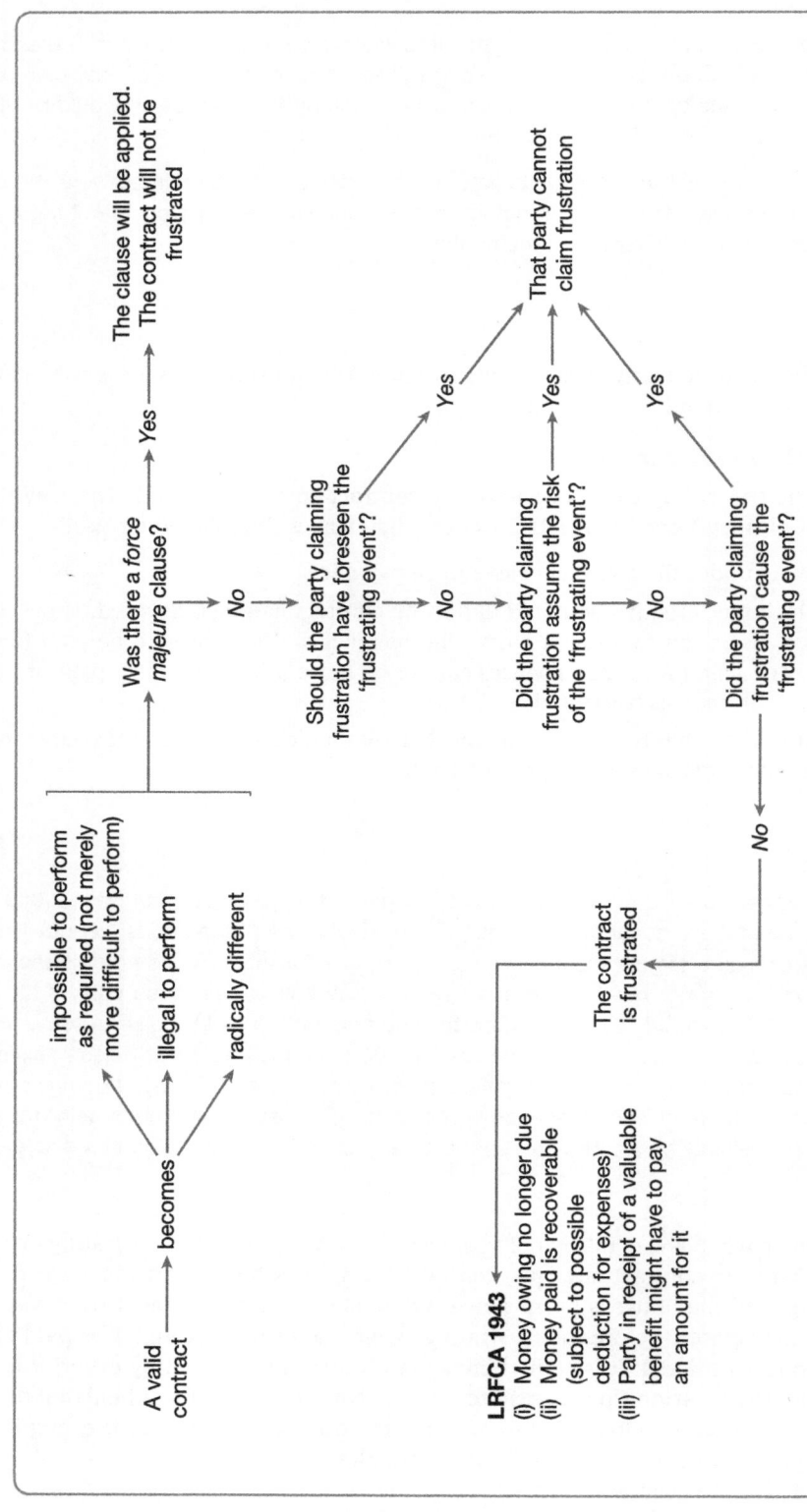

Figure 5.3 An overview of frustration

Discharge by breach

In an earlier chapter we considered the extent to which a party is entitled to treat a contract as discharged on account of the other party's breach of contract. (See conditions, warranties and innominate terms in Chapter 3.)

If a party shows an intention not to be bound by the contract, this is known as a repudiation of the contract. When one of the parties repudiates the contract before the time for performance of the contract is due, this is known as an anticipatory breach. The injured party can either accept the breach or keep the contract open. If the breach is accepted, the injured party can treat the contract as terminated and sue for damages. If the anticipatory breach is not accepted, the contract is still alive. The position then depends upon whether the anticipatory breach becomes an actual breach (because the contract is not performed when performance becomes due). If it does not become an actual breach (because the contract is properly performed in time), then there is no problem. If it does become an actual breach, the injured party can sue for damages for breach of contract. The following case demonstrates these principles.

 Hochster v De La Tour (1853)

In April 1852 the defendant contracted to employ the claimant as a courier for a three-month period which was to begin on 1 June. On 11 May the defendant told the claimant that he was not in fact going to employ him. The claimant immediately sued for damages.

Held The claimant was entitled to sue for damages because he had accepted the anticipatory breach. The claimant did not need to wait until the breach became an actual breach (which it would have done on 1 June).

In **Hochster v De La Tour** the claimant could have chosen to wait until the anticipatory breach became an actual breach. If the defendant had then changed his mind, and decided to employ the claimant after all, there would have been no breach of contract and no problem. If the defendant did not change his mind, and did not employ the claimant after all, then there would have been an actual breach on 1 June. However, there is a slight risk in waiting until an anticipatory breach becomes an actual breach. The contract might become frustrated, as the following case shows.

 Avery v Bowden (1856)

The defendant contracted to supply the claimant's ship with a cargo. The cargo was to be supplied at Odessa within 45 days. When the claimant's ship reached Odessa the defendant repeatedly told the claimant that no cargo would be delivered. The claimant kept his ship in Odessa, hoping that the defendant would change his mind. The Crimean War broke out before the 45 days had expired.

Held The outbreak of war frustrated the contract (because Odessa had become controlled by the enemy and it is illegal to supply an enemy-occupied country) and so the right to sue had been permanently lost.

Figure 5.4 gives an overview of discharge by acceptance of an anticipatory breach.

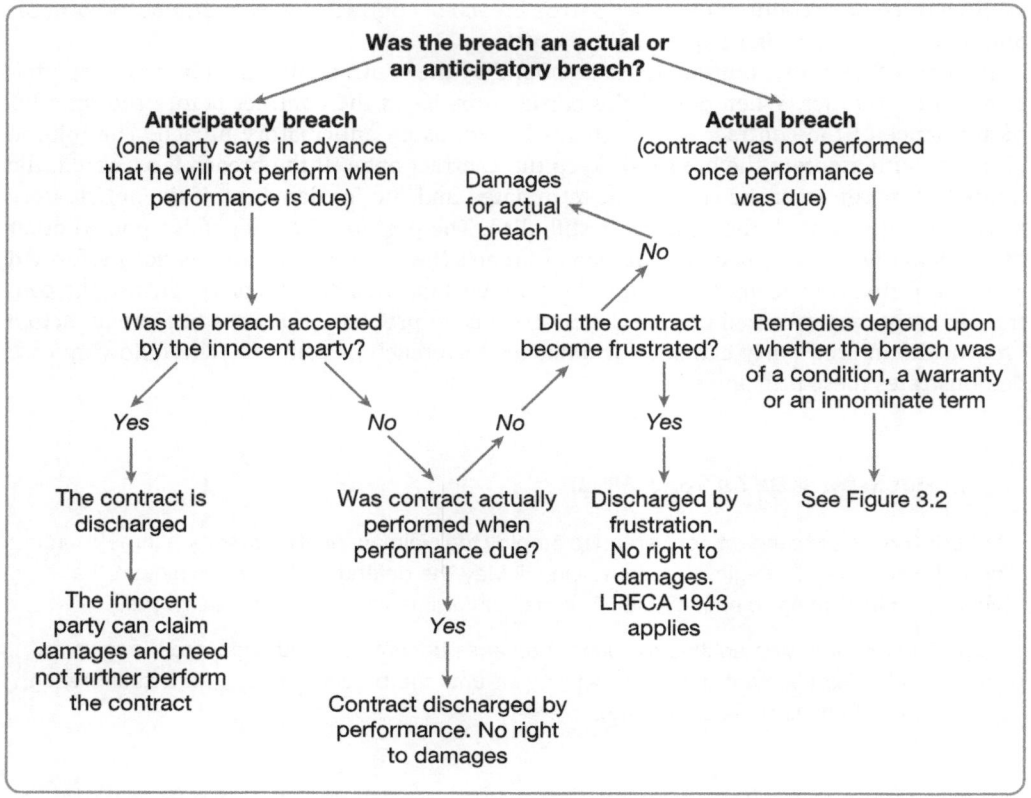

Figure 5.4 Discharge by acceptance of anticipatory breach

Legislation giving right to cancel concluded contracts

In certain circumstances legislation gives a consumer a 'cooling-off' period during which a concluded contract can be cancelled.

The Consumer Protection (Distance Selling) Regulations 2000 give a cooling-off period of seven days to consumers who buy goods or services from a supplier by means of a distance contract. A consumer is defined as a natural person (and therefore not a company) who is acting for purposes which are outside his business. A contract is a distance contract if it concluded solely by means of distance communications, that is to say without the consumer and the supplier ever actually meeting each other. The Regulations give the following examples of means of distance communications: letter, newspaper advertisement with an order form, catalogue, telephone, radio, television, computer, email, fax and television shopping. However, contracts to provide transport, accommodation, catering and leisure are not covered even if they were made exclusively by means of distance communications.

Regulation 8 provides that the supplier must inform the consumer of how to exercise the right to cancel the contract. Notice of cancellation must be made in writing or in some other durable medium. The Regulations specifically state that cancellation is to be regarded as having been properly given if it is posted to the supplier, left at the supplier's address, sent by fax or sent by email. If notice is given to a partnership, it can be sent to, or left with, any partner or any person who controls or manages the partnership. If it is given to a company, it can be sent to the company secretary or left at the address of the company. If the notice of cancellation is properly given, then the contract is treated as if it had never been made.

The cancellation period begins on the day when the contract was concluded. If reg. 8 was complied with, then the cancellation period ends seven working days after the day on which the consumer received the goods. If reg. 8 is not complied with at all, then the cooling-off period is extended by three months. If reg. 8 is complied with later than it should have been, then the seven-day period begins on the day after reg. 8 was complied with. The same time periods apply if the contract was to supply a service, except that the cooling-off period does not begin until the day after the contract was concluded.

In the following circumstances there is no right to cancel:

- If the contract was to supply a service and the consumer was told, before the contract was concluded, that cancellation would not be possible once performance of the contract had begun. (For example, a contract to have a house painted could not be concluded once work had begun if the decorator had informed the customer that this was the case before the work began.)
- If the price of the goods or services depends upon fluctuations in the financial market. (So a consumer could not cancel a contract to buy gold coins upon discovering that the price of gold had fallen.)
- If the goods were made to the consumer's specifications, or were clearly personalised, or could not be returned because of the nature of the goods, or were goods which were likely to deteriorate rapidly.
- If the contract was to supply audio recordings, video recordings or computer software and the consumer has broken the seal on the goods.
- If the contract was to supply newspapers or magazines.
- If the contract was for gaming, betting or lottery services.

A consumer who cancels must keep possession of the goods and take reasonable care of them. The consumer must also restore the goods by making them available for collection by the buyer.

The Cancellation of Contracts made in a Consumer's Home or Place of Work etc. Regulations 2008 (CCCHPW 2008) allow consumers to cancel contracts if they were made during a visit by a trader to a consumer's home or place of work, or to the home of another individual. The regulations apply whether the visit was solicited by the consumer or not. They also apply if the contract was made during an excursion organised by the trader away from his business premises, or after an offer made by the consumer during such a home visit or excursion. The Regulations apply to contracts to provide goods or services as long as they have a price of more than £35. The trader cannot enforce the contract unless, at the time of the contract, the consumer was given written notice of the right to cancel the contract within seven days. The consumer must also have been given a statutory cancellation form. The consumer does not need to use this form to cancel. However, the notice of cancellation must be in writing. Once written notice of cancellation has been given, goods supplied to the consumer must be made available for collection by the trader. The consumer gets back any money already paid and does not have to pay any money remaining due under the cancelled contract.

The Consumer Credit Act 1974 (CCA 1974) allows a debtor or hirer under a regulated consumer credit agreement to cancel the agreement within seven days of making the agreement if oral representations were made before the contract was made. This does not apply if the debtor signed the credit agreement at the creditor's place of business. (This right to cancel is examined in more detail in Chapter 16.) The Consumer Rights Directive, which must be implemented into UK law by December 2013, requires all of the current 7-day statutory cooling-off periods to be replaced with a 14-day cooling-off period.

The Timeshare Act 1992 allows a consumer who has made a timeshare agreement a 14-day cooling-off period.

Figure 5.5 gives an overview of statutory cooling-off periods.

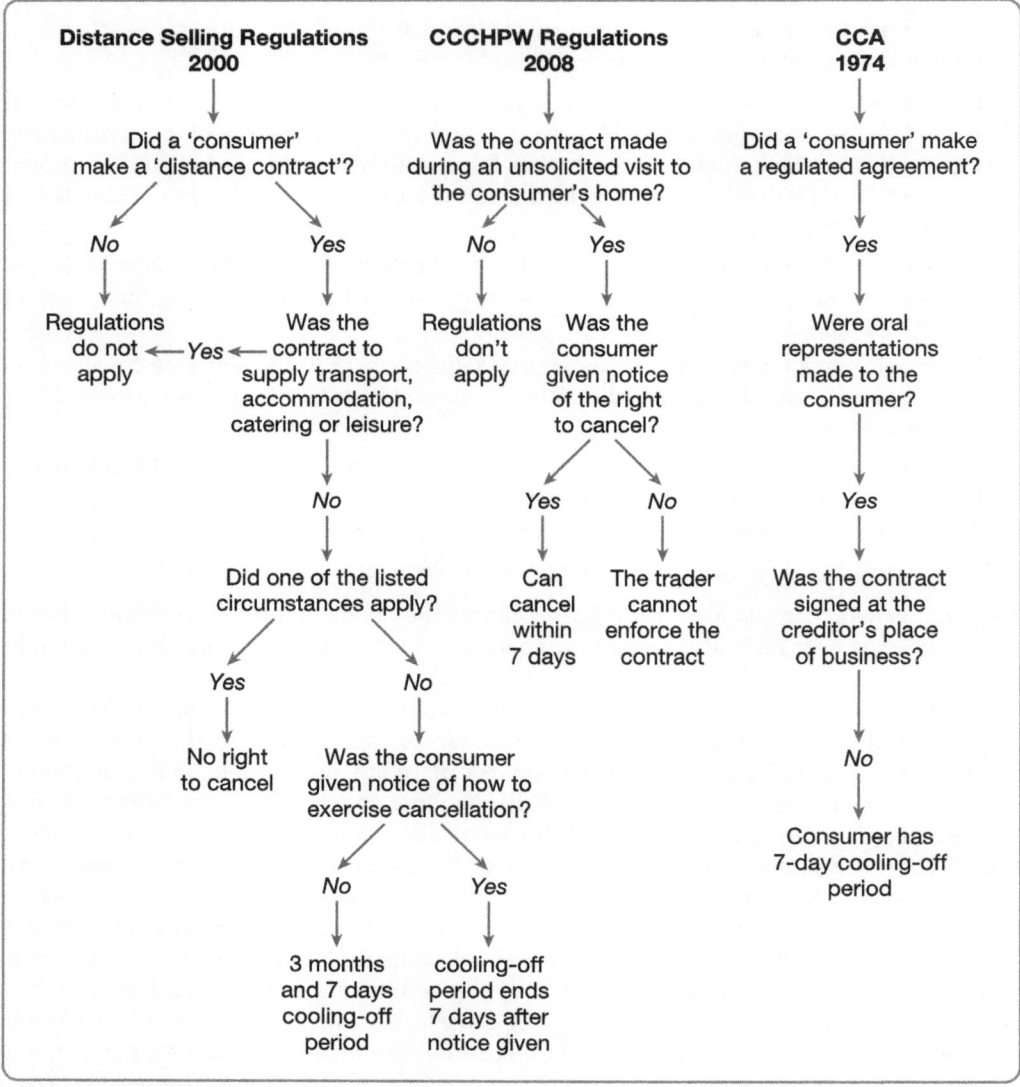

Figure 5.5 Statutory cooling-off periods

Remedies for breach of contract

Refusal to perform the contract

We have already seen that in some circumstances one party will be able to refuse to further perform the contract on account of the other party's breach of contract. We have seen that this will be possible if the other party repudiates the contract or breaches a condition of the contract. It will also be possible if the other party breaches an innominate term in such a way that this deprived the injured party of substantially the whole benefit of the contract. (See conditions, warranties and innominate terms in Chapter 3.)

Damages

Any breach of contract always allows the injured party to sue for damages. Contract damages are intended to put the injured party into the same position, as far as money can do this, as if the contract had been performed. It follows that if the injured party has suffered no loss as a result of the breach, only nominal damages will be available. Nominal damages are damages in name only, perhaps 5p or £1. It is also necessary that the defendant's breach of contract caused the loss being claimed for.

Remoteness of damage

When a contract is breached, substantial damages can be claimed only in respect of losses which fall within one of the two rules in **Hadley *v* Baxendale (1854)**. Other losses are regarded as too remote.

Rule 1 allows damages for a loss if the loss arose naturally from the breach of contract, in the usual course of things.

Rule 2 allows damages for a loss if the loss can reasonably be supposed to have been within the contemplation of the parties when they made the contract.

The rules on remoteness of damage provide an important limit on the amount of contract damages. A breach of contract can have many unforeseeable consequences. If there were no rules on remoteness, the person in breach of contract would always be liable for these consequences. This would make people unwilling to make contracts.

The following case shows how the two rules work.

 Victoria Laundry *v* Newman Industries (1949) (Court of Appeal)

The claimants agreed to buy a boiler from the defendants. The defendants knew that the boiler was to be used immediately in the claimants' laundry. They also knew that there was a big demand for general laundry services at this time. The defendants delivered the boiler 20 weeks late. Two claims for damages were made by the claimants. First, they claimed £16 a week, which represented the extra profit they could have made by doing more general laundry work with the new boiler. Second, they claimed £262 a week which had been lost on account of the claimants not being able to use the boiler to fulfil a very profitable contract to dye army uniforms.

Held The claimants were entitled to the £16 a week, under the first rule in **Hadley v Baxendale**. The £262 was not available under either rule. (It would have been available under the second rule in **Hadley v Baxendale** if the claimants had told the defendants, before the contract was made, that such a very profitable contract would be lost if the boiler was not delivered on time.)

In **Koufos v Czarnikow Ltd (The Heron 2) (1967)** Lord Reid held that, under **Hadley v Baxendale**, a loss was recoverable because it was 'not unlikely' or 'quite likely' to occur. Damages could be recovered for a loss if the loss was within the reasonable contemplation of the parties when the contract was made. The following case showed that although this is almost always the case, it is not the case if both parties would have thought that the contract breaker did not assume liability for the loss in question.

⚖️ Transfield Shipping Inc v Mercator Shipping Inc (2008) House of Lords

A ship owner, M, chartered a ship to T, a charterer. T was to redeliver the ship to M by 2 May 2004. On 20 April M chartered the ship out to another person, X, for about five months at $39,500 a day. If the ship was not delivered to X by 8 May, X had the right to cancel the contract. T breached the contract by redelivering the ship to M nine days late. This meant that X could refuse to be bound by the contract with M. Shipping rates had suddenly collapsed and M had to renegotiate the contract with X, so that X would pay only $31,500 a day. X took the ship from M for about five months at this price. T agreed to pay damages for the nine days that the ship was late. M also claimed the difference between the price which X had first agreed to pay, and the price which X actually paid, for the whole five months when X had the ship. This came to $1,364,584.

Held T did not have to pay the extra $1,364,584, even though it was 'not unlikely' that M would charter the ship to another person, and that the market rates would collapse. The potential liability of a charterer if such liability were to exist would be completely unquantifiable. The new contract might be for a week, a month or for several years. There was no legal precedent on the matter, but the evidence showed that everyone in the chartering business thought that a charterer did not assume liability to pay damages for this type of loss. All contractual liability is voluntarily undertaken, and the objective intention of the parties was that T would not have assumed this liability.

Having decided that a loss is within one of the two rules in **Hadley v Baxendale**, it must then be decided how much the damages should be.

Amount of damages

If the contract is a sale of goods, the Sale of Goods Act 1979 sets out rules which determine the amount of damages payable. These rules are examined later (see Chapter 7).

In contracts other than contracts of sale of goods, the damages are quantified on the basis that they are intended to put the injured party in the same position, as far as money can do this, as if the contract had been properly performed. Damages will therefore be available for putting right defects caused by the breach of contract. They will also be available for any other losses, such as loss of profits, as long as these were caused by the breach of contract and were within one of the rules in **Hadley v Baxendale**. If the defendant's breach of contract causes the claimant to pay damages to a third party, these damages paid are generally also recoverable.

> **Example**
>
> Jerry agrees to service Z Ltd's oven for £1,000. Jerry knows that Z Ltd need the oven to operate their bakery. Z Ltd tell Jerry that the service must be finished on time because otherwise Z Ltd will be in breach of a very profitable contract to do bakery for Y Ltd. Jerry performs the service so badly that Z Ltd's oven cannot work at all. Jerry cannot fix the problem. Z Ltd hunt around for someone else to fix the oven. The only person they can find is Tom, who fixes the oven one week after Jerry should have fixed it. As Z Ltd could not do the bakery for Y Ltd they are themselves in breach of contract and will have to pay Y Ltd £2,000 damages. Jerry will have to pay damages to Z Ltd as follows: (i) the cost of Tom putting right the fault which Jerry caused; (ii) the amount of ordinary business profit lost by Z Ltd as a consequence of not being able to use the oven for one week; (iii) the profit Z Ltd would have made if they had been able to perform their contract with Y Ltd; (iv) the amount of damages which Z Ltd had to pay to Y Ltd.

Mitigation

In the above example, Z Ltd might have incurred even more losses if they had not hunted around to find someone else to fix the oven. However, if they had not hunted around to find someone else, they could not have claimed more damages. A party who suffers a loss as a result of breach of contract must take all reasonable steps to mitigate (reduce) the loss. No substantial damages can be claimed in respect of a loss which could have been mitigated by taking reasonable steps.

> **Brace *v* Calder (1895)**
>
> The claimant was employed by a partnership of four people for a fixed two-year period. The partnership was dissolved when two of the partners left. The two remaining partners immediately agreed to employ the claimant on exactly the same terms as he had previously been employed. The claimant refused this offer and sued for breach of contract.
>
> *Held* There had been a breach of contract because the four partners had not employed the claimant for the full two-year period. However, the claimant was entitled to nominal damages only from the original partners. He should have mitigated his loss by accepting the alternative employment.

Damages are generally not available for injured feelings or disappointment. However, where the contract was to provide the claimant with enjoyment and relaxation (as in the case of a holiday) it is possible that damages can be awarded for disappointment and distress caused by a breach of the contract.

Mitigation and anticipatory breach

Earlier in this chapter we considered anticipatory breach. We saw that a person faced with such a breach can either accept the breach, and regard the contract as terminated, or elect to keep the contract open. A person who accepts an anticipatory breach must mitigate losses in the usual way.

A person who does not accept an anticipatory breach will generally also have to mitigate losses. However, in the following case the anticipatory breach was not accepted, and the injured party who continued to perform the contract had no duty to mitigate. The case was unusual in that the injured party could perform the contract without the co-operation of the party who committed the anticipatory breach.

 White and Carter (Councils) _v_ MacGregor (1962) (House of Lords)

The claimants were advertising agents who agreed to advertise the defendants' garage for a three-year period. On the same day that the contract was made the defendants wrote to the claimants asking them to cancel the contract. The claimants did not accept this anticipatory breach but began to advertise the defendants' business as agreed. One of the terms of the contract said that if any of the instalments which the defendants were required to pay became four weeks overdue, then the claimants could sue for the whole contract price. The defendants refused to pay any of the instalments. The claimants advertised the defendants' garage as agreed for the whole three-year period and then sued for the whole contract price.

**Held** The claimants were entitled to perform the contract and sue for the whole contract price. They were not bound to accept the repudiation and sue for damages. Nor did they have a duty to mitigate their losses.

**Comment** The principle in this case is unusual and will apply only where: (a) the contract can be performed without the co-operation of the other party; and (b) the injured party has some legitimate interest, other than claiming damages, in carrying the contract on.

Agreed damages

Sometimes, a term of the contract will fix the amount of damages payable in the event of breach of contract. Damages agreed in this way are classified as being either liquidated damages or penalties.

If the amount of damages fixed is the amount which the parties genuinely believed that the loss would be, then the damages agreed are liquidated damages. The amount of damages fixed by the term will then be the amount of damages awarded, no matter what the actual loss turned out to be.

If the amount of damages fixed is not the amount which the parties genuinely believed that the loss would be, but an excessively large amount, then the damages agreed will be a penalty. A penalty is ignored and damages are calculated as if the term setting out the penalty had not existed. Penalties are often put into a contract by the party with the greater bargaining power, to try to terrorise the other party into performing the contract. (Notice that a penalty clause will not amount to economic duress because it is not pushing a person into making a contract: it is saying what the damages will be if the contract is breached.)

Example

John, a builder, agrees to build a new shop which is to be completed by 1 March. A term of the contract states that if the shop is not completed on time, then the damages payable by John will be £500 a week for every week that the shop is not completed. John completes the work ten weeks late. If, when the parties made the contract, they thought that the actual loss to the shop owner would be £500 a week, then the agreed damages are liquidated damages. John would therefore have to pay £5,000 damages, no matter how much his breach of contract actually cost the shop owner. If, when the parties made the contract, they thought that the actual loss in the event of breach would be much less than £500 a week, then the term will be a penalty. The penalty will be ignored and damages will be calculated in the usual way to compensate the shop owner for the actual loss suffered.

Interest on damages

A contract might agree that interest on damages should be paid at a certain rate. If the parties do not make such an agreement, then the court will order that interest is payable from the date when the claim arose.

Figure 5.6 gives an overview of damages for breach of contract.

Suing for the contract price

When a seller sues for the contract price, this is not the same thing as suing for damages. When a claim is made for the payment of a debt, the amount claimed is said to be liquidated. As the claim is not for damages, the rules on remoteness, mitigation and quantification of damages will not apply. For example, let us assume that John agreed to build an office for Tony for £70,000 and completed the job properly. If Tony does not pay the contract price, then John can sue for it. The rules on remoteness, mitigation and quantification of damages will not apply. So there will be no need to consider the rules in **Hadley v Baxendale**, and John does not need to take any steps to reduce his loss. Nor will a court need to make calculations to find the amount being claimed, apart from working out any interest which is payable.

The Sale of Goods Act 1979 lays down the circumstances in which a seller of goods can sue for the contract price. These rules are examined later (see Chapter 7).

The Late Payment of Commercial Debts (Interest) Act 1998 gives all businesses the right to claim interest when a commercial debt arising from the supply of goods and services to another business or to a public sector body is paid late.

Interest becomes payable under the Act from the day after the date on which the supplier and purchaser expressly or impliedly agreed that it should become payable. If no such date is fixed, interest becomes payable 30 days after the supplier performed his obligations under the contract, or 30 days after the purchaser was given notice of the debt, whichever is the later. So interest would generally become payable 30 days after the goods or an invoice were delivered. The rate of interest is currently set at 8 per cent above the base rate.

The effect of the Act cannot be avoided by means of a contractual term unless there is a 'substantial' remedy available for the late payment of the debt. It is only possible for a contractual term to postpone the time at which a debt is created to the extent that the term satisfies the UCTA 1977 requirement of reasonableness. (The UCTA requirement of reasonableness was examined in Chapter 3.)

Specific performance

Specific performance is an equitable remedy which arises when a court orders a person to actually perform the contractual obligations undertaken. For example, if Mark agreed to sell an antique vase to Asif but then refused to go through with the contract, Asif might ask the

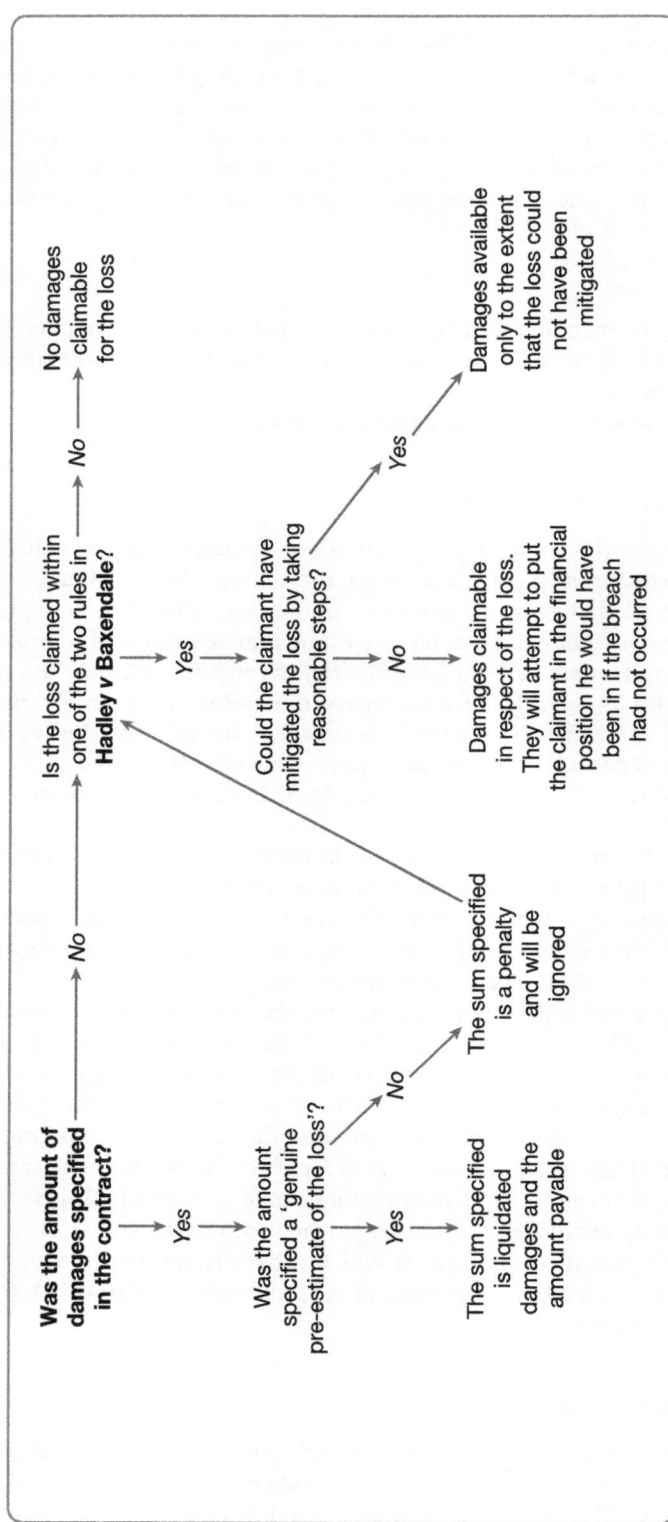

Figure 5.6 An outline of the availability of damages for a loss caused by a breach of contract

court for an order of specific performance. If such an order was made by the court, Mark would be ordered to go through with the contract and to let Asif have the vase. Disobeying such a court order would put Mark in contempt of court and liable to a fine or imprisonment.

Specific performance is rarely ordered by a court. It will not be ordered where damages would provide a good enough remedy. It will not therefore be ordered to make a seller hand over new mass-produced goods which could be obtained from another seller. Specific performance can be ordered where a seller refuses to hand over unique goods (such as an antique vase). All plots of land are regarded as unique and so specific performance will be ordered where a seller of land refuses to perform the contract.

As specific performance is an equitable remedy, it is only available at the court's discretion. The remedy will not be ordered in the following circumstances. First, where the claimant has behaved inequitably (unfairly). This reflects an old saying that: 'He who comes to Equity must come with clean hands.' Second, specific performance will not be ordered to enforce a contract which required personal services to be provided (such as a contract of employment). Third, it will not be ordered where to order it would cause excessive hardship to the defendant. Fourth, it will not be ordered for or against a minor (person under 18).

Injunction

An injunction is a court order which requires a person to do or not to do a certain thing. An injunction can be ordered, as an equitable remedy, to prevent a party from breaching a contract. However, an injunction will not be ordered where an award of damages would give a satisfactory remedy. In cases where specific performance could not be ordered, an injunction will not be ordered if it would have the same effect as an order of specific performance.

 Warner Bros Pictures Inc v Nelson (1936)

An actress, Bette Davis, made a contract with the claimants. She agreed that she would act for the claimants, and not act for anyone else, for a two-year period. The actress intended to act for another company. The defendants sought an injunction to prevent this.

Held An injunction was ordered to prevent the actress from breaching her contract by acting for another company. This did not amount to an order of specific performance of a personal service contract because the claimant was not compelled to act for the defendants. She could have earnt a living in some other way.

Comment An injunction forbidding the defendant from doing any other type of work would not have been ordered. Such an injunction would have forced the defendant to act for the claimants and would therefore have amounted to specific performance of a personal service contract.

Two special types of injunctions may be ordered, but only in very limited circumstances. A freezing injunction prevents a person from moving assets out of the jurisdiction of the English courts. A search order allows the claimant to take away or photocopy documents which the defendant might destroy. Both of these injunctions are granted only in very exceptional circumstances.

Rectification

Rectification is an equitable remedy which arises when a contract which has been concluded orally is then written down. If what is written down does not accurately reflect what the parties agreed orally, the court can allow the written document to be rectified (put right).

Quantum meruit (as much as he has earned)

A party who receives a *quantum meruit* payment is paid the amount deserved for work done. Such a right can arise in four circumstances:

(1) If the other contracting party prevented further performance of the contract.

(2) If the other contracting party voluntarily accepted partial performance of the contract.

(3) If the contract did not provide how much should be paid.

(4) If work was done and accepted under a void contract.

Time limits on remedies

The Limitation Act 1980 makes the following rules about the time span within which a remedy for breach of contract must be claimed.

A simple contract (one not made by a deed) must be sued upon within six years of the right to sue arising. The right to sue will arise when the contract is breached. A claim for personal injuries must be made within three years of the right to sue arising. Where a contract is made by a deed, a claim must be made within 12 years of the right to sue arising. Time does not run against minors until they reach the age of 18. Time does not run against a victim of a fraud until the fraud is, or should have been, discovered. Where the claim is for a debt, any written acknowledgement of the debt's existence will cause the time period to begin again.

The time limits set out in the Limitation Act 1980 do not apply to equitable remedies. However, an equitable remedy will not be granted to a party who has delayed unreasonably in asking for the remedy.

Essential points

- Contractual liability can become discharged in four ways: by performance, by agreement, by frustration or by breach.
- The general rule is that if one party fails to fully perform the contract, the other party need not perform the contract at all.
- Contractual obligations can be discharged by agreement, as long as both parties give some consideration to the other in return for being released from their contractual obligations.
- A contract may become frustrated if it becomes impossible to perform, illegal to perform or radically different from what the parties contemplated when they made the contract.
- When one of the parties repudiates the contract before the time for performance of the contract is due, this is known as an anticipatory breach.

- A party will be able to refuse to further perform the contract if a condition is breached.
- A party will not be able to refuse to further perform the contract if a warranty is breached.
- Any breach of contract always allows the injured party to sue for damages.
- Substantial damages can only be claimed in respect of losses which fall within one of the two rules in Hadley v Baxendale. Other losses are regarded as too remote.
- Hadley v Baxendale rule 1 allows damages for a loss if the loss arose naturally from the breach of contract, in the usual course of things.
- Hadley v Baxendale rule 2 allows damages for a loss if the loss can reasonably be supposed to have been within the contemplation of the parties when they made the contract.

Practice questions

1 Giles, a poultry farmer, agreed to supply Export Ltd with 5,000 turkeys. The contract said that the turkeys were for export to Ruritania and had to meet Ruritanian health standards. The contract price was £15,000. £5,000 was paid in advance and £10,000 was to be paid once all the turkeys had been delivered. After 1,000 turkeys had been delivered the exporting of turkeys was made illegal by a statute. Advise Giles of his legal position.

2 TeaSell Ltd, a retailer of high class teas, contracted last year to buy one tonne of Darjeeling tea from TeaGrow Ltd. The tea was to be delivered on 1 November. This year the weather in Darjeeling has been very bad and the annual tea crop has been disastrous. TeaGrow Ltd had expected to grow ten tonnes of Darjeeling but has only managed to harvest one tonne. On 1 September TeaGrow Ltd wrote to TeaSell Ltd, saying that it would not be able to supply the tonne of Darjeeling tea which it had agreed to sell. The letter explained that TeaGrow Ltd had no other existing contracts to sell the tea to anyone else, but that the price of Darjeeling teas has increased so substantially that it would be able to get a much better price from another buyer. Advise TeaSell Ltd of the following matters:

(a) Whether TeaGrow Ltd has committed a breach of contract.

(b) Whether TeaSell Ltd could prevent the sale of the one tonne of Darjeeling tea to another buyer.

(c) Whether TeaGrow Ltd could be ordered to deliver the one tonne of Darjeeling tea to TeaSell Ltd, as agreed in the contract.

(d) If TeaGrow Ltd do not deliver the tea, whether a claim for damages could be made in respect of the following losses:

　(i) Ordinary business profits lost by TeaSell Ltd as a consequence of their not being able to sell Darjeeling tea to regular customers.

　(ii) The loss of a very profitable contract to sell Darjeeling tea to a specialist café.

　(iii) Damages which TeaSell Ltd has had to pay because the lack of Darjeeling tea caused TeaSell Ltd to breach a contract to sell tea to a tea shop.

(iv) The managing director of TeaSell Ltd having a heart attack, and spending all of his money on private health care. The heart attack was caused by the stress of TeaGrow Ltd breaching their contract with TeaSell Ltd.

3 With reference to decided cases, explain the circumstances in which a contract may become frustrated. Explain also the legal consequences of a contract being frustrated.

Task 5

A friend of yours from abroad is considering setting up business in England. Your friend would like to know the ways in which contractual liability can be discharged and the remedies available for breach of a contract. Write a report for your friend, briefly explaining the following matters:

(a) How contractual obligations can be discharged by performance.

(b) How a contract can be discharged by agreement between the contracting parties.

(c) The ways in which a contract can become frustrated.

(d) The legal position when a contract is frustrated.

(e) The meaning of an anticipatory breach of contract, and the remedies available to a party faced with an anticipatory breach.

(f) How a court decides whether or not a loss caused by a breach of contract is too remote for damages to be claimed in respect of the loss.

(g) How a court quantifies the amount of damages payable for breach of contract.

(h) What is meant by mitigation of a loss.

(i) Whether the courts will apply a clause in a contract which sets out the amount of damages payable in the event of a breach of contract.

(j) What is meant by specific performance of a contract.

(k) How an injunction can be a remedy for breach of contract.

(l) What is meant by a *quantum meruit* payment, and the circumstances in which a contracting party will be entitled to a *quantum meruit* payment.

(m) The time limits within which a claim for breach of contract must be brought.

mylawchamber

Visit **www.mylawchamber.co.uk/macintyreessentials** to access tools to help you develop and test your knowledge of business law, including interactive multiple choice questions, practice exam questions with guidance, weblinks, glossary, glossary flashcards, legal newsfeed and legal updates.

Use **Case Navigator** to read in full some of the key cases referenced in this chapter with commentary and questions:

Carlill *v* The Carbolic Smoke Ball Co (1893)

Transfield Shipping Inc *v* Mercator Shipping Inc (2008)

13

Employment (1): The contract of employment, employment rights and dismissal

This is the first of two chapters on employment law. This chapter begins by considering how a contract of employment is formed and the terms such a contract might contain. It then considers several statutory employment rights, before concluding by considering rights which arise when an employee is dismissed or made redundant.

The following chapter considers discrimination in employment and health and safety at work.

The contract of employment

In an earlier chapter (see Chapter 9) vicarious liability was explained and the ways in which the courts decide whether a contract of employment exists were considered. Like other contracts, a contract of employment can be created orally or in writing, and will contain both express and implied terms. The express terms would be agreed by the parties, the implied terms would be implied by the courts.

Written statement of employment particulars

Section 1 of the Employment Rights Act 1996 (ERA 1996) requires an employer to provide all employees with a written statement of employment particulars. The statement, which has to be provided within two months of the employment beginning, must contain the following particulars:

- The names of the employer and the employee.
- The date on which the employment began.
- The date on which the employee's period of continuous employment began, taking into account whether any previous employment is to count as continuous employment. (Continuous employment is important in relation to dismissal and redundancy, as we see later in this chapter.)
- The scale or rate of pay and the method of calculation.
- The intervals at which payment is made (weekly, monthly, etc.).
- Any terms and conditions relating to hours of work.
- Any terms and conditions relating to holiday entitlement, sick pay or pensions.
- The length of notice which either party needs to give to end the employment.

- The job title of the employee, or a brief description of his duties.
- Where the employment is not intended to be permanent, the period for which it is expected to continue or, of it is for a fixed term, the date on which the term is to end.
- The place of work.
- Any trade union agreements which directly affect the terms and conditions of the employment.
- Where the employee is required to work outside the UK for a period of more than one month, the period for which he is to work outside the UK, the currency in which he is to be paid while working outside the UK and any additional salary or benefits to be paid on account of his being required to work outside the UK.

The written particulars are very strong evidence of the terms of the contract of employment. However, they are not the contract itself as this will already have been formed by the time the statement is provided. An employee who has not been given the particulars within the specified time period may complain to an employment tribunal. The tribunal will make a minimum award of two weeks' pay and a maximum award of four weeks' pay and order that particulars are given. For these purposes, the week's pay is capped at the limit of £430 which applies when calculating a redundancy payment.

Itemised pay statements

Section 8(1) ERA 1996 requires employers to provide a written itemised pay statement when wages or salary are paid. Section 8(2) provides that this statement must contain particulars of:

- the gross amount of the wages or salary;
- the amount of any deductions from the gross amount and the purposes for which they are made;
- the net amount of wages or salary payable; and
- where different parts of the net amount are paid in different ways, the amount and method of payment of each part-payment.

Implied obligations of the parties

Certain terms are implied into contracts of employment. Some of these impose obligations on the employee and some impose obligations on the employer.

Obligations imposed on the employee

The obligations imposed on the employee are as follows:

- To show mutual respect to the employer.
- To faithfully serve the employer.
- To obey lawful and reasonable orders.
- To use reasonable care and skill.
- Not to accept bribes.
- Not to reveal confidential information.

However, as regards the duty not to disclose confidential information, the Public Interest Disclosure Act 1998 protects 'whistleblower' employees who disclose certain information, such as that a crime is being committed or health and safety procedures are being ignored.

Such whistleblower employees must not suffer a detriment because of what they have done, and any dismissal in consequence of what they have done will be automatically unfair. Employees do not have a duty to disclose their own shortcomings. However, some employees, particularly those who are responsible for others, may have a duty to disclose the shortcomings of others.

Implied obligations of the employer

The implied obligations of the employer are as follows:

- To show mutual respect to the employee.
- To provide work, or pay the employee if there is no work.
- To pay wages.
- Not to reveal confidential information.
- To indemnify employees for expenses and costs reasonably incurred.
- To insure the employee.
- To take reasonable care and skill in preparing a reference. (However, an employer has no duty to provide a reference.)

It is possible that terms can be implied into a contract of employment by custom and practice, as long as the terms in question are well known, certain and reasonable. Works rule books are sometimes agreed by the parties to be included as terms of the contract of employment. In other cases, the rules in the workbook are imposed by the employer. If this is the case, then failure to obey the rules may be a breach of the duty to obey instructions.

Variation of the terms of the contract

Earlier (see Chapter 5) we examined the ways in which a contract can be discharged by agreement. We saw that one party cannot unilaterally alter the terms of a contract but that both parties must agree to the alteration. If an employer unilaterally imposes a significant change in an employee's terms and conditions, then this will amount to a repudiation of the contract and the employee can either accept the variation or not. An employee who does not accept the variation can regard the contract as terminated and himself as dismissed. (In technical terms, the employee accepts that the employer's repudiation has ended the contract.) However, the employee might accept the variation. If so, the old contract will have been discharged and the new one substituted. If an employee refuses to accept the new terms but continues working under protest, then, for a short time at least, the employee can still leave and claim to have been dismissed. An employee who continues to work without protesting will generally be taken to have accepted the unilateral change.

Figure 13.1 shows the employee's options.

Statutory rights of the employee

Maternity rights

Unless the contract terms give a more generous entitlement, all female employees have a statutory right to 26 weeks' ordinary maternity leave and 26 weeks' additional maternity leave. This right, which is set out in the Maternity and Parental Leave Regulations 1999, applies no matter how long the employee has worked for the employer.

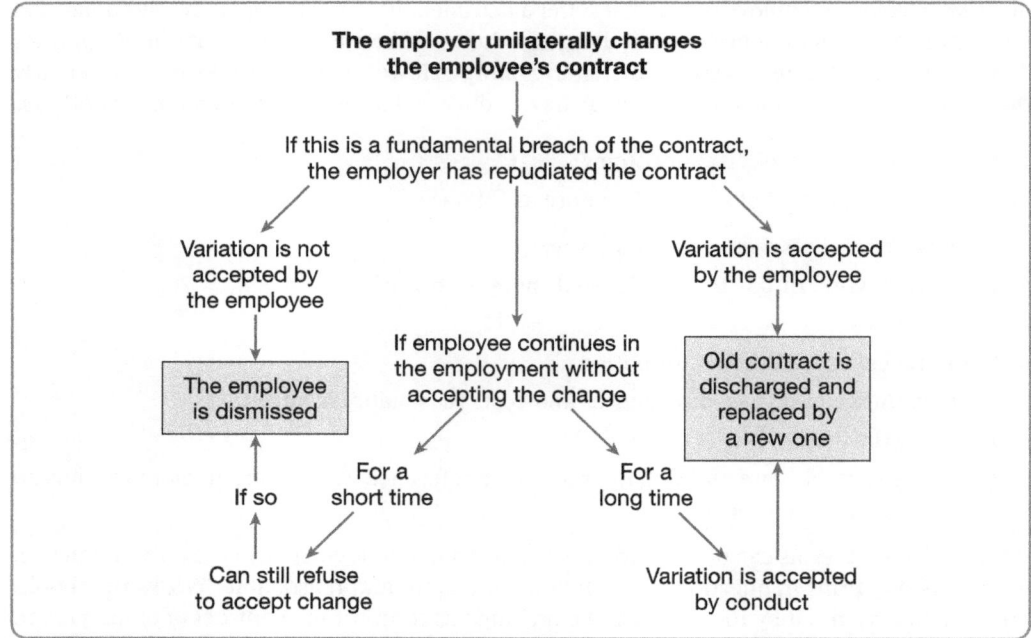

Figure 13.1 The effect of responses to a unilateral change of employment terms

A female employee will qualify for statutory maternity pay if she meets three conditions:

(1) She must have 26 weeks' continuous employment at a point 14 weeks before the expected week of childbirth.

(2) She must have stopped work due to the pregnancy.

(3) Her weekly earnings must not be so low that no national insurance contributions have to be paid.

Statutory maternity pay

An employee is entitled to statutory maternity pay for 39 weeks, beginning when she goes on ordinary maternity leave. However, this period must begin between 11 weeks and one week before the baby is due. The employee has to give 28 days' notice of an intention to go on leave or, if this is not possible, as much notice as is possible. The employer can ask for a medical certificate which confirms that the employee is pregnant and the date when the birth is due. Pregnant women are also allowed time off work to receive ante-natal care. There is no statutory right to maternity pay after the thirteenth week of maternity leave.

During the first six weeks of ordinary maternity leave the employee is entitled to 90 per cent of her normal weekly pay, which is calculated by looking at the weekly pay in the 12 weeks before the maternity leave began. For the next 33 weeks, the employee is entitled to a minimum of £135.45 a week or 90 per cent of her normal weekly pay, whichever is lower. However, if the employee does not qualify for statutory maternity pay, she may be entitled to a maternity allowance. Statutory maternity pay is subject to the usual deductions, such as tax and national insurance, and is paid at the same time as the employee would normally have been paid.

It is not only pay that the employee is entitled to, but also other contractual benefits of the job which she would normally have enjoyed.

Women who do not qualify for statutory maternity pay may be entitled to a Statutory Maternity Allowance of £135.45 per week, or of 90 per cent of their average weekly earnings, whichever is lower, for 39 weeks. To qualify the woman must have worked, either in employment or as self-employed, for at least 26 of the 66 weeks before the baby is due, and must have earned at least £30 for 13 of those 66 weeks. Statutory Maternity Allowance is paid by the Government. Employers can reclaim from the Government about 90 per cent of the amount which they have paid in statutory maternity leave.

Paternity leave and pay

Part II of the Paternity and Adoption Leave Regulations 2002 gives rights to paternity leave and paternity pay. In order to qualify for paternity leave, the employee must satisfy three conditions:

(1) The employee must have responsibility for the new child's upbringing or expect to have this responsibility.
(2) He must either be the biological father of the child or he must be the husband or partner of the child's mother.
(3) He must have at least 26 weeks' continuous employment 15 weeks before the baby is due to be born.

Paternity leave can either be for one week or for two consecutive weeks. It cannot be for parts of a week but it can begin midweek. The leave can begin either at the date of the child's birth or at some later date, but it must be completed 56 days after the child was born. If the mother gives birth to twins, no extra paternity leave is available. The rate of statutory paternity pay is currently either £135.45 a week or, if the average weekly earnings are less than £135.45, 90 per cent of average weekly earnings. Other contractual benefits must also be received. Employees who do not earn enough to pay any national insurance contributions are not entitled to statutory paternity pay.

Employees intending to take statutory paternity leave must inform their employers at least 15 weeks before the baby is expected. They must say when the baby is due, when they want the leave to start, and whether they want one week's leave or two weeks' leave. Employees are obliged to give the employer a completed self certificate which provides evidence of their entitlement to statutory paternity pay. A model certificate can be found on the DTI website: www.dti.gov.uk. Employees who take statutory paternity leave are entitled to return to work afterwards and must not be discriminated against for having taken the leave. Employers can reclaim from the Government about 90 per cent of the amount which they have paid in statutory paternity pay.

Adoption leave and pay

When a couple adopt a child, Part III of the Paternity and Adoption Leave Regulations 2002 entitles one member of the couple to time off work with statutory adoption pay. In addition, the other member of the couple, or a partner of an individual who adopts, may be entitled to paternity leave and pay.

In order to claim adoption leave, the employee must have worked continuously for the employer for 26 weeks and be newly matched with a child by an adoption agency. Such employees are entitled to 26 weeks' ordinary adoption leave, during which they are entitled to statutory adoption pay, and an additional 26 weeks' adoption leave. The leave can start either on the date of the child's placement or 14 days before the expected date of the placement. The rate of statutory adoption pay is £135.45 a week or 90 per cent of the normal weekly wage if this is less than £135.45. Adopters have to give notice of their intention to take adoption leave. Employers can also ask for a matching certificate from the adoption agency. Those taking time off are entitled to contractual benefits other than pay which they would normally receive, and have a right to return to work after the adoption leave. Employers can reclaim about 90 per cent of money paid in adoption leave from the Government. The statutory rates of maternity pay, paternity pay and adoption pay increase periodically.

Parental leave and time off for dependants

An employee with at least one year's continuous employment is entitled to take up to 13 weeks' unpaid parental leave, in respect of each child, to look after his or her child or to make arrangements for the child's welfare. In the case of disabled children, 18 weeks' leave per child can be taken. In the case of twins, both parents can have 13 weeks' leave for each child. The leave must be taken before the child's fifth birthday and can be taken in either long blocks or short blocks.

All employees are entitled under s. 57A ERA 1996 to take time off work to look after dependants in an emergency. The right can arise in the following circumstances:

- if assistance is needed when a dependant gives birth, is injured or assaulted;
- to provide care for a dependant who is ill or injured;
- when a dependant dies;
- when there is an unexpected disruption or ending of arrangements for the care of a dependant; or
- when an incident involving the employee's child arises unexpectedly during school hours.

Dependants include spouses, children, parents and people who live in the same house as the employee. It also includes people who reasonably rely on the employee. There is no entitlement to pay during the time off.

Flexible working for parents and carers

Section 80F of the Employment Rights Act 1996 has introduced a right for parents with children under 16 years old to apply for flexible working. In the case of disabled children the age limit is 18. The right is also available if the employee needs to look after a spouse, civil partner, relative or person with whom the employee shares an address. Employers have a statutory duty to consider these applications seriously but there is no automatic right to work flexibly. However, an employer should refuse an application only if there are good business reasons for doing so.

Only employees with at least 26 weeks' continuous employment can apply. They must either be the child's mother, father, adopter, guardian or foster parent or be married to such a person. They must be making the application so that they can care for a child for whom they have, or expect to have, responsibility for bringing up. Only one application can be made every 12 months and agency workers cannot apply.

The application can ask for a change of hours, a change to the times of work or to work from home. If the application is accepted, then the change will be permanent unless the parties agree otherwise. As a change in working pattern might involve a drop in pay, applicants need to think things through carefully before applying. Once the employer receives a written application, a meeting with the employee must be arranged within 28 days. At this meeting the application, and other possible solutions, are considered. Within 14 days of the meeting, the employer has to write to the employee, either agreeing to a new date on which a new work pattern starts or giving reasons why the application has been refused.

Transfer of employees

The Transfer of Undertakings (Protection of Employment) Regulations 2006 (TUPE) provide that when a business is transferred from one employer to another as a going concern the contracts of employment of all the employees are also transferred. These contracts then take effect as if made between the individual employees and the new employer.

If an employee refuses to accept the transfer, this ends the employment without a dismissal having taken place. (So the employee will have no remedy.) However, an employee can claim unfair dismissal if his refusal to be transferred was because the transfer would result in significant and detrimental change. Any dismissal made because of the transfer is automatically unfair unless it is made on account of the employee refusing to accept the transfer.

National minimum wage

The National Minimum Wage Act 1998 introduced new rights to a national minimum wage. The amount of the minimum wage depends upon the employee's age. The rate at the time of writing is £6.19 per hour for workers aged 22 or over, £4.98 per hour for workers aged between 18 and 21, and £3.68 per hour for those aged 16 or 17. These limits are increased periodically, roughly in line with inflation.

Employers must keep records relating to pay, and individual workers have a right to inspect, examine and copy their records. If this right is denied, an employment tribunal can award 80 hours' pay at the national minimum wage rate. However, the right to have access to records applies only if the employee has reasonable grounds to believe that there has been a breach of the Act's requirements and if it is necessary to see the records to establish whether this is the case.

A 'worker' is defined by the Act so as to include both employees, agency workers, Crown workers and home workers. The armed forces, prisoners, voluntary workers, the self-employed, some community workers and employees who live as part of a family, such as au pairs, are not protected. Nor are apprentices under the age of 19. The worker's hourly rate is calculated by looking at a 'relevant pay period'. This period is usually one month, and bonuses and performance-related pay count when calculating how much the worker has been paid. However, overtime and shift allowances do not count.

Example

Jane, aged 26, is paid £6 an hour basic pay plus a 20 per cent shift allowance. Her pay is below the minimum, even though it is £7.20 an hour. John is an 18-year-old salesman, who is paid £4.20 an hour basic rate. Every month he earns £400 additional commission. The Act has not been breached. When the commission is included, John's wage is well above the £4.98 minimum.

HMRC can enforce the Act on behalf of workers. It can also issue penalty notices. Employers in breach of the Act can be fined on a daily basis.

The Working Time Regulations 1998

These Regulations provide that no worker's working time should be more than 48 hours, including overtime, in each seven-day period when calculated over any 17-week period. It is the employer's duty to see that the limit is not exceeded. Any days which are taken off as annual holiday, sick leave or maternity leave are regarded as excluded days. When assessing the hours worked in a seven-day period, these excluded days are not counted and an appropriate number of days are added on to cater for them.

> **Example**
>
> Fred worked in a factory for 52 hours a week for 15 consecutive weeks. Fred then took two weeks' annual leave. Fred then worked 35 hours a week for two weeks. The annual leave is excluded. So Fred has worked 780 hours plus 70 hours = 850 hours in a 17-week period. The regulations have been breached because this averages out at 50 hours per week.

It is possible for a worker to agree that the 48-hour limit should not apply. However, such an agreement must be in writing to be effective.

Young workers (those who are under 18) cannot be made to work more than eight hours in any one day, or more than 40 hours in any one week.

Night workers

A night worker works a period of at least seven hours, at least three hours of which are between the hours of 11 p.m. and 6 a.m. No worker should be given night work unless the employer has first made sure that the worker has the opportunity of a free health assessment. Night workers must also be given regular opportunities to have a free health assessment. Over any 17-week period, with rest periods not counting, night workers should not work more than an average of eight hours in every 24 hours. If the night work involves special hazards, or heavy physical or mental strain, there is no averaging out over a 17-week period. These workers should never work more than eight hours in any 24-hour period.

Daily and weekly rest periods

If a pattern of work is likely to put a worker's health and safety at risk, the worker is entitled to a rest period of at least 11 consecutive hours in each 24-hour period of work. Workers under 18 (young workers) are entitled to 12 consecutive hours' rest. Work which is mono-tonous, or where the work rate is predetermined, is particularly likely to be such a pattern of work. Young workers are entitled to a 48-hour uninterrupted rest period in each seven-day period of work. Adult workers are entitled to a 24-hour uninterrupted rest period in each seven-day period of work, although the employer can insist that this is taken as one uninter-rupted 48-hour period in each 14-day period of work. Adult workers are entitled to a rest break of at least 20 minutes if their daily working time is more than six hours. Young workers have an entitlement to a rest break of 30 minutes if their daily working time is more than 4.5 hours.

Annual leave

Workers are entitled to at least 5.6 weeks' paid leave every year (28 days for those who work a five-day week), or the appropriate proportion of this if less than a year is worked. Where the employment ends before the leave has been taken, the employer can make a payment in lieu. Generally, a worker can take leave whenever he wants by giving the employer notice. However, the employer is entitled to give notice that leave must be taken on particular days.

Enforcement

In these Regulations, 'workers' are defined in much the same way as they are in the National Minimum Wage Act 1998. The Regulations are enforced by the Health and Safety Executive and by local authority inspectors. Employers can be prosecuted for breaching the Regulations. Employees can enforce their rights before an employment tribunal and must not be victimised for having done so. A dismissal in connection with the Regulations will be automatically unfair.

ACAS grievance procedure

When an employee raises a concern, problem or complaint with his employer, the ACAS Code of Practice should be followed. The Code advises that employers and employees should try to resolve disciplinary and grievance matters informally in the workplace, and should consider using independent third parties to help if necessary. However, where this is not possible the Code sets out procedures which aim to ensure fairness and a standard of reasonable behaviour.

First, the employee should formally raise the grievance with the employer, via a manager who is not the subject of the grievance. This should be done in writing and without unnecessary delay.

Second, the employer should hold a formal meeting with the employee, without unreasonable delay, to discuss the nature of the grievance. The employer and the employee should make every effort to attend the meeting. The employee should be given a chance to explain the grievance and how he thinks it should be resolved. The employer should consider adjourning the meeting to conduct any necessary investigation. The employer should allow the employee to be accompanied at the meeting by a companion, such as a fellow worker or a trade union representative.

Third, the employer should decide on appropriate action and communicate this to the employee in writing. The employee should also be told of the right to appeal against the decision.

Finally, the employer should allow the employee to appeal against the decision if he does not think that the grievance has been satisfactorily resolved. Appeals must be submitted in writing and without unreasonable delay. An appeal should be heard without unreasonable delay, preferably by a manager who has not previously been involved. The employee has the right to be accompanied at the appeal. The outcome of the appeal should be communicated in writing without unreasonable delay.

The grievance procedure does not apply when a recognised trade union, or other appropriate workplace representative, raises a grievance on behalf of two or more employees. In such cases the organisation's collective grievance procedures will apply. If an employee raises a grievance during a disciplinary process, the disciplinary process can be suspended until the grievance has been dealt with. However, where the disciplinary and grievance cases are related, both can be dealt with in the same proceedings. An ACAS Guide provides sample grievance procedures and sample letters which might be used by the employer.

The Code is not legally binding but is admissible as evidence and can be taken into account by the employment tribunal. A tribunal, if it considers it just and equitable, can increase any award to an employee by up to 25 per cent if it appears to the tribunal that the employer has unreasonably failed to comply with the Code. A corresponding power to reduce the award by up to 25 per cent exists where it is the employee who has unreasonably failed to comply with the Code.

Unfair and wrongful dismissal

A dismissed employee may be able to sue the employer for either unfair or wrongful dismissal. These are quite separate matters.

Unfair dismissal is a statutory remedy which gives the dismissed employee a right to a fixed payment.

An employee who sues for wrongful dismissal is simply suing for breach of contract. All contracts of employment give the employee an entitlement to a certain amount of notice after one month in the job. If an employee is wrongfully dismissed, without having been given this notice, the contract will have been breached and the employee will therefore be entitled to damages. In theory, an employer could sue an employee who left the employment without giving the required amount of notice but in practice this hardly ever happens.

Unfair dismissal

Figure 13.2 shows an overview of **unfair dismissal**.

Who can claim?

Section 94(1) of the Employment Rights Act 1996 gives an employee who has at least two years' continuous employment the right not to be unfairly dismissed. Section 212(1) ERA 1996 defines the weeks which count towards continuous employment:

> Any week during the whole or part of which an employee's relations with his employer are governed by a contract of employment counts in computing the employee's period of employment.

What is important then is not the kind of work done, but merely whether the employee continuously worked for an employer. It should be noticed that only employees are entitled to claim unfair dismissal. Independent contractors cannot claim unfair dismissal. (In Chapter 9 we examined the ways in which the courts distinguish between employees and independent contractors.) Employees who are over 65 can now claim unfair dismissal. However, discrimination on the grounds of age is permissible if it is a proportionate means of achieving a legitimate aim. So an employer's policy of compulsory retirement at a certain age could be lawful. But following the Supreme Court decision in **Seldon v Clarkson Wright and Jacques (2012)** the employer would have to prove that it was. The employer would have to show that the compulsory retirement was designed to achieve a legitimate aim, such as 'inter-generational fairness'. Even then, it would still be necessary for the employer to show that the aim in question was in fact the aim being pursued in the case before the court and that the aim was legitimate in the circumstances of the particular business. In addition, the means chosen to bring about the aim would have to be both appropriate and necessary, so that less discriminatory measures would not be possible.

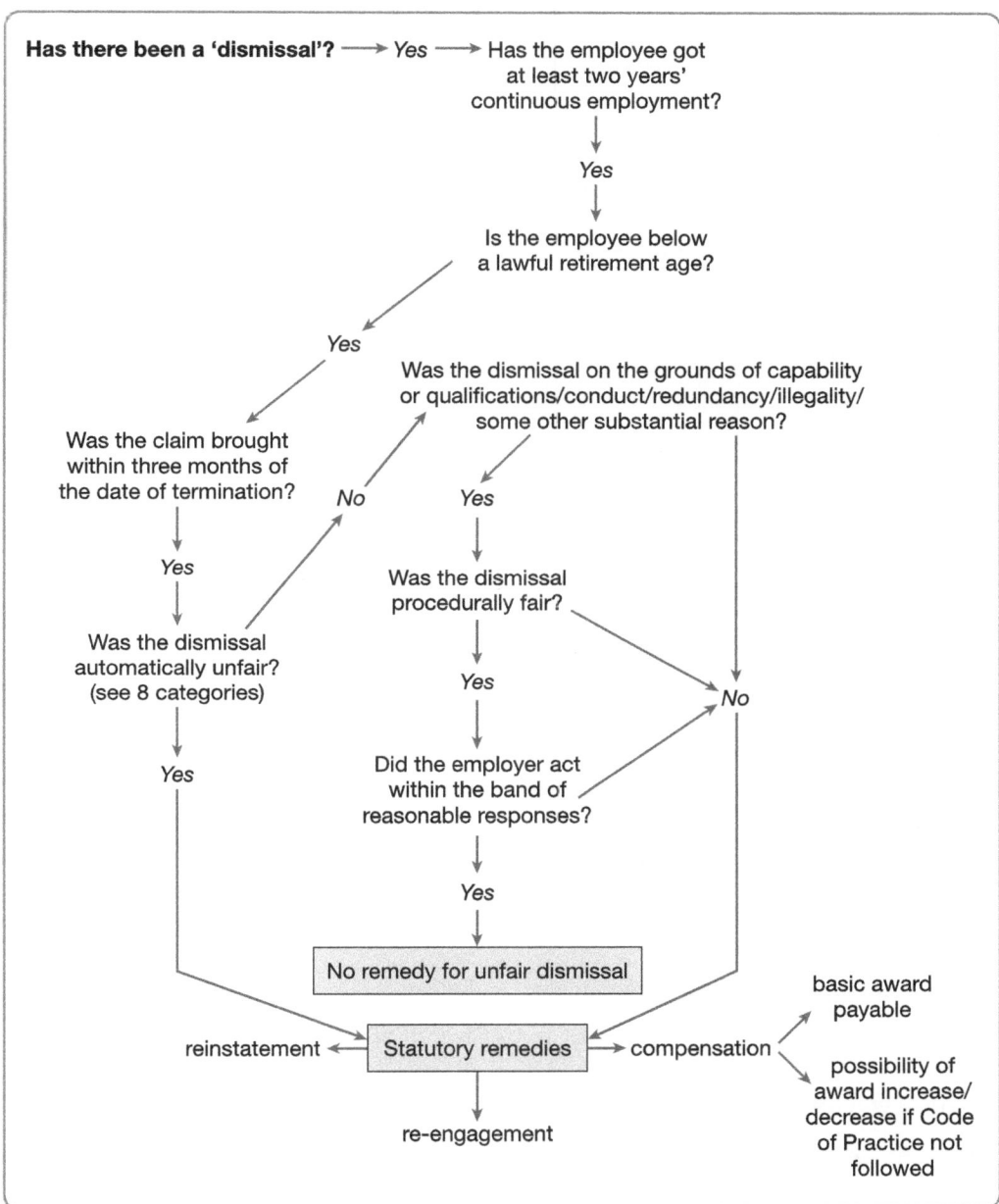

Figure 13.2 An overview of unfair dismissal

Section 212(3) ERA 1996 allows a week to count towards continuous employment, up to a maximum of 26 weeks, even if the employee was absent due to illness, or a temporary cessation of work, or absent by arrangement or custom. Weeks lost through industrial action do not break the continuity of employment, although they do not count as weeks of continuous employment either (s. 216 ERA 1996). If a business is taken over by a new employer as a going concern, weeks worked for the old employer count as weeks worked for the new employer (s. 218 ERA 1996).

What is a dismissal?

There can be a claim for unfair dismissal only if the employee is dismissed. Section 95 ERA 1996 provides that an employee is dismissed if:

- the employer terminates the contract, with or without notice;
- a fixed term contract ends and is not renewed; or
- the employee terminates the contract on the grounds of the employer's unreasonable conduct (this is known as **constructive dismissal**).

 In **Western Excavating *v* Sharp (1978)** Lord Denning explained the meaning of constructive dismissal:

> If the employer is guilty of conduct which is a significant breach going to the root of the contract . . . then the employee is entitled to regard himself as discharged from any further performance . . . He is constructively dismissed. The employee is entitled in those circumstances to leave at the instant without giving any notice at all, or, alternatively, he may give notice and say that he is leaving at the end of the notice.

If a contract is frustrated there will be no dismissal. The meaning of frustration, in relation to contracts of employment, is considered later in the chapter in relation to wrongful dismissal.

When is a dismissal unfair?

'Unfair' has a technical meaning here. Section 98 ERA 1996 provides that all dismissals are unfair unless the employer can justify the dismissal on one of following six grounds:

(1) The employee's capability or qualifications to do the job. (Dismissal for lack of qualifications is very unusual. Dismissal for lack of capability often arises because the employee is ill.)

(2) The employee's conduct, inside or outside the employment. (If the conduct is outside the employment, then it must be serious enough to have a detrimental effect on the employer's business.)

(3) That the employee was made redundant. (Redundancy is considered later in this chapter.)

(4) That it would be illegal to keep the employee on in the job.

(5) Retirement in accordance with the Equality Act 2010 (see Chapter 14).

(6) Some other substantial reason which would justify the employee's dismissal.

The last category is necessary to prevent the list of reasons from becoming too rigid. Usually the reason is a commercial one.

 Wilson *v* Underhill House School Ltd (1977)

Teachers were awarded a national pay rise. The school where the applicant was employed was in financial difficulties and could not meet the award in full. All the other teachers agreed to forgo some of their pay rise. The applicant would not agree to this and so she was dismissed.

Held The dismissal was fair.

Was the dismissal actually fair?

If the employer can show that the dismissal was for one of the six reasons which can be fair, then the tribunal will have to decide whether the dismissal actually was fair. The courts have adopted a test known as the band of reasonable responses. Under this test the tribunal will ask whether a reasonable employer could have acted in the same way as the employer who dismissed the employee. If the tribunal objectively considers that a reasonable employer could have acted in the same way, the dismissal will not be unfair. This test seems very favourable to the employer but it was affirmed by the Court of Appeal in **Post Office *v* Foley (2000)**.

In **British Home Stores Ltd *v* Burchell (1980)** the Employment Appeal Tribunal held that an employment tribunal should decide whether an employer had acted reasonably by establishing the following matters:

- The employer should believe in the employee's guilt or misconduct. Only the facts known to the employer at that time could be relevant here, not facts discovered later.
- The employer should have had reasonable grounds to believe in the employee's guilt or misconduct.
- The employer should have carried out as much investigation as was reasonable in all the circumstances. An employer who followed these three steps would have acted reasonably.

Disciplinary and dismissal procedure

Earlier in this chapter the new grievance procedures contained in the ACAS Code of Practice were considered. The Code also introduced new disciplinary and dismissal procedures. As is the case with grievances, both employers and employees should attempt to settle disciplinary matters informally, using outside third parties if necessary. They should also attempt to deal with matters promptly, without undue delay. The Code does not apply to dismissals by way of redundancy or to dismissals which occur when a fixed term contract is not renewed. The following five stages should be followed when a disciplinary issue cannot be resolved informally.

(1) The employer should establish the facts of the case. This should be done without undue delay and will involve carrying out necessary investigations. A preliminary investigative meeting with the employee may be required to achieve this but no disciplinary action should be taken at this preliminary meeting.

(2) The employer should inform the employee of the problem. If there is a disciplinary case to answer, the employee should be given details of the case in writing. The details should give the employee enough information for him to prepare an answer, and copies of any written evidence should be provided. As well as receiving written notice of the time and place of the disciplinary meeting, the employee should be informed of his right to be accompanied at the meeting.

(3) The employer should hold a meeting with the employee to discuss the problem. The employee must be given time to prepare his case but the meeting should otherwise be held without unreasonable delay. At the meeting the evidence against the employee should be explained and gone over. The employee should be given a chance to set out his own case and answer allegations and should also be given a reasonable opportunity to ask questions, present evidence and call witnesses. If either side intends to call witnesses, they should give advance notice of this.

(4) If the meeting could result in a formal warning being issued, or some other disciplinary action being taken, the employer must allow the employee to be accompanied by a

companion at the meeting. The companion could be a fellow worker, a trade union representative or an official employed by a trade union. The companion would have no right to answer questions on the employee's behalf. However, the companion would have the right to address the meeting in order to put and sum up the employee's case, to respond on the employee's behalf to any views expressed at the meeting and to confer with the employee during the meeting.

(5) The employer must decide upon appropriate action and inform the employee of this decision in writing. As regards most cases of misconduct or unsatisfactory performance, a first written warning would be the usual action taken, with the threat of a final written warning if there was further misconduct or a failure to improve performance. If the misconduct or unsatisfactory performance is sufficiently serious, a final written warning might be appropriate. A written warning should set out the employee's poor performance or misconduct, the change in behaviour or improvement required and the timescale for this. The employee should also be told for how long the warning remains in force and what the consequences of further misconduct or failure to improve might be. Even if there is gross misconduct which would justify dismissal without a warning, the disciplinary process should always be followed. Disciplinary rules should set out examples of gross misconduct. If the employee is persistently unwilling or unable to attend a meeting, without a good reason, the employer should make a decision on the evidence available.

(6) The employer should provide the employee with an opportunity to appeal. Appeals should be heard without unreasonable delay, preferably by a manager who has not previously been involved. The employee has the right to be accompanied at the appeal. The outcome of the appeal should be communicated in writing without unreasonable delay.

The Code is not legally binding but is admissible as evidence and can be taken into account by the employment tribunal. A tribunal, if it considers it just and equitable, can increase any award to an employee by up to 25 per cent if it appears to the tribunal that the employer has unreasonably failed to comply with the Code. There is a corresponding power to reduce the award by up to 25 per cent where it is the employee who has unreasonably failed to comply with the Code.

Under **Polkey v A E Dayton Services Ltd (1988)** a dismissal might be unfair, even if for one of the fair reasons specified and even if the employer acted within the band of reasonable responses, purely because the correct dismissal procedure was not complied with. In such cases the tribunal should reduce or eliminate the compensation payable, other than the basic award (see later in the chapter), to reflect any likelihood that the employee would have been dismissed even if the correct procedures had been complied with. Despite the **Polkey** ruling, there will have been no unfair dismissal if the tribunal concludes that the employer acted as a reasonable employer would have acted in taking the view that, in the exceptional circumstances of the particular case, the normal procedural steps would have been futile and were dispensed with because they could not have altered the decision to dismiss.

Automatically unfair dismissals

A dismissal is automatically unfair if it was:

- on the grounds of the employee trying to enforce a relevant statutory right;
- on the grounds of pregnancy;
- for being a member of a trade union;
- for being on strike, if the dismissal occurred in the first eight weeks of the strike;

- for being a union representative;
- for carrying out health and safety duties;
- for refusing to work on Sundays (some workers do not have this protection);
- in connection with a transfer of undertakings from one employer to another.

The effective date of termination

A claim must be brought before the employment tribunal within three months of the effective date of termination of the employment. The effective date of termination can also be important for calculating the amount of compensation. Section 97 ERA 1996 defines the effective date of termination as:

- Where the contract is terminated by notice, the date on which the notice ends. It does not matter whether the notice is given by the employer or the employee.
- Where the contract is terminated otherwise than by notice, the date on which the termination takes effect.
- Where the employee is employed under a contract for a fixed term, which expires without being renewed under the same contract, the date on which the fixed term expires.

Remedies for unfair dismissal

The three possible remedies for unfair dismissal are: reinstatement, re-engagement and compensation.

Reinstatement

If the employment tribunal orders reinstatement, then the employee must be treated as if he had never been dismissed. He will therefore get his old job back and recover back pay for any time that he has not been allowed to work. The employment tribunal will set the amount of back pay. Orders of reinstatement are rarely made.

Re-engagement

Here the employee is not given his old job back, but the employer is ordered to give him a similar job. The employment tribunal will set out the terms of the employment.

Like reinstatement, re-engagement is not awarded very often. If an employee takes the employer to the employment tribunal for unfair dismissal, this generally means that the implied term of mutual trust and respect has been permanently breached.

Compensation

The basic award is calculated in the same way as a redundancy payment. First, the relevant number of complete years of continuous employment is calculated. Then this figure is multiplied by the normal weekly wage:

- For years worked while under the age of 22, each year of continuous employment entitles the employee to half a week's pay.
- For years worked while over 22 and under 41 years old, each year of continuous employment entitles the employee to one week's pay.
- For years worked while the employee was over 41, each year of continuous employment entitles the employee to one and a half week's pay.

The week's pay is the gross pay which the employee normally earns, excluding overtime. However, there are two limits on the size of the award. First, the employee can only claim for up to 20 years' continuous employment. Second, the week's pay is capped at £430. (This amount is increased periodically to keep up with inflation.) There is no duty to mitigate loss because the basic award is not an award of damages. However, the award can be reduced if the tribunal considers that the employee's behaviour makes this equitable.

Example

Asif and Bill are both unfairly dismissed. Asif is 28 and has ten years' continuous employment. His normal weekly wage is £200 and the continuous employment started on his 18th birthday. The four years worked while under the age of 22 entitle Asif to two weeks' pay. The six years worked since becoming 22 entitle Asif to six weeks' pay. Asif is therefore entitled to eight weeks' pay, at £200 per week, which equals £1,600. Bill is 63. He has 40 years' continuous employment and earns £600 a week. Bill can count only 20 years' continuous employment. As his best 20 years were all worked while over the age of 41, this entitles Bill to 30 weeks' pay. Bill's normal weekly pay is capped at £430. Bill therefore gets the maximum basic award possible of £12,900.

There can also be a compensatory award of up to £72,300. In cases where discrimination has occurred, the amount of damages which can be awarded is unlimited. The compensatory award takes account of matters such as immediate and future loss of earnings, with no upper limit on the weekly pay, loss of statutory rights, loss of pension rights and a supplementary amount which can be awarded if the employer failed to go through an established appeals procedure. However, here the employee has a duty to mitigate any losses and so would have to take another suitable job if one arose. The award will also be reduced by the amount of jobseeker's allowance which the applicant has received. Section 123(6) ERA 1996 allows the award to be reduced on the grounds of contributory negligence. For the purposes of the compensatory award, the weekly pay received is the net pay rather than gross pay and there is no upper limit.

An **additional award** of between 13 and 26 weeks' pay can be made if the employer refuses to comply with a re-engagement or reinstatement order. If the dismissal was on the grounds of discrimination, the additional award is of between 26 and 52 weeks' pay. As regards these awards, the week's pay is still subject to the statutory maximum.

An employee who has been made redundant but who has refused an offer of suitable alternative employment will be entitled to an award of two weeks' pay.

Wrongful dismissal

An employee is summarily dismissed when he is dismissed without notice. The employee's behaviour might justify such a dismissal, in which case he will have no remedy. If an employee is summarily dismissed without a justifiable reason, however, then his contract of employment, which will entitle him to a period of notice, will have been broken. The employee can then sue the employer for breach of contract, and such an action is known as an action for wrongful dismissal. Of course, it is possible that the employer may lawfully dismiss the employee without notice. This would be the case if the employee had behaved so badly that he had committed a repudiation of the contract. The employer could accept the repudiation and dismiss the employee without committing a breach of contract. It is difficult to generalise from the cases, but employees have been held to repudiate the contract by refusing to obey lawful orders, by gross misconduct, neglect or serious breach of duty. However, it must be stressed that each of these matters will not necessarily amount to a repudiation which justifies dismissal. In each case the employment tribunal must consider the facts and come to a decision.

In general, an employer can escape liability for wrongful dismissal, but not for unfair dismissal, by giving the employee wages in lieu of notice.

Constructive dismissal

If the employer's behaviour is so bad as to amount to a repudiation of the contract, then the employee can resign, without giving notice, and sue for wrongful dismissal. (As we saw when considering unfair dismissal, the employee accepts the repudiation and this ends the contract.) This is known as constructive dismissal.

How much notice?

The contract of employment will usually state the amount of notice required. In addition, every employee is entitled to a reasonable period of notice, the length of which will depend upon a variety of factors, such as the nature of the position and the length of service with the employer.

ERA 1996 s. 86 lays down that employees are entitled to a minimum of one week's notice after they have been continuously employed for between one month and two years. After being continuously employed for two years or more, employees are entitled to one week's notice for every year of continuous employment (up to a maximum of 12 weeks). The effect of s. 86 is shown in Table 13.1.

There will be no right to sue for wrongful dismissal if the employer and employee agree to terminate the contract without notice. However, the employment tribunal would need to be satisfied that the agreement was genuine and that the employee was not pushed into it against his or her will.

Nor will there be a right to sue for wrongful dismissal if the contract was frustrated. Earlier (see Chapter 5) we saw that a contract will be frustrated if it becomes impossible to perform, illegal to perform or radically different from what the parties contemplated when they made the contract. A contract of employment can become frustrated by the imprisonment of the employee or by long-term illness. In **Egg Stores (Stamford Hill) Ltd *v* Leibovici (1977)** an employee of 15 years' standing was off work for five months after a car crash. After paying the employee's wages for two months, the employer stopped doing so when another employee was taken on. The Employment Appeal Tribunal held that, as regards a long-term employee, the employer should ask whether the time had arrived when the employer could no longer reasonably be expected to keep the employee's job open for him.

Table 13.1 The minimum periods of notice to terminate a contract of employment

Length of continuous employment	Notice entitlement
Less than 1 month	None
1 month–2 years	1 week
2–12 years	1 week per year worked
Over 12 years	12 weeks

This would require examination of matters such as: the length of employment, the nature of the job, the length and nature of the illness, the need for the job to be done, whether wages continued to be paid and whether the employer could reasonably be expected to wait any longer.

A person on a fixed-term contract who is dismissed when the contract ends is not wrongfully dismissed. (He could, however, have been unfairly dismissed.)

Wrongful dismissal is not a great deal of use to many employees because their notice entitlement is not long enough to result in large damages. It can be very useful to those who are highly paid and who are entitled to long periods of notice.

Earlier (see Chapter 5) we saw that the purpose of contract damages is to put the injured party in the position he would have been in if the contract had been performed as agreed. The injured party will be able to claim for any foreseeable loss which resulted from the

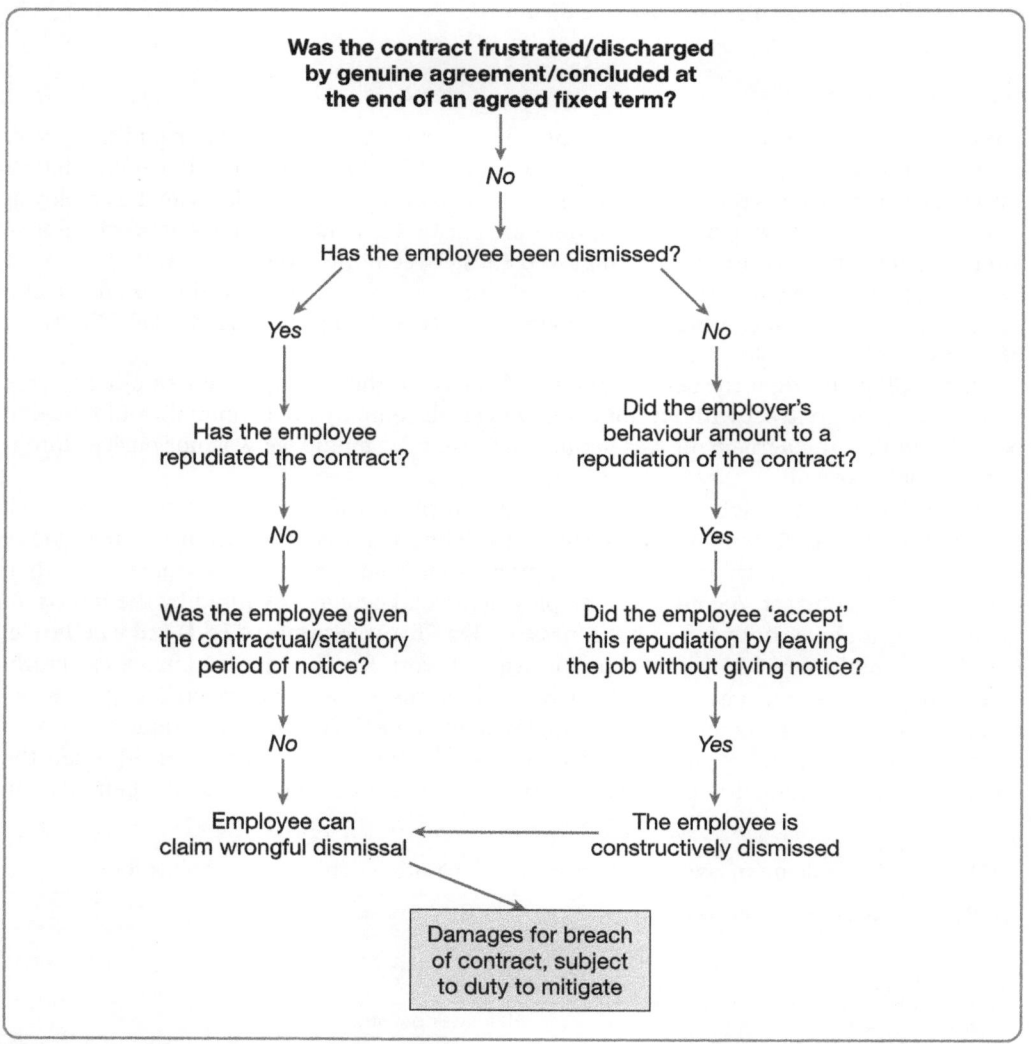

Figure 13.3 An overview of wrongful dismissal

breach of contract. Damages can only be claimed for matters which would have arisen if the employer had not breached the contract. So if the employee was contractually entitled to a bonus, damages could be claimed in respect of this. If, however, the bonus was discretionary, damages could not be claimed. The claimant must take all reasonable steps to mitigate the loss. If the dismissed employee receives jobseeker's allowance, this will be deducted from the damages.

The employment tribunal can award £25,000 damages for wrongful dismissal. If the wrongful dismissal claim is for more than £25,000, it must be pursued through the ordinary courts. Figure 13.3 gives an overview of wrongful dismissal.

Redundancy

Section 139(1) of the ERA 1996 explains that an employee has been made redundant if he was dismissed wholly or mainly because:

- the employer ceased, or intended to cease, to carry on the business; or
- the employer ceased, or intended to cease, to carry on the business in the place where the employee was employed; or
- the need for work of a particular kind to be carried on, or to be carried on in the place where the employee worked, had either ceased or diminished or was expected to do so.

Where the employer moves the place of business, whether or not the employees have been made redundant will depend upon how far the business moved and the amount of inconvenience caused to the employees by the move.

The meaning of the words 'work of a particular kind' have caused difficulty. In **Safeway Stores plc v Burrell (1997)** it was held that s. 139(1) involved a three-stage process:

(1) It should be asked if the employee has been dismissed.

(2) It should be asked whether the requirements of the employer's business for employees to carry out work of a particular kind had ceased or diminished or were expected to do so.

(3) It should be asked whether the dismissal of the employee was caused wholly or mainly by the state of affairs identified at stage two.

If the answer to the questions posed in the three stages was in each case 'yes', then the employee had been made redundant. This test was approved by the House of Lords in **Murray v Foyle Meats (1999)**.

Who can claim redundancy?

In order to claim redundancy, an employee must have at least two years' continuous employment. People who are ordinarily employed outside Great Britain cannot claim.

Offer of suitable alternative employment

If the employer offers the employee suitable alternative employment, and the employee unreasonably refuses to accept this, then the employee cannot claim to have been made redundant. The offer must be made within four weeks of the expiry of the employment and must be reasonable in all the circumstances.

Taylor *v* Kent County Council (1969)

A 53-year-old, who had been headmaster of a school for ten years, was made redundant when his school was merged with another school. He was offered alternative employment as a supply teacher at his headmaster's salary. He declined the offer.

Held He was made redundant. The alternative employment was not suitable.

Redundancy payments

A redundancy payment is calculated in the same way as the basic award for unfair dismissal. (See earlier in this chapter.) However, a redundancy payment cannot be reduced on account of the employee's conduct.

It is important to remember that what is being considered here is the right to a statutory redundancy payment. The terms of many contracts of employment agree that more generous payments should be made in the event of redundancy. Figure 13.4 gives an overview of redundancy.

Procedure for large-scale redundancies

In **Williams *v* Compair Maxam Ltd (1982)** five principles were laid out to be followed when a large number of people are to be made redundant:

(1) The employer should give the employees as much warning as possible.
(2) The employer should consult the trade union in order to be fair, and to cause as little hardship as possible.

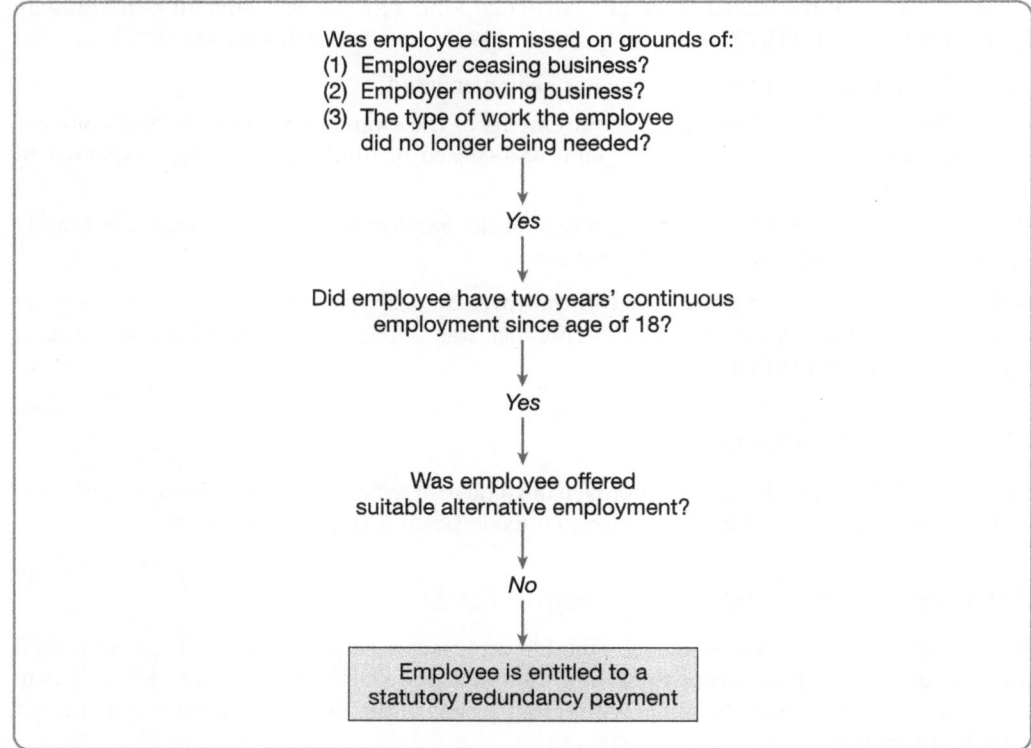

Figure 13.4 An overview of redundancy

(3) Subjective criteria should not be used. The process should be objective and matters such as attendance records and length of service should be considered.

(4) Union representatives should be consulted as to the appropriate criteria to be used.

(5) The employer should try to offer alternative employment instead of just making employees redundant.

If the employer does not follow these procedures, then it seems likely that the employees will not have been made redundant but will have been unfairly dismissed. This will be beneficial to the employees, as the tribunal may make a compensatory award. As we have seen, the basic award for unfair dismissal will be the same as a statutory redundancy payment.

Consultation on redundancies

An employer who intends to make 20 or more employees at one establishment redundant must consult with trade unions with a view to reaching agreement with them. If it is proposed to make at least 100 employees redundant at one establishment, the Secretary of State must be notified in writing.

Essential points

- Contracts of employment can be created orally or in writing and contain both express and implied terms.
- As a matter of law, implied terms of the contract of employment place obligations on both the employer and the employee.
- All female employees have a statutory right to 52 weeks' maternity leave.
- Those who qualify can take either one or two consecutive weeks' paternity leave.
- When a couple adopt a child, one member of the couple is entitled to time off work with statutory adoption pay.
- An employee with at least one year's continuous employment can take up to 13 weeks' parental leave, in respect of each child, to look after his or her child or to make arrangements for the child's welfare.
- All employees are entitled to take time off work to look after dependants in an emergency.
- Parents with children under 16 years old have the right to apply for flexible working. However, the employer need not grant this.
- When a business is transferred from one employer to another, the contracts of employment of all the employees are also transferred.
- All employees are entitled to be paid at least the national minimum wage. There is a minimum rate for workers aged 20 or over and lower rates for workers aged under 20.
- Workers should not work more than 48 hours a week. However, individual workers can agree in writing that this limit should not apply.
- Unfair dismissal is a statutory remedy which gives a dismissed employee with at least two years' continuous employment a right to a fixed payment.

- An employee is wrongfully dismissed when he is dismissed without having been given the notice to which he is entitled.
- In order to claim redundancy, an employee must have at least two years' continuous employment since reaching the age of 18.

Practice questions

1 Jane works for Ace Supplies Ltd. She has four years' continuous service and earns £20,000 a year. Jane has recently discovered that she is pregnant and that the baby is due in six months' time. Advise Jane of her rights to take maternity leave and the amount of any maternity pay which she will receive.

2 Jane's partner, Harry, wants to take paternity leave when Jane's baby is born. Explain the requirements which he will need to satisfy. Explain also the length of time which he will be able to take off and the amount of paternity pay which he will receive. Harry has worked for Ace Supplies Ltd for five years and earns £20,000 a year.

3 Explain the main differences between unfair dismissal and wrongful dismissal. Which remedy would be likely to be more useful to: (a) a very highly paid football manager; and (b) a long-serving factory worker if they were both wrongfully and unfairly dismissed?

4 On what six grounds can an employer justify a dismissal, so that the dismissal may not amount to unfair dismissal?

5 An employee is dismissed for the following reasons. Which of the reasons would mean that the employee was made redundant?

(a) Because the employer is going out of business.

(b) Because the employee was convicted of drinking and driving.

(c) Because the employee became too ill to do the job properly.

(d) Because the employer no longer did the type of work which the employee was employed to do.

(e) Because the employer is transferring his business to a new site several hundred miles away.

6 Calculate the amount of the basic award for unfair dismissal in the following cases.

(a) Farzana, a 21-year-old waitress with four years' continuous employment, who earns £220 a week.

(b) Gerry, a 42-year-old painter with one year's continuous employment, who earns £280 a week.

(c) Kevin, a 58-year-old football club manager with ten years' continuous employment, who earns £5,000 a week.

(d) Alex, a 40-year-old doorman with 18 years' continuous employment, who earns a basic weekly wage of £300 and earns an average of £100 a week in overtime.

7 Explain the difference between unfair dismissal and wrongful dismissal.

Task 13

A group of students from China are visiting England on a cultural exchange visit. Prepare notes for a presentation to be made to the visiting students. The presentation should cover, briefly, the following matters:

(a) The way in which a contract of employment is formed and the terms which are usually implied into such contracts.

(b) The way in which a contract of employment can be varied.

(c) The statutory procedure which must be followed when an employee brings a grievance against his or her employer.

(d) The essential differences between claims for unfair dismissal, wrongful dismissal and redundancy.

(e) The statutory procedure which must be followed when an employee is dismissed or disciplined.

mylawchamber

Visit **www.mylawchamber.co.uk/macintyreessentials** to access tools to help you develop and test your knowledge of business law, including interactive multiple choice questions, practice exam questions with guidance, weblinks, glossary, glossary flashcards, legal newsfeed and legal updates.

Use **Case Navigator** to read in full some of the key cases referenced in this chapter with commentary and questions:

Western Excavating *v* Sharp (1978)

Post Office *v* Foley (2000)

British Home Stores Ltd *v* Burchell (1980)

Business Ethics

CHAPTER 1

Perspectives on business ethics and values

Chapter at a glance

Chapter contents

- Learning outcomes
- Introduction
- Stories and business ethics
- The business case for business ethics
- Stakeholder theory
- Business and organisational ethics
- Boundaries of jurisdiction or spheres of justice
- Defining the boundaries of the economic sphere
- Reflections
- Summary

Case studies

- Case study 1.1 The *News of the World* story
- Case study 1.2 Biography and philosophy

Activities and exercises

- Activity 1.1 Is it ever ethical for a newspaper to use illegal means to expose political or commercial wrongdoing?
- Podcast 1.1 The limits of the economic sphere – post offices and the McCann story
- Typical assignments
- Group activity 1.1
- Useful websites

Having read this chapter and completed its associated activities, readers should be able to:

- Identify the good, tragic, comic, satirical and farcical elements in the way in which people and organisations deal with matters of ethics and morality.
- Explain the basic features of stakeholder theory.
- Evaluate the business case for business ethics and the validity of its claims.
- Give an account of the various arguments about the moral status of business, organisations and management.

Introduction

This chapter lays down the foundations of the book. Many of the foundations are stories and we start with stories that identify some of the issues, problems and dilemmas that form the subject of business ethics. We then tell one very important story about business ethics (at least in the UK and in the USA but not necessarily in other countries) in which there is a 'business case' for business ethics. In this moral tale, behaving well as a company has the fortunate consequences, according to the story, of increasing profits. The stories of business ethics have many characters, or in business speak – stakeholders; they are identified and their relative importance discussed in the next section. Finally there is a debate about whether all the stories of business ethics are about economics or whether moral, cultural and social perspectives should be included in the narratives.

Stories and business ethics

The study of business ethics begins with stories. Families and societies have always used stories to illustrate and reinforce their sense of values, justice and fairness. And so it is in business and organisations. There are the stories often found in organisational glossy newsletters of good deeds done by staff volunteering to work among disadvantaged groups and the benefits that the organisation has brought to the communities it works within. Then there are the more gossipy stories that are told, and half told, as episodes are interrupted by work or authority figures, that tell of jealousies and spites, corruption and abuse, lying and distortion.

Czarniawska (2004: 21) pointed out that there are four types of dramatic story in the European classical tradition – romances, tragedies, comedies and satires, each of which has its characteristic figure of speech. Each of them can represent different kinds of business ethics issues.

Figures of speech

Metaphor
Makes comparisons by referring to one thing as a different thing. So calling all the employees in an organisation 'assets' is a metaphor. If you said of a chief executive officer 'she is a Branson among business leaders', this would be a use of metaphor and a means of making a hero of the CEO. It could also be a kind of paralipsis in which attention is drawn to something – that the CEO is a woman and Branson a man – while pretending to pass over it. As a form of irony this paralipsis could be taken as a criticism of the CEO.

Metonymy
Uses an attribute of something to represent the thing itself. Chairpersons sit in a chair when they hold a board meeting. The chair is their attribute, so they become known as chairs. In tragedy a single attribute can undermine a person's integrity; a good person is often brought low because of a part of their behaviour or character.

Synecdoche
Uses a part of something to represent the whole. Business people wear suits and so that particular aspect of them comes to represent them and their role. Others refer to them as suits, as in 'are the suits arriving today to check us out?' Suits are also a means by which business people present a good image of themselves. In comedy synecdoche points out the comic pretensions between ambition and reality. The smartness of the clothes can emphasise the vacuity of the wearer.

Irony
Speaking or writing in such a way as to imply the opposite of what is being said. Often used to imply mockery or jest. It is therefore the basis of much satire.

Romances are based on the quest of a single individual to achieve some noble goal that is only achievable because human beings have an innate, if sometimes well disguised, goodness. The Quaker heroes of the past such as Joseph Rowntree, who built model factories and villages for model workers, or more modern heroes such as Anita Roddick, who sought, against the odds, to make selling beauty products a beautiful process, are good examples. Such heroes become metaphors for their particular brand of ethical management.

Tragedies tell of people who try to behave well but who, by challenging fate, come to personal grief. The stories of whistleblowers who reveal corporate wrongdoing but in so doing lose their families, their homes and their livelihoods are a good example. Tragedy is based on metonymy, as in the film *The China Syndrome* (Bridges, 1979) in which Jack Lemmon plays an engineer in a malfunctioning nuclear power station who is the only person to be troubled by a vibration felt as a test procedure is conducted. The vibration is a metonym for the potential cataclysm that is waiting to happen.

Comedies are stories about how human imperfections and weaknesses make the achievement of a happy ending difficult. The ways in which companies operating in a new country often get their attempts to integrate wrong are a strong source of comedy. The western businessmen, for it is mostly men who would do this, who ignorantly offend their Arab business partners by putting their feet up on their desk after concluding a deal in an attempt to show that the formal business is over and everyone can relax, and so revealing the soles of their shoes, have a degree of comic potential. The dirty soles of the shoes act as a synecdoche, a part of the businessman that stands for the unwholesomeness of the whole man.

Satires work ironically. By contrasting people's behaviour with their words, or by defining the context in which the words are said, it is made clear that people meant the opposite of what they said. When corporations are accused of not taking care of

- customers, by not closing the doors on the *Herald of Free Enterprise* (*see* p. 288), or

- employees, as in the Bhopal incident in which 20,000 people were killed or harmed by a chemical leak from an American owned chemical works in the city (*see* p. 465) (the leak could have been prevented if procedures, management and maintenance had been rigorous), or

- the environment when the oil companies are accused of despoiling the Niger Delta (*see* p. 471),

organisations often reply by saying that the objects and subjects they have damaged are in fact their top priority. They thereby make themselves the object of satire. People then take such claims as ironies. In the film *Super Size Me*, Morgan Spurlock (2004) tested McDonald's claim that its food is not intrinsically unhealthy by living for a month on its products. Of course such a diet made him an unhealthier person (that is irony).

Cross reference	The ethical issues raised by the film *Super Size Me* are discussed in Case study 2.24.

There is, in business ethics as in life generally, a narrow point of balance

- between romance and satire

- and between tragedy and comedy.

These tensions are the narrative dynamic behind business ethics issues. The heroes of romances can easily become the subject of satirists' scorn. In the struggles between heroes and villains the heroes can overreach themselves and believe they really do have magical powers, in some cases literally. In 1999, in the oil producing delta region of Nigeria members of a cult known as the *Egbesu* began a violent campaign against, as they saw it, the despoliation of their homeland by the oil companies (Ibeanu, 2000: 28). Members of the cult believed that the charms they wore made them impervious to bullets. The heroes may then become ridiculous and the villains begin to look more benign. Tragedy can, uncomfortably, have comic elements. As Marx (1963: 1) pointed out, history repeats itself, 'first time as tragedy, second time as farce'. Just as commonly comedy can descend into tragedy. The difference between an organisational comedy of incompetence and a tragedy may be no more than the operation of chance. If luck remains with the organisation then we can all laugh at its bumbling, but if luck runs out the story can become tragic, for some. In December 2004 (Harding, 2004) a Delhi schoolboy from one of the elite schools, doubtless anxious to show off his new mobile phone with built-in camera, used it to take a video clip of his girlfriend providing him with oral sex. Unfortunately for him within a few days the video clip was on sale on Bazee.com, the Indian version of eBay, and indeed owned by eBay. The company took the item off the website as soon as it became aware of it but nevertheless an uproar ensued in India and a mildly, if in poor taste, comic event turned serious. The boy was taken to juvenile court and expelled from school. Avnish Bajaj, the CEO of Bazee.com and a US citizen, was arrested and thrown into the notoriously overcrowded Tihar gaol. For three people at least tragedy was a tale of prosperity, for a time, that ended in wretchedness. The matter was debated in the Indian parliament and the Bharatiya Janata Party (BJP) denounced the incident as the result of American 'interference'. The American government in its turn was taking a serious interest in Mr Bajaj's imprisonment. Condoleeza Rice, the soon to be American Secretary of State, was reported to be furious at the humiliating treatment meted out to an American citizen. The Indian software industry association called for Bajaj's immediate release.

It would seem that the issues and problems that form the subject of business ethics can appear in different forms, sometimes as romances, sometimes as tragedies, sometimes as comedies and sometimes as satires. It follows that stories are a good mechanism through which business issues can be studied and understood. If we can understand how the plots of these stories can lead to either good or bad outcomes we can develop an intuitive knowledge of how to encourage more happy endings than bad ones. Or at least the stories might palliate, or help us come to terms with, the dilemmas we face (Kirk, 1974: 83).

Case study 1.1	The *News of the World* story

One of the major business ethics stories in Britain during 2011 concerned its leading Sunday newspaper, the *News of the World* (*NoW*). The newspaper's success might be related to its focus on publishing stories of scandal amongst the rich, the powerful and the ranks of media celebrities. It was famous for one of its reporters disguising himself as a rich Arab from the Gulf in order to lure the naïve and the famous to do things that would make a good story when published in the newspaper. The paper was part of *News International*, which in turn was the UK arm of *News Corporation*, which is Rupert Murdoch's international media company. This example can be used to illustrate business ethics stories as examples of romances, tragedies, comedies and satires.

The story had begun several years earlier when the newspaper's royal correspondent, Clive Goodman, was accused of employing a private investigator to hack into voice messages on the phones of members of the Royal Family. Such invasion of privacy is a crime. Both the private investigator and the reporter were found guilty and were given prison sentences. Andy Coulson, the editor of the paper at the time, said that he had no knowledge of this illegal hacking and that this case had been a one-off aberration. The story refused to go away, however. There was continued speculation that instead of being an aberration, phone hacking was in fact a normal

▶

part of the paper's working practices. A number of prominent people such as John Prescott, who had been deputy prime minister, claimed that their phones had also been hacked. Other prominent people in the media industry came to out-of-court settlements with News International and dropped their allegations that their phones had been hacked in return for a sum of money. The story rumbled on and Coulson resigned as the paper's editor whilst still claiming that he had not known of, or authorised, the hacking.

Although the phone hacking story remained alive it did not attract wide concern amongst the general population; that is until 4 July 2011 when *The Guardian* newspaper published the story that the *NoW* had listened to, and deleted, messages on the phone of murdered schoolgirl Milly Dowler whilst the police investigation into her disappearance was ongoing. Ironically, given that *The Guardian* was reporting journalistic malpractice, it had later to admit that the messages may have been deleted automatically and not by agents of *NoW*. However, at that time, that a newspaper had acted so crassly led to a wave of public disgust that had massive repercussions for News International. This was a particularly difficult time for News International. It was already a major shareholder of BSkyB the major subscription TV company in the UK and was seeking to acquire a controlling interest in the company. As News International's newspapers were seen as having great influence over the electoral prospects of political parties many felt that the company already had too much influence and were unwilling for it to accumulate more by gaining complete control over BskyB. In July 2011 the government was about to decide whether to accept News International's compromise proposal, that it would float the news operation as a separate entity from the parent company to ensure its editorial independence if it was allowed to acquire control of BskyB. It was anticipated that the deal would be accepted by ministers. The Milly Dowler story changed all that. In turn News International published a public apology and made a private apology to the Dowler family for its actions; it closed down the *NoW*, although Rebekah Brooks the CEO of News International, and one-time editor of *NoW* kept her job. Later the company withdrew its compromise deal related to the BSkyB purchase and therefore the government referred the deal to the competition authorities. As the public furore strengthened, Rebekah Wade retired and she, together with Rupert Murdoch and his son, were questioned by a Parliamentary Select Committee. Later Rebekah Wade, Andy Coulson and others were arrested and questioned by the police investigating whether crime has been committed.

Only the bare outlines of the story have been recounted above, and particular aspects of it can be drawn out to illustrate the different types of business ethics stories.

A Romance: a hero as a metaphor for ethical behaviour

A romance is a story that lauds a hero. There are those involved in the phone hacking story for whom the metaphor of hero can be used. They are, amongst others, Nick Davies a reporter on *The Guardian* newspaper and Alan Rusbridger the paper's editor. They deserve to be seen as heroes because they continued to investigate and report upon the phone hacking story despite pressure from many to drop the investigation. In particular they came under pressure from senior officers from the Metropolitan Police to change their reporting about the claim that, after the initial Goodman hacking case, the police had dropped the investigation rather than following up the evidence that they had gathered that suggested that the hacking had been more widespread. It was implied that the decision to drop the case had been made to avoid making life difficult for the *NoW*. The Commissioner, Assistant Commissioner and Director of the Metropolitan Police had meetings with Rusbridger in December 2009 and February 2010. They sought to convince the editor that the reporting of the story was 'over egged and incorrect' and that 'Nick's (Davies) doggedness and persistence in pursuing the story was displaced' (Dodd, 2011a).

After the revelations about the Dowler phone hacking *The Guardian* and Nick Davies received praise for their persistence.

A tragedy: a metonym tarnishes a hero

Associated with the romance story is a related tale that has the character of a tragedy. Sir Paul Stephenson was appointed as Commissioner of the Metropolitan Police in 2009. He was regarded as a safe pair of hands and someone who would bring stability and disinterestedness to the Metropolitan Police after the enforced resignation of the previous Commissioner. He had had an impressive career working his way up from constable to the most important job in the police service. However in July 2011 Neil Wallis, who had been a deputy editor of *NoW*, was arrested as part of the Metropolitan Police's re-opened investigations into the phone hacking case. It then emerged that after his resignation Wallis had been appointed as a part-time PR consultant to the Metropolitan Police; and that he had dined many times with senior officers from the force. This revelation identified that at the time that Stephenson and his colleagues were trying to persuade *The Guardian* to change its reporting on the *NoW* story the Metropolitan Police was employing a former *NoW* employee who had been at the paper when it was using hacking to source its scoops. It was claimed that Wallis had not been involved with the Metropolitan Police's dealings with *The Guardian* but there remained the problem that the Commissioner and his assistant had not revealed to *The Guardian,* or to the politicians responsible for the police, that the appointment had been made. The allegation was that the Metropolitan Police's relationships with the *NoW* were too close; in part perhaps because police officers were afraid they would be made the subject of critical news stories. A further revelation that the Commissioner had recuperated at a health spa, free of charge, after an operation on his leg, and that Neil Wallis was also a PR consultant for the spa added to the pressure on him to resign (Dodd, 2011b; Boffey & Townsend, 2011). On 17 July he did resign, saying that he had not acted improperly but that the media pressure was distracting him from doing his job; and that it would be better if he resigned and allow someone else to take forward the important work facing the Metropolitan Police. This work included preparing the security arrangements for the 2012 London Olympics. A successful career was tragically ended when aspects or parts of his behaviour, metonyms of his wider role, undermined his broader reputation as a policeman of integrity.

A comedy: a synecdoche points up the humour of a situation

An ethics story as comedy can be illustrated by a different aspect of the hacking scandal. The comedy arises from the contrast between those parts of a journalist's arguments that express a commitment to high-flown principles and other parts that relish the publication of seedy details about the lives of celebrities. The journalist in question is Paul McMullan who at one time was deputy features editor at the *NoW*. The celebrities are Steve Coogan, a British comedian, and Hugh Grant, a film actor. McMullan had been responsible for publishing stories about these two, most notably the story of Hugh Grant's encounter with the prostitute Divine Brown in Los Angeles in 1995, which, Grant and Coogan believed, invaded their privacy. McMullan thought it was legitimate to publish stories about the private lives of celebrities who avidly sought publicity to advance their fame and wealth, and that phone hacking was not wrong in every case. He argued that the public were not critical when it involved a 'game' between celebrities and the popular media (*Daily Telegraph*, 2011). During the *NoW* scandal Grant's car broke down and a passing driver stopped and gave him a lift. The driver was Paul McMullan. Grant said he would return and have a drink with McMullan, who by then was running a pub, to thank him. When Grant met McMullan he was wired and managed to record McMullan saying that he thought phone hacking was quite routine

▶

at the *NoW*. The story was published in *The New Statesman* and the tabloid journalist was humiliated by the same underhand techniques that he himself advocated (Greenslade, 2011). Further humiliation occurred when Steve Coogan and Paul McMullan came face to face on a BBC *Newsnight* programme, McMullan looked every inch the stereotype of a seedy hack – stubbled, necktie loosened, his shirt collar open; perhaps this late evening TV show was just the last of many interviews that day? Steve Coogan mounted a ferocious attack calling McMullan 'risible… morally bankrupt' and someone who published gossip and claimed this was necessary to defend the freedom of the press. McMullan attempted to fight back. He argued that without invasive techniques there would be no freedom of the press and corrupt politicians would remain undetected. But under pressure he expressed a further motive in a feature that is common in British culture; delight in a famous person being brought down. As he put it: 'You (Coogan) were in the Green Room talking about the number of houses you have bought this year. Oh, we all feel terribly sorry for you . . . we do these [kiss & tell] stories and five million people read the newspaper, and then when a good story comes along, when bad guys get exposed, five million people read it'. Coogan replied sarcastically 'Oh I didn't realize you were on a moral crusade. I am sorry' (Thorpe, 2011).

A satire: exploiting irony

A final aspect of the *NoW* scandal illustrates a satirical aspect of the story. As *The Sun* newspaper also belonged to News International there was speculation in the media about whether the bad habits practised by *NoW* reporters were also practised by *Sun* reporters. There was no evidence that this was the case, and on 20 July Trevor Kavanagh, the associate political editor of *The Sun* went on the Radio 4 *Today* programme to say so (BBC, 2011). He was asked whether, as associate editor, he had asked questions or made enquiries to discover if hacking was practiced at *The Sun*. He said that he had not and that no one senior in the company had asked him to do so. He explained that, as there were no accusations or information that suggested reporters were hacking, there was no need to investigate. In any case he believed that '*The Sun* did not do it' and so there was no need to investigate. He would expect to be told if it became known that someone was hacking phones. In any case, he said, his title was an honorary one and that he had no executive role in *The Sun* and did not work in the office. Therefore he could not know what was happening in the paper's newsroom. The irony, which makes the interview a self-satire, is that reporters are meant to be investigators who delve and question to discover the truth yet in this instance Kavanagh, a well-respected political reporter, saw no need to question what was happening even though problems had been identified in a sister paper.

Activity 1.1	Is it ever ethical for a newspaper to use illegal means to expose political or business wrongdoing

There are always arguments for and against, when deciding whether an action is ethical or not; unless of course you are a person whose values and standards, however eccentric they may be, cannot be challenged by evidence or argument. Can there be circumstances when it is right for the media to use information obtained illegally or dubiously? In recent times there have been many examples of issues being brought to light by information obtained in such a manner. The British MPs expenses corruption scandal, when some Members of Parliament were discovered to be claiming expenses falsely and improperly, only became known because confidential Parliamentary data had been leaked to *The Telegraph* newspaper. On a wider scale there is the example of Julian Assange and *Wikileaks*.

In what, if any circumstances would it be right for the media to use improper or illegal means to obtain information to publish a story? Identify the arguments for and against the practice.

One of the long-running business ethics stories concerns a moral decision that faces profit-seeking organisations. It is a conflict between public duty and self-interest. Should they only exercise their social and environmental duty if it coincides with the financial interests of their owners? In this case they will be heroes in the stories of the owners but villains in the tales of everyone else. Or should they pre-vent the organisation harming society and the environment, beyond the demands of the law if necessary, even if it will hurt the owners' immediate interests? In this case their ascription to the roles of hero and villain in the stories will be reversed.

Following the Asian tsunami in 2004 many Australian companies made donations to the appeal fund. Stephen Matthews, a spokesman for the Australian Shareholders' Association (ASA), criticised the companies, saying that they had no approval for their philanthropy. He implied that companies should not make such donations without expecting something in return.

Boards of directors don't have a mandate from their shareholders to spend money in this way. [ ] There is a role for business to make a contribution in relation to the tsunami, particularly those businesses who have activities up in South Asia. [ ] Where their businesses are dependent on those sorts of markets there could possibly be a benefit for shareholders in them making donations to relief.

(ABC News Online, 2005a)

Later the Association's chief executive tried to limit the damage of the ensuing public disdain by clarifying the statement. The ASA was not opposed to companies making donations because 'it is in everyone's interests that the affected commu-nities and economies recover as soon as possible'. Companies should, however, disclose to the shareholders the extent of their giving (ABC News Online, 2005b). Some commentators thought, uncharitably, that the rapid donations of cash and goods to the affected regions by some large companies was an attempt to have their brands associated with humanitarian good works (Simpson, 2005).

The story illustrates the question of whether a business case should be proven for acting in a socially and environmentally responsible way before it is necessary for an organisation to adopt the role. This is dealt with in the next section.

The business case for business ethics

Should private, profit-seeking organisations behave in a socially responsible and moral way, beyond the requirement of the law, because it is the right thing to do or because it pays them to do so? This might be seen as a moral dilemma; indeed in many ways it is the central issue in business ethics. If it is true that corporations that behave in a responsible and ethical manner do in fact make better returns for their owners than do those organisations that cut corners or behave badly, then the philosophical question of whether organisations ought to behave well is redundant. Do the well-behaved hero companies actually achieve their reward and despite their tribulations win through and enter into a successful long-term relationship with their investors and reach the top of the corporate financial performance league tables, or, in folk story terms, marry the princess and ascend the throne (Czarniawska, 2004: 78)? Several people have sought to answer this question.

There are sensible arguments that can be used to suggest that corporate bad behaviour can be bad for business. It would be logical to assume that a business that was seen to behave badly would lose the esteem and respect of its customers and so lose sales and profitability. A poor image would counteract the large sums that companies spend on developing their brands. Conversely if a company is associated with good behaviour, using renewable resources, not employing child labour in its factories in developing countries, and providing good training and development opportunities for its staff, this should be good for sales.

However, these benefits of good behaviour are not guaranteed. A brand untarnished by a poor reputation is most likely to affect the buying decisions of consumers, but less likely to influence business purchasers, who will rate a good deal before a sense of social responsibility. Bad corporate behaviour will only diminish reputation, and good behaviour boost it, if it becomes known. Many companies of course have PR departments and corporate communications departments that are designed to prevent harm being done to their brands and reputation. Making bad behaviour known requires that wrongdoing is seen and made public and that there are ways of measuring good behaviour so that credit can be given to those corporations that score well on some kind of ethics scale. There are measures of social, ethical and environmental performance, but these are mostly designed to meet the needs of the ethical investment community rather than consumers and purchasers.

Measures of corporate social, ethical and environmental performance

There are a number of standard measures, or more properly indices, that are available for assessing the social and environmental performance of corporations.

1. FTSE4Good

This index is calculated from a number of fators that cover the three areas of:

- working towards environmental sustainability;

- developing positive relationships with stakeholders; and

- upholding and supporting Universal Human Rights.

The factors are sometimes but not always measurable things. Judgments about whether a company is complying with international ethical standards are also included. A panel of experts meets to decide whether companies' performance entitles them to be included in the index.

2. Dow Jones Sustainability Indices

The DJSI tracks the financial performance of companies that have committed to long-term sustainability. It is a guide for those who wish to invest in companies that are ethical or that profess a philosophy of sustainability.

3. SERM Rating Agency

SERM rates companies on a scale of AAA+ to E according to how well the companies manage their environmental and socio-ethical risks. Twenty-five dimensions are used in three fields: environment, health and safety, and socio-ethical. The last category includes items such as use of corporate power, business practices and regard for human rights.

4. Ethical Investment Research Service

EIRIS carries out research on companies worldwide and provides information for those who wish to invest ethically. It is a charity set up in 1983 by churches and charities that did not wish to invest any of their money in ethically dubious organisations.

The indices are all professionally designed and include checks and tests to ensure that the judgments they contain are valid; this, however, makes starker the fact that they are judgments rather than measures of social and environmental outcomes.

Webley and More (2003) have sought an empirical answer to the question whether business ethics pays. They faced the technical problem that there is no single and definitive measure of ethical performance. They happily admit that they have had to choose proxy or surrogate measures that are indicative of whether a company is behaving in an ethical and environmentally protective way but not conclusive proof that they are. (Commentators have taken a satirical delight in the fact that Enron was often commended for its ethics policies.) Webley and More chose the following measures:

1. Whether a company has a published code of ethics that has been revised within the past five years.

2. Companies' SERM rating.

3. Companies' ratings on *Management Today*'s 'Britain's Most Admired Companies' survey, which is carried out by Michael Brown of Nottingham Business School.

Their analysis showed that companies that had a code of ethics had better ratings on both SERM and the 'Most Admired Company' league tables than those that did not. Therefore, to keep things simple all they needed to check was whether companies with a code performed better financially than those that did not.

It might have been anticipated that when Webley and More (2003) came to consider how to measure the financial performance of companies the task would be easier, but there is a wide range of possible measures. They chose:

1. Market value added (MVA) – This is the difference between what investors have put into a company over a number of years and what they would get from it if they sold it at current prices.

2. Economic value added (EVA) – This is the amount by which investors' current income from the company is greater or less than the return they would get if they had invested the money in something else of equal risk. In other words it is the opportunity cost of placing money in a particular company.

3. Price earnings ratio (P/E ratio) – This is the market value of a share in a company divided by the shareholders' earnings.

4. Return on capital employed (ROCE) – This is a measure of the return that the capital invested in a company makes for its owners.

The results of their research into the relationship between a company's ethical standing and its financial performance is shown graphically in Figures 1.1, 1.2, 1.3 and 1.4.

Two cohorts, each a little short of 50, of large companies were chosen from the FTSE 350 for the study. The results indicate, *prima facie*, that companies within the sample that have a code of ethics (and hence score better on the SERM ratings and the 'Most Admired Company' tables than those who do not) also achieved a better MVA and EVA over the four-year period 1997–2000. Between 1997 and 2000 companies without a code had a greater ROCE than those that did, but by 2001 the position had reversed and those with a code performed better. The P/E ratio was more stable over the period of the study for companies with codes than it was for companies without. There is a strong indication that having a code, managing the non-financial risks of a company (as measured by SERM), and being rated by one's peers as a reputable company are associated with higher and more stable financial returns.

1. **Is having an ethical code consistent with the generation of more added value?**

Chart 1: Average Economic Value Added (EVA) by year for major UK quoted companies

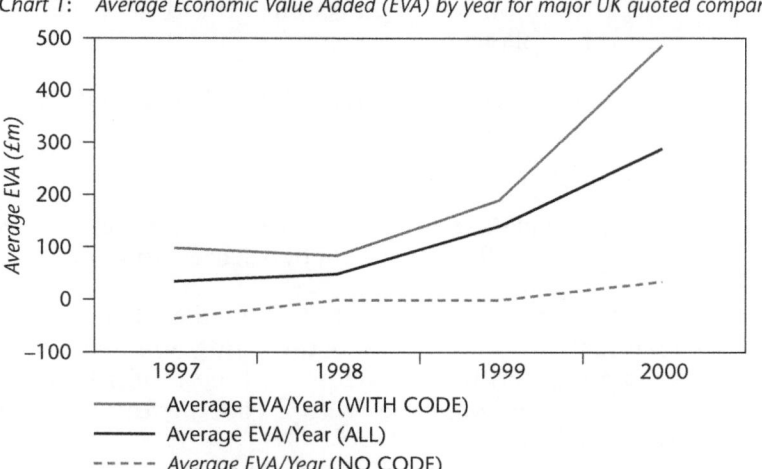

Figure 1.1 Does business ethics pay: does it add value?

Source: Webley and More, 2003

2. Is having an ethical code consistent with enhanced market value?

Chart 2:   Average Market Value Added (MVA) by year for major UK quoted companies

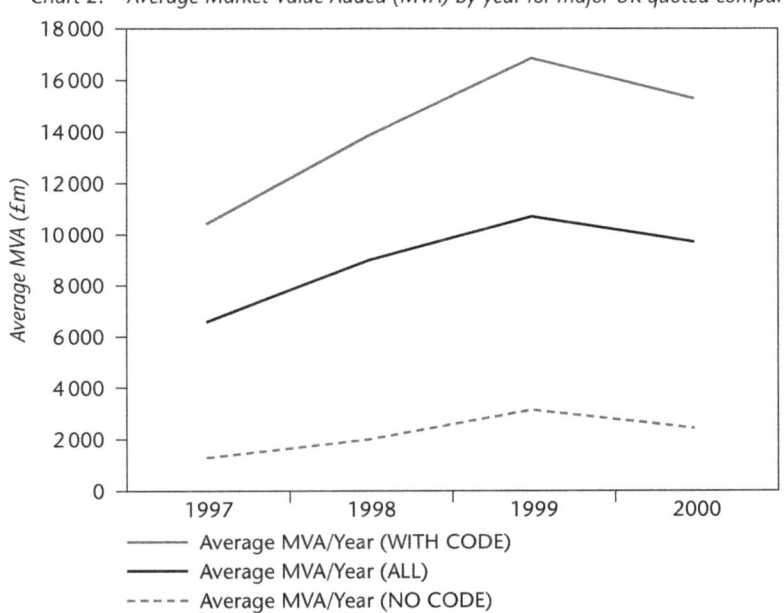

Figure 1.2 Does business ethics pay: does it enhance market value?

Source: Webley and More, 2003

3. Is having an ethical code consistent with an improved return on capital?

Chart 3:   Return on Capital Employed (ROCE) by year for forty-two major UK quoted companies

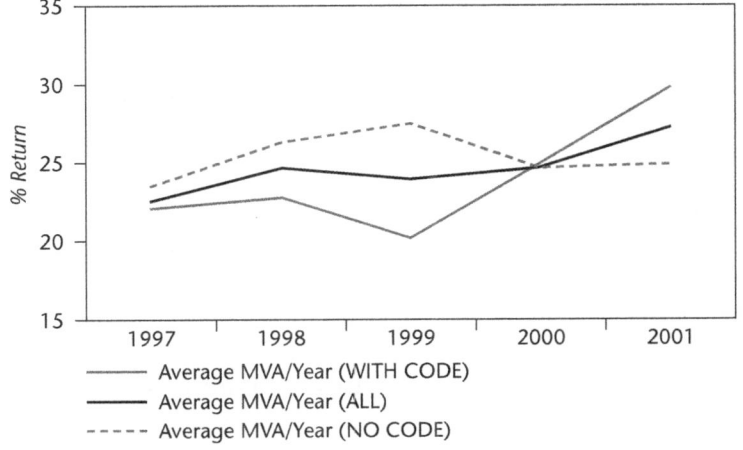

Figure 1.3 Does business ethics pay? Does it improve return on capital?

Source: Webley and More, 2003

4. Is having an ethical code consistent with a more stable Price/ Earnings Ratio?

Chart 4: Price/Earnings Ratio (P/E) by year for forty-two major UK quoted companies

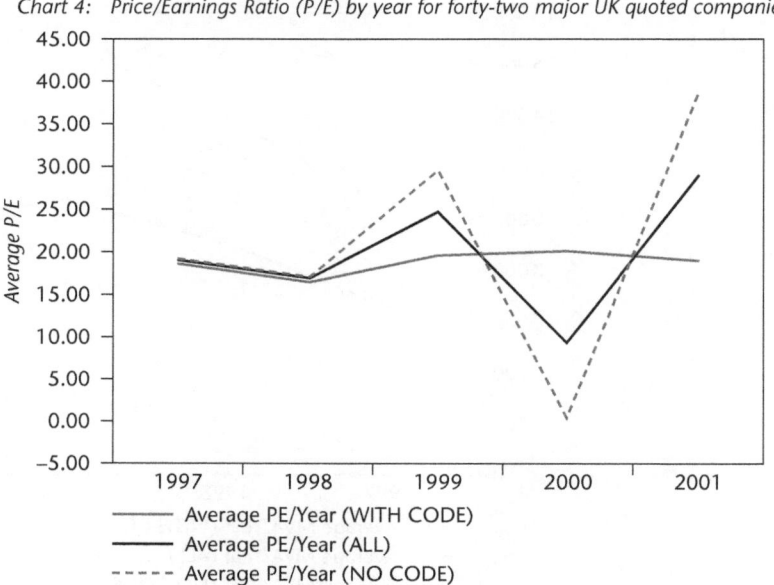

Figure 1.4 Does business ethics pay: does it improve the P/E ratio?

Source: Webley and More, 2003

However, this is not necessarily proof of the business case for business ethics. A statistical association does not mean that the adoption of ethical business practices is the cause of financial improvement. It could be the result of some different, and as yet unconsidered, factor. Moore (2001) conducted a study of the financial and social performance of eight retail supermarket companies in the UK over a three-year period. He found a number of statistical correlations but, because of the small sample size, only one was statistically significant. The social performance of companies was measured by a 16-factor index prepared by EIRIS (see p. 13). The correlations were:

■ That social performance got worse as financial performance improved.

■ But if social performance was compared with financial performance three years earlier the association was positive.

■ That older companies did better on social performance than younger ones.

■ And larger companies had a better performance than smaller ones; this was the one statistically significant finding.

These findings suggested that far from good social performance leading to improved financial effects the cause and effect relationship worked the other way around. That is to say, companies that do well financially find themselves with some money that they can spend on good works and improving their social and environmental performance. It takes time to implement these policies, hence the three-year time lag. The Institute of Business Ethics research could not be expected to identify this time lag because their key indicator, the presence or absence of a code of ethics, is not one that would fluctuate year on year, but the index that Moore used would. This direction of causation, from financial to social, is known as the Available Funding Hypothesis (Preston and O'Bannon, 1997). However, giving attention to these new social projects causes companies to take their eye off their main objective, making money. This distraction of attention, plus the fact that these projects can cost a lot of money, causes the financial performance to worsen. In response, companies return their efforts to financial performance. Commentators within the supermarket industry anticipated that as Sainsbury's and Marks and Spencer were performing less well financially, their social and environmental efforts would decrease.

These same commentators also speculated whether social and environmental performance might be related to the social class of customers (Moore and Robson, 2002: 27). Tesco and Morrisons served lower socio-economic groups (on average) who were less likely to be conscious of social and environmental concerns and so there would be no advantage to the company in taking a lead on such matters. The higher status groups who shopped in Sainsbury's and Marks and Spencer were more likely to be careful conservers of the natural and social world, and might begin to boycott the stores if they were not seen to be sufficiently interested in sustainability.

In a later study (Moore and Robson, 2002: 28–9) a more detailed statistical analysis was carried out between the 16 social performance indicators (instead of the aggregate result as in the first study) and an extended range of financial performance indicators. Negative, and statistically significant, correlations were found between growth in turnover and the league table rank of:

- the mission statements compared with those of others;
- the proportion of women managers compared with other companies;
- the environmental policy;
- the environmental management systems; and
- the social performance total.

In summary, this suggests that as companies increase their turnover their social performance worsens, or the obverse, that as their social performance improves their turnover declines. This adds support to the second part of the cycle suggested above, that social performance endangers financial performance, but does not of itself support the first part of the cycle, that companies flush with profits are inclined to spend some of the profits on social performance, even though, as we saw above, this is precisely what Sir Richard Branson says they should do. These results of course only apply to one industry – retailing and supermarkets.

There is an association between good social performance or ethical business practices and good financial returns. It is not clear, however, that it is the good social performance that increases profits. It may be the other way around. This conclusion is not necessarily dismissive of all concerns with business ethics from an organisational point of view. There may not be a financial case for actively and purposefully seeking to make a better social and environmental world. This does not mean that companies should not seek to minimise the potential costs of being found to have acted unethically or improperly. If a company or government department is sued for damages arising from its negligence or its bad behaviour, the costs of the case and the costs of the award can be very high. It may be wise to seek to avoid those actions and practices that could cost dearly; this management function is known as risk management. If a company can be shown through its risk management procedures to have taken every reasonable precaution to identify a potential malpractice or problem and to do what is reasonable to prevent it, then, even if the problem or malpractice happens and damages others, the company will have a legal defence.

So, unfortunately (although fortunately for textbook writers for if otherwise we would have to close the book at this point), it is not clear that there is a business case for business ethics, although on the defensive principle there is one for managing the financial risk of unethical or improper organisational behaviour. It is necessary to turn to other ways of deciding whether companies and organisations should act ethically and responsibly. This comes down to the question of whose interests companies and organisations should exist to serve. Should they serve the interests of society generally? Or should they serve the interest of particular groups within society? If so, which groups should they serve? It is the answer to these questions we now turn to.

Stakeholder theory

Cross reference	Stakeholder theory is a key and recurring theme in this book because ethics is concerned with the harm or good done to people. As different people may be affected differently by the same action then it is important to take these various impacts, some good and some bad, into account. The simplest way of doing this is to use stakeholder theory. The theory will be used and discussed in Chapters 9, and 11.

If we continue with the storytelling metaphor it is important to know who the characters in the story are. In terms of business ethics stakeholder theory provides an answer. It might be more accurate to say stakeholder theories, since there are various interpretations of what the term means. They share one attribute, however, which is that for any organisation there are a number of definable groups that have an interest, or a stake, in the actions of that organisation. There is more disagreement about what constitutes a stake. It is clear that the shareholders, the owners if it has any, have a legitimate stake in an organisation. So do its employees. At the other extreme the 'phishers', who fraudulently try to gain customers' bank account details through fake, spammed e-mails, obviously have an interest in the banks they attack; but it is hardly a legitimate one. So the issue is threefold:

■ What responsibilities or duties, if any, does an organisation owe to its stakeholders? The fact that a stakeholder group may have a legitimate interest does not, of itself, mean that the organisation owes anything to it. At one extreme of the spectrum of possibilities an organisation may be obliged to do what its stakeholder group requires. If that group is society at large, as it expresses its will through legislation, then the organisation should submit to it. At a level below this, stakeholders could have the right to participate in the organisation's decision making. This might be accepted in the case of employees who are expected to commit to the organisation's objectives and decisions. It might not be right in the case of a judicial system's obligations to those being tried in a court. A lesser obligation might be a stakeholder group's right to be consulted before major decisions are taken. If not this, then at least the group might expect the organisation to give it an account of why it did what it did. At the other extreme, the organisation might owe the stakeholder group nothing.

■ How should an organisation decide between its obligations to two or more stakeholders if they demand incompatible things from an organisation? What criteria should the organisation use when deciding which stakeholder group's wishes it should prioritise? Often in public service organisations the criterion used is a crude one – the group that shouts loudest is the one listened to. There is an interesting issue involved here. What if a constituency is not a person or persons but a thing or collection of things or ideas (these are known in sociological jargon as actants) such as rivers, nature reserves, spirituality? How can these things be given a voice? An easy answer might be that their voices are those of the lobby groups that support each particular cause. There is a problem here though. Some research indicates that, when lobby groups cause too much irritation to the organisation they are trying to influence, their reward is not to be listened to but to be shut out. If the cause of environmentalism is voiced by over-aggressive agitation then an organisation might close its ears to the problem when the cause itself is more deserving than its supporters' actions.

■ What legitimate interests justify a group of people being regarded as a stakeholder in an organisation? A criterion often proposed is that stakeholders are any group that is affected by an organisation's actions. But this would give a commercial company's competitors a voice in its activities because their performance would be affected by the organisation's performance, which would not seem fair.

So far the discussion has focused on fair and open debate of ethical matters. But the question of who should have a voice in the debate is also an important ethical matter. This question can best be considered by looking at the application of stakeholder theory to ethical matters. This theory proposes that, for every organisation, stakeholder groups can be identified:

■ who are affected by,

■ who can affect, or

■ whose welfare is tied into the actions of a corporation. It may be necessary to add a criterion of legitimacy to the identification of stakeholders. As Whysall (2000) pointed out, a shoplifter's welfare may be affected by a retailer's actions but that does not make them a legitimate stakeholder.

Donaldson and Preston (1995) presented four perspectives on the roles of stakeholder management.

- *Descriptive* – that the stakeholder theory describes what corporations are, i.e. constellations of interconnected interest groups.

- *Instrumental* – that if corporations adopt stakeholder management they will, all other things being equal, be more successful than those organisations that do not.

- *Managerial* – that the theory enables managers to identify options and solutions to problems.

But underpinning each of these roles was the fourth *normative* one: stakeholder theory can be used to develop moral or philosophical guidelines for the operations of corporations. In particular it forces corporations to make a broad ethical appreciation of their actions that considers their impact on communities as well as on the profit and loss account. Whysall used the case of companies that retail goods, at premium prices to affluent consumers, which were manufactured in sweatshop conditions in Third-World countries. A traditional management approach would only consider the benefits of the business model to the corporation and its customers. A stakeholder approach would also involve consideration of the impact upon the workforces, the communities and governments of the countries involved as well as activists and lobbyists.

The subject matter of business ethics is an attempt to answer these three questions. In the next section we consider four different answers, or perspectives, that are given in modern western, capitalist societies.

Business and organisational ethics

In this section four broad theories of the firm, and the assumptions and implications of these perspectives for prioritising the various stakeholders' needs and for the exercise of moral agency, are considered.

> **DEFINITION**
>
> **Moral agency** within organisations is the ability of individuals to exercise moral judgment *and behaviour* in an autonomous fashion, unfettered by fear for their employment and/or promotional prospects.

Organisation, in the sense we are using the term here, refers to any configuration of people and other resources that has been created to coordinate a series of work activities, with a view to achieving stated outcomes or objectives. At this stage we make no distinction as to whether an organisation is profit seeking, located within the public sector or is a charitable/voluntary organisation. The issues we discuss are largely, but not exclusively, sector-blind, although the intensity with which the issues are experienced may vary significantly between organisational types.

As will become evident as we progress through the chapters, the location of an organisation within the public sector does not make it immune from economic constraints, even economic objectives. Likewise, there is a growing body of opinion that argues forcibly that profit-seeking organisations should be more accountable to a body of citizens that extends considerably beyond shareholder-defined boundaries. While the distinctions between private sector and public sector, profit seeking and non-profit seeking, have become less clear-cut in recent years, we do not argue that all organisations are equivalent, and that the sector of the economy in which an organisation is located is irrelevant to understanding the ethical, political, economic and social constraints within which it operates. Penalties or sanctions for poor performance are possibly more obvious and severe in the profit-seeking sectors, but it can be argued that the multiplicity and complexity of the objectives managers are required to achieve in certain parts of the public sector make managing in such a context a far more demanding and ethically fraught role. Although each perspective assumes that organisational relationships are largely, if not exclusively, mediated by market dynamics, the extent to which 'the market' is relied upon as an exclusive mediating mechanism does vary.

Table 1.1 presents the schema of four perspectives to highlight the point that different imperatives and assumptions may underpin market-based, capitalist economies.

Within the four categories in Table 1.1 different assumptions are made about the relationships between:

- organisations and the state;

- organisations and their employees;

- organisations and their various stakeholder groups (i.e. beyond the employee group).

We need to understand these perspectives because they are helpful in appreciating the potential for, and the constraints we each face in exercising, moral agency within business contexts.

With the exception of the 'classical-liberal' category, each of the categories is an amalgam of a variety of theories, ideas and practices. The corporatist approach is referred to by Crouch and Marquand (1993) as 'Rhenish'. This latter term refers to a particular (German) approach to a market-based, capitalist-oriented economy, although the writers broaden their consideration beyond Germany to take in a wider group of non-Anglo-American market-based economies. Whilst the German approach displays important differences from the Japanese and the Swedish approaches, they have, for our purposes, been grouped together as representing a more corporatist approach, where the overt involvement of the state and employees in the running of individual organisations is an accepted practice.

This is not to say that the Anglo-American approach to economic development can be simply categorised within the 'classical-liberal-economic' group. Notwithstanding the rhetoric of various UK and US governments, state involvement has been required and forthcoming on many occasions in these two countries, often to overcome what is known as market failure. However, the common belief in the UK and USA leans towards the need for less, or minimal, government interference in business, and a drive towards market dynamics to facilitate organisational coordination.

Table 1.1   Theories of the firm and their ethical implications

Issue	Classical liberal economic	Pluralist (A and B)	Corporatist	Critical
Status of the category	1. For its advocates it is the only game in town, not merely the most efficient, but the most ethically justifiable	1. Type A. A stakeholder perspective is advocated in corporate decision making, with key interest groups physically represented on decision-making boards	Refers to the business relationships in countries such as Germany, Sweden and Japan (although the approaches adopted are not identical). The interests of employee groups, non-equity finance, and sometimes the state, are represented alongside the interests of equity shareholders, on senior decision-making boards	Ranging from descriptive theories category of the firm that portray how organisations appear to be (or are), rather than how they should be, to critical theorists who portray an organisational world beholden to the demands of capitalism or managerialism (these terms are not the same). Both approaches reflect messier and more ethically fraught worlds than tend to be suggested in the other three categories
	2. For others the 'pure' model must be tempered by interventions to (a) minimise problems of short-termism, or (b) correct power imbalances	2. Type B. Individual managers weigh the full ethical and social considerations of their actions and decisions. Stakeholder groups would not necessarily be present at decisions		
	3. Whilst for others the neo-classical model is a corrupting chimera that acts as a cover to camouflage the interests of the powerful			

Number of objectives recognised	One – meeting the demands of equity shareholders	Multiple – reflecting an array of stakeholder perspectives, although the actual mechanics remain problematic	A mix of equity shareholder, employee and non-equity finance perspectives, although the long-term economic interests of the firm are dominant	Multiple – reflected by the various coalitions and power groups within an organisation, particularly economic interests
Status of financial targets	Regarded as the organisation's primary or sole objective, because they will reflect the efficiency with which resources are being employed	Important, but do not dominate all other considerations. Ethical as well as multiple stakeholder perspectives are weighed in decision making	Important, but greater attention paid to the medium to longer-term financial implications of decisions than appears to be the general case in Anglo-American corporations	In highly competitive markets, or during periods of crisis, likely to be the dominant, although not the exclusive, organisational consideration. During periods of relative stability, other considerations will gain in significance and could dominate
Significance of ethical behaviour (both individual and corporate)	Defined by national and international laws, which are seen as both the minimum and maximum of required ethicality. The neo-classical model is argued to be the only approach that allows the primacy of individual interests to be reflected in economic and social coordination	At the heart of the debate for those who bemoan what is seen as the exclusive, or overly dominant, economic orientation of organisations	No clear evidence that ethical considerations feature more strongly in corporate decision making, although the lack of an exclusive shareholder perspective might offer greater potential for a broader societal perspective	An important, but variable, element in defining the reputation of the organisation. Will be shaped by the power of influential individuals and groups within and external to the organisation
Role of managers	Portrayed as functionalist, technicist and value neutral	Type A. Managers come into direct contact with specific sectional interest groups, which should affect decision making. Type B. Individual managers are required to have internalised a societal ethic into their decision making	The structures of organisations reflect a formal involvement of employee representatives, non-equity financiers and sometimes state representatives, alongside shareholder interests, on corporate decision-making boards	Complex, with competing and sometimes/often mutually exclusive interests and demands being required to be satisfied, including the managers' own agendas

Table 1.1 Continued

Issue	Classical liberal economic	Pluralist (A and B)	Corporatist	Critical
Status of employees	Resources to be used by the organisation in its quest to satisfy shareholder interests	Employees represent an important interest/stakeholder group within the organisation, although economic considerations are not ignored	Employee representation is guaranteed on some of the organisation's senior decision-making boards, e.g. supervisory boards in Germany	Operating within a capitalist mode of production, employee interests will vary between organisations, depending upon the power of individuals and groups of individuals
Values	Competition seen as the bulwark against power imbalances. Efficient resource allocation facilitated by profit-maximising behaviour	Inherently societal in orientation, but the views of those actually making decisions will be important	Those of the shareholders, employees, non-equity financiers (possibly the state) are likely to dominate	A complex interaction of multiple individual and corporate values. Critical theorists would single out the values that underpin capitalism
The possibilities for moral agency in organisations	The individual as consumer, as chooser, is the personification of moral agency, but the individual as moral agent when selling his or her labour is troublesome. The atomisation of society, which appears to be an inevitability of this form of individualism, is seen by many as leading to feelings of alienation and anomie	Type A. Multiple perspectives offer heightened possibilities, but medium to long-term organisational survival will dominate concerns. Type B. Very similar to Type A, but the confidence and integrity of individual managers becomes a critical issue	With employee representatives on the supervisory boards of organisations (as in Germany), the possibilities again appear stronger than with the liberal-economic perspective. However, economic considerations will remain dominant	Empirical evidence indicates that the suppression of moral agency might be more than minor and isolated aberrations in an otherwise satisfactory state of organisational affairs. Critical theorists would see these problems as an inevitable consequence of the demands of capitalism

The following is a closer examination of the four theories of the firm and their implications for moral behaviour within, and of, organisations.

The classical-liberal-economic approach

A classical-liberal theory of the firm places the organisation within an economic system that is made up of a myriad interconnecting but legally separate parts, and where relationships between these many parts are defined in terms of free exchange. Money acts as the facilitator of exchange, thus performing the role of the oil that greases the economic system's wheels. The 'invisible hand' that Adam Smith spoke of is the force that drives the mass of individual transactions. The argument is that, with no individual person or company able to affect price, the resulting transactions, and the prices that draw both suppliers and customers into the marketplace, reflect people's wishes. This is the strength of the claims for the ethicality of 'free' markets as espoused by writers such as Milton Friedman, Friedrick von Hayek and Ayn Rand. Individual choice, free of government coercion, is seen as the only ethical influence in shaping economic and social development.

Rand is probably the least well known of the three advocates of free markets mentioned above, although her advocacy appears to have been influential. She is reputed to be a favourite writer (she wrote novels rather than philosophical monographs) of Alan Greenspan, the Chairman of the American Federal Reserve from 1987 to 2006. Friedman's arguments in defence of a business world free of government or social obligations beyond those defined in law are considered in more depth in Chapter 8, so a little more time will be given here to consider some of the key thoughts of Rand on the subject of markets as the basis of economic and social coordination.

Ayn Rand was born in Russia in 1905, but she emigrated to America when she was 21, nine years after the 1917 Bolshevik uprising in Russia and four years after the civil war that followed the uprising. On arriving in America, Rand took a variety of low-paid, menial jobs. She is quoted as saying: 'I had a difficult struggle, earning my living at odd jobs, until I could make a financial success of my writing. No one helped me, nor did I think at any time that it was anyone's duty to help me'. Such snippets of historical and biographical features are helpful in understanding some of the factors that might explain an individual's philosophical position on key issues. Rand depicted man as 'a heroic being, with his own happiness as the moral purpose of his life, with productive achievement as his noblest activity, and reason as his only attribute'. Two of her novels have been recently republished (Rand, 2007a, 2007b). *The Fountainhead* first published in 1943 tells the story of Howard Roark, a ground-breaking, genius architect who has a clear vision of how buildings should be. He refuses to dilute the purity of his vision to suit the demands of clients and so business is bad and he becomes a manual labourer. But no matter, his integrity is preserved. He has many further setbacks. One of his buildings is built in ways that deviate from his design and so he blows it up. At his trial he expounds Rand's theories and is acquitted. As a recent reviewer (Crees, 2007) pointed out:

> Rand's characters make stands, but they rarely question themselves, and introspection is almost regarded as a form of serious thought-crime.

Her novel *Atlas Unshrugged* is was made into a film in 2011 but stars, such as Angelina Jolie, who were slated to be in it, were not.

Randianism (the term used by followers of Rand) rejects government in anything other than its minimalist form, i.e. that which can be justified to protect individual rights, such as the police, the law courts and national defence forces. All other functions can and should be operated by 'the people', preferably via market mediation, and paid for (or not) by choice.

Rand is credited with developing the philosophical position that is known as objectivism. Objectivism has three key elements:

Case study 1.2	Biography and philosophy

Bauman (1994) contrasts two philosophers, Knud Logstrup and Leon Shestov. Logstrup lived a tranquil and civilised life in Copenhagen. He wrote of human nature, 'It is characteristic of human life that we mutually trust each other . . . . Only because of some special circumstance do we ever distrust a stranger in advance . . . initially we believe one another's word; initially we trust one another' (Bauman, 1994: 1). Shestov, on the other hand, experienced great persecution during his life, under both the tsarist and anti-tsarist regimes and as a consequence had a far more pessimistic view of human nature, portraying the individual as one who is vulnerable and must at all times be ready to be betrayed. 'In each of our neighbours we fear a wolf . . . we are so poor, so weak, so easily ruined and destroyed! How can we help being afraid?' (Bauman, 1994: 2).

1. '*Reason* is man's [*sic*] only means of knowledge', i.e. the facts of reality are only knowable through a process of objective reason that begins with sensory perception and follows the laws of logic. Objectivism rejects the existence of a God, because it lacks (to date) empirical support. However, in America, some of the most strident advocates of free markets come from politically powerful religious groups.

2. *Rational self-interest* is the objective moral code. Objectivism rejects altruism (i.e. the greatest good is service to others) as an unhelpful and illogical human attribute. Individuals are required to pursue their own happiness, so long as it does not negatively affect anyone else's. This is compatible with negative freedom, one of Isaiah Berlin's two forms of freedom. It relates to a 'freedom from' approach that grants people a right to be free from interference by others, including, and in particular, government.

3. *Laissez-faire capitalism* is the objective social system. It is important to recognise that laissez-faire capitalism is referred to by its advocates as a social system, and not just an economic system. This is an important issue and one towards which critics of the approach feel unified in their opposition, although such opponents have differing views on how to respond. Some would argue for an overthrow of the capitalist ethic and practice, whilst others would retain a market-based framework, but define boundaries of relevance and ethical justification for markets. The latter is exemplified by writers such as Walzer (1983) and is discussed below.

> **Laissez-faire** means unrestricted. So laissez-faire capitalism **DEFINITION** refers to a preparedness to let markets 'sort themselves out', even during periods of disequilibrium and apparent malfunctioning. The belief is that a 'market' will self-correct in time (a natural law, or Darwinist view within economics). Self-correction rather than external intervention is deemed infinitely preferable in the long run for all concerned.

The attachment of modern-day libertarian-economists to a myopic focus upon competition can be criticised for ignoring two other significant elements of economic systems, which are:

■ *Command* (the extent to which power, coercion and hierarchy affect economic relationships), and

■ *Change* (the way that capitalism effects change and is itself affected by change).

These three central elements of capitalism – competition, command and change – have ethical and moral implications and it is argued here that they are interconnected, not subject to easy and simplistic separation. However, the classical-liberal perspective eschews these arguments and presents a schema in which the operations of the firm, both those within the firm and how it interacts with its external environment, are treated as if they are value neutral.

Within the simple competitive model of economic behaviour managers are expected to behave in ways that reflect what is known as economic rationality. This normative theory is open to challenge in terms of its descriptive rigour, hence the existence of alternative theories of the firm. Supporters of the neo-classical-economic perspective would accept that actual practice is likely to be variable around the preferred norm, but it is argued that economic rationality is the goal towards which organisations should strive. They argue that those organisations that get closest to the normative position will prosper, with competitors having to respond in a similar fashion, or wither on the economic vine.

The corporatist approach

The corporatist approach does not deny the primacy of competitive market forces, but an exclusive equity shareholder perspective is eschewed in favour of a broader-based set of perspectives in some of the organisation's decision making. These additional perspectives are those of employee representatives, debt financiers, and in some cases state interests. This broadening of the decision-making base is claimed, and appears to offer, a longer-term view to certain aspects of corporate decision making. For Crouch and Marquand (1993: 3):

> The system as a whole trades-off losses in the short-term efficiency on which the Anglo-American tradition focuses against gains in consensual adaptation and social peace. It owes its extraordinary success to its capacity to make that trade-off ... In a high skilled – or would be high skilled – economy, consensual

adaptation and social peace are public goods, for which it is worth paying a price in strict allocative efficiency.

The sphere of inclusion reflected in this approach goes beyond the exclusivity of the shareholder orientation of the classical-liberal perspective espoused by most Anglo-American corporations. Evidence suggests that the corporatist-type approach has avoided, or minimised, many of the worst effects of short-term economic 'adjustments' in world trade that have been experienced since about 1960. This is not to say that countries such as Germany, Sweden and Japan (examples of the corporatist perspective) can be immune from significant movements in world economic activity, but it is argued that significant economic lurches have been avoided in these countries, thus minimising significant rises in unemployment levels, with the attendant impacts upon social cohesion. The significant economic downturns experienced by a number of Asian economies in the late 1990s, including Japan, were associated more with structural factors within these economies than with inherent weaknesses in Japan's more corporatist approach to market coordination.

Whether the corporatist approach is preferred by some because it offers a greater likelihood of economic, and thus political, stability, with the greater apparent value placed upon the interests of individual citizens/employees merely an ancillary benefit, or whether the rationale for employing this approach is reversed (i.e. the ethics of the corporatist approach are argued to be the main reasons for its adoption), is not critical for our discussion. What is relevant is that both the 'classical-liberal-economic' and the 'corporatist' approaches can cite ethical justifications for their superiority as economic and social systems. The former can do so because of the primacy attaching to the notion of individual choice, the latter because of its attachment to social cohesion and the desire to avoid, or minimise, what might be deemed unnecessary social disruption and distress to individual lives during periods of economic correction or recession.

The pluralist perspectives

There are two main pluralist perspectives. The first (referred to as Type A pluralism) sees broad stakeholder interests being represented (as far as this is possible) by elected or appointed members of corporate boards. This is a development of the corporatist perspective, but with the stakeholder groups being drawn more widely. The corporatist approach is evident in the countries cited above on a reasonable scale, whereas the two pluralist perspectives currently exist as arguments and debates, rather than as practice. Companies such as The Body Shop are very much the exceptions that prove the rule.

In Type A pluralism stakeholder groups are required to do more than argue their particular, vested-interest, case. They are expected to be representative of societal interests. Clearly the extent to which the latter are adequately represented will depend upon the composition of the stakeholder groups. Thus, as compared with the classical-libertarian-economic perspective, where the unconscious forces of individual decisions are deemed to give expression to society's preferences, within

Type A pluralism societal preferences are given voice by the presence (or not) of stakeholder groups on company boards or committees.

The second pluralist perspective (referred to as Type B pluralism) does not dispute the possibility of stakeholder groups being physically represented within corporate decision-making processes, but this is neither a prerequisite, nor part of the basic arguments. This second variant of pluralism sees economic rationality being moderated by concerns for, and recognition of, wider social implications of corporate decisions, with these factors being weighed by individual decision makers. Type B perspectives can be presented as a continuum, with writers such as Casson (1991) at one pole, and Maclagan (1998), Maclagan and Snell (1992) and Snell (1993) at the other.

The perspective argued by writers such as Casson is that competition via market-based economies is the preferred economic system, but that reliance upon unadulterated economic rationality as the sole explanation of individual behaviour is both naïve and unhelpful. For the discipline of economics to retain relevance Casson argued that it must recognise behaviours that are explained by drives other than, or in addition to, economic rationality.

> These professional prejudices must be overcome if economics is to handle cultural factors successfully. They are the main reasons why, in spite of its technical advantages … economics has not contributed more to the analysis of social issues.
>
> (Casson, 1991: 21–2)

Classical-libertarian economics retains a view of human behaviour that sociologists would describe as 'under-socialised' (i.e. unrepresentative of the complexity and variability of actual human behaviour). Type B pluralism argues for a recognition of the realities of everyday market conditions, but also a more socialised set of assumptions of human behaviour. Whilst a market-based economy is seen as the foundation upon which organisational coordination takes place, structural issues and problems within markets are recognised, e.g. power imbalances between competitors; information asymmetry between producers and customers; and the capricious nature of (the owners of) capital. Greater responsibility, ethicality and humanity are required of corporate decision makers.

In a similar vein, but with less of Casson's implicit instrumentalism, Etzioni (1988) employed a moral justification for an overt recognition of broader perspectives beyond short-term profit motives. In the following quotation Etzioni used the term 'deontological'. This is an important word in any consideration of business ethics and it is considered in more depth in Chapter 3. However, we offer a brief definition of the term here to allow you to understand the argument that Etzioni was making.

A **deontological** approach to moral behaviour is one that believes **DEFINITION** that moral reasoning and action should be guided by universal principles that hold irrespective of the context in which an ethical dilemma might exist.

Instead of assuming that the economy is basically competitive, and hence that economic actors (mainly firms) are basically subject to 'the market' possessing no power over it (monopolies are regarded as exceptions and aberrations), the deontological 'I & We' paradigm evolved here assumes that power differences among the actors are congenital, are built into the structure, and deeply affect their relationships. We shall see that power differentials are gained both by applying economic power (the power that some actors have over others, directly, within the economy) and by exercising political power (the power that some actors have over others, indirectly, by guiding the government to intervene on their behalf within the economy). These fundamentally different assumptions make up what is referred to here as the I & We paradigm (one of the larger possible set of deontological paradigms). The term [I & We] highlights the assumption that individuals act within a social context, that this context is not reducible to individual acts, and most significantly, that the social context is not necessarily wholly imposed. Instead the social context is, to a significant extent, perceived as a legitimate and integral part of one's existence, a whole of which the individuals are constituent elements ... The deontological paradigm evolved here assumes that people have at least some significant involvement in the community (neo-classicists would say 'surrender of sovereignty'), a sense of shared identity, and commitment to values, a sense that 'We are members of one another'.

(Etzioni, 1988: 5)

Etzioni continued:

The issues explored here range way beyond the technical, conceptual matters of what constitutes a workable theory of decision-making in economic and other matters. At issue is human nature: How wise are we, and what is the role of morality, emotions and social bonds in our personal and collective behaviour.

(Etzioni, 1988: xii)

Progressing along the continuum, past Etzioni's position, one moves towards those who argue for Type B pluralism on the grounds that a broader ethic than that required by classical-liberal economics is desirable, even essential, on the grounds that society as a whole needs organisational decision makers who understand and can exercise moral judgment in complex situations (Maclagan, 1996, 1998; and Snell, 1993). These writers see management practice as essentially a moral practice, set in a complex and challenging arena (business organisations), for individual moral development.

Thus, our pluralist continuum moves from writers, such as Casson, who argued for theories of decision making to recognise actual human behaviour and instincts in order to make economic theorising more relevant and realistic, to the arguments of writers such Maclagan and Snell, who justify the inclusion of the moral dimensions within business decision making on the grounds of the ethical demands of society as a whole.

The critical perspective

The critical perspective is composed of many different theories about human and collective behaviour, including the politics of organisations (Simon, 1952, 1953 and 1955); expectation theory (Vroom, 1964); the use of ambiguity and hypocrisy as managerial tools (Brunsson, 1986 and 1989); the theory of coalitions (Cyert and March, 1992); the exploitation of people (Marcuse, 1991); the benefits that people seek at work and the importance of these benefits (Maslow, 1987); power and identity in organisations (Knights and Willmott, 1999); and the range of strategic resources that individual managers draw upon to allow them to cope with managerial life (Watson, 1994). This is far from an exhaustive list, but it gives a flavour of the range of research and theories that have been developed to explain actual behaviour within organisations. What these works share is a picture of organisational life that is far more complex and messy than classical-liberal economics would prefer to work with. The behavioural and critical theories are not normative theories (i.e. theories of how things should be, such as the classical-libertarian-economics perspective), but what are referred to as descriptive theories, i.e. theories of how things actually appear to be. However, behavioural theorists and critical theorists do vary in terms of the intentions of their respective arguments.

Behavioural theories are amoral in their stance in that, unlike the liberal-economic, corporatist and pluralist perspectives, they do not put forward a preferred ethical foundation for their theorising. They might, however, highlight examples of laudable, contentious or downright immoral behaviour. They do so by acting as organisational windows through which we can observe the ways in which employees at all levels in organisations appear to react, and behave, when faced with ethically complex situations. For example, you become aware that a friend and work colleague, who you know has a very difficult financial situation at home, unlawfully takes a small toy (a company product) home to one of their children. Such situations could involve divided loyalties between either colleagues or concepts, where the ethics of a situation are not clear-cut or neat; or where moral agency is compromised by power imbalances that jeopardise future employment and promotional prospects.

Critical theorists, however, have an avowed commitment to societal change, for the emancipation of employees from the shackles of capitalism. However, critical theorists make different analyses (for example, Foucaudian perspectives, e.g. McKinley and Starkey, 1998, and neo-Marxist perspectives, e.g. Alvesson and Willmott, 1996) and there is no consensus on the preferred replacement for market-based societies. Habermas (whose ideas are discussed in Chapter 3) does, however, outline the necessary conditions for a societally acceptable economic set of relationships to develop.

Boundaries of jurisdiction or spheres of justice

The fear of market-based relationships as the bedrock upon which all societal and interpersonal relationships are based is articulated by a number of writers. Walzer (1983), for example, wrote:

> One can conceive of the market as a sphere without boundaries, an unzoned city – for money is insidious, and market relations are expansive. A radically laissez-faire economy would be like a totalitarian state, invading every other

sphere, dominating every other distributive process. It would transform every social good into a commodity. This is market imperialism.

(Walzer, 1983: 119–20)

Taking his cue from Walzer, Keats (1993) argued that:

It is as if their [liberal economists'] theoretical energy has been so fully utilised in demonstrating the virtues of the market that little has been left to deal with the arguably prior question of what it is that defines the nature – and hence limits – of that 'economic' domain with respect to which market and state are seen as the chief rival contenders.

(Keats, 1993: 7)

As a way of handling this problem Walzer argued that societal life should be seen as a series of spheres, which contain and constrain differing elements of societal existence. One of these spheres is the economic, in which markets are recognised as the most effective mediating mechanism, and competition the most defensible form of organisational coordination. Whilst markets, contract and competition are seen as appropriate mediating elements, their relevance is largely constrained within this sphere. Within the spheres representing non-economic interpersonal relationships we find notions of trust, care, welfare, sharing, friendship, leisure and possibly even altruism (although this is not highlighted by Walzer). There is some similarity between Walzer and the earlier work of the German philosopher Hegel (1770–1831) who also used the notion of spheres to conceptualise the social world (Singer, 1983). Hegel spoke of the spheres of state, family and civil society, and to these Walzer adds the economic as worthy of consideration.

McMylor comments upon the development of market-based capitalism from feudal societies. He presented the development from non-market societies as a process whereby the economic moved from being enmeshed 'within other dominating frameworks' to a situation in market societies when:

the economy, with a capital 'E' is no longer so embedded. The market means that there is in some sense, a differentiation of economic activity into a separate institutional sphere, no longer regulated by norms that have their origin elsewhere. The individual economic agent is free then to pursue economic self-interest, without 'non-economic' hindrance.

(McMylor, 1994: 100)

From a moral perspective one of the problems with dividing the human world into separate spheres is that it might suggest the spheres are independent to the point of allowing differing forms of behaviour to prevail within each. Behaviour might be accepted, or at least tolerated, in one sphere that would not be acceptable in another. It has been argued that this is a recognition that people sometimes act (or feel they need to act), when in 'business mode', in ways that they would not employ within their private, domestic lives. Walzer recognised this and argued that the spheres should not be seen as totally autonomous and independent. Rather, he portrayed a dynamic set of relationships between the spheres in which shifts between spheres of particular facets of societal life do happen, and that a sphere's scope and importance may wax and wane. Boundary conflict thus becomes endemic:

> The principles appropriate to the different spheres are not harmonious with one another, nor are the patterns of conduct and feeling they generate. Welfare systems and markets, offices and families, schools and states are run on different principles: so they should be.

> (Walzer, 1983: 318)

However, Walzer went on to say that 'the principles must fit within a single culture' (1983: 318). This is highly problematic, unless the single culture is one that recognises difference, a multiplicity of cultures. Within such a complexity of perspectives, the notion of wisdom becomes an important mediating factor, but this has to be an active wisdom, i.e. it is always in a state of emerging through dialogue and debate. Within this perspective the dynamic of change is recognised, is debated and matures through processes that are demanding but which, it must be stressed, are subject to 'social capture' by active groups and voices if participation is shirked by the general polity.

> **Social capture** is a term used to describe a mechanism, e.g. a **DEFINITION** committee, a regulatory body or a political process, which is established to oversee a particular facet of social life, but which becomes dominated by, or heavily influenced by, the very sectional interests the mechanism was intended to monitor or control. The original intentions behind the creation of the mechanism thus become at best neutralised, and at worst subverted.

To minimise the risk of social capture and other such distorting influences within political, economic and social systems requires an active citizenry, prepared to be interested in, even involved in, micro- and macro-level debates about equity and justice – the very morality of life's various spheres. Hegel spoke of the dialectic, the processes of debate and argument that are required to surface and (possibly) resolve differences of view and contradictions. The dialectical approach is to be found in the teachings of Socrates, certainly in the way that Plato presents the work of his master. Billig (1996) makes a plea for a resurgence of the practice of rhetoric, not in the pejorative sense in which the term tends to be viewed in contemporary society, but as a return to an engagement in debate and argument, for these are the mechanisms and processes by which civilised societies develop and progress.

Podcast 1.1

The limits of the economic sphere – Post Offices and the McCann story

Podcasts explaining how today's business news relates to the topics discussed here will be updated in an ongoing process. Podcast 1.1 refers to two current issues to illustrate the drawing of boundaries between different moral domains or spheres. To listen to this podcast, other archived podcasts or recent additions, please visit the companion website at www.pearsoned.co.uk/fisherlovellvalerosilva.

Defining the boundaries of the economic sphere

One of the principal virtues of competitive markets, as the mechanisms by which business and social interaction is mediated, is that the 'invisible hand' of the market is amoral, i.e. value neutral. Although some may suffer as a result of market-based outcomes, through unemployment or loss of capital, the outcomes are not intended from the start. They are simply the unintended consequences of the multitude of transactions that comprise a free market. Sir Keith Joseph, a notable politician of the 1970s and 1980s and an architect of the political period and philosophy referred to as Thatcherism, was a devotee of Hayek and Friedman. As Heelas and Morris (1992: 19) observed:

> Policies designed to effect more equal distribution of resources, Joseph claims, are not only coercive and threaten individual liberty but are counter-productive and give rise to a series of negative consequences (economic, psychological, moral and political). . . . Liberty is primarily to be exercised by the self-interested consumer in the market place, including the political, educational and medical 'markets'.

Plant (1992), taking up the theme of markets being the most appropriate mediating mechanism for medical services, explored the possibilities for a free market in body parts (human organs), as well as the justification for a market-based ethos replacing a service ethic in non-voluntary, public service organisations. With regard to a market for human body parts Plant (1992: 91) observed:

> On a strictly capitalist view of market principles, it is very difficult to see why there should not be such a market. The scope for a market is clearly quite wide. There could be a market in blood and blood products; in kidneys; in sperm; in renting out a uterus for surrogate pregnancy; and so forth.

Plant argued that, from a market perspective, at least three principles would favour a market in these areas:

1. There is a clear demand.

2. The current donor system is failing to meet demand.

3. Ownership of the human organs is clear and would not be undertaken by the donor if it were not in their personal interest.

Despite strong advocacy for such markets, broad public support was (and appears to continue to be) lacking. Plant argued that this reluctance reflected a boundary being drawn by society, with human organs currently residing outside the boundary that defines the limits of market application.

Titmuss (1970), in a seminal work on the marketisation/commercialisation of blood donor services, observed, when responding to arguments that blood should be seen as a commodity and thus private blood banks should be introduced to improve the productivity of the blood giving process:

In essence, these writers, are making an economic case against a monopoly of altruism in blood and other human tissues. They wish to set people free from the conscience of obligation. Although their arguments are couched in the language of price elasticity and profit maximisation they have far-reaching implications for human values and all 'social service' institutions . . . . The moral issues that are raised extend beyond theories of pricing and the operations of the marketplace.

(Titmuss, 1970: 159)

Titmuss worried about the wider implications of commercialising the blood donor service in the UK. If the altruism that, it is argued, is reflected in the voluntary and unpaid giving of blood is replaced by a commercial relationship, what, asked Titmuss, fills the space that used to be occupied by the sense of community inherent within the existing system?

There is nothing permanent about the expression of reciprocity. If the bonds of community giving are broken the result is not a state of value neutralism. The vacuum is likely to be filled by hostility and social conflict, a consequence discussed in another context . . . the myth of maximising growth can supplant the growth of social relations.

(Titmuss, 1970: 199)

Titmuss discussed four economic and financial criteria, excluding the much wider and unquantifiable social, ethical and philosophical aspects to concentrate upon those aspects that economists (the focus of his criticism) would recognise. These were:

1. Economic efficiency.

2. Administrative efficiency.

3. Price – the cost per unit to the patient.

4. Purity, potency and safety – or quality per unit.

On all four criteria the commercialised blood market fails. However, paradoxically ... the more commercialised a blood distribution system becomes (and hence more wasteful, inefficient and dangerous) the more will the GNP be inflated. In part, ... this is the consequence of statistically 'transferring' an unpaid service (voluntary blood donors, voluntary workers in the service, unpaid time) with much lower external costs to a monetary and measurable paid activity involving costlier externalities.

(Titmuss, 1970: 205)

The discussion so far in this chapter has laid out the arguments for claiming that the market system is:

■ The only defensible economic and social system for protecting the freedom of the individual to exercise personal choice, which allows the development of economic and societal relationships that are free from government coercion and intervention. This is the liberal-economic perspective.

- Something that is preferable to alternative economic systems, but which needs to be carefully watched and, if necessary, modified from time to time to ensure that the economic system is compatible with broader societal aims. This incorporates the corporatist and pluralist perspectives.

- An intrinsically corrupting system that pits human beings against each other, with only an elite few dictating the life chances of the many. This is the critical perspective.

The argument has been about the place of ethics in business life, and the place of business in the ethics of life.

Descriptive, normative and reflective approaches

Two ways of discussing ethical matters, normatively and descriptively, are often proposed. Normative discussion is concerned with rules and principles that ought to govern our thoughts and actions. Normative arguments are focused in particular on how such prescriptive claims can be shown to be legitimate or valid. Descriptive discussion focuses on how things *are* rather than how they should be. A descriptive approach to ethics would give an account of the values and ethics of particular groups and try to explain how they have emerged. It would analyse value systems to look for norms and the tensions between them. The word normative is troublesome in a subject such as business ethics, which spans both philosophy and sociology. In sociology, normative refers to that which is the norm within a group or society. The term is both descriptive – the norms are those of a particular group, and also normative – they define right and wrong within that group. In philosophy normative and descriptive are seen as opposing terms. In this book normative will be used in its philosophical sense.

Many business ethics textbooks take a normative approach. They identify ethical difficulties in business, rehearse the arguments about what should be done about them and then present a resolution or a set of principles. Rather than taking a normative and prescriptive approach this textbook takes a descriptive and analytical approach. It attempts to describe how people in organisations interpret and respond to ethical issues at work. It does not propose solutions to the many ethical dilemmas and problems that face managers and organisations. However, by explaining how others think about and respond to ethical matters, and by providing you with the appropriate tools for thinking, we hope the book will enable you to analyse the issues and to come to your own conclusions.

The intention of the book brings us to a third way of talking about business ethics, the reflective and reflexive approach. Reflection implies careful consideration of ethical issues. Reflexive means to turn back on one's own mind and to consider one's own values and personality. This textbook therefore tries to help you examine your own positions and thoughts. This can be done in part by reflecting on the material in this book and other publications. But this is vicarious learning, piggybacking on the experiences of others. Reflexive learning occurs when you use your values to challenge your actions and your experiences to challenge your values.

Reflections

One of our concerns in this book is the possibility of the existence of moral agency and ethical practice within organisations. Integrity is one of the concepts that would form part of any definition of business ethics. The importance of integrity within organisational life in general, and executive decision making in particular, is discussed by Srivastva and Cooperrider (1988), although they stress that the way forward is not easily mapped. It can only be navigated and negotiated through dialogue, reflection, learning, tolerance and wisdom.

> Executive integrity is dialogical. Executive integrity is more than the presence of morality or the appropriation of values; integrity involves the process of seeing or creating values. Whereas ethical moralism is blindly obedient, integrity represents the 'insightful assent' to the construction of human values. In this sense, organisation is not viewed as a closed, determined structure but is seen as in a perpetual state of becoming. Dialogue is the transformation of mere interaction into participation, communication, and mutual empathy. Executive integrity is, therefore, a breaking out of a narrow individualism and is based on a fearless trust in what true dialogue and understanding might bring, both new responsibilities and new forms of responsiveness to the other.
>
> (Srivastva and Cooperrider, 1988: 7)

The big weakness of a heavy reliance upon the notion of a dialectic transformation of society is that the associated processes are subject to the risk of social capture. The best chance of minimising this possibility is for all of us to take ourselves seriously and to believe that our individual voices count in shaping the societies in which we live.

We end this opening chapter on a qualified, optimistic note. Spaemann (1989) refused to accept that conscience is either purely instinct or exclusively a function of upbringing:

> In every human being there is the predisposition to develop a conscience, a kind of faculty by means of which good and bad are known.
>
> (Spaemann, 1989: 62–3)

However, Spaemann went on to say that conscience has to be nurtured and supported – shown good practice in order for it to flourish and mature. Fail to do this and the development of a strong conscience becomes 'dwarfed'. The term 'dwarfing' is used by Seedhouse (1988) when discussing the growing attention to a 'business mentality' within UK health care, at the expense of a prioritising of the individual. Both Spaemann and Seedhouse saw the individual as central to any challenge to the primacy of business interests, although, as you will see in Chapter 6, conscience is often the victim of the need to maintain organisational and personal relationships.

Hannah Arendt (cited in Bauman, 1994) also placed the individual at the centre of any developments towards making ethics a live and legitimate subject for debate within organisations. Arendt wrote, 'there are no rules to abide by ... as there are no rules for the unprecedented'. Bauman continued in other words, no one else but the moral person themselves must take responsibility for their own moral responsibility.

(Bauman, 1994: 14)

With this in mind, this book is intended to inform your understanding of some of the key issues that bear upon this critical element of modern society – the possibilities for business ethics.

Summary

In this chapter the following key points have been made:

- Business ethics issues can be illustrated through stories; sometimes these are expressed as romances, as tragedies, as satire, as comedies and sometimes as farces.

- Many writers, and indeed organisations, argue that there is a business case for companies to behave ethically and responsibly. There is an association between the two, but whether good companies are profitable because they are good, or good because their profitability means they can afford to be, is not easily proven one way or the other.

- Many business ethics issues are best understood by using a stakeholder approach.

- Four different perspectives: the classical-liberal, the corporatist, the pluralist and the critical, on the question of whether organisations, and their role within market systems, are ethically proper.

- The doubts about the classical-liberal model place a premium on the role of the moral agency of individuals within organisations. Moral agency involves reflection on what is right and wrong and working for the good within organisations.

Typical assignments

1. Is there an effective 'business case' for corporations acting in a socially, ethically and environmentally responsible way?

2. Compare and contrast the four approaches to the involvement of stakeholders' business decision making (classical-liberal, pluralistic, corporatist and critical) outlined in this chapter.

3. How should a company decide which interest groups should be treated as stakeholders and which should not?

4. What can we learn about business ethics issues at work by studying the stories in which they are reported?

Group activity 1.1

A delphi exercise on reasons to be an ethical organisation

Delphi is a technique for creating a consensus on difficult matters of prioritising or forecasting. In this instance it will be used to answer the question:

Why should organisations choose to behave ethically and socially responsibly?

The exercise needs the group to divide into groups of between five and eight people. Each group should then follow these steps.

1. Each person, working on their own, should think of as many reasons as they can why an organisation should behave ethically and socially responsibly. Write each reason down on a Post-it note and make a pile of them.

2. Everyone then posts their Post-its in random order on a convenient board.

3. The group should gather around the Post-its and sort and cluster them, putting similar points together, until the mass of Post-its has been reduced to about five or six clusters of reasons.

4. The group should then write a simple, one-page questionnaire that lists the five or six reasons and asks respondents to score each reason according to its importance. The scoring should be done using percentages, the larger the percentage the more important the reason. Photocopy a batch of the questionnaires (or, if you are inclined, create a small spreadsheet).

5. Each member of the group then completes the questionnaire on their own.

6. The scores are then totalled and averaged and presented to the whole group.

7. Each group member then completes a new questionnaire taking into account the average scores of the whole group.

8. The process continues through cycles of individual scoring and group feedback until the group reaches a consensus, or nearly does, on the scoring and importance of the five or six reasons.

9. You will then have decided why organisations should behave ethically and socially responsibly.

10. Discuss in the group how the arguments you have identified are similar to or differ from those presented in this chapter.

Useful websites

Topic	Website provider	URL
Global business ethics issues.	World Economic Forum	http://www.weforum.org/issues
Business ethics and etiquette guide	Youngstown State University	http://maagblog.ysu.edu/business-ethics/web/
A useful website for keeping up to date with business ethics issues	Institute of Business Ethics	http://www.ibe.org.uk
FTSE4Good Home page	FTSE	http://www.ftse.com/index.jsp
Assessing firms' sustainability performance	Dow Jones Sustainability Indexes	http://www.sustainability-indexes.com/
Another ratings agency for sustainability	Ethical Investment Research service (EIRIS)	http://www.eiris.org/

CHAPTER 2

Ethical issues in business

Chapter at a glance

- Case study 2.16 Economy with the truth when dealing with the tax authorities
- Case study 2.17 Fraudulent corporations – Parmalat, Satyam and Madoff
- Case study 2.18 Lord Black and Hollinger International
- Case study 2.19 BAT and allegations of cigarette smuggling
- Case study 2.20 The retention of dead babies' organs in hospitals
- Case study 2.21 British Airways and Virgin Atlantic
- Case study 2.22 The hospital consultants
- Case study 2.23 Supermarkets' treatment of their supply chains
- Case study 2.24 The *Super Size Me* sales promotion
- Case study 2.25 Sexual harassment
- Case study 2.26 The Firestone Tire recall issue
- Case study 2.27 Huntingdon Life Sciences

Activities and exercises

- Video clip 2.1 Bullies on the job
- Video clip 2.2 Fired for being fat
- Discussion activities 2.1–2.27 Discussion points arising from the case studies
- Typical assignments
- Group activity 2.1
- Recommended further reading
- Useful websites

Learning outcomes

Having read this chapter and completed its associated activities, readers should be able to:

- Describe the range of ethical and moral issues that arise in management, business and organisations.

- Distinguish between ethical, moral and legal wrongdoing and assess the importance of a particular misdeed.

- Analyse the complex consequences and motives that typically attend ethical and moral issues in management, business and organisations.

Introduction

Identifying the range and variety of ethical issues in business and management is the main focus of this chapter. It includes many case studies and so is longer than the other chapters. The case studies are provided because understanding theoretical issues, which are not dealt with until the next chapter, is made easier if the reader first has some concrete examples to which to refer. They also provide resources that will be referred to in other chapters. When reading this chapter it is not necessary to read all of the case studies. Only read those that have taken your interest or where you feel you need to think some more about the general issues raised. To make the chapter more manageable it has been divided into five parts.

- Part one: The map of business ethics issues

- Part two: Encouraging goodness

- Part three: Creating a level playing field, benignness

- Part four: Preventing indifference to others

- Part five: Discouraging badness

Part one: The map of business ethics issues

If the variety of business ethics issues is going to be explained we need a map, and that in turn requires a set of coordinates to explain how the range of issues relate to each other. In practice the field of business ethics has been divided into specialist fields dominated by academics and consultants with backgrounds in different forms of knowledge.

- Corporate social responsibility (CSR) – dominated by social policy experts and environmentalists

- Corporate governance – largely dominated by lawyers and accountants

- Corporate citizenship – lawyers

- Sustainability – environmentalists

- Ethical investment – market analysts

- Employment rights and human rights – human resource management specialists and lawyers

- Fair trade and the regulation of international trade – economists

- Risk management – accountants

- Reputation management – marketing and public relations specialists.

We will not divide the issues between these sub-fields because it prevents the holistic approach that business ethics issues commonly demand. Our map will use two coordinates:

- Degree of morality, or from bad to good.
- Legality, illegality and justice.

Good and bad

The semiotic square

The semiotic square, under the name of the square of opposition (Parsons, 1999), has been used by philosophers since classical times as a tool for logical analysis. It was reinvented in the twentieth century by Greimas (1987) as a method for analysing the structures in stories and narratives. We will use it to identify the structures within stories about business ethics matters. It has been popularised in the UK by Chandler (2001). All semiotic square analyses begin with a key theme and continue by plotting three types of relationships that necessarily stem from it (*see* Figure 2.1). As we are dealing with ethics we will begin the semiotic square with the notion of good.

The first type of relationship is opposition or contrariety. If we begin with good its opposite is bad. Both of these two terms then has its contradiction – the second form of relationship. Contradictions are represented by the diagonal lines in Figure 2.1. In the semiotic square opposites and contradictions are not the same thing. Contradictions occur through particulars and practicalities that negate formal, universal terms. An example is the poet Edna St Vincent Millay's remark 'I love humanity but I hate people'. In other words, in formal, general terms Millay approved of humanity, but her dislike of individuals in all their, sometimes unpleasant, diversity contradicted that belief. If the good is negated we are left with an absence of good, which is not the same as the bad; it may be mere indifference. Indifference however, in its connection with 'bad', represents the third kind of relationship – complementarity – because, as in the quotation famously (but probably incorrectly) attributed to Edmund Burke, 'the only thing necessary for the triumph of evil is for good men to do nothing'. Indifference may permit badness but is not the whole of it. It is, to use the term of the original square of opposition,

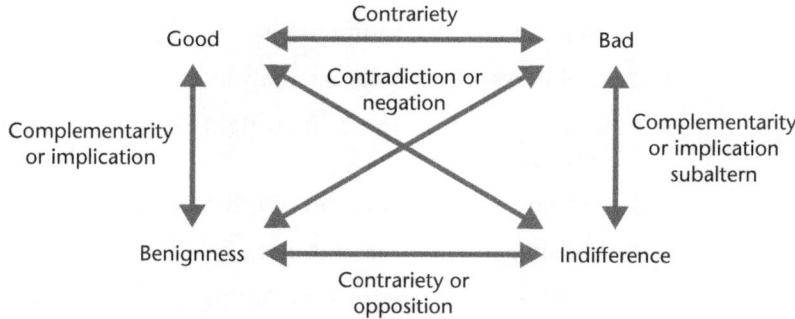

Figure 2.1 A semiotic square analysis of the concept of 'good'

subaltern to it. The most complex relationship is now left, which is the contradiction of 'bad', the negation of the negation. If we absent the bad we are left with benignness (as incorporated in the famous precept 'first of all do no harm'). This is the opposite of indifference. Benignness allows the good to occur and avoids the bad, but on its own does not constitute the good. Benignness may only consist in avoiding the doing of harm and not concern itself with doing good.

The semiotic square identifies four degrees of rightness and wrongness in behaviour, which in order of goodness are:

- the good;
- benignness;
- indifference; and
- the bad.

These four categories, which form a scale from good to bad, are the first dimension in Table 2.1, which will be used to illustrate and explain the range of ethical issues facing businesses, organisations, managers and those affected by them. The scale from good to bad may also be seen from a different perspective. In terms of moral action what is required at the 'good' end of the spectrum is encouragement, or prescription, while at the 'bad' end distraint, or proscription, is necessary. Some writers (Vardy and Grosch, 1999, Taylor, C., 2001) distinguish between the terms ethics and morality to point up this contrast. Ethics is focused on doing good. It deals with defining the good life for humankind. Morality in contrast is a concern for justice, which is about preventing wrongs and making restitution if wrongs are done. Ethics, in these terms, can be thought of as developmental whereas morality is judgmental. In Christian terms the Ten Commandments represent morality but ethics is represented by the Beatitudes. The Ten Commandments specify what it is wrong to do, for example commit murder or adultery (Deuteronomy, 6). The Beatitudes are the virtues that Jesus commended in a sermon to his followers. They include meekness, mercy, pureness of heart and peacemaking (Matthew, 5.7). Just to confuse the issue some writers make the same distinction, between the effort to prevent bad behaviour and the effort to encourage positive behaviour, but use different terms to describe the two ends of the spectrum. Caza et al. (2004: 172) describe a focus on the positive as ethos and virtuousness but use the terms ethics and integrity for the other pole of the spectrum; thereby giving the word ethics an entirely opposite meaning to that ascribed to it by Vardy and Grosch (1999). Despite the confusion of vocabulary the distinction is an important one.

Legal, illegal and just

The second dimension in Table 2.1 is based on the following categories, which can be used to judge the rightness of actions:

- things that it is legal to do but which the law does not require to be done;
- things that must be done or not done according to law; and
- things that are illegal but that may well be justified (i.e. a requirement of justice).

Table 2.1 Illustrative cases of the major issues in business ethics

Ethics — Prescribing the good life → | **Morality** — Proscribing bad actions

	Good Positive action for good or to prevent harm being done		**Benign** Avoiding doing harm, supports the doing of good but takes no positive action to do good		**Indifferent** Ignoring harm done by or to others and disregarding the rights of others		**Bad** Taking action to do harm / Taking no action to prevent harm being done	
	Social development and caring	Social responsibility and supporting	Reciprocity	Fairness	Lying and dishonesty	Cheating and selfishness	Bullying and social irresponsibility	Harming and social and environmental disengagement
Legal, but not a legal obligation	*The Nationwide Foundation.* Case study 2.1, p. 52	*AIDS drugs and patent rights in South Africa.* Case study 2.4, p. 56	*Paying for staff's professional training.* Case study 2.7, p. 62	*Providing new drugs for MS sufferers.* Case study 2.10, p. 67	*BAT, Nottingham University and the honorary professor.* Case study 2.14, p. 78			
Legal	*British Sugar and Sunday trucking.* Case study 2.2, p. 53 *Farepak.* Case study 2.3, p. 54	*Child labour in developing countries.* Case study 2.5, p. 58	*Executive fat cats.* Case study 2.8, p. 63 *The oil companies and the 2000 fuel crisis.* Case study 2.9, p. 65.	*The British railway system: priorities, profits and governance.* Case study 2.12, p. 70	*Economy with the truth when dealing with the tax authorities.* Case study 2.16, p. 80	*The retention of dead babies' organs in hospitals.* Case study 2.20, p. 87.	*The hospital consultants.* Case study 2.22, p. 90. *Supermarkets' treatment of their supply chains.* Case study 2.23, p. 91.	*The Firestone Tire recall issue.* Case study 2.26, p. 95. *The Super size Me sales promotion.* Case study 2.24, p. 93.
Illegal				*Discriminating against employees.* Case study 2.11, p. 68.	*The case of Shell's missing oil barrels.* Case study 2.13, p. 75. *The Lord Browne.* Case study 2.15, p. 78.	*Fraudulent corporations – Parmalat, Satyam and Madoff.* Case study 2.17, p. 81. *Lord Black and Hollinger International.* Case study 2.18, p. 83. *BAT and allegations of cigarette smuggling.* Case study 2.19, p. 85.	*British Airways and Virgin Atlantic.* Case study 2.21, p. 88. *Bullies on the job.* Video clip 2.1, p. 88.	*Sexual harassment.* Case study 2.25, p. 95. *Fired for being fat.* Video clip 2.2, p. 95.
Illegal but just?	*David Shayler and whistleblowing on MI5.* Case study 2.6, p. 58.							*Huntingdon Life Sciences.* Case study 2.27, p. 97.

Legality and illegality are defined by the criminal or civil law. A criminal offence is one so grievous that the state takes action to protect society. Civil law is concerned with the compensation that people who are damaged by others (by tort or breach of contract) may seek. Four combinations of legality and justice are identified.

1 Actions that are good and legal but not a legal obligation

Some actions may raise ethical issues because, although they are good and legal, people do not take them because the law does not require them to do so. The question is whether people, and corporations, should do them even though they are not obliged to do so.

2 Actions that are wrong and illegal

In the next category ethical or moral questions arise because an action is both wrong and illegal. Such actions ought to be straightforward to condemn. However, on issues that many would place in this category, others might argue that the action is neither wrong nor illegal.

3 Actions that are legal but not necessarily just

Another category includes actions that may be legal but are also, arguably, bad. Many of the moral and ethical issues that affect business and management fall into this category. They are a reflection of the big question, raised in Chapter 1, of whether business has moral obligations beyond the proprietary claims of the shareholders. The claim that there are no ethical obligations on a private company other than to obey the law and meet the demands of their shareholders was most famously articulated by Milton Friedman (1970).

Cross reference	Milton Friedman is an economist who is one of the major participants in debates about business ethics. His views are discussed in Chapter 9.

Friedman's position can be criticised from several perspectives. Solomon's (1993) critique is based on the Aristotelian idea of virtue (*see* p. 131). He argued that the belief that business is simply about the financial 'bottom line' is untrue. However, he claimed this misconception has generated many false metaphors for business that hide the truth from people. The idea of cowboy entrepreneurs who are driven by greed and profit and who see themselves as loners in competition with all others is one such metaphor. Rather, he argued, the purpose of business is to provide for the prosperity and happiness of the community. This cannot be achieved if people make a distinction between their business and their personal lives. People are social animals but their social needs are ignored if their business lives are focused on the individualistic pursuit of profit. The problem is intensified if working lives are associated with necessary drudgery in contrast to the pleasure that can be had from personal and social lives. Virtues, according to Aristotle, are formed from the ability to find a sensible mean between such extremes as dreary work and pleasurable personal lives.

The bottom line of the Aristotelian approach to business ethics is that we have to get away from the 'bottom line' thinking and conceive of business as an essential part of the good life, living well, getting along with others, having a sense of self respect, and being part of something that one can be proud of.

(Solomon, 1993: 104)

There is a religious objection to the Friedmanite view of business that can be exemplified from the Roman Catholic position as expressed in the encyclical *Centesimus Annus* (John Paul II, 1991). Humans, it argued, have a capacity for transcendence – the ability to give themselves away to others, and to God. The role of capitalism and profit seeking has to be seen within this context.

The church acknowledges the legitimate role of profit as an indication that a business is functioning well. When a firm makes a profit, this means that productivity factors have been properly employed and the corresponding human needs have been duly satisfied. But profitability is not the only indicator of a firm's condition. It is possible for the financial accounts to be in order and yet for the people, who make up the firm's most valuable asset, to be humiliated and their dignity offended ... In fact the purpose of a business firm is not simply to make a profit, but it is to be found in its very existence as a community of persons who in various ways seek to satisfy their basic needs and who form a particular group at the service of the whole society.

(John Paul II, 1991: §35)

Large companies, such as Shell, are adopting forms of accounting that attempt to balance traditional financial accounting with a concern for environmental sustainability and social justice. This is known as triple bottom-line accounting, which provides output and performance measures in the, potentially contradictory, fields of financial, social and environmental performance. The idea, similar to that of the balanced scorecard, is to make it obvious if financial success is only being achieved at a social and environmental cost. The technical problem of identifying measures that can illuminate a company's performance on environmental quality and social justice is difficult. Comparing the many possible measures against each other and against financial performance is a matter of judgment rather than of accountancy calculation (Elkington, 1999).

Cross reference	The triple bottom-line reporting concept is discussed in more detail in Chapter 9.

The issues that arise from legal, but unethical, managerial and business actions all reflect one or more of these criticisms of the Friedmanite perspective.

4 Actions that are just but illegal

The final category of the dimension is one that will always generate controversy. It concerns actions that may be illegal but are morally or ethically good. It concerns the perennial question of when a law can be said to be immoral and when it is justifiable to break or defy it. Campaigning against a law one disapproves of is acceptable within a democratic system; the ethical problem only emerges when a person moves from campaigning to disobedience. The dilemma is twofold.

The first problem is to define the conditions or circumstances in which it would be proper to defy the law. In a democratic system does a general acceptance of governmental authority imply that it is never acceptable to disobey a particular law? Political obligation does not exhaust moral obligation. This is the case with conscientious objectors, for example, who refuse to take a combatant role in a war. But before refusing to obey a law the person needs to consider carefully the balance between their political and moral obligations (Raphael, 1970: 115–16). If in general the state seeks to achieve justice and the common good, and if the law has been passed with the assent of the majority and according to the rule of law, then there is a presumption in favour of complying with the law. Conversely where laws are arbitrary and the state is not just, the contrary presumption may hold. Lyons (1984: 214) argued that the presumption should be that a legal system does not automatically deserve respect. Respect has to be earned. Greenawalt (1987: 222), however, pointed out that there are no plain rules available to guide people on when it is proper to disobey a law.

The second problem is the nature of the defiance, which can extend from passive civil disobedience through to violent direct action. Gandhi, in his campaigns against British rule in India, practised passive resistance. His belief was that people should disobey immoral laws but should not resist when the forces of the law took action in response. His concept of *Satyagraha* was based on the Hindu Vaishnavite principle of *ahimsa* (or non-violence) and the importance of suffering (Brown, 1972: 6). He believed that passive resistance would eventually cause the authorities, through shame, to right the injustices. This increasingly appears to be the position of the Catholic Church. The Pope wrote, concerning the fall of the Soviet bloc:

> It seemed that the European order resulting from the Second World War and sanctioned by the Yalta Agreement could only be overturned by another war ... Instead it has been overcome by non-violent commitment of people who, while refusing to yield to the force of power, succeeded time after time in finding effective ways of bearing witness to the truth.
>
> (John Paul II, 1991: §23)

At the other extreme some anarchist and other radical groups argue that harming property, and in some cases people, can be justified by the importance of their cause. As will be seen in Case study 2.27 some animal rights activists argue that the evil of vivisection, practised by some pharmaceutical companies, justifies violent action against those companies, their employees and backers.

Deciding when, if ever, violence against an organisation is justified is similar to arguing about which circumstances can make war just. The concept of the just war has concerned theologians since the time of St Augustine. St Thomas Aquinas set down the main tests of a just war in the thirteenth century. They were:

- The war must be declared by a lawful authority (*auctorprincipis*).

- The cause must be just (*justacausa*).

■ Those going to war must intend to advance the good and avoid evil (*recta intentio*) (D'Entreves, 1965: 159).

■ The test of 'proper means' (*debitomodo*), which requires that minimum force be used in accordance with the rules of war and that peace should be established at the end of the conflict, was added to the list later.

An additional requirement, that all other means of resolving the issue should have been exhausted before resort is made to violence, seems to be a twentieth-century addition.

In considering the question of the justness of violent action against organisations, rather than war between states, the first criterion does not apply. If the actions that people condemn as immoral also happen to be legal then the state could not be expected to take action against the company. However, the criterion does alert us to the dangers of validating violent action that is not carried out in the name of some legitimate body. Allowing self-legitimating groups the right to define who is evil and to use force to attack them could lead to the intolerance displayed by fascism. Sometimes civil associations or non-governmental organisations (NGOs), such as Greenpeace, take this legitimating role upon themselves.

The cause of militant animal rights activism can illustrate the impact of the other criteria. Even if the cause, for sake of argument, were just, its narrow focus on destroying an alleged evil, rather than the creation of a peaceful solution, violates the requirement that the violence should serve the establishment of long-term peace. Nor do the movement's tactics meet the requirement for minimum use of force and adherence to the 'rules of war'. Actions have included intimidating 'civilians' such as investors and bankers who had only an indirect connection with vivisection. These also violate one of Greenawalt's (1987: 235) considerations for disobeying a law: that the law objected to and the laws being broken are closely connected. The final criterion has not been met in the case of violent actions in support of animal rights because, in a democratic society there are always non-violent means of protest that can be adopted. Pacifists of course object to the notion of a just war and would claim that, as violence begets violence, its use to stop evil is never justified.

The business world of Russia since the collapse of the Soviet Union provides an example of the issues that surround behaviour that may be illegal but just. Tax evasion (not just legal tax avoidance) is rife among companies in Russia. Corporations evade their tax liabilities by constructing the accounts so as never to show a profit, by transferring the company's income to a third-party organisation a few days before the tax is due, providing loans and insurance cover for employees to reduce the taxable revenue and so on. These practices are clearly illegal, but in a study into Russian executives' views on these practices Meirovich and Reichel (2000) reported that 36 out of 40 interviewees regarded such practices as ethical while the remaining four took the neutral position that the practices were neither ethical nor unethical. Their arguments in support of this view were that:

■ the legal and environmental conditions for businesses in Russia are draconian and businesses would not survive if they paid tax at 90 per cent on all their profit;

■ the government itself is corrupt and inefficient and it merely wastes or embezzles the taxes received, therefore it is good to deny the government the money and instead direct it to society at large by enabling economic growth.

There are, of course, suitable counter arguments such that the illegal behaviour of private organisations further encourages the growth of corrupt institutions. Also the loss of revenue to the government prevents it from meeting the many pressing social needs of the Russian population.

Cross reference	The battle between the Russian government and the oil company Yukos is instructive on this matter. It is described in Chapter 12. Some see it as a proper attempt by the Russian government to make large corporations pay their taxes, which can then be used for the good of society at large. Others see it as an attempt by the Russian government to renationalise a major industry and curtail the growing political power of the oligarchs – businessmen who have become very rich after they bought many state enterprises during the time of privatisation.

The cases

Table 2.1 plots some classic, and some recent issues in business against the two dimensions just discussed. The cases (presented later in this chapter) are located in positions on the grid according to whether, on the face of it, they are examples of goodness, benignness, indifference or badness and whether they represent actions above and beyond legality, conformance to the law, illegality or unjust legality. These grid positions are not indictments of the people and organisations discussed in the cases. The cases are located at certain coordinates in the grid because it forces us to ask questions about legality, morality and ethicality, not because they are definitive illustrations of good or bad behaviour.

Part two: Encouraging goodness

Social development

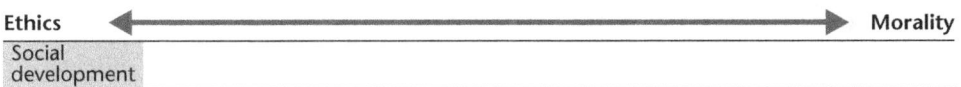

Social development is defined as actions taken by an organisation or company that are designed to improve the social, economic, cultural or environmental conditions of a society. In an earlier period such actions would have been termed philanthropy. Andrew Carnegie, who was a poor Scottish immigrant to the USA in the nineteenth century, provides a classic example. He built an industrial empire and when he sold his business he was thought to be the richest man in the world. He disposed of his wealth philanthropically. A particular interest was the public libraries, of which he founded 2,509 throughout the English-speaking world. He thought libraries important because of the role they could play in helping the poor to participate in what he saw as a meritocratic society in which people could become successful through learning. He also saw libraries as a means by which immigrants such as he could learn about the countries in which they had chosen to live.

Between 1985 and 2000 the generosity ratio of UK companies (the percentage of their philanthropic donations to their pre-tax profits) rose from 0.10 per cent at the start of the period to 0.40 per cent at the end (all statistics are from Moore, 2003). This rate of growth in the ratio was much faster than it had been in the previous decade. There is a Percent Club in the UK, an association of corporations committed to giving 0.5 per cent of their pre-tax profits to good causes, though none of the members has yet achieved this. In the USA where there is a form of social contract, which requires low corporate tax rates to be offset to some degree by higher levels of philanthropy, the average level of donations is five times higher than in the UK, although the generosity ratio is in decline there.

A company's social development activities need not be directly connected with its business activities. However, even if they are not it may be argued that organisations are hoping to improve the standing of their business indirectly as a result of their good works. Motives, corporate and philanthropic, are nearly always mixed and this should not detract from the value of development activities. Other organisations, such as NGOs, have social development as their prime purpose.

Corporate citizenship is sometimes used as an alternative term for social development. British Airways, for example, define its citizenship objective as 'To succeed in partnership with the communities in which we work, not at their expense' (British Airways, 2000: 26). It has provided high-profile sponsorship, in the tourism field, for the Millennium Dome (which probably did little for BA's reputation) and the British Airways London Eye (which probably did much for the company's reputation). BA's (2000) corporate social responsibility report mentions, among other things, charitable work in Kenya and Bangladesh, and its Community Learning Centre at Heathrow. Many of its initiatives stem from voluntary work by its staff and volunteering is an important theme in its activities.

Case study 2.1 reports on an organisation that is seeking to respond to social problems and raises the question of whether philanthropy necessarily must arise from altruism or whether the point is to bring social good from strategic necessity.

Case study 2.1	The Nationwide Foundation

Building societies are mutual organisations. Their customers own them. This reflects their origins as self-help organisations designed to help people buy their own homes. In the 1990s, and into the twenty-first century, there was a move to demutualise building societies. This process involved converting a society into a public limited company (plc). The new plc would give the previous owners (the customers) shares in the new company to compensate them for their loss of ownership. The new owners could either keep or sell these new shares. If they sold them they would make a windfall profit. They would receive a cash sum for a property that had cost them nothing except the constraint of saving with, or accepting a mortgage from, that particular building society. Some building societies wished to remain as such. The pressure to demutualise is more keenly expressed by their customers.

The Nationwide Building Society wished to remain mutual. In 1997 it created the Nationwide Foundation to become the channel for its charitable giving. Everyone who became a member of the society from November 1997 onward also became a member of the foundation and agreed to assign to the foundation their rights to any future conversion payments. This meant that should the society demutualise or be taken over in the future then any connected payment of any sort, which would otherwise be received by the society members, would be passed to the foundation to create a fund for charitable giving. Bluntly, there would be no windfall payments. A number of the society's members who had been members since before 1997 also agreed to become members of the foundation.

None of the building societies that became banks by demutualising survived the financial collapse of 2007–2008. They were either obliged to merge with other banks or become part nationalised. The Nationwide, however, survived and continued as a building society and its Foundation supports schemes throughout the UK using money donated by the society, its staff and its members. Its strategy for 2009–2012 focuses on addressing the housing and financial capability problems of the survivors of domestic abuse and disadvantaged elderly people.

(Source for further information: www.nationwidefoundation.org.uk)

Discussion activity 2.1

Does the use of the fund as a means of meeting the society's own purpose, of remaining a mutual institution, detract from the worth of its activities?

Case study 2.2 is about a company that was accused of disengaging from the largely rural community within which it operated. Although its plans were legal it drew back from implementing them because people objected to the disruption they would cause to the pattern of weekend life in East Anglian villages.

Case study 2.2   **British Sugar and Sunday trucking**

East Anglia is sugar beet territory. There is an annual sugar beet harvest that lasts for five months when the crop has to be taken to British Sugar's factories for processing. For many years there had been an agreement between British Sugar and the National Farmers Union (NFU) that deliveries would take place for five-and-a-half days each week with no lorries on Saturday afternoons or Sundays. Most residents in the villages through which the large and heavy beet lorries rumble accept the beet harvest as part of country life. In 2000 British Sugar in an attempt to diminish the queues of lorries that formed during the mornings at the factories, decided to switch to seven-day-a-week deliveries and it came to an agreement with the NFU to do so. There was immediate outcry. As a resident in one of the affected villages said, 'We do appreciate that they have a job to do. The noise of these lorries is quite considerable. All we want is for them to leave us in peace for one day of the week.' The hauliers who delivered the beet met at Peterborough and came out against seven-day deliveries. As one of them said, 'Imagine big sugar beet lorries driving past country churches on a Sunday morning while people are trying to worship. It simply won't work – we won't do it.' The campaign against the additional deliveries carried on and within a few weeks British Sugar announced that it was suspending its agreement with the NFU to deliver beet for seven days each week.

(Sources: Moore, 2001; Bradley, 2000; Pollitt and Ashworth, 2000)

Discussion activity 2.2

Was British Sugar right to forgo the efficiency and cost benefits that could have been gained from a seven-day working week?

The next case study considers whether a bank should have been more generous in the name of social responsibility.

Case study 2.3   Farepak

Farepak was a part of the savings economy that people had forgotten about; but which was very important to the many people on low incomes or benefits for whom it was a way of saving for Christmas. It began as a Christmas Club in a butcher's shop in 1969. By 2007 it was part of the European Home Retail (EHR) group. Customers made monthly or weekly cash payments to self-employed agents, who were often their relatives as well as being savers within the scheme themselves. In return before Christmas the customers received hampers and vouchers to spend in high-street stores. By 2006 the EHR group was in financial difficulty. Money that Farepak customers had paid in was not protected or ring fenced as would have been the case with deposits in banks or other regulated institutions. Instead the money went into EHR's accounts, from where it was used to offset the company's overdraft with HBOS (Halifax/Bank of Scotland). Eventually in October 2006 HBOS refused to extend the overdraft and EHR called in the administrators. As Farepak's funds had been drained away its 150,000 customers looked as if they would receive as little as 4p in the pound when the company was wound up; and, of course, there were no Christmas hampers or presents. There was much argument over who was to blame. The Farepak management said it was HBOS for refusing to accept rescue plans and extend the overdraft. Others blamed HBOS for insisting that EHR use customers' savings to pay off the overdraft, even though this was perfectly legal. Some commentators pointed out that savings clubs were one part of the financial industry that was unregulated. The government did not see it as their job to protect club customers' savings; although a year later when Northern Rock collapsed it moved swiftly to protect that bank's customers' deposits. The MP Frank Field claimed that HBOS had a 'pivotal role' in the collapse of Farepak. He argued that the bank had been acting as a 'shadow director' and therefore bore responsibility; HBOS argued that they were 'bankers to EHR, we did not run the company'. A public fund was opened to provide some compensation to those who had lost their savings. By the end of November 2006 £6m had been saved by the administrators. As savers had lost £40m they would receive about 15p in the pound from this fund. HBOS donated £2m to the fund without admitting liability and said it would pay no more. One Scottish MEP demanded that other banks should donate to the fund. One big bank, the Royal Bank of Scotland said it would not.

However, five years later the claims had still not been settled and in 2011 it was reported that there was a fund of £5.53m to pay compensation to customers but the cost of winding up the company had been greater at £8.2m.

(*Sources*: BBC News Online, 2006a; Warwick-Ching, 2007; Bolger, 2006)

Discussion activity 2.3

Did the banking sector generally, and the banks in particular, have a responsibility for this unregulated savings industry? Should they have paid more into the Farepak compensation fund? Does the fact that Farepak's customers were often from the poorest groups of society make a difference?

Social responsibility

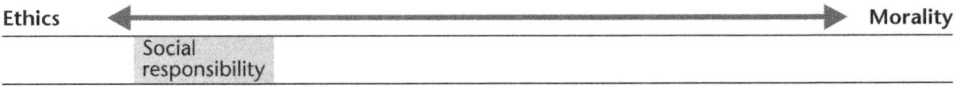

Social responsibility, in the way the term is used in this chapter, covers a narrower canvas than social development. It can be defined as conducting the business of an organisation in a manner that meets high social and environmental standards. It differs from social development in not requiring organisations to do good works beyond the commercial purposes of the organisation. Also social responsibility affects fewer arenas than social development. Social responsibility excludes the social and cultural good works that are appropriate to social development. Social responsibility is important to organisations 'not least because of the devastating impact that even isolated acts of wrong doing can have on an organisation's reputation among its stakeholders' (Arthur Andersen and London Business School, 1999). Many large companies report their performance as socially responsible organisations; for an example see British Petroleum's social and environmental report (BP, 2001).

The nature of a socially responsible approach to redundancy illustrates some of the factors that distinguish social responsibility from social development. It is possible to argue that redundancies, especially on a large scale, are morally wrong because they harm individuals, families and communities. The counter argument is that the welfare of families and communities is not the concern of a company or organisation. Another possible defence is that the loss of some jobs protects the jobs and livelihoods of many more. Social responsibility would suggest a middle position. It would argue that redundancy may be justified but that a responsible organisation will take trouble to help those affected. This might involve using outsourcing consultants to provide counselling and career advice to those losing their jobs. It could involve setting up agencies or funds to encourage the introduction of new businesses in affected localities, or helping those made redundant to start their own companies. Social responsibility is an obligation to minimise the collateral harm caused by the organisation's actions and decisions.

Case study 2.4 provides an example of assertive public and governmental opinion, which judged companies' protection of their patent rights as socially irresponsible. The pressure of global media scrutiny became such that the threat to the companies' reputations became greater than the economic loss caused by the challenge to their patents.

AIDS drugs and patent rights in South Africa

There is an epidemic of AIDS in southern Africa. There is therefore a great need for drugs (anti-retro-viral – AVR) with which to treat the disease. One of the drugs, Ciprofloxican, cost South Africa's public health sector 52p for each pill when bought from the company that had developed it and that held the patent. A generic version of the drug could be imported from India for 4p a pill. The cost of these drugs was a heavy burden on the health service and the South African government proposed a new law that would allow the cheaper generic drug to be imported. The world's largest pharmaceutical companies opened a lawsuit against the South African government to claim that their property and patent rights were thereby put at risk. However, in May 2001, as the case was about to commence in the South African High Court, the pharmaceutical companies withdrew the claim.

The following article from the *Financial Times*, which includes an interview with the chief executive of one of the major pharmaceutical companies, rehearses the arguments.

FT Very sick people need drugs. The world's largest pharmaceutical companies charge plenty for them but they channel that money into research to find new medicines. The companies, now suffering an unprecedented onslaught over the prices they charge and lack of access to their medicines, want to refocus public attention on what they see as the main issue. 'You can kill the golden goose', says Hank McKinnell, chief executive of Pfizer, of demands for lower prices. 'You'll eat well today but the cupboard will be bare in future.'

Mr McKinnell is a staunch defender of the prices that his company, the world's largest drugs group, charges. He is also very aware that a humanitarian and economic disaster is unfolding in Africa, where 27m Africans are now HIV-positive and only a fraction of them have access to or can afford even deeply discounted western AIDS medicines. But in an interview he points out that AIDS was first identified by medical researchers in the early 1980s. By 1987, he says, there was one treatment. Now, 64 AIDS drugs are available and more than 100 are in development. 'What was the right thing to do in 1981?' asks Mr McKinnell. 'Say the prices are too high and take away the incentives for the research? That doesn't help patients or their families.'

But many believe this is an argument the drugs industry will never win. Companies are supplying AIDS drugs in Africa at up to 90 per cent discounts but they face demands for larger cuts. This is on the grounds that the products are still unaffordable for almost all HIV-positive patients or their governments. Meanwhile, companies in countries such as India and Thailand are making cheap, often illegal, copies of western drugs and promising to save thousands of lives at a fraction of the cost. And in the US there is speculation that it will not be long before patients lose patience and refuse to pay up to 10 times the price for treatments. Whichever way they turn, Mr McKinnell and his peers will be accused of placing a different value on the lives of people on different continents.

Pfizer's chief executive concedes the industry appears to have lost its way trying to formulate a response to the unprecedented wave of bad publicity. Changing that is one of his new responsibilities. This month he became chairman of the Pharmaceutical Research and Manufacturers of America, the industry's most powerful lobby group. Drugs companies have been caught off-guard by the sheer size of the attack. As well as being criticised for their drugs pricing policy in sub-Saharan Africa, they have endured closer scrutiny of pricing and patent regimes worldwide.

Federal and state regulators in the US have been investigating abuses of marketing to physicians and consumers. Influential Washington politicians have proposed revisions to US patent law that make it easier for cheap copies of drugs to come on the market. Meanwhile, Mr McKinnell says, Indian companies have been lobbying the World Trade Organisation to preserve their ability to break patent laws being ushered in as part of the WTO's Agreement on Trade Related Intellectual Property. He has little sympathy: 'The Indian companies have been making billions of dollars stealing our technology and selling it, not only in India but any place around the world they can get away with it.'

He believes the pharmaceutical industry has convinced people it genuinely wants to help, particularly in Africa. Last week, in a high-profile dispute, 39 pharmaceutical companies abandoned their case against the South African government in which they had said their patent rights were in danger. Bad publicity was an important factor behind the decision to drop the case and the companies have escaped a disastrous legal situation. Mr McKinnell says the companies have also been increasing their efforts to work with aid agencies, non-governmental organisations and local governments to improve distribution.

'Unfortunately, we haven't expanded them rapidly enough', he says. 'But there is now a realisation that if we don't provide access, we're going to stay as part of the problem ... I think we've been pretty successful in becoming part of the solution.'

But prices are still too high in countries where any price is unaffordable. The answer, says Mr McKinnell, is to forge partnerships with agencies and governments to bring in more resources. 'If the sole problem is the high price of drugs, you give up. But the industry has been smart enough to take that off the table. When the drug is free or at cost, now what's the problem? It's national will, it's distribution, and it's medical treatment.' In other words, drugs companies have knocked 90 per cent off the price but it is up to someone else to find the rest and to help deliver the drugs.

(*Sources*: Inside Track: Big pharma and the golden goose, *The Financial Times,* 26 April 2001 (Michaels, A.), Copyright © The Financial Times Ltd.; McGreal, 2001; Clark and Borger, 2001)

The main pharmaceutical companies began to cut their prices for ARV drugs in developing countries. Glaxo SmithKline reduced the price of its main drug three times in 2003. The large companies also began to come to understandings with the generic drug producers in India and began to license generic producers in South Africa (Dyer, 2003a). In some cases regulatory bodies such as the South African Competition Commission argued that the international companies were breaking competition rules by over-charging and threatened to force the companies to grant generic licenses to local producers (Dyer, 2003b). Much of the movement on the issue was attributed to pressure from institutional investors, who were worried that the damage being done to the reputation of the pharmaceutical industry might reduce its ability to charge premium prices in industrialised countries. The focus of the debate shifted more to the ability and commitment of governments in some African countries to take action against AIDS. It took the South African Government, for example, a long time to agree to a programme to provide free ARVs and in 2004 there were criticisms that the roll-out of the programme was being delayed (DegliInnocenti and Reed, 2004).

New drugs, known as 'second line' treatments, have emerged since the pharmaceutical companies started providing AVRs to Africa at not-for-profit prices. The supply of these new drugs has again been hampered by patent problems; a situation exacerbated because India has tightened up on its patent laws and so the supply of generic new drugs from Indian companies is restricted. However, several African countries are now establishing their own pharmaceutical companies in an attempt to reduce their reliance on international pharmaceutical companies (BBC News Online, 2006b).

Discussion activity 2.4

What are the arguments for saying that knowledge that is medically beneficial to humanity should not be private property?

Case study 2.5 raises similar issues to those discussed in Case study 2.3 as it reviews why a company acted more responsibly than was required by law.

Case study 2.5 Child labour in developing countries

The use of child labour by multinational companies in their factories in the Third World to produce cheaply the products they sell in western markets became an international issue in the 1990s and the first decade of the new millennium. The United Nations' Convention on the Rights of the Child and the International Labour Organisation's Declaration of Fundamental Principles and Rights at Work (United Nations, 1989) condemn the use of child labour. NIKE in particular has been the subject of public campaigns against its labour practices in South East Asia.

Although the issue has been high on the agenda for many years problems still occasionally emerge. In 2007 a 10-year-old boy was filmed in India by *The Observer* newspaper making clothes for the fashion chain Gap. The newspaper was told that the boy had been sold to the factory owner by his family in payment of a debt; that he had worked without pay for four months and would not be allowed to leave the job until his family's debt had been paid off. Gap has a code of Vendor Conduct (Gap Inc., 2007), which states in relation to child labour, that factories which supply goods for Gap:

■ will employ only workers who meet the applicable minimum legal age requirement or are at least 14 years old, whichever is greater; and

■ must maintain official records that verify the workers' dates of birth.

The code also encourages factories to provide apprenticeships and educational programmes for its younger workers. Once the company became aware of the problem it investigated and discovered that the vendor had subcontracted the production of one particular garment to an unauthorised subcontractor (contrary to the Vendor Code). The order for the garment, a smock blouse, was withdrawn and the product was withdrawn from sale and destroyed. The company also said that it would hold meetings with its suppliers in Asia to reinforce its policies (BBC News Online, 2007a).

Discussion activity 2.5

What action do you think companies should take when they find their suppliers use child labour contrary to their company policy? Why do you think Gap destroyed the garments made by the unofficial subcontractor?

The next case introduces a new aspect of social responsibility, which considers when it is proper for a person to break their duty of confidentiality to their employer if they know that their employer is acting irresponsibly.

Cross reference   This issue, also known as whistleblowing, is discussed in detail in Chapter 7.

Case study 2.6   **David Shayler and whistleblowing on MI5**

David Shayler is an ex-employee of MI5. He alleged that the service had plotted to kill the President of Libya. Having made the allegation he fled to France where attempts by the British government to extradite him were unsuccessful. However, he decided to return to Britain where he was arrested and charged. As a member of MI5 he had signed the Official Secrets Act of 1920, which banned him from revealing official secrets for life. The Public Interest Disclosure Act (*see* p. 285), which gives some limited protection to whistleblowers, does not apply to the security services. Shayler's intention was to use the Human Rights Act 1998, which incorporated the European Convention on Human Rights into English law, in his defence. The Act provides a right to freedom of expression and if a court makes a declaration of incompatibility between the Human Rights Act and a particular piece of legislation, such as the Official Secrets Act, the government would have to consider amending the law. Some of the issues are raised in the following leading article from the *Financial Times*.

FT Here's a paradox for Britain's spymasters. Three years ago, David Shayler, the former secret agent, fled to Paris after claiming that the security service had tried to kill President Muammar Gadaffi of Libya. Robin Cook, the foreign secretary, said the allegation was 'pure fantasy'. Yesterday on his return to Britain, Mr Shayler was arrested. But he would only be guilty in relation to the Gadaffi affair under the Official Secrets Act if what he said about his former employment was fact, not fiction.

The authorities seem to have avoided this difficulty by charging him with unauthorised disclosure related to his other allegations of mess-ups and impropriety in the service. Even so, the case shows up a huge problem for spymasters in dealing with former agents who talk too much. In James Bond's world, the solution was easy – perhaps something nasty with an exploding cigar, or a shark.

Outside spy fiction, the authorities face harder options. They may dismiss mud-slinging agents as mercenary fantasists. But then some of the mud may stick. If the authorities prosecute the agent for a serious disclosure, they risk giving credence to his allegations. If they bring charges for a technical breach, they look heavy handed. If they mount a full investigation into the agent's allegations, they risk further embarrassing revelations – even if the allegations prove false. If true, the agent faces huge difficulties in proving them in court.

Clearly the secret services must be allowed to keep their secrets. But such secrecy is only tenable in peaceful democracies if the agencies are seen to act within the law and the principles of civil liberty. This requires a good deal more openness than they have shown in recent decades – and more vigorous scrutiny by the parliamentary committee set up to watch over them 11 years ago.

In the present case, the authorities must show that they have not done a shabby deal by promising to soft-pedal charges in exchange for silence. If Mr Shayler has revealed important secrets – as the authorities appear to believe – he must be prosecuted vigorously, however embarrassing his defence might prove.

▶

Equally, the police, who are now investigating his charges against the service, must find ways to demonstrate that they are doing the job properly. Mr Shayler's accusations may be found eventually to be insubstantial or wildly exaggerated. But if the authorities take Mr Shayler seriously enough to prosecute him, there must be a presumption that his allegations against the service deserve, at the least, serious investigation.

(*Source*: Leader: Spy Trap, *The Financial Times*, 22 August 2000, Copyright © The Financial Times Ltd.)

Shayler appeared in Court in August 2002 and was charged with passing on information without the consent of his employers. He pleaded not guilty but was found guilty and sentenced to six months in prison. He appealed on the grounds that he was acting in the public interest but he was denied this defence by the Court of Appeal and by the House of Lords.

Discussion activity 2.6

Was David Shayler's whistleblowing justified?

Were the British authorities acting in a socially responsible way in choosing the offence David Shayler was charged with?

Part three: Creating a level playing field, benignness

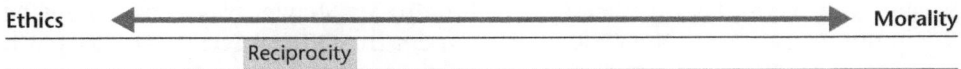

Ethics ⟵⟶ Morality

Reciprocity

Reciprocity

If the avoidance of doing good and behaving well is irresponsibility, then selfishness is doing harm through a pursuit of self-interest. This section discusses human beings' inclinations to act either selfishly or altruistically. The assumption that selfishness is the norm in the behaviour of human beings may be unsafe. Research into the evolution of insects and animals suggests that altruism, sacrificing oneself to benefit others, may be the result of evolutionary selection. Reciprocity is perhaps a more appropriate term than altruism because such behaviour anticipates a future benefit for the individual's near relatives, if not for the individual. One form of reciprocity is called kin selection. It accounts for the altruistic behaviours found among ants, bees and wasps. Individuals in these species, it is suggested, forgo their own opportunity to breed in order to support the queen, their sister, in rearing large numbers of offspring. By doing this they will increase the total number of offspring that are born bearing genes similar to their own. This characteristic is particularly noticeable among bees, ants and wasps because their odd genetic system means that they are more closely related to their sisters than they are to their offspring. Reciprocity can also be a successful evolutionary allele (genetic trait) in animal evolution. Some writers, such as Dugatkin (2000), have argued, controversially, that studies of altruism in animals and insects can provide clues for improving human cooperation. Of course, this behaviour will only develop if in the long run 'cheats' (individuals who accept but do not return the favour) are 'punished'. This issue is most often studied through the medium of a game theory scenario known as the Prisoners' Dilemma.

DEFINITION

The **Prisoners' Dilemma** involves two imaginary prisoners who have jointly committed a murder. They have been arrested by the police and put in separate cells. They have not been able to talk to each other since the murder and the police make sure that they cannot communicate in the police station. The police have inadequate information to charge them with murder but they could charge both of them with possessing illegal weapons. The two prisoners are interrogated separately. They have a choice of two options, to confess or to keep silence. The consequences of each option, in terms of number of years in gaol, are shown in the pay-off figure (Figure 2.2).

If both prisoners confess they will each receive the normal sentence for murder of six years' imprisonment. If they both keep silent the police have insufficient evidence and they will be charged for the weapons offence for which the sentence is two years in prison each. This is the best option for both of them. However, if one confesses after doing a deal with the police, he will only get one year in prison, while the one who keeps silent will have the book thrown at him and will receive the maximum penalty of 10 years. Neither prisoner knows what the other will do because they cannot communicate. If each prisoner feels they can trust the other then neither will confess and both will receive a relatively light tariff of two years' prison each. However, if one keeps silent, but the other 'cheats' and confesses, the silent one will receive a harsh 10 years. If a prisoner feels he cannot trust the other then the best bet is to confess. The worst that can happen is six years in prison but the worst that can happen if he does not confess is 10 years. This is the Prisoners' Dilemma, whether they can trust each other enough to achieve the best outcome for both of them by both not confessing.

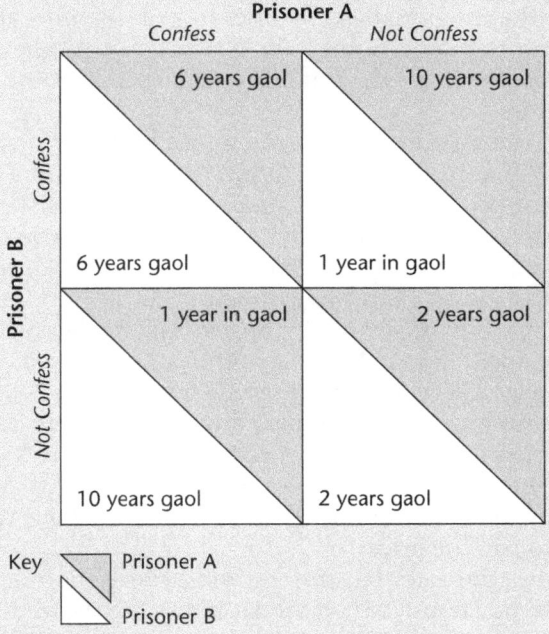

Figure 2.2 Pay-off table

The Prisoners' Dilemma can only be avoided if the players exist in a continuing community in which cheats are punished. In these circumstances the players have to continue to meet, which enables trust to develop. Selfishness will occur, on this analysis, where there is a lack of trust or where people do not see themselves as being in the same community as those whom they harm by their selfishness.

These issues can be seen in the following case studies. In Case study 2.7 altruism was present because all the players saw themselves as part of the same community and there were opportunities for the altruism to be reciprocated. But even in this situation the person explaining the situation found it hard to decide whether the recipients were trustworthy and who was likely to reciprocate his altruism.

Case study 2.7	**Paying for staff's professional training**

Extract from an interview with a partner in an accounting firm responsible for the professional training of new staff

Well, treating people properly and fairly is always an interesting one; it is a very subjective area. In my role as training partner there are undoubtedly incidents every time anybody doesn't pass an exam; we have to decide what to do about it. Whether to terminate their contract, or whether to pay for absolutely everything. There is a whole spectrum of solutions. Yes, and there is never, I don't think, a right or wrong answer. Well, we had a situation a few weeks ago where we had two students, sat the same exams, got very similar results, both marginally failed.

One of them had cruised through the year, not really done enough, but was a bright lad. The other, a girl, had sweated blood throughout the year and still wasn't quite good enough. Then you get a situation where, some people would think, well, Claire deserves another chance because she worked so hard, some people think you should treat Chris better, he is the brighter one, he will be the more marketable one, he will be more use to us. Some people think you should treat them the same. Some people think that people should be allowed to keep sitting exams at our expense for as long as it takes. Some people think we should just terminate people's contracts for failure.

So, I suppose, I take a business decision basically, rather than a moral judgment when anyone fails. I would say that in practically no instance would more than a small minority agree with my decision, some people think they should be treated harsher, some people think they should be treated more leniently. I gave them both a week's study leave and I paid for their exams, so it gave them both another week and a half to find out of their holiday and about £200 to find for the course. It was a close call, it was a difficult call.

But what you have to do as well is consider the impact on the other students, what message it sends to them. I will have a dilemma within the next year, because I have only been training partner for just over a year. The exam results here; I don't believe they are good enough. I don't think they have been good enough basically because there has been tolerance of failure in the past and I have said repeatedly that in certain circumstances I will terminate people's contracts for failing. That has not happened here for about five years. Sooner or later I am going to have to do it, otherwise people won't believe me. I will only have to do it once. The difficulty is, one person has got to pay the price.

Everyone knows the rules but no one will believe the rules. Now the brighter one of those two, the one who had cruised, the Monday when I spoke to them about it, I was in a foul mood.

I didn't terminate his contract – the only reason I didn't – I was sorely tempted to, because (a) I think he deserved it and (b) it would have made an example of him – the reason I didn't was because I was in a bad mood and I thought, there is a risk that I could let my mood take my decision. Had I been in a good mood, I think I would have terminated his contract.

(*Source*: Research interview conducted by the authors)

Discussion activity 2.7

Why do you think the training partner acted altruistically when, by not supporting the trainees, he might have better met the (selfish) needs of the firm?

In Case study 2.8 it is clear that highly paid executives do not feel they need to act altruistically towards the generality of employees because they see themselves as belonging to a small elite group of world-class CEOs. This is the market argument, which holds that executives are entitled to whatever salary they can command on the international market. This argument only holds good of course if the market is an open and fair one. The second argument in support of high executive rewards is that it can be justified if they secure good performance and results for the organisation. Researchers from two Business Schools (Erturk et al., 2004 cited in Caulkin, 2004) studied chief executive pay in a sample of FTSE 100 companies. They reported that between 1978/9 and 2002/3 CEO pay in those companies rose by 536.9 per cent but net profits only increased by 118.9 per cent. At the same time the differential in remuneration between the CEOs and average employees rose. CEOs now earn on average 50 times as much as ordinary employees but 20 years ago the figure was only nine times average pay. Case study 2.8 was written at a time when the question of executive pay had long been a matter of public concern and debate.

Case study 2.8   Executive fat cats and bankers' bonuses

The question of whether corporate executives are being paid too much, which has always been referred to as the 'fat cat' issue, has been a topic of debate since the late 1990s (Skapinker, 2001). It became an even more explosive topic when bankers seemed to retain their large bonuses after the financial collapse of 2007–8.

In 2006 The Trades Union Council (TUC) in the UK reported that from 2000 to 2006 the remuneration of directors of FTSE 100 companies rose by 105 percentage points above the rate of inflation. The earnings of other employees rose by only 6 percentage points (Taylor, 2006). In 2011 the median pay of the CEO of these companies had increased to £3.5m when most of their employees had received either no, or only very small pay increases. The gap between the median pay of the average worker and their top managers has been increasing and continues to increase. Top managers also have greater opportunities than normal employees for avoiding paying tax on their incomes. They can become non-domiciled (a non-dom), even though working in the

UK, for tax purposes and thereby reducing liability for UK tax. In 2012 it was reported that some top public sector managers were having their salaries paid into private companies that they owned, thereby paying the lower rate corporation tax on their income rather than the higher rate income tax.

Such practices highlight the first ethical concern with high executive pay. It can be argued that too big a gap between the pay of the average employee and that of the top managers is unfair. Directors and executive are not the owners of a company (though as individuals they may well hold shares in the company) and like all other employees are servants of the company. This essential equality would mean that if the company can afford to increase earnings then it would be fair for all grades of employees to benefit in the same proportion. Large discrepancies between top and median pay can also be seen as unethical because they diminish any sense of community and common purpose within the organisation. Others would argue that this is just envy and that people should not worry about the rich getting richer. The more common argument is that as most companies operate in a global market they have to constrain average salaries and increase top salaries. The claim is that there is a limited pool of executive talent that they have to compete for in the world market and if top remuneration is not offered companies will not obtain the leadership they need.

A further ethical consideration is whether the pay increases are actually justified, or not, by the performance of the office holder or the organisation they are managing. Following the financial and banking crisis of 2007–8 the level of banker's bonuses did fall but soon began to return to previous levels (see Table 2.2) even though the banks were not often performing well and the rest of the economy was still coping with the recession that the banks had triggered. In 2011, under Project Merlin, the British Treasury reached an agreement with four of the largest UK banks that the size of the annual bonus pot should fall. The Office of National Statistics reported that in 2010–11 the financial and insurance sector (a broader sample that that reported on in Table 2.2) paid out £14bn in bonuses, unchanged from the year before (Groom, 2011).

Table 2.2   **City bank bonuses 2001–9 and projections for 2010–12 (£m.)**

2001	2002	2003	2004	2005	2006	2007	2008	2009	2010	2011	2012
3.921	3,329	4,893	5,695	7,130	10,059	10,241	4,008	6.012	6,654	7,098	7,546

(*Source*: CEBR, 2009)

Another trend is to pay executives a bonus for completing a one-off transaction, such as an acquisition, or as a retention payment to keep them with a company whilst it goes through a major change. In 2007 Tesco announced plans to give its chief executive 2.5m in shares for the success of its American 'Fresh & Easy' chain. Many investors were concerned that a chief executive should receive a bonus for one part of the business when he was already remunerated for running the whole business. There was a protest vote against the package at the AGM but the vote was not binding (Rigby, 2007). In March 2008 there were reports that sales at the Fresh & Easy stores were falling short of expectations. Tesco denied the reports (Birchall and Braithwaite, 2008). A particular issue arises when an executive achieves a target in one year but the bonus for their success is paid in arrears; and it is actually distributed in a subsequent year when the company's performance is poor. A sensible senior executive always ensures that they have a good severance deal included in their contract should they fail and the company wishes to replace them quickly (Donkin, 2007).

Discussion activity 2.8

Are chief executives inclined to selfishness? If they are, is that a problem?

Is the high pay of top ranking professional footballers more morally acceptable than that of CEOs and bankers? If so, why?

Does it matter if the gap between top incomes and average incomes widens if everyone is earning more?

Case study 2.9 raises questions about whether there is an obligation on companies to avoid selfishness in times of national crisis.

Case study 2.9	**The oil companies and the 2000 fuel crisis**

The UK experienced an oil crisis in July 2000. A combination of self-employed lorry drivers, owners of small haulage companies and farmers objected to the high price of petrol (the bulk of the price of which in the UK is determined by the excise duty). In a Poujadist protest they used their mobile phones to create a network of supporters, who blockaded the country's oil storage depots and led slow-moving convoys up and down motorways causing traffic queues. Any modern country depends on the internal combustion engine and the shortage of fuel caused by the action soon threatened chaos. The National Health Service was put on red alert and businesses could not carry out their normal business. There were fears that food would not be delivered to the supermarkets.

The government was caught unawares. The Prime Minister declared that the situation would be back to normal within 24 hours; but it was not. It looked for scapegoats and blamed the international oil companies for selfishness. The government argued that the oil companies should take strong action to break the blockades and ensure that oil was delivered to the nation's petrol station forecourts. The oil companies argued that it was not their responsibility to take risks with the safety of their employees. They would not order their drivers to drive through the pickets if there was a danger that they might be hurt. The oil companies were suspected by some politicians of secretly agreeing with the protestors. It was reported that there was a 'chummy camaraderie' between the protestors blockading a refinery and the management within it; even to the extent that the protestors were served tea and bacon sandwiches from the canteen within the refinery (Weaver, 2000). The oil companies claimed to make only small profits of a penny a litre on retailing petrol, and if the protest led to a reduction in excise duties it could only be of benefit to the industry. Oil transport was outsourced to small independent companies and self-employed drivers (some of whom had been sacked by the companies only to be re-employed as independents for less pay) who did have real complaints about the cost of the diesel that fuelled their lorries. The oil companies had little leverage to force these drivers to break the blockade. The view of the *Observer* (2000) leader writer was that the oil companies were too concerned with maximising their shareholders' returns by carrying low contingency stocks of oil and using a just-in-time logistics system, which meant there was no buffer in the case of a crisis. There was a view that the companies owed an obligation to the wider community when they traded in a material that was so vital to the functioning of society.

▶

The blockade melted away as quickly as it had formed as people began panic buying at the supermarkets. The Prime Minister said he would not be forced into cutting the duty on fuel.

There was a minor replay of this issue in April 2008 when rising world oil prices and a strike at an oil refinery caused some truck drivers to protest in Whitehall about increasing fuel prices. Again in 2012 tanker drivers voted to go on strike for better pay and conditions. The government responded by saying that it was training soldiers so that they could take over fuel deliveries if the strike went ahead.

DEFINITIONS

Poujadism is a set of political beliefs named after Pierre Poujade, a small-town shopkeeper in France in the 1950s. It objects to state interference such as taxation, the investigation of tax evasion and any regulation of small businesses. It also opposes big corporations and large-scale labour organisation.

Discussion activity 2.9

Do the oil companies have a moral obligation to maintain fuel supplies in a country?

Fairness

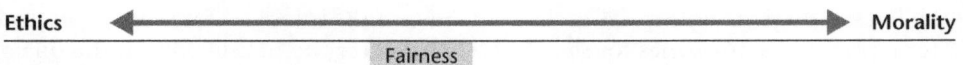

Fairness concerns the proportions in which resources are distributed between people or causes. The resources can be money, respect or any possession that a community can allocate among its members. Aristotle expressed the central concern, about the appropriateness of the proportions, in a system of distributive justice. He saw it as a matter of algebra in which there are at least four terms: two persons and two shares. A just distribution is one in which the ratio between the first person and the first share is equal to the ratio between the second person and the second share. If Fred is twice as worthy as Jane then Jane's portion should be half of Fred's. In this case the two ratios will be the same. The arithmetic is fine but the question is how the two people involved are to be assessed. Aristotle said it should be done by assessing their merit. But he admitted that people define merit in different ways.

> People of democratic sympathies measure degrees of merit by degrees of freedom, oligarchs by degrees of wealth, others judge by good birth, those who believe in the rule of the 'best' go by moral and intellectual qualifications.

(Aristotle, 1976: 146)

This does not exhaust the possibilities. Marx measured it according to need, 'From each according to his ability, to each according to his needs' (in Marx and Engels, 1962: 24). Others might measure merit by personhood and insist that, since all are equal in this particular aspect, then everyone should receive equal shares.

The debates under the ethical heading of fairness concern the appropriate measure of a person's merit and the fairness of the ratios between one person's merit and share and those of others. The case studies in this section give examples of these debates. Case study 2.10 focuses on need, 2.11 on personhood and 2.12 contrasts the property rights of shareholders with the needs of customers.

| Case study 2.10 | **Providing new drugs on the NHS to people with multiple sclerosis** |

Multiple sclerosis is a debilitating and incurable disease. A new drug, with the generic name of beta interferon, has been shown to alleviate the effects of the disease but it costs £10,000 per patient per year. The National Institute for Clinical Excellence (NICE) in the UK investigated the drug to see whether, on clinical and economic grounds, it should be made freely available on the NHS. The belief of those who suffer from the disease, and of those who support them through membership of lobby groups, is that it would be unfair to deny this drug to sufferers. The following article from the *Financial Times* identifies some of the politics and anger that surround the issue.

FT The National Institute for Clinical Excellence has put off a decision on the use of beta-interferon, the drug for multiple sclerosis sufferers, until at least July next year. The decision to delay has been taken to allow a publicly available economic model of the costs and benefits of the drug to be built. The delay brought a furious reaction from the Multiple Sclerosis Society that accused the institute of putting back the decision to ensure that it came after the likely date of the general election. Peter Cardy, the society's chief executive, described the decision to delay as 'astonishing' and 'breathtaking bungling' given that beta-interferon and glatiramer, another MS drug, have been reviewed by the institute for almost a year.

Mike Wallace, a former managing director of Schering, which manufacturers beta-interferon, said: 'I find it appalling. You have to wonder what these guys are playing at. I feel desperately sorry for the people with MS who have had their hopes raised and dashed and raised and dashed again by the NICE process.'

The institute initially judged that MS drugs were not cost effective and should be supplied only to patients already receiving them. Appeals led to that decision being reconsidered, but the institute is unhappy with the economic models that Schering and Biogen have supplied. The appeals committee described as 'flawed' a model built by Biogen that claimed the drug might save money when the cost of working days lost by patients and carers was taken into account. Schering has submitted a new model, but has told the institute that it is commercially sensitive – a stance which appraisal committee members say makes it difficult for the institute to explain its objections to the model's conclusions.

The committee has, therefore, decided to build its own model – an approach that may force manufacturers to reveal more of the assumptions behind their results. Mr Cardy said it was 'impossible to understand why NICE has only now decided to look at the cost effectiveness of these drugs in a different way'. He demanded that Alan Milburn, the health secretary, 'sort NICE's ineptitude out'. Andrew Dillon, the institute's chief executive, said: 'The evidence relating to the cost effectiveness of these medicines is critically important in this appraisal.' It was 'of the utmost importance that the institute's guidance is both evidence-based and seen to be fair', and the delay to achieve that was in the best interest of those with MS. The appraisal committee originally said that a big price reduction would be needed before the drugs became cost effective. The process of deciding what would go into the institute's model, and the commissioning and evaluation of its results would be transparent, said Mr Dillon. The results would be published in full, with interested parties free to comment on it.

(*Source*: National News: Medicines arbiter delays decision on beta-interferon: Clinical Excellence Multiple Sclerosis Society angry that drug ruling is only likely after election, *The Financial Times*, 23 December 2000 (Pilling, D. and Timmins, N.), Copyright © The Financial Times Ltd. Additional material from Barlow, 2001; NICE, 2001 and 2002.)

In 2002 NICE decided it would not recommend beta interferon or glatimirer for the treatment of MS.

Discussion activity 2.10

Should the decision whether or not to provide these drugs to MS sufferers be based solely on clinical grounds or should cost-effectiveness criteria also be considered? What influence should powerful lobby groups have on such decisions?

Case study 2.11 raises the issue of unfair discrimination at work. In the last three decades of the twentieth century this was one of the major areas of ethical concern in business and organisational life. In the UK discrimination on grounds of race has been illegal since the Race Relations Act 1975 was passed. The Sex Discrimination Act came into force in 1975; it was amended and broadened in 1986. The Equal Pay Act took effect in 1975 and was amended in 1984. In 1995 an Act of Parliament made discrimination on the grounds of disability illegal. There is currently much debate about discrimination on the grounds of age but at the time of writing this was not illegal.

Case study 2.11 — Discriminating against employees – the Metropolitan Police Service

One of the most high-profile cases of race discrimination at work involves the Metropolitan Police. It was accused of institutional racism by the McPherson report into the police's investigation of the murder of Stephen Lawrence (Burns & Shrimsley, 2000). This case had a major impact on the force, which sought to establish that it was an equal opportunities employer in practices as well as in policy. Many thought that the service had worked hard to become multicultural and to reduce racial discrimination.

The issues of discrimination later became focused on the case of Superintendent Ali Dizaei, who was Iranian born and one of the most senior officers in the Metropolitan Police from an ethnic minority background. In 1999 he became officer in charge of operations at Kensington Police Station. The Metropolitan Police made him the subject of an undercover operation called 'Helios', which investigated suspicions that he was involved in drugs and prostitution. This enquiry became the most expensive ever undertaken against a single officer. Dizaei was suspended from office in 2001. He was eventually charged with attempting to pervert the course of justice, misconduct in public office and submitting false expenses claims. In April 2003 he was found not guilty of perverting the course of justice and in September of the same year the prosecution withdrew the expenses charges. His lawyers claimed that the prosecution had been a 'witch hunt' and a campaign of 'Orwellian proportions' (Tait, 2003).

The criminal proceedings being concluded, the Metropolitan Police service then began a disciplinary process against Dizaei. In 2003 nine allegations were identified and an investigation began. Subsequently the National Black Police Association (NBPA), of which Dizaei was once president, called for a boycott of the Metropolitan Police Service by anyone from the ethnic minorities who might have considered joining the service. This was something of a blow when the service was intent on increasing the proportion of its officers from the ethnic minorities. Before the investigation was completed the Home Secretary urged Dizaei and the Metropolitan Police to come to a settlement. A deal was brokered by the Arbitration and Conciliation Advisory Service. Under this deal Dizaei admitted that his conduct had fallen 'far below the standards expected of a police officer' and he agreed not to take his employer to an employment tribunal. In return he received £80,000 compensation, a statement that his integrity was intact and a return to work (BBC News Online, 2004a). The NBPA dropped its boycott. However, the Police Complaints Authority (PCA) was unhappy that the disciplinary process had not taken its proper course and had been pre-empted by a private agreement between the parties. The chairman of the PCA stated,

> Every police officer should face a consistency of treatment as far as the disciplinary process is concerned – we can't have one officer getting special treatment because he is a senior black officer and because there are concerns about race in the police service.

(Source: BBC News Online, 2004b)

The Metropolitan Police resisted the demand to continue disciplinary action against Dizaei and in March 2004 the PCA directed the Metropolitan Police to take disciplinary action. However, the PCA was then replaced by a new body called the Independent Police Complaints Commission (IPCC). This organisation reconsidered the issue. It was also unhappy about the private deal but thought it not in the public interest to pursue the disciplinary action. It beleived the charges against Dizaei were capable of proof but that if he were found guilty any penalty would likely be modest. It pointed out that he had admitted errors and was to receive 'Words of Advice from his Chief Officer'. It therefore revoked the instruction to continue the disciplinary proceedings (IPCC, 2004). A separate enquiry by another Police Force into Operation Helios continued.

Dizaei said his re-integration into the Met would not be easy – he thought there might be some backlash from others in the service; but that he had never had an easy time in the force (Dodd, 2011a). Nevertheless in 2008 he was promoted to Commander. There continued to be tensions between him and other senior managers. He became involved in the case of Inspector Ghaffur, who was accusing the Commissioner of racism. The situation became confused when it emerged that Ghaffur's solicitor, a Mr Mireskandari, had a criminal conviction and his practice was shut down by the Solicitors' Regulation Authority. It emerged that Mireskandari was Dizaei's best man when he married his third wife and there were claims that Dizaei had advised Mireshkandari's clients, including a Russian millionaires who killed a man in a hit-and-run crash. Dizaei was cleared of any wrongdoing.

▶

Further problems arose when Dizaei was involved in a brawl over an invoice for work on his website, and he had his protagonist Mr al-Baghdadi arrested. Allegations were made that he had 'fitted up' al-Baghdadi. Dizaei was tried, convicted and dismissed from the Metropolitan Police in 2010. Dizaei's wife investigated al-Baghdadi's background and discovered that he had lied to the court about his identity and had been defrauding the social benefits system. On appeal Dizaei's conviction was quashed and he was released from prison after having served a year. However the appeal judges recommended a retrial. Dizaei said 'When I clear my name it is my intention to go back to the Metropolitan Police and serve my time" (Dodd, 2011b). In September 2011 he was reinstated but then was immediately suspended. His retrial started in 2012 and resulted in Dizaei being sentenced to three years' imprisonment.

In a link with another business ethics issue in 2011 it was claimed that Dizaei's phone had been hacked into by the *News of the World* (See Case study 1.1).

The story of Ali Dizaei is picaresque; a series of accusations and challenges. Each time he is cleared there are claims that he is the victim of racism.

Discussion activity 2.11

It is probably impossible for those without detailed knowledge to come to a definitive view on the Dizaei case; but it does raise a range of interesting issues.

Does an individual case, such as that of Ali Dizaei, suggest that an organisation is institutionally racist despite its policies and principles?

To what extent do formal process of discipline and grievance exacerbate rather than solve problems of discrimination?

Case study 2.12 considers whether Railtrack, the company that oversaw the operations of the British railway system, was fair in its treatment of its stakeholders, in particular the travelling public, in relation to its solicitude towards shareholders.

Case study 2.12   The British railway system: priorities, profits and governance

In May 2001 Railtrack, the company responsible for running the infrastructure of Britain's rail system, published its financial results. It made a worse than expected loss of £534m. This was largely due to the cost of renewing the permanent way after the Hatfield crash in 2000. Despite a disastrous year the company maintained the dividend payment to its shareholders. It was argued that it had to keep the confidence of the financial markets because it would need to borrow millions of pounds in the future to invest in the rail system.

The following leading article was published in the *Financial Times*.

 That profits conflict with safety on the railways can no longer be in doubt. The draft report of the official inquiry into the Hatfield derailment reveals a catalogue of management and engineering failures.

After privatisation in 1996, the top executives of Railtrack, the infrastructure company, focused too much on immediate value for shareholders and too little on maintenance of the track. This might have been predicted; for although the rail regulator set targets for infrastructure improvement, every pound saved on maintenance helped to increase dividends.

Railtrack would have been entitled to keep such savings if they had resulted from extra efficiency. But the inquiry shows that it lacked managerial and technical skills, was slack in its maintenance discipline and communicated poorly with subcontractors. New management brought in after the fatal crash has admitted past failings and has made some progress towards putting them right. But broader remedies are needed. The company must be subject to a new set of incentives that more explicitly recognises its status as a public service utility in receipt of large government subsidies.

At the time of privatisation, it was decided to adopt the regulatory model used in the gas, electricity and telecommunications industries. This sets a price that the utility may charge, leaving an incentive to make extra profits from greater efficiency.

It is now obvious that this was a bad model for the railways – partly because of the importance and unpredictable costs of safety and partly because the fragmented structure of the industry creates perverse incentives. If Railtrack closes a line for unexpected safety work, for example, it must pay penalty charges to train operating companies.

Regulation should move closer to the US model. That would involve tighter supervision and replace the profit motive with the guarantee of a 'fair' rate of return – provided the company does its job properly. There are disadvantages: the spur to efficiency is blunted and, when the return is assured, managers may try to over-invest.

But since Railtrack has failed to convince its shareholders, the markets and the general public that it can find the right balance between profit and maintenance expenditures, stronger regulation must be the way ahead.

(*Source*: Leader: Changing track, *The Financial Times*, 9 May 2001, Copyright © The Financial Times Ltd.)

The case raises the question of whether public utilities, which are necessities of a civilised life, are ethically different from other products and services. The chairmen of UK regulated utilities, according to a survey (Brigley and Vass, 1997: 164), thought they were not, and that the ethical obligations on a private utility company should be no different from those placed on any private company.

In 2001 Railtrack plc was declared insolvent and placed into administration. The shareholders demanded that they should be compensated by being paid the value of the Railtrack shares when the company was floated on the stock exchange. The government retorted that taxpayers' money would not be used to spare shareholders the consequences of their poor investment.

The successor body is called Network Rail. It is a not-for-profit public interest company. It has no shareholders but it does have 116 members. It was thought that a company devoid of shareholders would be run for the benefit of the whole railway network and its customers and not simply for the financial benefit of the shareholders. The members have no financial interest in the company and receive neither dividends nor capital. Nevertheless they are expected according to Network Rail to ensure that 'Network Rail is managed in line with high standards of corporate governance' (House of Commons, 2004). Two-thirds of the members are members of the public who were appointed from those chosen from 1,200 applicants by a membership selection panel that was appointed by Network Rail. The public members therefore are the appointees of Network Rail. Some public members represent special interest groups, such as The Royal Society for Disability and Rehabilitation (Gosling, 2004). In addition the key industry stakeholders, franchise holders who actually run the train services, railway undertakings and operators of railway assets who look after the rolling stock and property such as stations are represented. The Parliamentary Select Committee on Transport (House of Commons, 2004: §59) argued that this structure would create no strong accountability to the public interest.

> We were also concerned that the industry members were virtually self-appointing. These members include contractors [to Network Rail] and while members may have a duty to the company, there was always some possibility of the appearance of a conflict of interest. Finally the public members are appointed by the Board of the company and represent no one but themselves.

There was much scepticism regarding whether members without a financial interest would have sufficient influence on the Board. The rail regulator thought the members would not have the motivation to drive down costs. It is arguable that such a consequence reflects a better balance of influence between stakeholders, and between the demand for profit and other demands such as safety. If this argument is correct then the governance of Network Rail might be a powerful new model of governance. In 2008 the Office of the Rail Regulator fined Network Rail £14m after it failed to complete engineering works on schedule and caused massive delays for rail passengers.

Iain Croucher left his job as chief executive of Network Rail in 2010 after he had been the subject of criticism that reflected on the corporate governance of the organisation. The allegations were that there was not enough constraint on the chief executive's power. One illustration of this was the debate about executive bonuses that many thought were excessive. The Board approved the payments by 37 votes to 31. Fewer than half of the 'public' members of the Board voted for the bonuses. The chairman of Network Rail said that the decision had been a good demonstration of the management being held to account (BBC News Online, 2010).

Discussion activity 2.12

What is a fair balance between interests of the owners of a company that provides a public utility and the interests of the customers? Was Railtrack right in its approach? Will the structure of Network Rail, which has no shareholders, redress the balance?

Part four: Preventing indifference to others

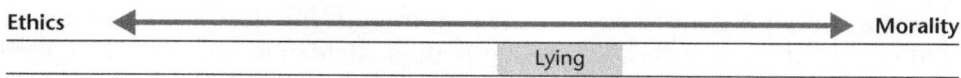

Ethics ⟵————————————————————————⟶ Morality

Lying

Lying

Lying is wrong; except that in everyday usage it is not always so. The acceptability of a lie depends partly on the context in which it is made. Perjury, lying under oath in a court of law, is not acceptable; indeed it is a crime that carries heavy punishment. In the context of business negotiations lying, in the form of bluffing, may be acceptable as Carr argued (1968) in a classic article. Lies, in such a context, may be no more than putting a spin on an unpalatable truth.

> **DEFINITION**
>
> Winston Churchill used the phrase **terminological inexactitude** in a speech on Chinese labour in South Africa. The phrase was not actually used as a euphemism for a lie. He argued that although the labourers' contracts might not be proper or healthy they could not be classified as slavery without 'some risk of terminological inexactitude'. However, Alexander Haig, the American politician, is credited with saying, 'It is not a lie, it's a terminological inexactitude'.

The reprehensibility of a lie may also depend upon its nature. Telling an absolute untruth is often worse than failing to tell the whole truth. A cabinet secretary to a British government famously objected to a suggestion that he had lied. He had, he claimed, merely been 'economical with the truth'. Managers often find difficulty when they have to keep silent about privileged or confidential information, as when they know there are proposals to make people redundant but have been required to say nothing until the plans are finalised and can be announced. Their loyalty to their staff conflicts with their commitment to their company's needs. Conflicts of interest are a particular problem for professionals and public officials whose judgment should be seen to be free of private or opposing interests. They should be open about any such conflicts. Recruitment consultants finding new jobs for staff being made redundant would be regarded with suspicion if they received fees from both the organisation buying the out-placement service and the company in which they placed the redundant staff. The Nolan Committee's (1995) seven principles for public life are all focused on ensuring that private or sectional interests do not prejudice people's decisions on matters of public interest.

> ## The Nolan principles
> **DEFINITION**
>
> **Selflessness**
> Holders of public office should act solely in terms of the public interest. They should not do so in order to gain financial or other benefits for themselves, their family or their friends.
>
> **Integrity**
> Holders of public office should not place themselves under any financial or other obligation to outside individuals or organisations that might seek to influence them in the performance of their official duties.
>
> **Objectivity**
> In carrying out public business, including making public appointments, awarding contracts, or recommending individuals for rewards and benefits, holders of public office should make choices on merit.

▶

Accountability

Holders of public office are accountable for their decisions and actions to the public and must submit themselves to whatever scrutiny is appropriate to their office.

Openness

Holders of public office should be as open as possible about all the decisions and actions that they take. They should give reasons for their decisions and restrict information only when the wider public interest clearly demands.

Honesty

Holders of public office have a duty to declare any private interests relating to their public duties and to take steps to resolve any conflicts arising in a way that protects the public interest.

Leadership

Holders of public office should promote and support these principles by leadership and example.

Another test of the dishonesty of a lie is its purpose. There is a range of names for acceptable lies, including fibs and white lies, that are intended to avoid giving offence or causing distress to individuals. Not all managers see such lying as acceptable, as one told us in a research interview.

> I think for me the most important thing is honesty and what I find difficult is when managers maybe are doing something for one reason but are telling staff it's for another reason. Something like that I would find, and do find, quite difficult. Rather than actually saying to staff, you didn't get the job because your performance isn't as accurate or whatever else; what they give is fairly obscure reasons rather than actually facing the real reason.

A lie involves intent to deceive; if there is no such intent there is no lie. We fill our conversations with figures of speech such as hyperbole ('I'm so hungry I could eat a horse') and metaphor ('That man is a pig'), which do not lead people to accept the literal truth of what we are saying. Advertising is a common area in which companies may seek to deceive their customers. The Advertising Standards Authority, in a typical example, criticised Virgin Trains for claiming in their advertisements that all fares were half price when conditions meant that many were not (Milmo, 2001).

Sometimes organisations simply lie. In 2007 Southern Water, which provides water and waste water services in the south-east of England, was fined £20.3m by the water industry regulator. Water companies have to provide performance information to the regulator and it was discovered that Southern Water had deliberately misreported information, to make its performance look better than it was, on its response times, billing enquiries and service complaints. Because the industry is a regulated one, and because the increase in retail prices it is allowed by the regulator partly depends on its performance, the company had been able to increase its prices more than was justified. It had to pay back £500,000 to its customers (BBC News Online, 2007c).

Case study 2.13   **The case of Shell's missing oil barrels**

The Royal Dutch/Shell company, or rather group of companies, has been accused of being over-large, out of control, secretive and hidding behind a bland façade. These claims have centred on the story of Shell's missing oil reserves.

The problem began in the late 1990s. One of the figures used by observers of the oil industry is the reserve replacement ratio (RRR). Shell's RRR was one of the poorest in the industry. It was not finding new sources of oil fast enough. Managers assumed that the policy for 'booking' new reserves was too restrictive. There was a fashion in management at the time for using problem-solving teams to come up with radical and creative solutions, and Shell established four such teams to improve the exploration and production function, which was led by Sir Phillip Watts. New guidelines for booking reserves were implemented. In Shell's 1998 annual report there was a brief note reporting that 'Estimation methods have been refined during 1998'. The RRR consequently increased by 40 per cent and the director was rewarded for im-proving the efficiency of his directorate. Shell had adopted the system of determining senior managers' rewards and bonuses according to their performance against critical performance indicators. Rewards were triggered by numbers and targets, and not by the rounded judgments of appraisers.

In 2001 the American Securities and Exchange Commission (SEC) published new guide-lines for assessing the commerciality of new oil discoveries. These were to be used to deter-mine whether finds were certain enough to be accounted as a reserve. Shell's booked reserves in Australia, Norway and Nigeria did not comply with the new SEC guidelines. However, there was great pressure within Shell to keep the RRR as high as possible. Nor was there much internal auditing pressure to review the reserve figures, the auditing of which was done part-time by one engineer who had no staff to back him up.

It is clear that several top executives within Shell knew of this problem by 2002. However, nothing was made public. This was largely a result of feuds between senior managers, particu-larly between Sir Philip Watts (who had been promoted to chairman) and Walter van de Vijver, head of exploration. After what van de Vijver considered an unfair performance appraisal from Sir Philip Watts the former sent the latter an e-mail stating 'I am becoming sick and tired about lying about the extent of our oil reserves issues and the downward revision that needs to be done because of far too aggressive/optimistic bookings'.

On 9 January 2004 the Shell group announced through its investor relations staff that they had downgraded their reserves by 20 per cent, or 3.9 billion barrels of oil. The markets were not happy and the stock market valuation of Shell dropped to £2.9bn. That the announcement had not been made by Sir Philip Watts personally increased investors' anger. The pressure led to Watts and van de Vijver resigning. At first it was reported that Watts left by mutual consent, although later it was admitted that he had been pushed. Nevertheless he received a £1m com-pensation package for the breaking of his contract. Jeroen van der Veer from Royal Dutch be-came the new chairman. There was some negative comment in the business press that the new chairman was an insider, although given the reported friction between the British and Dutch wings of the group Shell insiders would be more likely to see the appointment as a Dutch *coup d'état*. The finance director resigned in July. There was no question of financial impropriety on her part but there were questions about her effectiveness in ensuring compliance with good accounting practice.

▶

Shell argued that the differences between its criteria for booking reserves, and those of the SEC, are largely a technical matter. It pointed out that the de-booking of reserves does not mean that the oil is not there and it anticipates that 85 per cent of the missing barrels will prove to have been there all along. Shell's approach to internal control is on a risk assessment basis, which is designed to manage rather than to eliminate the risks to achieving the company's objectives. In September 2004 Sir Philip Watts announced that he planned to challenge the UK Financial Services Authority (FSA) in the Financial Services and Markets Tribunal (the appeal court for FSA decisions). He was claiming that he was treated unfairly by the FSA, which criticised him implicitly in its report, although not by name, and did not give him an opportunity to rebut the criticisms (Hosking, 2004).

Shell's audit committee instigated an internal review, which was carried out by external accountants. There was pressure for an independent inquiry both in the UK and the USA. In the UK the charge was that the company had breached Stock Market regulations by not reporting in good time matters and information that could have an impact on the share price. The FSA started an investigation, as did the SEC in America.

Shell cooperated fully with the investigations. In August 2004 the FSA fined the company £17m and the SEC fined it £66.29m. The FSA accused Shell of 'unprecedented misconduct' and a failure to put internal controls in place to prevent misleading information being given to the market. In its agreement with the SEC Shell did not admit any illegality but it did agree to spend nearly £3m on developing better internal compliance systems. These official punishments may be only the start of the problem for Shell as lawyers in the USA are clamouring to start class actions against the company on behalf of various pension funds, which believe that the misinformation caused them financial losses. Shell may be one of the first cases to feel the weight of the Sarbanes–Oxley Act, which was passed in the USA following the Enron and WorldCom cases. Under this Act's provisions the senior managers of the company signed a declaration concerning the 2002 annual report that 'based on my knowledge, this annual report does not contain any untrue statement of a material fact'.

Royal Dutch Shell has an unusual, but not unique structure. It is a dual listed company. This means that the Shell group operates as a single organisation but legally it is two organisations: the Royal Dutch Petroleum Company, which is based in Holland and listed on the Dutch Stock exchange, and the Shell Transport and Trading Company, which is based in London and whose shares are listed on the London Stock Exchange. These two companies are the parent companies. The shareholders of Royal Dutch are mostly Dutch and those of Shell Trading mostly UK based, although there is a substantial block of American depository receipts (ADR) held in the USA. A series of legal agreements governs the relationship between the two parent companies. This arrangement dates from 1907 when Shell (which was founded in 1833 as a shop selling seashells to naturalists) merged with the Royal Dutch Company for the Exploration of Petroleum Wells in the Netherlands East Indies. Under this deal Royal Dutch controls 60 per cent of the group's assets and Shell Trading controls the remaining 40 per cent.

Royal Dutch and Shell Trading do not undertake any operations. Instead they own the shares of two holding companies, Shell Petroleum NV and the Shell Petroleum Company Ltd. These in turn own the large number of companies that carry out the group's operations around the world. The two parent companies each have a board of directors (Royal Dutch has a supervisory board as well) that have different memberships. The combined group is overseen by an executive board known as the committee of managing directors (CMD). The members of the CMD are appointed by the boards of the parent companies. In such a structure there is clearly tension as to who has the greatest influence and who carries oversight and responsibility for the organisation's compliance with laws and conventions. It appears that Royal Dutch is the dominant partner. The supervisory board of Royal Dutch controls a number of foundations that own 'priority shares', which confer voting rights but no economic benefit. These enable the supervisory board to control nominations to both parent company boards and thus to the CMD. The CMD is not formally covered by the joint venture agreement, which defines the merged company, and so it has no formal authority over the parent companies' assets.

Investors have complained that the legal structure of Royal Dutch/Shell makes it difficult for shareholders to gain information from the group and to influence its policy. This, taken together with the divisionalised structure of the group, which leads to a high level of decentralisation, raises questions about the effectiveness of internal control. This said, the group has the full panoply of policies, codes of ethics and operating principles, which all large companies have, to ensure good governance. Economists have studied the tensions between insider ownership and insider control (through such devices as priority shares) in dual class companies. Some have suggested that when the insiders, in this case the Dutch boards, have great voting muscle they use it to support their own position as against the interests of outsiders such as shareholders. This tendency itself would make it difficult for shareholders to hold the company to account. Although it can equally be argued that the system in Royal Dutch/Shell, which gave the managers low ownership but high voting rights, contributed to the development of a strong and flexible corporate culture.

The reserves revaluation has led to calls for changes in corporate governance of Royal Dutch/Shell to prevent the reoccurrence of similar problems. Shell has now adopted a single board structure. In 2005 Shell announced the largest profit ever made by a British based company, largely attributable to the increase in world oil prices in 2004.

(Sources: Doran and Mansell, 2004; Gompers et al., 2004; The Guardian, 2004a
and 2004b; Harrington, 2003; Harris and Michaels, 2004; Morgan, 2004; Plender,
2004; Shell Group, 2004; Watchman, 2004)

Discussion activity 2.13

- In your opinion did Shell lie?
- If you believe it did what were the factors and influences that may have caused it to lie?
- Is this a good news story because the regulatory agencies punished Shell?
- Why did Shell's shareholders get so vexed about the corporate governance issues?
- What changes in corporate governance, if any, might be necessary?

Refusing to be true to one's own beliefs can be a form of self-deception. This can happen when a person justifies continuing their connection to an organisation even though they object on ethical grounds to the organisation's behaviour.

Case study 2.14   BAT, Nottingham University and the honorary professor

In 2011 Nottingham University accepted £3.8m from British American Tobacco (BAT), the world's second biggest tobacco company, towards setting up an international Centre for Corporate Responsibility. There was, of course, nothing illegal about the gift but many individuals and groups thought it was wrong. The problem was that Nottingham University carried out medical research into cancer and its treatment, some of it funded by medical charities. This was thought to fit badly with accepting money from a company that sells products known to cause cancer.

Richard Smith was editor of the *British Medical Journal* (BMJ) and an unpaid honorary professor of medical journalism at Nottingham University. He believed the university's acceptance of BAT's money was a 'serious mistake'. He polled readers of the BMJ to discover their views on whether he should resign from his post at Nottingham University. Of the 1,075 votes cast 84 per cent said the university should return the money and 54 per cent said that Professor Smith should resign if the university did not do so. The latter vote was closer than had been anticipated and this was because some argued that the professor should stay within the university and argue his case internally. The professor did resign, both because he said he would abide by the result of the poll and because he firmly believed the university was wrong in its actions.

(*Source*: Meikle, 2001)

Discussion activity 2.14

Is it better to retreat and live to fight another day or to take a stand on a matter one sees as an injustice?

The next case study concerns a senior manager who told what was, of itself, an inconsequential lie; but one that nevertheless had great consequences because of the context in which it was told.

Case study 2.15   Lord Browne of Madingley

Lord Browne was appointed chief executive of British Petroleum (BP) in 1995 when the company was valued at £24.4m. By 2007 it was worth £108.3bn. He was an internationally respected executive with access to senior politicians. He was due to retire, and be lauded with praise at the end of 2008. However, on 1 May 2007 he announced his immediate resignation. Lord Browne had been in a four-year relationship with Jeff Chevalier. Lord Browne supported his partner by encouraging him to enrol for a postgraduate course, helping him set up a business and taking him to BP functions. When the relationship ended in 2006, Chevalier found the transition from a luxury lifestyle to a more normal existence difficult. Chevalier offered to sell his story to the *Daily Mail*. This story included a number of allegations, such as that Lord Browne had allowed Chevalier to use his BP laptop computer for his personal e-mails and that he had talked openly about issues he had discussed with senior politicians. BP and Lord Browne denied the allegations. Lord Browne applied for an injunction to prevent publication of the story and it was granted on 6 January. He announced the following week that he would be retiring in July 2007 instead of the end of 2008. Even the date in 2008 was earlier than Browne had originally wanted but was the result of a battle with the chairman of BP over succession. The *Daily Mail* took the case to the House of Lords. During the hearing Browne lied when he said that he had met Chevalier whilst exercising in Battersea Park. The judge said he was not prepared;

> to make allowances for a 'white lie' told in circumstances such as these – especially by a man who prays in aid of his reputation and distinction.

Once the judgment had been published and the judge's comments became known, Lord Browne resigned. By resigning before the end of his contract he lost a pay package worth nearly £16m. The lie may have been a small one, and Browne's sexuality of no relevance to his job; but lying in court was a diminution of his honesty and integrity. The CEO's integrity would have been an issue had he stayed on; especially as there were legal proceeding taking place against BP in the USA over the Texas City oil refinery explosion that killed 15 people. In October 2007 BP admitted being guilty of a felony in not maintaining proper safety standards and paid fines of $373m (Grant et al., 2007).

(*Sources*: Crooks, 2007; Hawkes, 2007)

Discussion activity 2.15

Can a white lie be acceptable to protect one's privacy?

In the Lord Browne case, the judge's remarks that Lord Browne was willing to lie and 'trash' the reputation of Mr Chevalier to protect his reputation and avoid personal embarrassment hints at what was known in ancient Greek tragedy as hubris.

Hubris, nemesis and catharsis   DEFINITION

The first two terms represent the themes of Greek tragedy and the third is the experience of the audience watching the play. **Hubris** is a great pride and belief in one's own importance. **Nemesis** is a deserved punishment that cannot be avoided; and **catharsis** is the release of strong emotion caused by the experience of fear, albeit only expressed on the stage. These terms can be illustrated by the story of Jonathan Aitken, a prominent politician and one-time Minister of State for Defence. In 1993 he stayed at the Paris Ritz. *The Guardian* newspaper took an interest in this visit and enquired why a cabinet minister was staying at a very expensive hotel at someone else's expense. Aitken said he had paid for the stay himself. He lied. But at the time there was no proof he had. *The Guardian* kept running the story, believing the weekend was connected with an arms deal involving Saudi Arabia, and Aitken, saying that he was going to fight 'the cancer of bent and twisted journalism . . . with the simple sword of truth', sued the newspaper for libel – his hubris. He persuaded his wife and his daughter to lie in support of the claim that he had paid for the stay himself. When documents were presented that showed that he had lied on oath in the court the libel case collapsed. He was charged with perverting the course of justice and perjury in 1998 and sent to prison in 1999 – his nemesis. That the public found this cathartic is suggested by his availability as a public speaker (SpeakersUK, 2005). Rumours that Aitken was planning to become a priest after finishing his 18-month sentence were denied by him. He did enrol to study theology at Oxford. This may be his catharsis.

(*Sources*: *The Guardian*, 1999; Harding, 1999; Wilson, 1999)

Many of the issues related to lying, as in the following case study, concern the failure to tell the whole truth rather than the telling of falsehoods.

Case study 2.16	**Economy with the truth when dealing with the tax authorities**

Extract from an interview with the finance director of a private company
Most of the ethical issues revolve around disclosure to the revenue and tax authority. The issues are whether we should disclose all the material facts and secondly, when arguing a case with the revenue, whether we should make a case even when we know it is weak. The rule is 'we will make a case as long as we have one argument – however obtuse'. As long as we have an arguable position we won't be embarrassed.

I have just had a conversation with someone on an issue . . . actually tax again, on whether we give the Inland Revenue a letter or not at this particular point in time. It could be slightly prejudicial, only slightly, to our case, and as we are going to have a meeting and it may settle it, do I need to give it to him [the tax inspector] now? This is a question of timing. If I can settle it without giving it to him I might do.

It's just to do with tax planning and why we actually had done a transaction. It may make the revenue renege on something they have just agreed. Unlikely, but you don't want to raise doubts in somebody's mind who has actually spent some time looking at it. Tax is always slow anyway, so why shouldn't I delay sending the letter? We are likely to have a meeting in July. I would see how that went and if they decide they still want the correspondence – we'll give it to them. It is actually the fact that we know we have got a meeting due that enables us to prevaricate.

(*Source*: Research interview conducted by the authors)

Discussion activity 2.16

In what circumstances might it be right not to tell the whole truth?

Cheating

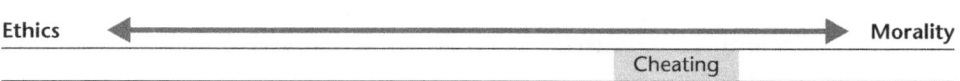

This category of ethical issues concerns keeping the rules. However, for many in organisations the important question is whether the benefits of bending the rules are high enough, and the chances of being caught low enough, to justify taking a risk. This ethical calculation can be made both at a corporate level and as a matter of individual discretion.

Rules are not always bent to benefit the person doing the bending. In bureaucratic systems rules are often bent to protect people who would otherwise be harshly treated by the system. One example we came across during our research concerned a production-line worker in a factory that made prepared foods for supermarkets. The employee was diabetic and, on the day of the incident, had been careless of his diet. Consequently at work he felt the start of a hypoglycaemic attack and took, and ate, one of the products from the production line. This prevented him from collapsing. But he was threatened with dismissal because company rules made theft of company property punishable by instant dismissal. The personnel officer thought the man had been foolish but thought it unjust to sack him. The rules were ignored.

In many cases, however, rules are broken and lies are told by people who simply seek their own benefit at others' expense. The case of the rise and fall of Parmalat provides a major example. The Tanzi family, who were the major shareholders, benefited themselves to the cost of bond holders and other investors. More recently there have been the cases of Bernie Madoff and Satyam.

Case study 2.17	**Fraudulent businesses – Parmalat, Satyam and Madoff**

This case study considers three examples of fraudulent accounting by companies.

In 1961 Calisto Tanzi started a milk pasteurisation plant to supply milk to the Italian city of Parma. From that starting point it grew to become a multinational, publicly owned corporation in the food and milk business. Until December 2003 Tanzi led the company, which employed 36,200 people in 146 plants in 30 countries on five continents. In December 2003 Parmalat defaulted on payment of a €150m bond despite having €4.2bn of liquidity. Tanzi handed over control to a company doctor. Then the Bank of America announced that the claim that Bonlat, a Parmalat subsidiary, had an account in the Cayman Islands with €2.95m was untrue and that Parmalat had a €4.9m hole in its accounts. Parmalat sought bankruptcy protection and the Italian Prime Minister Silvio Berlusconi said he found the revelations 'almost unbelievable' but pledged to save the company, which was Italy's eighth largest corporation (CNN International, 2003). As time went on the financial hole in the company was discovered to be larger – €14.8bn (Kapner 2004a). Parmalet had created false accounts to hide the losses

The company's operating principle seems to have been that ensuring the long-term survival of the firm by acquiring influence among local politicians was more important than making a

▶

profit. In this, of course, it was proved wrong. However, it applied this system in countries other than Italy. A *Financial Times* investigation identified that Parmalat considered, but never completed, a deal to buy a near-bankrupt Nicaraguan Bank in 2001 in an effort to 'build influence in Central and South America' (Barber and Parker, 2004).

A letter writer to the *Financial Times* generously saw Parmalat's policy of subsidising European farmers (by making a loss of between €350m and €450m per year in the late 1990s) as more efficient than the European Union's Common Agricultural Policy. He pointed out that the farmers received a subsidy at no cost to European taxpayers because the financial strain was being borne by largely American Parmalat bond holders. So the farmers were better off, as were the taxpayers, and the consumers were no worse off (Carter, 2004).

When this policy proved expensive and the company was making losses the Tanzi family, several of whom apart from Calisto were arrested, tried a number of devices to cover up the losses and protect their own interests. One technique was to transfer money from the publicly owned Parmalat to family-controlled companies, such as the travel firm Paratours (Kapner and Minder, 2004). They also used sophisticated and legal financial devices. In one deal with a bank called Buconero (black hole in Italian) the bank made an 'investment' in Parmalat of €117m in return for a share of the company's net profit. By setting up the loan as an investment Parmalat's borrowing costs were made to look smaller than they were (ExecutiveCaliber, 2004). On occasions the company resorted to plain lying and forgery. When the auditors enquired about the money in the Cayman Islands branch of the Bank of America they received a reply from the bank, confirming the existence of the account, which had in fact been forged at Parmalat's headquarters.

Calisto Tanzi was sentenced to 10 years imprisonment for market rigging. He remained free while other legal processes took place. He was subsequently charged with fraudulent bankruptcy and criminal association and was given a sentence of 18 years in 2011. However while he appeals against the sentence he continues to live on his estate near Parma. It is in any case unusual for elderly people, Tanzi is in his seventies, to go to prison in Italy. Sixteen other Parmalat executives were found guilty on various charges.

Satyam Computer Services is an international information technology services company based in Hyderabad, India. It was presented as a paragon of the new Indian outsourcing industry that was successful, innovative and focused on developing its employees. In four years it had increased the number of its employees from 9,000 to 42,000. Satyam is structured around 1,773 business units, each headed by its own chief executive. Ramalinga Raju the founder and chairman of the company argued that innovation is the key to satisfying the customer and that learning, at both the individual and at the organisational level, is what drives change. The company had a strong official culture known as the Satyam way, which is made available to all associates as a book.

On 7 January 2009 Raju published a letter in which he admitted that he had falsified the company's accounts. He had entered fictitious assets, equivalent to $1.5bn. He said that it had started with an initial cover-up of one quarter's poor performance and then escalated. He wrote in the letter:

> It was like riding a tiger, not knowing how to get off without being eaten.
> I sincerely apologise to all Satyamites and stakeholders, who have made Satyam a special organisation, for the current situation. I am confident they will stand by the company in this hour of crisis.

> (Times Online, 2009)

By 2011 Raju was in judicial custody and his repeated appeals to be granted bail had been refused. Satyam's American Depository Shares had been traded on the New York Stock exchange and in 2011 Satyam, which by now was trading under new management, and its former auditor PricewaterCoopers agreed to pay fines to the SEC in the USA of $17.5m.

Bernie Madoff was a highly rated financial advisor and investor. He used his charm to attract investors and his fame became such that people were begging him to invest their money in his company. He took deposits, not only from individuals, but also from financial institutions and hedge funds. However in December 2009 his sons reported that Madoff had confessed to them that his business was a massive Ponzi scheme. (Both Raju and Madoff eventually confessed their crimes – is this a feature of fraudsters who believe they are about to be found out?) A Ponzi scheme is a very simple scam. The conman takes in deposits but does not invest them. Instead new deposits by new investors are used to pay the dividends and capital gains to earlier investors. As the scheme grows the conman can find no new investors and at that point the whole inverted pyramidal structure collapses. Few of Madoff's investor queried how he managed to provide consistently better returns than the market average. It was this misplaced confidence that kept the scheme afloat for many years. Investors lost an estimated $18bn. In 2009 Madoff pleaded guilty to various charges and was sentenced to 150 years' imprisonment.

Discussion activity 2.17

Neo-institutionalism is a theory which argues that societies have templates of formal and informal rules, values and acceptable ways of behaving; and that organisations in those societies fit in with, and organise themselves to fit in with, those institutional templates. The technical name for this process is iso-morphism. Can the story of Parmalat be interpreted using this theory? Can it be argued that Parmalat's way of operating by keeping local politicians and others happy reflected the institutional world of a small company in Italy in the 1960s, but that it was too risky to sustain when Parmalat had become a huge multinational corporation?

The next case study tells a similar story but the history and motivations were probably very different from those seen in the Parmalat case study.

Case study 2.18 — Lord Black and Hollinger International

At the beginning of 2004 Conrad Black, Lord Black of Crossharbour, was chairman and chief executive of Hollinger International, an organisation based in the USA that owned many newspapers including the *Daily Telegraph* in Britain and the *Chicago Sun-Times* in the USA. On 3 March 2008 he started a six-and-a-half year jail sentence in Florida after being convicted on three counts of fraud and one of obstructing justice.

The group has a complex structure. Hollinger International Inc. is the holding company that oversees the group's assets and operations. Hollinger Inc. (a Canadian registered company) holds 18.2 per cent of the equity in Hollinger International; and 80 per cent of Hollinger Inc. is held by Ravelstone which is a private company belonging to Lord Black. One particular feature of

▶

the structure is that although Hollinger Inc. only owns a small part of Hollinger International it owns 68 per cent of the voting rights. This was possible because Hollinger International has a dual class of shares. Those held by Hollinger Inc. were super-voting shares carrying more votes per share than ordinary shares. This discrepancy between ownership and control gave Black control of the main company and control over appointments to the board.

This situation led to a conflict between Lord Black and the rest of the board of Hollinger International. In 2003 Lord Black lost his position as CEO of Hollinger International but remained chairman. However, Lord Black's announcement in January 2004 that he had made a deal, to sell the *Daily Telegraph* to the Barclay brothers, which prevented the ordinary shareholders of Hollinger International benefiting from the sale, brought the crisis to a head. The 'non-interested' board members challenged the deal by setting up a corporate review committee to scrutinise the deal. Lord Black responded by using his controlling interest to change the company's by-laws by written consent, a technique that bypassed the other shareholders. The new by-laws abolished the review committee and put practical constraints on the board's freedom to act. The matter went to court in Delaware and Lord Black lost the case.

After these battles the board of Hollinger International commissioned a detailed investigation into Lord Black's business affairs in relation to Hollinger International. The investigation was conducted by Richard Breeden, a former chairman of the SEC. The Breeden report, which arose from the investigation, was published in September 2004 and accused Lord Black of 'fiduciary abuses' and fraudulent acts. According to Breeden, Black had taken £223m from the company in a six-year period up to 2003. This represented 95.2 per cent of its entire adjusted net income. Most of this money, it was claimed, came in the form of excessive management fees paid to Black and his associates and in expense claims. Lord Black challenges these claims and has hired forensic accountants to work on his case. He argues that there was no misconduct and that his actions were approved by the board.

One of the main accusations was that Lord Black and Mr Radler, a former deputy chairman, broke their fiduciary duties to the company's shareholders by causing Hollinger International to pay them unjustifiable management fees through Lord Black's private company Ravelstone. This matter was the cause of Lord Black losing his position of CEO in 2003 when he was found to have overcharged for his services by $32m, a sum that he subsequently repaid to Hollinger International. Some of the fees were paid to shell companies registered in Barbados, which does not tax dividends and charges only 2.5 per cent income tax. One particular device that was used by Black was non-compete payments that were made between 1999 and 2001. When Hollinger International wished to sell one of its publications Black and his associates would demand a fee to sign a non-competition agreement with prospective purchasers, which ensured that they would not enter the competition to buy the titles. The Breeden report considered this a conflict of interests because, as a board member of Hollinger International Black had responsibilities to maximise the sale price of the company's assets. If these non-competition deals had not been made then the fee paid to Black (as compensation for not acquiring the assets) would most likely have gone to pay a higher purchase price to Hollinger International.

The second main charge against Black made by the Breeden report was that Black and Radler and their families had used Hollinger International as a 'piggy bank'. The company paid for much of their living expenses, their housing expenses and their personal travel. Radler was given a private aircraft by the company, worth $11.6m, and Black had a Gulfstream IV leased for him at a cost of $3m–$4m a year. The running costs of these aircraft between 2000 and 2003 were $23m. Two of the more high-profile items mentioned in the report were $43,000 spent by the company on Lady Black's birthday party and the $2,436 handbag she was given as a gift.

KPMG, who were auditors for Hollinger International, Hollinger Inc. and Ravelstone, did not initially question or raise with the company's audit committee the matter of whether the management fees and non-compete contracts contradicted Lord Black's fiduciary duties to Hollinger International. However, it did so in late 2003 and resigned as auditors in December.

Some of the journalists who worked and socialised with Conrad Black saw him as an intelligent and scholarly man, who acted with propriety in editorial matters concerning the papers he controlled. Some saw him as leading a revival of newspapers in Canada. The journalist who uses the pseudonym Taki (2004) wrote:

> Conrad Black took the *Telegraph* company, which was moribund, and turned it into a powerful weapon for the values we conservatives believe in. He was a great proprietor, but more important, a great visionary. He and his wife should get their good name back and the sooner the better.

Black was rewarded in 1999 when he was made a British peer, though the Canadian Prime Minister forced him to renounce his Canadian citizenship in order to accept the honour. Black was also a generous host.

> (*Sources*: Burt (2004); Hollinger International Inc. (n.d.), Investor Responsibility Research Centre (IRRC) (2004); *Observer* (2004); Paris et al. (2004); Parker (2004); Rees-Mogg (2004); Rubin (2004))

Discussion activity 2.18

- Can a greedy person be a good visionary and corporate leader?

- What ethical problems might flow from dual-voting structures and 'super shares'?

- Conrad Black was the effective owner of Hollinger International; could he not do as he wished with his property?

- What rights, if any, did or should the minority shareholders have in such companies?

- Have you ever manipulated your expenses or used organisational resources for personal benefits?

Case study 2.19   BAT and allegations of cigarette smuggling

An oddity in the world market for cigarettes was discovered in 1997. When global exports were compared with global imports one-third of the total inventory was unaccounted for. The reason was not hard to find. Up to one-third of cigarettes sold are smuggled. The charge made by investigators and journalists against BAT was that it colluded with tobacco smuggling and factored the sales of smuggled cigarettes into its strategic planning. The charge was not that BAT employees actually took cigarettes across borders without paying the excise duties. It was that they sold

▶

cigarettes to distributors whom they knew would avoid paying tax. This conclusion was drawn from a study of BAT's internal documents, which were made public as a result of legal cases in the USA and in the UK.

BAT used a series of euphemisms for smuggling in its documentation. They included DNP (duty not paid), GT (general trade) and transit goods. Legal goods were known as DP – duty paid. One extract from the documentation illustrates the process. It concerns a 1995 dispute in Colombia between BAT and Philip Morris over the ownership of a cigarette brand called Belmont. One memorandum proposed a contingency plan to be used in the event that BAT lost the case. The plan was 'to launch a new brand in DP and maintain Belmont in a GT channel'. One problem with selling Belmont through GT was that the 'company could not support Belmont in GT through advertising'. Advertising a product that was not officially imported might have caused the revenue authorities to ask questions.

Kenneth Clarke, the deputy chairman of BAT, and a one-time Chancellor of the Exchequer who had been responsible for UK duties on tobacco, responded to these criticisms when they were published in *The Guardian*. He pointed out that smuggling was a major problem in the tobacco business. Cigarettes are easily transportable and of high value. These factors, combined with the high rates of duty and the high differentials between the taxes of neighbouring countries, provide incentives for smuggling. He pointed out that BAT was always willing to cooperate with governments that wished to crack down on smuggling. He added:

> However, where governments are not prepared to address the underlying causes of the problem, businesses such as ours who are engaged in international trade are faced with a dilemma. If the demand for our brands is not met, consumers will either switch to our competitors' brands or there will be the kind of dramatic growth in counterfeit products that we have recently seen in our Asian markets. Where any government is unwilling to act or their efforts are unsuccessful, we act, completely within the law, on the basis that our brands will be available alongside those of our competitors in the smuggled as well as the legitimate market.

Audrey Wise, a Member of Parliament and a member of the House of Commons Health Committee, said of BAT's policy:

> If there was ever a case of being within the letter of the law but clearly outside the spirit of the law then this is a gem. Smuggled goods are illegal goods, so if you're deliberately making your goods available for smuggling knowingly and deliberately you are an accessory to the fact.

(*Sources*: Center for Public Enquiry, 2000; Clarke, 2000; Maguire, 2000)

Discussion activity 2.19

Should companies accept being placed at a competitive disadvantage by following the spirit as well as the letter of the law?

The next case study raises a large number of ethical issues. One is whether doctors used people's ignorance of the law and the regulations to 'cheat' parents grieving for their dead children.

| Case study 2.20 | **The retention of dead babies' organs in hospitals** |

When a child dies in the UK the coroner can order a post-mortem examination to discover the cause of death. A hospital can also order a post-mortem with the parents' consent to study the disease that killed the child. After post-mortems, organs from the child are often retained for research or educational purposes. Doctors assumed, wrongly, that a coroner's request for a post-mortem allowed them to retain organs. In other cases the law merely required that the parents should not object. Over a period of years a collection of 50,000 organs from dead children was established in a number of English hospitals. The general public were unaware of these collections; more importantly the parents of the children were not aware the organs had been retained. Even where parents had given consent to post-mortems they were not necessarily aware that the hospital could remove and retain the organs. The parents had not been given the opportunity to give full and informed consent. This is a form of cheating that arose, as Professor Kennedy argued, 'from a type of professional arrogance that ignored – indeed did not acknowledge, the views and voices of parents'.

The issue exploded into the public's consciousness because of the Alder Hey hospital case. Professor van Velzen at that hospital had developed an obsession with organ retention. The Redfern report into Alder Hey found that van Velzen had ordered illegal retention of children's organs, had falsified records and had failed to catalogue the specimens. The identification of this particular example of illegal activity triggered the investigations that revealed a culture of mendacity over organ retention in many hospitals. The issue released raw emotions, as parents who believed they had buried their dead child requested that they be allowed to bury their child's retained remains.

The impact of these new stories was a tightening-up of rules for organ retention and an unwillingness of the public to allow organs to be retained. Researchers began to complain that research into cancers was being prevented because of the difficulty of obtaining human material for use in trials and experiments. The pharmaceutical companies were removing clinical development from UK to Europe because of the difficulties in obtaining materials for work on breast and prostate cancers.

(*Sources*: Anon., 2001; Boseley, 2001a; Boseley, 2001b; Redfern Report, 2001)

| Discussion activity 2.20 |

Was the general practice (rather than the particular practice of Dr van Velzen) of retaining organs without proper consent a case of actions being ethical but illegal?

Part five: Discouraging badness

Bullying

In organisations bullying is the misuse of power to abuse, humiliate or cajole others. Unlike bullying in the school playground, which may also involve physical harm, organisational bullying is more likely to be social. Some bullying may be too insignificant or transient to be turned into an issue. But where should the line between the insignificant and the significant be drawn? At what point does proper assertion, within a negotiation for example, become an improper use of aggression? The problem is made worse by people's differing perceptions of acceptable, and unacceptable, behaviour. What may be harassment from a supervisor, from a subordinate's point of view, may be an effective example of leadership from the team leader's perspective.

Video clip 2.1	**Bullies on the job**
	The clip deals with bullying and harassment at work.
	To view the video clip please visit this book's companion website at www.pearsoned.co.uk/fisherlovell.

One answer to the problem of bullying is to allow the victim to define it. This empowers the weak against the strong by accepting that if someone says they are being bullied then they are. If a legal perspective were to be taken this would put the burden of proof on the accused and not on the victim. The accused would have to prove they were innocent. This, of course, is the opposite of the legal custom that the accused is innocent until proved guilty.

The following case may not look like bullying but it is an example of a company using its dominant position to control the actions of its agents. It raises the question of when assertive marketing and selling practices cross the line and become illegal.

Case study 2.21	**British Airways and Virgin Atlantic**

British Airways (BA) and Virgin Atlantic have for many years been in intense competition. In 1993 Virgin had accused BA of 'dirty tricks' that discouraged customers from buying tickets from Virgin. In the subsequent libel proceedings BA paid Richard Branson, the chairman of Virgin, £610,000 to settle the case. Virgin started proceedings in the United States courts seeking damages for BA's unfair and illegal marketing practices.

The core of Virgin's complaints was that BA, by far the larger of the two airlines, was using its dominant position in the market to coerce travel agents to sell its flights. This was done by only paying agents certain commissions when they had sold a quota of BA flights, and by packaging discounts on flights. People who travelled to destinations where BA had little competition were offered additional discounts if they bought BA connecting flights in areas where there were many alternative carriers. In November 1997 Virgin formally complained to the European Commission that these 'illegal' practices were in breach of Article 86 of the Treaty of Rome, which covers abuse of dominant market position.

In 1998 BA accused Virgin Atlantic, in its in-house magazine *BA News*, of using similar marketing techniques to those that BA was accused of using. In November of that year Sir Colin Marshall, chairman of BA, apologised to Richard Branson for the accusations and destroyed all copies of the magazine.

In 1999 the European Commission fined BA £4.5m for operating an anti-competitive loyalty scheme with travel agents. The Competition Commissioner said, 'It is well established in community law that a dominant supplier cannot give incentives to its customers and distributors to be loyal to it, so foreclosing the market from the dominant firm's competitors'. BA announced it would appeal. In October of the same year a New York judge threw out Virgin Atlantic's claim against BA. One lawyer pointed out that the notion of a 'dominant company' did not exist in American law.

At the end of 1999 it appeared that BA's ticketing practices were illegal in the European Union but legal in the United States.

(*Sources*: Anon., 1997; Anon., 1999a; Anon., 1999b; Skapinker, 1998)

The story entered the mythology of business and Sir Richard Branson did his best to keep it fresh; especially as in one version first published in 1994 (Gregory and Rufford, 1994) he was presented as a hero – a combination of a 'corporate Peter Pan' and a 'misty eyed Corinthian' (Tilney, 2000). (Unfortunately Corinthian has a range of meanings from 'a wealthy sports enthusiast', through 'a fashionable man' to 'someone given to elegant dissipation'.) Virgin republished the book in 2000. In 2003 Richard Branson sought to take over the operation of Concorde from BA when the latter announced it would be taken out of service. BA announced this intervention as a 'stunt' and Branson retorted that BA was acting in ways reminiscent of its dirty tricks campaign in the 'bad old days' (Done, 2003).

The ill feeling between the two companies has also had significant commercial effects. The case of airline routes to India is an example. The commercial flights between India and the UK have long been constrained and controlled by a bilateral treaty. Consequently the supply of direct services was much less than the demand. In 2004 the two countries agreed a new deal that would increase the number of flights between them from 19 to 40 a week. BA had held the rights to all of the flights under the old treaty and Virgin only provided a limited service to Delhi through a deal with Air India. The Civil Aviation Authority held a competition for the new services because BA had applied for all 21 and Virgin for 18 (Done, 2004). BA were awarded seven, Virgin ten and British Midland four.

For 17 months from August 2004 and January 2006 it looked as if the two companies were collaborating. Executives from both companies met to agree the prices they would charge for the fuel supplements that were necessitated by increases in fuel prices. Of course, this was against competition law because they should have been competing on fuel surcharges and not making life comfortable for each other by ensuring one did not undercut the other. It appears that both companies were willing participants in the cartel. Then Virgin blew the whistle and informed the competition authorities about the collusion. Companies who blow the whistle on such practices are given immunity against prosecution. The result was that Virgin escaped all penalties whilst all the opprobrium was laid at the door of BA, which was also fined £121.5m by the Office of Fair Trading (BBC News Online, 2007b).

Discussion activity 2.21

Is corporate bullying as common as personal bullying? Is it more or less of an ethical wrong than personal bullying?

This next case involves powerful individuals within an organisation exploiting their strength.

Case study 2.22   The hospital consultants

Extract from an interview with an accountant in a hospital

You will be aware I am sure, through the media, that the government this year has made available an extra £500 million or £600 million for trying to reduce the waiting lists [of patients awaiting treatment]. What that means with a hospital like this is that suddenly you have got to do an extra lot of work, very quickly over a short period of time and it doesn't really give you time to get additional staff employed. You are really talking about expecting either existing staff to do overtime or to get some agency staff in to help. Also we haven't had confirmation that this money will be recurrent, although it is likely to be. But because we haven't had that specific guarantee, hospitals are reluctant to employ people on open-ended contracts.

One of the problems we then face is with consultant surgeons, a lot, if not all, of whom have private work as well, and there are some of them who say, 'Right, I will do this extra work, provided I am paid such and such a rate'. The rates that they are inclined to quote will be what they would charge privately. I think they forced the hospital's arm into agreeing to it. They got what they wanted then ... They will see their job probably in a wider context than just their work in the NHS, because it is regular, their private work. What their stance of course is, if you are wanting me to do this extra NHS session, in theory I am foregoing doing a private session somewhere else, so I want to be compensated at least somewhere near the level of income that I would have earned.

It causes me some unease. I suppose in terms of unfairness. If we haven't got additional nurses in the hospital prepared to do extra hours, then we won't get the operations done because it needs a team in the operating theatres, both the consultants and the nurses. But, of course, the nurses haven't got the option of doing private work and being able to earn more money so they haven't got the clout. Yeah, I think, I am sure whoever you speak to, they will see it is the consultants who have got the most clout in the hospital. It is them who can bang the table. Why is it that they can do this? Is it right that they should do this? Don't get me wrong, I am not saying that every surgeon in the hospital has taken a slider, some think the stance taken by most people is totally wrong and unjustified. I know that when there was a meeting of surgeons to discuss it, one particular [consultant] said 'well, he didn't think that any of the surgeons should get additional money for this extra work because they all earned quite enough anyway'. In some ways it can be helpful, because in theory you can maybe marginalise those that have taken a more extreme stance, but that depends really if they are very forceful personalities within the hospital; it depends then whether the hospital management wants to stand up to them.

(*Source*: Research interview conducted by the authors)

Were the consultants exercising their market power legitimately or were they bullying the hospital management?

The bullies in the next case study were organisations rather than an individual or a group.

| Case study 2.23 | **Supermarkets' treatment of their supply chains** |

In recent years there have been many criticisms of the power that the major supermarket chains exercise in the UK. Among these criticisms were the charges that they were using oligarchic power to keep prices to the consumer high and that, by building large out-of-town stores and requiring people to drive to them, they were damaging the environment. The Competition Commission investigated several of these arguments. They found that the market was competitive and that profits were not excessive. However, they did uphold the claim that the big supermarkets did bully (to use our word, not theirs) the farmers and smaller companies locked into their supply chains. The following extract from a *Financial Times* article rehearses some of the arguments.

FT The relationship between food suppliers and retailers will again come under the microscope. In the meantime, ministers want to use a new code of practice between supermarkets and suppliers, one of the recommendations of the Competition Commission report, to clamp down on some of the extreme practices, such as retailers imposing retrospective price cuts to contracts.

A draft code has been drawn up by the Office of Fair Trading with the supermarkets. Food suppliers are being consulted on the results and have signalled their dissatisfaction with what they have seen so far. Instead of calling a halt to some of the practices criticised by the Competition Commission, such as asking suppliers to meet the cost of shop refurbishment or staff hospitality, the code suggests retailers should not 'unreasonably' ask suppliers to foot the bill. But Whitehall officials expect the code to be toughened up during the consultation process. 'The code has to be robust. It has to end the practices the Competition Commission criticised, not just say it would rather they didn't happen. If there is no confidence in the new code, a future government may have to consider further legislation,' said one. Colin Breed, Liberal Democrat agriculture spokesman, believes the code will not help suppliers stand up to supermarkets. 'The only sensible way to proceed is to appoint an independent retail regulator who would not be in the pockets of the supermarkets,' he said.

The industry may also come under the scrutiny of the [House of] Commons' trade and industry committee. Members have praised the sector for helping to deliver lower food prices through fierce competition, but say they are aware suppliers further down the chain often pay the price. Martin O'Neill, committee chairman, said there could be room for an inquiry around the time of the planned sweeping review of the farming industry. 'I would hope that review will spark off a broad debate about the future of retail and the protection of consumer choice just as much as consumers' rights', he said.

▶

Retailers are, of course, keen to avoid any inquiry that focuses directly on their role, although all say they are happy to take part in any wider-ranging review of the supply chain. Inquiries are costly and time consuming. They can also depress share prices across a sector. For many retail analysts, constant carping about supermarket profits risks damaging the industry, leaving it susceptible to overseas predators. 'One day people are weeping and wailing about the fact that Marks and Spencer does not make £1bn profits any more,' said one analyst. 'The next thing, they are complaining that Tesco does just that. Do they want a successful retail industry in this country or not?'

(*Source*: Supermarkets facing more scrutiny after election, *The Financial Times*, 11 April 2001 (Bennett, R. and Voyle, S.), Copyright © The Financial Times Ltd.)

A few years later the Competition Commission did undertake a full-scale investigation and its provisional findings were published in 2007. They again found that overall the market and competition in the grocery trade were working to the consumers' advantage. They did identify some areas of concern. They concluded that the buying power of the large supermarkets was a contributory factor to the decline in farm profitability but that other factors were equally important. However, they found that large suppliers with powerful brands could counter the supermarkets' buying power. They reported that supermarkets adopted various supply chain practices, which transferred risk and unexpected costs from themselves to their primary producers. Although if the code of practice discussed in the above article had not been in place the situation would have been worse (Competition Commission, 2007: § 8.25, § 9.5). In their final report the Commission proposed that an Ombudsman be set up to deal with complaints about purchaser/supplier problems.

A Code of Practice for regulating the relationships between supermarkets and their suppliers was developed by the Competition Commission and the Government agreed in 2010 to establish an independent adjudicator to investigate breaches of the code. However, in 2011 the debate continued as a committee of MPs claimed that the sanctions available to the adjudicator were too weak.

Discussion activity 2.23

How easy is it for supply chain partnerships, which are proposed as a new and better way to manage procurement, to become abusive relationships? How might this tendency, if true, be prevented?

Harming

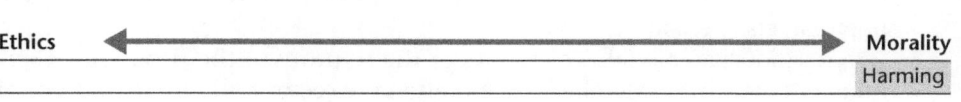

This category involves questions of harm to individuals, animals, institutions, organisations or the environment. One area of controversy is whether a degree of harm is acceptable if the overall results of the harmful action are good. Another concerns the accuracy of the forecasts of the amount of harm and good a particular action will do. An interesting case, which involved such judgments, was that of the Brent Spar oil platform. The issue was whether it was safe to dump the disused platform at sea or whether it would be better to take it ashore and dismantle it. Some time after the issue had been resolved the environmental group Greenpeace admitted that it had exaggerated the amount of environmental harm the sinking of the platform would have done.

Many of the examples of harm being done within or by organisations concern harm to individual employees, as in the following case study.

Case study 2.24	**The *Super Size Me* sales promotion**

The film *Super Size Me* was directed by Morgan Spurlock (2004) and gives a cinematic account of the results of living for 30 days by eating only the food he bought from McDonald's. The question of whether a sensible person would eat such a monotone diet is at the centre of the ethical issue raised by the film. It was a question that had been considered by the American courts in 2002. Ashley Perelman, aged 14, and Jazlyn Bradley, aged 19, were both obese and had many of the health problems associated with the condition. They also ate hugely at McDonald's restaurants. They blamed the McDonald's Corporation and sued it. The judge pointed out that this was a conflict between personal responsibility and public health, and thought the girls were sufficiently knowledgeable and rational to realise that eating too much of what they fancied would not do them good. But the judge's rejection of the girls' claim was not an unalloyed victory for McDonald's (United States District Court, Southern District of New York, 2003). He pointed out that in certain circumstances it could be possible to show that McDonald's might be responsible for its customers' obesity-related ill health. If restaurants do nothing to encourage people to overeat, and provide all the proper nutritional information, then if the customers still decide to eat more than they should that is the customers' problem. If, however, it was shown that any restaurant intended and encouraged customers to eat its food at dangerous rates then 'proximate cause' could be established. Many American restaurants do encourage gluttony by offering a free dessert if a customer can eat, for example, an impossibly sized steak. If it could be shown that McDonald's staff were encouraging people to eat a meal far larger than anyone should eat at a single sitting then the legal situation might be very different. The judge commented,

> The plaintiffs fail to cite any advertisement where McDonald's asserts that its products may be eaten for every meal of every day without any ill consequences [and] if plaintiffs were able to flesh out this argument in an amended complaint, it may establish that the dangers of McDonald's products were not commonly well known and thus that McDonald's had a duty towards its customers.
>
> (United States District Court, Southern District of New York, 2003: 12, 17)

This comment must have acted as the trigger that led Spurlock to make his film, in which there were three rules he chose to follow.

1. He had to eat everything on the McDonald's menu at least once.

2. He could only consume what was on offer at McDonald's, including the water.

3. Whenever McDonald's offered him the option to super size his meal by the addition of extra French fries and sodas he had to take it.

▶

At the start of the month he was fit, healthy and slim; he was checked by doctors who confirmed his healthy condition. Thirty days later he was 35 pounds heavier, with a liver in poor condition and all the symptoms of addiction – twitches, chest pains, headaches. He was also impotent. Some of the latter symptoms, it may be supposed, could have been reinforced by his need for a good film narrative. As one reviewer pointed out,

> Obviously the more rapidly his health deteriorates; the better it is for his career. [ ] When one of his doctors tells him that his liver is malfunctioning and he must stop the diet at once, he keeps a straight face; but we can tell that inwardly he is cheering.

(Wilson, 2004: 17)

The film was a critical success and McDonald's felt it necessary to take out advertisements in the daily newspapers in the UK arguing that it was irresponsible for anyone to eat such an imbalanced diet; and that no sensible person would eat their products alone. They pointed out that eating at McDonald's, if part of a balanced diet, would not cause people problems. They also pointed out that the company had introduced healthy options into its menus, though others pointed out that if the dressings provided with the salads were eaten then the meals had as many calories as the burgers. The messages were reinforced by a special website set up to counter the film's claims (*www.supersizeme-thedebate.co.uk*). It did, however, cease the *Super Size Me* promotion. As Wilson concluded her review of the film,

> The best the food giant can do is to accuse Morgan Spurlock of having acted 'irresponsibly' – by eating too much of its own food.

(Wilson, 2004: 17)

Discussion activity 2.24

1. To what extent should people be protected against their own ignorance and frailties? (This by the way is a standard revealing question because it gives away the feelings of the writer – so you might wish to reframe it.)

2. Is there a litigation culture developing in other regions of the world following US precedents? Is it a bad thing?

Case study 2.25 — Sexual harassment
Extract from a research interview

I mean I haven't had it personally but a very close friend of mine was a secretary in a very large organisation in London and worked for the Assistant Chairman and she felt she was being harassed. Well she was being harassed and when she actually spoke to her personnel department they said, 'Well yes, you're probably right, we've had complaints before but nobody in this organisation will remove the Assistant Chairman. We will help you find another job.' So their compassion went to the individual in getting her another job because their knowledge was, what could they do? The organisation would not support [her], whatever claim she put in, at the end of the day it would not result in his dismissal. It may have resulted in a rap over the knuckles but she could not work for him and . . . sometimes you know that that is the approach you are going to have to take. Fortunately I've never been in that sort of situation of something quite as clearly wrong.

(*Source*: Research interview conducted by the authors)

Discussion activity 2.25

What are the longer-term consequences of not confronting behaviour such as that discussed in the case study?

Video clip 2.2

Fired for being fat

The clip considers whether it is acceptable to fire cocktail waitresses and waiters if they become too fat and no longer match the company's image and values.

To view the video clip from the interview please visit this book's companion website at www.pearsoned.co.uk/fisherlovell.

The next case describes the harm that can be caused by corporate inaction, although in this example there is a dispute as to which of two corporations was culpable. It also raises the question, to be discussed in Chapter 8, of when harm done by corporate indifference can, or should, invite criminal charges as well as civil liabilities.

Case study 2.26

The Firestone Tire recall issue

In August 2000 Ford and Firestone announced the product recall of 6.5 m tyres used on Ford's sports utility vehicle (SUV), the Explorer. The recall was limited to tyres made at Firestone's plant at Decatur in Illinois. Tyres made at other plants were not recalled. The problem was that the treads on the tyres were prone to separate in hot weather; this could cause a loss of control of the vehicle, which could result in a rollover accident. Over 180 people had died in such accidents in the USA and 700 people had been injured.

It was alleged by commentators that Firestone knew the problem was not simply a quality systems fault at Decatur but a general problem that affected all of Firestone's SUV tyres. It was therefore alleged that Firestone, far from putting things right, was replacing the faulty tyres with equally dangerous ones.

The situation was made more complex by the desires of both Ford and Firestone to blame each other for the rollover accidents and the deaths. While Ford blamed Firestone, Firestone

▶

partly blamed design faults in the Explorer. In a report on the accidents Firestone identified some problems for which it was responsible, but also claimed that Ford's recommendation that the tyres should be inflated to a pressure significantly below the tyres' maximum capacity (to overcome a design fault in the Explorer) increased the temperature of the tyres and increased the possibility of tread separation. Ford, in its 'root cause' report, claimed that design problems played no role in the crashes and that under-inflation was not a contributory factor. The argument continued during 2000 and was the subject of Congressional hearings.

On 22 May Firestone announced that it would no longer be a supply partner of Ford, ending a relationship that had lasted nearly a century. On the same day Ford announced that it was recalling 13 m tyres at a cost of $2.1 b. On the previous day it had recalled 47,000 of its SUVs because of fears, unconnected with the Firestone issue, that tyres had been damaged on the production line.

The case paralleled that of the Pinto model, which exercised Ford in the 1970s (De George, 1999: 240–1). The Pinto was a car produced in a hurry. When it was tested for rear-end impact it was found to be below the standard of comparable cars. There was a danger, because of the positioning of the fuel tank, that the tank could be punctured in a crash and the car would explode. Ford undertook a cost-benefit analysis. They estimated that the cost of inserting a protective baffle was greater than the cost of legal claims that might arise from deaths attributable to the design fault. The design of the car was not changed between 1971 and 1978 and the customers were not informed of the potential problem. Between 1976 and 1977 13 Pintos exploded after rear-end crashes. The cost of the legal compensation proved to be much greater than the cost of the alteration and in 1978 the cars were recalled and protective baffles were fitted.

(*Sources*: Turner, 2001; Firestone Tire Resource Center, n.d.; Bowe, 2001)

Discussion activity 2.26

Had Ford's strategic attitude to safety fears concerning its vehicles changed in over 20 years?

This last case study concerns when it might be right to break the law to prevent an organisation doing harm. It also, as it centres on the issue of the moral status of animals, questions the definition of harm.

Case study 2.27   Huntingdon Life Sciences

This case raises questions about whether there are situations in which it is appropriate to take illegal action because either the law is immoral or the law has to be broken to prevent some greater harm being done. This case study concerns Huntingdon Life Sciences (HLS), a company that carries out pharmaceutical testing on laboratory animals. The company's activities are highly regulated by government agencies and the testing it does is legal.

Animal rights activists argue that testing drugs on animals is cruel and immoral. The case raises difficult questions about whether animals have rights. The traditional view was that animals are not accorded moral status or rights because they lack the power to reason. The obvious response is that this does not prevent them from suffering. This argument may justify minimising the pain caused during experiments, but it does not necessarily mean that the experiments are bad in themselves, especially if they contribute to a greater benefit for humanity through the development of better drugs and medical treatments. The arguments around this issue, which are not primarily the concern of this text, can be explored in Tester (1991) and Scruton (2000). When people claim the existence of rights they may be exhibiting emotivism. This simply means claiming something is right because it feels right. Moral judgment becomes a subjective emotional reaction to a situation.

Animal rights activists believe they are justified in using violence, or the threat of violence, to stop vivisection. The shareholders of HLS, as well as its managers and employees, have been intimidated. The activists threatened to identify and protest to the shareholders. Various institutional shareholders decided in consequence to cease investing in HLS and a number of brokers advised shareholders to sell after threats from activists. Two of HLS's market-makers had also withdrawn and this made it difficult for investors to trade their shares. The company responded by proposing to set up a rarely used shareholding structure to keep investors' identities anonymous and to protect them from intimidation. The proposed corporate nominee scheme is within the rules set out by the FSA.

The government felt it had to take action, as described in the following article from the *Financial Times*, to protect a legitimate business.

FT The authorities on Thursday stepped up their fight against animal rights activists with the launch of a police hit squad and a top-level government committee. The two measures are aimed at preventing violent attacks against companies that carry out medical research, their customers and financial backers. The police announced the creation of a squad 'to target the ringleaders of animal [rights] extremist activity who are organising and taking part in serious criminal offences'.

The group will draw officers from different police forces and will work under the National Crime Squad. It aims to prevent attacks such as those suffered by directors, staff and customers of Huntingdon Life Sciences, the drug-testing group. Over the past year, activists have set fire to Huntingdon workers' cars, sent hate mail to staff and assaulted Brian Cass, its managing director. No one has been arrested in connection with these attacks.

The Association of Chief Police Officers denied that the police had acted slowly in dealing with animal rights extremists. It would 'not say [the squad] was late. We felt this was the right time to act.' The squad will liaise with the new government committee, which includes five ministers and is chaired by Jack Straw [at the time, Home Secretary]. The committee will co-ordinate government action against the activists. The home secretary, who on Thursday visited Huntingdon's laboratories in Cambridgeshire, said: 'We will not tolerate a small number of criminals trying to threaten research organisations and companies.' Some 15 protesters stood outside the gates but were denied a meeting with the Home Secretary. Greg Avery of Stop Huntingdon Animal Cruelty said the campaign group had no involvement in the violent attacks.

(*Sources*: Hit squad to tackle animal rights activists by F. Guerrera, www.FT.com, 27 April 2001, Brands feel the impact as activists target customers by E. Alden, *The Financial Times*, 18 July 2001. Copyright © The Financial Times Ltd.)

Discussion activity 2.27

In what situations do you think it might be justified to break, or defy, the law, to end an injustice?

Reflections

This chapter has presented a panorama of the ethical and moral issues that affect managerial and organisational life. Some patterns can be seen to emerge from plotting the case studies on the matrix in Table 2.1. Many of the issues that cause difficulty and controversy in the business and organisational world concern actions that are, arguably, wrong but legal. These cover the range of matters from the ethical to the moral. Issues that centre on actions that are wrong and illegal mainly concern questions of morality rather than ethics. They are about stopping organisations doing harm. Conversely, issues arising from actions that are good and legal, but are not legal obligations, rest mostly at the ethical end of the spectrum in Table 2.1. The most contentious issues, and perhaps the least common, are those concerning illegal actions that are ethically and morally justifiable.

All the case studies are matters of controversy; every claim that an act is illegal or wrong can be challenged. As Watson (2002: 455) argued, ethical ambiguity and ethical dilemmas are inevitable in organisational and managerial life.

Summary

In this chapter the following key points have been made:

- The major virtues of corporate and organisational behaviour are:
  - **Doing good**
    - social development
    - social responsibility

  - **Acting benignly**
    - reciprocity
    - fairness

- The major vices are:
  - **Ignoring harm done to others**
    - lying and dishonesty
    - cheating and selfishness

  - **Doing harm**
    - bullying and social irresponsibility
    - doing social and environmental damage

- Under each of these headings issues at work may raise questions about what is right and what is wrong. What is right may in many cases also be legal but not necessarily a legal obligation. In other cases what is right may not be legal. Conversely, things that the law allows might not be right.

- Ethical issues are not easy to categorise. They appear as dilemmas in which arguments can be made for all sides. The protagonists in the cases, however, may see and present only a single point of view.

Typical assignments

1. In what circumstances might it be right to break the law in an effort to prevent a company behaving in a way that is legal, but, in the eyes of some, immoral?

2. Discuss the proposition that companies should behave in a socially responsible manner but are not obliged to contribute to social development.

3. Are there degrees of lying? Can some forms of lying be acceptable in business and management practice?

4. Should dual class share systems (in which some shares carry more voting weight per share than others) be made illegal? Illustrate your reasons from recent cases.

Group activity 2.1

Locating issues on the grid shown in Table 2.1 is not straightforward. An issue may involve several of the moral and ethical problems identified. It might, for example, exhibit an unfair distribution of resources as well as lying and bullying. It might also be possible to argue about which categories of rightness and legality the issue best fits. Different readings of the facts of the case might lead to different opinions about whether an action was, *prima facie*, illegal or not.

In class identify current business ethics issues that are being discussed in the media. Identify as best you can the facts of the issue and discuss where, on the grid in Table 2.1, the issue might best be placed. It might be necessary to plot different aspects of the issue in different places on the grid.

Recommended further reading

A good review of issues in business ethics is P.W.F. Davies (ed.) (1997) *Current Issues in Business Ethics*, London: Routledge. Allhoff and Vaidya (2008) *Business in Ethical Focus: An Anthology*, Ontario: Broadview, is a more recent review of business ethics topics. D. Winstanley and J. Woodall (2000) *Ethical Issues in Contemporary Human Resource Management*, London: Macmillan, is a very useful guide to ethical issues related to human resource management.

Useful websites

Topic	Website provider	URL
A business ethics blog	Chris McDonald	http://businessethicsblog.com/
A website that reports on current business and human rights issues	Business and Human Rights Resource Centre: a charitable not-for-profit organisation set up to promote discussion of human rights issues in business	http://www.business-humanrights.org/Home
John Entine is a controversialist who first came to prominence by criticizing the business ethics of *The Body Shop*	An online magazine edited by John Entine	http://www.ethicalcorp.com/
Most of EIRI'S services are subscription based but it does provide press releases which identify emerging business ethics issues	EIRIS (Ethical Investment Research Service)	http://www.eiris.org/publications.html
A London-based organisation concerned with human rights in business	The Institute for Human Rights & Business	http://www.ihrb.org

CHAPTER 3

Ethical theories and how to use them

Chapter at a glance

Chapter contents

- Learning outcomes
- Introduction
- A map of ethical theories
- Applying ethical theories
- Reflections
- Summary

Activities and exercises

- Video clip 3.1 Interview with the Canon Precentor of St Paul's Cathedral, London. Priorities and human flourishing
- Discussion activity 3.1 Conscience
- Discussion activity 3.2 Kantian ethics
- Discussion activity 3.3 Rawlsian justice
- Discussion activity 3.4 The 'do no harm' perspective
- Discussion activity 3.5 Utilitarian ethics
- Discussion activity 3.6 Corporate Social Responsibility
- Discussion activity 3.7 Ethical egoism & objectivism
- Discussion activity 3.8 Virtue ethics
- Discussion activity 3.9 Decency
- Activity 3.1 The Ethical Corporate Decisions Toolkit
- Activity 3.2 Prioritising your ethical principles
- Activity 3.3 The TI Ethics Quick Test
- Typical assignments
- Group activity 3.1
- Recommended further reading
- Useful websites

Learning outcomes

Having read this chapter and completed its associated activities, readers should be able to:

- Compare and contrast 10 approaches to ethical thinking.
- Describe the implications of different ethical theories for businesses, organisations and management.
- Apply the theories to ethical issues in business, organisation and management.

Introduction

In Chapter 2 the range of ethical issues that can affect businesses, organisations and managers was plotted and examples were given that you were invited to think about. This chapter will give you tools for ethical thinking that you can use to analyse such issues. We have called them ethical theories because they are speculations or mental conceptions about how one should think about ethical matters. They should help you to move from an intuitive response to ethical matters to a systematic and analytical approach; a shift from system 1 to system 2 thinking as Kahnemann (2011) terms it. However, the theories do not provide an easy resolution. One reason for this is that there are many theories and it may not be obvious which should be applied to any particular set of circumstances. A second reason is that the theories are general. It is not always clear how they should be applied or interpreted in specific cases. The fact that some of these theories have been the subject of philosophical debate for many centuries implies that there is no consensus, or final resolution, to be had on these questions. It may be best to consider that the theories provide means of legitimating the stances you take on an issue rather than as sources of definitive or authoritative solutions.

A map of ethical theories

A map or framework of ethical theories is shown in Figure 3.1. Any fans of Madonna may recognise the form of the diagram as the Ten Sefirot of Kabbalah, of which Madonna is, or was, an enthusiast. Kabbalah is a system of medieval Jewish mysticism that in the twenty-first century has been revived as an aspect of New Age philosophies. The authors of this book are not New Agers. We have not adopted the diagram of the Sefirot for mystical reasons but because it expresses a convenient logic for explaining how the various ethical perspectives that we shall use in this chapter link together. Towards the end of the chapter this framework will be used as the basis of a corporate ethical decision-making tool.

In Figure 3.1 each of the ovals represents a particular ethical perspective or way of thinking. Each of these will be explained in detail in this chapter. At

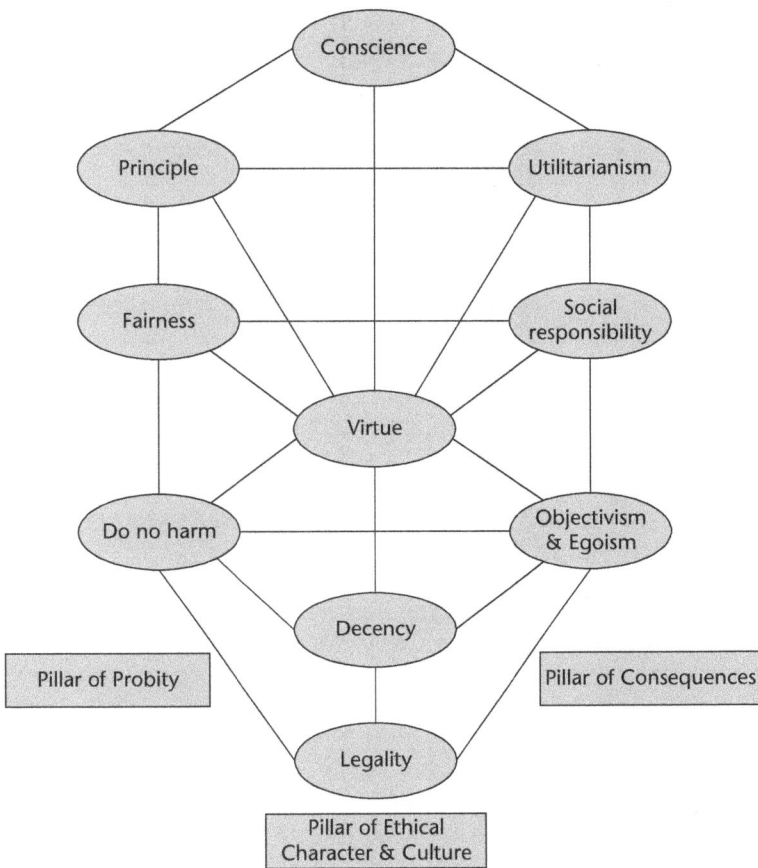

Figure 3.1 A framework for ethical theories

the end of the chapter they are used as the foundation of a toolkit designed to help people make ethical corporate decisions. The 10 ethical perspectives are divided into three columns or pillars. On the left is a pillar of probity, on the right a pillar of consequences and in between them a pillar of ethical character and culture. The two outer pillars are in tension with each other. As in the original Kabbalah version of the diagram the left-hand pillar is concerned with constraint and proper behaviour. In the terms developed by Dworkin (1977: 48) this pillar includes standards that have to be observed, not because they will advance an economic, political or social situation, but because they are a requirement of fairness or justice or some other dimension of morality. They take no regard of the consequences of an action as in 'let justice be done though the heavens fall', a maxim of Roman law that was famously used in 1772 by Lord Mansfield during a legal case concerning slavery. Whereas the right-hand column is focused on action and impact. It is a policy-focused pillar and is defined by considering the goal to be reached, generally an improvement in some economic, political or social feature. The middle column has the function of mediating between these opposing imperatives. The balance is achieved by people, either as individuals or as participants in an organisational culture, exercising their ethical judgment and moral imagination in deciding what the right thing to do is, and willing it into action. These three pillars can also be associated with a commonly made distinction in ethics between:

- Deontology – the pillar of probity
- Teleology – the pillar of consequences
- Virtue ethics – the pillar of ethical character and culture

Deontology is the study of the right action, which it is it is the duty of all to do, even if there are sometimes bad consequences. Teleology derives from the Greek word *telos*, which means an end to be achieved. Therefore teleology means that the rightness or goodness of an action is not intrinsic to that action but can only be judged by its consequences. These theories are sometimes therefore called consequentialist. Virtue ethics is concerned with finding a balanced position between extremes.

A brief description of the framework can be started by looking at the middle pillar of character and culture. At the top and bottom of this pillar are conscience and legality, respectively. All the pillars are hierarchical in that the higher positions exhibit a higher level of ethics than the lower ones. For example simply conforming to the law shows a lower level of ethical development than acting according to conscience. In between these two positions are virtue ethics proper, and below that, but above legality, is decency. Decency is a minimal form of ethical behaviour. A decent person does not seek to constrain or harm others but neither do they show any positive concern for other's welfare. The pillar of probity has a sequence of standards of behaviour. The lowest one requires no more than that a person does no harm. The next position up, fairness, requires as a principle that those who are worst off in a society should not be made worse off to the benefit of the best favoured in society. At the top of this pillar is principle, which is the most demanding expectation on this column, and which obliges people to apply certain universal principles in all their actions. At the apex of the pillar of consequences is utilitarianism, which seeks the greatest good of the greatest number. Below that is corporate social responsibility, which is also concerned with a balance of beneficial consequences but with a narrower remit, concerned only with those parts of society with which a company or organisation is involved. At the lowest point on this pillar is objectivism, which is narrower still and only concerns what is good for the organisation, or perhaps narrower yet what is good for the owners of the organisation.

Each of these ethical perspectives will be discussed in turn.

Legality

At the bottom of the ethical framework in Figure 3.1 is legality. This subject has already been discussed in Chapter 2. Legality is at the bottom of the framework because it requires someone to make only a minimal ethical effort. When evaluating or proposing an action a person simply has to discover whether that action is legal or illegal. Laws of course seek to be definitive but the complexity of actions and society means that sometimes it is not known whether something is legal or not until it has been tested in the courts. Again, should the situation arise, the ethical choice is made by the courts and not by the individual. It can be argued that the principle of the Rule of Law reinforces individual's lack of responsibility for thinking through the ethics of a thing themselves. The Rule of Law means that no one is above the law, as long as the law has been promulgated in a legitimate and transparent manner. The principle developed out of the need to protect individuals against arbitrary government. However, it also implies that people should not disobey a law even though they think it wrong or bad. They do though have the democratic right to use legitimate processes to seek to change a law of which they disapprove.

In terms of business ethics legality can be extended to include the rules, regulation and policies of the organisations within which people work. These do not have the same force as national or international laws and therefore the grounds on which organisational rules can be broken, if they are considered unethical, will be slighter than those needed to justify disobeying laws on the grounds of their immorality.

Conscience

Conscience can be seen from a psychoanalytical perspective but in this section conscience is viewed as a way of reasoning about whether a particular act is ethical or not. For this purpose it is placed at the top of the framework in Figure 3.1. It is also in this position because all the other ethical perspectives in the framework are subordinate to conscience. To illustrate the type of thinking conscience may involve we will use, what Arjoon (2007) names, triple-font theory. This is not a new approach but is closely based on the theology and philosophy of St Thomas Aquinas who lived between 1225 and 1274. His philosophy, called Thomism, is at the core of Roman Catholic teaching.

Cross reference	You can find a discussion of conscience from a psychoanalytical perspective in Chapter 5.

The three fonts that are used to judge whether an action can be taken in good conscience are:

- moral object;

- intention; and

- circumstances.

The test of moral object asks whether the end or purpose of a proposed action is good. Moral object is concerned with the moral form or kind of the act as determined by some absolute moral precepts. Intention refers, not to the object of an action but to the motive of the person who proposes carrying it out. Intention is concerned with people's will to act and whether their intentions are moral. Finally circumstances may change the moral nature of an act. By circumstances is meant the particular setting and context within which an act is being considered. These can include the condition of the person, whether for example they are suffering a mental illness, or whether they are being prevented from acting morally by some insuperable force. Some circumstances are aggravating factors that do not change whether an action is moral or immoral but simply either increase or decrease the degree of goodness or badness. There are also specifying circumstances that change the ethical nature of an action rather than simply emphasise its goodness or badness. The reason why someone plans or undertakes an act is a specifying circumstance, although this is seen as separate from the person's intention (Smith, n.d.: Arjoon, 2007: 399–400). A company seeking its own self-interest by cutting costs, of itself, is a matter of moral indifference; but the circumstance of doing it in a way that does harm, by say bullying partners in a supply chain, would make it unethical.

A consideration of circumstance may identify that an action will have a mixture of both good and bad consequences. The double-effect principle is proposed by Arjoon (2007) to deal with situations where an action can have both good and bad consequences. If four conditions, developed by Aquinas, are met an action that has bad effects as well as good effects can be ethical. The conditions are that the action itself must be moral, the good effect must not be achieved through the bad effect, the bad effect must not be an intention and finally, there must be sound reasons for tolerating the bad effect. The principle of double effect allows the aggravating, mitigating or justifying circumstances of an action to be taken into account when judging the action's morality.

Cross reference	A particular example of this manner of reasoning, applying the princicple of double effect, is Aquinas' discussion of the Just War. This is discussed in Chapter 2.

Trolleyology and the double-effect principle

The trolley problem is a thought experiment that can be explained by the double-effect principle. It was developed by Phillippa Foot and Judith Jarvis Thomson and its study has expanded so much as to become an 'ology'. Imagine there is a fast train racing down a track towards five people who will certainly be killed. But before the train reaches them there is a spur track that will divert the train from its otherwise inevitable victims; and you have the button that will switch the points. The only snag is that on the spur there is a man chained to the rails. So, here is the ethical dilemma; do you switch the points and so condemn one man to death but save five others or do you do nothing and stand back as five die? Then consider a slightly different situation. This time there is no spur track, but standing beside you on a bridge over the rails is a fat man who, if you push him onto the track, will stop the train and so save the lives of the other five who are still in danger further down the track. Although the cold morality of the two situations is the same;

should you sacrifice one life to save five, most people say they would throw the points but they would not push the fat man onto the track (Edmond, 2010). The double-effect principle can be used to explain this preference. If you switch the points in the spur line scenario the act is good, even though there is also a bad effect (the death of the individual man), because it is not your intention to kill him, because and because the overall effect of the act is good. In the fat man scenario, however, the act of pushing your neighbour onto the track requires an intention to kill him. The double-effect principle therefore says this act cannot be moral. Some people have argued that the double-effect principle is a neurological imperative that we cannot easily overcome; which is, conveniently, quite a good definition of conscience.

Amongst Catholic philosophers there is a debate about the impact that circumstances can have on the nature of moral norms. The proportionalists argue that ethical rules cannot be absolute if they are influenced by circumstances. The Papacy declares that there are absolute moral principles and that the proportionalists are guilty of error. This orthodoxy argues that circumstances may change a person's culpability for a bad act but they cannot make a bad act good. They also claim that the proportionalists focus on intention and circumstances but ignore moral object. However, this argument requires claiming that circumstances may not always be circumstances; but may be a part of the form of the moral object (Smith, n.d.). It can be claimed that the orthodox start from the position that there are absolute moral norms and then struggle valiantly to interpret Thomist philosophy in a way that supports that view. If it is believed that there are, at least some, absolute values then conscience cannot be above principle, as it is shown in Figure 3.1; and it ought to have been included in the next section that deals with principle. If principles have to be weighted, or put into proportion, in response to circumstances then conscience involves judging object, intention and circumstances to come a conclusion about the morality of an action.

Discussion activity 3.1   Conscience

Apply the triple-font test to Michael Shayler's whistleblowing described in Case study 2.6. Was the action a moral one? If it was were there circumstances that diminished his culpability?

Principle; Kantian ethics

One of the most important western philosophers of duty and principle was Immanuel Kant who came from Konigsberg in Germany, now known as Kaliningrad in Russia, and lived between 1724 and 1804. His ethical principles are the basis of the highest position on the column of probity in Figure 3.1

Kant's ethical philosophy was that actions must be guided by universalisable principles that apply irrespective of the consequences of the actions. In addition an action can only be morally right if it is carried out as a duty, not in expectation of a reward. From a Kantian perspective, principles exist *a priori*. By this is meant that, knowing what to do in a situation will be determined by a set of principles that have been established by deductive reasoning, independent of, or before, the specifics of the decision in hand have been considered. Indeed, for Kantian ethics the context and consequences of a decision are irrelevant. Lying, for example, is invariably employed to illustrate the inflexibility of Kantian ethics. Lying, irrespective of the context, is wrong. So, for Kant, truth telling, even if the telling of a lie would save a human life, has to be strictly adhered to – no deviations, no exceptions.

For Kant actions have moral worth only when they spring from recognition of duty, and a choice to discharge it. The 'duties' to which Kant refers were a response to the question, 'What makes a moral act right?' They were formulated around the concept of the 'categorical imperative'.

Categorical imperative   DEFINITION

Categorical means unconditional (no exceptions), while imperative means a command or, in Kantian terms, a principle. Thus a categorical imperative refers to a command/principle that must be obeyed, with no exceptions. If the categorical imperative is conceptually sound we should be able to will all rational people around the world to follow this particular law. This is the concept of universalisability.

The Ten Commandments of the Old Testament are written in the form of categorical imperatives, i.e. 'Thou shalt not . . .', although the extent to which they are universalisable is problematic. (The commandment 'thou shalt not kill' is debated below.)

For Kant an act is morally right if it can be judged by all reasoning people to be appropriate as a universal principle of conduct, irrespective of whether they are to be the doers, receivers or mere observers of an act. The issue of putting oneself in a state of ignorance as to one's own position within a situation is an interesting one, and one to which we will return when we discuss the ideas of John Rawls.

The 'Golden Rule', which is normally expressed as 'do unto others as you would have done unto yourself', is an example of a categorical imperative. It is a rule that can be willed as universalisable. Indeed, Shaw and Barry (1998) cited the scriptures of six world religions, which go back over millennia, identifying quotations from each that are examples of the 'Golden Rule'.

Bowie (1999), in his proposal for business organisations built upon Kantian principles, provided three formulations of the categorical imperative.

1. The first is that universalisability provides a theory of moral permissibility for market interactions. Interactions that violate the universalisability formulation of the categorical imperative are morally impermissible. This might appear reasonable, but it must be remembered that under this rule someone who is prepared to allow others to exploit, harm and cheat him could, within the universalisability principle, proceed to exploit, harm and cheat others. Bowie tackled this issue when he cited Carr (1968), who argued for a different set of rules and morality for business. Carr observed:

The golden rule for all its value as an ideal for society is simply not feasible as a guide for business. A good part of the time the businessman is trying to do to others as he hopes others will not do unto him . . . The game [poker] calls for distrust of the other fellow. It ignores the claim for friendship. Cunning, deception and concealment of one's strength and intentions, not kindness and open-heartedness, are vital in poker. And no-one should think any worse of the game of business because its standards of right and wrong differ from the prevailing traditions of morality in our society.

(Carr, 1968: 145–6)

A further example of this attitude is provided by Pava (1999) who, drawing upon the work of Badaracco (1997), referred to the case of the pharmaceutical company, Roussel-Uclaf, and its chairman, Edouard Sakiz. The case concerned the abortion drug, RU 486. Sakiz wished to market the drug, but a range of powerful interest groups opposed the drug's sale, including Roussel-Uclaf's majority shareholder, the multinational Hoechst organisation. One of Hoechst's drugs (Zyklon B) had been used by the Nazis in their pogrom against the Jews in the Second World War. Since then the company had committed itself to 'placing our energy, our ideas and our dedication to the service of Life' (Pava, 1999: 82). Sakiz is claimed to have employed a devious and high-risk strategy, in which he forced a vote of the executive committee on the drug's launch, voting against the decision himself. However, in so doing he compromised the French government, which was keen to see the drug launched. The French government threatened to move production of the drug to another company, which forced Roussel-Uclaf to reconsider its decision. This it did, but now 'under the seeming protection of the government' (Pava, 1999: 83). Pava observed:

Sakiz obtained his ultimate goal and avoided the pitfall of publicly proclaiming his real intentions. Badaracco justifies such seeming hypocrisy by stating that public leaders must follow a 'special ethical code', one that differs from their private morality and from Judeo-Christian ethics. Badaracco elaborates that 'only a naive manager would think otherwise'.

(Pava, 1999: 83)

A Kantian refutation of this argument would avoid a consequentialist assessment, that businesses could not work effectively if lying and deviousness was the universal norm, on the basis that Kant refused to allow considerations of consequences to enter into issues of ethics. Instead a Kantian refutation would take the form of a rebuttal of the logic of the attempted categorical imperative, 'always lie, always be devious'. If everyone always lied or was devious, there would be no point in listening to what anyone had to say. Conversation, language even, would be meaningless and would therefore become redundant. Thus, 'always lie, always be devious' cannot be universalised. Because categorical imperatives are derived deductively, they can be successfully challenged, if flawed.

2. Bowie's second formulation of the categorical imperative is 'respect for humanity in persons'. This is normally taken to mean treating fellow human beings as ends not means. However, Bowie's formulation is looser than this, and might fail to achieve this objective. Bowie's argument is that this formulation provides the basis for a moral obligation in the employment of people. Employees would cease to be commodities. Everyone involved in market transactions – employees, suppliers, customers and indeed all stakeholders – should be treated with respect. However, this presupposes that it is not possible to treat a commodity with respect. If it is possible to do so, then this formulation fails to achieve its stated aim – to treat people as ends not means. The ultimate test of this formulation would be the reaction of the Kantian organisation to a dramatic fall in demand for its goods or services. If the economics of the situation demanded cost-cutting measures for the firm to survive, with redundancies high on the agenda, the people-as-ends-not-means philosophy is severely tested. It is possible to show respect to those who are being made redundant, for example by providing as generous a financial severance package as is feasible, providing counseling sessions and assistance in interviewing techniques, but, in the end, the redundant employees are redundant because they are judged to be a resource that can no longer be justified (economically) by the firm. They are ultimately a means, not an end.

This particular circle can only be squared if it is acknowledged at the outset that a market-based economy is the backdrop against which the Kantian firm is located. Thus, it is within the actions permitted by market dynamics and economic logic that the Kantian perspective is being argued. In which case, short-term pressures from financial markets to protect the company's share price are likely to take precedence over desires to accept lower profit figures in order to protect employment levels. Any significant deviation from this set of relationships would require a different set of institutional arrangements between a business and its significant investors from that which currently exists. These issues are taken up further when we discuss the stakeholder perspective later in the chapter.

3. The third formulation is an attempt to further minimise or remove the 'people-as-means' accusation. It is an argument for greater democracy in the workplace – the moral community formulation. For example, by involving all employees (or at least their representatives) in corporate decision making, as with the 'Type A' pluralist model discussed in Chapter 1, the Kantian firm will seek out the most equitable solution when faced with a severe downturn in its markets, arriving at a 'way forward' that reflects the views of the employees. Whether this will be the majority view, or some other formulation, would presumably be left to the firm to decide.

The criticisms leveled at Kantian ethics, over the rigidity of the categorical imperative, are challenged by both Beck (1959) and Bowie (1999). Kant is partly to blame for the criticism, argued Beck, because of the examples he used to illustrate his principles (Kant actually argued for truth telling in a situation in which a lie would save an innocent life). One possible way out of this cul-de-sac is to create a hierarchy of categorical imperatives. In this way the categorical imperative of 'always tell the truth' would be inferior to the categorical imperative of 'lie if it will save an innocent life'. Whether this form of hierarchical formulation is permissible, within a strictly Kantian categorical imperative perspective, is debatable. The notion of categorical imperatives being ranked contains a logical inconsistency. If categorical imperative 'A' can be overridden on occasions by categorical imperative 'B', then it cannot be a categorical imperative because it is not universalisable. We will return to this issue when we discuss *prima facie* obligations, but for the moment we will concentrate upon those writers and arguments that have sought to stay true to an undiluted version of the categorical imperative, but have offered ways of overcoming its rigidity.

De George (1999) offers one such resolution. The scenario depicted by De George addresses the truth-telling categorical imperative. It involves the shielding of an escaped slave who is being pursued by his slaveholder. For De George an untruth that might be told to the slaveholder to throw him off the scent would *not* be construed as a lie, on the basis that slavery is immoral, irrespective of what the law of the land might say. The slaveholder is not judged to have a legitimate interest in the information being sought. Under this interpretation the telling of an untruth is not lying if the person seeking information has no legitimate (ethically acceptable) interest in the information.

This approach is arguing that the telling of an untruth to someone who does not possess a morally legitimate interest in the information being sought is not merely acceptable, but accordingly not actually a lie. The enquirer's lack of moral legitimacy does not warrant the same level of truthfulness from the respondent, as would be required if the enquirer had possessed a legitimate interest.

Kant's use of truth telling has created many problems for the principle of categorical imperatives. The above, rather tortuous, attempts to try to overcome them are not altogether convincing. Purposely misconstruing known facts is a lie, to whomever the lie is to be told, and whatever the justification for the lie. By adopting a pure Kantian perspective, the concealer of the slave is left with no option but to reveal the whereabouts of the slave. However, if the protection of an innocent person is judged more important than telling an untruth, at a *universalisable* level, then there is something wrong with making truth telling a categorical imperative.

The critical question with regard to the truth-telling example used by Kant thus becomes: is the flaw within the principle of a categorical imperative, or is the problem the use of truth telling as an example of a categorical imperative? Whilst Kant did indeed cite truth telling as an example of a categorical imperative, this is not to say that the example is an appropriate or helpful one. If the way out of this difficult situation is simply to reject truth telling as an example of a categorical imperative, then further questions arise, namely:

(a) Is it possible to identify a categorical imperative? and/or

(b) Is it not possible to think of at least one exception to every categorical imperative that might be suggested, thereby nullifying its claim to being universalisable?

You might, for example, suggest 'one should not kill another human being' as a categorical imperative. But would a mother be morally wrong to respond to the pleas of her child who was being attacked by someone intent on taking the child's life? The killing of the assailant might be unpremeditated, unintentional even, but in an unequal struggle between mother and crazed assailant, how does the mother defend her child and herself? This is not to say that the killing of the assailant is the only outcome possible from such a scenario, but what is the status of a categorical imperative of 'no-taking-of-life', if the mother does ultimately stab or shoot the assailant? This is an extreme example, but a categorical imperative is intended to be universalisable and must therefore be able to withstand such tests.

Writers such as Ross (1930) have felt the need to develop a more flexible form of principled reasoning, but remaining emphatically within a non-consequentialist perspective. Ross employed an approach known as *prima facie* obligations.

> **DEFINITION**
>
> A literal translation of the Latin term *prima facie* is 'at first sight' or colloquially 'as it seems'. '*Prima facie* evidence' is a legal term that refers to evidence that is deemed sufficient to establish a presumption of truth about an incident, unless or until counter-evidence is discovered. Thus, we can define a *prima facie* obligation as one that should be respected in one's practice, unless and until a different *prima facie* obligation, with a superior claim for adherence, is presented.

Thus, whilst supporters of *prima facie* obligations would see truth telling as a *prima facie* obligation, in a situation where truth telling would lead to the probable death of an innocent human being (e.g. by revealing the whereabouts of an innocent fugitive), the *prima facie* obligation of 'lying to protect a wrongly or unjustly accused person' would override the obligation to tell the truth.

> **Discussion activity 3.2**   **Kantian ethics**
>
> Employing a Kantian perspective, briefly analyse Case study 2.20 (*The retention of dead babies' organs in hospitals*).
>
> 1. Can you develop a categorical imperative that would be appropriate for this case?
>
> 2. Would *prima facie* obligations be more helpful? If so, what would they be?

Notwithstanding the above problems, Kant and others who argued for principle-based ethics did so out of a belief that there are certain principles upon which societies need to be based if they are to develop in positive ways. With the emphasis on the atomised individual in modern society, non-consequentionalists feel that principle-based ethics are particularly relevant in the present day. At the root of consequentionalist concerns are the issues of justice and human rights. It is to these issues that we now turn.

Fairness; justice as fairness

In 1971 John Rawls published a book (revised in 1999) that has had a significant impact upon debates about theories of justice. His theory of justice as fairness is the basis of the middling position on the column of probity in Figure 3.1.

While Rawls does not argue that his theory is a practical one for everyday decision making, it presents a normative approach to deciding what a just society would look like in what he describes as 'the original position'. It offers a reference point against which contemporary social, political and economic systems can be contrasted. We then have to decide, as individuals and as societies, what we want to try to do about the differences between these two states – the should-be and the actual.

The original position is an artifice of Rawls that allows each of us to contemplate a 'just' society without the burden of our life experiences and prejudices tainting our views. We are required to envisage a situation in which we have no knowledge of who we are. The distinctive personal characteristics that we will ultimately possess (assuming we will actually have some bestowed upon us) are unknown within the original position. We have no knowledge of any natural or social advantages, or disadvantages, we might ultimately possess. We do not even know where in the world we would live, and therefore under which type of political system we might be governed. We do not know our ethnic origins; whether we will have a privileged or deprived upbringing; whether we would be intelligent or slow-witted; male or female; be sexually abused or lead an idyllic childhood; be short or tall; born with profound physical disabilities or be an Olympic-grade athlete; or experience a very poor or excellent educational system. We are placed behind what Rawls refers to as a 'veil of ignorance'.

From this position of total ignorance we are then asked a series of questions about the type of society we would like to live in. We are expected to employ actual knowledge of the chances of being placed within a privileged or elite position when answering a series of questions relating to issues such as social, political and economic governance; health care; education; social norms; wealth distribution and hereditary wealth; race, gender and religious equality; and employment opportunities. It must be emphasised again that the world we construct from the original position is a world in which we do not know where we will ultimately fit.

Faced with this challenge, Rawls argued that the rational person would adopt a maximin strategy. This is a risk-averse strategy that works on the basis of studying all the worst-case scenarios that exist within each option before us. Having identified all the worst-case possibilities, we then select the one that is the least worse. Thus, we opt for the option that gives us the greatest possible benefit, assuming we were unfortunate enough to be dealt a position at the bottom of the economic and social ladders in any of the choices with which we are confronted. The following illustrates the approach.

The veil of ignorance

You are in the 'original position' and the choice of political systems in which you will live are feudal, dictatorship, democracy and anarchy. You can imagine a range of outcomes for yourself in each system. In a feudal state, a dictatorship or a centrally controlled state, history has shown that the lives of those in power can be privileged ones, and that such an outcome is a possibility for you. However, maybe only a few can be expected to enjoy such lives. For the rest of the population, life is likely to be miserable. In a democracy the distribution of power will be far greater, going beyond political democracy and taking in workplace democracy. The opportunities to exercise moral agency should be higher than in the other options, although the opportunities to enjoy the sumptuous lifestyle of the elite of the feudal or dictatorship systems would be slight. Anarchy might possess certain attractions, but the uncertainty surrounding the notion of anarchy is likely to prove unappealing to you. Remember, Rawls anticipates that you are a calculating, risk-averse individual. Thus, considering the options before you, Rawls assumes you will judge that if you were to be one of the general members of the public (and there is a 90–99 per cent chance that this will be the case), it would be better for you to live in a full democracy.

A way of rationalising Rawls' original position is to see it as a mechanism to free each of us from our personal prejudices and life experiences. By removing us from the shackles of the inequities of how things are, it can enable us to focus upon what we believe distributive justice would/should look like, without the distortions born of history or fate.

Flowing from the assumption that the individual in the original position will desire not to be dealt a station in life that is unpalatable, Rawls argued that there are two guiding principles that will explain the reason for each choice made. These are:

1. Each member of society would be entitled to the same civil and political rights; and

2. Open competition for occupational positions exists, with attainment being based upon merit, but with economic inequalities being arranged so that 'there is no way in which the least advantaged stratum in the society could as a whole do any better' (Barry, 1989: 184).

The second principle is referred to as Rawls' difference principle. This is because Rawls was not arguing that everyone could be or should be the same. He recognised that differences relating to qualities such as intelligence, acumen, technical skills, physical abilities and so on will exist. However, he viewed the arbitrary and random distribution of social and natural attributes as no justification for the individuals blessed with these attributes prospering to the detriment of others less fortunate. Rawls thus rejected Nozick's entitlement theory. As Shaw and Barry observed,

Rawls' principles permit economic inequalities only if they do in fact benefit the least advantaged.

(Shaw and Barry, 1998: 114)

In dealing with differences in personal attributes and qualities, Rawls argued that contingencies must be set in place to handle the issues raised by such differences. These contingencies would be mechanisms, established at the original position, built upon cooperation and mutual respect.

We are led to the difference principle if we wish to set up the social system so that no-one gains or loses from his arbitrary place in the distribution of natural assets or his initial position in society without giving or receiving compensating advantages in return.

(Rawls, 1971: 101–2)

Thus, before you would be asked questions about your preferred political system, education, corporate governance, etc. (and still in a state of ignorance about your personal position), you would have to identify the mechanisms that would need to be in place to minimise the worst effects of the differences that would exist between individual members of society, and between societies, when the final allocation of roles was made.

You may have detected a form of schizophrenia within Rawls' theory, inasmuch as the first principle has a strong socialist egalitarian moral perspective, while the second principle clearly assumes market-based, self-interest-driven behaviour. Rawls has been challenged on this 'inconsistency' from a variety of sources. Meade (1973) observed:

In my view the ideal society would be one in which each citizen developed a real split personality, acting selfishly in the market place and altruistically at the ballot box . . . [It] is . . . only by such altruistic political action that there can be any alleviation of 'poverty' in a society in which the poor are in the minority.

(Meade, 1973: 52)

Rawls also acknowledged that there have to be limits to what people can reasonably be expected to do on behalf of others less fortunate than themselves. He termed this limit the 'strains of commitment'. In doing so Rawls accepted that there would be boundaries to the demands that the least privileged could make of those more fortunate than themselves. However, Rawls' theory does demand far more of individual citizens than that advocated by free-market theorists. The 'hidden hand' of Adam Smith delivers an impoverished form of justice from a Rawlsian perspective. Incentives are acknowledged, albeit in a reluctant way. As Barry observed:

Inequalities are not ideally just, but . . . once we concede the need for incentives, inequalities permitted by the difference principle are the only defensible ones.

(Barry, 1989: 398)

> ### Discussion activity 3.3
>
> Briefly analyse Case study 2.4 (*AIDS drugs and patent rights in South Africa*) from a Rawlsian perspective.

The principle of 'do no harm'

The lowest point on the pillar of probity is the principle of 'do no harm'. It is at the bottom of the pillar because it is a default principle, to be used in the absence of any higher imperative. It requires that, if you cannot act well, you should at least avoid acting badly. The principle is historically associated with Hippocrates, the Greek philosopher (c460 BCE – c370 BCE) who is often called the 'Father of Medicine' because he has given his name to the Hippocratic oath, which it is commonly believed that all medical doctors take. The oath is the subject of many myths; not least that it is required to be taken by doctors, though some do take a modern version. Nor does it contain the words 'First, do no harm' that are attributed to it (National Institute of Health, n.d.). It does however include pledges amongst other things, not to give medicines that may do harm or not to take the knife to patients (surgery) when one does not have the skill to do so.

The principle takes the form in business and policy matters of the precautionary principle, which is expressed through the techniques of risk management. The concept emerged out of concern about environmental pollution but it is now seen as a useful guide to ethical behaviour in many different fields. The principle focuses on the prevention of harm rather than rectification after the harm has been done. It also requires that action should be taken to stop or limit the likely causes of a harm, even if there is a lack of definitive scientific knowledge that they are the true causes of the harm. The World Commission on the Ethics of Scientific Knowledge and Technology (2005: 14) give the following working definition of the precautionary principle:

> When human activities may lead to morally unacceptable harm that is scientifically plausible but uncertain, actions shall be taken to avoid or diminish that harm.

The failure to diminish the risks of exposure to asbestos by industry and governments identifies the damage can be done if the precautionary principle is not applied. Evidence that exposure to asbestos was injurious to health was known, if not proven to be so, and was available as early as 1898–1906. It was not until 1993 that asbestos was banned in the European Union. One Dutch study suggested that in that country alone 34,00 people could have avoided harm if the ban had been introduced 18 years previously (The World Commission on the Ethics of Scientific Knowledge and Technology, 2005: 11).

| Discussion activity 3.4 | **Do no harm** |

Briefly analyse Case study 2.26 (*The Firestone Tire recall issue*) from the point of view of the precautionary principle and the need for risk assessment in industry.

Utilitarianism

Utilitarianism, which is at the top of the pillar of consequences in Figure 3.1, accepts utility, or the greatest happiness principle, as the foundation of morals. It holds that actions are right in proportion, as they tend to promote happiness, wrong, as they tend to promote the opposite of happiness. Or as Jeremy Bentham, the eighteenth-century philosopher who proposed the principle, put it:

> The greatest happiness of the greatest number is the foundation of morals and legislation.

> (Bentham, 1994: 142)

The term utilitarianism, however, was coined by John Stuart Mill, a nineteenth-century writer, and not by Bentham. One interesting question that arises from utilitarianism is, 'What is happiness?' Most philosophers were at pains to suggest that it is not simply sensual pleasure. As J.S. Mill argued, 'It is better to be a human being dissatisfied than a pig satisfied' (Mill, 1998: 140). The importance of the higher pleasures over the lower has long been a theme in western ethics. St Augustine recognised that worldly pleasures were not of themselves bad but that they were insufficient to achieve an admirable life. He saw the sensual, material world as but part of human experience that has to be understood within the wider context of the intelligible world, which is one of clear and enduring ideas. Utilitarianism, according to Mill, who took a similar view, is not concerned only with material and sensual pleasures.

Utilitarianism is a calculating approach to ethics. It assumes the quantity and quality of happiness can be weighed. Bentham (1982) identified the following features of happiness that ought to be considered when measuring it:

- Intensity.
- Duration.
- Certainty – the probability that happiness or pain will result.
- Extent – the number of people affected.
- Closeness (propinquity) – pleasure or pain now or deferred in time.
- Richness (fecundity) – will the act lead to further pleasure?
- Purity – is the pleasure unalloyed or is it mixed with pain?

It is often assumed, in a business context, that maximising happiness is the same as maximising profit or return on capital invested. Plainly, improved profitability will generate happiness for some. But to apply the utilitarian principle properly one must consider the possibility that the pleasure derived from increased profitability has been achieved at the cost of a greater pain to other people. Mill (1998: 151) pointed out that most of the time someone applying the utilitarian principle need only concern themselves with their private interest. This is not necessarily so when the 'person' in question is a corporation.

Cost-benefit analysis is a natural tool of a utilitarian approach because it measures not only the direct costs and benefits to an organisation but also externalities. Externalities are defined in economics as social costs and benefits that are not reflected in the price of a product because they do not accrue directly to the organisation concerned. When people smoke the cigarettes produced by a tobacco company they are more likely to fall ill and so create costs for health-care systems. But the costs of that health care are not reflected in the costs of the cigarettes because the medical bills are not the tobacco company's responsibility. In the USA, however, the claim that tobacco companies misled their customers as to the harmful effects of smoking led the courts to require the companies to reimburse states with the cost of the medical treatment of smoking-related diseases. In this case an externality was converted into a private cost of the companies.

Cost-benefit analysis is a form of project appraisal. The costs   **DEFINITION**
and outputs of the project are identified and priced. If the outputs will arise over an extended period of time, and inputs are needed over a similar time span, the benefits and costs are discounted. If the benefits are greater than the costs then investment in the project would be sensible. If the project were, for example, a malaria control programme in a poor country, it is clear that the benefits would be widespread. Many lives would be saved; the health of the population would be improved. But these benefits are intangible and difficult to measure in financial terms. It might be thought that the costs of such a project would be easier to identify. Some, such as the cost of the labour and the insecticide, would be. But there may be wider, and less easy to measure, costs such as increased costs of education because more children survive and are fit enough to attend school.

Cost-benefit analysis is based on the premise that both elements in the equation can be measured in monetary terms. To do this some limitations have to be accepted. An example of a study undertaken by Lambur et al. (2003) illustrates the point. The question was whether a programme of nutrition and health education in schools created more benefits than costs by altering children's eating habits in ways that made them healthier and less prone to illness. The costs of the programme were tangible and could be measured. Three main types of benefits were anticipated:

1. Direct tangible benefits – the savings on medical treatment of people who would have become ill had they not changed their eating patterns. These benefits could be measured financially because the costs of treating medical conditions are known.

2. Indirect tangible benefits – the additional economic productivity that is achieved by preventing or delaying the onset of illness.

3. Intangible benefits – these are such things as the improved quality of life and improved self-esteem associated with healthier eating. The analysts in this case, as do all cost-benefit analysts, listed the intangible benefits but did not measure them or include them in the quantitative analysis.

Analysts have to make further, technical, choices, about how to conduct the analysis. There are three main issues:

1. Cost-benefit ratio. This is the monetary value of the benefits per pound or dollar or euro spent. If the ratio is greater than one then benefits exceed costs.

2. Discount rate. The value of money to be spent or received at some future time is less than money spent or received in the present. In cost-benefit analysis it is necessary therefore to choose a rate at which future income will be discounted.

3. Net present value. This is a way of showing the result of a cost-benefit analysis in present-day values. The streams of benefits and costs in future years are discounted, using the chosen discount rate, so that all costs and benefits are presented in terms of their present value.

In the study we are looking at it was decided that the cost-benefit ratio was the appropriate method and it was found to be $10.64 worth of benefits for every $1 spent. There are two problems that emerge from this form of analysis.

1. So many assumptions have to be made, and so many things have to be left out of the calculation that the validity of the results is brought into question.

2. A cost-benefit analysis may show, as indeed the example given does, that the expenditure would be worthwhile. But it does not show whether that expenditure is affordable or what its priority is in relation to other projects that could be undertaken, unless the simple criterion is used that priority should be established according to the cost-benefit ratio, with projects with higher ratios having the greater priority. Fisher (1998) has argued that establishing priorities is a more complex matter.

One danger of utilitarianism, which cost-benefit analysis is designed to address, is that organisations seek to maximise *a good* rather than *the good*. In the British National Health Service, for example, the government set a target for reducing the size of the waiting lists for treatment, maximising a good – the number of patients treated. However, many hospitals achieved this by treating patients with minor problems that could be quickly and cheaply resolved and leaving those who needed lengthy and difficult treatment at the back of the queue, and so they failed to maximise the overall good.

In the case of public policy, public, and not simply private, good has clearly to be taken into account. Kemm (1985) used a utilitarian approach in a discussion of the ethics of food policy. He was interested in the ethical issues involved in modifying the eating habits of the population through regulation, facilitating measures (such as differentially taxing foods) and education. He argued that a policy is ethical if it produces more beneficial outcomes than harmful ones. But his suggestions about how policy makers might analyse issues sheds light on the limitations of technical means such as cost-benefit analysis.

Kemm stressed the interconnections between subjective and objective thinking in assessing the outcomes of policies. The three stages in this process are:

1. Determining the inherent goodness or badness of an outcome. This is a subjective value decision such as that involved in stating that dental mottling is less bad than carcinoma of the colon.

2. Measuring the probability that the desired outcome will be achieved. This is a scientific and objective activity.

3. Assessing the degree of certainty with which the probability of the outcomes has been estimated. This is a matter of judgment rather than measurement.

The subjective element can be illustrated by an example from the first item in the above list. Utility's concern for populations makes these subjective judgments difficult. How, for example, should moderate good for the majority be weighed against great harm to the minority? Fortifying chapatti flour would provide some health benefit for most chapatti eaters, but for the rare individual with vitamin D sensitivity it might cause serious vitamin D toxicity. The ethical problem can be exacerbated by the fact that the majority may not be aware that they have received benefits from the fortified flour. To give another example, if food policies increase the amount of fibre in the diet this will benefit people by protecting them from diverticulitis. However, they will not be aware of this. But those who suffer from flatulence as a result will be in no doubt that they have suffered, albeit the pain is not critical.

> Most would take the view that a very small harm to a very few individuals could be outweighed by a sufficiently large benefit to a sufficiently large number of individuals.

> (Kemm, 1985: 291)

One of the criticisms of utilitarianism is that it is unconcerned with equity. As Sen said:

> The trouble with [utilitarianism] is that maximising the sum of individual utilities is supremely unconcerned with the interpersonal distribution of that sum.

> (Sen quoted in Barr, 1985: 177)

The problem of forecasting future consequences, as identified in the last two items of Kemm's list, is a general difficulty with utilitarianism. If people cannot make accurate predictions about the consequences of particular actions then it is hardly worth the bother of weighing the anticipated pleasures and pains. Common experience, as expressed in Murphy's Law (if it can go wrong it will), suggests that people's forecasting skills are not to be overestimated. There is psychological evidence that people are overconfident when they make predictions. Fischoff, Slovic and Lichtenstein (1977) asked people a series of general knowledge questions (e.g. is absinthe (a) a liqueur or (b) a precious stone?) and found that when people said they were 100 per cent certain they had given the right answer they had in fact only done so on 80 per cent of occasions.

The form of utilitarianism that has been discussed so far is known as act utilitarianism, which calculates the net pleasure or pain to be obtained from a particular act. One of the practical problems with it is that the calculations it would require are too many and too complex. Let us consider a decision over whether 25 per cent of a company's employees should be made redundant to reduce costs and prevent the company going into insolvency. Table 3.1 lays out the calculations that might be required. The example is fictitious and the numbers are invented; the purpose of the table is to explain the nature of the calculations required.

The first step in the calculation is to identify the groups, stakeholders, who would be affected by a decision to make people redundant and the ways in which they might be affected. The following have been chosen although doubtless other groups could be identified.

- The shareholders who own the company. If the company becomes bankrupt they face losing their investment. If making people redundant saves the company then their capital is secured and they might even make slightly higher returns on it in future. Even if the company is saved from insolvency the situation would have increased their worries about the long-term future of the company.

- The managers will have to decide who to make redundant and also tell people that they have lost their jobs. The psychological effect of this on some managers will be to cause them much anxiety and worry because they dislike inflicting distress on others. Some managers, however, will gain a psychological boost from the event because it will confirm their self-impression that they are strong managers capable of making tough decisions.

- Those employees who will keep their jobs will have a weight of worry lifted from their shoulder but this may be balanced by feelings of guilt that they kept their jobs while their friends and colleagues lost theirs. They may also feel less confident about the long-term prospects of keeping their jobs. There would also, of course, be pleasure that they are still receiving a salary and in response to both these feelings they may work harder.

- The people made redundant would suffer a degree of psychological trauma and suffer a loss of self-esteem. Some may find a new and better job quite quickly, or discover that a different lifestyle not based on employment is more to their liking. These people would gain some pleasure from having been made redundant. Those who only find a worse and less well-paid job or remain unhappily unemployed will only experience pain.

- The families of those who lost their jobs will also share some of the psychological and economic impact. They may all become more stressed yet not be able to afford a holiday to help them relax.

- Finally, in this list, the taxpayers may have to pay for additional social security benefits for those who have lost their jobs.

Table 3.1 A utilitarian calculation concerning making employees in a company redundant to prevent bankruptcy

Stakeholder	Impact Positive (+) or Negative (−)	The probability that the impact will happen	Amount of pleasure or pain (JOLLIES) per person	No. of people who might be affected	Intensity and duration Scale 1–5	Propinquity Scale 1–5	Purity Scale 1–5	Fecundity Scale 1–5	Net totals (millions of JOLLIES)
Shareholders	Insolvency is avoided (+)	0.6	5	2,000,000	2	5	3	1	66
	Financial returns are increased (+)	0.4	3	2,000,000	2	3	4	2	26.4
	Worry about long-term future of the company (−)	0.7	−2	2,000,000	3	1	2	3	−25.2
Managers	Psychological pain at dismissing staff (−)	0.7	−20	150	3	5	2	2	−0.0252
	Psychological benefit from seeing oneself as able to make the tough decisions (+)	0.3	20	150	2	5	4	4	0.0135
Employees who keep their jobs	Removal of worry and anxiety (+)	0.5	30	60,000	2	5	1	4	10.8
	Continued receipt of salary (+)	1.0	50	60,000	2	5	1	3	33
	Work harder in gratitude (+)	0.6	5	60,000	3	5	1	3	2.16
	Sense of guilt at having kept their job (−)	0.7	−20	60,000	2	4	3	2	−9.24
	Fear that may lose job in future (−)	0.3	−10	60,000	4	1	3	4	−2.16
Employees made redundant	Psychological trauma (−)	0.9	−50	20,000	5	5	4	4	−16.2
	Quickly find a better job or lifestyle (+)	0.15	100	20,000	3	3	5	4	4.5
	Find a job that is worse than the one you lost	0.50	5	20,000	4	2	1	4	0.55
	Find no job and suffer a loss of income (−)	0.35	−100	20,000	5	5	5	5	−14
Families of those made redundant	Psychological and economic impact on families of those who lost jobs	0.8	−40	50,000	3	5	2	4	−22.4
Taxpayers	Additional social security benefits paid and loss of revenue	1.0	−0.001	29,400,000	2	2	3	1	−0.2352

TOTAL

The JOLLIES calculator

The next two tasks involve identifying the number of people in the stakeholder groups who may experience the impact of the downsizing; and the probability that they will. Some of these groups are large. In the UK, for example, there are 29.4 million income tax payers and it is certain (a probability of one) they would all have to bear a portion of the increased public expenditure on social security caused by the redundancies. Other groups are quite small. In this fictitious example, there are only 150 managers who have to make the redundancy decisions. The fictitious company has 80,000 employees and the proposal to make 25 per cent redundant would result in 20,000 job losses. In the table it is estimated that 90 per cent of them would suffer symptoms of psychological trauma. It is also estimated that 15 per cent would find a better job, 50 per cent would accept a new job that was less good than their previous one and 35 per cent would fail to find a new job (accounting for 100 per cent of those made redundant).

A further element needed in the calculation is a unit of measurement for pleasure and pain. We will have to invent one. In cost-benefit analysis in health care, health economists created a measure called QALYs (Gudex, 1986) to measure the consequences of medical and surgical interventions. In a similar spirit we have invented the JOLLIES (Judged, Outcome Leveraged, Life Improvement Expected Sum – OK, we admit – it is a joke). Pleasure is measured by positive JOLLIES, the greater the pleasure the more JOLLIES. Pain is measured in negative JOLLIES. In Table 3.2 the number of JOLLIES per person caused by each consequence of the redundancies is assessed. Some consequences are obviously high but some are very low. For example, because there are so many taxpayers, the extra amount of tax an individual would have to pay to cover the cost of extra social security payments would be so low that it might not even be noticed. Consequently, the pain caused to an individual is very small.

Utility

In economics the measure of happiness or satisfaction received from an act – mostly goods and services – is known as utility. It is the formal term for what we have jokingly called JOLLIES, which would cover a wider range of acts than simply the provision of goods and services. Utility is of course difficult to measure and so economics is largely based on preferences, which can be measured. In plainer language there is no objective way to measure the happiness I get from a shot of vodka. It is, however, possible to measure whether I prefer vodka to tequila. So it is not possible to measure the amount of happiness gained from the drinks, which is what utilitarianism requires, but preferences can be put into rank order even though we cannot know the happiness gaps that separate them.

The other economic approach to the problem of measuring utility is to use money as a proxy measure. In other words we can assume that the more money we have the more it enables us to put ourselves into positions that make us happy. This assumption is the basis of much cost-benefit analysis because it allows things that cannot be measured directly to be incorporated into formal economic analysis. The problem is that there are disputes about what the exact relationship between the intensity of happiness and money is. It is generally thought not to be a straight line; increase of wealth suffers from diminishing marginal returns in the amount of pleasure it delivers but the shape of the relationship is not proven (Lane, 1995: 276–8).

The first calculation to be done is to multiply the number of people who might be affected by the probability that they will be affected. This number can then be multiplied by the number of JOLLIES to identify the amount of pleasure or pain caused by the redundancy decision. This is not the end of the calculation, however. As we have seen, pleasure and pain have different qualities (*see* p. 129) intensity, duration, certainty, extent, propinquity, fecundity and purity. The total, raw quantity of pleasure and pain has to be weighted by these factors. In Table 3.2 each of these factors is assessed on a five-point scale on which one equals very low and five equals very high. We will give a few examples.

■ The intensity and duration of shareholders' relief at the avoidance of insolvency is marked but it will not last long as their minds move on to other issues and concerns. The psychological impact of redundancy on those made redundant, however, is likely to be intense and last a long time and so this has been scored high at five.

■ Propinquity is concerned with whether the pleasure or pain is felt immediately or only occurs at some future time. The managers' delight at confirming their self-estimation as tough managers will be close in time to the decision. Contrarily, the psychological impact of redundancy may only emerge some time after the family member has been made redundant. The guiding principle involved is similar to that of discounted cash flow – pleasure and pain deferred to the future carry less weight than that experienced immediately. Future pleasure and pain carry lower weighting therefore in the calculation.

■ Purity is concerned with the degree to which pleasure and pain are alloyed with each other. The pleasure those who keep their jobs feel will be mixed with anxiety about how much longer their jobs will be secure, and so this scores low on purity. Those who find themselves in a better position since being made redundant will experience a relatively pure pleasure and so this is scored high at five.

■ Fecundity concerns the extent to which an act will create future pleasure or pain. The psychological stress caused to the job losers is likely to create more problems for them in the future and so this is scored high, whereas the typical short-sightedness of investors will mean that their pleasure at receiving increased dividends will not produce much future pleasure because they will be hungry for the next reward.

In the next stage of the calculation the raw total of JOLLIES is multiplied by all the weighting factors added together (and then divided by a million to keep the numbers manageable). As the purpose of a utilitarian analysis is to balance the total amount of pain caused against the total amount of pleasure, the final calculation is to add up the total JOLLIES, remembering that the pain JOLLIES are negative to get the net impact. If the result is positive then the pleasure outweighs the pain and the act is ethical; if the total is negative the act would result in more pain than pleasure and so would be unethical. In Table 3.2 the total is positive and so the redundancies would be an ethical act.

We have written a simple Excel spreadsheet to do the calculations in Table 3.2 and it would not be too difficult to devise a small program that prompted users to make the various judgments needed and then perform the calculations. The example also identifies some of the limitations of this approach to ethics.

- If all the stakeholders and all the impacts that an act may have upon them were included then the matrix of data and calculations would become very large. One obvious one that has been ignored in the example is the impact on local businesses and economy of making 20,000 people redundant.

- People are not good at judging the consequences of actions and so it is quite likely that the probability figures in the third column are wrong.

- There are many problems in creating a measure of pleasure and pain because these are essentially subjective. The system of QALYs mentioned earlier used a matrix of pain and mobility to make the assessment and a large sample survey. A real measure such as a QALY or a fictitious one such as JOLLIES can only give an average value for the pain or pleasure caused by a particular event and cannot capture the individual experience.

- The weighting scales for the features of pleasure and pain are also subjective and so will suffer the problem of inter-rater comparability; in other words different raters may make different assessments on these scales. The overall problem is that it is difficult to identify precise and agreed numbers to put into the calculations. This means that each number has a large margin of error and if calculations were done using one extreme of the range the act might be calculated as ethical, yet if numbers at the other extreme were used the act might be shown to be unethical.

Cross reference	It seems unlikely that managers go through such a complex calculation whenever they have to make a decision. Indeed, psychological research suggests they use an intuitive, heuristic approach that reduces the complexity of decisions and restricts the amount of information that is brought to bear upon it. Heuristics in decision making are the subject of Chapter 4.

Some writers have tried to overcome this difficulty by proposing rule utilitarianism. This approach looks at the general consequences, in terms of pleasure and pain, of particular rules of conduct. The rule, the following of which produces the best results, is the best rule to follow. This approach does not, however, necessarily make matters simpler. A rule such as 'you should always keep your promises' would probably have to be followed by so many exceptions that it would be no simpler than act utilitarianism.

A further criticism of utilitarianism is that it is implicitly authoritarian. This tendency can be illustrated by the public debate, in the early part of the nineteenth century, over the sources and mechanisms of revenue collection in the Indian provinces ruled by the East India Company. James Mill, the father of John Stuart Mill, was at the centre of this debate and through him the utilitarian philosophy of Bentham became a dominant theme in the argument. The utilitarians argued that the company had a duty to decide how best to spend the tax revenue of the country. As Holt Mackenzie argued in 1820:

Holding 9/10ths of the clear rent [revenue] of the country as a fund to be administered for the public good, the government may, I think, justly be regarded as under a very solemn obligation to consider more fully than has hitherto been usual, how it can dispose of that fund so as to produce *the greatest sum of happiness*.

(Stokes, 1959: 113, emphasis added)

There was a clear authoritarian and paternalistic strand in the thinking of these utilitarians. They believed they had a mission to transform India, but this mission could only be achieved by strong government. They would decide how the revenue should be spent. Utilitarianism requires the presence of a powerful figure who can calculate where the happiness of the country lies and then take the necessary action to bring it about. This strain of thought can be found in Bentham's own writings in which he argued that the will of the executive should not be checked by constitutional or popular devices (Stokes, 1959: 72, 79). It can also easily take root in companies and organisations where management become the judges of utility.

Despite the criticisms that can be made of utilitarianism its core ideas are commonly expressed by managers when they talk of 'business cases'. These are arguments that a thing should be done because it would be good for the business; the good of the wider society is not always considered.

Discussion activity 3.5	**Utilitarian ethics**

Briefly analyse Case study 2.10 *(Providing new drugs on the NHS to people with multiple sclerosis)* from a utilitarian perspective.

Corporate social responsibility

The notion of corporate social responsibility (CSR) is discussed in detail in Chapter 10. In Figure 3.1 CSR is positioned in the middle of the pillar of consequences. The CSR perspective is subsidiary to utilitarianism on the pillar because organisations can expand or restrict their areas of responsibility. A company's commitment to act responsibly only requires it to consider the consequences of its own actions and it is not responsible for the actions of others. Whilst a company may have a social responsibility to its employees, for example, it does not have an obligation towards those employed by other, independent organisations.

On occasions the emphasis may be on palliating or mitigating harm caused by organisational actions rather than on doing positive good. It may be necessary for an organisation to downsize its work force by making people redundant. In broad utilitarian terms this may produce the best balance of good and bad outcomes. However a socially responsible organisation would take action to minimize the disadvantages to those who lose their jobs by, for example, training those made redundant for new jobs or helping them establish small businesses. In this section we want to look at CSR as a criterion for judging whether a proposed action or decision is ethical or not.

As a yardstick for evaluating actions CSR is concerned with whether the actions of a company or organisation assists with the development and sustainability of individuals, communities and the environment. Ideally this implies that organisations should

- form themselves so that they are learning organisations in which the individuals within it can develop to their own potential;

- help the communities in which they operate develop and grow;

- increase the sustainability of the environment they draw upon. This will be dealt with in chapter 10.

What role should organisations have in helping its employees develop? Covey's (1992) *The Seven Habits of Highly Effective People* can stand as an example. He argued that people develop their character ethic through a process of deep self-reflection. He distinguished character ethic from personality ethic (Covey, 1992: 18–21). The character ethic proposes basic principles of effective living, things like integrity, fidelity, humility, courage and so on. These are hard precepts to live by. In contrast the personality ethic proposes 'quick-fix solutions' drawn from a public relations approach, which aims to present a good image of oneself and easy behavioural tricks used to manipulate others. It is the character ethic that people should concentrate on, and which responsible organisations would encourage employees to develop. Covey (1992: 36) adopted the 'principle of process' of personal growth in the spheres of emotion, human relationships and character formation. These processes cannot, he argued, be short-circuited; people have to go through the necessary stages to achieve greater effectiveness. He applied these lessons not only to people's personal lives but also to working lives. His book became a very popular guide for managers.

Senge, in his book *The Fifth Discipline* (1990), also stressed the importance of individuals' learning, which he saw as necessary for the development of learning organisations. These, he argued, were the only kind of organisation that will be successful. For Senge learning is not simply an acquisition of useful information; it is a personal moral development. He used the classical Greek term *metanoia* (Senge, 1990: 13–14) to describe the sort of learning that learning organisations should aspire to. It means a shift of mind. The word was used by the Gnostics who, in the early years of Christianity, saw gnosis, or knowledge, as an awareness of a person's relationship with God. Gnosis involves relating to the divine power of creativity by truly learning to know oneself (Pagels, 1982: 133–4). Senge's view of organisational development parallels this view of learning as ethical and spiritual growth.

> Real learning gets to the heart of what it means to be human. Through learning we recreate ourselves. Through learning we reperceive the world and our relationship to it. Through learning we extend our capacity to create, to be part of the generative process of life.

> (Senge, 1990: 14)

Individual growth and learning is not simply learning how to use new leadership or financial appraisal techniques. It is a process of becoming aware of one's ethical potential. Learning becomes an ethical end in itself that responsible learning organisations support

The communitarian approach to ethics is a reaction to the liberal view that sees the individual as more important than social groups. The communitarian approach argues that people are inherently social and that they can only achieve their moral potential by being part of growing and developing communities. By contributing to the ethical growth of a group people also become ethical individuals. These communities may be based on place, such as a neighbourhood, on shared group memories, such as in immigrant communities, or on a host of voluntary associations such as golf clubs, parent teacher associations, churches and so on. A tenet of the communitarian perspective is that different communities might be expected to develop their own values and moral principles. The universalism of liberalism's claim, that democratic, free market systems are the correct solution for all societies, as argued by Fukuyama (1993) in his book *The End of History*, is false. This acceptance of particularism or relativism will become important when we discuss international business in Chapter 11. Amitai Etzioni (1993) is the most high-profile advocate of a communitarian approach.

It follows from a communitarian point of view that anything that limits the potential for communities to grow and be responsible for themselves is reprehensible. Such threats may come either from the political left, with its concern for creating centralised, bureaucratic welfare structures for dealing with social problems, or from the right, whose protagonists do not see why granting rights such as flexible working hours, parental leave and childcare facilities to support families should be tolerated in a free-market system.

Communitarian ethics raises a number of questions for businesses and organisations:

- Should business try to create a homogenous world in which everyone consumes the same products and shares the same values? This would maximise industry's efficiency. Or should business respond to the particularities of different societies and groups by diversifying their products and business models?

- To what extent should businesses and organisations contribute to the growth and development of local communities? Should they provide resources and managerial expertise to encourage the development of self-help groups in the communities in which they work? Should such support be philanthropic or be part of commercial sponsorship deals? The development of 'family friendly' employment practices (Elshtain et al., n.d.) is important from a communitarian perspective. These matters of corporate citizenship are considered in Chapter 8.

- Should organisations attempt to create themselves as communities? The Foster Architectural Partnership has long sought to design office buildings that encourage the development of community bonds, as well as employment relationships, between the staff. Their buildings include 'streets', cafés, restaurants, swimming pools and games areas so that in one building the staff described working in the building as 'homing from work' (Foster, 2001: 206). The commercial pressures on organisations mean that such facilities are often converted to a more directly productive use.

Discussion activity 3.6   A CSR perspective

Briefly compare Case study 2.1 (*The Nationwide Foundation*) with Case study 2.3 (*Farepak*) from a CSR perspective.

Objectivism or ethical egoism

J. S. Mill praised those who would sacrifice their personal happiness to gain a greater happiness for others. Ethical egoists would not understand such an act. They argue that an individual should pursue their own interests by applying their reason to the task of identifying and achieving their own best interests. Objectivism is located, in Figure 3.1, at the bottom of the pillar of consequences because this viewpoint only considers the benefits of an action to an organisation and its managers. We will consider this view by looking at the ideas of Robert Nozick and the objectivist philosophy of Ayn Rand.

Robert Nozick (1974) was a leading advocate of the libertarian position on justice and rights. The libertarian perspective adopts the notion of negative freedoms. That is, it holds as its primary tenet the individual's right of 'freedoms from'. The most significant of these is freedom from government interference in all but the most critical of property rights protection systems, for example, police forces for private property and military forces regarding property of the realm. From a libertarian perspective, there is little outside the maintenance of property rights that represents legitimate government activity. Differences in personal wealth, talent, physical attributes and intelligence are seen as being obtained in the 'natural' sense, in that their ownership owes nothing to social or political institutions. If they are obtained in this way, nothing can deny the owner possession of them, or the value that derives from that ownership. Differences caused to the life-chances of individuals by the possession, or not, of these qualities/characteristics are not seen as justifying the meddling of governments in attempts to redistribute some of the associated benefits.

Within the libertarian frame of reference, and as long as what an individual wishes to do is within the law, then nothing should prevent the individual from fulfilling those desires. It is for this reason that taxation (and particularly the taxes levied on inherited assets) is such a vexed subject. From a libertarian perspective, taxation is the forcible, involuntary withdrawal of economic resources from individuals to be spent by governments in ways that might fail to satisfy or be compatible with the desires and values of the taxed individuals.

Nozick coined the term 'entitlement theory' to express the view that what has been acquired legally and fairly (although fairly is an ill-defined concept) cannot be taken away within a libertarian concept of justice. This is despite the fact that practices that are regarded as immoral and illegal today, for example, slavery, have not always been so, yet they represent an important factor in explaining the present distribution of wealth that shapes so many people's life-chances. Interestingly, in his later works, Nozick recognised the problems associated with resources obtained or lost by dubious methods and modified his views a little with respect to inherited wealth, an example being the plight of the American Indians. However, inherited resources and life-chances remain central issues within this debate.

Entitlement theory attempts to draw a veil over the means by which wealth may have been acquired. The ramifications of being denied an equal opportunity to education, health care, legal justice are seen as irrelevant within a libertarian conception of justice, or at least a greater injustice would be to transfer 'legally' acquired assets from those that have to those that have not. With no limits attached to what individuals can achieve in a liberal society, it is for every individual to improve their own life chances.

Objectivism gained popularity in America during the twentieth century through the novels of Ayn Rand (1905–1982), who has already been discussed in Chapter 1. Her ethical stance is known as objectivism. It gives primacy to people's capacity for rational thought. This facility, when applied to knowledge of the world gained through the senses, leads to an objective understanding of the world that leaves no room for the sceptical belief that all knowledge is mere opinion. The theory's ethical position is that each individual should seek their own happiness through a productive independent life in which their own rational judgment is their only guide. The main virtues of objectivist thought are independence, integrity, honesty, productiveness, trade and pride. It encourages a robust belief in self-help and accepts that people who cannot or will not take responsibility for themselves would have to bear the consequences. They should not expect the state or society to bail them out. An individual should not sacrifice themselves to others or expect others to sacrifice themselves for him.

We will illustrate the main themes of objectivism through Kirkpatrick's (1994) defence of advertising. He used objectivism to counter the social criticisms made of advertising, which are that advertising can be manipulative and offensive. His broad argument is that laissez-faire capitalism is good because, according to Rand, the principle of trade is the 'only system consonant with man's rational nature' (Kirkpatrick, 1994: 28). If capitalism is good then advertising, which is a necessary part of it, must also be good. Kirkpatrick blames Kant for the common mistake of seeing advertising as unethical. He attributed to Kant the ideal that human reason cannot objectively comprehend reality because reason is always affected by the innate structures of a person's mind. If this were so then human reason would not be adequate to cope with the blandishments of advertising. But he argued that Kant is wrong and Rand is right. Objective knowledge is possible and human reason is capable of properly evaluating the advertisers' messages. As to the charge of offensiveness, he argued that values are not intrinsic to objects. So a cigarette for example is not in itself a bad thing; only the way people use it can make it good or bad. If cigarettes are not intrinsically immoral and individuals have free will then 'tobacco advertisers defraud no one' (Kirkpatrick, 1994: 80).

The only necessary constraint on advertising is the common law one against fraud. 'Anything less than that turns both marketers and consumers into victims of subjective law, that is, of "rule by men" [i.e. by bureaucrats] rather than the "rule of law"' (Kirkpatrick, 1994: 51). The American-ness of the argument was emphasised when he quoted Daniel Boorstin arguing that advertising is the American epistemology – the way in which Americans learn about things. Kirkpatrick's argument for advertising only stands, of course, if objectivism is held to be objectively true.

The difficult question for ethical egoism is how far self-interest would cause individuals to give away some of their independence in order to accommodate others. Kirkpatrick argued that obeying the common law should be the limit of the surrender. Hobbes, who wrote in the seventeenth century, identified the key problem. People are very similar in wit and strength and therefore,

> If two men desire the same thing, which nevertheless they cannot both enjoy, they become enemies; and in the way to their end, which is principally their own conservation, and sometimes their delectation only, endeavour to destroy, or subdue one another.

(Hobbes, n.d.: 81)

Self-interest, therefore, would cause people to

> be willing, when others are so too, as far-forth, as for peace, and defence of himself he shall think it necessary to lay down this right to all things; and be contented with so much liberty against other men, as he would allow other men against himself.

> (Hobbes, n.d.: 85)

Of course, in modern business terms, it is a matter of dispute as to the degree of liberty a person, or a company, would rationally agree to forgo.

| Discussion activity 3.7 | **Ethical egoism** |

Briefly analyse Case study 2.22 *(The hospital consultants)* from an ethical egoism perspective.

Although this discussion has largely focused on individuals, which is intrinsic to an egoist philosophy, Rand does acknowledge the importance of organisations. Corporations, Rand argues, should be associations of individuals who freely choose to cooperate together on the basis of shared rational ideas and principle (Rand, 1995). In the world that we are focusing on in this book therefore objectivism becomes a concern for meeting the needs of the owners of a corporation, normally a focus on shareholder wealth.

In the toolkit at the end of this chapter a focus on the self-interest of organisations and companies is considered from both a short-term and a long-term perspective. From a philosophical objectivist point of view only a long-term orientation is appropriate for a person seeking the rational development of their potential. A fixation on the short term would be a degenerate, if not uncommon, form of objectivism.

Virtue ethics

Virtue ethics is located on the central pillar of character and culture in Figure 3.1, below conscience but above the perspective of decency.

Virtues are not 'ends'; rather they are 'means'. They are personal qualities that provide the basis for the individual to lead a good, noble or 'happy' life. Whilst the notion of what is virtuous behaviour has changed over time, the person most associated with virtue ethics is Aristotle, a philosopher of great eminence who lived in Greece between 384 and 322 BC. Not only have the characteristics of a virtuous life undergone significant changes, but the meanings attached to the terms used to describe particular characteristics are also a source of difference.

The Greek word, ευδαιμονία (eudaemonia) is loosely translated as 'happiness'. However, as MacIntyre (1967) pointed out, in Greek the term actually embraces the notion of both behaving well and faring well. Its use in ancient Greece was not concerned with hedonistic notions of happiness. It concerned itself with the individual's behaviour, and thus the way others perceived the individual. The latter was an essential ingredient to personal happiness. The 'good life' had, and retains, strong connotations of a 'whole' life, and places the individual within a social context. Even though social structures were deeply class-ridden during Aristotle's life, within the social and political elite there was a strong sense of being part of a whole.

Aristotle, reflecting the ideas of his age, placed the 'great-soul-man' on a pedestal. As you will see, the great-soul-man displays those virtues that were regarded as of the highest order. In ancient Greece the views of one's peers were critical to feelings of self-worth. Whilst the individual is the focus of Aristotle's attention, it is an individual within a society. Some social commentators, like MacIntyre (1967, 1987), have argued that since the eighteenth century liberalism has placed the individual outside of society. In this latter context, society is at best the sum of its parts. At worst, in Margaret Thatcher's famous words, 'there is no such thing as society'.

Virtue ethics is not a system of rules, but rather a set of personal characteristics that, if practised, will ensure that the individual is likely to make the 'right' choice in any ethically complex situation. Thus, the question for the individual, caught in the maelstrom of an ethically complex situation and appealing to virtue ethics as a guide for action, would ask, 'What would a virtuous person do in this situation?'

Plato, Aristotle's teacher, had identified four virtues, those of wisdom, courage, self-control and justice. For Aristotle, justice was the dominant virtue, but he expanded upon the number of personal qualities that could be regarded as virtues. Thus, into the frame came qualities such as liberality (the virtuous attitude towards money); patience (the virtuous response to minor provocation); amiability (the virtue of personal persona); magnanimity, truthfulness, indifference (in relation to the seeking of public recognition of achievement) and wittiness. It must be stressed that these virtues were not seen as of equal merit. The original Platonic virtues were seen as central to the attainment of a 'good' life, whereas the other virtues were seen as important for a civilised life. To understand the nature of a virtue we must understand how they are derived, and to do so we introduce the concept of the 'mean'.

For Aristotle, those personal qualities that were regarded as virtues were reflected in behaviours that represented a balance, or mean, in terms of the particular personal quality being considered. Thus, if the response of an individual to the threat of 'danger or significant personal challenge' was being considered, we can envisage a continuum with cowardice at one extreme and recklessness at the other (as in Table 3.2). Neither of these personal qualities (what Aristotle termed 'dispositions') is appealing as they are both likely to lead to detrimental outcomes in the long run. In the face of danger the 'noble' or 'great-soul-man' (and it was always the male that was considered in ancient Greece) would have to overcome his fears (i.e. suppress feelings of cowardice), but avoid acts of rashness, which would be likely to reduce the chances of success. Thus, an intermediate-point is required. This mean, or disposition, in this context is termed 'courage'.

Table 3.2 Aristotle's moral virtues

Context	The vice of deficiency	Virtue (mean)	The vice of excess
Danger or a significant personal challenge	Cowardice	Courage	Rashness
Physical pleasures	Indifference (being unable to recognise the joy that physical pleasures can offer)	Self-control (knowing when and where to enjoy oneself)	Greed
Wealth	Meanness	Liberality (discriminating generosity)	Profligacy
Money	Miserliness	Magnificence (knowing when to spend, how much and on what)	Spendthrift
View of self	Meekness	Magnanimity (being able to feel and display personal pride when it is deserved, but without vanity)	Vanity
Personal recognition	False modesty	Indifference (good deeds are done for their own sake and not for personal recognition)	Careerist
Minor irritants	Defeatism	Patience	Irascibility
Personal demeanour	Obsequious (fawning and grovelling)	Amiable	Quarrelsome
Sincerity in expression	Self-deprecating	Truthfulness	Boastfulness
Sociability	Boorishness	Wittiness	Buffoonery

Video clip 3.1

Interview with the Canon Precentor of St Paul's Cathedral, London. Priorities and human flourishing

The Canon Precentor discusses the notion of human flourishing. To view the video clip from the interview please visit this book's companion website at www.pearsoned.co.uk/fisherlovellvalerosilva.

Aristotle also considered modesty (used by Aristotle to mean 'respect', or 'sense of shame') as a possible virtue, but he dismissed it, other than as a virtue in the younger man. In the latter case, Aristotle saw it as a curb on youthful indiscretion, but he considered that the virtuous mature man should not require modesty for he should not commit acts of which he could be ashamed.

For Aristotle, the 'great-soul-man' was magnanimous, which was defined as 'possessing proper pride, or self-control' (Aristotle, 1976: 153). It is not surprising that, in the class-ridden society of ancient Greece, the virtues described by Aristotle were only available to the elite of society. McMylor (1994), citing MacIntyre, observed:

> Certain virtues are only available to those of great riches and high social status, there are virtues which are unavailable to the poor man, even if he is a free man. And those virtues are in Aristotle's view ones central to human life.
>
> (McMylor, 1994: 103)

Wealth, however, was not a necessary prerequisite of a magnanimous man.

> It is chiefly with honours . . . that the magnanimous man is concerned; but he will also be moderately disposed towards wealth, power, and every kind of good or bad fortune, however it befalls him.
>
> (Aristotle, 1976: 155)

Indeed when discussing the virtuous approach towards wealth Aristotle identified liberality as the virtue (the mean). Illiberality or meanness was one extreme vice, while prodigality or profligacy was the other. However, Aristotle did not regard the two extremes as vices of equal unacceptability, judging profligacy as less objectionable than meanness. This ranking of profligacy over meanness underscores the slightly lower importance attached to money and wealth, although this is not to say that wealth was unimportant.

Magnanimity was not equated with self-deprecation or undue humility. These were seen as approximating to vices, but so too were vanity and boastfulness. Being *rightly* proud of who you were, or what you had achieved, was not a vice; only unjustified high self-esteem was unacceptable.

> A person is considered to be magnanimous if he thinks that he is worthy of great things, provided that he is worthy of them; because anyone who esteems his own worth unduly is foolish, and nobody who acts virtuously is foolish or stupid.
>
> (Aristotle, 1976: 153)

The point about this statement is that it is the perception of others that determines whether behaviour is vain or deserving. In one sense a person can be both vain and deserving, but for Aristotle vanity implied a degree of exhibitionism above that which could be justified by one's achievements or social standing. Thus, vanity becomes a relative term in this context, relative to the state of deservingness attached to the achievement of the individual or his position in society.

Virtue and justice

Aristotle gave justice prominent consideration, but the notion of justice in ancient Greece was quite different from that which we articulate today. As is further explored below, the accepted standards of ethical behaviour are a product of their times, notwithstanding that notions of justice feature in most philosophies of ethics. Aristotle, while he spent some time differentiating between differing forms of justice, nonetheless offers a less than precise definition of justice, with the notion of the 'mean' again featuring strongly.

> To do injustice is to have more than one ought, and to suffer it is to have less than one ought and justice is the mean between doing injustice and suffering it.
>
> (Aristotle, 1976: 78)

This concentration upon the notion of justice as the bedrock of ethical behaviour is not universally shared, with the invisibility and muteness of women within such debates a cause for concern.

The role of women in ancient Athenian society did not register on political and social seismographs. Thus, the virtues as articulated by Aristotle can be said to be virtues from a masculine perspective. This is a relevant observation when we consider, as we do later, the work of psychologists, such as Lawrence Kohlberg, who developed a hierarchy of moral reasoning, based upon the assumption that justice is the ultimate test of the superiority of one form of moral reasoning over another. Within this framework, hard choices can be made between competing claims using justice as the decision criterion. The hypothetical scenarios employed by Kohlberg during his studies presented research subjects with choices to be made, but compromises were not available. Under this approach, one claim could be successful, while all others would fail.

Gilligan (1982), a former student of Kohlberg, has taken issue with the use of justice as the pre-eminent determinant of moral reasoning. Within Kohlberg's studies fewer females than males have displayed the form of moral reasoning that has allowed them to be classified as reasoning at the highest levels of Kohlberg's hierarchy. Gilligan has argued that this should not be interpreted as a lower level of reasoning than is possible, rather that the form of reasoning often displayed by women is *different* from that held by men. It is argued that women's early socialisation processes (particularly observing their mothers) encourage them to seek out compromises, not to allocate blame exclusively to one side or another, nor to distribute prizes or plaudits exclusively to only one member of a group. Rather the resolution of competitions, games or arguments is achieved with a sense of 'everyone gets something'. This approach is adopted with one eye on the medium to long term, that is, if a family is to develop cohesively there must be give and take from all sides at one time or another. From Gilligan's perspective the wisdom of Solomon involves more than the simple application of all-or-nothing justice to resolve a family dispute. Gilligan's argument contains a strong sense of the wisdom of the female perspective that she referred to as 'care'.

The need for wisdom to temper justice is possibly best exemplified in recent times by the approach adopted by President Mandela's government in South Africa when, on coming to power, it established the Commission for Truth and Reconciliation. The Commission was charged with investigating the myriad of stories and accusations of atrocities, murder and brutality inflicted upon the black and coloured communities by individuals, the police and the army during the apartheid years. Under the chairmanship of Archbishop Desmond Tutu, the Commission for Truth and Reconciliation continues to investigate a wide range of cases, with the accused giving evidence in the knowledge that they will not be prosecuted for their crimes. It is hoped that the truth relating to each case will thereby emerge (a critical issue for the bereaved), and gradually the nation's shame will be exorcised. In the process a potential bloodbath of retribution will have been avoided.

Whether the Commission's work has satisfied everyone is a moot point, but it represents an understanding that justice, if exercised exclusively in the form of retribution ('an eye for an eye'), would be unlikely to serve the longer-term interests of the people of South Africa.

Gilligan argued that the concept of 'care' should be regarded as highly as justice when interpreting responses of research subjects to moral reasoning scenarios. This is not care (which is too often interpreted as compromise) born out of an 'anything-for-a-quiet-life' approach. Rather, care is reflected by an approach that seeks to find a way forward that not only provides some form of equitable resolution to a conflict (although not necessarily reflecting 'full' justice in an Aristotelian or Kohlbergian form), but also holds out the possibilities for maintaining a working relationship between the protagonists, so that future cooperation might be possible. This is not to deny that there are times when guilt or success should be identified with individuals, to the exclusion of all others. Gilligan's argument is that such an approach is undoubtedly appropriate on occasions, but not as a universal maxim.

If we think about this issue from an Aristotelian perspective, we can employ the notion of a mean as in Figure 3.2. You may wish to consider this perspective when you tackle Activity 3.1.

Changing perceptions of virtue

The notion of virtue is heavily dependent upon the period in which the concept is being considered. As MacIntyre (1967: 174) observed,

> it [virtue] always requires for its application the acceptance of some prior account of certain features of social and moral life, in terms of which it has to be defined and explained.

As centuries have passed, so shifts can be detected in what becomes regarded as virtuous behaviour.

- In the time of Homer (who lived some 400 years before Aristotle and during a period of constant hostilities), the warrior was the model of human excellence and achievement.

- During the Greece of Aristotle's time, with its relatively stable Athenian city-state, the virtues embodied in the privileged, Athenian gentleman were paramount.

- From a western perspective, the rise of Christianity, as reflected in the New Testament, brought with it a fundamental shift in the perception of virtuous behaviour. Contra Aristotle, the New Testament presents an image of goodness that is unattainable by the wealthy and the privileged. Only the poorest are

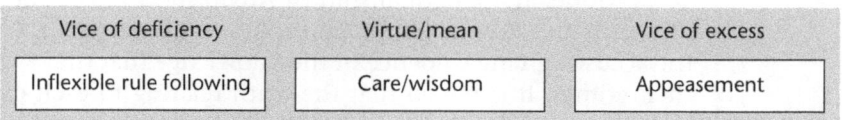

Vice of deficiency	Virtue/mean	Vice of excess
Inflexible rule following	Care/wisdom	Appeasement

Figure 3.2 Care and wisdom as a virtue

deemed worthy, with slaves (the lowest class within Aristotle's Athenian society) more likely to be seen as virtuous than the rich.

■ The coming of the Industrial Revolution, in the eighteenth century, found new personal qualities becoming valued. Benjamin Franklin, for example, espoused the virtues of cleanliness, silence and industry, as well as punctuality, industry, frugality, plus many others, but always with utilitarian motives (McMylor, 1994).

■ Solomon (1993: 207–16) identified honesty, fairness, trust and toughness (having a vision and persevering in its implementation) as the important virtues for managers in modern corporations.

The Aristotelian and Christian perspectives recognise different virtues but both link means and ends. Unethical means cannot be justified by good outcomes. A good deed is not a good deed if it is done with bad motives, for example, to avoid pain, or to ingratiate oneself with the recipient. In Aristotelian terms, a virtuous life is one that allows individuals to achieve their *telos*, or end, to its full potential. Practice of the virtues makes this potential realisable. The emphasis is thus upon both means (virtues) and ends (*telos*). From this perspective the relationship between means and ends is an internal one, not external. Both are within the control of the individual.

For Franklin, however, virtue was dependent upon some specified notion of utility. Achievement of socially acceptable ends (which have increasingly become articulated in material terms) can justify less than virtuous means. Understanding the values, social structures and key discourses of an era is crucial to understanding what will be regarded as virtues.

Within the Franklinian conception of virtues we have some of the seeds of what troubles many people about juxtaposing ethics and business. Some of the virtues articulated by Franklin can be achieved most effectively by the suppression of individual rights, for example, silence and industry, whilst others, for example, punctuality and cleanliness, are regarded as virtues, not primarily because they benefit the individual concerned, but because they contribute to the economy and efficiency of business. Thus, whilst the ends (punctuality and cleanliness) can be regarded as beneficial in themselves, they would not be regarded as virtues from an Aristotelian perspective, because they are driven by a concern with ends and not means.

Discussion activity 3.8   **Virtue ethics**

Briefly analyse Case study 2.15 (*Lord Browne of Madingley*) employing a virtue ethics perspective.

1. Which virtues would you prioritise?

2. Are there any personal characteristics that so far have not been mentioned that you would regard as virtues and that might contribute to addressing the issues raised in the case?

Decency

Decency is one of those words that in English carries great emotional power but is hard to define. The decency of behaviour is intuitively judged. It is placed below virtue ethics, but above legality, on the pillar of character and culture in Figure 3.1. Decency is the minimum degree of respect that we should give to others in our dealings with them. It is the basic expectations that we need to have of others in order to be able to do business with them.

Elaine Sternberg (2000) has argued strongly that private companies' ethical responsibilities only extend to serving the interests of the shareholders, or owners; and that it is unethical for them to dissipate their energies trying to meet the contradictory demands of the large range of interest groups, often called stakeholders, who are involved with companies. But she does not argue that companies should be wholly unrestrained in seeking their own interests. She argues that companies must act in a decent manner. She attributes two qualities to decency. The first is acting in a legal manner. This is dealt with elsewhere in this chapter; and so in this section we shall deal only with the second quality of decency, which is acting in a manner that establishes and maintains trust between the company and its customers, suppliers, distributors and all the others it comes into contact with. She defines decency as the honesty, fairness, and the avoidance of coercion or threat, that are necessary for an organisation to earn profit over the long term.

Discussion activity 3.9	**Decency**

Briefly analyse Case study 2.23 (*Supermarkets' treatment of their supply chains*) to assess whether the supermarkets treat their supply chain partners decently.

Applying ethical theories

As you are now aware there are many ethical theories. Even if you find it easy to discount some of them, because you think them trivial or ill-founded, several will remain. This raises a question for someone who wishes to think ethically. Should all or several theories be applied when thinking about an issue or should one approach be adopted that seems best suited to the matter in hand? Petrick and Quinn (1997: 55–6, 63) argued that those managers who are temperamentally attached to one of the theoretical perspectives on ethics 'fanatically rush to judgement'. They claimed that there can be no 'quick fixes' when dealing with matters of managerial integrity and that managers ought to use the ethical insights to make balanced ethical decisions.

If all, or at least several, ethical perspectives need to be applied when trying to make a decision that is ethical then debate and discussion is inevitable. It may be that debates between a group of people are necessary or it may simply be that an individual needs the debate the issues with themselves within their own heads. This brings us to the topic of discourse ethics and in the next section an account of it will be given. Discourse ethics has not been included in the diagram in Figure 3.1 because it is the approach to ethics that frames Diagram 3.1 and so it cannot also be an element within Figure 3.1. This next section is followed by an introduction to a toolkit for making ethical decision that you can access on this book's companion website.

Discourse ethics

Discourse ethics is a normative approach that deals with the proper processes of rational debate that are necessary to arrive at a resolution of ethical questions. It does not lay down what is right and wrong but it does distinguish right and wrong ways of arguing about right and wrong. It is an ancient idea that the process of argument, or rhetoric, is key to discovering the truth. Some, such as Protagoras, argued that there are always two sides to any argument (Billig, 1996: 72). This implies that dialogue cannot lead to a definitive truth because there are always arguments to be made for or against any proposition. However, Protagoras was prepared to argue, as reported by Socrates, that although opposing arguments could be presented some were more useful than others. Whether or not argument and debate can lead to true or useful statements about what is right and wrong, these classical concerns established an importance for forensic debate, and the classification of rhetorical techniques, that has remained in western culture.

The approach in modern times is most closely associated with Jürgen Habermas, of the Frankfurt school of critical theorists (Pusey, 1987). Habermas built upon the philosophical heritage of Kant. However, he breaks with Kant, in his belief that knowledge develops through social interaction and discourse. Knowledge is not, as Kant argued, a matter unaffected by social and cultural processes. Habermas holds that disagreement can be resolved rationally through debate that is free of compulsion, in which no disputant applies pressure to another, and in which only the strength of the arguments matters. This calls for linguistic skill but it also requires a critical self-reflection in which those involved in a debate challenge their own arguments at:

- The objective level – at which a statement is tested against an observed state, checking for example whether the statement that 'the balance sheet does not add up' is true.

- The inter-subjective level – when a statement is made and heard it creates a social relationship between the hearer and the speaker. At the inter-subjective level it has to be questioned whether this relationship is legitimate. If the statement that the balance sheet does not add up implies, without evidence, that the listener is accused of cooking the books the relationship may be unfair, especially if the speaker is the listener's boss.

- The intra-subjective level – at which a speaker has to consider whether their speech sincerely or authentically mirrors their internal thoughts and values.

It is these processes of validation that Habermas refers to as discourse. The application of these in organisations would be very difficult. However, writers have attempted to put these ideas into operation. Some have focused on the skills of debate. Schreier and Groeben (1996) looked at the advice, given in popular books on how to persuade and influence people, about which tricks of presentation were unfair. They asked a panel of experts to categorise 84 of the rhetorical tricks against four ethical categories that are used to assess whether an argument in a debate was proper. Using the results they were able to identify some possible rules or tests for assessing the ethical integrity of any debate. A few examples follow.

- **Formal validity** – Are the arguments logically rigorous? *e.g. do not select only those cases to use in your argument that support your point of view.*

- **Sincerity/truth** – Are the arguments intentionally misleading, inconsistent or economical with the truth? *e.g. misrepresenting an opponent's position or exaggerating a point.*

- **Content justice** – Treating your opponents unfairly or imposing impossible requirements on them. *e.g. ad hominem attacks on an opponent in which the opponent is vilified rather than his or her arguments criticised. Making mutually exclusive demands on an opponent.*

- **Procedural justice** – Preventing an opponent from fully and freely participating in the debate. *e.g. unnecessary use of technical jargon in a way intended to confuse the opponent.*

Steinmann and Lohr (quoted in Preuss, 1999: 414) also propose the use of discourse to achieve a consensus on ethical business issues. They simplified the characteristics of ideal discourse, against which actual discussions may be assessed, as:

- impartiality;
- non-coercion;
- non-persuasiveness; and
- expertise.

They had an opportunity to put these guidelines into practice when they organised and chaired a series of corporate dialogues within Procter & Gamble on the question of self-medication by selling over-the-counter cold medicines. Others have proposed rules and procedures for debate. This has been particularly common in the field of public policy making. Fischer (1983) made a case for forensic skills to be applied to the process of evaluating public policy options through ethical discourse. He drew upon a method he called normative logic. This was based on studies of how people discuss and decide normative issues in everyday speech and life. He concluded that despite the lack of final ethical truths, people resolved value matters by combining questioning based on empirical knowledge with a lawyer-like process of marshalling a supportable case, by drawing upon their knowledge of:

- the consequences of the different positions or actions they may take;
- the alternative positions and actions open to them;

■ established norms, values and laws;

■ the facts of the situation;

■ the network of circumstances that preceded the situation; and

■ the 'fundamental needs of humankind'.

People can construct defensible cases for taking particular actions or positions by answering the questions just listed. However, according to some philosophers this process is untenable because it requires decisions, about what ought to be, to be derived from descriptions of how things actually are, and this they claim is illogical.

Cross reference

In philosophy this argument is known as the naturalistic fallacy, as is discussed further. Fischer's response is argued from the point of view of pragmatism, which is explained.

Fischer's response was to say that the purpose of drawing up guidelines for debate is not to establish ultimate values but to arrive at pragmatic resolutions through a rigorous, if ungrounded, process that is not anchored in immutable values.

The mention of pragmatism brings us to the basis of the toolkit for making ethical decisions that will be discussed shortly. Pragmatism can be contrasted with Habermas' theories of discourse that have just been discussed. Habermas was not so much concerned with everyday decision making, which he called pragmatic discourse. In his writings this is the lowest of the forms in the hierarchy of discourse. He was interested in how, through discourse, a community could establish fixed and general ethical principles that would form the framework for the resolution of specific ethical conundrums. Such a consensus may not commonly exist in organisations, which are the focus of this book, and it cannot be assumed that organisations are moral communities with agreed moral standards. The pragmatist philosopher Richard Rorty takes a different view of discourse; and it his view that informs the ethical decision-making toolkit. As can be seen from the discussion of pragmatism later in the book (see p. 160) the pragmatists argue that it is not possible to define a fixed and valid objective truth. The nature of language disbars such an achievement. Rorty argues that because of this humans need to maintain a dialogue. If there is no definable objective truth then, without dialogue societies will either lapse into cynicism or allow fundamentalists, who believe they do have the truth, to dominate all others. Therefore, as Mounce (1997; 185–9) noted we must keep the conversation going. According to Rorty the absence of absolute truth or standards does not prevent people living in a civilised and well-mannered condition, as long as dialogue is kept open. He calls this a re-educative process in that people's desire for validated norms and standards should be replaced by a wish for solidarity for others; something that Habermas regards as inadequate (Habermas, 1999: 348). Rorty's retort is that Habermas should drop the idea of the 'better argument' and accept that there is only 'the argument which convinces a given audience at a given time' (Rorty, 1985: 162).

The toolkit for ethical decision-making builds upon Rorty's ideas. It takes the form of a maze. The toolkit user is asked a series of questions about the action or decision they are thinking of taking. These questions are based upon the different ethical perspectives that have been outlined in this chapter. The answer the user gives leads to further questions. In a Rortyean sense this sequences of question, answer and subsequent question might continue endlessly; but as Rorty points out it is only necessary to convince a given audience, perhaps temporarily, at a given time, and so at certain points the toolkit makes a recommendation about whether the action or decision should be accepted or rejected.

Activity 3.1	The ethical corporate decision toolkit

The Ethical Corporate Decision Toolkit is based on the framework shown in Figure 3.1. You can access it at www.pearsoned.co.ukfisherlovellvalerosilva. In order to use the toolkit you have to frame the action or decision you want to evaluate. The toolkit does not compare a series of options at a go; rather it evaluates single options against a set of ethical criteria. At the start of the maze you will be asked a few questions about the context of the decision. Then you will be asked to consider the action from a number of ethical perspectives.

Like many aids to ethical decision making the Ethical Corporate Decision Toolkit uses a screening process by which decisions are tested against a sequence of ethical positions. There are various such decision aids you can explore. Cavanagh et al. (1981) proposed three criteria in their process, namely, utility, rights and duties, and justice. In response to feminist criticism they added (Cavanagh et al. 1995) a fourth test of caring. Post et al, (1996: 125) reverted to the three-test model in their framework. Carroll & Buchholtz (2000; 157) also used a threefold screen, but in their framework the tests were, firstly, conventional (is the proposed action acceptable to a range of conventional norms and standards) secondly, principle and thirdly ethical tests (is the action acceptable to one's conscience or sense of oneself as a good person). The apparent simplicity of the Carroll & Buchholtz three-test model is undermined by the presence of a variety of sub-tests within the categories. The principle test for example incorporates a diverse set of criteria such as justice, rights, utilitarianism and the 'Golden Rule'. Brooke Hamilton et al. (2009) developed a specialist decision aid for companies considering whether they should remain or quit a country that did not allow them to operate to their own, higher, ethical standards.

An alternative to the screening approach to making difficult ethical choices is to choose one ethical approach and to ignore others, or at least to put the approaches into rank order of preference. Carroll (1990) proposed a simple exercise (Activity 3.2) for people who wish to reflect on the relative importance they give to a range of ethical perspectives. The list of principles he proposed included both normative approaches, methods for thinking about the right response and norm approaches, which invite a person to accept the values and standards of a particular group. The categorical imperative, the Golden Rule and the utilitarian principle are all methods for normative thinking whereas the disclosure rule, the organisation ethic and the professional ethic concern decisions about which social group one wishes to belong to. These norm-based questions could be seen as an application of a stakeholder analysis.

Activity 3.2	Prioritising your ethical principles

Here are a number of 'principles'. Identify your top three and rank them 1, 2, 3 in order of importance/relevance to you and your decision making. Then mark your least relevant 9, 10 and 11.

Principle	Description	Rank
Categorical imperative	You should not adopt principles of action unless they can, without inconsistency, be adopted by everyone else	
Conventionist ethic	Individuals should act to further their self-interest so long as they do not violate the law	
Golden Rule	Do unto others as you would have them do unto you	
Hedonistic ethic	If it feels good, do it	
Disclosure rule	If you are comfortable with an action or decision after asking yourself whether you would mind if all your associates, friends and family were aware of it, then you should act or decide	
Intuition ethic	You do what your 'gut feeling' tells you to do	
Means-ends ethic	If the end justifies the means, then you should act	
Might equals right ethic	You should take whatever advantage you are strong enough and powerful enough to take without respect for ordinary social conventions and laws	
Organisation ethic	This is an age of large-scale organisations – be loyal to the organisation	
Professional ethic	You should only do that which can be explained before a committee of your professional peers	
Utilitarian ethic	You should follow the principle of 'the greatest good for the greatest number'	

Source: Principles of business ethics: their role in decision making, *Management Decision*, Vol. 28, No. 8, Fig. 2, p. 21 (Carroll, C. B. 1990), © Emerald Group Publishing Limited, All rights reserved.

Carroll used the list in Activity 3.2 as the basis of a research project and found that the Golden Rule was given the highest ranking by his respondents. The disclosure rule came second in the study.

Some ethical checklists, such as the Texas Instruments Ethics Quick Test, emphasise the social acceptability of an ethical decision rather than the philosophical correctness of the mode of thought used to achieve it. Use the questions of the Quick Test to decide whether an action you are planning to take is right.

Activity 3.3	**The TI Ethics Quick Test**

- Is the action legal?

- Does it comply with our values?

- If you do it, will you feel bad?

- How will it look in the newspaper?

- If you know it's wrong, don't do it!

- If you're not sure, ask.

- Keep asking until you get an answer.

(*Source*: Texas Instruments, 2001)

Reflections

This chapter has provided the formal, philosophical tools that can be used when you have to think about an ethical problem. These tools are not, however, easy to handle. There is first the problem of which theories you are going to use. If all the theories were to give the same answer to a problem then admittedly there would be no problem. But this is not always the case and then you have the difficulty of choosing which theories to ignore or deciding how much weight to give to the various theories. Once you have chosen a theory there remains the difficulty of applying it to the particular circumstances of the issue confronting you. It may be these problems that make the TI Ethics Quick Test (Activity 3.3) look so attractive. The 'quick and dirty' approach it uses leads us into the matter of how people actually decide about ethical issues – which is the subject of the next chapter.

Summary

In this chapter the following key points have been made:

- Ethical issues at work might be best approached by concentrating on developing people who are virtuous and have the judgment to be able to make moral decisions and act upon them when faced with ethical problems.

- Ethical issues at work might best be approached by seeing organisations as networks of individuals who learn personally and collectively through experience, reflection and the sharing of that learning. Learning about learning, learning how to deal with ethical issues, is more important than learning pre-packaged solutions.

- Ethical issues at work might best be tackled by applying sound moral principles, which should guide our actions.

- Ethical issues at work might best be tackled by forecasting which actions will bring about the greatest amount of good.

Typical assignments

1. How relevant to business and management is a Kantian approach to ethics?

2. Discuss the use of child labour in factories in developing countries from two different ethical perspectives (you might choose between virtue ethics, Kantian ethics, Rawls' theory of justice or utilitarianism).

3. It is sometimes argued that a major flaw of utilitarianism is that it is only concerned with maximising the total amount of good and is not concerned with the distribution of that good between people and groups. Is this true?

4. How might an organisation implement the practices implied by discourse ethics?

Group activity 3.1

Form into groups. As a group, choose one of the case studies from Chapter 2. Each member of the group should then choose a different ethical perspective – utilitarian, fairness, ethics of care and so on, and individually produce an analysis of the case from that perspective. Come back together as a group and debate the issue.

Recommended further reading

P. Vardy and P. Grosch (1999) *The Puzzle of Ethics*, London: Fount, is a good introduction to the main ethical theories. Simon Blackburn's (2001) *Being Good. A Short Introduction to Ethics*, Oxford: Oxford University Press, is an elegant reflection on the main issues in ethics. Anne Thomson's (1999) *Critical Reasoning in Ethics*, London: Routledge, is a good guide to the application of theories to issues.

Useful websites

Topic	Website provider	URL
Ethics Updates. This site provides some helpful materials on all the major ethical theories and perspectives. It is a general ethics site rather than a business ethics site.	Edited by L.M. Hinman, The Values Institute, University of San Diego	http://ethics.sandiego.edu/about/editor/index.asp
Some useful material and quizzes on ethical decision making	Centre for Ethics and Business, Loyola Marymount University	http://www.ethicsandbusiness.org
A website on virtue ethics, and a pdf file on virtue ethics. The website provides a link to a virtue ethics scale	A website provided by Michael Cawley III, James Martin and John Johnson, Penn State University	http://personal.psu.edu/faculty/j/5/j5j/virtues/Virtue.pdf & http://www.personal.psu.edu/faculty/j/5/j5j/virtues/
An ethical decision-making tool. Other toolkit items are available on this website	The Ethics Resource Centre, a non-profit research organisation	http://www.ethics.org/resource/plus-decision-making-model
A fan site for Ayn Rand	Centre for Ethics and Business Leonard Peikoff	http://www.peikoff.com/
The Bentham Project, University College London Jeremy Bentham's auto icon (his embalmed and preserved body, although the head is waxen, the original having decayed), bequeathed in his will for the inspiration of future generations, can be seen in the south cloisters of the main building of University College. Use the link for an image of the auto icon.		http://www.ucl.ac.uk/Bentham-Project
A framework for ethical decision making	Markula Center for Applied Ethics, Santa Clara University	http://www.scu.edu/ethics/practicing/decision/framework.html

CHAPTER 4

Personal values and heuristics

Chapter at a glance

Chapter contents

Case studies

Activities and exercises

- Recommended further reading
- Useful websites

<hr>

Learning outcomes

Having read this chapter and completed its associated activities, readers should be able to:

- Define values and distinguish them from attitudes and beliefs.

- Explain the idea that a set of values may be fragmented or integrated.

- Explain how traditionalists, modernists, neo-traditionalists, postmodernists and pragmatists may have different perspectives on their values; and consider which position might explain their own stance.

- Understand how values, acting as heuristics, affect decision making and judgement about what is ethical.

Introduction

It is difficult to discuss ethics in a business and organisational context without talking about values. As both are central themes in the book, it is necessary to distinguish one from the other.

The broad distinction we wish to make is that ethics is a branch of philosophy and is therefore concerned with formal academic reasoning about right and wrong, but values are the commonsense, often taken-for-granted, beliefs about right and wrong that guide us in our daily lives. Imagine a situation at work where you have to decide whether to take action against a manager who you know to be fiddling their expenses. Ethics provides principles and arguments, drawn from ethical theory, for thinking about the issue. The emotional force of your values in contrast would lead you to an intuitive feel for the right thing to do. Of course, how much weight you give to your analysis and your emotions is another matter.

Ethics and values have different sources. Ethics are drawn from the books and debates in which philosophical theories about right and wrong are proposed and tested. Ethics have to be studied. Values are acquired informally through processes of socialisation. We acquire values from our interactions with our friends, family and colleagues and, most importantly for our purpose, from the organisations we work for or belong to. Values are learned, not studied. It is true that our employing organisations may make formal attempts, through induction courses and corporate videos, to inculcate their formal values. We are not required to study them, which would involve a critical engagement with them; we are simply required to 'buy into them', to 'mark, learn and inwardly digest' them. If values are learned rather than studied, they must be few and simply expressed so that all in a society can understand them. Ethics in contrast need to be studied, not simply learned, because they are more complicated.

Video clips 4.1 	**The Dilley six pack** The clip deals with the impact of nature and nurture on human personality by considering a family of sextuplets. To view the video clip from the interview please visit this book's companion website at www.pearsoned.co.uk/fisherlovellvalerosilva.

There are overlaps between ethics and values. The processes through which values are formed, adopted and modified within groups and societies may be influenced by debates between philosophers. Equally the rational discourses of ethics may be swayed by the emotional undertow beneath the participants' arguments. Within a group of philosophers social learning, conforming to the group's norms may be more emotionally comfortable than challenging it. Conversely, critical study and the reading of books may challenge the values people have acquired through life. Nevertheless the distinction between learned values and studied ethics is still a useful one.

It follows from the above argument that values are social. They exist and are communicated through social connections. Rokeach defined values as:

> a small number of core ideas or cognitions present in every society about desirable end-states.

(Rokeach, 1973: 49)

DEFINITION

Values are core ideas about how people should live and the ends they should seek. They are shared by a majority of people within a community or society. They are simply expressed generalities, often no more than single words such as peace and honesty. As they are very broad, they do not give guidance on how particular things should be evaluated.

Attitudes, like values, are evaluations of whether something is good or bad. But unlike values they are evaluations of particular things, issues, people, places or whatever. Attitudes, because they relate to specific circumstances, are more changeable than values.

A **belief** is an acceptance that something is true or not. This acceptance does not imply any judgment about whether that thing is good or bad.

Rokeach's work is helpful because it distinguishes between different types of values that might affect thinking about ethical issues.

- *Moral values* – concern interpersonal behaviour, e.g. being honest is desirable.

- *Competence values* – concern one's own valuation of one's behaviour, e.g. behaving imaginatively is desirable.

- *Personal values* – concern the ends, or terminal states, that are desirable for the self, e.g. peace of mind.

■ *Social values* – concern the ends that one would desire for society, e.g. world peace is desirable.

The first two items in this list concern instrumental values that are about how a person should live and behave. The second two items are terminal values that concern the ends or purposes that we should be striving for. Table 4.1 lists the instrumental and terminal values identified by Rokeach's survey of a sample of Americans.

The rank orders in Table 4.1 are averages, and individuals will, to a greater or lesser extent, have different views on the proper order of the values. Billig has also pointed out (1996: 240) that Rokeach's view of values is positive and aspirational. He argued that values may be negative. We may, for example, all agree that cruelty is bad.

Table 4.1   The instrumental and terminal values of Americans

Terminal values	Rank order (females)	Rank order (males)	Instrumental values	Rank order (females)	Rank order (males)
A comfortable life	13	4	Ambitious	4	2
An exciting life	18	18	Broadminded	5	4
A sense of accomplishment	10	7	Capable	12	8
A world at peace	1	1	Cheerful	10	12
A world of beauty	15	15	Clean	8	9
Equality	8	9	Courageous	6	5
Family security	2	2	Forgiving	2	6
Freedom	3	3	Helpful	7	7
Happiness	5	5	Honest	1	1
Inner harmony	12	13	Imaginative	18	18
Mature love	14	14	Independent	14	11
National security	11	10	Intellectual	16	15
Pleasure	16	17	Logical	17	16
Salvation	4	12	Loving	9	14
Self-respect	6	6	Obedient	15	17
Social recognition	17	16	Polite	13	13
True friendship	9	11	Responsible	3	3
Wisdom	7	8	Self-controlled	11	10

Note: 1 represents the highest value and 18 the lowest.

| Activity 4.1 | **Terminal and instrumental values** |

Put the two lists in Table 4.1 (terminal values and instrumental values) into rank order according to your personal preferences. Compare these with the American average scores (male or female as appropriate) by subtracting the American ranking from your ranking (and ignoring whether the result is positive or negative). For example, equality is ranked 9 by American men. If my ranking was 12, the difference is 3. Then total up all the differences. The smaller the number, the greater the similarity between my ranking and that of Americans. If the difference is zero, then the two sets of rankings are almost certainly (but not entirely, because there may be differences that cancel each other out) identical. Ask some friends or colleagues to do the ranking. Compare their average score with yours.

Consider: Is the difference between your ranking and the American's ranking greater or lesser than that between you and your friends?

Different organisations, different groups, different cultures and different countries may have different values. Ethical theory, however, is disdainful of societies. It does not matter to the validity of a theory if it is not accepted by the generality of people. The truth of an ethical theory cannot be judged by an opinion poll. It will be a constant theme of this book that in business and organisation there can be great tensions between how an ethical theory says people should behave and how their social values incline them to behave.

| **Cross reference** | The diversity of values relating to business and management in different countries and societies is explored in Chapter 11. |

Perceptions of values

Just as in the first chapter we discussed different views on whether there is a normative ethical order that applies to business so we can ask similar questions about the nature and role of values. It is convenient to do this by using the notion of fragmentation to explain the nature of values. Fragmentation is the idea that things in the social world are disordered and disconnected. A fragmented view of values would see them as diverse, various and expressed through conflict between different views and opinions. There are no wholes in a fragmented social and ethical world, only discordant parts that clash against each other. The philosopher Thomas Hobbes expressed this view in the seventeenth century. He argued that even a single person's view could be fragmented.

Nay, the same man, in divers times, differs from himself; and one time praiseth, that is, calleth good, what another time he dispraiseth, and calleth evil: from whence arise disputes, controversies, and at last war.

(Hobbes, n.d.: 104)

The contrary view is the one we have already noted that Rokeach expressed. He claimed that values, far from being fragmented, are simple and whole. Billig (1996: 240) agreed that the values of a group or society are simple and whole. But he pointed out that this makes them difficult to apply to particular situations. A society may have clear views on the importance of telling the truth and on loyalty. However, there may be situations in which such simple nostrums do not help much. There are two reasons for this.

1. The demands of truth telling and loyalty may conflict in a particular case. Should a government spokesman tell the truth about a military operation if it would cause danger to the soldiers who might expect him to show them loyalty? In such cases, the simplicity and wholeness of values is broken by not knowing which value should be applied.

2. Simple and whole values can only provide general guidance. When it comes to dealing with specific situations, values need interpretation. Can there be situations, as the behaviour of politicians often implies, when truthfulness can be interpreted as not telling lies but equally as not telling the whole truth? Once interpretation is necessary, values that were simple and whole become fragmented.

Ambiguity can arise in organisations when simple values are inadequate because they cannot deal with new circumstances or are in conflict with other values. When ambiguity occurs, those who seem to offer a resolution gain power and they bring with them their new values and ideologies (Weick, 2001: 47). Weick sees this as a process of sense-making in which, through communication and interaction, people interpret and construct a view of their organisation and their roles within it. From this perspective, values do not exist prior to and separate from organisational life (as Rokeach would suggest); instead they emerge and become pervasive in organisations as a consequence of a dynamic process within organisations. In his earlier book, Weick (1995) identified seven properties of sense-making. These can be illustrated by considering how values about telling the truth (or not; manipulating performance measurement information for example) might emerge from a sense-making process.

- **Identity construction.** When someone considers deceiving others at work by manipulating performance statistics, they will consider how they see themselves: whether they believe themselves to be macho managers, who will change the management information to give a better impression of their efforts, or whether they value themselves as truthful individuals who can bear the truth even if it hurts them.

- **Retrospective sense-making.** According to Weick, sense-making will occur after people have acted – in other words, values follow actions and do not precede them. The case of the Russian business people (*see* p.00) who justified their avoidance of taxes by arguing that they only did this because the state was too corrupt to be the rightful guardians of tax revenues is a good example.

- **Sense-making is done through enactment.** People make sense of things by taking action. If people decide to manipulate performance management information, they do so by choosing an action that fits with their environment (they might decide that to actually change the performance numbers might be unacceptable), but by their choice of method of deception (say, hiding the poor figures in a great many other numbers), they also change the environment by creating a climate where that particular form of deception becomes acceptable.

- **Sense-making is social.** If people talk with their colleagues about what they have done then the practice may become accepted through use. It has been discovered that different occupational groups have different perceptions of right and wrong. Different occupational groups as a consequence may have different views about what is and is not acceptable behaviour. Some groups of programmers, for example, think it more acceptable than other groups to violate intellectual property rights (Stylianou et al., 2004), probably because they are great users of the Web, which diminishes the idea of property rights in knowledge by making it so accessible.

- **Sense-making is ongoing.** As situations change, for example, if a member of staff is dismissed for violating intellectual property rights, then people will reformulate their position on the matter in discussion with each other.

- **Sense-making is focused on 'extracted cues'.** This means that people in an organisation will concern themselves with some things in the daily stream of events and ignore others. Those cues become the raw material from which a view and actions are taken. The vicarious experience of others (e.g. whether others who are known to have deceived the performance management system flourish or are caught and punished) will become part of the sense-making process.

- **Sense-making is driven by plausibility.** The process of sense-making is based on personal assessments of risk and benefit. It is not a process of fine judgment based on incontrovertible facts. In other words, people take a calculated gamble. When deciding to manipulate performance management systems, they are chancing that the benefits of doing so will be great enough to outweigh the probability of being caught and the severity of the punishment.

This brief review would suggest that values can be seen as something that emerge from dynamic processes of sense-making as well as being one of the process inputs. Agreed sets of values in organisations can be changed through this process. Values express a potential tension between wholeness (wanting a consensual set of values) and fragmentation (the value sets are broken up and reformed). People's responses to this tension and their method of making sense of it can be classified under five headings:

- Traditionalist;

- Modernist;

- Neo-traditionalist;

- Postmodernist; and

- Pragmatist.

The traditional view of values

From the traditional viewpoint, a group – whether a work group, an organisation, a profession or a country – is defined by its possession of shared values. The idea of value fragmentation therefore is considered anathema and a contradiction in terms. A group's values either derive from the ancient traditions of the group or are presented as if they did. In organisations these traditional values are often presented as those of the firm's founder. In companies that were not blessed with a charismatic founder, a mythical one is sometimes created for public relations and advertising purposes and to act as a fount for the values the company wishes to present (Mr Kipling of Kipling's Cakes is an example). A group based on traditional values sees them as a whole. By turning their gaze inwards and not outwards to other groups and societies, they fail to recognise the fragmentation and diversity of values that surrounds them.

This inward-lookingness identifies a disapproval of questioning as a feature of traditionalism. Education and training are seen as the processes of attaining knowledge burnished by age. To challenge that knowledge by asking why it should be so is unacceptable. In broad historical terms it can be argued that the Enlightenment, which occurred in Europe in the eighteenth century, was a time when thinkers began to challenge with empirical observation and study things that had long been accepted as unchallengeably true because they were stated in ancient religious and classical texts (Sloan and Burnett, 2004). A consequence of the lack of questioning is that traditionalism is often experienced as a moral traditionalism that defines which behaviours are acceptable in and beyond organisations. This may be seen in the movement in the Bible Belt of the USA to run businesses according to fundamental Christian precepts. Riverview Bank in Minnesota, for instance, was set up as America's first evangelical bank. Its founder believed it to be a good commercial proposition because born again Christians do not smoke or gamble or drink and are dedicated to their families, all of which make them a good credit risk (Doran, 2004).

The Enlightenment	DEFINITION

This was a historical period during the eighteenth century when academics and writers began to question truths and beliefs that had been long held because they were sanctified by the Church or by the ancient writings of Greek philosophers. Traditionally it was thought to have been dominated by European philosophers such as Immanuel Kant (*see* p. 000) who defined the Enlightenment (*die Aufklärung* in German) as emancipation from humankind's self-incurred immaturity. But it was also seen in the work, for example, of antiquaries and amateur geologists who began to discover and collect fossils, rocks, minerals and finds from what we would now call archaeological sites. The study of these objects began to raise doubts about the previously accepted fact that the world was created in 4004 BC, a date that Bishop Ussher had calculated from the Bible. From such practical activities, rational analysis based on observation began to undermine traditionalism's criteria of antiquity and the Bible as the tests of truth. It was also a period when morals drawn from these sources were challenged by rational analysis in such works as Mary Wollstonecraft's (1995) *Vindication of the Rights of Women* published in 1792.

The modernist view of values

The modernist position is that the twentieth and, so far, the twenty-first century have been characterised by value fragmentation. However, this is seen as a transitory phase and it is thought that, through the application of reason, the pieces can be put back together and true values defined. Those who take this position believe that values are tangible, and can be unambiguously stated and defined through formal and rational debate. They accept deductive reasoning that allows truths to be logically developed from first principles. The modernist believes that values can be determined by ethical study. Jürgen Habermas, for example (Pusey, 1987: 78ff.), constructed a complex theory of communicative action that defines how the validity of spoken understandings between people can be tested. Modernism sees this as an individual task. Progress, both moral and technical, is thought possible through individual effort and rationality.

> [modernist identity] is epitomized by the notion of the self-developing individual, rootless yet constantly evolving to new heights.
>
> (Friedman, 1994: 39)

At the least, other modernists believe that values can be defined and clarified (Kirchenbaum, 1977; Smith, 1977) as a preliminary to rational discussion about an organisation's mission and core values.

Cross reference	Habermas' idea of communicative action is discussed within the general framework of what is known as discourse ethics in Chapter 3.

The rationality that Habermas talks about is not the same as that spoken of by many managers. The former can be labelled as critical and emancipatory whereas the latter is instrumental rationality. Instrumental rationality is focused on achieving a set of given aims. Much managerial effort, for example, goes into maximising return on capital or increasing the number of hospital beds without giving much thought to whether these ends are in themselves the right ones. Questions about whether growth at all costs is a good thing, or whether, for example, a focus on preventive health measures might not be better than simply building bigger hospitals, are forgotten. Emancipatory or critical rationality (Legge, 1995: 288) asks these deeper questions. It challenges the conventional wisdoms of modern life so that people become aware of the constraints that deform their lives. Both forms of rationality have a place in the modernist perspective. Between them they develop the 'cognitive adequacy' (Giddens, 1985: 100–1) that organisations and societies might use to improve and unify their values.

The neo-traditional view of values

The neo-traditional approach emphasises the function of culture as a device for mediating the tensions between fragmented values and the need of societies and organisations for a common purpose and mutual understanding. Neo-traditionalists see values in the context of organisational and social cultures; indeed, cultures are defined by the values that characterise them. They argue that the fragmentation of values can be overcome and that organisations and societies can have unified values. But such an end cannot be achieved by rational analysis, which sees values as objects for analysis and not as shared myths, which is how neo-traditionalists view them. Myths can act as the glue that holds an organisation or society in unity because of their simplicity (which needs no sophisticated explanation) and because of their ability to finesse dilemmas. Sometimes the glue is weak and sometimes strong. There is agreement, however, among neo-traditionalists that values, presented as vision and myth and not as cold rationality, are the keys to overcoming fragmentation. This perspective is a form of 'back to basics' and traditional values. Historically, this may be dated to the publication of Peters and Waterman's (1982) *In Search of Excellence*. This book advocated replacing the 'paralysis by analysis' of modernism, with an emphasis on values and organisational culture. Those who take this approach stress that organisations are culture-creating mechanisms and that cultures can change. This thought leads to the notion that culture may be a critical lever or variable with which managers can lead or direct their organisations. As Smircich put it,

> Overall the research agenda arising from the view that culture is an organisational variable is how to shape and mould the internal culture in particular ways and how to change culture, consistent with managerial purpose.

> (Smircich, 1983: 346)

Values, from this view, can be deliberately used as a means of overcoming fragmentation and improving organisational effectiveness. As Smircich also pointed out, there is an alternative view that cultures are too complex for managers to be able to mould them into a desired form.

A second form of neo-traditionalism can be seen in the wave of interest in 'New Age' therapies and philosophies that encourage the spiritual growth of individuals through the rejection of materialism. It might be thought that this would fit ill with the self-interest of organisations but Covey's work (1992 see p. 127) has led to many agreeing that concerns with individual and organisational growth can be combined.

The postmodern view of values

The postmodern stance sees nothing in the social and intellectual world as tangible or fixed. At this vantage point, fragmentation is accepted as part of the human condition. In Lyotard's (1988: 46) famous phrase, there is 'incredulity towards metanarratives'. This means that the large ideological schemes, such as capitalism and communism, that used to dominate people's thinking no longer have credibility. In the postmodern view there are no eternal truths or values. What we think of as objectively true emerges through discourses that are embedded in power and knowledge relationships where some have more influence on the outcomes of the discourses than others. But what emerges is in any case uncertain because the language we use is opaque and carries no single, clear message (Legge, 1995: 306).

The words we use to express our values have no fixed meaning. Statements of value have to be treated as texts and deconstructed. *Différance* is Derrida's device for exploring the limitless instability of language. One aspect of *différance* is that no word has a positive meaning attributed to it; it only has meaning to the extent that it is different from other words. Another aspect is deferral because the meaning of one word is always explained by reference to another and the search for meaning can involve a complex chain of cross-references as one chases a word through a vast thesaurus. Let us take an innocuous statement about public management:

> The first steps to achieving accountability for performance must be to clarify objectives and develop a recognised approach to measuring and reporting performance.
>
> (Dallas, 1996: 13)

This is enough to cause a deconstructionist to salivate. Most of the words in the sentence do not have an unambiguous or uncontested meaning. Accountability, for example, can only be defined by relating it to other words such as hierarchy, responsiveness, transparency and so on. Accountability may be viewed from different discourses such as political accountability, audit and accounting, consumer rights, and investigative journalism. If we had the time to explore this sentence in detail and to plot its webs of signification, we would find that the sentence could mean almost anything.

The search for meaning may not be endless; but the end will be terminal confusion rather than clear understanding. The function of deconstruction is to reach a final impasse. This can be seen in Derrida's view of ethical decision making. He recognises that decisions have to be made but points out that any decision is 'haunted by the ghost of undecidability' (Painter-Morland, 2011: 130). By which is meant that sense of discomfort that remains after any decision we make because we know we may have misunderstood the issues, or are simply aware of the impossibility of having made a fully rational decision because we chose between options which themselves will have been incomplete or poorly founded.

Deconstruction is not intended to overcome fragmentation but simply to map the instabilities, paradoxes and aporetic states that define it. From this position, there is no hope that the fragmented values can be put back together again. As Harvey (1989: 45) expressed it, disapprovingly, postmodernism

> swims and even wallows in the fragmentary and chaotic current of change as if that was all there was.

The political passivity of postmodernism annoyed him:

> The rhetoric of postmodernism is dangerous for it avoids confronting the realities of political economy and the circumstances of global power . . . metatheory cannot be dispensed with.
>
> (Harvey, 1989: 116)

This form of postmodernism could be called hard postmodernism because it seems to lead to the impossibility of business ethics, or any other kind of ethics, in a world that desperately needs it. However, as Derrida (Derrida with Bennington, 1985: 221) said, to deconstruct the enlightenment project (which seeks to raise humanity's moral status through the application of reason) is not necessarily to criticise it. Just because someone points out that the language used, when people attempt to analyse the realities of global power, is inadequate does not mean the task is unworthy. As Gustafson (2000: 648) emphasises, Derrida does not say that all ways and options are of equal value, though it is not possible to say that there is one best way. This softening of the stereotypical view of postmodernism does allow postmodernists to have an ethical agenda, but this will be described in the next section under the more suitable heading of pragmatism.

The pragmatic view of values

The pragmatism of this stance is that of the American philosopher Richard Rorty (1989, 1990). He shares the postmodernists' scepticism about the possibility of an objective truth and of a fixed hierarchy of values. In this circumstance, the issue for Rorty is not how to represent, or mirror, the world in our thinking but how to cope with its ambiguity:

> All descriptions (including one's self description as a pragmatist) are evaluated according to their efficacy as instruments for purposes, rather than their fidelity to the object described.
>
> (Rorty, 1992: 92)

The notion of usefulness is a hermeneutic one. If a belief helps us to interpret our other beliefs and vice versa then it is useful. The justification of belief is therefore conversational. A dialogue between developing beliefs is necessary, not because it will bring us to an ultimate truth, but because it keeps the conversation going (Mounce, 1997: 185–9). The line taken by pragmatists is that the inability to ground our values in some grand overarching theory such as Christianity, Marxism, Islam or capitalism does not prevent people making sensible and practical arrangements for living a civil and well-mannered life. As Rorty expressed this view,

> No such metanarrative is needed. What is needed is a sort of intellectual-analogue of civic virtue – tolerance, irony and a willingness to let spheres of culture flourish without worrying too much about their 'common ground', their unification, the 'intrinsic ideas' they suggest or what picture of man they presuppose.
>
> (Rorty, 1985: 168)

He argued that the lack of a metanarrative could be overcome by dealing with the concrete and practical concerns of a community and by finding ways of harmonising, but not abolishing, the conflicts of values within the community.

Zygmunt Bauman (1993) developed a pragmatic notion of ethics that he called, adding to the confusion surrounding the term, postmodern ethics. (The title of one of his other books – *Life in Fragments* (Bauman, 1995) – reinforces the importance of the idea of fragmentation in a postmodern sensibility.) He saw the techniques of rational analysis and technological development, as proposed by modernism, as part of the problem of business ethics. Organisations take a bureaucratic approach to the matter by defining rules and regulations that deny and quash employees' natural tendency to act morally towards each other. Such rules enable them to settle for the lower standard of obeying the regulations rather than aspiring to the higher level of behaving well. The failure of rationality to solve ethical problems does not mean that we should not continue to try to solve them. The contribution of postmodern ethics, however, may lie more in asking important questions than in finding the answers.

Gustafson (2000: 652–4) identifies a number of characteristics of postmodern (though we would prefer to call it pragmatic) ethics.

■ Not separating personal values and principles from those applied at work. Dividing one's life into a series of disconnected boxes is a typical modernist way of reducing complexity and ambiguity to a seeming sense of order. A postmodernist would much rather face up to the conflicts between their personal values and those they are called upon to apply at work.

■ As postmodernists do not accept any grand metanarrative ethical theories, they have to look instead at particulars and circumstances. These can only be expressed in stories and myths that express humanity's fears, confusions and expectations. Concrete illustrations of moral issues are a more assured route to ethical awareness than mental abstractions divorced from substance. Some people have gone as far as to recommend that we should return to meditation upon the lives of saints to help us deal with the ethical dilemmas and tensions that we experience (Wyschogrod, 1990: xiii). As the medieval historian Gervase of Canterbury wrote in the twelfth century:

There are many people whose minds are induced to avoid evil and to do good more easily by example than by prohibition and precepts.

(Bartlett, 2000: 629)

■ A disbelief in Utopian ideas. As Bauman expressed it, a postmodern thinker uses history (particularly that of the twentieth century and even more specifically of the Holocaust) as evidence of modernists' belief in instrumental thinking and technological development is wrong. Even on a more mundane level the belief held in the 1960s that technological development would lead to a world in which everyone would have huge amounts of leisure has proved false.

■ Finally, Gustafson sees postmodern ethics as a 'tempered quest'. By this he means that the search for ethical answers to the problems of business ethics is conducted with the one item of knowledge that is certain – that no definitive answer can be found.

Living in an ungrounded ethical system may call upon people's resources of humour and tolerance. These are needed because value conflict will be endemic in such a situation. Irony is helpful because people's purposes may require them to act in ways that seem naïve in the absence of a metanarrative that justifies simple behaviours. Let us explain this point by quoting Umberto Eco (1985: 67). In his reflections on his best-selling novel, *The Name of the Rose*, he used the example of the pragmatist lover. The lover wishes to say to his partner, 'I love you', but he cannot do so because everyone is aware that the proliferation of romantic novels has devalued that particular metanarrative. He would feel too naïve and unsophisticated if he said that simple sentence even though it is the emotion he wishes to express. Being a pragmatist he does not give up, and stalk away undeclared. Instead, he says, 'As Barbara Cartland would say "I love you"'. He has thereby expressed his purpose but in a way that reveals his knowledge that such sentiment can no longer be justified by reference to transcendental values. Irony, by which an apparently straightforward statement is undermined by its context, is essential to the pragmatist's stance.

From a pragmatic view, in summary, it is recognised that there is confusion and conflict over the ends of a good organisation or society and that the meanings people ascribe to values change and develop as they debate and discuss issues with others. Nevertheless the pragmatist believes that by maintaining the conversation with good humour and irony it is possible to make organisations and societies more bearable.

The five stances can be characterised in relation to their position on ethical fragmentation. A traditionalist sees a unified world united by time-hallowed values. From the other four positions, the ethical world is seen as fragmented but with different responses to this perception. The modernist believes that unity can be restored through rational development of individuals. The neo-traditionalist believes unity can be restored only by a return to concern for neglected values. The postmodernist accepts the inevitability of fragmentation and enjoys it. Pragmatists learn to live with fragmentation. The following exercise is designed to test your understanding of the five stances. Read Case study 4.1. Although it is an invented case study, many of the incidents have been taken from interviews with managers. Then answer the questions in Activity 4.2.

| Case study 4.1 | Chris's managerial development: a fable |

Chris is a newly qualified social worker. She didn't start training until she was in her late twenties but she had much previous experience of acting as an unpaid worker with a voluntary agency. In her first role as a field social worker, she brought much of the enthusiasm and motivation that she developed during her early experience and training. She liked to see her clients as whole persons and she tried to spend as much time with them as possible so that she could come to a proper understanding of their situation from their point of view. It is important, she believed, not to take action without the full and active consent of the client.

After some years the pressure of Chris's caseload made it difficult to find the time she needed to spend with clients. She often felt frustrated that she had to foreshorten important discussions with them. On occasions this frustration caused her to be short and less than helpful with those clients who seemed to enjoy creating their own misfortune and yet were ungrateful for any help she provided. Although some of her clients were often short-changed on the service they received because of this reaction, it did not undermine her essential belief in the need to work with her clients in a way that maintained and developed their dignity.

After a few years, Chris was promoted to team leader and she became responsible for the management and professional supervision of a team of workers. In a small way, her attitude towards the clients changed. She no longer spent the bulk of her time working face to face with them. She also had the managerial responsibility of dividing her staff resources between all the clamouring demands for service. Her attitude towards clients was more objective. She made sure that careful, measured and objective assessments were made of all clients so that those with the greatest needs received priority.

A few years later, Chris was appointed as a services manager for a particular category of clients in the northern area of the county. Two important themes within her new job were service quality (as expressed by performance indicators) and budgets. Cost-effectiveness became a worrying issue. She had to convince her managers that she was providing value for money and this caused her to question whether the range of services was not too wide and whether some of them could be ended or reduced. There was talk within the department about only providing the high 'value added' services. She came to the view that better IT, better information and more rational decision-making processes would improve the service's effectiveness. She was studying for an MBA and its heavy emphasis on IT and management science convinced her that the department needed to put more effort into producing a computer-based needs profiling and resource allocation system. She started, in a small way, to produce such a system for use within her own locality.

A few years later Chris was still a services manager, but she had moved sideways and was now working with a different client group. The move made her realise the differences in professional values between people who worked with different client groups. It was the failure to address these differences, she thought, that was at the root of organisational conflict within the department. She came to believe that it was very important that everyone in her area subscribed to a central vision and mission that would motivate and inspire all staff. To this end she organised a couple of away-day sessions at which she and her fellow managers tried to hammer out some key goals and core values for the service as a whole. The software she had developed in her previous job had proved very valuable but it had failed to deliver easy solutions to the resource allocation problems. As a result of this experience, Chris thought that focusing the department on some basic core values was a better way of managing than relying too much on IT systems.

After a few years in this job, Chris was more aware of its political dimension. Managers seemed to spend their time fighting their corner and the person who shouted loudest got the most. For example, whilst the IT system optimised the allocation of staff to clients, it caused as many problems as it solved. It gave some groups of clients a very low priority ranking. Some managers felt that this was correct ('it would be more effective to pay for them all to go to Lourdes', as one senior manager put it) but there was a powerful and critical lobby from the relatives of the clients.

When she was trying to develop core values she began to see it as a game. People were trying to control the language that was to be used in framing the values. It was also clear that when they wrote a core value everybody bought into it while retaining the right to define it in their own way. Everyone was smart enough to play the language games of anti-oppressive practice but there was no consensus about its meaning. Indeed at meetings Chris thought they were playing a circular word game in which *client focus* was identified with quality of service, which in turn was defined as providing equal opportunities, which in its turn was seen as responding to the diversity of clients. The debates' ends were their beginnings. The inconclusive debates over policy documents often led to a point where everything seemed ineluctably confused.

▶

Some years later Chris was a senior manager. Her enthusiasm for the importance of social services was undimmed but her expectations were less ambitious. She was aware that things in organisations do not always work as planned. She no longer believed that the answer to organisational management was more and better computers; nor did she think that the publication of a nicely printed and laminated card proclaiming the Mission Statement actually meant that everyone shared the same values. She saw the organisation as having many stakeholder groups, internal and external, and the task of managers was to keep them sweet. But this ironic awareness did not mean that Chris became cynical, although this is precisely what has happened to some of her colleagues. Chris continued to work for improvement (whatever that is) but perhaps in a different way. She came to believe in proceeding on a Ready – Fire – Aim basis. This meant trying things out in a small way, without too much prior planning, and building on them if they worked, and modifying or abandoning them if they did not. No more rational master plans. She no longer believed in acronyms (such as CFI – Clients First Initiative) any more. Truth lay in aphorisms not acronyms. Aphorisms are a statement of a general principle memorably expressed in a condensed form. For example, 'He who is too busy doing good finds no time for being good' (Tagore quoted in Gross, 1987: 197). Aphorisms make you think about fundamental issues, acronyms just require blind acceptance. Chris accepted both the fragmented nature of the managerial role and the plurality of values within the organisation, and she could become a little manic-depressive as a result. Nevertheless, Chris tried to maintain manners and tolerance when managing the service. Her attitude was 'pessimistic wishful thinking'.

| Activity 4.2 | Analysing Chris's managerial development |

The fable implies that managers' responses to value issues at work may change as their careers progress. In this fable can you detect the periods when Chris's approach was:

(a) traditional,

(b) modernist,

(c) neo-traditional,

(d) postmodern, and

(e) pragmatic?

We will give one possible interpretation of the fable in Case study 4.1. You may have made a different reading of it. Chris starts her career as a field social worker as a traditionalist. She had acquired a set of values about how social work clients should be treated. To some extent these would have been absorbed as she grew up and from her voluntary work. They would have been reinforced by her social work training. She had picked up the traditional values that are associated with her chosen profession. As her workload pressures increased, she found it increasingly difficult to apply these values. Her next two jobs gave her responsibility for setting priorities, managing budgets and achieving performance targets. In response she began to adopt a more modernist stance. She had to assume that clients' needs can be objectively measured and ranked in order of importance so that she could make sure the neediest would receive services. She extended this view into a belief, fostered by doing a master's degree in management science, that the difficult decisions about the rationing of services, when need exceeds the resources available to meet it, could be made easier by more data and more rational decision making. Up to this stage in her career, Chris had been working in the same specialist field. Her next job took her into a different one and she realised that different groups have different values and norms. This, together with the failure of more data and better software systems to solve the management problems, led her to take a neo-traditionalist stance and to try to make the service more effective by developing an organisational set of values that everyone could 'buy into'. However, this proved to be more difficult than she had expected as attempts to create a unified organisational culture floundered on organisational politics. Chris began to view things from a postmodern perspective and observed wryly the games playing with language that went on in the organisation. However, by the time she had become a senior manager she had become a pragmatist, who saw no quick fixes to organisational problems, but nevertheless continued to work to improve things, even though progress, even if everyone could agree it was progress, was slow and piece meal. Success, she felt, lay in maintaining the importance of concern for others and for good manners even though this seemed an endless task.

Values and ethical thinking

The next part of the chapter considers how people think about and make ethical decisions in practice. It is in contrast to Chapter 2, which considered how philosophers and writers on ethics argue that people should think about ethical matters. The central theme of the chapter is the role of heuristics in human thinking. The argument is that people do not use a comprehensively rational process when they come to a view on moral matters. Rather, it will be argued, people use heuristics to ease the process of arriving at a view or taking a decision, and to simplify the mass of competing views and information that surround any issue.

The account of ethical thinking provided in this chapter is to some extent speculative. It presents an argument about how people might make up their minds on ethical matters. The argument is based on well-established ideas as well as on newly emerging theories, but their application to thinking on ethical matters is incomplete. Unusually for a textbook therefore it remains for you to make up your mind on the arguments presented.

DEFINITION

Heuristics are a means of discovering or finding out something. They are mental tricks of the trade or rules of thumb that are used, almost unconsciously, to simplify the process of decision making. They are cognitive devices that limit the need to search for, and evaluate, further options. The term also carries with it the idea of discovering things by trial and error rather than by systematic analysis of all appropriate information.

Heuristic thinking

The idea of heuristic thinking can be illustrated by contrasting it with a rational approach to making a non-ethical decision such as choosing a car to buy. If this decision were to be approached from an analytical and rational position, you would have to go through the following stages.

- Identify all the cars available on the market.

- Identify all the factors that are important to you in a car, such as cost, reliability, acceleration, colour and so on.

- Decide on the relative importance to you of the above criteria by either putting them into rank order or assigning weights to them.

- Research each car on the market and decide how they score against each of the criteria.

- Calculate the degree to which each car would satisfy your wishes by combining the cars' performances against each criterion with the criterion's importance, so that cars that do well against the more important criteria will have the higher scores.

- Choose the car that scores highest in these calculations.

The process just described is called subjective expected utility. This is because the decision maker makes a personal (subjective) assessment of both what is important to them about a car (utility) and the chances (expected) that any particular car would actually provide that value.

This is obviously a time-consuming process. A heuristic approach would simplify it. A large number of heuristics could be involved in deciding which car to buy. Here are just a few. To begin with, you would probably not evaluate every car available on the market but simply focus on those you have been made aware of by advertising. This is the availability heuristic. The recency heuristic might mean that a pleasurable trip last weekend in a friend's new car weighs heavily in your preference for that model. Your dislike of the colour purple might mean that the purple car you have been considering seems to have a lot of factors that turn you against it. This is an example of the halo and horns heuristic that is explained on p. 169. The application of one or more of these heuristics will leave you with a narrow range of cars from which to choose and an intuitive inclination to buy one particular car.

Let us move on to consider decision making about ethical matters. Benjamin Franklin proposed, in the eighteenth century, the use of a moral algebra to resolve such issues (Gigerenzer et al., 1999: 76). This was similar to the rational and analytical model, described above, for choosing a car. He would divide a sheet of paper into two columns and head one 'Pros' and the other 'Cons'. He would then identify the factors for or against a particular course of action. On further consideration, he would strike out some pros and cons because they cancelled each other out. If two cons were, in his view, equal to one pro he would strike out all three.

As a result of this process he would come to a balanced view about the right thing to do.

If we applied moral algebra to an ethical question we might find, but not necessarily, deontological pros ranged against consequentialist cons. Rights would have to be weighed against justice and equity and the virtuous mean might be hard to find. Giving equal consideration to potentially mutually exclusive ways of thinking about ethical questions may lead to confusion. Some writers (Kaler, 1999) suggest that the way business schools teach business ethics ('well, you could look at it from a deontological viewpoint or alternatively from a consequentialist position') encourages such confusion. It will be argued, contrarily, that people tend not to combine all the ethical perspectives on an issue but choose one and use it in a heuristic manner.

It is further argued in this chapter that values and emotions can perform the role of decision-making heuristics. Two examples of the role of values as heuristics in ethical decision making are provided to illustrate the process.

- The first example focuses on priority setting and uses the case of resource allocation in health-care management.

- The second example concerns ideas of integrity and loyalty as decision-making heuristics. Each of these is explained, and illustrated by an activity.

Decision-making heuristics

The idea has long been recognised that people do not possess the capacity to obtain and process the amounts of information necessary in order to take a rational approach to decision making. Herbert Simon's (1983) concept of bounded rationality is the classic formulation of this viewpoint. Search behaviour is the process of looking for the information and options necessary to make a decision. Bounded rationality sets limits on the extent of such searches. He introduced the concept of satisficing, which is the process of searching for and evaluating options until one is found that is good enough. He accepted that this solution may not be the best or optimal one. If the decision maker had continued to identify and assess options, better ones might have been found. But, he argued, once a solution has been found that will do, the psychological and practical costs to the decision-maker of looking for the best solution outweigh the additional benefits of a best solution that may not, in any case, be found. Simon's work emphasised that fully rational decision making was at best an aspiration and that the way people actually made up their minds about things was less analytical and was based more on trial and error – which is one definition of a heuristic.

Some examples might give a clearer understanding of heuristics. In the 1970s, psychologists, among them Kahneman et al. (1982), studied the exercise of judgment. In particular, they investigated how people made estimates about the probability or likelihood of situations and events. The research was carried out using questionnaires. The box below presents an example of the questions they asked.

Blue taxi or green taxi?

A taxi was involved in a hit-and-run accident at night. Two taxi companies, the green and the blue, operate in the city. You are given the following data:

(a) 85 per cent of the taxis in the city are green and 15 per cent blue.

(b) A witness identified the cab as blue. The court tested the reliability of the witness under the same circumstances that existed on the night of the accident and concluded that the witness correctly identified each of the two colours 80 per cent of the time and failed 20 per cent of the time.

What is the probability that the cab involved in the accident was blue rather than green?

(Source: Kahneman et al., 1982: 156–7)

This example identifies a heuristic (known as base-rate neglect) that leads people to pay more attention to immediate sources of information (the witness's statement) and to ignore background information (such as the relative frequency of the two types of cabs). The correct answer, derived from Bayes' theorem (which takes both items of data into account), is 0.41.

DEFINITION

Bayes theorem includes both prior and current information when calculating a probability. It is not necessary for you to know the mathematics but for those who are curious there is a useful Bayes' theorem calculator on the Web at http://faculty.vassar.edu/lowry/bayes.html.
 If you put into this calculator:

■ the probability that the taxi will be blue, which is 0.15 (P(A)),

■ the probability that the witness will correctly identify the taxi as green if it is green, which is 0.68 (P (B|~A) = 0.8 × 0.85), and

■ the probability of the witness identifying the taxi as blue if it is blue, which is 0.12 (P (B| A) = 0.15 × 0.8)

it gives the probability of the taxi being blue as 0.41.

Most people, when asked to answer this question, however, ignored the data in point (a) because they were considered too general and distant from the event, and produced an answer around 80 per cent, which was based on the information given in point (b) alone.

In this classic research conducted by Kahnemann and his colleagues, the research questions were constructed so that if a heuristic were present respondents would misuse or neglect important information and give incorrect answers. The inference was then drawn that heuristics were a source of bias and prejudice in judgment. In hind sight it can be objected that the questions were so deviously constructed that they did not represent the kinds of judgment people have to make in real life. If so, the possibility remains that in everyday situations the heuristics might not be a cause of error.

A large number of heuristics are identified in Hogarth (1980). Just a few will be mentioned here. The recency effect was mentioned in the example of the car-buying decision mentioned above. This heuristic causes people to put more weight on information they have collected recently and to undervalue things they may have learned in the past. The halo and horns heuristic has long been known to selection and recruitment specialists. This heuristic leads people to latch on to one aspect of an interviewee to which they have a strong like or dislike. It may be the fact that the interviewee has a moustache or is wearing blue suede shoes. This one feature then dominates the recruiter's whole assessment of the individual. They might think that a man with a moustache cannot really be trusted, or that anyone who wears blue suede shoes must be just the sort of creative person the company needs. The heuristics-and-biases programme of research established the existence of heuristics in judgment but suggested that they were a problem.

A more recent programme of research led by the ABC research group, based in Berlin, has revisited heuristics and come to the conclusion that far from being a distortion of decision making, they are both necessary and effective. The programme is intended to 'capture how real minds make decisions under constraints of limited time and knowledge' (Gigerenzer et al., 1999: 5). It rejects the rational, subjective, expected utility model as a description of decision making and instead proposes the idea of fast and frugal heuristics. These are rules for limiting the search for information and options, and for making choices, that employ a minimum of time, knowledge and computation. It argues that fast and frugal heuristics are bounded rationality in its purest form.

The working of fast and frugal heuristics can best be explained by an example. One of the heuristics is the recognition heuristic that applies to situations where a person has to decide which of two objects has a higher value on a particular criterion. The heuristic is defined as follows: 'If one of the two objects is recognised and the other is not, then infer that the recognised object has the higher value' (Gigerenzer et al., 1999: 41). In an experiment students at the University of Chicago and the University of Munich the question, 'Which city has more inhabitants: San Diego or San Antonio?' Sixty-four per cent of the Chicago students got the answer right, but 100 per cent of the Munich students gave the correct answer. Why did the German students do better? They had heard of San Diego but not of San Antonio. They applied the recognition heuristic and got it right. The American students recognised both cities and could not apply the recognition heuristic. They had to search their memories for further clues as to the right answer. The additional information merely confused them. There is of course logic to the recognition heuristic; cities of which you have heard are more likely to be bigger than those that are unknown to you. The heuristic uses this logic as the basis of a very simple decision rule. But because of the logic the heuristic is not only simple; it is effective.

Of course there are many situations in which the recognition heuristic cannot be used because both of the options are recognised. Gigerenzer et al. (1999: Chapter 4) used a computer simulation to evaluate some simple heuristics for searching through data for solutions in such circumstances. As in their work reported above, the simulation was based on the task of deciding which, of pairs of cities, was the larger. They built into the simulation a series of 10 cues or clues about each of the cities. Whether a city was a capital or not was one clue. In the database of information, which was to be searched in the simulation, the cue was recorded as positive (if it was a capital city) because a capital city was likely to be larger than a city that was not, as negative (if it was not) or as a 'don't know'. Some additional information was included about the reliability of each cue (how often its use could give the right answer) and how often it would prove useful (as only one city can be a capital city you will not often have an opportunity to use it to discriminate between pairs of cities). In the simulation, six search strategies were tested. The first three were based on heuristic principles.

1. *Minimalist.* Choose one of the 10 cues at random. If one of the pair of cities you have to decide between scores a positive on this cue and the other a negative, then choose the positive city as the larger one. If not go on trying cues randomly in turn until one provides an answer.

2. *Take the last.* Choose whichever cue worked well last time this kind of decision had to be made.

3. *Take the best.* In this strategy, some of the information about the reliability and usefulness of the cues is used to decide which cue is likely to provide the most accurate answer.

The other three search strategies were all based on the rational model. They were:

■ Franklin's rule

■ Dawe's rule

■ Multiple regression.

We will not explain each of these in detail. It is sufficient to point out that they all shared one common feature, that, when choosing between two cities, they aggregated all 10 cues about each city in order to decide which was likely to be bigger. The heuristic strategies, in contrast, only used cues one at a time and when a decision had been reached ignored all the other cues.

The results from the simulation are shown in Table 4.2. The results suggest that not only are heuristics efficient because they give answers by using less information than the rational strategies, but they are also as accurate as the rational techniques. The fast and frugal researchers see heuristics as (generally) effective strategies for making decisions. This leaves open the possibility that ethical thinking, as well as judgment, might be a heuristic process.

Table 4.2 The results of the simulation comparing heuristic and rational research strategies

Type of strategy	Strategy	Frugality (no. of cues looked up)	Accuracy (% of correct answers)
Heuristic	Take the last	2.6	64.5
	Minimalist	2.8	64.7
	Take the best	3.0	65.8
Rational	Franklin's rule	10.0	62.1
	Dawe's rule	10.0	62.3
	Multiple regression	10.0	65.7

Values as heuristics in ethical reasoning

In this section, we want to move away from what is established in the literature and to speculate about how the fast and frugal heuristics may apply to ethical decision making. The argument is that heuristics operate in ethical decision making and that values are the basis of these heuristics.

Gigerenzer et al. (1999: 30) pointed out that, while most of the fast and frugal research concerns cognitive heuristics, emotions and social norms can also act as heuristics. For example, a social norm such as 'copy the choices made by your social peers' acts as an efficient heuristic for stopping further searching for other options. This heuristic might be particularly powerful in academic recruitment procedures in which academics apparently appoint those whom they think their colleagues would approve of. Emotions, such as love for one's child, prevent wasteful ethical dithering. If a child screams in the night, the emotional response forces the parent to get out of bed and comfort the child. Such parents do not calculate whether the greatest utility is achieved by this action or whether staying in bed so that they might be fresher for work the next day might do greater good. Kahneman (2011) has written in his new book that in the past the role of emotion as a decision-making heuristic has been underrated and that the affective heuristic is one of the most important amongst heuristics.

Four categories of moral emotions have been identified (Haidt, 2003) that, once elicited by some event, act as a trigger or create a tendency to act in a particular way. They are:

- Other condemning – contempt, anger and disgust.
- Self-conscious – shame, embarrassment and guilt.
- Other suffering – compassion.
- Other praising – gratitude and elevation.

If emotions and social norms can act as heuristics, then it is possible that values can also do so. This is because values are closely related to emotions and social norms. Values are like emotions because people find it hard to give a rational account of why their values are important to them; they just are (Eden et al., 1979). The link with social norms derives from the fact that values are acquired as part of the process of growing up and becoming socialised in a society. It is this early acquisition of values, according to Rokeach (1973: 17–18), that makes values simpler and more robust than attitudes.

Values acting as heuristics

The ways in which values may act as heuristics can be illustrated by considering a well-known management development exercise called *Cave Rescue* (Woodcock, 1979, 1989: 81). In this exercise, groups have to decide how to allocate scarce resources between people who are described in thumbnail sketches, which are deliberately brief and partisan. *Cave Rescue* concerns six volunteers in a psychological experiment that requires them to be in a pothole. The cave is flooding and the research committee in charge of the experiment has called for a rescue team. When the team arrives, it will only be able to rescue one person at a time because of the narrowness of the cave's entrance. The committee has to decide the order in which the volunteers will be saved from the cave when the rescue party arrives. The exercise provides a good opportunity to study the values that are articulated in such debates.

Observations of people doing the exercise suggest that they used their preferred values to select the information from the thumbnail sketches that they consider useful. Each of the characters in the *Cave Rescue* exercise has positive and negative aspects included in their thumbnail sketches. Some material about each of the characters has to be edited out for other information to become useful in making the necessary ranking decisions. A number of different values are used that include:

- Maximising the number of people who are saved by rescuing first those likely to panic and hamper the rescuers.

- Maximising the happiness of society by rescuing first those who can make the greatest contribution to society (utilitarianism).

- Rescuing first those who have the most family or other dependants.

- Rescuing the youngest first because the oldest have already had their opportunity for life.

- Rescuing the morally worthy before the morally unworthy.

The heuristic use of values can be illustrated by reference to volunteer Paul who, according to the information given to the participants, has been convicted of indecent assault. But he also has, in his working notes, details of a cheap cure for rabies. People who used the morality criterion to choose whom to rescue assumed that the cure could be understood from the working notes (and that in any case he was bound to have a research assistant who understood and could continue the work) and that there was, consequently, no barrier to using his behaviour to decide his order of rescue. Other people, using a utilitarian value, assumed that it was impossible to make sense of the working notes. This allowed them, when making their decision, to ignore Paul's criminal activities and concentrate on his potential contribution to society. People edited out, or rationalised into insignificance, that information which inhibited the application of their preferred values.

How values are used as heuristics

So far, the argument seems straightforward. Values are simple but strongly held beliefs such as the importance of honesty. People, it is suggested, use values as filters to reduce the amount of information they take into account when making a decision. Values may act as a fast and frugal heuristic for limiting the amount of search behaviour. To the three heuristic search strategies proposed by Gigerenzer et al. (1999, see p. 87) might be added another one: choose a cue that you like because it fits with your values.

If people do not change their values, ethical decisions ought to be easy. But it is not. Ethical issues are often seen as dilemmas that are not easily resolved. According to Billig (1996: 238–47), values may be simple in themselves but in at least two ways they are complex matters of controversy.

- The first concerns the interpretations of the values. Their very simplicity makes them banal. This in turn means that they have to be interpreted before they can be of use in making decisions. An example can be taken from health-care management. Everyone in the field would agree that patients come first. But different health-care professionals may make sense of this value in different ways. For some it would mean improving the patients' clinical condition. Others might say it is empowering the patients to take control of their treatment and their condition. Yet others might claim it means making the patient physically comfortable and at psychological ease.

- The second source of argument and conflict over values is the multiplicity of conflicting values in any given society. Ambition, for example, may clash with honesty. Ethical issues are often difficult because it may not be certain which value, from a variety of contradictory values, should be applied in any given situation.

The problem for someone faced with an ethical matter is to choose which of many values to apply to the situation. This brings us back to a feature of fast and frugal heuristics as described by Gigerenzer et al. (1999: 30). They proposed that people are equipped with a psychological adaptive toolbox that is filled with a jumbled collection of one-function tools. Just as a mechanic manages to choose the right tool to repair a car, so people choose the best heuristic to hand to help them make their mind up or take a decision.

<table>
<tr><td>Video clip
4.2
</td><td>**Nepotism**

The clip deals with nepotism – taking family connections into account when recruiting staff. Is this a good and appropriate value to apply or not?

To view the video clip from the interview please visit this book's companion website at www.pearsoned.co.uk/fisherlovellvalerosilva.</td></tr>
</table>

In the next two sections we explore the ways in which particular values might be used.

Value heuristics and priority setting

Resource allocation is a particular form of priority setting. It involves deciding which things are more important and which less. In this section, it is argued that right answers to problems of priority setting cannot be found by technical means. Priority setting is a matter of values. The person setting the priorities has to decide which values they will use to determine relative importance. Whether a particular set of priorities is right or wrong depends upon the values used to judge it. This makes that priority setting an ethical matter.

This section explores the use of values as heuristics for making decisions in ethical matters, using a simulation exercise called *Monksbane and feverfew*. The exercise is based on a problem in health-care management. A limited budget has to be divided between two health-care programmes, one aimed at the diagnosis and treatment of monksbane and the other at the diagnosis and treatment of feverfew, both dangerous, if fictitious, diseases. The problem is to decide which programme should be given priority. Fisher (1998) identified six values concerning priority setting in the allocation of resources. They are listed here but will be defined later in the chapter:

1. utility

2. individual need

3. deservingness

4. ecology

5. fairness

6. personal competence and gain.

In *Monksbane and feverfew*, there are opportunities to apply each of these values in setting your priorities between the two programmes. Whichever you choose will lead to a different allocation of resources. It may be that you will change your mind as you work through the simulation. Do Activity 4.1 now and then the different values will be explained.

Activity 4.3	Monksbane and feverfew: a diagnostic instrument about values and priority setting

Go to the companion website for this book (www.pearsoned.co.uk /fisherlovell) where you will find both an interactive, web-based version of the activity as well as a hard-copy version that you can print off. The interactive version calculates your scores for you. If you use the hard copy you will have to do the scoring yourself.

Transfer your score from the *Monksbane and feverfew* exercise to the grid to the below by placing ticks in the appropriate cells.

Heuristic	Low	Medium	High
Utility			
Individual need			
Deservingness			
Ecology			
Fairness			
Personal competence and gain			

Source: Fisher (1998)

The value heuristics of resource allocation

Each of the six value heuristics for resource allocation will be explained by reference to the information provided to the decision maker in *Monksbane and feverfew*.

Utility

Utility is a value concerned with allocating resources in a way that maximises the common good (or the beneficial impact of services). Utility values the maximisation of the quantity of good done. It is a form of utilitarianism.

In Section 1 of *Monksbane and feverfew*, you are given enough information to apply utility as a value. If the graph is studied carefully it is clear that at any point money spent on feverfew will always save more lives than will be saved by spending it on monksbane. The way to save the most lives is to spend all the money on feverfew and none on monksbane. Those who make this decision are using the utility value. Not everyone can bear to do this. Those who know that rationally any money spent on monksbane costs the lives of feverfew sufferers, who might otherwise have been saved, may still find themselves unable to spend nothing on monksbane at all. They therefore decide to spend a small amount on its treatment. This suggests that they are not entirely at ease with the utility value.

Utility is the heuristic that underwrites much management theory, and management science in particular. The development of QALYs, in health-policy studies, provides an illustration of this approach. QALY stands for quality-adjusted life years (Gudex, 1986) and is a measure of the benefit, to the average patient, of a medical treatment in terms of additional years of life and of the quality of life. Once the benefit of a medical intervention is measured, its cost can be calculated to produce a ranking of treatments in cost-effectiveness terms. Haemodialysis produced a cost per QALY of £9,075 while for scoliosis surgery the cost was £194. The latter treatment will therefore produce more benefit for any given sum of money than the former. There have been many criticisms of the utilitarian QALY approach, as reported in Pereira (1989) and Baldwin et al. (1990), but it is still persuasive to many.

Cross reference The heuristic of utility relates to the general ethical tradition of utilitarianism that is discussed in Chapter 3.

Individual need

Individual need is a value that can be triggered by the cues and information given in Section 2 of *Monksbane and feverfew*. This value holds that resources should be allocated in proportion to people's needs. Needs can of course be attributed to groups of people but those who adopt this value prefer to consider people as individuals. Needs are not the same as wants or demands, however. A need can only be defined by an expert in the field, in the cases of monksbane and feverfew by a doctor. Needs have two further characteristics: they can be objectively described, which means that it is possible for someone to have a need they do not know about, and, secondly, they can be ranked so that some are seen as more pressing than others.

The information provided in Section 2 of *Monksbane and feverfew* suggests that people who suffer from monksbane have greater need than those ill with feverfew. Monksbane patients are much more likely to die if not treated than feverfew patients. The information in Section 2 also highlights another aspect of individual need. It is the belief that if there are the means and the technology to improve people's lot, then we are obliged to use them. In a medical setting it is the belief that everything that can be done, that has some chance of providing some benefit to the patient, should be done. It is to be noted that more can be done to treat people with monksbane than can be done for those with feverfew. If someone adopts the individual need value therefore, they will decide to spend significant sums of money on the treatment of monksbane.

The problem with individual need as a value is that it wills the expenditure of money without any regard for the availability of that money.

Deservingness

The deservingness heuristic, which is made available in Sections 3a and 3b of Activity 5.1, divides people into two moral classes, the deserving and the undeserving. When resources are being distributed according to the deservingness heuristic, the favourable allocation is given to the former and the unfavourable portion to the latter. Deservingness is an Edwardian concept. This traditional view saw the provenance of poverty and need in individual moral failure and indolence. The growing depersonalisation and alienation of social life, caused by nineteenth-century industrialisation, made this view untenable, and a distinction was drawn between the deserving poor, brought low by social and economic factors beyond their control, and the undeserving poor, whose failure was of their own doing. New possibilities for morally classifying people have emerged since Edwardian times. People can be allocated to moral categories according to whether they are, on the one hand, greedy, truculent and ungrateful or, on the other, meek, humble and full of gratitude. A further moral criterion of deservingness is group membership. The deserving person is one of us; the undeserving person is an outsider.

In more recent times, the debate about the funding of treatment for sufferers from AIDS suggests that the distinction between the morally deserving and the undeserving is still current, and indeed is experiencing a renaissance. Academic writing on the subject has been concerned with whether the treatment of AIDS sufferers is cost effective (Eastwood and Maynard, 1990). But there were arguments put forward, particularly in the press, which suggested that AIDS patients should be seen as 'less eligible' for treatment because they had visited the illness upon themselves through homosexual behaviour or drug abuse. It is, perhaps, the effect of deservingness that accounts for the different public perceptions of the plights of haemophiliacs, who acquired the disease through the necessary treatment of their primary illness, and that of homosexuals who, more likely, acquired it as a result of chosen behaviours. Whilst the UK government was initially curmudgeonly in the question of compensation for haemophiliacs, who had become HIV positive from being treated with infected blood products, public opinion clearly thought they should be compensated quickly (Mihil, 1990). There was a popular temptation to see haemophiliacs as deserving, and homosexuals as undeserving, and to fund their programmes accordingly.

In *Monksbane and feverfew*, you are informed that people with the disease to which you have given the biggest share of the budget are ungrateful and truculent and that their behaviour has contributed towards their condition. If you are attracted to the value of deservingness, you will have little patience with these people and decide to spend less on their treatment. However, if you do not hold this value, you will probably regard all the information given in this section as irrelevant to the problem and decide to leave the budget allocation unaltered.

Cross reference	The heuristic of deservingness has some connections with the largely American philosophy of objectivism that is associated with Ayn Rand, whose ideas are discussed in Chapter 3. This philosophy emphasises the moral independence of individuals. Those who do not rise to this challenge are undeserving.

Ecology

The apologists for the ecology heuristic take a very different approach. They see clients as morally autonomous agents who are not passive recipients of services but actors within the resource-allocation process. Put simply, the ecology value states that the voices of all the parties interested in a decision should be heard. Those who value this perspective are pluralists who assume there will be many different points of view that have to be accommodated.

The ecology heuristic is concerned with identifying the different perceptions of the many groups involved with a service and trying to create a consistent policy from that variety. Ultimately, this concatenation is achieved by giving more weight to the views of those who are most closely involved with the service. Some groups, particularly the most powerful with respect to the decision makers, will be listened to more intently than others. In other words, an ecological resource allocation is one that meets the expectations and aspirations of the most significant interest groups. But such allocations also have to meet the minimum requirements of all the interest groups. If they do not, then those disregarded groups will seek to make themselves more significant to the organisation and so reach a condition in which the decision makers have to listen to them.

Section 4 of *Monksbane and feverfew* provides enough clues for people who adopt this value to act upon it. Some very powerful interest groups are pressing for more money to be spent on the monksbane programme. People who accept ecology respond by putting another five or ten thousand pounds into the programme. Most of those who reject ecology as a value simply ignore the demands of the pressure groups. Some respondents, however, are so incensed by what they see as bullying by the pressure groups, that they reduce the expenditure on monksbane to punish those who would seek to bring pressure to bear.

Fairness

Fairness is concerned with impartiality between individuals. Fairness emphasises the importance of giving everyone equal access to services or at least an equal chance of access. This makes the use of arbitrary mechanisms for allocating scarce resources possible. Some managers, for example, when faced with too many job candidates, all of whom fit the employee specification, believe the only fair way of choosing the successful candidate is to draw lots. People who apply the fairness heuristic are interested in the standardisation and consistency of services to customers and clients. One of the clearest definitions of fairness, as it is defined here, can be found in a medieval Islamic story.

> A child and an adult both of the True Faith are in Heaven, but the adult occupies a higher place. God explains that the man has done many good works whereupon the child asks why God allowed him to die before he could do good. God answers that he knew the child would grow up to be a sinner and so it was better that he die young. A cry rises up from the depths of Hell: 'Why O Lord did you not let us die before we became sinners?'

> (Russell, 1985: 85)

The Lord was obviously working on an ad hoc basis, dealing with individuals as they appeared before him for judgement. For some reason this child was noticed and saved while many others were not, a lapse on God's part that those in Hell naturally thought unfair. Fairness therefore must operate according to universally applied rules. Either all potential sinners die young or none.

Fairness is only concerned with equality of access and opportunity, not with equality of outcomes. In Section 5 of *Monksbane and feverfew*, the table shows that if £10,000 is spent on feverfew and £60,000 on monksbane then 30 per cent of sufferers from feverfew and 30 per cent of sufferers from monksbane would be identified and treated. This would be fair because, irrespective of which disease a person had, their chances of treatment would be the same. This does not of course mean that they would all have the same chances of being made well. Some people favour the value of fairness but would not wish to impose it by dividing up the budget 10:60. Section 6 of *Monksbane and feverfew* therefore provides another option for applying the fairness heuristic. In this section you are given the opportunity to leave the allocation of resources between the two treatment programmes to chance. This is done by treating patients as they present themselves, irrespective of their diagnosis, and by stopping all treatments when the budget is spent. This alternative puts everyone in a queue and so everyone is dealt with in the same way – fairly.

Personal competence and gain

Personal competence and gain is a heuristic which, when applied to the allocation of resources, causes decisions to be made to the decision maker's benefit. The benefit can be of two different kinds. The first is the sense of worth and self-esteem that can come from having done a job properly. This implies that the decision has been made using appropriate methods and that no short cuts, which offend against the decision maker's beliefs, have been used. The second sense relates to personal advantage. In this sense, the decision makers allocate resources in a way that brings some material or personal benefit to them – this may be an increase in organisational influence, professional satisfaction, something which eases the burden of daily life, cash or a bottle of whisky. Personal gain does not necessarily imply gain for the decision maker because they may value being able to help their friends or family, but it does imply that decisions are made according to private rather than public considerations.

In *Monksbane and feverfew*, respondents are invited to respond to this value in Section 7. It suggests that someone very dear to the respondent is suffering from the disease that is being given the smaller amount of money. Clearly that person's chances of recovery would be better if more money were spent on the screening and treatment for that disease. If the respondent increases the money allocated to the disease of the person close to them, they are using the personal gain value. A range of other factors could of course trigger this value. The person making the decision might, for example, have a research or clinical interest in the treatment of one of the two diseases. We do not necessarily think people will answer this part of the simulation honestly. We suspect people do not know how they would behave in such a situation until they are in it. However, Section 7 does illustrate how this value could be used as a heuristic for making the decision.

We are suggesting that *Monksbane and feverfew* illustrates how values can oper-ate heuristically in the way that people search for solutions to a priority-setting problem. It is suggested that the six value heuristics identified in this chapter can be seen in any priority-setting or resource-allocation decision. They can be seen, for example, in decisions about the allocation of budget cuts or increases between departments, in deciding whom to make redundant in a round of downsizing and in decisions about responding to different market segments. Although it does not prove that people use values heuristically when making real-life decisions, it does provide some interesting issues for you to think about.

Integrity and loyalty as value heuristics

There are two other values that, it will be argued, can play an important role as heuristics for deciding what to think, say or do in an ethical matter. They are in-tegrity and loyalty. A commitment to either loyalty or integrity can act as a heuris-tic for deciding what should be done in a situation. The process may be related to the extent of a person's ethical horizon, which is a personally set boundary within which a person seeks to act with integrity. When dealing with those considered to be beyond that boundary, a person shows loyalty to those within their ethical horizon. All of these issues need to be explained in more detail.

Defining integrity and loyalty

Integrity is defined as basing action on sound judgment and seeking a unity or wholeness of thought and action. The medieval scholar Aquinas, after Aristotle, argued that the practice of virtue requires people to act knowingly, voluntarily and according to a fixed principle or habit (D'Entreves, 1965: 147–8). Winstanley and Woodall reflected these ideas when they argued that

> The development of integrity [is] based upon ethical judgement and a sense of responsibility, the development of appropriate virtues.

> (Winstanley and Woodall, 2000: 285)

Integrity therefore is defined by its possessor's self-reflection and awareness. As C.P. Snow, quoted by Adair (1980: 171), epigrammatically expressed it:

Give me a man who knows something of himself and is appalled.

Video clip 4.3

Ethical communication

The clip deals with the importance and nature of integrity in business communication. To view the video clip from the interview please visit this book's companion website at www.pearsoned.co.ukfisherlovellvalerosilva.

A sense of self-doubt, as well as the tension between integrity and loyalty, can be illustrated by an account of an incident given during a research interview we conducted. The interviewee was a senior manager. His company required all managers to attend a series of development workshops that were designed to apply the precepts of an eastern mystical tradition to modern management practice. The respondent was a man of strong Christian belief who believed the philosophy of the seminars was contrary to his Christian principles. He felt that he should not in conscience attend the seminars. He was aware that taking this stance to maintain his integrity was at odds with his sense of loyalty. His loyalty was not particularly directed at the company but was focused on the rest of the management team who would be going to the seminars. The other team members told him that they thought him an important team member and they wished him to attend the seminars. The respondent reported that the issue caused him to think deeply about his beliefs and his responsibilities to others. His final position on the issue spoke of a self-conscious attempt to meet the demands of both integrity and loyalty. He attended the seminars but made a personal statement at the commencement in which he stated his personal objections to the values that informed them.

In contrast to integrity, loyalty is an unthinking faithfulness to a person, group or purpose. If a loyal person were to reflect on their actions they would have to question whether they were being loyal to the right thing. As Snell (1993: 82) characterised it, loyalty can range between a high commitment, analogous to a marriage, and a low level, which requires only the performance of actions contractually agreed. In a situation where high loyalty is demanded, but there is no opportunity for developmental openness (which would allow an individual to develop their own values and ethical reasoning),

Unquestioning conformity is expected of members: one must suppress individuality, ignore one's own arguments and perspectives and accept what one has to do.

(Snell, 1993: 82)

The unreflective nature of loyalty can be illustrated by another account of an ethical issue given by a manager in a finance department. When he moved to a new job he asked a colleague, with whom he had previously worked, to move with him and to support him in his new role. The manager was aware that the colleague was a discharged bankrupt who had invested unwisely when he had worked in the City. The financial accountant, who also reported to the manager, warned him of suspicions about the colleague's use of the credit card that the company had given him for business expenses.

> I had to take a view whether to expose him or to bring him to account, make him pay it back, and to carry on . . . Either to keep it to myself and the financial accountant, or to let other people know. I think there was enough going on that could have cost him his job: and I chose the latter. I had known him for a number of years, he was an extremely hard working individual, played hard as well, and played hard sometimes in my time. But if someone is working for me I take a balanced view. I don't expect them to work like an automaton . . . He was always getting phone calls at home in the early hours of the morning from the department, 'can't do this and can't do that', and he solved it . . . he was also being hounded by the CSA [Child Support Agency] so he wasn't having an easy time. All this encouraged me to take a lenient view. I also knew of his background and he was probably finding life a bit tough.

The colleague had spent £600 improperly using the credit card. The manager challenged him privately and, instead of starting disciplinary proceedings, made him pay the sum back within two weeks. The manager's loyalty towards the employee was at a cost to his honesty and integrity. He thought the colleague reciprocated the feeling of loyalty:

> I felt that as he was working for me he would behave himself and he would not wish to implicate me. I thought I was entitled to more consideration than somebody he didn't know.

However, within a short space of time the colleague had found himself a new, better-paid, job with a different company and in his last few weeks of his old employment he again misused his credit card.

> And so I felt as if I had paid my dues . . . I had no loyalty to him then once he had done it twice . . . On many occasions I have gone back and questioned my initial judgment. I find it quite difficult to think of abstract examples and decide what I would do, *because most things are instinct*. I am nearly forty-six years of age and so I have had a fair amount of experience; I am not sure I would do the same thing again.

> (Research interview: our emphasis)

Loyalty, in this account, is seen as a matter of instinct and experience and not as a matter of self-reflection. The instinctive wish to act loyally can easily be destroyed, as here, by an act of betrayal by the person to whom loyalty is given.

Ethical horizons

People in organisations may experience conflicts between behaving with integrity within a group they belong to and their inclination to defend this chosen group to those beyond it, even if that group has acted badly. Let us imagine that someone is a member of a professional body that has acted unethically. Within that group, they may well seek to put right the thing badly done, in short to act with integrity; but when someone outside of that body challenges it for its wrong doing, that same person could well defend the body, even though they know it has done wrong. The issue is well illustrated by a conversation imagined by Watson (1998: 266).

> *David:*   Alright for the sake of argument, imagine we set up a business to murder people.
>
> *Colin:*   Murder Incorporated.
>
> *David:*   OK; it's been done. But say we did this and we followed all the culture and empowerment stuff. We could have democratic management, lots of trust and all that. There's good pay for everybody, welfare arrangements, good pensions, and Christmas parties for the kiddies. There's a moral code – just like the Mafia – that holds everything together. Everything we have said so far makes this a moral business. But it is not. Murder isn't moral is it?

Legge expressed the dilemma, raised by this thought experiment, in a more formal way when discussing human resource management (HRM):

> If capitalism is, or has the potential to be viewed as ethical, then HRM similarly has a good chance. If not, it is difficult to imagine how an ethical system for managing people at work can emerge from an essentially unethical economic order.
>
> (Legge, 1998: 166)

The dilemmas in these two quotations hinge on the question of ethical horizons. An ethical horizon represents a person's belief about the extent of their ethical world. For some the horizon may be very close and focused on themselves alone or their immediate family and associates. For others their ethical horizon might be so wide as to include global society as a whole. Within the ethical horizon, people seek to act with integrity; beyond the horizon, they believe, it is not necessary to act with integrity but it is important to show loyalty to those within the ethical horizon.

The concept of an ethical horizon can be used to explain the issues in the examples of the fictitious conversation about organised crime, and Legge's discussion of capitalism. To take the mafia conversation first. If people's horizon is local and only encompasses the organisation, then they are only required to act with integrity within the organisation. Outside of the organisation, they are not required to act with integrity and can engage in criminal activities, as long as they show loyalty to the organisation. However, if the ethical horizon is drawn very broadly to include society as a whole, then such criminality would be unacceptable because people would be expected to display integrity in all their actions. In the example of Legge's

The Cynocephali

An example from the Middle Ages can illustrate the idea of an ethical horizon. In medieval maps of the world, there can often be seen on their margins images of people, normal in all respects, except that they have dog's heads. They are the cynocephali. It was thought they lived far to the east. Theologians were worried about how to treat the cynocephali when contact was eventually made with them. Should they be treated the same as the rest of humanity, with respect and with care for their souls? Or should they be seen as less than human in which case they could be treated as chattels and be exploited for humanity's benefit? Their problem was where the horizon of the ethical universe should be drawn. Should the cynocephali be within it or beyond it? If they were beyond it then the normal moral standards would not apply to how they should be treated.

analysis of HRM, she makes a similar point. If the ethical horizon is drawn widely then HRM is not ethical if capitalism is not; but if it is drawn only around the function of HRM then integrity is not required in the wider capitalist system. It is argued therefore that whether people think they should show loyalty or integrity, when it is not possible to do both, is affected by the extent of the subject's ethical horizon. A simplified analysis of the range of ethical horizons is shown in Box 4.1.

The ethical horizons of loyalty and integrity

Four levels of ethical horizon

1. The ethical horizon is drawn around the self and close associates

   - When people are acting within this narrow horizon, people are expected to focus on themselves, family and associates. Within the horizon they are expected to treat others properly and with integrity, as defined by their social norms. This may be represented by the alleged judgment on many East End gangsters that they were essentially good because they 'were good to their mothers'.

2. The ethical horizon is drawn around a person's networks and associations within civil society

   - Within this horizon, people are expected to act with integrity within their civil associations. When they are acting in the space beyond this horizon, they must defend and show loyalty to those associations. This is perhaps exemplified by E.M. Forster's (1975) remark, 'If I had to choose between betraying my country and betraying my friend, I hope I should have the guts to betray my country'.

3. The ethical horizon is drawn around a person's employing organisation

   - A person who perceives the organisation as their ethical horizon should act in an ethical manner within it but show loyalty to it if it is criticised or attacked from beyond the horizon. As the Civil Service code of ethics states, 'Civil servants owe their loyalty to the duly constituted government' (Cabinet Office, 2004).

4. The ethical horizon is set at its widest extent to include global society

- When the horizon is drawn at its widest, there is no space beyond the horizon so that loyalty has to exist within rather than beyond the horizon. This means that loyalty and integrity become one. To be loyal to global society you have to act with integrity.

The first level in the hierarchy of ethical horizons in Table 4.3 is the broadest one and encompasses a concern for the well-being of society as a whole. At this level, people see themselves as parts of the whole, as flakes of rock chipped from the mountain. Such a sense of personal inconsequence, yet commitment to society, creates a willingness to sacrifice the self for the greater good. As, when the horizon is drawn this wide, integrity and loyalty are one, a person would be willing to resist any wrongdoing. Such an action would exhibit both integrity and loyalty to wider society.

When ethical horizons are set around membership of a civil association or an organisation, people seek to behave integrity within the organisation or association but will sacrifice their integrity in order to show loyalty to that body when acting in the world beyond it. Imagine a situation where someone has discovered that the organisation or association has done something seriously wrong. Within the horizon people will try to act with integrity and put the wrong right, or at least to convince others in the organisation to put things right. However, when dealing with people outside of the organisation, the same person will put their concerns to one side and protect and defend their organisation against criticism. In short, they will show loyalty. The degree to which they will sacrifice integrity to show loyalty will vary with the degree of their emotional identification with the organisation or association. At a minimal level, loyalty may just be keeping silence about the wrongdoing. At a further level, people may be prepared to lie to protect the organisation. At the extreme a person may be willing to become a scapegoat for the wrongs of the organisation or association. In the biblical origin of the term the scapegoat is not killed but is allowed to escape into the wilderness. This is an appropriate image for the ways in which modern organisations 'let go' those who carry the taint of organisations' bad behaviour.

When the ethical horizon does not extend beyond the self, the focus of actions will be on the protection and improvement of the self's position. Protecting the self's integrity can be achieved in two ways. The first involves drawing the ethical horizon so tightly around the self that any wrong action is kept beyond it. In plainer terms the subject claims or feigns ignorance of the wrongdoing. This approach to integrity has similarities with the concepts of ethical closure and ethical bracketing (Jackall, 1988; Kärreman and Alvesson, 1999). However, if the situation makes this stance untenable then people can maintain their integrity, not by attempting to put things right, but by removing themselves, by resigning from the organisation. When a person acts with integrity, by resigning from an organisation that they cannot prevent from behaving unethically, they sacrifice their material well-being, their job and their salary, to protect their ethical well-being. Loyalty to the self involves sacrificing integrity for material benefits. In the scenario described in Activity 4.4, it is represented by using knowledge of the organisation's wrongdoing to gain advantages for the self. The subject believes their integrity justifies self-seeking behaviour, and that the self-seeking legitimates their integrity.

In summary, what has been argued is that a focus on a particular ethical horizon can act in a heuristic manner. A person's ethical horizon constrains the range of actions open to them. How then does a person choose between them? You can see which values you favour, at least under simulated conditions, by completing Activity 4.4.

Activity 4.4	**Dilemma: a diagnostic inventory of managers' ethical horizons**

Go to the companion website for this book (www.pearsoned.co.uk /fisherlovellvalerosilva) where you will find both an interactive, web-based version of the activity and a hard-copy version that you can print off. The interactive version calculates your scores for you. If you use the hard copy you will have to do the scoring yourself. Have a go at the activity.

Discussion of the *Dilemma* simulation in Activity 4.4

The exercise you have just completed has been tested on a sample of undergraduate business students. Studying the sequence of choices they made as they worked their way through the action maze can identify their ethical horizons. In the first section of the maze, just over half of the respondents chose integrity in the organisational arena and tried to convince the management to admit the tax liability and to regularise the situation. Nearly 30 per cent continued with this position when the management at first refused to concede. A small percentage of respondents (5.8 per cent) found themselves in a closed loop, by continuing to suggest, despite the management's intransigence, that the tax liability should be admitted. But most of the respondents, when rebuffed by the management, chose integrity at the level of self and resigned from the organisation. Twenty-five of the 30 respondents who chose resignation subsequently took a position of integrity at the civil-association horizon, by whistleblowing on the organisation, when urged by their professional peers to do so. The most common route through the maze took, at every opportunity, a path of integrity rather than loyalty, but the ethical horizon changed as circumstances changed. Practising managers may not share undergraduates' commitment to integrity.

A minority of respondents took the route of loyalty but changed the focus of their loyalty. Nineteen per cent of the respondents initially opted for loyalty to self, by using their knowledge of the tax liability to gain advantage for themselves. But in Section 5 of the maze, most of those who had chosen loyalty to self changed their focus to loyalty to the organisation as they helped in the cover-up.

People's commitments to the sometimes competing demands of loyalty and integrity illustrate the importance of values as heuristics in decision making on ethical questions.

Cross reference	The issue of whistleblowing, raised in Activity 4.4, is explored more fully in Chapter 6.

Reflections

Our values are our ethical anchors. However, we each may find our values difficult to pin down. Schein (1993) has argued that we each have a 'career anchor', a value that is so important to us that we would rather lose our jobs, or in some other way be disadvantaged, rather than offend against it. The problem is that we may be uncertain about what that anchor, among our many professed values, may be until we are actually tested by some crisis or hurtful dilemma. At the same time, we have argued in this chapter that when we fail morally at work we tend to fail in a way that is characteristic of our temperament and our stance. In other words, it is not just what our values *are* that matters, but also how important those values are to us. Cathexis is a term from psychoanalysis; it refers to the strong sense of attachment that people may have towards their values and it is this commitment that drives people to act in the world (Young, 1977). The nature of a person's emotional attachment to a particular value may have many forms. A particular value may be:

- something we keep to ourselves and use only to manage our personal lives (a stance known as quietism);

- things that we are aspire to for others (a modernist stance);

- straightforward truths that we do not question (traditionalists and neo-traditionalists);

- things over which we agonise and debate (the position of pragmatists); or

- things that we can conveniently and playfully use to persuade people in arguments at work (as postmodernists think).

All of these possibilities indicate that our connections with our values are not straightforward. This suggests that the belief, often put forward by management writers, that the role of senior management is to promulgate a mission and a set of values that everyone can accept, looks naïve. People's response to their organisation's published values will be complex. They may accept them, for example, as ones they can work with even though they are not the same as their personal values. Or they may accept them ironically or mockingly such that their listeners are not sure whether they actually agree with them or not. More commonly they may agree with the values but doubt whether the top managers who published them have committed to, and are willing to act in accordance with, them. Such qualified acceptance of an organisation's values by managers and staff might not be a bad thing. As has been argued in the case of Enron, the over-enthusiastic acceptance of an organisation's values may give it the characteristics of a cult, and that carries its own dangers. The Enron case also reminds us that there is no particular reason to believe that people who reach the top of organisational career ladders will be particularly ethical and therefore capable of being ethical leaders.

The complexities of people's connections with their values and with those of their organisations also raise doubts about the value of ethical leadership. Employees may consider their leader a good ethical role model who exhibits, what Blanchard and Peale (1988) argued were, the cardinal virtues for organisational leaders: the five 'Ps' – pride, patience, prudence, persistence and perspective. The employees may not follow their leader's example to the extent of becoming role models themselves, or indeed even follow their leader's good example. The very act of putting a leader on an ethical pedestal may indicate that such good behaviour is only for those special enough to be leaders, and who can aspire to such ethical behaviour, and that other more ordinary people cannot possibly emulate them.

People do not simply 'have' values. Their values are constantly being redefined and prioritised as they find themselves in different situations and talking to different people. It is rare for people to be driven to such extremes that they discover what their value anchors, to misquote Schein, actually are. This analysis means those who believe an organisation should and can be managed so that everyone accepts the organisation's values are misguided. The term often used for such acceptance – buy-in – suggests a limited form of engagement. You only buy into something because you think it will be advantageous, not because you think it is right.

Many textbooks on business ethics have relatively little to say about values. When they are discussed, it is in the context of corporate codes of ethics or statements of organisational core values. The materials and arguments put forward in this chapter suggest that values may be central to people's thought processes when they are deciding what to say or do in response to an ethical issue. There is a paradox, however. Values can be used heuristically to *simplify* the process of making up one's mind, but the problem of which particular value to apply to an issue, when there are many values within organisations and society, all of which are valued but which conflict with one another, is *complex*.

The account of values as heuristics in this chapter may provide a good description of how people make decisions on ethical issues. This does not imply that this is how such decisions should be made. Indeed, if heuristics are more a matter of habit than conscious thought, they may merely be ways of avoiding complex value and ethical choices. Choices involve thinking about what we ought to do, not recalling what we normally do. In the next chapter we will explore these tensions between taking habitual stances on ethical issues, bred from our upbringing and experiences, and having to knowingly challenge our habits because the ethical matters we face contain novel circumstances or inconvenient facts.

Summary

In this chapter the following key points have been made:

■ Ethics represents an intellectual approach to matters of morality at work whereas values represent a response based on beliefs that people hold with emotional attachment. Both perspectives need to be considered when dealing with business ethics matters.

■ People may take one of five viewpoints on the role of values in business ethics: the traditional, the modernist, the neo-traditional, the postmodernist and the pragmatist. The position they take will reflect their responses to ethical issues at work.

■ Which of these they adopt will depend, among other things, on their career history and experiences in organisation and on their education and training.

■ Rational and analytic theories explain how decision making ought to be done.

■ Heuristic theories probably explain how people make decisions in practice.

■ Research into heuristics used to see them as sources of bias and distortion; the fast and frugal research programme sees them as efficient and effective procedures for decision making.

■ Values probably act in a heuristic manner in decision making about ethical matters.

■ Values can be used to limit and stop decision makers' searches for further information and options.

■ In decisions such as setting priorities and deciding how to respond to wrong-doing in an organisation the problem is to choose which of many mutually exclusive values should be applied.

Typical assignments

1. Compare the traditional view of values, as exemplified, for example, by the work of Rokeach, with the view that values emerge from a process of sense making. Which view might be more helpful in understanding the role of values in management?

2. How might people with different sensibilities (traditional, modern, neo-traditional, post-modern and pragmatist) understand the nature and role of values in organisations?

3. What criticisms can be made of a postmodern view of organisations and management? Are they justified?

4. 'The commonly accepted idea that management should define and publish a set of organisational core values may create as many problems as it resolves.' Discuss vigorously.

5. Compare rational and heuristic models of decision making (that is to say contrast system 1 – thinking fast, with system 2 – thinking slow, as Kahneman (2011) terms them). How might the heuristic model be applicable to decision making on ethical matters?

6. Loyalty or integrity: which should be the most important to organisational employees?

7. Analyse a resource allocation decision that has been taken in an organisation by reference to the six resource allocation heuristics.

8. What role do emotions and value play in an individual's decision making on ethical matters?

Group activity 4.1

The Rice Orientation Test (ROT)

This test was devised by our colleague Chris Rice. It is designed to alert you to your approach to ethical issues. It uses a distinction between hedonism, moralism and pragmatism. It is not a statistically validated test and so its results must be used as a trigger for reflection and no more.

Think about each of the headings in the boxes in turn. Decide whether that term causes you to think in terms of:

A – right and wrong

B – pleasure or pain

C – success or failure

Then decide whether the concept (A, B or C) that you have chosen is of High (Hi), medium (Me) or low (Lo) importance in your thinking about the headword in the box.

Then place a tick in the appropriate cell of the grid within the box. If you think about the lottery in terms of pleasure or pain but that this is only of medium importance in your thinking, then place a tick in the central cell in the grid.

Carry on to complete all the boxes.

The National Lottery

	Hi	Me	Lo
A			
B			
C			

Trades Unions

	Hi	Me	Lo
A			
B			
C			

David Cameron

	Hi	Me	Lo
A			
B			
C			

Competition

	Hi	Me	Lo
A			
B			
C			

Richard Branson

	Hi	Me	Lo
A			
B			
C			

Management

	Hi	Me	Lo
A			
B			
C			

Higher education

	Hi	Me	Lo
A			
B			
C			

Manchester United FC

	Hi	Me	Lo
A			
B			
C			

Profit

	Hi	Me	Lo
A			
B			
C			

Gordon Brown			
	Hi	Me	Lo
A			
B			
C			

The Welfare State			
	Hi	Me	Lo
A			
B			
C			

Parliament			
	Hi	Me	Lo
A			
B			
C			

Scoring Instructions

Add up the number of ticks placed in each of the cells in the above matrices and transfer the totals into the table below. Calculate the weighted totals, and their percentage of the grand total, for each of the three rows in the table. The percentages show the relative importance to the respondent of moralism, hedonism and pragmatism.

Scoring ROT						
	Hi (N × 3)	Med	(N × 2)	Low (N × 1)	Total	%
A = Moralism						
B = Hedonism						
C = Pragmatism						

Discuss your results with your colleagues in the group.

Group activity 4.2

Obtain a copy of the *Cave Rescue Exercise*, which can be found in Woodcock (1979, 1989: 81) and in the appendix to Fisher (1998). Another version of this exercise can be found in Francis and Young (1979). Both are variations on a classic management game theme, of which *The Kidney Machine* is another popular version (Jones and Pfeiffer, 1974).

Divide into groups of between six and ten people and do the exercise.

Recommended further reading

Milton Rokeach's (1973) *The Nature of Human Values* is the classic work on the subject but pages 239–47 of Michael Billig's (1996) *Arguing and Thinking* provides a contrary view on the subject. The whole book is worth reading because it offers a new perspective based on the idea that thinking is entirely an argumentative process in which there are no fixed points, only constant debates, both within our heads and with other people. An implication of this is that the arguments never come to a definitive end, although people might have the last word on a particular occasion. This view has interesting implications for the role of values in business ethics that are followed up in Chapters 5 and 6. Terry Eagleton (1996) is not a management writer but he provides an intriguing introduction to postmodernism, *The Illusions of Postmodernism*. It is particularly relevant to the themes of this chapter because he treats postmodernism as a sensibility, a particular way of looking at the world, rather than as a set of philosophical ideas, although he also discusses many of these with a degree of humour. If you want to read a critique of the more (mostly French) extreme writings in a postmodernist mode then Sokal and Bricmont's (2003) *Intellectual Impostures* is good fun. An interesting book that explores management issues from a postmodern perspective is Gibson Burrell's *Pandemonium: Towards a Retro-organizational Theory* (1997, London: Sage). It has the distinction of being capable of being read back to front as well as in the normal direction.

For a wider account of how values can be fragmented or integrated in societies, see Jonathan Friedman's (1994) *Cultural Identity and Global Process*. On the topic of the role of values in management, see Paul Griseri's (1998) *Managing Values*. There is an excessive number of 'how to manage with values' books. Two worth looking at are Rabindra Nath Kanungo and Manuel Mendonca's (1996) *The Ethical Dimensions of Leadership* and Stephen Covey's (1991) *Principle-centred Leadership*.

If you are interested in the role of heuristics in decision making, see G. Gigerenzer, P. Todd and the ABC Research Group's (1999) *Simple Heuristics That Make us Smart*, Oxford: Oxford University Press. Daniel Kahneman, who won a Nobel prize for his work on heuristics has published a book on the topic for the general reader; D. Kahneman (2011), *Thinking Fast and Slow*, London: Allen Lane Penguin. On the topic of the role of values in management, see P. Griseri (1998) *Managing Values*, London: Palgrave.

Useful websites

Topic	Website provider	URL
A useful overview on values and the issues of moral education and development	Huitt, W. (2004). Values. Educational Psychology Interactive. Valdosta, GA: Valdosta State University	http://www.edpsycinteractive.org/topics/affect/values.html
Home page of the ABC Centre, which researches heuristics and decision making	Centre for Adaptive Behaviour and Cognition	http://www.mpib-berlin.mpg.de/en/forschung/abc/index.htm
A good interactive guide to heuristics and decision making	Elliott Hammer	http://cat.xula.edu/thinker/decisions/heuristics/
Thinking about risk. Information on some of the heuristics of judgment	Centre for Informed Decision Making	http://www.cygnus-group.com/CIDM/risk.html
A very simple interactive questionnaire for identifying your personal values	MAS Management Advisory Service	http://www.mas.org.uk/quest/ivp2.htm

CHAPTER 8

Compliance and integrity: an organisation's internal accountability

Chapter at a glance

Chapter contents

- Learning outcomes
- Introduction
- An overview of the pressures upon organisations for ethical development
- Codes of conduct and codes of ethics
- Factors that will affect the impact of a code
- Writing a code of ethics
- Arguments against the employment of codes of conduct and ethics
- The difficulties of writing codes of conduct – the ethics of e-communication
- Ethical culture and ethos
- Reflections
- Summary

Activities and exercises

- Podcast 8.1 The ethical standards of BAE
- Activity 8.1 The negative consequences of developing codes of ethics
- Activity 8.2 Designing a code of conduct for e-mail and internet use at work
- Typical assignments
- Group activity 8.1
- Recommended further reading
- Useful websites

Having read this chapter and completed its associated activities, readers should be able to:

- Discuss the pressures upon organisations to employ codes of practice.
- Differentiate between various types of codes.
- Describe the practical problems faced when drafting codes.
- Understand the arguments for and against the employment of codes of practice within organisations.
- Show an awareness that codes of practice can sometimes conflict with one another, creating organisational tensions.
- Understand the significance and power of organisational culture and unwritten codes of conduct.
- Evaluate the role of ethical leadership.
- Evaluate the role of public pressure on maintaining organisational good behaviour.

Introduction

The previous chapter looked at an organisation's accountability to others outside of itself. This chapter looks inwards at how organisations seek to encourage, and ensure compliance with, good standards of behaviour and ethics. Initially codes are considered but then ethical leadership and ethical organisational cultures are discussed.

The International Labour Organisation (ILO) argued that worldwide interest in corporate codes of conduct was initially awakened in the 1980s by scandals in the US defence industry and the overt greed that was displayed on Wall Street. The ILO sees business ethics as a way for companies to promote self-regulation, thereby deterring government intervention and possible regulatory action.

Corporate interest quickly led to the institutionalisation of business ethics programmes, consisting largely of codes of conduct, ethics officers and ethics training. However, Brytting (1997) cited the Zeiss organisation as having a recognisable code of conduct for its employees in 1896, and Mill, writing in 1861, but cited by Warren (1993: 187), observed that 'it is the business of ethics to tell us what our duties are or by what test we may know them'. It has been argued that the more recent increase in the growth of corporate codes of conduct relates to the potential for such codes to reduce corporate exposure to punitive damages in claims of negligence. As Warren (1993: 109) observed in terms of the situation in the USA,

> The 1984 Sentencing Reform Act and the US Sentencing Commission's 1991 Federal Guidelines for Sentencing Organisations, allow for a fine on a corporation to be reduced by up to 95% if it can show that it has an effective program to prevent and detect violations of law.

Attempts to reduce negligence claims are not the only reason for organisations to be seen to be addressing the ethicality of their practices. Multinational corporations (MNCs) are not only increasingly powerful, but also open to critical scrutiny of any of their practices in all parts of the world. MNCs thus have a vested interest in harmonising and standardising practices throughout their respective organisations in order to minimise the risk of aberrant behaviour. We consider later in this chapter the initiatives being employed by MNCs to address concerns about their practices and those of their supplier networks.

An overview of the pressures upon organisations for ethical development

Figure 8.1 reflects the differing pressures on organisations to institute and formalise their ethical practices. Of all the connections depicted in Figure 8.1, the only unbroken line is that between 'Governments' and 'The organisation'. This reflects the mandatory nature of laws, as opposed to the other relationships that are characterised by frameworks, agreements, codes, understandings or memoranda, none of which is legally binding. The agreements, or framework documents, between governments and MNCs reflect the dilemma faced by many governments, particularly those of developing countries. The presence of MNCs within the host country can bring the prospect of accelerated economic development, but the

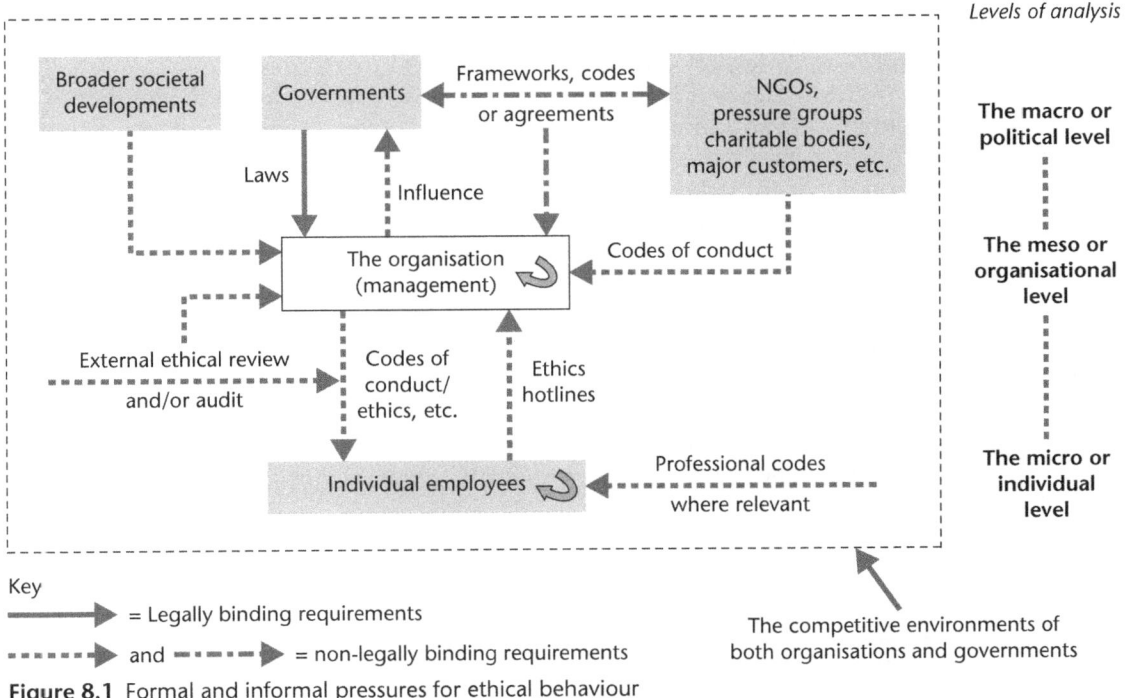

Figure 8.1 Formal and informal pressures for ethical behaviour

support, incentives and conditions that must be agreed to by the host government, in the face of alternative offers by other countries to the MNCs, can weaken the host government's bargaining powers. In such circumstances, legislation is unlikely to be deemed 'appropriate' to control the operations of the MNCs, and more adaptive, negotiable instruments such as framework agreements, or codes, become the norm. The non-legally binding agreements or codes of practice may be developed with or without the involvement of pressure groups and interested charitable bodies.

In turn, non-governmental bodies (NGOs), pressure groups and charitable bodies can exert pressure upon organisations independently of governments by developing their preferred codes of practice for business organisations and then contrasting these codes with the behaviour of specific organisations. These comparisons can reveal considerable discrepancies between espoused and actual behaviour and, given the glare of national and international publicity, can involve discussions about change. These relationships are reflected in the additional lines emanating from the 'NGOs, pressure groups' box and going towards the 'The organisation' box. Organisations such as Greenpeace, Friends of the Earth and the International Baby Food Action Network (IBFAN) are notable in this field.

Business organisations do not have to wait for external pressure before they act to enhance their own practices and behaviour. We illustrate below examples of ethical initiatives that appear to have come from within organisations, although the initiatives may have been in anticipation of government or pressure group involvement if the organisation did not respond in some way to an ethical issue.

There are examples of cooperation and collaboration between governments and pressure groups, between pressure groups and organisations/industries and between governments, pressure groups and business organisations, that appear to be addressing matters of ethical concern in effective ways. We also highlight, however, examples of apparent 'good' practice, which, when carefully scrutinised, are possibly less effective than they might at first appear.

Within Figure 8.1, the introduction of a corporate code of conduct by an employing organisation is shown by the downward-pointing arrow, aimed at 'Individual employees'. This is because such codes are invariably the result of a 'top-down initiative', with relatively little, or no, involvement from non-senior managerial staff. These codes tend to be statements of how employees are required to behave by the company/senior management.

Cross reference   However, companies can also incorporate 'ethics hotlines' to allow those employees with concerns about the ethicality of particular business practices to express their concerns, as we discussed in Chapter 6. These organisational vents can be both important mechanisms for concerned employees to express their worries, and effective early warning systems for organisations about potentially damaging practices and behaviour.

Both the ethics hotlines and the codes of conduct can be supported by external ethical review, for example, an annual or periodic ethics audit, but because all of these mechanisms are optional they are shown as broken lines.

An important point to emphasise is that the 'Codes of conduct, etc.' link between 'The organisation' and 'Individual employees' is not just about codes of conduct. The 'etc.' encompasses a range of other ways of communicating, inculcating and nurturing corporate values. McDonald and Nijhof (1999) cited:

- training;
- storytelling;
- reward systems;
- monitoring systems;
- communication channels;
- job design;
- ethics officers;
- information systems;
- recruitment and selection policies and processes; and
- organisational strategies

as further examples of ways in which organisations can influence the values and practices that become accepted as 'the ways things are done around here'. Many of these elements come within what is known as organisational culture. A consideration of some of the important issues of organisational culture for values and ethics, and vice versa, is undertaken towards the end of this chapter.

The arrows within 'The organisation' and 'Individual employees' boxes that appear to turn on themselves indicate that neither organisations, nor individuals, should expect or passively wait for developments on ethical behaviour to be externally imposed or influenced. If terms such as 'learning organisation' and 'reflective practitioner' are to mean anything, they will need to be evident in the critical reflection of both organisations and individuals on their respective practices. In many respects, the integrity with which organisations and individuals reflect upon notions of ethicality are fundamental elements of Figure 8.1. If change is only ever externally stimulated, rather than the result of internal reflection and action, then such change is subject to whims and pressures that will not necessarily be rooted in well-argued principles and values.

Podcast 8.1

The ethical standards of BAE

Podcasts explaining how today's business news relates to the topics discussed here will be updated in an ongoing process. Podcast 8.1 discusses the report by Lord Woolf on the ethical standards of the major defence company BAE. To listen to this podcast, other archived podcasts or recent additions, please visit the companion website at www.pearsoned.co.uk/fisherlovellvalerosilva.

The arrow moving from the 'The organisation' to 'Governments' acknowledges that business organisations are not passive or disinterested bystanders in the development of laws affecting corporate practice. This arrow acknowledges the quite significant influence that specific organisations and industrial/commercial sectors can have on governments and the laws that are passed. Equally, it must be emphasised that the whole of Figure 8.1 sits within a commercial and competitive environment that bears upon the practices of individuals, organisations and governments.

Codes of conduct and codes of ethics

In market contexts where competitive forces are significant, consistency in all aspects of an organisation's operations is imperative. In order to stimulate, foster and maintain consistency in the behaviour of employees, consistency that also reflects the standards of behaviour that an organisation wishes its employees to adopt, organisations often develop codes of conduct and ethics. A distinction can be made between codes of ethics and codes of conduct that is helpful in examining the roles these types of statements perform. Although this distinction is not universally employed, indeed you may find some organisations employing codes of ethics that by our definition would be classed as codes of conduct, it offers some insight into the purpose of such codes. A study by Farrell and Cobbin (1996) discusses variations between codes of conduct and codes of ethics and the findings of this study add support to the distinction. A much higher level of prescription was found in the codes of conduct studied (average number of rules equalled 30.6), compared with the average number of rules contained in the codes of ethics (16.5).

> **DEFINITION**
>
> *Codes of conduct* tend to be instructions, or sets of rules, concerning behaviour. As a result they are likely to be reasonably prescriptive and proscriptive concerning particular aspects of employee behaviour. They identify specific acts that must be either adhered to (prescription), or avoided (proscription). However, the extent to which all possible situations can be addressed within a code of conduct is problematic.
>
> *Codes of ethics* tend to be reasonably general in their tenor, encouraging employees to display particular characteristics such as loyalty, honesty, objectivity, probity and integrity. They do not normally address specific types of decisions; rather they encourage the application of what might be called 'virtues', although, as noted in Chapter 3, what are regarded as virtues can vary over time. While notions of honesty and integrity remain fairly constant over time, concepts such as justice and loyalty are more contentious.
>
> The distinction between codes of ethics and conduct is similar to that used by Cadbury (2002: 17), in relation to corporate governance, when he distinguished principles and provisions. He explains:
>
>> The question to ask of principles is how companies have applied them, while the equivalent question over provisions is how far they have been complied with.

From these definitions it is evident that, where all possible scenarios that an employee might face can be predicted with a high degree of confidence, as well all the circumstances relating to those scenarios, then a specific code of conduct might be possible, because ethical judgment becomes redundant. However, where the likely scenarios that an employee might face cannot be predicted in the requisite detail, then reference to general qualities and principles will be preferred, that is, codes of ethics become more appropriate.

The risk of confusing these two general positions is that, if a code of conduct fails to address a particular scenario that an employee actually faces, then the silence of the code on the matter in question might be interpreted by the employee as an indication that the employing organisation is at best indifferent to the ethics of the decision in hand. In this discussion, the employee might be said to be (or be treated as) morally immature, requiring a code of conduct or ethics to act as a reference point in times of need, but that is just what codes imply. By issuing such codes, a company is stating that it does not have sufficient confidence in all of its employees to be able to view a code of conduct or ethics as unnecessary. This is an implication that some, perhaps many, employees might find objectionable, but for an organisation that straddles many countries and cultures in its operations, the need for an articulation of expected behaviour and practices throughout its operations can be overwhelming.

The purposes of codes of conduct and ethics

At one level, codes of conduct and ethics can be seen as legitimate and necessary devices for senior management to develop in order to specify expected codes of behaviour of all employees. Each employee of an organisation will be seen as a representative of that organisation by others external to the organisation. Thus, it is important that employees reflect behaviour that is commensurate with the persona and reputation that the organisation wishes to project. In this context, some writers see codes of conduct as principally manipulative control devices to achieve managerial ends. Stevens (1994: 65) argued that 'some ethical codes are little more than legal barriers and self-defence mechanisms; others are intended to influence and shape employee behaviour'. These were observations that had been made earlier by, among others, Mathews (1988) and Warren (1993).

Developing and adding to the work of Bowie and Duska (1990), we have listed below eight roles for corporate codes. These are:

- *Damage limitation* – to reduce damages awarded by courts in the event of the company being sued for negligence by one of its employees.

- *Guidance* – the 'reference point' role, similar to what Passmore (1984) referred to as 'the reminding role'. An aide-memoire for employees when faced with an ethically complex situation.

- *Regulation* – this is the prescribing and proscribing role that will stipulate specific qualities that are essential, for example, independence, objectivity, etc., or acts that are prohibited.

- *Discipline and appeal* – this is the role of a code as a benchmark for an organisation or professional body to decide whether an employee/member has contravened required conduct and what form of punishment might ensue. In addition, the code can form the basis of an appeal by the accused.

- *Information* – a code expresses to external audiences standards of behaviour that can be expected of employees/members.

- *Proclamation* – this has echoes of 'information', but it relates more to the role of codes of conduct developed by professional bodies. To achieve 'professional' status, trade associations are normally required to assuage public concerns over the granting of monopoly rights to specific areas of commercial/social activity (e.g. auditing, doctoring, etc.). Ethical codes will attempt to reassure that these monopoly powers will not be abused.

- *Negotiation* – this is not dissimilar to *guidance* in that codes can be used as a tool in negotiations and disputes with and between professionals, colleagues, employers, governments, etc.

- *Stifling* – this is the creation of internal procedures for handling the ethical concerns of employees that are more concerned with management keeping a lid on internal dissent than acting as a conduit for internal debate and examination. Hunt's (1995 and 1998) work on whistleblowing in the health and social services reflects a number of examples of this use of codes of conduct and internal whistleblowing processes.

The attention paid to codes of conduct by both organisations and researchers does presume both that codes are a 'good' thing and that they do have a positive impact upon individual and corporate behaviour. With regard to the latter, Mathews (1988) was able to identify only a weak link between the existence of ethical codes and corporate behaviour. This latter point was taken up by Cassell et al. (1997: 1078), who argued that:

> An important, if implicit, assumption of many writings on corporate codes . . . is that such codes do have a 'real' effect upon behaviour. This tends to be something that is taken for granted, but it is not empirically validated by subsequent investigation . . . recipients of the code: those who are required to make sense of it, and respond to it, often as one more instance of managerially-inspired change, amidst a plethora of pre-existing formal and informal control processes within which the impact of the code must be located. As with any example of formal organisational control, the actual, as opposed to the intended, effect may be subject to processes that entail negotiation and bargaining.

Stevens' (1994) observations were that codes were:

- primarily concerned with employee conduct that might damage the firm, that is, they were thus skewed towards self-protection; and

- preoccupied with the law.

The legalistic orientation of many codes has been noted by a number of writers, including Farrell and Cobbin (1996). The latter identified differences between American, Australian and UK corporate codes of conduct. They concluded that, of the codes they studied, the Australian codes tended to concentrate upon a reiteration of the legal environment within which individuals and organisations operate, emphasising the importance of not doing anything to harm the employing organisation's reputation. American codes included, but went beyond, this orientation, emphasising customers, equal opportunities and insider dealing, while the UK codes made more frequent reference to the community, customer welfare and the environment than the Australian or American codes. However, all of these are relative terms, 'the level of specific guidance on ethical content in each country's codes was very low' (1996: 54). As lawyers were identified as the most frequent developers of such codes (30 per cent), a legalistic orientation to the codes was not surprising.

Factors that will affect the impact of a code

Cassell et al. (1997), combining the work of Hopwood (1974) and Kelman (1961), identified three possible explanations why individuals might display behaviours that conform with desired organisational behaviours. These are:

1. *Internalisation*, in which the behaviours are accepted by the individual as their own, even though they are set externally. This does suggest, however, that the ethical values displayed will be subject to, and influenced by, further external forces, unless the organisational values are held by the individual at a profound and deep level.

2. *Compliance*, in which the displayed behaviour is associated with the desire to achieve some form of reward, or avoid an identifiable punishment. This form of behaviour will last as long as the punishment or reward is regarded as both significant and realisable by the individual/s concerned, but not beyond. This form of behaviour is thus not ethically based, but instrumental, calculating and unreliable.

3. *Identification*, in which behaviour is shaped by, and mirrors, the behaviours of significant others with whom the individual wishes to identify. Again because of the instrumental and externally located locus of a behaviour's rationale, the reliability of the behaviour in question is problematic.

Of these three possible explanations, only the first holds out the prospect of consistency for the organisations, the other two being unreliable due to external corruption. If this is so, then the individual must absorb the organisation's values in a conscious and knowing way because either:

■ The individual's existing values correspond closely with those espoused by the organisation and, thus, little change is required to the individual's own ethics; or

■ The individual recognises in the organisation's values a set of principles that transcend their own and to which they wish to aspire.

Alternatively the internalisation is not conscious, but unconscious, achieved by the constant drip-drip of organisational images and rhetoric. This might seem a very distant possibility in the current day and age, but one of the authors is reminded of an ethics workshop he held for a group of managers on a Master's programme. One of the managers worked for a well-known and respected retail organisation, respected among other things for the apparently strong employee benefits and care provided by the company. However, during the course of the workshop all the participants reviewed aspects of their organisation's practices, and this particular manager gradually shifted from a view of his employing organisation's paternalistic care as benign, to one that saw it as more oppressive and manipulative. This change in interpretation came not from questioning by the tutors, but from a series of interactive exercises with other members of the course. The manager in question had worked for the retail organisation for over 15 years and during that time had accepted the organisation's house journal, the management conferences he attended and other practices as evidence of his employer's good intent. His now more critical interpretation did not suddenly make his employers 'bad' employers, when for the previous 15 years they had been 'good' employers. What unsettled him was how uncritical he had been in accepting a particular interpretation of some of the organisation's actions and decisions over the years, some of which did not square with his original uncritical, 'rose-tinted' description of his organisation.

Using Goffman's (1959) dramaturgical metaphor, individuals can be said to 'act out' their preferred view of themselves on the stage of life. Information likely to enhance others' opinions of oneself is kept 'centre stage' rather than 'in the wings'. The concept of impression management pervades the literature on business ethics, and is particularly apparent in ethnographic accounts of how managers deal with ethical problems (e.g. Jackall, 1988; Toffler, 1991; Schein, 1992; Watson, 1994). Interestingly, the 'management' and 'organisational behaviour' literature is a much richer and a more academically robust source of material on this point than much of the business ethics literature.

Jackall (1988) argued that the unethical actions of managers do not result from the individual's moral deficiencies, but rather from the bureaucratic structures of modern organisations, which encourage managers to behave unethically. This view has been echoed by others within the literature. For example, Liedtka (1991) concluded that many of the managers in her study found themselves forced to choose between preserving their relationships within the firm (operating within the organisational political model) and following their own values (using a value-driven model). We will conclude our consideration of this issue with a quote from Cassell et al. (1997: 1088):

> It is our contention that although individual psychological and demographic factors play a role in influencing behaviour in relation to codes, that role is relatively minor given the significance of the organisational context and culture within which behaviour takes place.

Cassell et al. (1997) identified three factors they argued would determine the influence a code would have upon the behaviour of organisational members, namely:

1. The nature of the code, its content and the processes by which it has been designed, developed and implemented.

2. The organisational control mechanisms (both formal and informal). For ex-ample, will the employees see the introduction of a (new) code as just another mechanism by which the employing organisation wishes to determine indi-vidual behaviour, or a genuine attempt to help employees cope with complex ethical issues that they will face during their day-to-day practice?

3. Individual influences which focus upon perceptual and self-control processes.

Thus, if the individual employee acts in keeping with required organisational behaviour out of either compliance or identification motives, and is sceptical about factors (1) and (2) above, the prospects for a newly introduced code of conduct or practice are likely to be unpredictable and variable throughout an organisation, two outcomes the code was presumably intended to obviate.

Writing a code of ethics

The difficulty of writing a code of ethics is that, when such codes are completed they look banal and people comment, 'Well, that is all just common sense'. Their commonplaceness is intensified when they are reduced to their basic content and provided to all employees as laminated cards that can be stored alongside credit cards in wallets and purses. Commonplaces, of course, are mostly true and important statements about trust, integrity, honesty and fair-ness. The intention is clearly that employees should carry these cards around with them as reminders, thus implying that the staff need constant admo-nition to be honest and so on. In our research interviews, one respondent reported a debate in a focus group set up to discuss what should be included in the new code of ethics. One side of the argument was that 'Employees should act honestly' should be included. The contrary view was that this was such an obvious requirement that it did not need stating, and that if it was it implied that the management thought their employees potentially dishonest. It was decided not to include it.

Most organisations go to great trouble to ensure that their code of ethics is par-ticular to them and their business and circumstances. Yet most codes of ethics look alike. It is unusual for codes to go against convention or the norms and institu-tions of the surrounding society. Table 8.1 attempts to illustrate this phenomenon by comparing elements from an ethical codes for the conduct of pharmaceutical medicine developed by Johnson and Johnson with that of the Covenant of the Goddess (Center for the Study of Ethics in the Professions, 2003), which is an association of white witches.

As there is much common ground between different organisations' codes of ethics, it is possible to identify the topics and themes most commonly mentioned. In the analysis in Table 8.2, the examples are taken from Johnson and Johnson's Credo, the UK Civil Service Code of Conduct (The Cabinet Office, 2004), BP's busi-ness policies and the statement of core values of Carbo Ceramics (2002) (this last example was more or less chosen at random from the many company statements available); note that none of these uses the term code of ethics, but nevertheless that is what they are.

Table 8.1 A comparison of elements from typical codes of ethics for the conduct of pharmaceutical medicine and of the Covenant of the Goddess Code of Ethics

Common theme	Ethical codes for the conduct of pharmaceutical medicine	Covenant of the Goddess ethical code
Credo based	The ethical codes of the pharmaceutical company Johnson and Johnson (n.d) are famously based on a Credo, which is a statement of basic values and principles to which everyone in the company must subscribe.	'Members of the covenant should ever keep in mind the underlying unity of our religion as well as the diversity of its manifestations.' 'These ethics shall be understood and interpreted in the light of one another, and especially in the light of the traditional laws of our religion.'
The credos are of similar antiquity	Credos, and similar statements, often date back to the origin of a company or to a founding father. The Johnson and Johnson Credo was first published in 1943	Modern witchcraft was probably invented as a religion in the 1920s and 1930s when there was a fashion for magic and druidism.
Do no harm	Most ethical codes in the fields of pharmacy and medicine include a classic command – above all do no harm, or something similar, which has its origins in the Hippocratic Oath, which in turn has its origins in ancient Greece	'An ye harm none, do as ye will.'
Respect the differences and autonomy of others	Most companies' codes have a statement that they respect the rights of individuals and recognise and value the diversity of their employees.	'Every person associated with the covenant shall respect the autonomy and sovereignty of each coven, as well as the right of each coven to oversee the spiritual, mental, emotional and physical development of its members and students in its own way, and shall exercise reasonable caution against infringing upon that right in any way.'
A position on openness and secrecy	At a time when governments are concerned with the cost effectiveness of drugs, pharmaceutical companies may commit to transparency or perhaps to a more limited commitment to providing fair, balanced accurate and comprehensive data.	'All persons associated with this covenant shall respect the traditional secrecy of our religion.' OK so the White Witches do not believe in transparency but they do have a principled position on the issue.
Right to a fair return	The belief that a fair return on investment is morally acceptable is core to the belief of commercial organisations.	'All persons have the right to charge reasonable fees for the services by which they earn their living, so long as our religion is not thereby exploited.'
Professional standards of those who practice the activity	Companies recognise the professional standards that apply to medicine and pharmacy and accept a responsibility to adhere to the principles of good clinical practice.	'Since our religion and the arts and practices peculiar to it are the gift of the Goddess, membership and training in a local coven or tradition are bestowed free, as gifts, and only on those persons who are deemed worthy to receive them.'

Source: The Covenant of the Goddess Code of Ethics and Johnson and Johnson Credo

Table 8.2 Common themes in codes of ethics

Theme	Example	Source of example
Integrity	The constitutional and practical role of the Civil Service is, with integrity, honesty, impartiality and objectivity, to assist the duly constituted Government [ ] whatever their political complexion, in formulating their policies, carrying out decisions and in administering public services for which they are responsible.	UK Civil Service Code
	We conduct our business with the highest ethical standards. We are truthful and honor our commitments and responsibilities.	Carbo Ceramics
Loyalty	Civil servants are servants of the Crown. Constitutionally, all the Administrations form part of the Crown and, subject to the provisions of this Code, civil servants owe their loyalty to the Administrations in which they serve.	UK Civil Service Code
No harm and risk management	We believe our first responsibility is to the doctors, nurses and patients, to mothers and fathers and all others who use our products and services. In meeting their needs, everything we do must be of high quality.	Johnson and Johnson
	We will regularly identify the hazards and assess the risks associated with our activities. We will take appropriate action to manage risks and hence prevent or reduce the impact of potential accidents or incidents.	BP
Respect for individual employees	We are responsible to our employees, the men and women who work with us throughout the world. Everyone must be considered as an individual. We must respect their dignity and recognize their merit. They must have a sense of security in their jobs. Compensation must be fair and adequate, and working conditions clean, orderly and safe. We must be mindful of ways to help our employees fulfil their family responsibilities. Employees must feel free to make suggestions and complaints. There must be equal opportunity for employment, development and advancement for those qualified. We must provide competent management, and their actions must be just and ethical.	Johnson and Johnson
Respect for the law	We will respect the law in the countries and communities in which we operate.	BP
Trust	Our commitment is to create mutual advantage in all our relationships so that people will trust us and want to do business with BP.	BP
Relationship with stakeholders	We will enable customers, governments, communities and our own people to participate in a new constructive dialogue. We aim for a radical openness – a new approach from a new company, transparent, questioning, flexible, restless and inclusive.	BP
	Our suppliers and distributors must have an opportunity to make a fair profit.	Johnson and Johnson

▶

Table 8.2 Continued

Theme	Example	Source of example
Developing communities	We are responsible to the communities in which we live and work and to the world community as well.	Johnson and Johnson
	We must be good citizens – support good works and charities and bear our fair share of taxes.	Johnson and Johnson
	We must encourage civic improvements and better health and education. We must maintain in good order the property we are privileged to use, protecting the environment and natural resources.	Johnson and Johnson
Goals and achievement	We set aggressive goals and strive to exceed them.	Carbo Ceramics
	We value and celebrate a high level of individual achievement and team performance.	
Return to shareholders	Our final responsibility is to our stockholders.	Johnson and Johnson
	Business must make a sound profit.	Johnson and Johnson
Environmental sustainability	We are committed to [ ] demonstrating respect for the natural environment and work towards our goals of no accidents, no harm to people and no damage to the environment.	BP
Political activity and contributions	BP will never make political contributions whether in cash or in kind anywhere in the world.	BP
Personal advantage	Civil servants should not misuse their official position or information acquired in the course of their official duties to further their private interests or those of others. They should not receive benefits of any kind from a third party which might reasonably be seen to compromise their personal integrity or judgment.	Civil Service Code
Commitment to external standards or assurance	BP supports the principles set forth in the UN Universal Declaration of Human Rights and will respect the 2000 International Labour Organisation, the 'Tripartite Declaration of Principles Concerning Multinational Enterprises and Social Policy' and the 2000 OECD 'Guidelines for Multinational Enterprises'.	BP

Sources: The Cabinet Office; Johnson & Johnson; BP plc; Carbo Ceramics

Activity 8.1	The negative consequences of developing codes of ethics

Although our consideration of codes of conduct and ethics has identified limitations in practice and referred to evidence that casts doubt upon the actual impact of codes 'on the ground', we have not suggested that the development and introduction of a code would be a negative development. There are, however, such arguments, and before discussing these we would like you to think through what these might be.

Identify as many negative aspects as possible associated with the development of a code of conduct or ethics.

Arguments against the employment of codes of conduct and ethics

While the employment of codes has an intuitive appeal, we can identify five possible objections to their development and employment.

1 Justification

This relates to the lack of any universally accepted set of common principles and ethics. If 'everything is relative' is taken to its logical conclusion and codes can only ever be culturally and socially specific, the notion of universal laws is rejected and with it the argument that a corporation can have a single code of conduct. If a multinational organisation produces a code of conduct that reflects a basic set of values, by definition this implies there are certain basic concepts that it wishes to universalise, at least within its own worldwide operations, but is this possible? The question might become one of distinguishing between negotiable and non-negotiable values – how and when does one balance local customs and traditions with one's own sense of values when the two are in conflict? For example, when is a gift a bribe?

Jensen et al. (2009) analysed codes of ethics using actor network theory, which amongst other things, considers the impact of non-human and virtual objects such as codes on human sense making. The writers of codes inscribe certain values and constraints into them; and they expect the code will be understood uniformly throughout the organisation. However, as the codes are received in different contexts (the authors say 'heterogenous materialities'), the codes of ethics 'oblige us humans to oblige them and as the chain of translation unfolds several versions of morality circulate in the organisation' (Jensen et al., 2009: 539). The case study the analysis was based on explored how a code of ethics in an American multinational company was re-interpreted within its Swedish subsidiary.

2 The inability of rules to govern actions

If codes cannot change behaviour for the better, and the empirical evidence for this is very limited, will the negative signals being sent out to employees, that the organisation does not trust them, be the abiding impact of the introduction of a code? If so, then the overall impact of a code is likely to be negative. This was a possible conclusion from a large-scale survey by Kaptein (2011) in which people were asked their opinions on various aspects of ethical codes in the organisations they worked in. The study looked at:

- whether a code of ethics was present or not;
- frequency of formal communication about the code;
- quality of communication about the code; and
- the embedding of the code by senior and local management.

The statistical analysis of the data suggested that in some circumstances the presence of a code was associated, counter-intuitively, with higher levels of unethical behaviour. It was also found that the simple presence of an ethical code was not associated with a lack of unethical behaviour. However, when some of the contextual factors just listed were in play, and added their influence to the simple presence of a code, the incidence of unethical behaviour was lower (Kaptein, 2011: 244–5).

3 Support structures

There is a need for, but a paucity of, support structures within organisations for employees to feel able to act in accordance with specified codes of behaviour. Where codes of conduct do exist, Warren (1993: 189) argued that:

> All too often ethical codes are handed down to employees from the executive above and the importance of trying to create a community or purpose within the company is ignored.

Warren (1993) referred to the field of industrial relations where evidence indicates that rules governing industrial relations need collective agreement if they are to be honoured in the observance as well as in the breach (e.g. Terry, 1975). This perspective is supported by Bird and Waters (1989: 83). They argued that just talking about ethical issues is unlikely to enhance the significance of the issues unless mechanisms are found for 'connecting this language with the experiences and expectations of people involved in business'. Taking this argument forward, Bird and Waters (1989: 84) argued that:

> Business people will continue to shun open discussions of actual moral issues unless means are provided to allow for legitimate dissent by managers who will not be personally blamed, criticised, ostracised, or punished for their views.

They found that talking to managers individually revealed that the managers had many concerns of an ethical nature. However, when asked if these issues were ever raised among managerial colleagues, either formally or informally, the managers replied that they were not. The managers identified a range of explanations for the collective managerial muteness on ethical issues. Such talk was perceived to be a threat to:

- efficiency (i.e. the imposition of rigid rules and regulations);
- the image of power and effectiveness (i.e. previous attempts had resulted in the dissenting manager being shown to be organisationally impotent); and

- organisational harmony (i.e. discussion of moral issues at work was perceived to be dysfunctional).

Thus, the introduction of a code of conduct requires an environment in which expressions of concern over particular practices are not perceived as simplistically 'anti-company' or 'wimpish'. Without such an environment, cynicism is likely to be fuelled, and the overall impact of the code will be negative.

4 The marginality of codes

Codes tend to be treated as 'add-ons', as constraints upon action, and thus act at the margins of corporate activity. To be effective, codes need to be at the centre of corporate beliefs. More particularly, a code becomes redundant if the corporate culture encapsulates those values and beliefs that would be reflected in a corporate code of conduct or ethics. If left at the margins, a code might be interpreted as a necessary accoutrement (garnish) to corporate activities, but one that can be circumvented, or 'negotiated' in certain circumstances. If so, then cynicism about corporate motives would be heightened and the overall effect of the code would be negative.

One particular way in which codes can become marginalised has been termed distancing. In a study by Helin and Sandstrom (2010: 594–6), it was noticed that when an American multinational forced upon its Swedish subsidiary an American code of ethics that had not been adapted to local law and norms, the staff all signed it even though they disagreed with it. This apparent paradox was explained by the staff distancing the code in how they made sense of their work and putting it to the edge of their daily practices. The organisation's staff thought that the code was so American, and so separate from their context, that there was no harm in signing it. A second distancing mechanism was to ignore the detailed content of the code by saying 'it's all common sense'; and thinking therefore that if you worked to that sense of local common sense, little engagement with the details of the code was necessary. A third distancing mechanism was to say that the code was unnecessary because the local systems were adequate and so, as the code would not come into play, it could be signed and ignored.

5 The diminution and ultimate invisibility of individual responsibility

Codes that specify behaviour in particular situations seek to take judgment out of ethically charged situations. Whilst this has the advantage of standardising behaviour throughout an organisation and potentially minimising the risk of behaviour that is unacceptable, there is also the risk of the individual using the 'I was only following orders' defence in the event of an enquiry into a dispute over a particular incident. This shifting of responsibility has been termed by Bauman (1994) as 'floating responsibility' and was discussed in Chapter 6. It becomes an organisational defence against individual conscience. The following of rules and adherence to the commands of superiors makes identification of responsibility difficult to isolate. Identification of responsibility for a particular action or inaction falls between the cracks of job descriptions and responsibilities, and codes of conduct. Morality (or the defining of it) thus becomes someone else's responsibility. The actions of individuals become automatic, with little thought or judgment on the part of the individual required. Whilst actual situations will often present complexities and nuances that take the individual into contexts not addressed adequately by a code, the existence and 'failings' of the code present the individual with an escape route from responsibility. To obey instructions is less demanding and far less risky than exercising moral judgment.

Bauman (1994) identified a second tendency, that of organisational actions being deemed amoral, that is neither good nor bad, only correct or incorrect. In this context codes of conduct can be used to make what could be transparent opaque. Codes might be expressed, not so much in moral terms, but in technical terms, implying a moral neutrality to the issues being addressed in the code.

The difficulties of writing codes of conduct – the ethics of e-communication

With the coming of new forms of electronic communication and diffusion of information, in particular e-mail and the Internet, new forms of ethical problems have appeared in organisations. As this has happened, organisations have tried to develop new codes of conduct governing e-communications, to minimise abuse. Their attempts to respond to new problems illustrate many of the problems and difficulties with codes of conduct discussed in the previous section. The matter is not an inconsequential one. In 1998, an IT manager was sacked from her job because she had booked her holiday on the Internet, using the company's computers, during work time (Wakefield, 1999). In 2003, four lawyers lost their jobs at a top London law firm after circulating an e-mail about oral sex among their colleagues; at some point it was e-mailed to a further 20 million people worldwide. A year later, 10 clerical workers at the Royal Sun Alliance in Liverpool were dismissed after e-mailing a risqué cartoon involving Bart Simpson and a donkey (Observer, 2004). People have no control over what they are sent by e-mail, and they may inadvertently, or so they will claim, download a pornographic image, for example. Even if they delete it immediately a record will remain, in this networked age, that they received the image. It might be difficult for them subsequently to disprove that they were simply an innocent dupe.

As access to e-mail and the Internet grows so the ethical issues become more important. The main problems are listed below.

1 Misuse by employers

■ Employers have the capacity, but not always the inclination, to monitor every action that employees take while using networked computers at work.

Employees' net surfing and e-mail correspondences are all logged. The question is the extent to which such surveillance is ethical and legitimate and when it could be claimed to break an employee's right to privacy. In 2003, the UK government passed the Regulation and Investigatory Powers Act, which made it illegal to monitor employees' e-mails without their consent. Guidelines issued by the Department of Trade and Industry, however, construed the act as allowing surveillance if contracts of employment included a clause that allowed employers to monitor e-mail and internet usage. The employers argued that they needed this right as all e-mails sent from their systems were their legal responsibility, which is why most e-mails now sent from organisational systems have a disclaimer (often longer than the message) denying any such responsibility.

■ Employers may assume that by e-mailing all staff they have exhausted their responsibility to communicate effectively with their staff.

2 Misuse by employees

■ Stealing employers' time by surfing the net when they should be working.

■ Using the e-mail and internet facilities for improper purposes, such as distributing racist messages or obscene materials.

■ Conducting a personal business using their employer's systems.

■ Harassing or stalking other employees by e-mail, a practice that has been recognised by Industrial Tribunals as illegal behaviour (Taylor, D., 2001).

■ Sending an internal e-mail communication to an external body. For example, an aggrieved employee who had taken Prince Charles to an Industrial Tribunal complaining of sex discrimination used an internal e-mail from the Prince's household as evidence in support of her case.

■ Misusing online selection and recruitment testing to misrepresent oneself to a potential employer. In 2003, 6 per cent of organisations were using some form of online testing for recruitment and selection purposes (Czerny, 2004).

3 Abuses of good communication

■ E-mail communication is anomalous; on the one hand it is seen as quick and informal yet on the other it is a recorded form of communication that can be used in a court of law. This leads people to show a lack of courtesy in their communications with others that they would not think of exhibiting on the telephone or in face-to-face communication (Taylor, D., 2001).

■ People often use e-mails to avoid giving news, often bad, that ought to be given personally. There was in 2004 a case of a large number of employees being informed by e-mail that they had been made redundant.

■ The informality and distance of e-mails encourage people to be ruder, especially when they are angry, than they would be if addressing the subjects of their disgust directly. Reliance Industries (RIL) is a very large family firm in India. When the founder died there was a power struggle between his two sons, which was conducted almost entirely in e-mails and leaked to the media. The directors of the company thought the dispute would never be resolved by e-mails and said,

> [we do] not find the mode of e-mail suitable. Instead of e-mail it should be love mail. It is better to sit and talk.

> (*Hindustan Times*, 2004: 1)

■ The extreme e-mail discourtesy is when someone writes an e-mail complaining about some hurt from another and then copies it to the entire company. Such a practice may have a beneficial aspect, such as when an e-mail that affects all staff, but which was intended to be confidential to a select group, is forwarded by one of that group to all employees. This can lead to a vigorous and democratic debate about the issue between all staff. E-mails can be an effective forum for rapid debate.

■ Overusing mailing lists and the 'cc' function to flood people with e-mails that are of little interest to them.

One of the difficulties of writing a code of conduct to cover these issues is that most employers wish to draw a sensible balance between the employees' rights and those of the companies. Most organisations are happy to allow their employees to use e-mail and internet access for personal use, but, as one code expresses it,

> this should not interfere with or conflict with business use. Employees should exercise good judgement regarding the reasonableness of personal use.

This particular employer provided a junk mail group so that employees could post messages such as 'looking to rent' or 'something to sell'. Only a few organisations go to the extreme of prohibiting all personal use of the Internet and e-mail. One American University did, and incurred the wrath of its academic staff (Woodbury, 1998). One of the reasons for employers to exercise some discretion is that the custom and practice, the work culture, of many occupational groups does not see personal use of ICT as an ethical wrong. Stylianou et al. (2004) conducted research that shows that R&D staff think it is right to violate both intellectual property (IPR) and privacy rights (when using ICT) to favour open access to data and knowledge.

Programmers, more restrictively, think it acceptable to plagiarise (ignore IPR) but not to breach an employee's right to privacy. Some of the standard clauses in a code of conduct on the use of e-mail and the network might be as follows.

■ No e-mail or communication should violate the law or company policy.

■ Employees should take care to maintain the security of their passwords.

- Accessing and using copyright information in ways that break the law is a disciplinary offence.

- Confidential internal messages should not be posted outside the organisation.

- Chain messages should not be originated or passed on.

- E-mails should be brief, courteous and only sent to individuals with an interest in them, and not en bloc to groups.

- Employees should be informed of the level of monitoring of their e-mail and internet usage that will be carried out.

- The monitoring of an individual's private e-mails will not be routinely conducted unless it has been specifically authorised by a senior manager in support of a specific allegation of wrongdoing. (This is a particularly contentious clause.)

- Employers should give warnings to staff about misuse and make the penalties clear. Cronin (2004) has carried out some intriguing research on the efficacy of such warnings.

Of course, once someone starts to draft such regulations, the creation of a rule to prevent one problem, not using email to distribute political messages to staff for example, quickly creates another. Does this mean that Trade Union officials cannot use organisational email to send messages to its members? The other problem is the rate of innovation in e-communication. Each new development probably creates a new opportunity for misuse that had not been anticipated by the writers of codes (*see* the story of the Delhi schoolboy, p. 7).

Activity 8.2	**Designing a code of conduct for e-mail and internet use at work**

In what ways, if any, might a code of conduct designed to govern e-mail and internet use at work in:

- a research and consultancy company with a small staff of professional IT employees; and

- a large call centre dealing with service and other enquiries differ?

  If they do differ, why?

When codes of conduct collide

A fundamental problem within many types of organisation, but particularly those in the public and non-profit seeking sectors, is the issue of the codes of conduct of differing professional groupings and the potential conflicts that the respective codes can create. For example, the role of internal accounting information as a management information support system places the role of accountants within the managerial structures. This does not of itself set accountants and those professionals located within an organisation's managerial structures against those professionals who are outside those structures, but it creates the possibilities of conflict. One of the six principles upon which the International Federation of Accountants' Code of Ethics is based, and which is reflected in the codes of conduct of all the UK professional accountancy bodies, is that of confidentiality. The duty to protect the confidential nature of corporate information is underscored, even after a contract of employment is terminated.

A consideration of the codes of conduct or ethics within which other professionals must operate indicates the potential for conflict. For example, the United Kingdom Central Council for Nursing, Midwifery and Health Visiting (1996) states that 'each registered nurse, midwife and health visitor shall act, at all times, in such a manner as to safeguard and promote the interests of individual patients and clients'. In an environment that has seen health care subjected to considerable financial strictures over the past 20 years, a number of cases have highlighted the extremely difficult situations healthcare workers face in delivering effective and appropriate medical care 'that is in the interests of individual patients and clients'. The creation of managerial posts for medical staff such as nurses has only served to emphasise these tensions. Hunt (1995, 1998) recounted cases in healthcare and social services where individuals have tried to speak out about their concerns, but found their actions thwarted and future career progression blighted.

The very nature of the codes of conduct of nurses and accountants maps out the territory of potential conflict. While the nursing code requires patient advocacy, the accountants' code reflects an orientation of organisational loyalty. Indeed, in the cases of the codes of conduct developed by the American Institute of Internal Auditors and the (American) Government Finance Officers Association (Harris and Reynolds, 1993), explicit reference is made to loyalty to the employer. Even the HR managers interviewed in the Fisher and Lovell (2000) study displayed a greater organisational orientation than the stereotypical portrayal of HR managers might suggest.

The respective codes of conduct under which professional accountants and health-care workers must operate are both understandable and defensible when viewed separately. However, when placed within a single organisational context, the potential for conflict is evident.

Even within a code of conduct, tensions often exist. Proctor et al. (1993: 166) highlight the contradictory situation that confronts social workers:

> The preamble to the Code itself acknowledges that multiple principles could bear on any practice situation . . . thus, the potential for conflict is inherent in the profession's values and is reflected in its Code of Ethics.

At least the code of the social workers' professional body recognises these tensions. For accountants, the needs both to respect the confidentiality of corporate information and to respect the public interest are not usually formally recognised as posing any particular dilemma for accountants.

Interestingly, Article IV of the code of conduct of the Project Management Profession (1996: 2) contains the following clause:

> Project management professionals shall protect the safety, health and welfare of the public and **speak out** against abuses in the areas affecting the public interest [emphasis added].

Some would argue that more than a pinch of salt needs to be on hand when considering the pronouncements of aspiring professional associations, but it is quite clear that this aspiring professional body expects its members to take public stands when appropriate. This is an unusually explicit statement from a trade association.

The above discussion has introduced an additional dimension, that of the ethics codes of professional associations. Much has been written on the rise of the professions (*see* Durkheim, 1992; Koehn, 1994; and Larson, 1977, for a discussion of these issues) and the roles of codes of ethics have been influential in this rise. Any trade association that gains the statutory right to control the membership of a particular aspect of human activity (e.g. the British Medical Association and doctoring; the Law Society and particular legal work; and certain professional accountancy bodies and auditing) will possess a code of ethics for its members to follow. The existence of a code of ethics will have been an essential element of the trade association's submission to control the membership of those who wish to practise as specific 'professionals', such as doctors, lawyers and auditors, etc. This is because the trade associations will need to assuage public concern that their state-granted monopolies will not be abused. The 'professional' bodies concerned will commit their members, above all else, to act 'in the public interest' whenever there is a clash of interest.

The 'public interest' is a very slippery concept. It refers to the interests of the public at large, not in a simplistic majority-type way, but rather in terms of what should be in the general interest of civic society if a rational, objective, long-term assessment of a situation is taken. Major scandals involving professional people cast very long shadows over the veracity and intentions of codes of conduct when employed by so-called professional bodies. Examples include the involvement of the international firm of accountants, Arthur Andersen, in the Enron affair. Shortly after Enron's collapse and the complicity of the auditing arm of Andersen's was revealed, this part of the company collapsed. Other examples are the failure of the accountancy profession to respond in any meaningful way to the travails of its senior members, or the way that doctors appear to have placed the interests of their profession and fellow colleagues' status above that of the public interest in cases such as the Bristol Heart Surgery Unit, or the body-parts shambles (*see* Case study 2.20, p. 87). Yet to stay within the membership of a 'profession', the individual member must attempt not to bring the profession into disrepute. As mentioned above, individual professional codes of ethics, while defensible when considered on their own, can present a conflict situation when juxtaposed in particular organisational contexts.

In the Fisher–Lovell (2000) study, few of the accountants and HR professionals had studied their respective professional bodies' code of ethics and little weight seemed to be placed on them. In some senses, the issue of the codes of ethics of professional associations has diminished in its relevance as an area of interest and study, as the mantle of professional bodies has slipped, and their claims to be acting in the public interest are seen as little more than façades behind which opaqueness is maintained and vested interests are concealed.

Given the arguments posed in this section against the use of codes, the question might be asked, 'So do codes have a future?' Judging by the increase in the number of organisational codes in evidence, codes certainly have a present. A survey conducted by Arthur Andersen and London Business School (1999) contrasted the prevalence of codes of conduct in 1996 and 1999. Whereas 59 per cent of companies surveyed in 1996 acknowledged the use of a code of conduct, the figure had grown to 78 per cent by 1999, and 81 per cent of companies surveyed in 1999 had values or mission statements. Thirteen years after the Andersen survey, it can be supposed that all large organisations will have a series of ethics codes and policies. The question is whether this recent upsurge in interest is anything more than a defensive reaction against potential legal claims, or, as in the case of public sector bodies, merely a necessary response to the outcome of the Nolan Committee reports. Does managerial attention to codes of conduct represent anything more than the latest management fad – after quality circles, business process re-engineering, the balanced scorecard, the learning organisation, etc.?

Cross reference	The Nolan principles, which were published in the First Nolan Committee Report on Standards in Public Life, can be read in Chapter 2.

So far we have focused upon organisational responses to ethical issues by way of the development and employment of a range of different forms of codes of practice. We now move to a consideration of less overt, more subtle, but possibly more effective ways of shaping behaviour within organisations. This is the notion of corporate cultures, either singular or multiple. The development of a particular culture does not preclude the employment of a code of conduct; indeed the unwritten understandings that invariably comprise a particular culture often act as inviolate rules of conduct. All organisations will have 'ways of working', although those ways may be many and varied, with espoused behaviour sometimes deviating from actual behaviour.

Ethical culture and ethos

There are ethical issues about the propriety of using culture as a device for encouraging people to behave in one way rather than another. However, if we assume for the moment that it is acceptable for managers to foster a culture that encourages ethical behaviour, what would such a culture look like? Snell (1993, 2000) used the term moral ethos, rather than ethical culture, when he discussed this issue. He defined moral ethos as comprising a set of 'force-fields',

> all of which impinge on members' understandings, judgements and decisions concerning good and bad, right and wrong.

> (Snell, 2000: 267)

Snell argued that the moral ethos emerges from the interactions of such forces. For example, if the demand for loyalty is low, this may encourage openness within an organisation that supports criticism and acting with integrity. Contrarily, an organisation's demand for loyalty may inhibit the exercise of integrity. From an organisational perspective, loyalty is possibly the most important behaviour to cultivate among employees. Willmott (1998: 83) highlighted the contentious nature of codes of conduct and the implicit role of loyalty within them when he observed:

> the value ascribed to the adoption of codes is made conditional upon their contribution to business objectives. This implies that, in principle, the codes will be refined or discarded according to calculations about their continuing contribution to these objectives.

Integrity is less amenable to codes of conduct. For example, a code or rule to respect the confidentiality of corporate affairs in all circumstances might conflict with a broader social perspective of integrity.

Paralleling Kohlberg's stages of moral reasoning, Snell (1993: Chapter 6) identified six types of moral ethos that could arise within organisations. They are:

1. *Fear-ridden ethos.* Behaviour that is characterised by coercion, blind obedience and a myopic focus on organisational survival at any cost.

2. *Advantage-driven ethos.* Employees are rewarded for getting the best for the organisation even if this might involve deception, gamesmanship and exploitation of others if necessary. The ethos encourages private alliances, secrecy and personal advantage.

3. *Members-only ethos.* This ethos demands loyalty and a shared concern to present a good image to those outside the organisation. Clever upstarts are to be tamed and brought into the fold. Internally the focus on group membership can encourage paternalism, sexism and racism.

4. *Regulated ethos.* Regulation and accountability are typical of this ethos. Codes of conduct are written and employees are often expected to self-certify that they have obeyed the rules.

5. *Quality-seeking ethos.* This ethos seeks to encourage everyone to work to the highest ethical standards. Training and development encourages debate and argument about what those standards should be. The ethos can create a sense of arrogance and over-commitment.

6. *Soul-searching ethos.* The organisational ethos supports a spiritual learning community that emphasises integrity and an ongoing ethical dialogue.

Given that corporate cultures can be employed in manipulative ways, the issues of ethicality that pervade this area ultimately resolve themselves around

> the process of moral thought and self-scrutiny that precedes it. This understanding of ethics puts weight on the process of thought that precedes action, to qualify behaviour as ethical.

(Sinclair, 1993: 69)

Thus, the ethicality of a decision lies not in the behaviour displayed, or the decision taken, but in the forethought that preceded the behaviour or decision. This suggests that we need to think more critically about notions of culture. The 'forces' that Snell referred to can be seen at the visible level (e.g. the behaviour of individuals) or at more subtle, less visible levels (e.g. assumptions and beliefs that inform behaviour). Thus it is argued that culture operates at different levels, with important implications for business ethics.

Cross reference	Kohlberg's staged theory of moral development is discussed in detail in Chapter 5, if you wish to confirm the parallels between his theory and Snell's stages of development of ethical ethos.

Levels of culture

Schein (1992) offered an analysis that reflects three levels of culture, each with a different level of visibility. The top or first level is the most visible level of culture. Within this category would be included evidence such as signs, symbols, written codes, forms of address (i.e. how seniors, peers and juniors are expected to be addressed), clothing (formal, informal), stories and myths (usually about past leaders), rituals, architecture and décor of the company's premises. These visible signs, practices and images are described as artefacts of culture. Schein argues that while these are the most visible evidence of culture, they are not always easy to decipher by the external observer. Forms of initiation and 'apprenticeship' are often required before the full significance of these artefacts is revealed.

The second level of culture is represented by the espoused values of a group. These are the beliefs that are articulated, that are audibly expressed. Sometimes these beliefs can be represented by a 'go-get-'em' philosophy, with staff encouraged to 'take the moment' or to 'go for it'. Whether these values are wholeheartedly believed is a matter of question, but if the stated values or beliefs tend to deliver the outcomes sought, then the credibility of the beliefs will grow and become accepted as 'the way things are done around here'. An interesting example of how language is used to create particular attitudes and cultures is reflected in the refusal of one leading security firm to allow its employees to use the term 'failure'. This reflects a refusal by the senior management to accept any level of underachievement by employees, or for the employees to see any demand as unattainable.

Schein referred to the third level as basic assumptions. These are the unspoken beliefs that exist within an organisation. They are the least visible, yet the most pervasive, form of culture because they represent deeply embedded ways of thinking about such questions as the nature of human nature, humanity's relationship with the environment, the nature of truth and of human activity. Basic assumptions are difficult to bring to the surface and challenge. Consequently they operate below the level of consciousness and can undermine the idea of moral agency, which requires conscious deliberation. If corporations are capable of subliminal influence on their employees' basic assumptions, then this would be a potent threat to moral agency. There is much debate (Smircich, 1983), however, about whether top managers do have this power or whether any attempts they make to guide cultures lead only to unanticipated changes. That corporations can shape employees' beliefs is not questioned; whether those influences can be controlled to the organisation's benefit is doubtful, at least in the short term.

How to develop the ethical ethos of organisations leads us to a consideration of ethical leadership.

Ethical leadership

In many large organisations, responsibility for ethical leadership is given to a new category of managers, which first emerged in the 1990s, called ethics & compliance (E&C) officers, although many other job titles are used for this role. They are often responsible for ethics education, ensuring compliance with codes and standards, advising top management and running corporate social responsibility programmes. As Adobor (2006) reported, the role is an ambiguous and contradictory one. He identified ten propositions about the skills and competencies that might make an E&C officer more effective. Some of these could be seen as undermining each other, such as the requirement to be morally developed but also to have good political influencing skills. Others could be tautological, such as the proposition that E&C officers are more effective in organisations with a good ethical climate, where presumably the demands upon them are smaller. One major problem is that an E&C officer may at times be required to challenge their top managers; an activity that would require them to be tolerated by their superiors in much the same way as fools and jesters would be allowed to challenge their sovereigns in medieval courts. This brings us to a consideration of the ethical leadership role of top managers.

The direction and example presented by senior management in terms of what is considered to be acceptable practice within an organisation must inform and shape the behaviour of others. Most textbooks argue that it is a leader's role to define the vision and core values of an organisation. The UK government, through an agency called the CSR Academy, has published a set of CSR competencies. These can be seen as a tool for establishing a set of behaviours and core values within organisations that would support the development of a CSR culture within an organisation. In Schein's terms, they would be cultural artefacts. The competencies are intended to make CSR an integral part of business practice not only in large companies but also in small ones. The competencies (CSR Academy, 2004):

- focus on the personal qualities, attitudes and mindsets that managers need to learn and which will in turn drive improvements in business performance;
- should become embedded into the education, training and development of managers and staff; and
- are a tool for assessing performance in all business functions.

The competencies are:

1. Understanding society and business's roles and obligations within it.
2. Building capacity within an organisation to work effectively in a responsible manner.

3. Questioning business as usual.

4. Stakeholder relations.

5. Strategic view and ensuring that social and environmental concerns are considered in broad decision making.

6. Harnessing diversity.

Alongside these competencies are a set of benchmark indicators that can be used to assess whether people in the company:

- are aware of CSR;

- understand the issues around CSR;

- apply the competencies at work;

- integrate the competencies into the culture of the company; and

- provide leadership on CSR across the organisation.

Competencies have normally been defined as an ability to do something. Distinctively, these CSR competencies are about understanding at the lower levels of attainment and only about action at the higher levels. As a cultural artefact, the extent to which the competencies will affect the levels of values and basic assumptions in organisations is limited. They are probably best seen as a way of raising the priority given to CSR in businesses, especially smaller ones, and of creating a market for training courses in CSR.

Kanungo and Mendonca (1996) pointed out that employees will not believe leaders who lack ethical integrity and the leaders' values will not be accepted. They suggested that ethical leadership has to be altruistic, putting the well-being of others in the organisation before self-interest. However, they noted that western culture was better known for its emphasis on egoism than on altruism. The HR management function has been identified (Connock and Johns, 1995: 159) as the natural repository of organisations' consciences, although a survey found that, in those companies that allocated business ethics to a particular department, responsibility was given to a range of departments (Arthur Andersen and London Business School, 1999: 19).

To suggest that where there is a virtuous set of senior managers all employees will automatically follow their examples of desired practice would be naïve. However, negative examples of immoral behaviour by senior executives can act like a cancer on ethical behaviour throughout an organisation, as the example provided in Case study 6.6 (*see* p. 240) illustrated. The organisation in question appeared to harbour unpalatable practices and beliefs at a senior level, which created moral indifference within the headquarters.

A significant problem for any organisation that publicises its commitment to high ethical standards in all its business dealings is that any one single departure from such standards is likely to attract considerable media attention and cast doubt upon the full range of the organisation's activities. If this does happen, the reaction could be both unreasonably harsh (depending of course upon the nature and scale of the alleged infraction), and also a somewhat disingenuous approach to the analysis and reporting of the incident. Even if the infraction in question is finally judged to be an intentional and knowingly unethical act on the part of the individual employee concerned (however senior), the individual transgression might be just that, an individual's error of judgment. It might not be a revelation of institutionally entrenched unethical practices. In such a situation, the more telling test of organisational commitment to a broadly accepted notion of corporate ethical behaviour would be how the organisation's senior management respond to the transgression and the steps it takes to remedy the problem. In short, no one is perfect, but when errors are made, or misjudgments are revealed, how do we as individuals and corporations react and respond? The openness of individuals and organisations to acknowledge an error or problem, and the learning that ensues from the incident in question, are more likely to reflect the depth of commitment to ethical practice than are pious claims to high ethical standards made in mission statements or corporate reports. It is at times of tension or challenge that ethical credentials are more likely to be revealed. Organisational learning is a much vaunted but also a most demanding and challenging notion. The processual model of managing is commensurate with such an approach, and Bucholz and Rosenthal (1998) adopt it to explain their view of moral development within organisations.

> The adjustment between the self and the other is neither assimilation of perspectives, one to the other, nor the fusion of perspectives into an indistinguishable oneness, but can best be understood as an 'accommodating participation' in which each creatively affects and is affected by the other through accepted means of adjudication . . . because of these dynamics, the leader does not 'stand apart' from a following group, nor is the leader an organizer of group ideas, but rather leadership is by its very nature in dynamic interaction with the group, and both are in a process of ongoing transformation because of this interaction.
>
> (Bucholz and Rosenthal, 1998: 418–19)

Such a processual and 'accommodating participatory' approach would represent a fundamental change of perspective for the type of managers represented in the studies reported by Bird and Waters (1989) and Lovell (2002). The processual perspective offers, on the one hand, the prospects for moral chaos, but, on the other, possibly the best hope for moral agency. The former because the type of leadership implied in the processual model requires a degree of maturity and humility, but also a strength of belief and conviction that might be beyond many managers and leaders. However, if some form of accommodation is achievable in ways that eschew indoctrination, the debates that would be evident might do much to address many of the concerns raised throughout this book.

An important caveat with respect to greater openness and transparency in corporate dealings is the issue of litigation. The greater demands made of public corporations in terms of their various impacts are in many respects a sign of a maturing society. However, there has been an attendant increase in the propensity of members of the public to take legal action against corporations when infractions occur. In such a context, it should not be surprising that corporations become very wary of revealing their 'failings' in public for fear of how such information might be employed. These complex issues can only be moved forward by debate and a developing sense of balance between:

- on the one hand, reparation for any 'injuries' experienced as a result of sub-standard performance by an individual or organisation, where culpability is evident; and

- on the other, a recognition that 'things' will and do go less than satisfactorily on occasions and that if the 'failing' was innocent, and all reasonable measures had been taken to avoid its occurrence in the first place, then retribution should be avoided, to encourage and foster learning from the experience.

These words are easy to say and write, but much more difficult to put into practice. Yet this is the challenge facing organisations. No easy compromise or solution is on offer, only the prospect of continued action and attention to the levels of behaviour deemed acceptable within our societies.

Reflections

Thomas Hobbes, a seventeenth-century philosopher, took a pessimistic view of humanity. From the Hobbesian view of human behaviour, that people will not behave morally without the fear of retribution, flows the necessity for rules, of which codes of conduct are an obvious example. Bauman saw rules and codes, based upon reason, as leading to a morality associated with law – the laws of business and bureaucracy. This adherence to procedural rationality requires that

> all other emotions must be toned down or chased out of court . . . the most prominent of the exiled emotions are moral sentiments; that resilient and un-ruly 'voice of conscience'.

> (Bauman, 1994: 8)

Interestingly, Bauman argued that when the term ethics appears in the vocabulary of bureaucracy, it is invariably in connection with 'professional ethics'. The latter term is considered to be breached when a member shows disloyalty either to the organisation or to (organisational) colleagues. A qualified notion of honesty thus becomes of critical importance, that is, the keeping of promises and contractual obligations. This leads to predictability and consistency in organisations, an extremely important managerial need. When this is coupled with the notion of 'floating responsibility', an escape route is provided for those seeking a quiet life in the face of an awkward organisational issue.

People's instrumentalism is seen as something to be encouraged by Clutterbuck (1992: 100–1) as he exhorted organisations to reward exemplary behaviour, possibly with cash payments, and to 'punish breaches of the code publicly; use the key motivators of influence, promotion and access to resources'. This simplistic view of human nature and notions of managing assumes that instrumentalism is the only determinant, or at least the dominant explanation, of human behaviour. From a purely instrumental perspective, it is also an expensive option. In the governing of human relationships, trust is a far less expensive option than contractualism or financial incentives. But the problem remains of whether trust can be relied upon. When associated with notions of loyalty, it becomes increasingly problematic. For example, in a situation where it has become known to you that a product of your employing organisation poses health risks to consumers, which is paramount, your loyalty to:

- your work colleagues;
- your employing organisation;
- your family (who depend on your income);
- the consumer; or
- the general public?

The converse of the loyalty question is which of these groups has the right to trust you and your actions in such a situation.

Maybe the least that can be said for codes of ethics is that they give the principled employee a reference point should times become ethically challenged and certain organisational practices give rise to serious cause for concern. At its best, a code can reflect an honestly expressed expectation about moral conduct within an organisation, with the code probably written in terms of principles rather than in a prescriptive or proscriptive fashion. Employees would be encouraged to act with moral agency and the codes would be supported by mechanisms that would allow concerned employees to raise concerns in a neutral and anonymous forum, preferably using external counsellors.

Within the complex arenas that are modern business corporations, codes of conduct, codes of ethics and the prevailing culture/s will be important reference points for many of the players involved with, or affected by, the activities of the corporation. At different times, the eight roles of codes discussed in this chapter will be seen in operation. Yet if ethics is at the heart of an organisation's practices and its *raison d'être*, embedded within its culture/s, written codes become less important. They become less defensive in terms of their tenor, being essentially codes of ethics.

Summary

In this chapter, the following key points have been made:

- While not universally or uniformly recognised, distinctions between codes of conduct and codes of ethics help crystallise the intended purpose of a code.
- Codes of practice can be important mechanisms that allow business corporations to negotiate their position in a society.
- Codes of practice have multiple roles within organisations, which will not necessarily be mutually exclusive.
- The development of a code of practice is, at one and the same time, an understandable development by a corporation, but also a reflection of a lack of trust in the integrity and reliability of its employees.

- There are arguments against developing codes of practice that require ethical practice to be at the heart of an organisation's activities and 'ways of working'.

- Organisational cultures and leadership are critical to understanding an organisation's actual (as distinct from espoused) values.

Typical assignments

1. Why have codes of ethics become so commonplace in corporations and how useful are they?

2. Draft a code of conduct to cover e-communications (e-mail, web use and so on). Explain and justify your proposed code.

3. What are the drawbacks and problems associated with codes of ethics?

4. Discuss the role of leadership and organisational culture in developing a socially responsible company.

Group activity 8.1

Search the World Wide Web to find a code of ethics that you can download. The easiest way might be to think of a company you have heard of and track down its code. Analyse it by answering the following questions.

- Is it a code of ethics, a code of conduct or both?

- Does it look like a standard code, the same as everyone else's, or does it look as if it has been tailored to that organisation?

- Is it a code that recognises that some things within it are likely to be aspirations?

- Is it clear and unambiguous or does it leave lots of 'wriggle room'? If it does, is such a 'fudge factor' necessary?

- Does it look like a PR document or one that will be helpful to employees?

- If you were an employee of the organisation what would you think the code implied about the organisation's view of its staff?

Recommended further reading

A useful text is R.A. Buchholz and S.B. Rosenthal (1998) *Business Ethics: The Pragmatic Path Beyond Principles to Process*, London: Prentice Hall. Deborah Smith's pamphlet, *Demonstrating Corporate Values – Which Standard for Your Company?*, published by the Institute of Business Ethics in 2002 is an excellent comparative guide to the various codes and standards of ethical business available to organisations. The following articles will be of interest to those who wish to study the topic further: C. Cassell, P. Johnson and K. Smith (1997) 'Opening the black box: Corporate codes of ethics in their organisational context', *Journal of Business Ethics*, 16, 1077–93; G. McDonald and A. Nijhof (1999) 'Beyond codes of ethics: An integrated framework for stimulating morally responsible behaviour in organisations', *Leadership & Organisation Development Journal*, 20(3), 133–46; R.C. Warren (1993) 'Codes of ethics: Bricks without straw', *Business Ethics: A European Review*, 2(4), 185–91. See also S. Srivastva and D.L. Cooperrider (1988) *Executive Integrity: The Search for High Human Values in Organisational Life*, San Francisco: Jossey-Bass Inc., pp. 1–28.

Useful websites

Topic	Website provider	URL
The CSR Competency framework	Business in the Community (BITC)	http://www.bitc.org.uk/cr_academy/cr_practitioner_competency_map/
This is a good place to find copies of professional, governmental and organisational codes of ethics. Particularly fun is the code of ethics for witches (the Covenant of the Goddess). Most of the codes on this site are utterly serious	Centre for the Study of Ethics in Professions, University of Illinois	http://ethics.iit.edu/research/codes-ethics-collection
This link takes you to the quick test but TI's whole ethics website is an interesting corporate ethics website	Texas Instruments	http://www.ti.com/corp/docs/company/citizen/ethics/benchmark.shtml
A useful website on a wide range of business ethics issues.	Business for Social Responsibility	https://www.bsr.org/en/tag/governance-accountability
Home page of the professional association for Ethics & Compliance officers	ECOA	http://www.theecoa.org/imis15/ECOAPublic/
Shell's corporate principles, but you can Google most large organisations for their statements of values and principles	Shell	http://www.shell.com/home/content/aboutshell/who_we_are/our_values/sgbp/